Dear Mrs. Colman שתחי׳

This is a little token of appreciation for your warmth and kindness you extend to Moshe שיחי׳.

„As water mirrors a face, a heart responds to another" ‭Proverbs 27:1‬

Moshe שיחי׳ loves to come to school. This is certainly a reflection of the atmosphere you create for him there.

Your effort in giving him the proper ingredients for life so that he can grow and prosper is truly appreciated.

Sincerely,
Mendel and Basya Deutsch

Dedicated to

REBBETZIN CHAYA MUSHKA SCHNEERSON ע״נ

of blessed memory
5661-5748
(1901-1988)

Daughter of the previous Lubavitcher Rebbe
RABBI YOSEF YITZCHOK SCHNEERSOHN ע״נ

Wife of יבלחט״א the Lubavitcher Rebbe,
RABBI MENACHEM M. SCHNEERSON שליט״א

Her life will continue to enrich
and inspire us all.

*May the Al-mighty comfort
her illustrious husband
and strengthen and bless his untiring efforts
on behalf of world Jewry.*

Rabbi Yosef Yitzchok Hakohen and Stera Gutnick
and family שיחי׳

"And The Living Should Take It To Heart..."

(*Ecclesiastes* 7:2)

REBBETZIN CHAYA MUSHKA SCHNEERSON was born in 1901, and was destined from an early age to a life of pre-eminence in the Jewish world. In the house of her father, Rabbi Yosef Y. Schneersohn, the previous Lubavitcher Rebbe, and of her grandfather, Rabbi Sholom Dovber Schneersohn, the fifth Lubavitcher Rebbe, this always meant dedication to others and striving for the well-being of the Jewish people. Through Czarist and Stalinist oppression and through the Nazi horror, the Lubavitcher Rebbes displayed unparalleled courage and self-sacrifice to strengthen and preserve Torah and *mitzvot*.

Throughout these difficult years, Rebbetzin Chaya Mushka grew into a young woman of striking intelligence, courage and sensitivity. She discreetly supported the efforts of her father in planting the seeds for Jewish survival, and he chose her to accompany him when he was exiled by the Russian government to the remote city of Kostroma.

She married Rabbi Menachem Mendel Schneerson, the present Lubavitcher Rebbe, in Warsaw in 1928. When her father, Rabbi Yosef Y. Schneersohn, passed away in 1950, the Rebbetzin, continuing in her family's tradition of selfless dedication to the Jewish people, strongly encouraged her husband to assume the mantle of leadership of the world-wide Chabad-Lubavitch movement. For the next thirty-eight years, she stood beside the Rebbe in his incessant efforts on behalf of Jews the world over.

Rebbetzin Chaya Mushka Schneerson was an exceptionally brilliant and erudite woman. Her striking regal bearing, her gentle sense of humor and her compassionate, considerate and sensitive manner, endeared her to all. She carried the mantle of her revered and exalted position in a most humble and unpretentious manner.

It is written, "The glory of the king's daughter is on the inside..." (Psalms 45:14) In Rebbetzin Chaya Mushka we have seen the epitome of this statement. While avoiding publicity to an incredible extent, the Rebbetzin was a source of strength to the Rebbe in all his endeavors. Her devotion to the Rebbe's welfare and her personal self-sacrifice so that the Rebbe could give so totally of himself to world Jewry has benefited all of us.

Her passing on the 22nd of Shvat, 5748, left a void that cannot be filled. The *Rebbe, shlita* has said on many occasions that "the living should take it to heart" — meaning that our response to her passing must be an effort to bring ever more life and light into the world. We can truly say that we are all her children spiritually, and that in spreading Torah and *mitzvot* in all ways possible we are perpetuating the heritage which she bestowed. She will be eternally remembered.

SPICE
and
SPIRIT

The Committee

EDITORIAL

Executive Board
Esther Blau
Cyrel Deitsch
Cherna Light

Editors
Tzivia Emmer
Tzipora Reitman

Associate Editor
Leah Lederman

Home Economist
Rivkah Katzen

Administrative Assistant
Luba Ashurov

Production Staff
Eta Morris
Aksana Waldman

Recipe Copy Editors
Suzanne Zavrian
Margaret Wolf

Contributing Editors
Bassie Morris
Shulamis Nadler

ADVISORY

Rabbinical Board
HaRav Y. K. Marlow
  Head of Beis Din Tzedek
  of Crown Heights
Rabbi G. Avtzon
Rabbi B. Bell
Rabbi H. Greenberg
Rabbi D. Shepard

Advisory Board
Rabbi Y. Friedman
Rabbi B. Klein
Rabbi Y. Krinsky
Rabbi A. Serebryanski
Rabbi A. Shemtov

Consultants
Adela Bernstein
Leah Klein
Batsheva Shemtov
Esther Sternberg

Marketing Consultants
Barbara Oka
Mashi Taurog
Nohum Waxman

Advisors
Mr. and Mrs. Leon
  Hershbaum, Esq. ע״ה

PRODUCTION

Design and Graphics
Avrohom Weg

Art Director
Asher Hecht

Design Concept
Al Sokol
Ilana Peerles

Illustrations
Fruma Stern

Type Director
Meyer Bendet

Typesetters
Chaya Sara Cantor
Cirel Neumann

**Production
and Printing**
Gary and Michelle Gluckow

Preface

Spice and Spirit: **The Complete Kosher Jewish Cookbook** is more than a collection of recipes - it is a very special form of communication, encompassing the entire cycle of Jewish holidays and occasions. We hope to reach out beyond our community to share the experience of cooking for our families, friends, and guests in the context of living a fully Jewish lifestyle.

We present the "spice" — a treasurehouse of kosher dishes, against the backdrop of the "spirit" — the rich tapestry of Jewish life. These two elements are inseparably intertwined; the delicious "spice" of kosher food derives its unforgettable flavor from its "spirit" — the occasion for which it was prepared and the people with whom we shared it.

Jewish food characteristically draws Jewish people together. This phenomenon has persisted throughout the centuries in countless locales. Jews have in fact lived in nearly every nation and culture in the world, and have picked up many food traditions and recipes along the way. The unifying theme has been *kashrut*, for eating Jewishly means eating kosher.

In the center stands the Jewish woman — creating, organizing, cooking, talking, teaching. The more we learn about Jewish life, the more we realize that the world of our great-grandmothers is not lost in the pages of history or embalmed in museums. Jewish homes around the world today are vibrant with *mitzvot*. Every Jew can prepare and experience Shabbat this very week. Every one of us can celebrate the next Pesach, Shavuot or other Yom Tov as the Torah describes it. Everyone can begin to keep kosher.

Kosher Cuisine: A Contemporary Approach

Spice & Spirit meets the needs of today's Jewish woman by responding to several trends. The resurgent interest in authentic Judaism continues to grow, with ever more people seeking to create the unique atmosphere of the traditional Jewish home in their own lives. At the same time, our culinary horizons have broadened. We have become, as a society, more sophisticated and knowledgeable about food, with more people taking an interest in gourmet cooking, in healthful eating, and in new cuisine styles.

Our over 800 recipes represent kosher cookery at its best. Each recipe, whether for a simple dish or a complex specialty, is given a clear and straightforward treatment to ensure the most delicious results. These carefully selected recipes range from blintzes and chicken soup to Szechuan chicken and aduki-squash soup. They are from the kitchens of women who are as different from one another as sushi is from gefilte fish, yet who have in common an expertise in cooking and an excitement about sharing their knowledge of kosher cuisine.

The recipes themselves are identified with logos which classify them as to style and complexity. For quick reference, for those times when a Yom Tov is almost here, the soup is boiling over and the guests are about to arrive, you will find a handy checklist at the end of each Yom Tov section listing the main *mitzvot* and customs for that day.

Using This Book

This book represents the outgrowth of our original cookbook, *The Spice & Spirit of Kosher-Jewish Cooking*, which met with overwhelming success. After producing fourteen printings and selling 60,000 copies of the original book, we are excited to offer a brand new cookbook, **Spice and Spirit: The Complete Kosher Jewish Cookbook**. It is the latest addition to our series of publications, Kosher Living Classics.

Spice and Spirit provides the important information needed for observing many basics of Jewish life. The comprehensive yet clearly presented sections on *kashrut*, Shabbat, and the

Jewish Festivals provide an enriching dimension to the experience of preparing kosher dishes throughout the year.

Each festival is discussed in light of its historical context and spiritual content. All laws and customs have been carefully researched by our staff and approved by a prominent Rabbinical Board. Many Hebrew and Yiddish words are defined in the Glossary. Those readers interested in further exploration of topics touched upon here can consult the Suggested Reading List.

For more extensive coverage of *kashrut*, refer to a previous volume of Kosher Living Classics, *Body & Soul: A Handbook For Kosher Living*. It offers insights and perspectives on *kashrut*, and includes information not covered here. We recommend that everyone, whether commencing a return to Judaism or already observant, have a Rav, a competent Orthodox Rabbi, who can answer questions and give further guidance in all areas of Jewish life.

The information in **Spice and Spirit** was culled from a variety of sources, both English and Hebrew. Where customs vary from one community to another we have made note of this fact. The "inner spirit" which informs this book throughout is that of *Chabad Chassidut*, the philosophy first revealed by Rabbi Schneur Zalman of Liadi (1745-1812) and taught in our time by the revered Lubavitcher Rebbe, *shlita*, Rabbi Menachem M. Schneerson. *Chassidut* shows how every concept in Judaism relates to the inner development of each individual Jew. The Rebbe's guidance and inspiration has been our steady beacon throughout the creation of this book.

A Community Project

A book of this scope can have been produced only through the cooperative efforts of many individuals. We would like to express our deep appreciation to those who generously granted so much of their time and talent to aid in the development of this book. Their steadfast support throughout the many phases of producing the book has contributed to its beauty and quality. Our many talented recipe contributors are listed in the back of the book. This book is one of the many projects accomplished through the dedication of hundreds of women who participate in the activities of the world-wide Lubavitch movement.

We are forever grateful to our many gracious sponsors whose generous support represents the backbone of this project. We are touched by their friendship and encouragement, and we hope they share in our pride.

To our community and to the many other friends of *Chabad* who helped make **Spice and Spirit: The Complete Kosher Jewish Cookbook** a true communal effort, we extend our heartfelt thanks.

The Editors

RECIPE LOGOS

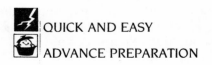QUICK AND EASY
ADVANCE PREPARATION

TRADITIONAL
NATURAL

INTERNATIONAL
GOURMET

Table of Contents

Kashrut: Spiritual Nutrition

Kashrut Basics
The Kosher Kitchen
Kashrut Supervision
Blessings on Food

The world of *kashrut* encompasses the history of a people and enriches countless Jewish homes around the globe. The *mitzvah* of *kashrut* transforms food into a vehicle for holiness, making the kitchen the spiritual hub of the home.

The Jewish home is a miniature sanctuary and its table is like an altar. For the Jewish woman, the kitchen is the field in which she sows the seeds of national survival, the fertile ground in which she implants Jewishness in her family. Here, by following the dietary laws given in the Torah, she nurtures the future Jewish nation.

The laws of *kashrut* detail the permitted and forbidden animals, fish, and fowl, and describe the separation of dairy and meat. A significant part of Jewish observance is associated with food, from the dietary laws to the saying of blessings before and after eating, from the celebration of holidays to the agricultural laws governing food from Israel. *Kashrut* is an all-encompassing way of life, whether at home, on the job, or eating out. Through *kashrut* observance, every activity associated with food becomes an opportunity for spiritual refinement.

Kashrut is one of three *mitzvot* entrusted especially to Jewish women, which are the separation of *challah*, lighting candles for Shabbat and Yom Tov, and observing the laws of marital purity, including immersion in a *mikvah*. The *mitzvah* of separating *challah*, a small portion of dough, symbolizes the entire realm of *kashrut*. *Kashrut*, together with the other two *mitzvot*, strongly affects the foundation and essence of the Jewish people.

These special *mitzvot* embody the idea that the mission of a Jew is to sanctify and elevate everyday life, bringing awareness of the Creator into all of our activities. One's profession, talents, accomplishments and interests can all serve as vehicles for accomplishing this goal. But for both men and women, the most important edifice in Judaism and in life is the home. This is the edifice built by the Jewish woman, not with nails and hammer, nor with fabrics and colors, but with *mitzvot*, love, Torah knowledge and wisdom.

Why Keep Kosher?

Not too long ago, nearly all Jews adhered to the dietary laws without ever asking, "Why keep kosher?" It was the Jewish thing to do. Only those who deliberately rebelled against the ways of their parents and grandparents would have eaten *traif*, non-kosher food. Today the situation has largely reversed, in that Jews who have no thought of rebellion and even identify proudly as Jews eat every kind of non-kosher food. It requires thought and effort to keep kosher.

Our thinking has changed to the extent that we no longer know why Judaism places such emphasis on eating and drinking, basic necessities shared not only by all mankind but by animals as well. We ask, "Does G-d really care what I eat?" Without a satisfactory explanation for *kashrut* and without the simple faith based on Torah values that characterized former generations, many Jews conclude that keeping kosher is simply obsolete — that it is based upon ancient health precautions which no longer apply to modern life.

We therefore offer some of the insights into the *mitzvah* of *kashrut* provided by Jewish tradition. These insights satisfy our need for understanding and motivate us to keep the *mitzvot* of the Torah in the face of opposing values from contemporary culture. Nevertheless, it should be understood that the commandments are Divine in origin and can never be fully comprehended by human intellect. We keep the *mitzvot* because they are G-d's gift to the Jewish people.

"Religion," as everyone knows, deals with prayer, meditation, charity, ethics and sometimes various forms of self-denial. Judaism, however, encompasses every aspect of life. Our most ordinary daily activities become imbued with holiness when we follow the Torah dictum to "know Him in all your ways." (Proverbs 3:6)

Kashrut represents the meeting of body and soul. The Torah tells us not to reject the physical but rather to sanctify it. We sanctify the act of eating with kosher food and blessings before and after eating. Kosher food is the diet of spiritual nutrition for the Jewish *neshamah*, (soul). It is designed to bring refinement and purification to the Jewish people.

What does this mean? Modern nutritional science recognizes what Judaism has always taught that to a large extent we are what we eat. We know that the food we eat is absorbed into our flesh and blood. Forbidden foods are referred to in the Torah as abominations to the G-dly soul, elements that detract from our spiritual sensitivity. Birds of prey and carnivorous animals, having the power to influence the eater with aggressive attributes, are among the foods that are forbidden. For a Jew, all non-kosher food diminishes one's spiritual sensitivity, reducing the ability to absorb concepts of Torah and *mitzvot*. Both mind and heart are affected.

It is easy to see why *kashrut* is often considered the most far-reaching of all the *mitzvot*. History demonstrates that when *kashrut* observance is strong, Jewish identity remains strong.

To explain the power of kosher food, we must turn to Chassidic teachings based upon the mysticism of the Ari-Zal (Rabbi Yitzchak Luria). The Ari-Zal gave a literal interpretation of the verse, "Man does not live by bread alone, but by the word of G-d" (Deuteronomy 8:3). He explained that it is not the food itself which gives life but rather the spark of G-dliness -- the "word of G-d" -- that is in the food. All matter has within it some aspect of the "G-dly sparks" that give life and existence to the world. When we eat, the digestive system extracts the nutrients while the *neshamah* extracts the G-dly spark found in nature.

The Divine energy in the food is thus the actual source of its ability to sustain and nourish the body. Kosher food has a powerful energy that gives spiritual, intellectual and emotional strength to the Jewish *neshamah*, while non-kosher food does the opposite. The kosher diet is truly the health-food diet for the soul, containing the spiritual nutrition necessary for Jewish survival.

A Little Help From Above

The kitchen takes on a new dimension when we think of the awesome responsibility involved in providing kosher meals for one's family. Children, especially, because they are still developing, require purely kosher food. The affect on their *neshamah* is strongly felt, just as some medicines and foods affect children more powerfully than they do adults.

The Jewish wife and mother, as the provider of kosher food, occupies a special position in Jewish Law. In most areas of *halachah*, verification is based upon the testimony of two witnesses. However, throughout Jewish history, the Jewish woman alone has been entrusted with carrying out the detailed practices involved in keeping a kosher home, even if she had no formal education and had learned about *kashrut* only at her mother's side.

This responsibility may seem awesome, but we can and should approach it with happiness and confidence. Our human efforts are boosted to success when accompanied by "a little help from above" — G-d's blessings.

A time-honored Jewish way of eliciting G-d's blessings is by generously sharing our blessings with others. In a recent address to Jewish women and girls, the Lubavitcher Rebbe, Shlita, suggested that we put coins into a *pushka* (charity box) while we are in the kitchen, thus linking our food preparation with the provision of food for the poor. In this way, we elicit G-d's blessing that our time spent in the kitchen will result in superior and truly kosher meals. The Rebbe further explained that the *pushka* should be attached to the wall or cabinet of the kitchen, thereby becoming a structural part of the home and making the act of *chesed* (kindness), one of the home's foundations.

Kashrut: A Universal Jewish Recipe

The *pushka* is one small but significant detail which identifies a kitchen as being uniquely Jewish. Together with a *mezuzah* on the doorpost and the "standard equipment" of *kashrut* - e.g. separate working areas for dairy and meat - the Jewish kitchen is the workshop for both the Jewish body and soul.

In the sections that follow, we offer a thorough guide to practical *kashrut* observance in the home and beyond. Kosher living is a lifelong journey, a source of challenge and enjoyment throughout the years.

Kashrut Basics

Keeping kosher is an intrinsic part of the daily life of a Jew. Understanding the fundamentals of *kashrut* is basic to the functioning of the Jewish home.

Kosher foods are divided into three categories: meat, dairy and *pareve*. One of the basic principles of *kashrut* is the total separation of meat and dairy products. Meat and dairy may not be cooked or eaten together. To ensure this, the kosher kitchen contains separate sets of dishes, utensils,

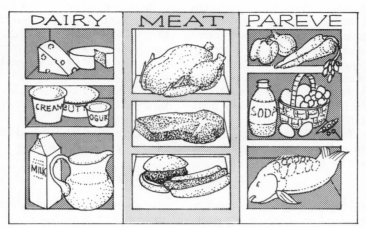

cookware, and separate preparation areas for meat and dairy. A third category, *pareve*, is comprised of foods which are neither meat nor dairy and may therefore be eaten with either.

The following section gives a detailed description of meat, dairy, and *pareve* foods, and offers practical guidelines for cooking and serving the foods within each category according to *kashrut* specifications.

MEAT, DAIRY AND PAREVE

Meat

The category of meat includes meat, fowl and their byproducts, such as bones, soup or gravy. Any food made with meat or fowl, or with meat or fowl products, is considered "meaty;" also called *fleishig* (Yiddish). Even a small amount of meat in a food can cause it to be *fleishig*. All meat, fowl and meat parts in any product, including items such as liver pills, must meet the following requirements to be considered kosher:

☐ Meat must come from an animal that chews its cud and has split hooves. Cows, sheep and goats are kosher.

☐ Kosher fowl is identified by a tradition handed down from generation to generation and universally accepted. The Torah names those species of fowl that are forbidden, including all predatory and scavenger birds. Kosher fowl include the domesticated species of chickens, Cornish hens, ducks, geese and turkeys.

☐ The animal or fowl must be slaughtered and examined according to the dietary laws by a *shochet*, an individual skilled and extensively trained in kosher slaughtering.

☐ The permissible portions of the animal and fowl must be properly prepared before cooking. All utensils must be kosher.

For more information regarding kosher meat, see the introduction to the meat and poultry section, page 185. See also Laws of Kosher Meat and Fowl, page 187.

Dairy

All foods derived from or containing milk are considered dairy, or *milchig* (Yiddish). This includes milk, butter, yogurt and all cheese -- hard, soft and cream. Even a small amount of dairy in a food can cause the food to be considered dairy. All dairy products require *kashrut* certification. They must meet the following criteria in order to be certified kosher:

☐ They must come from a kosher animal.

☐ All ingredients must be kosher and free of meat derivatives. Non-kosher dairy products are often made with ingredients of animal origin. For example, hard cheese is made with rennet, yogurt sometimes contains gelatin, and butter may contain non-kosher additives.

☐ They must be processed on kosher equipment.

Many kinds of "non-dairy" creamers, candy, cereal and margarine do contain milk derivatives, as do some low-calorie sweeteners. Dairy ingredients whose names appear on many product labels include caseinate, lactose and whey.

Commercial bread containing dairy ingredients presents *kashrut* problems. Consult an Orthodox Rabbi before purchasing or using any dairy bread.

More information about *kashrut* and dairy products can be found on page 67. See also Chalav Yisrael, page 68.

Pareve

Foods that are neither meat nor dairy are called *pareve*. This means that they contain no meat or dairy derivatives, and have not been cooked or mixed with any meat or dairy foods.

Eggs, fish, fruit, vegetables, grains, and juices in their natural, unprocessed state are common *pareve* foods. Other *pareve* foods include pasta, soft drinks, coffee and tea, and many types of candy and snacks. Products that have been processed in any way should be bought only if they bear reliable *kashrut* certification.

Although *pareve* foods present fewer *kashrut*-complexities than either meat or dairy foods, certain points must be kept in mind:

☐ *Pareve* foods may lose their *pareve* status if processed on dairy equipment or when additives are used. The label may give no indication of this processing. There is a further problem in that such products are not *chalav Yisrael*. Chocolate, cookies and other snacks should not be used with meat or meaty foods unless they are certified *pareve*.

☐ Certain fruits, vegetables and grains must be checked for the presence of small insects and larvae (page 259).

☐ Eggs must be checked for the presence of blood spots (page 75).

Separating Meat and Dairy

Meat and dairy foods may not be cooked together or eaten together. One may not even derive benefit from a combination of meat and dairy foods; for example, selling such a combined product or feeding it to a pet.

To ensure this total separation, the kosher kitchen requires the use of separate utensils, accessories and appliances for meat and dairy. It is useful to have some separate *pareve* utensils as well.

For a complete guide to setting up and maintaining the separation between meat and dairy see The Kosher Kitchen, page 20.

The Waiting Time Between Eating Meat and Dairy: The laws of *kashrut* require that we wait a specified period of time between eating meat and eating dairy.

☐ After eating dairy and before eating meat, it is necessary to eat something *pareve*, which does not stick to the palate. Then one must rinse one's mouth, or take a drink, and wash one's hands. (*Chabad* custom is to wait one hour between dairy and meat.) After eating certain hard cheeses, a six-hour waiting period is required.

☐ After eating meat foods, it is necessary to wait six full hours before eating any dairy. The six-hour waiting period is standard for all Jews, except those groups which have *halachically* established other customs. For people on special dairy diets, and for children under nine years old, consult an Orthodox Rabbi for guidance. If there are no special problems involved, it is advisable to train children at an earlier age in the practice of waiting between meat and dairy foods.

If a small piece of meat is discovered between the teeth, it is necessary to remove it and rinse the mouth, but an additional waiting period is not required (even if six hours have elapsed since eating meat). If even the smallest amount of food is chewed or swallowed, the full waiting period becomes necessary.

☐ If food is tasted but immediately eliminated from the mouth before chewing or swallowing, then no waiting period is required. One should rinse the mouth well.

NOTE: Meat and dairy foods may not be eaten in the same meal, even if they are in separate dishes and even if the waiting time elapses.

Serving Pareve Food

Pareve food can generally be served with either meat or dairy meals. Some kitchens have serving and mixing bowls, pots, and knives used exclusively for *pareve* food. These are always washed separately from meat and dairy dishes. One should also have separate dish sponges, dish towels, and draining boards.

If a *pareve* food, however, is cooked or mixed together with any meat or dairy products it becomes respectively either meat or dairy and all laws pertaining to meat and dairy apply, including the required waiting times.

If the *pareve* food has only *touched* the meat or milk food, then washing the food is sufficient to keep it *pareve*, if the two items that made contact are room temperature, and neither was a sharp or spicy food (such as those mixed with onion, lemon, pickles, etc., see Sharp and Spicy Pareve Foods, below). If washing is impossible, one must cut off a layer from where the foods came in contact.

Pareve Foods Cooked In Meat or Dairy Utensils: When a *pareve* food has been cooked in a clean meat pot, one is generally required to serve that food only on meat dishes. A waiting time is not required before eating dairy food. Similarly, *pareve* food cooked in a clean dairy pot is generally served only on dairy dishes, and a waiting time is not required before eating meaty food.

If one cooks a *pareve* food in a clean meaty pot and wishes to serve it during a dairy meal, or vice versa, one should consult an Orthodox Rabbi as to whether the circumstances would make it permissible.

An important factor to bear in mind is whether the pot or utensils used to prepare the *pareve* food have been used with hot meat, or washed in hot water together with meaty dishes, within the last twenty-four hours. If so, this *pareve* food may certainly not be eaten with dairy products. The reverse is also true; if the pot or utensil used to prepare a *pareve* food has been used with hot dairy, or washed in hot water together with dairy dishes within the last twenty-four hours, then this *pareve* food certainly cannot be eaten with meat products. The waiting period, however, is not necessary.

Sharp and Spicy Pareve Foods: Using sharp and spicy foods such as onions, garlic, lemons, and pickles may change the *pareve* status of the food with which they are prepared. Sharp and spicy foods which are cut with a meaty knife are considered as a meat dish and may not be used with dairy foods, and vice versa.

If a sharp or spicy *pareve* food is cooked in a meaty pot or prepared with meaty utensils, even if the meaty pot or utensil was not used for hot meat food or washed in hot water together with meaty dishes within the last twenty-four hours, that *pareve* food may not be eaten with dairy. The reverse is also true; if the pot is dairy, the sharp or spicy *pareve* food cannot be eaten with meat. Concerning the waiting period for such foods, and the precise application of the terms sharp, spicy and hot, consult an Orthodox Rabbi.

The Kosher Kitchen

A kosher home is an important element in the foundation of Jewish life. Whether you are embarking on the exciting step of setting up a newly kosher kitchen or have been keeping kosher for years, the following step-by-step guide will prove most helpful.

The decision to make one's home kosher is indeed a big one, but it need not be overwhelming. Help is available at all stages. Before long, "keeping kosher" will be second nature to you, an integral part of your life as a homemaker and as a Jew.

Becoming Kosher: Any kitchen can be made kosher. Whether your kitchen is up-to-the minute in fashionable design or a relic of the 1920's, whether you have a spacious "great room" or a tiny galley kitchen, you can readily adapt it to kosher practices.

Read the following guide and the preceding pages carefully. Then contact a qualified person to answer any questions you may have and help you take the next steps. The *Chabad* representative in your area will be happy to assist you in transforming your kitchen, as will most Orthodox Rabbis. Often it is the Rabbi's wife or a knowledgeable woman with the practical, hands-on experience of keeping kosher who will provide the most help.

How to Begin: Even before your kitchen is made kosher, begin preparing for the change. Buy only foods which are certified kosher. Begin to keep meat and dairy separate. Many people use disposable utensils just before going kosher. Remove all questionable foods. Before making the kitchen kosher, discard all foods prepared in the pre-kosher kitchen.

Inventory of Kitchen Items: One of the first things that the person who is helping you to become kosher will do is divide all the items in your kitchen into two categories: those which can no longer be used in a kosher kitchen, and those which can be used after undergoing the various procedures of *kashering* (making kosher). Some new purchases will undoubtedly be necessary. New items may include dishes, some additional pots, plastic drainboards, and basins for the sink.

Many dishes and utensils require immersion in a *mikvah* before being used. See Tevilat Kailim, page 22. Decide which cabinets you will use for the newly separated meat and dairy dishes. Labeling these storage areas is a good idea.

Kashering Utensils: Many of the utensils in your kitchen will continue to be used after undergoing a process called *kashering*. There are several methods of *kashering*, including heating the item with a blowtorch or immersing in boiling water. The method used depends upon the type of utensil and how it has been used. After deciding with your Rabbi which utensils will be *kashered*, an appointment should be made for him to come and *kasher* your kitchen.

To prepare for this procedure, clean all parts of the kitchen well. Counters, tables, ovens, stoves and refrigerator should be perfectly clean. Scrub utensils and set them aside. Twenty-four hours prior to *kashering*, the stove, oven and broilers should not be turned on, and hot water should not be poured into the sink.

KITCHEN PLANNING

While a kitchen remodeled or designed for *kashrut* observance with two sinks, two stoves, and separate working areas is certainly a great convenience, it is by no means a necessity.

"Milchigs" and "Fleishigs:" In keeping with the total separation of meat and dairy required in the kosher kitchen, separate sets of dishes, pots, silverware, serving dishes, bread trays and salt shakers are needed. These different sets should be kept in separate cabinets. Also necessary are separate sets of draining boards, draining racks, dish sponges, scouring pads, dish towels, and tablecloths. Dish soap, cleanser, and scouring pads used for dishes and pots must have a *hechsher* (*kashrut* certification).

A very practical and widespread practice in Jewish homes is to plan the different sets of meat and dairy utensils around a color scheme. A traditional example is red for *fleishig* (meat) and blue for *milchig* (dairy). Draining racks, sponges and dish towels are key elements in this color system. Choose your own color scheme and use it as a reminder for yourself and anyone else who will be working in your kitchen. (The dishes themselves need not conform to a strict color scheme, but should be readily distinguishable.)

One must be especially careful to mark utensils that look similar for both meat and dairy, such as knives, ladles or wooden spoons. Distinguish between such utensils by having a different color or design, or paint a line on the handles according to the color scheme. Plastic tape, color-coordinated signs, or paint of the same color may be used to mark other items.

Kitchen Surfaces And Appliances

The separation of meat and dairy must be maintained throughout the kitchen. Consult your Rabbi as how to clean and *kasher* surfaces or appliances that were non-kosher.

The Sink: Separate sinks for washing dishes and preparing foods are recommended. If the two sinks are adjoining, there should be an effective separation between them so that no water or food splashes from one sink to the other.

If there is only one sink, it may be used after it has been completely cleaned, but the inside of the sink should be regarded as non-kosher. No food or dishes should be put directly into non-kosher sinks. There should be separate dish pans and slightly elevated racks under the dish pans for both meat and dairy. Similarly, two sinks which were used before the kitchen was kosher should also be regarded as non-kosher, unless they are stainless steel and were *kashered*. If the two sinks were *kashered*, one should be designated for meat and one for dairy.

Tables: A table can be used at different times for meat and dairy if one uses different tablecloths or placemats. A new table or a table surface that was *kashered* can be used for one category and a tablecloth or placemats used for the other.

Countertops: Designate separate countertops or work areas for meat and dairy. If one area must be used for both, separate coverings must be used.

Refrigerators and Freezers: These may be used for all food types. However, separate areas should be designated for meat and dairy foods. Sometimes a shelf or the door of the refrigerator or freezer is kept for dairy. If dairy is kept on a shelf inside the refrigerator, one should cover the shelf with aluminum foil or a plastic liner to prevent leakage onto other foods. If dairy drips on the foil, the foil must be carefully removed and replaced. Similar care must be taken with meat products inside the refrigerator.

One should avoid placing hot meat or hot dairy foods in the refrigerator as this may affect the other foods in the refrigerator and cause *kashrut* problems.

The Stove Top: Where heat is involved, the laws concerning the accidental mixture of meat and dairy foods become much more complex. Therefore, strict precautions are taken concerning the use of the stove and oven for meat and dairy products.

The ideal set-up in the kosher kitchen is to have two separate stoves. A practical alternative is to use the full size range for meat, and a portable gas or electric range or cooktop for dairy. Where one stove is used, separate burners designated for milk or meat use are preferable. If this is not possible, extra care must be taken to keep the burners very clean.

It is best to avoid cooking both types of food at the same time since the steam or food in one pot might splatter or escape to another, creating serious *kashrut* problems regarding the food and pots involved.

If it becomes necessary to cook both meat and dairy foods in separate pots at the same time, utmost care should be taken that the lids are secured tightly at all times and that an upright sheet of tin or other metal separates the pots. Be careful to avoid lifting lids of both meat and dairy pots at the same time. If the lids must be lifted to check the food or add any ingredients, raise the lid only slightly off the pots, tilted away from the opposite pots. It is best to have the meat and dairy pots well separated, to keep the steam or liquid from coming in contact with each other.

The Oven and Broiler: It is best to use the oven for only one type of food: meat, *pareve* or dairy. If only one oven is available, the use of portable broilers or toaster-ovens for other food types is advisable. Meat and dairy foods can never be baked or broiled in one oven at the same time, even in separate bakeware.

If you wish to keep the oven *pareve*, then meat or dairy foods cooked in that oven (at separate times) must be tightly covered all around, including the bottom. It is advisable to place a piece of foil under the pan and to change it for meat or dairy use. The pan may be opened for testing only when it is completely removed from the oven.

Dairy foods should not be baked in a meaty oven, and vice versa. *Pareve* foods baked in a meaty oven (or broiler) should not be served on dairy dishes or eaten with dairy foods, unless the following conditions are met:

☐ The oven, racks, and broiler are thoroughly clean. (It is helpful to put a piece of foil under the bakeware to ensure the cleanliness of the oven racks.) This might be difficult to achieve without a self-cleaning oven.

☐ 24 hours have elapsed since the oven was used for meat. For example, if meat is baked in the oven, and then you wish to bake a cake which can be served with milk, first be sure the oven and racks are clean, then wait 24 hours before baking the cake. The same conditions apply if one wishes to bake *pareve* in a dairy oven. It is advisable to have separate bakeware for *pareve*.

If the oven is clean, the waiting periods between milk and meat is not required for *pareve* foods baked in a meat or dairy oven.

To use an oven for both meat and dairy at separate times, consult an Orthodox Rabbi.

All of the above also applies to broilers which are on the bottom of the oven. Regarding the use of self-cleaning and microwave ovens, consult an Orthodox Rabbi.

Portable Electric Broilers: These must be used for either meat or dairy exclusively because they cannot be properly *kashered*.

Small Appliances: An electric mixer, blender or grinder do not require a separate motor in order to be used for meat and dairy. However, one must buy separate attachments if the appliance is to be used for more than one food type (meat, dairy, or *pareve*). Even when using separate attachments, the machine should be cleaned well on all sides after each use.

Dishwashers: These should preferably be designated for the exclusive use of either meat or dairy. If you have further questions, consult an Orthodox Rabbi, as there are many factors involved.

Kashrut Questions In The Kitchen

In any kosher kitchen, it is only natural for questions to arise. What happens if you stir a pot of chicken soup with a dairy spoon? How are the spoon, pot and food affected? Can you *kasher* a particular type of pot, and if so, how must it be done? Whether one has just begun to keep kosher or has been doing so for years, it is important to ask a *sha'alah* (question in *halachah* or Jewish Law) of a Rabbi competent in *halachic* matters each time a situation in *kashrut* or any other area of Jewish life needs clarification.

Until the question is answered, set aside the utensils and/or food in question. For example, if a dairy knife was inadvertently used to cut meat, remove the knife from the meat and wipe off all traces of meat from the knife, then set aside both the meat which was cut and the knife which was used. When there is a question, use only cold water. Never rinse these utensils with hot water.

Consulting A Rabbi: When a question regarding a utensil or food arises, consult an Orthodox Rabbi as soon as possible.

Keep in mind the circumstances and details involved in the situation. The Rabbi will tell you whether the utensils need to be *kashered*, and how to do it. (See Kashering Utensils above.) He will also indicate if the food is permitted. Some of the circumstances to describe to the Rabbi are:

☐ type(s) of food involved,

☐ type(s) of utensils, dishes or pots involved,

☐ the manner in which food was prepared (cooking, frying, broiling, etc.),

☐ whether the mix-up occurred in dishes or in cookware, and before or after the cooking process,

☐ the temperature of food or utensils: whether hot, cold, or room temperature,

☐ when the utensil was last used prior to the mix-up, and for which foods it was used,

☐ the amount of food involved.

Another type of question that can arise is when a *pareve* utensil comes in contact with hot meat or dairy foods, in which case it may become *fleishig* or *milchig*. In this situation, a *sha'alah* should be asked.

With each situation that arises, a new question should be asked, for the answer to each case is determined independently. One should not draw one's own conclusion based on an answer to a previous *sha'alah*.

TEVILAT KAILIM — IMMERSION OF VESSELS

The Jewish table is likened to an altar, its holiness compared to that of the *Beit Hamikdash*. Before dishes and utensils can be used in the kosher kitchen, they must acquire an additional measure of holiness which is conferred through the ritual immersion in a pool of naturally-gathered water, or *mikvah*. A *mikvah* is a specially constructed ritual pool connected to a source of pure rainwater. Vessels may also be immersed in certain natural bodies of water such as the ocean.

The procedure is known as *toiveling* (derived from the Hebrew *tovel*, to immerse).

Immersion in a *mikvah* is required only for utensils that were manufactured or ever owned by a non-Jew. Even those that were previously used without having been immersed still require immersion, after thorough cleaning, and *kashering* if necessary.

Preparation for immersion consists of the removal of any substance that would intervene between the water of the *mikvah* and the surface of the utensil, such as dirt, rust, stickers, glue from labels, and price markings. Steel wool and/or acetone (nail polish remover) are sometimes needed to remove all traces of surface markings.

Types of Vessels Requiring Immersion: A vessel made of metal or glass with which one eats, drinks, cooks, roasts, fries, or heats up water for drinking, requires immersion with a blessing. Examples of vessels requiring immersion with a blessing include: Correlle dishes, silverware, pots and pans, glazed china, kettle, and those parts of a mixer or blender which come into direct contact with food.

When immersing several items at the same time, only one blessing is said. If one is unsure as to whether or not an item requires immersion with a blessing, it should preferably be *toiveled* together with utensils requiring a blessing is:

BA-RUCH A-TAH ADO-NOI ELO-HAI-NU
ME-LECH HA'O-LAM A-SHER
KID-SHA-NU B'-MITZ-VO-TAV V'TZI-VA-NU
AL TE-VI-LAT KE-LI (KAI-LIM).
Blessed are You, L-rd our G-d, King of the Universe, Who has sanctified us with His commandments, and commanded us concerning the immersion of a vessel (vessels).

Items Made of Two or More Materials: When a utensil is made of two different materials, only one of which requires immersion, immersion is usually required. (Examples include glazed earthenware, pans with a non-stick coating, wooden-handled utensils and Thermos containers.) However, the blessing is not always said. Consult an Orthodox Rabbi for information about immersing any of these types of utensils.

Utensils Made From Plastic: As regards to plastic items, the need for immersion varies according to the type of plastic. Therefore, it is preferable to immerse plastic items without a blessing.

Utensils that do not require *tevilah* are: (1) those made of wood, paper, bone, or unglazed earthenware; or (2) disposable utensils such as plastic cups or plates which are not fit for long-term use and which one normally discards after using.

Immersion of vessels may be done by a man or a woman and during the day or night, but may not be done on Shabbat or Yom Tov.

THE KOSHER KITCHEN ON PESACH

A new dimension is added to *kashrut* observance during Pesach, when we may not eat, derive any benefit from, or possess any *chametz*, leavened food. Only kosher for Pesach foods may be eaten for the eight days of the holiday.

The kitchen is extensively prepared before the holiday to conform with the Pesach laws. All leavened foods are removed from our possession, and all dishes and utensils used for *chametz* are stored away. Special Pesach dishes, cutlery, and cookware are used exclusively during the holiday and then stored separately until the following Pesach. The laws of Pesach are complex, requiring further study, and the guidance of an Orthodox Rabbi.

More details on these laws can be found in the section on Pesach, page 523. For a complete description on preparing the home for Pesach, refer to our other publications, *Body & Soul: A Handbook For Kosher Living*, and *The Spice & Spirit of Kosher – Passover Cooking*.

Kashrut Supervision

Knowing the basic laws of *kashrut* and their application in the kosher kitchen sets the stage for the part of keeping kosher that is sometimes the most challenging: buying kosher food. Although there are many more kosher products available to us than there were to our mothers and grandmothers, there are also many more questions that need to be asked.

Hundreds of foods labeled "kosher" dot our supermarket shelves, but many factors that we cannot see complicate the process of guaranteeing a product as kosher. Over 2,800 additives not known fifty years ago are legally present in our foods, including colorings, flavorings, and preservatives. Huge factories manufacture enormous quantities of many types of food using processing techniques of which we know little or nothing.

Furthermore, these food factories often incorporate ingredients and agents which have been manufactured at still other plants and which often contain previously processed ingredients.

As many ingredients used by local food-processing factories are imported from countries which do not have reliable supervising agencies, supervising Rabbis sometimes find themselves on worldwide journeys when determining whether a single product is kosher.

The enormous quantities of food manufactured by these industrial methods poses another difficulty for the kosher consumer. Often, a seemingly kosher product is processed on equipment also used for non-kosher foods - making the previously kosher food non-kosher. Other requirements of *kashrut*, which must be scrupulously upheld (such as meat and dairy separation) are often submerged in the busy, come-and-go routine of factory personnel who are limited in their knowledge of *kashrut*.

For these and other reasons, it is necessary to have reliable Rabbinical supervision and certification of kosher foods.

SUPERVISION SERVICES

All processed food products must be carefully supervised throughout the many phases of production: cooking, baking, freezing, bottling, and canning. This supervision is performed by a party independent of the manufacturer, at the latter's expense.

*K*ashrut supervision is provided by either a national agency, a local board of *kashrut*, or an individual Orthodox Rabbi. Most large *kashrut* organizations have a registered symbol or logo. This appears on the package and signifies their endorsement of the product. (This is quite different from a mere "K," see below.) Sometimes only the name of a particular Rabbi or city *kashrut* board appears.

The certification of *kashrut* is called a *hechsher*.

When an organization or individual puts a *hechsher* on a product they attest to the fact that the contents and manufacturing meet their standards of *kashrut*. Not every *hechsher* is considered reliable.

The Letter "K": A "K" appearing on a label does not necessarily mean that the product is kosher. It may signify *kashrut* certification, or it may have been put there by the manufacturer as his own claim that the product is kosher. To find out who or what is behind the "K" on a product, write to or call the manufacturer. Keep up with the newsletters published by the major certifying agencies listing the products under their supervision.

THE NEED FOR RELIABLE SUPERVISION

Reading The Label - Why The Ingredient List is Not Enough: Label-scanning becomes a habit for the kosher-conscious as well as for the health-conscious consumer. Looking for the *hechsher* and for the statement of whether a product is dairy, meat or *pareve*, or for questionable ingredients listed on the label, are necessary procedures. But the ingredient listing alone, without *kashrut* certification, cannot be used to determine whether the product is kosher. Some factors which could cause a seemingly innocent product to be non-kosher are:

☐ A food may be processed in a factory where non-kosher products are also prepared and the same machinery is used for both. The food produced in such a factory is non-kosher, unless a reliable *mashgiach* supervises the *kashering* of this equipment.

☐ Many additives used to enhance the flavor, texture and color of food are not kosher. Their names are often technical or vague (e.g. "natural flavors"), with the result that we do not know exactly what they are. All additives must also be processed on kosher equipment for the product to be kosher. (For further discussion of additives, see below.)

☐ Only "ingredients" must appear on the label. Processing agents, release agents, and other substances, often of animal origin, are technically not considered "ingredients" and usually are not listed. For example, oils and fats used to coat the pans for baked goods are not listed as ingredients and are often not kosher.

☐ Oils or shortening must be certified kosher and *pareve*. According to government standards, an ingredient may be listed as vegetable oil or shortening even when containing a small percentage of animal fat.

☐ Not all ingredients are necessarily listed. If an ingredient falls below a certain percentage of the content, the government does not require it to be listed on the label.

☐ The ingredients of a product may have been slightly altered, yet the manufacturer is allowed to continue using the same labels until new ones are printed.

☐ Manufacturers of certain products, such as ice cream, are not required to list ingredients at all, and therefore may list them selectively.

☐ Israeli products, which need special supervision (see Food From Israel, page 27), are often used by large companies. We would never be aware of their presence simply by reading the label.

How Food Technology Affects Kashrut

We can see from the preceding examples that our foods are often not one hundred percent what they appear to be. Even "pure apple juice" or "pure apple cider," with "no artificial ingredients or additives," may not be kosher. Apple juice is a good example of what may happen to a "natural" product when nature meets technology, so we will explore it in further detail.

"Pure apple juice" generally has gelatin (made from the skin, cartilage, bones and meat of non-kosher animals) added to remove the pectin from the juice and to give it a clear appearance. The pectin attaches itself to the gelatin and both are filtered out. *Kashrut* problems can arise in the filtering method or if the juice is heated before filtering. Even a "cloudy" juice, which would seem to indicate that no clarifying agent has been added, sometimes indicates the opposite: the gelatin has been added, but not totally removed, in order to give it a "natural" appearance.

In addition, the FDA (Food and Drug Administration) currently approves a number of different food colorings. Many are of natural origin, including fairly common red dyes derived from insects — which may be completely "natural" but are not kosher. Nutritional additives such as proteins, amino acids or vitamins may also be non-kosher or render a *pareve* product dairy. For example,

some tuna fish is made dairy by virtue of the type of protein added. When buying tuna, be sure it bears a reliable *hechsher*. One must still carefully examine the list of ingredients to be sure that no dairy ingredients are included. Sometimes, but not always, dairy products are marked with a "D" next to the *hechsher*.

These few examples should provide us with ample reason to insist upon reliable *kashrut* certification when shopping for food, even for foods considered "natural."

Staying Informed: It is more important than ever for the kosher consumer to be aware of new information, because changes in *kashrut* supervision and in food production occur almost daily.

Sometimes these changes are misleading to the consumer. A manufacturer, for example, may change a product's ingredients and yet keep the same label with its *kashrut* symbol. *Kashrut* agencies often remove or add their certification. Mistakes are sometimes made in the labeling of ingredients, indicating, for example, that a product is *pareve* when it is really dairy, or vice versa.

To keep up to date in the complex world of *kashrut* one should keep in touch with those who are knowledgeable and also read some of the magazines or newsletters devoted to keeping the public informed in matters of *kashrut* supervision.

SPECIAL KASHRUT REQUIREMENTS

The following paragraphs outline special requirements for kosher wine, milk products, baked goods, and food from Israel. Many commercially prepared products also fall under the category of cooked foods, which has its own set of special *kashrut* requirements. It is particularly important that all of these products bear a reputable *hechsher*.

Companies owned and operated by *kashrut*-observant Jews are likely to be the most stringent in upholding these special requirements. In the case of nationally-known *hechsherim*, the standards vary widely. The best policy is to look for the most widely-respected *hechsher* on the foods that are available.

Wine and Grape Products

Wine, more than any other food or drink, represents the holiness and separateness of the Jewish people. It is used for the sanctification of Shabbat and Yom Tov and at Jewish *simchot*. In the *Beit Hamikdash* wine was poured upon the Altar together with the sacrifice.

However, since wine was and still is used in many forms of idolatrous worship, it has a unique status in Jewish Law, which places extra restrictions on the making and handling of wine. This includes wine used for non-ceremonial purposes.

The production and handling of kosher wine must be done exclusively by Jews. Wine, grape juice, and all products containing wine or grape juice must remain solely in Jewish hands during the manufacturing process and also after the seal of the bottle has been opened. We are not allowed to drink any wine or grape juice, or any drink containing wine or grape juice, which has been touched by a non-Jew after the seal of the bottle has been opened.

Yayin Mevushal: (Boiled Wine). Kosher wine (or grape juice) which has been boiled prior to the bottling process is called *yayin mevushal*. In the time of the *Beit Hamidash*, boiling wine rendered it unfit to be brought upon the Altar.

Yayin mevushal is not considered "sacramental wine" and is therefore not included in the prohibition against being handled by non-Jews. This wine must, as with all kosher wines, bear a reliable *hechsher* and it should say *yayin mevushal*.

A wide variety of domestic and imported kosher wines under reliable supervision has been added to the sweet Concords traditionally associated with kosher wines. Many of these wines are *yayin mevushal*, as indicated on the label. Whether for *Kiddush*, dining, or a *simchah*, you are sure to find a fine kosher wine to suit your taste.

Grape Ingredients In Processed Foods: All liquids produced from fresh or dried grapes, whether alcoholic or non-alcoholic, such as grape juice and wine vinegar, are in the same category as wine in Jewish Law. Therefore, foods with grape flavoring or additives must always have a reliable *hechsher*; examples are jam, soda, popsicles, candy, juice-packed fruit, fruit punch, and lemonade.

Alcoholic drinks such as cognac and brandy have wine bases. Liqueurs and blended whiskeys are often blended with wine. All such beverages require *kashrut* supervision, as does herring in wine sauce.

Cream of tartar is made from wine sediment and needs Rabbinical supervision.

Baked Goods

All baked goods must have reliable *kashrut* certification. Some bakeries in Jewish communities carry the certification from a local Orthodox Rabbi or the *kashrut* board in that city.

In addition, bread, cake and other baked goods from a Jewish bakery with reliable *kashrut* certification often ensures not only the *kashrut* of these products but also that they are *pat Yisrael*. It is preferable to use *pat Yisrael* products whenever possible. This means that a Jewish person has baked or assisted in the baking of the products. Even if he simply lit the oven he is considered as having assisted.

Non-commercial bread and cake that is completely baked by an individual non-Jew is called *pat akum* and may not be eaten.

Under certain circumstances, baked goods prepared with kosher ingredients in a non-Jewish bakery (not by an individual) may be permitted. Such bread is called *pat palter*. The conditions under which *pat palter* may be used are 1) that the bakery is under reliable Rabbinic supervision to ensure that the ingredients, utensils and all substances coming in contact with the food are kosher, and that 2) comparable *pat Yisrael* baked goods are unavailable. Many packaged baked goods sold in supermarkets are *pat palter*, even if certified kosher.

For spiritual reasons, many Jews do not use *pat palter* even in cases where it is permitted. All should avoid its use during the days between Rosh Hashanah and Yom Kippur. A *hechsher* on packaged baked goods does not mean the product is *pat Yisrael* unless it is labeled as such. NOTE: Commercial breads often contain milk or milk derivatives; check the label to make sure it states that the product is *pareve*. If bread is dairy, even if it is known to be kosher, there are various problems involved which make it necessary to consult an Orthodox Rabbi.

For more information on the *kashrut* of baked goods, see pages 37 and 343.

Cooked Foods

Certain foods which were completely cooked by a non-Jew (*bishul akum*) may not be eaten, even if the foods are kosher and are cooked in kosher utensils.

Foods that generally come under the category of *bishul akum* are: 1) Foods that cannot be eaten raw, such as meat or grains. (This excludes foods that can be eaten either cooked or raw, such as apples or carrots.) 2) Foods that are considered important, "fit to set upon a king's table." There are various opinions regarding what are considered "royal foods."

The way the food is prepared (boiled, steamed, pickled, etc.) can also affect its status regarding these laws.

If a Jew has supervised and assisted in the cooking of these foods, such as by lighting the fire of the oven or stirring the food, such food is considered *bishul Yisrael* and is permitted.

These laws affect many commercially prepared foods. Some supervising services write the words *bishul Yisrael* on their *hechsher*. One should consult an Orthodox Rabbi for further clarification. These laws must also be kept in mind when enlisting the help of a non-Jewish housekeeper or cook.

Dairy Products

Jewish law requires that in the production of dairy products, a *mashgiach* or Jewish supervisor must be present from the beginning of the milking to the end of processing to ensure that only milk from kosher animals is used. Where supervised milk is unavailable, some Rabbinic authorities permit government inspection as sufficient assurance (although not in all countries). All agree, however, that actual supervision is preferable. Milk with such supervision is known as *chalav Yisrael*.

Jewish tradition stresses the importance of using *chalav Yisrael* products exclusively, and emphasizes that using non-*chalav Yisrael* dairy products can have an adverse spiritual effect. Even when *chalav Yisrael* is very difficult to obtain, many people, aware of its positive effect on a Jew's spiritual sensitivity, go out of their way to acquire these products. Certainly, where they are readily available, one is required by Jewish Law to use these products exclusively.

Food From Israel

Several Torah commandments involving agricultural practices in the Land of Israel apply even when the products are exported to other countries. Recent articles report that Israel exports over 7 billion dollars worth of agricultural products per year, all subject to the Torah's agricultural laws.

Any food from Israel, whether fresh or packaged, requires a reliable *hechsher*. Israeli produce has become common in American supermarkets. Jaffa oranges are the most famous, but one can also find Israeli tomatoes and other produce. Packaged and processed foods from Israel such as crackers, soups, and candies are also widely available. All of these foods must comply with the following agricultural laws:

T'rumah and Ma'aser: *Gifts for those who served in the Holy Temple.* When the Jewish people settled in the land of Israel, eleven tribes received a portion of land as an inheritance. The twelfth tribe, Levi, comprised of *Levi'im* and *Kohanim*, did not receive portions of land. Their lives were to be devoted to serving G-d in the Holy Temple, not to working the land. The other tribes, known collectively as Israelites, were commanded to give to the tribe of Levi the "first fruits of corn, of thy wine, and of thine oil, and the first of the fleece of thy sheep." (Deuteronomy 28:4)

By giving a portion of the land's produce to the *Kohanim* and *Levi'im*, living representatives of G-d and the Torah, the Jews made tangible the concept that material possessions must be used in the service of spiritual life.

In addition, a certain percentage of the crops were to be designated for the poor (*ma'aser oni*) and a certain part to be eaten only in Jerusalem (*ma'aser sheni*).

Even today, fruits, vegetables, and grains grown in the Land of Israel are subject to the laws of *t'rumah* and *ma'aser*. Although these special portions are no longer consumed, the food may not be eaten until the portions of *t'rumah* and *ma'aser* are separated. Consult an Orthodox Rabbi for practical guidance in applying these laws.

Shmittah: *A year of rest for the land.* Every seventh year in the Land of Israel is a "sabbatical" year for the land, just as every seventh day is a Sabbath day for each individual Jew: "You may plant your land for six years and gather its crops. But during the seventh year, you must leave it alone and withdraw from it. The needy among you will then be able to eat from your fields just as you do..." (Exodus 23:10-11)

Farmers in Israel who observe the *shmittah* year proclaim their faith in G-d, Who promised to give a blessing in the sixth year so that their needs would be more than met in the seventh. No food may be grown or cultivated during this year, and all poor or needy people are welcome to collect any crops remaining in the fields. It is forbidden to eat food grown by a Jew in Israel during the *shmittah* year,

Orlah: *The fruit of young trees.* Fruit which has grown in the first three years of a tree's existence is called *orlah* and may not be used. Even in the fourth year certain restrictions apply. A *hechsher* is therefore necessary on fruit from Israel. However, for fruit grown outside of Israel, only that fruit which is definitely known to be *orlah* is prohibited.

FOOD ESTABLISHMENTS REQUIRING SUPERVISION

Eating only kosher food when visiting, dining out, vacationing or traveling is, of course, just as important as eating kosher at home. Food, wherever it is eaten, has an affect on the *neshamah* (soul). Therefore, we must be very careful to patronize only those food establishments which conform to our expectations and standards of *kashrut*. Acquaintances and friends may not always understand our unwillingness to eat in all restaurants, but most people will respect us for upholding our principles.

Restaurants, Caterers And Hotels

When food is prepared in large quantities with many different ingredients, and a number of people are working in the kitchen, the task of maintaining high standards of *kashrut* is greatly enlarged. Add to this the pressure of commercial considerations, and the need for *hashgachah* (*kashrut* supervision) becomes apparent. A *mashgiach* (*kashrut* supervisor) is essential and may be required to be on the premises at all times.

The *mashgiach* must be present to check all products brought into the establishment, and must also be present during the preparation of the food. Before you dine out, find out who is responsible for the *kashrut* of the premises. Trustworthy kosher establishments are always willing to answer your questions about the *kashrut* of their restaurant or service.

The proprietor should be a Shabbat observer, for Shabbat observance is a criterion often used to determine a person's commitment to the Torah and its laws. If the establishment is a hotel, or a restaurant kept open for the purpose of serving holiday meals, the reservations and payment must be taken before the Shabbat or holiday begins.

Meat Restaurants: Like all commercial food manufacturers, meat restaurants require proper supervision. A reliable *mashgiach* is a necessity. All laws pertaining to kosher meat (*shechitah*, permissible cuts, salting, *treibering* and separation from dairy) must be strictly observed.

In addition, incoming food orders must be strictly supervised in order to prevent the use of foods which are non-kosher or dairy. Further, personnel involved in handling the food require careful supervision because they may not be fully aware of the special requirements of kosher meat. Most meat restaurants also serve fish which, besides having its own special *kashrut* requirements, may not be mixed with meat. A reliable *mashgiach* is a necessity.

For more information on the *kashrut* of meat and fowl, see page 185. For the laws of the separation of meat and dairy, see page 18.

Vegetarian and Dairy Restaurants: Do not assume that a restaurant is kosher simply because it does not serve meat. In addition to the requirements for a *mashgiach* and for Shabbat and Yom Tov observance, any of the following may cause problems in a vegetarian restaurant:

□ All fish must be kosher; otherwise the pots, dishes, dishwashers, etc. become non-kosher, and foods prepared in such utensils may not be eaten.

□ All *pareve* and dairy ingredients must also be kosher in order to maintain the *kashrut* of utensils and all other foods. All oil or shortening used must be made of pure vegetable products and be Rabbinically approved.

□ Certain vegetables and grains must be carefully washed and checked for insects and worms. Eggs must be inspected for blood spots.

□ Food which is usually not eaten raw, and which was prepared for consumption entirely by a non-Jew, is not permitted even if cooked in kosher utensils. Such food is called *bishul akum*. If a Jew assists, such as only by lighting the flame, the food is not *bishul akum* and may be eaten.

Airlines: Most airlines will readily arrange, upon request, a pre-packaged kosher meal at no extra cost. When making your reservation, be sure the kosher meal has a reliable *hechsher.* The food must be brought to you complete with its wrappers still sealed. It may not be warmed in the airplane's oven once the original wrapper is removed, and may not be handled with non-kosher utensils.

Experienced kosher travelers find that it is wise to call the airline the day before the flight to confirm your request for a kosher meal. Even with these precautions, it is advisable to pack some carry-on snack food just in case.

Hospitals: Most hospitals have available, or are willing to obtain, pre-packaged kosher meals like the ones served by airlines. Again, the food must be warmed in its original wrapper and be brought to you still sealed. The nursing staff will often be quite helpful and may allow you to keep some food in the refrigerator. This food should be clearly marked and sealed.

Some hospitals even have kosher kitchens. It is important to ensure that there is *kashrut* supervision. Often a *mashgiach* is available on the premises and will be ready to answer your questions.

Blessings on Food

"*Blessed are You L-rd our G-d, King of the Universe... Who brings forth bread from the earth... Who creates various kinds of sustenance... Who creates the fruit of the vine...of the tree...of the earth... by Whose word all things came to be.*"

With these words, recited before eating any type of food, we express gratitude to the Creator for the manifold blessings He bestows upon us for our sustenance. These blessings are our recognition that the earth and its fullness belong to G-d. After acknowledging this fact, we may then enjoy the bounty and riches of the land.

These blessings are not mere verbalizations, but are an essential part of our spiritual service. Saying a blessing, a distinctly human ability, is an opportune moment to meditate on G-d's greatness as provider and Creator. This moment of spiritual awareness, represented by saying the blessing, transforms the commonplace activity of eating into a holy act.

Chassidic teachings explain that all food contains a G-dly spark of holiness. When we say a blessing before eating, and eat with the intention to serve G-d, we actually elevate the physical substance of the food into holiness. This holy spark, which is inherent in the food, becomes reunited with its Divine source.

Six different *brachot* (blessings) correspond to the various categories of food. They belong to the type of blessing called *bircat ha'nehenin* (blessings of pleasure) which are required before we derive physical pleasure from G-d's creations.

Children, from the time they are old enough to speak, are taught to say blessings over food. In this way, we nurture in them a sense of appreciation for G-d's bounty.

After we eat, we must also remember G-d as the ultimate source of our sustenance, as the Torah commands: "And you shall eat and be satisfied and you shall bless *Hashem*, your G-d, for the good land which He has given you." (Deuteronomy 8:10)

This command was given to the Jews prior to entering the Land of Israel, after wandering in the desert, where G-d sustained them with the miraculous manna. Even in times of great prosperity, when we might be tempted to delude ourselves into believing that our wealth is due only to our own efforts, we are reminded through the blessings to acknowledge G-d's mercy.

BLESSINGS BEFORE EATING

Before partaking of any food, a *brachah rishonah* (preceding blessing), is said. There are six different blessings, each beginnning with the same words, BA-RUCH A-TAH A-DO-NOI ELO-HAI-NU ME-LECH HA-O-LAM, *Blessed are You, L-rd our G-d, King of the Universe,* and concluding with a few words related to the type of food eaten. Following is a transliteration, and translation of each Hebrew blessing, with examples of foods requiring that blessing.

I. BA-RUCH A-TAH A-DO-NOI ELO-HAI-NU ME-LECH HA-O-LAM HA-MO-TZI LE-CHEM MIN HA-A-RETZ.
Blessed are You, L-rd our G-d, King of the Universe, Who brings forth bread from the earth.

Examples: bread, bagels, challah, matzah, pita and rolls made from any of the following five grains: wheat, barley, rye, oat or spelt.
NOTE: Many of the above foods, especially bag-

els, pita and rolls, may require a blessing of *mezonot*, depending upon their ingredients. (See Regarding ''Mezonot'' Bread, page 60.)

2. BA-RUCH A-TAH A-DO-NOI
ELO-HAI-NU ME-LECH HA-O-LAM
BO-RAI MI-NAI ME-ZO-NOT.
Blessed are You, L-rd our G-d, King of the Universe, Who creates various kinds of sustenance.
Examples: cakes, cereals, cookies, cupcakes, doughnuts, and pasta — if made of one or more of the five grains listed under the first blessing.

3. BA-RUCH A-TAH A-DO-NOI
ELO-HAI-NU ME-LECH HA-O-LAM
BO-RAI PRI HA-GA-FEN.
Blessed are You, L-rd our G-d, King of the Universe, Who creates the fruit of the vine.
Examples: wine and grape juice.

4. BA-RUCH A-TAH A-DO-NOI
ELO-HAI-NU ME-LECH HA-O-LAM
BO-RAI PRI HA-AITZ.
Blessed are You, L-rd our G-d, King of the Universe, Who creates the fruit of the tree.

Examples: all fruits from permanent trees, such as apples, oranges, and peaches, even if these fruits are dried; also grapes, raisins, and all nuts, except peanuts which are a legume.

5. BA-RUCH A-TAH A-DO-NOI
ELO-HAI-NU ME-LECH HA-O-LAM
BO-RAI PRI HA-A-DA-MAH.
Blessed are You, L-rd our G-d, King of the Universe, Who creates the fruit of the earth.

Examples: all vegetables and greens from the ground, peanuts, legumes, and some fruits such as bananas, melons, and pineapples.

6. BA-RUCH A-TAH A-DO-NOI
ELO-HAI-NU ME-LECH HA-O-LAM
SHE-HA-KOL NI-H'YAH BI-D'VA-RO.
Blessed are You, L-rd our G-d, King of the Universe, by Whose word all things came to be.

Examples: candy, dairy, eggs, fish, liquids, meat, mushrooms and everything else which is not included in the first five blessings above.
NOTE: The above blessings apply to foods in their basic form; however, the blessings may vary when the form is changed through processing, or when foods are combined.

Some Basic Laws

The rules of blessings on foods are intricate, requiring careful study. Following are some of the most basic rules. In addition to knowing the correct blessings to say over various foods, many other laws apply.

☐ A blessing is required whenever eating even a small amount of food.

☐ Before beginning to say a blessing, one should know the correct blessing to say.

☐ The food over which the blessing is being said should be held in the right hand (if the person is right-handed) at the time of the blessing.

☐ Do not talk from the moment of beginning a blessing until swallowing the first bite.

☐ As the name of G-d is mentioned in each blessing, and we are not allowed to say G-d's name in vain, we should never say a blessing unnecessarily. However, when teaching blessings to a child, one may pronounce G-d's name if necessary.

☐ Answer *Amen* immediately after hearing a blessing being concluded by another person. (Do not say *Amen* after your own blessing.)

''SHEHECHIYANU'' A *Special Seasonal Blessing*:
BA-RUCH A-TAH A-DO-NOI
ELO-HAI-NU ME-LECH HA-O-LAM
SHE-HECH-I-YA-NU V'KI-MA-NU
V'HI-GI-YA-NU LI-Z'MAN HA-ZEH.
Blessed are You, L-rd our G-d, King of the Universe, Who has granted us life, sustained us and enabled us to reach this occasion.

This blessing is said the first time each year one eats a fruit or vegetable which is seasonal, i.e., one which grows only at a certain time of the year. The *shehechiyanu* should preferably be said before the regular blessing on the fruit, although some have the custom to say it afterwards. A *shehechiyanu* is said only if the fruit is ripe. Examples of seasonal fruits over which one can say this blessing: kiwi, fresh figs or dates, pomegranates, cherries, tangerines, cantaloupes, and strawberries.
NOTE: This blessing is also said the first time a *mitzvah* is done each year, such as lighting the Chanukah candles, reading the *Megillah* on Purim, and taking the *lulav* and *etrog* on Sukkot.

When Eating A Meal With Bread

The blessing *hamotzi*, said at the beginning of a meal, is inclusive and exempts one from saying additional blessings over the other foods eaten at the meal. (For exceptions, see below.)
Washing One's Hands: Before eating bread it is necessary to wash the hands ritually. When washing the hands in this manner, be sure the hands are clean and free of rings or anything else which might intervene between the fingers and the flow of water. It is preferable to use a special

two-handled cup, although any large cup can be used. The water is poured first on the right hand, two or three times according to one's custom, then on the left hand for the same number of times. If one will be eating at least two ounces of bread, one says the blessing:

BA-RUCH A-TAH A-DO-NOI
ELO-HAI-NU ME-LECH HA-O-LAM
A-SHER KID-SHA-NU B'MITZ-VO-TAV
V'TZI-VA-NU AL N'TI-LAT YA-DA-YIM.
*Blessed are You, L-rd our G-d, King of the
Universe, Who has sanctified us with His
commandments and commanded us concerning
the washing of the hands.*

Then rub the hands together and dry them. After drying the hands, say the blessing *hamotzi* over the bread. Do not speak or engage in other activities between washing the hands and saying the blessing.

Other Blessings During The Meal: After the blessing of *hamotzi* is said, do not say blessings on the other foods in the meal, with the following exceptions:

□ A blessing is said on wine, unless the meal was preceded by *Kiddush*.

□ A blessing is required for some *mezonot* desserts, depending on the ingredients. Consult an Orthodox Rabbi for guidance.

□ A blessing is said on all other desserts (e.g. ice cream, compote).

If in doubt, one can first say *Bircat Hamazon* (Grace After A Meal) and then eat the dessert, saying the appropriate blessings before and after the dessert.

After concluding a meal in which at least one ounce of bread was eaten, we say *Bircat Hamazon*. NOTE: Some breads and rolls require the blessing *mezonot* because of their ingredients. See Regarding "Mezonot" Bread, page 60, for the many *halachic* factors concerning these breads.

**Blessings
Before
Various
Foods
Without
Bread**

Whether eating a snack or a complete meal without bread, one must be aware of and know the appropriate manner in which to say blessings over individual foods.

□ When eating several different foods in the same category, say only one blessing. For example, when eating apples, oranges, and peaches, say only one blessing *ha-aitz*. The blessing is made over the preferred item, with the intention of including all foods of that category.

□ When eating several foods from different categories, say a separate blessing over each type of food. For example: *mezonot* on crackers, *ha-adamah* on coleslaw, *shehakol* on eggs.

Order Of Blessings: When one is eating foods requiring different blessings, the priority of the blessings is as follows: 1) *mezonot*; 2) *ha-gafen*; 3) *ha-aitz*; 4) *ha-adamah*; 5) *shehakol*. For example, first say *mezonot* on crackers and then *ha-aitz* on grapes; or *ha-adamah* on celery and then *shehakol* on milk.

Two exceptions are:

1. On Shabbat and Yom Tov, *Kiddush* over wine precedes the blessing over bread or cake.

2. When eating foods requiring the blessing of *ha-aitz* and *ha-adamah*, such as an apple and a banana, say the blessing over the preferred food first.

□ After saying the blessing *borai pri hagafen* over wine, additional blessings before and after other liquids or drinks are not necessary.

Blessings On Combined Foods: When a dish contains different kinds of food from different blessing categories mixed together, the following criteria apply:

□ If one food is clearly the main food, then even though many other types are combined, a blessing is made over the main food only. For

example, for tuna salad with vegetable bits added, the blessing is said over the tuna.

□ If the different foods are equally important, then the blessing is made on the one that constitutes the majority of the dish.

□ When foods contain *mezonot* ingredients, the *mezonot* is considered the main ingredient even if it is the minority ingredient. The blessing *mezonot* is then said over the entire dish and includes the other ingredients. Examples are fruit pie and macaroni and cheese.

□ If the *mezonot* ingredient is present only for the sake of binding, thickening, or adding color, the blessing is determined by the other ingredients. An example is, flour added to thicken soup.

When Food Is In Changed Form: Most juices and totally strained or ground foods require the blessing *shehakol*. However, if the food still resembles its original form and is conventionally eaten in such a manner, we say the blessing which would be made over the food in its raw form, such as *ha-aitz* on chunky applesauce.

When In Doubt As To The Correct Blessing: The following options apply:

□ Wash hands ritually and eat bread, saying *hamotzi*. The food in question may then be eaten during the course of the meal. If the food over which there is a question is a fruit, then at least the first bite should be eaten in the same mouthful with the bread.

□ If in doubt as to which of two blessings should be said over a particular food, you can first eat a bite of two different foods, one for each blessing, having in mind also the food in question. Then that food may be eaten.

□ If one said the blessing *shehakol* instead of

the specific blessing that applies to a particular food, then one has fulfilled the requirement for saying the blessing. However, this alternative may be used only if there are varying opinions among *halachic* authorities as to the proper blessing for this food. One must make an effort to know the correct blessings to say.

BLESSINGS AFTER EATING

After eating at least a *k'zayit* of food (approximately 1 ounce) or a *revi'it* of liquid (approximately four ounces), a *bracha acharonah* (after-blessing) is said. After-blessings should be said as soon as possible after one finishes eating. There are three different after-blessings. The text of these can be found in any *siddur* (prayer book).

In order to say the after-blessing, the above-mentioned minimum amount of food must be eaten within approximately six minutes. If it takes longer, such as when slowly sipping a hot drink, it is questionable whether one is allowed to recite the after-blessing. Consult an Orthodox Rabbi for the relevant laws.

Borai Nefashot

This brief blessing is said after eating a variety of foods.

☐ It is said after eating one or more foods belonging to the categories of *ha-aitz* (fruit), *ha-adamah* (vegetables), and *shehakol*.

☐ When more than one food requiring *Borai Nefashot* is eaten at one sitting, the after-blessing is said only once. For example: meat and vegetables, potato chips and milk, coffee and eggs.

Bircat M'ain Shalosh

Bircat M'ain Shalosh is a short paragraph with variations in wording that adapt it to the following three categories:

☐ "*Al hamichya*", is said after foods made of any of the five grains - wheat, barley, rye, oat, spelt;

☐ "*Al hagafen*" is said after wine and grape juice;

☐ "*Al ha-aitz*" is said after one or more of the five fruits with which Israel is blessed - grapes, figs, pomegranates, olives or dates.

When more than one of these foods is eaten, the after-blessing is said only once, incorporating the appropriate sections as indicated in the prayerbook. On Shabbat, Yom Tov, or *Rosh Chodesh*, an additional sentence mentions the special day.

If a food or foods requiring the after-blessing of *Borai Nefashot* are eaten along with those requiring *Bircat M'ain Shalosh*, then *Bircat M'ain Shalosh* is said before *Borai Nefashot*.

Two exceptions are:

☐ After drinking wine and other liquids, say only the after-blessing on wine. *Borai Nefashot* need not be said for the other liquids.

☐ After eating one or more of the five fruits of Israel together with other fruits, say only the after-blessing on the fruits of Israel.

Bircat M'ain Shalosh should be said sitting, immediately after eating, in the same place where one ate.

Bircat Hamazon (Grace After A Meal)

This special blessing is said after concluding a meal in which a *k'zayit* (approximately 1 ounce) of bread was eaten. It contains several paragraphs originally instituted by some of our great Sages thanking G-d for giving us food. No other after-blessing need be said. Saying *Bircat Hamazon* is known as *bentching*, from the Yiddish word *bentch*, to bless.

☐ *Bircat Hamazon* should be recited seated at the same place where one ate, unless at the time of saying *hamotzi* one intended to complete the meal elsewhere.

☐ Before saying *Bircat Hamazon*, men should rinse the fingertips and lips slightly. The water used for this is called *mayim achronim* (final waters). This may be done at the sink, but is often done at the table, using a special vessel. The water should be removed from the table before beginning the *Bircat Hamazon*.

☐ When three or more men over the age of *Bar Mitzvah* recite *Bircat Hamazon* together, this is known as a *mezuman*. A short introductory paragraph is recited.

☐ On Shabbat, Yom Tov, Chanukah, Purim and *Rosh Chodesh*, there are special additions inserted in the *Bircat Hamazon*.

Challah
and Bread

Bread, fresh from the oven, fills the house with a tantalizing aroma, evoking warm feelings of home, hearth and family. Before Shabbat, golden braided challah loaves hint at the culinary and spiritual delights to come.

The busy homemaker will find that challah and bread baking is easier than ever in the modern kitchen. Mixers and dough hooks help cut down the time and effort involved, while a freezer allows you to begin the process in one session and finish it at another. The baking hints that follow provide all the information that both the neophyte and the experienced baker need to produce delicious challahs from the recipes in this section.

Baking bread in a uniquely Jewish way, we perform the special *mitzvah* of *hafrashat challah* - the commandment to separate a small portion of the dough, called *challah*. It recalls the time when this *challah* portion was given to the *Kohanim*, descendants of Aharon who were responsible for the service performed in the *Beit Hamikdash*.

Although we no longer give the *challah* portion to the *Kohanim*, we must still observe the *mitzvah* by removing a piece of the dough before baking. We then burn the piece of dough because it is no longer ours, and we may not derive any benefit from it.

Challah is taken from a dough when several require-ments are met. These relate to the type and amount of flour used and the liquid content of the dough.

Separating *challah* is one of the three *mitzvot* entrusted especially to Jewish women and cherished by them throughout the generations. It highlights one of the many ways a Jew can serve G-d through physical actions in daily life. See The Mitzvah of Separating Challah, page 47, for further information about this commandment.

Challah and bread may not be baked with dairy ingredients unless the loaves are formed into a dis-tinctive shape to ensure that they will not be mistakenly used at a meat meal. Bread used at a meat meal should not be served later with dairy foods or vice versa, since bread is often handled and mixed with other foods during mealtime. It is preferable to bake challah and bread in a *pareve* oven.

When eating bread it is necessary to wash the hands ritually and follow with the blessing of *hamotzi* ("Who brings forth bread..."). After eating bread, or a meal including bread, we conclude with the *Bircat Hamazon* (Grace After A Meal).

The Shabbat Loaves

The word *challah* refers to both the portion of dough

that is separated and to the special braided loaves eaten at Jewish festive meals. This bread has become symbolic of Shabbat itself. Two loaves, a gleaming candelabra, wine and a silver Kiddush cup laid out on an elegant white tablecloth create the timeless setting for the Shabbat and Yom Tov meal.

Why do we use two *challot*? These two loaves remind us of the double portion of *mahn*, manna that the Jews received each Friday during the time they wandered in the desert. After the Jews left Egypt, their supply of *matzah* was soon exhausted. Then G-d Himself sent each family a daily portion of manna, "bread from heaven."

Our ancestors were fortunate to receive a powerful reminder each day that man is dependent on G-d for his daily sustenance. On Friday they received a double portion of manna, for on Shabbat they were not allowed to gather any at all.

When the manna (which yielded any taste desired by the person eating it) fell to the ground, it was protected by a layer of dew above and a layer of dew beneath. This is one reason that the challah rests on a tablecloth and is covered with a special cloth, the *challah deckel*. From the Biblical description of the manna it seems to have resembled whitish poppy seeds. Many people therefore sprinkle the top of their *challot* with poppy seeds before baking them.

The challah loaves are often shaped into six-stranded braids so that the total number of strands equals twelve. This recalls yet another miracle, one which took place both in the Mishkan, the Sanctuary, the Jews carried with them in the desert, and later in the Beit Hamikdash in Jerusalem. Each week, twelve loaves of bread called "showbread" were placed on special open shelves. A miracle occurred: Despite the fact that every Shabbat when the Kohanim removed these loaves from the shelves, they were as fresh and as warm as when they had been placed there a week earlier.

At our own tables, we begin each Shabbat and Yom Tov meal with the recital of Kiddush, followed by the blessing of *hamotzi* on two whole loaves of challah. Round *challot* in a spiral shape are often used for Rosh Hashanah.

Challah and Bread Baking
Professional Techniques

Baking bread is both a science and an art. The same recipe used by different cooks, or even by the same cook on different days, may result in a different bread. Understanding the various factors that affect the process will ensure a successful baking experience.

INGREDIENTS

☐ YEAST is a living organism needing warmth and water to grow. It makes the dough rise by giving off gas that expands the cells held together by the *gluten*. Sugar speeds up this process; salt slows it down.

☐ SALT inhibits yeast. Too much salt slows its action; too little salt allows the yeast to expand before the flavor has developed. Salt also gives bread a good flavor and acts as a preservative.

☐ SWEETENERS, such as sugar or honey, are food for the yeast. A little bit of sweetener feeds the yeast, while a little more gives a sweet flavor without harming the growth of the yeast. More sugar will make the yeast grow faster, but too much will slow it down. Sweet breads generally require more yeast to compensate for the extra sugar. Sugar will also give a browner crust.

☐ FLOUR is the body of the bread. The amount of flour needed for a particular recipe will vary because the amount of water the flour absorbs is not constant. It will vary according to the weather on the day you are baking, the variety of wheat used, and when the wheat was harvested.

☐ GLUTEN, found in the innermost part of the wheat, holds everything together. The yeast gives off gas that expands the cells. Gluten then holds them in the expanded condition. It is developed by mixing, kneading and rising. Underdeveloped gluten will give a heavier loaf. The amount of gluten in different types of flour is in descending order as follows: gluten flour, bread flour, all purpose white flour, whole-wheat flour, rye flour.

A white flour dough allowed to rise too many times will become light and dry, more like bakery challah. Whole-wheat bread, dense and moist to begin with, becomes lighter with extra rising.

☐ EGGS and OIL add richness to the challah or bread and act as a preservative. They also shorten the gluten strands, giving a more tender texture.

When opening eggs examine each one *before* combing with the recipe to make sure there are no blood spots. If a blood spot is found, discard the egg, and rinse out the cup or dish with cold water.

PREPARING THE DOUGH

☐ Add 1 tablespoon of sugar to a small amount of lukewarm water. Dissolve yeast in the water. Let stand for 8 to 10 minutes.

☐ Add the remaining ingredients according to the recipe. The last four cups of flour should be added gradually, as needed. When using a mixer, follow directions, adding each ingredient into the mixer and beating. If all the flour doesn't fit in the bowl, remove the dough to a larger bowl and continue adding flour. Mix until stiff and smooth.

☐ Place the dough on a well floured board and gather it into a ball. Knead it away from you. Give it a one-quarter turn and knead it again. Continue kneading in this way about five to seven minutes, until the dough feels smooth and elastic. Sprinkle your hands and the board with more flour as necessary. If any dough sticks to the board, scrape it up and add it to the rest of the dough, putting more flour on the board. Use firm but gentle kneading motions, trying not to tear the dough. When it springs back when poked with your finger, the dough is ready to rise.

RISING

Usually, dough is allowed to rise at least twice before being baked. The first rising takes place after the dough is kneaded and before it is shaped into loaves. The following instructions apply to the first rising.

☐ Place the dough in a large, well-oiled bowl, turning over once so that it is completely oiled. Cover bowl with a damp cloth.

☐ For best results, place dough in a warm location, such as the top of the refrigerator, stove, or radiator. Another option is to pre-heat the oven, turn it off, and place bowl on opened oven door.

☐ Dough should be allowed to rise until doubled in bulk, usually 1-2 hours.

SHAPING

The following guidelines apply no matter what shape you plan to use.

☐ When your dough has risen to its proper size according to the recipe you choose, begin cutting off pieces to shape. (Don't forget to separate a piece first. See The Mitzvah of Separating Challah, page 47.)

☐ The amount of dough needed to shape an individual loaf depends on the size of the pan. The dough should be about two-thirds the size of the baked loaf. Since the challah expands a good deal in the baking process, don't let the shaped, raw dough touch the sides of the pan.

☐ Oval-shaped challah and braided challah look best in individual oval-shaped pans. However, if you do not have this size pan you can place them in square pans or on a large baking sheet, spaced well apart to allow for growth.

☐ Round loaves come out best in round, shallow cake pans.

☐ Place 8 to 10 small rolls on a standard cookie sheet, leaving space between them.

☐ Final rising: After shaping, let rise in the pan in a warm place until double in bulk.

GLAZING

A few minutes before putting the dough in the oven, glaze the tops and sides using a small basting brush. Some different glazes are:

> 1 egg yolk
> 1 egg yolk plus 1 teaspoon sugar
> 1 egg yolk plus a few drops of water
> 1 whole egg
> 1 whole egg plus 1 to 1½ teaspoons sugar

In all of these above glazes, beat the egg well before spreading. One egg can glaze quite a few loaves.

After glazing, poppy seeds or sesame seeds may be sprinkled on the loaf.

BAKING METHODS

☐ Bake in a preheated oven at 375° for 35 to 45 minutes. Small loaves take about 20 minutes.

- Another method is to skip the final rising in the pan. Place the dough in a cold oven. Turn temperature to 350° for 50 minutes for large loaves and 20 minutes for rolls.

- To save time and for exceptionally soft challah, do not let loaves rise after they have been shaped. Glaze with eggs and poppy seeds. Place in a preheated 400° oven for 10 to 15 minutes. Lower oven to 350° and bake an additional 30 minutes.

- Loaves are done when they are nicely brown and pull away from the sides of the pan. They should sound hollow when tapped on the bottom. To prevent bottoms from getting soggy, remove the loaves from the pans and cool on a rack.

STORING

- If loaves will not be used immediately, they may be frozen.

- When thoroughly cooled, they should be put in a plastic bag and tightly closed. Care should be taken that they be completely sealed to avoid stale "freezer" taste.

- Large challahs take about 4 to 6 hours to defrost. Small challahs take about 2 hours.

- Heating them in the oven for 10 to 20 minutes gives them a fresh-out-of-the-oven taste, especially when wrapped in aluminum foil.

- If you should forget to defrost the challahs before the meal, don't panic. They can be sliced and set out at the table. Each slice will defrost in about 5 to 10 minutes.

FREEZING UNBAKED DOUGH

Occasionally it is more convenient to prepare dough either many hours or days in advance of the actual baking. For best results:

- The dough should rise once. *Challah* should be separated. The loaves should then be shaped, carefully placed in plastic bags and sealed well.

- Place the loaves carefully in freezer on a flat surface to allow them to freeze straight. Once loaves have frozen solid they can be stacked.

- To bake, remove from freezer and allow 3 to 6 hours for defrosting and rising depending on size of *Challahs*.

- Remove from plastic bags and place on a greased baking sheet.

- Cover with a cloth and allow to rise until doubled.

- Glaze with beaten eggs, sprinkle with poppy or sesame seeds if desired, and bake according to recipe.

HELPFUL HINTS

- To substitute honey for sugar, use half the amount of sweetener.

- Whole-wheat and rye flour give a heavier loaf. If a lighter loaf is desired, mix in white flour or add 1 tablespoon gluten flour for each cup of whole-wheat or rye.

- When adding flour, add the last 4 to 6 cups gradually. Flour absorbs different amounts of water depending on the weather, the type of flour and how it was stored.

- To store yeasted dough that you won't bake in one day, keep leftover dough in the refrigerator. Grease the top of the dough well. Cover with wax paper and then a damp cloth. Keep the cloth damp. Storage time is up to three days. Dough may also be frozen; defrost before shaping or baking.

AVOIDING UNWANTED RESULTS

If your bread or challah doesn't come out just right, one of the following factors may be responsible:

☐ The dough doesn't rise:
The room may be too cool. Place the dough in a warmed oven.
The water for the yeast was too hot or too cold.
The yeast was bad.
There was too much sugar or salt.

☐ The dough rises and then falls:
It may have been allowed to rise too long.
Salt may have been omitted.
Too much yeast was used.

If this happens, re-knead the dough and shape into loaves. It may rise, but even if it doesn't, it will still have a good flavor.

☐ Crust too thick:
Too slow baking at too low temperature.

☐ Loaf too crumbly:
Too much rising or too little rising and kneading.

The Art of Shaping Challah

Whether baking for Shabbat, Yom Tov or a Simchah, the traditional shapes of challah enhance and grace a table. The beauty of a glazed, well-shaped loaf contributes as much to its total effect as its flavor. The following are illustrated, hands-on instructions for shaping challah, from the most basic three-braided to the most complex six-braided.

THREE-BRAIDED CHALLAH ILLUSTRATED

This is the most classic of all challah braids and extremely easy to make. Start braiding from the middle in order to bring more fullness to the loaf.

1 Divide dough into three portions. Roll out each piece into long uniform strands. The pieces should be a bit longer than the pan in which the challah will be baked.
Place three strands side by side.

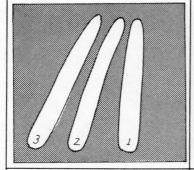

2 The strands will be braided from the center down and the center up.

At the center take the strand on the outer right (#1), cross it over middle strand (#2) and bring it into the middle.

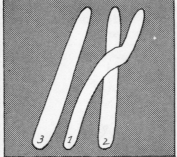

3 Take the one on the outer left (#3), cross it over the middle strip (#1) and let it rest in the middle.

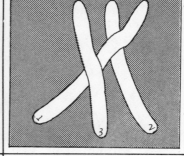

4 Repeat this procedure, alternately bringing the one on the outer right to the middle, and then bringing the one on the outer left to the middle, to the bottom.

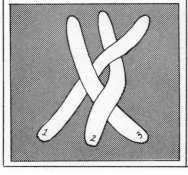

5 Reverse loaf so free ends point downward and finish braiding in the same manner.

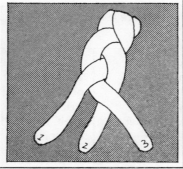

6 Tuck ends under to finish.

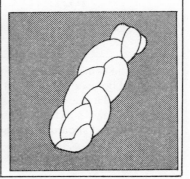

FOUR-BRAIDED CHALLAH ILLUSTRATED

Braiding with four strands is very simple and produces a beautifully full challah.

1 Divide dough into four portions. Roll out each piece into long uniform strands. They should be an inch or so longer than the pan to be used for baking.

2 Place strands side by side and press together at the top.

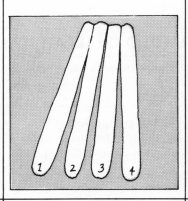

3 Beginning from the left and working to the right, take the outside strand (#1) and weave it over the next strand (#2) and under the next (#3) and over the last on the right.

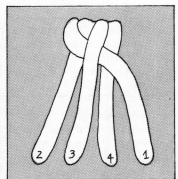

4 To continue, from the left take outside strand (#2) and weave it over the next strand (#3) and under the next (#4) and over the last on the right.

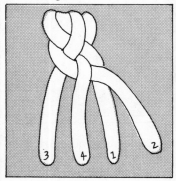

5 Proceed as above weaving each strand once and under other strands until ends of strands are reached. Connect ends and tuck under.

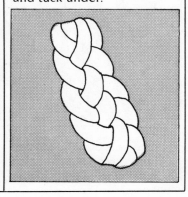

ROUND CHALLAH ILLUSTRATED

A Rosh Hashanah specialty, these challot are quick to make. Knead in raisins to symbolize our wish for a sweet year.

1 Use the same amount of dough that would be used to make a Three-Braid Challah. Roll it out into a long strip approximately 18-inches long by 3-inches wide. One end should be tapered thinner.

2 Place thicker end in center of pan and coil strip around itself. Tuck ends under challah.

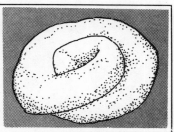

SIX-BRAIDED CHALLAH ILLUSTRATED

Although somewhat complex to explain, the six-braided challah is also relatively simple to make once the technique is mastered. The fullness of the body of the challah and the beauty of its appearance make your efforts worthwhile.

1 TO BEGIN: Divide dough into six portions. Roll out into 12-inch uniform strands. Lay strands next to each other and pinch together at the top. Push three strands on the left (1, 2, & 3) further to the left and push three strands on the right (4, 5, & 6) further to the right.

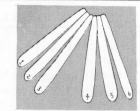

2 TO MAKE FIRST CROSSOVER: With right hand take strand on extreme left (#1), and with left hand take strand on extreme right (#6). (*Left hand is crossed over right hand.*) Moving right and left hands simultaneously bring strand in left hand (#6) over strand in right hand (#1), laying it in the right middle next to strand #4. AT THE SAME TIME strand in right hand (#1) is brought over pinch and above.

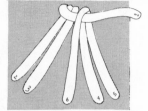

3 NOTE: From now on the right and left sides will have two or three strands alternately with one strand above the others. TO MAKE LEFT CROSSOVER: In right hand take uppermost strand (#1) and in left hand take strand furthest to the right (#5) and bring left hand over and up, across the pinch so that #5 is uppermost above. Bring right hand with strand #1 to left middle next to strand #3. Now right side has two strands left side three and strand #5 is above the left side.

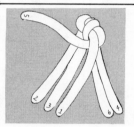

4 TO MAKE RIGHT CROSSOVER: In left hand take uppermost strand (#5) and in right hand take strand further to the left (#2). Bring right hand with strand #2 over and up across the pinch so that strand #2 is uppermost above. Bring left hand with strand #5 down to right middle next to #6.

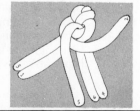

5 REPEATING THE PROCESS: All the steps thereafter take on the same pattern, merely alternating between left and right sides. The right side group has three strips when the left has two. The left side group has three strips when the right has two. The outermost strip of the three-strip side is always placed on top of and beyond the pinch, while the strip which was on top of the pinch is always brought to the innermost place of the two-strip side, thus making it a three-strip side.

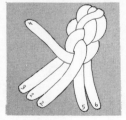

6 COMPLETING THE CHALLAH: To complete challah continue repeating left crossover and right crossover until all strands are finished. Tuck ends under to finish.

SMALL CHALLAHS ILLUSTRATED

Small challahs are very popular. They are made in order to place lechem mishnah *in front of each person making* Kiddush *at the Shabbat table, or in order to place a roll by each setting at a* simchah. *There are various shapes and each roll usually weighs 2 to 3 ounces.*

SMALL BRAID	QUICK TWIST	ROUND

1 Divide dough into three small portions and roll into strands 4 to 6-inches. Braid according to directions for Three Braided Challah (page 43).

1 Roll a piece of dough into a strand 6 to 8-inches long by 1-inch wide. Cross one side over the other with a small hole in the middle.

1 Place a piece of dough weighing about 2-ounces in the palm of your left hand. With right hand, pull sides gently towards you into a pinch at the top. Gently pushing in middle of pinch continue smoothing sides up into top. The sides resting in palm of left hand until bottom is very smooth.

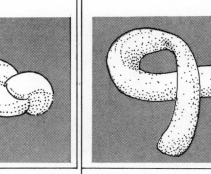

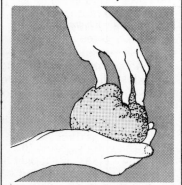

2 Take the tip (about 2-inches) of the upper half and bend it under the lower half and pull up through the hole so that it extends about ½-inch above the top.

2 Turn over so pinch is on bottom and top is a smooth sphere.

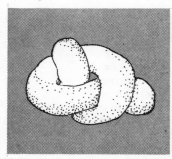

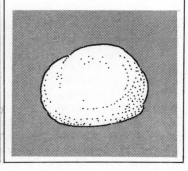

The Mitzvah of Separating Challah

"Separate the first portion of your kneading as a dough offering. . .In future generations, give the first of your kneading as an elevated gift to G-d."

(Numbers 15:30-21)

When the Jewish people first inhabited the Land of Israel, one of the many gifts they were commanded to give to the *Kohanim* (priestly tribe), who served in the *Beit Hamikdash*, was a portion of their dough -- "the first and the best." This gift of food is known as *challah*, from which the name of our Shabbat loaves is derived. Since the destruction of the *Beit Hamikdash*, we may not give this dough to the *Kohanim* of today. However, in remembrance of this gift and in anticipation of the future Redemption and the third *Beit Hamikdash*, we still observe the *mitzvah* of separating the *challah* portion.

The *mitzvah* of *hafrashat challah*, separating *challah*, is one of the three *mitzvot* entrusted especially to the Jewish woman. As the *akeret ha-bayit* (mainstay of the home), the woman not only prepares the physical sustenance for the family, but by observing this *mitzvah*, she imparts a spiritual message as well. The *mitzvah* of *hafrashat challah* embodies the belief that all of our sustenance truly comes to us through G-d's hand. Just as we may not use the bread dough unless we have separated *challah*, so too, a portion of our livelihood is always reserved for the giving of charity, which is given freely -- of "the first and the best."

Observing the *mitzvah* of *hafrashat challah*, our Sages tell us, "will cause a blessing to rest on your house." The woman, so influential in shaping the values and attitudes of her family members, brings blessings upon her home and family through this *mitzvah* and instills faith in G-d within those around her. The *mitzvah* of separating *challah* is symbolic of the entire practice of kashrut, with its emphasis on elevating the physical and mundane to the realm of holiness.

Jewish women have traditionally baked their own challah loaves in preparation for Shabbat and Yom Tov, treasuring the opportunity to perform this special *mitzvah*. This *mitzvah* is especially significant on *erev* Shabbat. Before separating *challah*, many women put a few coins into a *pushka* (charity box) designated for needy Jews, particularly Torah scholars in Israel.

Separating the *challah* portion is easy to do, but an understanding of the measurements and other criteria involved is necessary. Not all dough will require the separation of *challah*. The following paragraphs provide a guide to the requirements for separating *challah*.

A Blessing In The Home

FLOUR AND LIQUID REQUIREMENTS FOR SEPARATING CHALLAH

In regard to separating *challah*, there are three possibilities. One may be required: to separate *challah* with a blessing; to separate *challah* without a blessing; or not to separate *challah* at all. Whether *challah* is to be separated or not depends upon the type of and amount of flour, and liquid contents of the dough.

Type Of Flour: *Challah* is separated when the dough is made of one of, or a combination of, the following five grains: wheat, rye, barley, oat and spelt. Other types of flour such as rice, soy, corn, and buckwheat, when used without "the five grains," do not require the separation of *challah*. If they are used in combination with flour from one of the five grains, consult an Orthodox Rabbi as to the requirements for *hafrashat challah*.

The amount of flour also determines whether or not the separation of *challah* is necessary, and if so, whether a blessing is said, (see Amount of Flour, below).

Liquid Contents: To separate *challah* with a blessing, the majority of the liquid contents of the dough should be water, provided that the flour requirements are met. If the majority of the liquid content is comprised of liquids other than water (such as oil, eggs, honey, etc.), *challah* is separated without a blessing.

In order to take *challah*, even without a blessing, at least some water should be mixed into the dough before the flour and liquid are well mixed together. If the recipe does not call for water, it is *halachically* advisable to add a drop of water.

Amount Of Flour: The amount of flour used determines whether *challah* is separated a) with a blessing, b) without a blessing, or c) whether *challah* is not separated at all. This depends upon the flour's weight. The measurements below, given in grams, are those established by Horav Hagaon Rabbi Avrohom Chaim Noah, of blessed memory.

NOTE: One may not bake with less than the required quantity of flour with the intention of avoiding separation of *challah*. However, if only a small amount of flour from the five grains is available, or the recipe calls for only a small amount of flour, it is not necessary to increase the amount in order to separate *challah*.

Flour Requirements in Grams/ Pounds

A. **Do not separate** *challah* when using flour weighing *less* than: 1230 grams or 2 lbs. 11 oz.

B. **Separate** *challah* **without a blessing** for flour weighing: *between* 1230 and 1666.6 grams or *between* 2 lbs. 11 oz. and 3 lbs. 11 oz.

C. **Separate** *challah* **with a blessing** when using *more* than the following amounts of flour: 1666.6 grams or 3 lbs. 11 oz.

DIAGRAM I - Flour Requirements for Separating Challah

g = grams	2 lb., 11 oz. 1230g		3 lb., 11 oz. 1666.6g	
	DO NOT SEPARATE CHALLAH	SEPARATE CHALLAH WITHOUT A BLESSING		SEPARATE CHALLAH WITH A BLESSING
1000g 1100g 1200g	1300g 1400g 1500g 1600g		1700g 1800g 1900g 2000g	

APPLYING THESE MEASUREMENTS WHEN BAKING

Most recipes give the amount of flour in cups, not weight. Therefore, before using a recipe, one must know how to determine whether or not to separate *challah*.

The best way to determine the amount of flour being used for baking is to weigh it (in a bag or container) on a scale (preferably one with gram measurements).

However, since most cooks find it more practical to deal with the cup equivalents of the required amounts, we have attempted to translate these amounts to cups.

Many factors can affect the results when converting the gram or pound measurements (weight) to cups (volume). Whether or not the flour is sifted is a major factor. Different methods of sifting can produce varying cup measurements due to changes in volume. Whole-grain or high-gluten flours yield different cup equivalents. Seasonal changes, moisture content, and handling can also slightly affect the cup measurements.

Therefore, it is not possible for us to present exact cup equivalents for the flour requirements in Diagram I, but we offer the following suggested methods for applying these measurements in your kitchen.

Practical Methods For Measuring Flour

When using any of the methods, bear in mind that variables, including imprecise kitchen scales and seasonal changes in flour, make it impossible to rely completely on the resulting measurements. It is therefore advisable, when baking, to allow a "margin" by adding or subtracting some flour in order to be certain about whether or not to separate *challah* and whether or not to say the blessing.

Scale Method: If you are unsure whether or not separation of *challah* is required, place the flour being used for baking in a plastic bag, weigh it on a scale, and refer to Diagram I.

Container Method: This requires a one-time use of a scale.

Place an empty container (such as a plastic canister or a jar) on a scale, and note the weight of the container.

Add the type of flour you use to bake challah, and when the flour weighs 1230 grams (2 lbs. 11 oz.) on the scale, mark a line on the container. Up to this line, do not separate *challah*.

Continue to fill the container until the flour weighs 1666.6 grams (3 lbs. 11 oz.). Mark another line. When using amounts of flour up to this line, separate *challah* without a blessing.

When using amounts of flour above the higher mark, separate *challah* with a blessing.

When you bake challah or large quantities of cake, you can measure the flour in this container to determine whether or not to separate *challah*, as long as you use the same type of flour and the same method (sifted or "unsifted") each time. As mentioned above, do not rely completely on your container measurements; either add or subtract some flour so that it is well below or above the lines on the container.

"**Mathematical Calculation**" **Method**: Use a 5 lb. bag of flour, a dry cup measure and a calculator. Using the dry cup measure, count how many cups are in 5 lbs. of flour (2268 grams). Divide 2268 by the number of cups. This equals "grams per cup."

To know the maximum number of cups of flour which can be used without separating *challah*, divide 1230 by your above "gram per cup."

To know how many cups of flour are needed to separate *challah* with a blessing, divide 1666.6 by your above "gram per cup."

When using amounts of flour between the above two figures, separate *challah* without a blessing.

The following measurements are based on repeated kitchen tested experiments with different brands of white all-purpose flour. (Whole grain flours such as whole-wheat, rye, oat, and barley will yield different results.)

Nowadays, most packaged, all-purpose white flour is presifted, as indicated on the package. For practical purposes, we use the term "unsifted" to refer to presifted flour used from the bag, and "sifted" to refer to flour which is resifted at home.

For "unsifted" flour, a dry measure cup was used to scoop flour from the bag; for "sifted" flour, flour was sifted into a large bowl and spooned lightly into the dry measure cup. In both cases, the flour in the cup was leveled. Then, the flour in the cups was weighed in gram measure.

Our experiments resulted in the discovery that the number of cups of flour varied from one 5 lb. bag of flour to another, producing a range of cup measurements rather than a single standard one. Among the many factors which cause these variables are seasonal changes, moisture content of flour, and handling. Therefore, it is not possible for us to give exact cup measurements.

5 lbs. "unsifted" flour yielded a range of 14 1/2 -16 cups.

5 lbs. sifted flour yielded a range of 18 - 20 cups.

Both a scale and mathematical calculations were used to obtain the cup measurements in the diagrams below.

The following diagrams show when A) not to separate *challah*; when B) to separate *challah* without a blessing; and when C) to separate *challah* with a blessing.

The white areas clearly indicate whether or not to separate *challah* and when a blessing should be said.

The gray areas indicate amounts which may fall into one category or another; avoid using this amount of flour if possible. If the recipe calls for that amount of flour the only way to be sure about whether or not to take *challah* is to weigh the flour used. If no scale is available one should separate *challah* without a blessing.

The striped areas indicate 1/4 cup "margins" above and below the required amounts. It is best to avoid these areas to account for slight differences in volume based on how the flour was measured.

Approximate Cup Measurements For White All-Purpose Flour

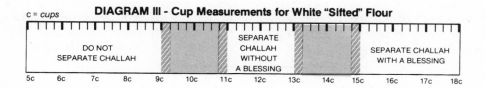

DIAGRAM II - Cup Measurements for White "Unsifted" Flour

DIAGRAM III - Cup Measurements for White "Sifted" Flour

If using the approximate cup measurements as a guide, we recommend the following:

☐ When measuring flour, use a dry measure cup (rather than a liquid measure) cup.

☐ When adding extra flour to achieve the desired consistency or to flour the board, use the measuring cup to keep track of flour being added.

☐ Avoid using "borderline" measurements in the striped areas by allowing a margin of 1/4 cup above or below the determined amount. For example, to be sure that separating *challah* is not required, use no more than 7 1/2 cups "unsifted" flour; to be sure that you are required to separate *challah* with a blessing, use at least 12 cups "unsifted" flour.

Using The Diagrams

HOW TO SEPARATE CHALLAH

Challah is separated after the flour and liquid are well mixed together, while the dough is still whole, before it has been divided and shaped into loaves. Before the piece of dough is separated, the following blessing is said:

BA-RUCH A-TAH A-DO-NOI ELO-HAI-NU
ME-LECH HA-O-LAM A-SHER
KID-SHA-NU B'MITZ-VO-TAV
V'TZI-VA-NU L'HAF-RISH CHAL-LAH.
Blessed are You, L-rd our G-d, King of the Universe, Who has sanctified us with His commandments and commanded us to separate challah.

Then remove a small piece, approximately one ounce, from the dough. Immediately after separating *challah*, (whether or not a blessing is required) say, "*Harai zeh challah*," (this is *challah*).

Today, since we cannot give the *challah* to the Kohanim and since we may not use it ourselves, the prevailing custom is to burn this piece separately (e.g. in a piece of aluminum foil). It should be burned in the oven (preferably, in the broiler). However, if one burns the *challah* inside the oven, it should not be burned at the same time as the loaves or cakes are being baked, or for that matter, when any other food is being cooked in that oven.

NOTE: Although separating *challah* is one of the three *mitzvot* given especially to women, anyone over *Bar* or *Bat Mitzvah* age may also separate *challah* if necessary.

Combining Doughs

When repeating a recipe which calls for less than the required amount of flour, the doughs should be combined after they are mixed, if together they fulfill the requirements for *hafrashat challah*. For example, most mixers do not hold enough dough to require *hafrashat challah*, making it necessary to prepare the dough in two or more batches. These doughs should then be combined, as described below.

All the doughs should be put into one container. Then cover it on top to make it appear as "one dough," making certain that the sides are covered by either the container or the covering. *Challah* is then taken with a blessing from one of the doughs.

Separating Challah After Baking

There are times in which *challah* is separated after baking:

□ If the batter is loose and one cannot separate *challah* prior to baking, such as with many cakes.

□ If one forgot to separate *challah* before baking.

Challah is separated by placing all of the baked loaves or cakes into a box or container, covering with a cloth, and then taking a piece from one of the loaves, saying the blessing when applicable.

This procedure should be completed before using the baked goods.

When Challah May Be Separated On Shabbat or Yom Tov: Ordinarily, one may not separate *challah* on Shabbat or Yom Tov. An exception to this is if one actually kneads and bakes the bread on Yom Tov, in which case it is permitted to separate *challah* on Yom Tov. In this instance, one should set aside the *challah* and burn it after Yom Tov.

However, if one forgets to separate *challah* and becomes aware of the mistake on Shabbat or Yom Tov, it is still possible to use the baked loaves in the following manner: When eating the loaves, a small amount, or slice, should be left over from each loaf. The leftover pieces should be reserved until the conclusion of Shabbat or Yom Tov. A small amount is then removed from each slice of reserved bread (saying the blessing if required), thus fulfilling the *mitzvah* of separating *challah*.

NOTE: On Shabbat or Yom Tov in Israel, if one forgot to separate *challah* one may not use the above method. One must wait until after Shabbat or Yom Tov, to use the bread when *challah* can be separated. If the bread was kneaded and baked on Yom Tov, *challah* may be separated.

Dough That Is Not Used For Bread

Separating Challah When Baking Cakes, Cookies, and Pastries: When baking large amounts of dough other than for bread or challah, the laws of separating *challah* may apply. The types and amounts of flour and liquid are the same as those given for bread.

As water comprises the minority of liquid in most cake recipes, even if the recipe calls for over 1666.6 grams of flour, *challah* is separated without a blessing.

Separating Challah For Cooked Or Fried Dough: If one kneads a dough with the intention of cooking it or frying it (e.g. for noodles or dumplings), *challah* should be separated without a blessing. However, if the dough is kneaded with the intention of baking even part of it, and part of it is in fact baked (even a small amount), then *challah* is separated with a blessing as long as the entire dough meets the minimum requirements.

Challah

Challah freshly baked from the oven fills the air with the fragrance of Shabbat. Throughout the generations, Jewish women have cherished the tradition of baking challah.

BEFORE YOU BEGIN

☐ Before baking, it is very important to know the laws of *hafrashat challah*. See The Mitzvah of Separating Challah, page 47.

☐ The following recipes indicate when *challah* should be taken and if a blessing is said. If you increase or decrease the amount of flour used, or sift the flour, consult the chart of Requirements for Separating Challah, page 48.

☐ For a variety of shapes, glazes, and other baking tips, see Challah and Bread Baking, page 39.

CLASSIC CHALLAH

One of the most universally popular challot to grace the Shabbat and holiday table.

2 ounces fresh yeast or
4 packages dry yeast
3½ cups warm water
¾ cup sugar
1½ Tbsps. salt
13 to 14 cups flour
6 eggs, slightly beaten
1 cup oil

GLAZE
1 egg, beaten
Poppy or sesame seeds

USE: Baking sheets
or loaf pans
YIELDS: 4 to 6 loaves

Dissolve yeast in warm water in a large bowl. When dissolved, add sugar, salt, and half of the flour. Mix well.

Add eggs and oil, then slowly stir in most of the remaining flour — dough will become quite thick. (Until the kneading stage, dough can be mixed in an electric mixer.)

When dough begins to pull away from sides of bowl, turn onto floured board and knead for about 10 minutes. Add only enough flour to make dough manageable. Knead until dough is smooth and elastic and springs back when pressed lighty with fingertip.

Place dough in a large oiled bowl. Turn it so the top is oiled as well. Cover with a damp towel and let rise in a warm place for 2 hours, punching down in four or five places every 20 minutes.

Separate *challah* with a blessing. Divide dough into four to six parts and shape into loaves; place in well-greased bread pans or on greased baking sheet. Let rise until double in bulk.

Preheat oven to 375°.

Brush tops of loaves with beaten egg and sprinkle with poppy or sesame seeds. Bake for 30 to 45 minutes or until browned. Remove from pans and cool on racks.

VARIATIONS
☐ Substitute 1 cup whole-wheat flour and ½ cup wheat germ for equal amounts of regular flour.

☐ Add 2 teaspoons vanilla extract to dough before kneading.

TRADITIONAL CHALLAH

This challah has an unusually smooth taste and texture.

2 ounces fresh yeast and
2 packages dry yeast
1 cup warm water
3 cups boiling water
¾ cup margarine, softened
2 Tbsps. salt
1½ cups sugar
5 eggs
14 to 15 cups flour

GLAZE
1 egg, beaten
Poppy seeds

USE: Baking sheets
or loaf pans
YIELDS: 6 medium challahs

In a small bowl, dissolve both fresh and dry yeast in 1 cup warm water, with one tablespoon of sugar taken from the 1½ cups. Let stand until it foams.

In a large bowl, pour 3 cups boiling water over margarine and stir until margarine is melted. Add salt and sugar. Let cool for a few minutes and beat in eggs. Add the bubbling yeast. Gradually add flour and knead for 10 minutes. If dough is too moist, add a little more flour.

When dough is kneaded, oil the top of the dough, cover, and let rise 1 hour.

Separate *challah* with a blessing. Shape dough and place in greased pans or on baking sheets. Let rise another hour.

Preheat oven to 350°.

Brush loaves with beaten egg to glaze and sprinkle with poppy seeds. Bake 1 hour for large challah, 35 to 40 minutes for medium challahs. Remove from pans and cool on racks.

BASIC CHALLAH

2 packages dry yeast
2½ cups warm water
½ cup honey
1 Tbsp. salt
¾ cup oil
4 eggs
9 cups flour

GLAZE
1 egg yolk, beaten
1 tsp. water
Poppy seeds

USE: Baking sheets
or loaf pans
YIELDS: 3 loaves

Dissolve yeast in water in a large bowl. Add honey and let stand 2 minutes, until yeast foams. Add salt, oil, and eggs and mix well.

Gradually add flour, 2 cups at a time, mixing after each addition. As mixture gets stiff, use floured hands and begin kneading. Knead for 7 minutes, turning dough over often.

Let rise in greased bowl until doubled in size, approximately 1 hour. Punch down dough. Separate *challah* without a blessing.

Divide dough into thirds, shape as desired, and place in greased pans or on baking sheet. Let rise again until doubled in size.

Preheat oven to 375°.

Brush with glaze. Bake for 45 minutes to 1 hour or until brown. Remove from pans and cool on racks.

NOTE: Do not let dough rise longer than 1 hour. If unable to shape loaves after first rising, punch down dough and let rise again.

RAISIN CHALLAH

4 cups warm water
2 Tbsps. dry yeast
4 eggs
½ cup oil
½ cup honey
2 cups raisins
(or less, to taste)
14 to 15 cups flour
1 Tbsp. coarse kosher salt

GLAZE
1 egg, beaten
Poppy seeds

USE: Baking sheets
or loaf pans
YIELDS: 6 loaves or
4 loaves and 12 rolls

Pour warm water into a large mixing bowl. Stir in yeast, and then add eggs, oil, honey, and raisins. Mix well and add about half of the flour. Stir well.

Let mixture rest 45 minutes to 1 hour until the yeast is bubbly. This is the first rising.

Add the salt and most of the remaining flour. Mix and knead on a lightly floured board, adding only as much flour as necessary to be able to handle the dough. The dough should be soft. You may let the dough rise again for 1 hour, if desired.

Separate *challah* with a blessing. Divide dough, and shape loaves.

Place challah in greased pans and let rise 45 minutes to 1 hour.

Preheat oven to 350°.

Brush tops of loaves with beaten egg and sprinkle with poppy seeds. Bake for about 45 minutes to 1 hour for loaves, or 30 minutes for rolls. Remove from pans and cool on racks.

TASTY CHALLAH

The addition of a little whole-wheat flour and wheat germ creates a richer look and flavor.

1 Tbsp. sugar
½ cup warm water
1½ ounces fresh yeast
3 eggs
¾ cup sugar
¾ cup oil
¼ cup wheat germ
2 cups hot water
12 cups flour
plus
½ cup whole-wheat flour
1 Tbsp. salt

GLAZE
1 egg, beaten
Poppy seeds

USE: Baking sheets
or loaf pans
YIELDS: 4 loaves

In a large bowl, dissolve sugar in ½ cup warm water. Crumble yeast into sugar-water, mix, and let stand until it begins to foam. Add eggs and mix well. Add sugar, oil, and wheat germ, and mix again.

Slowly add hot water, flours and salt, alternating liquid and dry ingredients. When dough forms a single ball, place on floured board and knead until smooth.

Place in oiled bowl and turn so top is oiled. Cover with towel and let rise 30 to 45 minutes until doubled in bulk. Punch down. Let rise again until doubled.

Punch down. Separate *challah* with a blessing. Divide dough into four parts and shape loaves. Place in greased pans and let rise 15 minutes.

Preheat oven to 400°.

Brush loaves with beaten egg and sprinkle with poppy seeds. Bake at 400° for 5 to 10 minutes, then lower temperature to 350° and bake for 35 to 40 minutes, until brown. Remove from pans and cool on racks.

KITCHENAID CHALLAH

This special KitchenAid process produces a perfect taste and texture.

2 ounces fresh yeast
1¾ cups warm water
½ cup sugar
3 egg yolks
7 cups flour
¼ cup oil
1 Tbsp. salt

GLAZE
1 egg, beaten
Poppy seeds

USE: Baking sheets
or loaf pans
YIELDS: 3 loaves

Put yeast, warm water, and sugar in the KitchenAid bowl. Let stand until yeast bubbles. Add egg yolks, 5 cups of flour, oil, and salt. Put on Speed 2 and mix with dough hook until ingredients are combined. Add 1 more cup of flour and mix for 2 more minutes on Speed 2. Repeat with next cup of flour until all flour has been added. Then knead on Speed 2 for 10 minutes.

Remove bowl from machine. Oil the top of the dough, cover and let rise for 1 hour.

Separation of *challah* is not required when using this amount of flour.

Divide dough into thirds. Shape and place in greased pans, cover and let rise another 45 minutes.

Preheat oven to 350°.

Brush loaves with beaten egg and sprinkle with poppy seeds, if desired. Bake until brown, 45 minutes to 1 hour. Remove from pans and cool on racks.

WHOLE GRAIN CHALLOT *are a welcome and nutritious alternative on the Shabbat table. For a light and flavorful effect, combine whole grain flours with unbleached white flour.*

RYE-OATMEAL CHALLAH

6 packages dry yeast
2 cups warm water
2 Tbsps. honey
1½ cups honey
3 cups warm water
7 eggs, beaten
1 cup oil
6 Tbsps. caraway seeds
3½ Tbsps. salt
3 cups rye flour
4 cups rolled oats
7 - 8 cups whole-wheat flour
3 cups white flour

GLAZE
2 eggs, beaten
Poppy seeds or
sesame seeds

USE: Baking sheets
or loaf pans
YIELDS: 7 medium loaves

In a small bowl mix yeast, 2 cups warm water, and 2 tablespoons honey and set aside. In a large bowl, mix honey, warm water, eggs and oil. Add caraway seeds and salt. When yeast mixture foams, add it to mixture in large bowl.

Stir in rye flour, oats, whole-wheat flour and white flour. Turn dough out on well-floured board and knead for 15 to 20 minutes.

Place dough in well-oiled bowl, turning to coat all surfaces with oil. Let rise 1½ to 2 hours. Punch down dough and knead for 5 to 10 more minutes.

Separate *challah* with a blessing and divide dough into seven pieces. Shape dough and place in greased pans. Let rise 1 to 1½ hours.

Preheat oven to 350°.

Brush loaves with beaten eggs and sprinkle with poppy or sesame seeds. Bake for 45 to 50 minutes or until hollow-sounding when tapped on the bottom. Remove from pans and cool on racks.

HALF-AND-HALF CHALLAH

3 ounces fresh yeast
1 cup warm water
8 cups white flour
6 cups whole-wheat flour
⅔ cup sugar
1 cup oil
2 Tbsps. salt
4 eggs, slightly beaten
3 cups warm water

GLAZE
1 egg yolk, beaten
1 tsp. water
Poppy seeds

USE: Baking sheets
or loaf pans
YIELDS: 5 loaves

In a small bowl dissolve yeast in 1 cup warm water and set aside. Put white and whole-wheat flours in a large bowl and make a well in the center. Add sugar, oil, salt, and eggs.

Add 3 cups warm water and the yeast mixture. Mix and knead until smooth, approximately 5 to 10 minutes. Place in greased bowl and oil the top of the dough lightly. Cover and let rise in a warm place for 2 hours. Punch down, knead again 2 to 3 minutes, oil as before and let rise 1 hour.

Separate *challah* with a blessing. Divide dough into five pieces, shape each challah and put in greased pan. Cover, let rise 1 hour.

Preheat oven to 350°.

Brush loaves with egg glaze and sprinkle with poppy seeds. Bake for 45 minutes or until brown. Remove from pan and cool on rack.

HONEY AND WHOLE-WHEAT CHALLAH

6 packages dry yeast
4 cups warm water
1 Tbsp. honey
1 cup oil (preferably safflower or sunflower)
5 eggs
¾ cup honey and
¼ cup molasses or
1 cup honey
3 Tbsps. salt
12 cups whole-wheat flour
8 cups white flour

GLAZE
1 egg, beaten
Poppy or sesame seeds

USE: Baking sheets
or loaf pans
YIELDS: 7 loaves

In a large bowl dissolve yeast in 2 cups warm water mixed with 1 tablespoon honey. Set aside 5 to 10 minutes. Add oil, eggs, honey, and remaining 2 cups warm water, and mix well.

Gradually add dry ingredients and knead dough until elastic and not sticky, 5 to 10 minutes. (If necessary, add more flour, ⅛ cup at a time. If too stiff, add more water, a little at a time.)

Place dough in an oiled bowl, turning to coat all sides with oil. Cover and let rise 1 to 2 hours.

Punch down and let rise 1 hour. Divide dough into seven pieces. Separate *challah* with a blessing. Shape dough as desired and place in greased pans. Let rise another hour.

Preheat oven to 350°.

Brush loaves with beaten egg and sprinkle with poppy or sesame seeds. Bake until brown, 45 minutes to 1 hour. Remove from pans and cool on racks.

EASY WHOLE-WHEAT CHALLAH

4 cups warm water
3 Tbsps. dry yeast
½ cup oil
½ cup honey
4 eggs
12 to 13 cups whole-wheat flour
1 Tbsp. coarse kosher salt
2 Tbsps. cornmeal

GLAZE
1 egg, beaten
Poppy seeds

USE: Baking sheets
or loaf pans
YIELDS: 4 to 6 loaves
or 4 loaves and 12 rolls

Pour water into large mixing bowl. Add yeast and stir. Add oil, honey, and eggs. Stir in about 5 cups of the flour.

Let the mixture rest about 45 minutes to 1 hour until it bubbles. This is the first rising.

Add salt and stir in most of the remaining flour. Lightly flour a board, and knead dough 7 to 10 minutes until mixed. As you work, add only as much flour as necessary to allow you to handle the dough.

Separate *challah* with a blessing. Lightly grease pans and sprinkle with cornmeal. Shape the dough into loaves and rolls. Place loaves in pans and let rise 45 minutes to 1 hour.

Preheat oven to 350°.

Brush loaves with beaten egg and sprinkle with poppy seeds. Bake until brown, 45 to 50 minutes for loaves, 30 minutes for rolls. Remove from pans and cool on racks.

WATER CHALLAH

A good challah for the dieter. It's low in sugar and oil and contains only one egg.

2 envelopes dry yeast
2¾ cups warm water
2 Tbsps. sugar
3 Tbsps. oil
1 egg plus
1 egg white
1 Tbsp. salt
9 cups flour

GLAZE
1 egg yolk plus
1 Tbsp. water
Poppy seeds

USE: Baking sheets
or loaf pans
YIELDS: 3 loaves

In a large bowl, sprinkle yeast over warm water. Add sugar and let stand until yeast starts to bubble. Add oil, egg, egg white, salt, and 3 cups flour. Beat with a wooden spoon. Add remaining flour one cup at a time until dough can be kneaded.

Knead dough 5 minutes on a floured surface until smooth and elastic. Lightly flour dough and place in a clean bowl. Cover and let rise in a warm place until doubled in bulk, 1 to 2 hours.

Knead again for 4 to 5 minutes.

Separate *challah* without a blessing. Divide dough into three portions and shape into loaves. Place in lightly greased and floured pans. Let rise, covered, until doubled in bulk, ½ hour.

Preheat oven to 350°.

Mix egg yolk and water and brush on loaves. Sprinkle with poppy seeds. Bake for approximately 35 to 45 minutes, or until brown. Remove from pans and cool on racks.

Breads and Rolls

Bread, the staff of life, varies widely in its flavors, textures and shapes. Try a sourdough for its distinctive tartness, or onion pletzel for a nostalgic treat. Experiment with combinations of different types of flour — the results can be pleasing.

BEFORE YOU BEGIN

☐ Before baking, it is very important to know the laws of *hafrashat challah*. See The Mitzvah of Separating Challah, page 47.

☐ The following recipes indicate when *challah* should be taken and if a blessing is said. If you increase or decrease the amount of flour used, consult the chart of Requirements for Separating Challah, page 48.

☐ For baking tips, see Challah and Bread Baking, page 39.

BEST-EVER ONION ROLLS

2 packages dry yeast
1¼ cups warm water
¼ cup sugar
¼ cup oil
2 eggs
1 Tbsp. salt
5 to 5½ cups flour

FILLING
2 to 3 medium onions, chopped
¼ cup margarine
2 Tbsps. nondairy creamer
2 Tbsps. beaten egg

GLAZE
1 egg, beaten
Poppy seeds

USE: Baking sheets
YIELDS: 2 dozen rolls

In a large bowl, sprinkle yeast over warm water. Mix in sugar and wait until bubbles begin to form. Add next four ingredients in order, forming a stiff dough. Knead several minutes until smooth and elastic. Cover and let rise about 1 hour until doubled in bulk.

FILLING: Prepare filling, mixing all ingredients well in medium bowl.

Divide dough into twenty-four pieces. Shape each piece into a ball and flatten. Place on greased baking sheets.

Make a small hollow in the center of each roll with fingers and place a tablespoon of filling in each hollow. Brush rolls with egg and sprinkle with poppy seeds. Let rise about 45 minutes until doubled in bulk.

Preheat oven to 400°. Bake 12 to 16 minutes or until golden brown.

VARIATION
☐ **New Yorkers:** After first rising, roll out dough and cut into rectangles. Spread filling in center of each rectangle and sprinkle with poppy seeds.

Fold two sides of rectangle over center and place seam side down on greased baking sheet. Brush with egg and sprinkle with poppy seeds. Let rise 45 minutes.

Preheat oven to 400°. Bake 12 to 16 minutes or until golden brown.

RYE BREAD

This is an excellent, slightly heavier rye bread — much more like the European variety. Very little yeast is used, but it is compensated for by the extra rising time. Challah is not separated when using this small amount of flour.

3 cups rye flour
2 cups whole-wheat flour
1 cup white flour
1½ tsps. salt
3 Tbsps. oil
⅓ tsp. dry yeast
½ cup warm water
2 cups water

GLAZE
1 egg yolk, beaten
1 Tbsp. caraway seeds

USE: Baking sheets
YIELDS: 2 to 3 medium loaves

Prepare the dough in the evening. Mix the flours and salt in a large bowl. Add oil and rub it in well with your hands to break up lumps.

Dissolve yeast in ½ cup warm water, let it foam, and add to flour mixture. Mix well. Add 2 cups water slowly and mix it in by hand.

Knead for about 5 minutes until dough does not stick to sides of bowl. Place dough on floured surface and knead 5 minutes more. Place in well-oiled bowl and cover with a wet towel. Let stand overnight.

In the morning, knead 5 more minutes. Divide dough into two or three portions and shape into loaves. Place on oiled baking sheet and cover with a damp cloth. Let rise 2 hours.

Preheat oven to 375°.

Brush tops of loaves with beaten egg yolk and sprinkle with caraway seeds. Bake for about 50 minutes or until done.

ONION PLETZEL

These tasty onion specialties conjure up childhood memories.

1 cup warm water
1 package dry yeast
2 tsps. sugar
1½ tsps. salt
2½ to 3 cups flour
¼ cup margarine, melted
1 cup chopped onion
2 tsps. paprika

USE: 2 9-inch round
cake pans
YIELDS: 2 rounds

Pour warm water into warm mixing bowl and sprinkle yeast over water. Stir until dissolved. Add sugar, 1 teaspoon salt, and 2 cups of the flour and mix until well blended. Add additional flour to make a stiff dough.

Turn onto lightly floured board and knead until smooth and elastic, about 5 minutes.

Place in well-oiled bowl, turning to coat all sides with oil. Let rise in warm place until doubled in size, about 1 hour.

Punch dough down and divide dough in half. Cover and let rest for 5 minutes.

Place into two greased 9-inch round cake pans. Brush tops with melted margarine. Sprinkle with onion, pressing onion into dough with fingertips. Let rise uncovered in warm place about 45 minutes.

Preheat oven to 450°.

Sprinkle tops of loaves with paprika and ½ teaspoon salt. Bake for 20 to 25 minutes. Cool in pans on wire racks.

SOURDOUGH RYE BREAD

SOURDOUGH STARTER
1 package dry yeast
2½ cups warm water
2½ cups rye flour
1 tsp. sugar
1 medium onion, peeled

BREAD
4 packages dry yeast
6 cups water
2 cups starter
¼ cup sugar
¼ cup salt
¼ cup oil
4 cups medium rye flour
2 to 4 Tbsps. caraway seeds
14 to 16 cups white flour
White cornmeal

GLAZE
1 egg white mixed with 1 Tbsp. water
Caraway seeds

USE: 3-quart container
Baking sheets
YIELDS: 8 1-pound loaves or
4 2-pound loaves or
8 dozen rolls

STARTER: Combine all ingredients in a 3-quart container. Cover with cheesecloth or leave lid slightly ajar. Let mixture stand at room temperature for 48 hours, stirring down several times. Discard onion.

Cover and store starter in refrigerator. (A plastic container should be used. Do not use glass as it might explode if covered too tightly.)

NOTE: After each time starter is used, add equal amounts of water and rye flour to remainder of starter and leave at room temperature for 12 hours before refrigerating again.

BREAD: Dissolve yeast in water in very large bowl. Add 2 cups starter, sugar, salt, oil, rye flour, and caraway seeds. Mix well.

Gradually add enough white flour to form a firm dough. Knead until smooth and elastic, about 10 minutes. Cover and let rise 1 hour.

Separate *challah* with a blessing. Divide dough and shape into loaves or rolls. To make loaves, roll out dough into a rectangle, then roll *very tightly*, as for a jelly roll. Seal edges and tuck ends under.

Place on baking sheets that have been sprinkled with cornmeal. Slash tops of loaves diagonally in about three places. Let rise 1 hour.

Preheat oven to 400°.

Place a pan of water on lower oven rack while preheating and leave there for first 10 minutes of baking time. Brush loaves with egg white mixture and sprinkle with caraway seeds. Bake for 30 minutes or until golden brown. Remove from pans and cool on racks.

VARIATION
☐ Substitute whole-wheat flour for part of white flour.

GARLIC BREAD

Here is an interesting way to enhance the flavor of ordinary bread for the dinner table.

1 loaf "Italian" bread
2 Tbsps. margarine
1 tsp. garlic powder or 2 cloves pressed garlic
1 tsp. paprika
1 tsp. parsley

USE: Baking sheet
YIELDS: 4 servings

Slice bread three-fourths of the way through, lengthwise.

Mix margarine with garlic and spread on cut surfaces of bread. Sprinkle with paprika and parsley. Return bread to original shape and wrap whole loaf in aluminum foil.

Preheat oven to 350°.

Bake for 10 to 15 minutes.

Serve warm.

"Mezonot" Bagels and Variety Breads

Bagels and English muffins are perfect for Sunday brunch or any weekday meal. Toast them, or fill them with lox or cream cheese. Fresh pita bread stuffed with salad, meatballs, falafel or sauce make a delicious "meal in a pocket."

REGARDING "MEZONOT" BREAD

☐ The recipes in this section, although resembling those for bread and rolls, etc. require the blessing *mezonot* because of their ingredients. When the proportion of combined liquids (including eggs, oil, margarine, juice, honey, etc.) is greater than the amount of water, the blessing *mezonot* is said. (According to many Rabbinic authorities, sugar is included in the liquid measurement.)

☐ However, it is *halachically* questionable and best to avoid making a meal of *mezonot* products. When they are eaten as a meal to the point of satiation, or when more than a certain quantity of "*mezonot*" bread is eaten, it may be necessary to first wash the hands ritually, say the blessing *al n'tilat yadayim*, and say the *hamotzi* blessing on a piece of "regular" bread before beginning the meal.

☐ The above often applies when eating several slices of pizza, falafel sandwiches, or meals on *mezonot* rolls. Consult an Orthodox Rabbi regarding the proper use of *mezonot* rolls, bagels, breads, pizza and the like.

☐ Many of the following recipes include instructions for conversion to *hamotzi* bread in order to avoid these *halachic* questions.

BEFORE YOU BEGIN

☐ Before baking, it is very important to know the laws of *hafrashat challah*. See The Mitzvah of Separating Challah, page 47. In most of the following recipes, *challah* is not separated due to the small amount of flour used. However, if increasing the amount of flour, consult the chart of Requirements for Separating Challah, page 48.

☐ As water comprises the minority of liquid in these *mezonot* recipes, even if the recipe calls for over 1666.6 grams of flour, *challah* is separated without a blessing.

QUICK AND EASY BAGELS

½ **cup warm water**
1 **package dry yeast**
2 **Tbsps. sugar**
1 **cup apple juice**
2 **tsps. salt**
4¼ **cups flour**
Poppy seeds or sesame seeds (optional)

USE: Baking sheet
YIELDS: 1 dozen bagels

Pour warm water into bowl. Sprinkle yeast and stir until dissolved. Add apple juice, sugar, salt, and 4 cups of flour. Knead about 10 minutes, and add flour as needed until smooth and elastic.

Place in a greased bowl. Cover and let rise in warm place for 15 minutes.

Punch down and roll on lightly floured board into a 9 x 5-inch rectangle about 1-inch thick. Cut into twelve equal strips, 5 inches long. Roll each strip into a ½-inch thick rope about 6 inches long. Fasten ends to form circle. Place on greased baking sheet, cover, and let rise in warm place for 20 minutes.

➤

Preheat the oven to 375°.

Bring 1 gallon of water to a boil, lower heat, and place four bagels in the simmering water. When bagels float to the top after about 3 to 4 minutes, remove and place on ungreased baking sheet.

Repeat for all remaining bagels. Sprinkle with poppy seeds or sesame seeds if desired.

Bake for 30 to 35 minutes until brown.

NOTE: To convert this recipe into "*hamotzi*," substitute 1 cup warm water instead of 1 cup apple juice.

TASTY BAGELS

1 ounce fresh yeast
½ cup water
1 tsp. salt
4 eggs
2 Tbsps. sugar
½ cup oil
6 cups flour

USE: Baking sheet
YIELDS: 18 bagels

In a large bowl dissolve yeast in water. Combine all ingredients and knead well until smooth. Let rise in warm place until doubled in size. Punch down and let rise again.

Shape dough into bagels or knots by pinching off pieces and rolling these into "ropes" between the hands. Pinch the ends together to form bagels or knots. Bring large pot of water to a boil, with salt to taste.

Drop bagels in, several at a time, and let boil for 3 minutes. Remove from water.

Preheat oven to 400°.

Place on ungreased pan. Bake for 15 to 18 minutes.

ENGLISH MUFFINS

½ cup lukewarm water
¼ cup oil
1 Tbsp. sugar
1 package dry yeast
½ cup apple juice
3 cups flour
1½ tsps. salt
4 Tbsps. cornmeal

USE: Griddle or skillet
YIELDS: 10 to 12 muffins

In a large bowl, combine first four ingredients. Gradually add apple juice, salt, and flour, and mix until well blended.

Cover and let rise 15 minutes. Roll dough out on floured surface to ¼-inch thickness. Cut out 3- to 3½-inch rounds. Place on baking sheet sprinkled with 2 tablespoons cornmeal. Sprinkle tops with remaining cornmeal.

Let rise 1 hour.

Transfer with spatula to hot ungreased griddle or frying pan. "Bake" about 7 minutes on each side, or until browned.

NOTE: To convert this recipe into "*hamotzi*", substitute ½ cup lukewarm water for ½ cup apple juice.

CINNAMON RAISIN BREAD

2⅓ cups warm water
3 packages dry yeast
⅔ cup sugar
¾ cup oil
1 Tbsp. salt
6 eggs
9 cups flour

FILLING
½ cup sugar
3 Tbsps. cinnamon
Raisins
3 Tbsps. oil
Margarine, melted (optional)

USE: 9 x 5-inch loaf pans
YIELDS: 3 medium loaves

Pour warm water in large mixing bowl. Sprinkle yeast over water and add sugar. Mix well. When bubbles begin to form, add oil, salt, eggs, and then flour.

Knead until smooth and elastic. Cover and let rise until doubled in size, about 1 hour.

Separate *challah* without a blessing.

Punch down dough and divide into three pieces. Roll out each piece into a 9 x 12-inch rectangle.

FILLING: Combine sugar, cinnamon, and raisins in small bowl. Spread 1 tablespoon of oil over each rectangle. Sprinkle each with a third of combined filling, leaving a ½-inch margin at edges. Roll up dough tightly as for a jelly roll. Pinch ends and seam to seal tightly.

Grease pans. Dip seam side of loaf into flour and place in pan, seam side down. Cover and let rise about 45 minutes.

Preheat oven to 350°.

Bake for 30 minutes. Remove from pans and cool on racks.

OPTIONAL: For soft crust, brush tops with melted margarine as soon as the loaves come out of the oven.

DANISH SALTY CARAWAY CRESCENTS

1 Tbsp. sugar
⅔ cup warm water
2 packages dry yeast
1 tsp. salt
½ cup oil
1 egg plus 1 egg yolk
3½ cups flour

GLAZE
1 egg white, beaten
Coarse salt
Caraway seeds

USE: Baking sheet
YIELDS: 16 crescents

In a large bowl mix sugar into ⅔ cup warm water. Sprinkle yeast over water. When yeast bubbles, add salt, oil, egg, egg yolk, and flour. Mix to form a heavy dough.

Knead dough 3 to 4 minutes on a lightly floured board. Lightly sprinkle dough with flour, cover with a towel, and let rest 20 minutes.

Divide dough in half and roll each half into a circle. Cut circle into eight wedges. See Rugelach Illustrated (page 421). Pat wedges to ¼-inch thickness and roll up from the wide side to the point. Curve the ends of the rolls inwards to form crescents. Place on a greased and floured baking sheet. Cover and let rise 30 minutes in a warm place.

Preheat oven to 375°.

Brush with beaten egg white and sprinkle with coarse salt and caraway seeds.

Bake for 15 minutes. Remove from sheet and cool on racks.

VARIATION
☐ For extra flavor, sprinkle additional coarse salt and caraway seeds onto wedges before rolling.

PITA BREAD

½ cup warm water
2 packages dry yeast
¼ tsp. sugar
6 cups flour
3 Tbsps. olive oil
2 tsps. salt
2 cups apple juice

USE: Baking sheets
YIELDS: 15 pitas

Combine ½ cup warm water with yeast and sugar. Stir until yeast dissolves and begins to foam. Let stand for 5 minutes.

Sift flour into large mixing bowl. Add oil, salt, and 2 cups apple juice and stir with a wooden spoon. Add yeast mixture and mix thoroughly.

Turn dough onto floured board and knead for about 10 minutes until dough is smooth and no longer sticky. Oil a bowl and place dough in it to rise, turn to coat with oil.

Cover and let rise in a warm place until dough doubles in size, about 2 hours. Punch down and knead 3 minutes. Roll and stretch dough into a thick tube shape about 15 inches long and 3 inches wide.

Cut roll into fifteen equal pieces. Shape each piece into a ball. Pat each ball into a 6-inch circle about ⅛-inch thick. Place circles on baking sheets and let stand about 1 hour to rise again.

Preheat oven to 500°.

Place baking sheets on lowest shelf of oven. Bake 3 to 5 minutes until puffed and slightly brown. Don't overbake!

NOTE: To convert this recipe to "hamotzi", substitute 2 cups warm water for 2 cups apple juice.

Dairy

Breakfast and Light Lunches
Dairy Soups
Entrees and Accompaniments
Pastries and Desserts
Sidelights

A dairy meal can be elegant and satisfying. From blintzes to French onion soup, dairy dishes add variety and pizazz to the weekly menu. A green salad, together with quiche or a fondue, makes a complete, light dinner. Grated cheese sprinkled on a vegetable casserole transforms it from a side dish to a tasty main course.

In the kosher kitchen, dairy meals assume a special role. Dairy and meat foods may not be cooked, served or eaten together. Separate utensils are used exclusively for dairy, and a separate oven is recommended for baking or toasting dairy dishes.

Even a small amount of milk-derived substance in a food can make it a dairy food according to Jewish Law. All dairy products require a reliable certification of *kashrut*. When planning dairy meals, be sure six hours will have elapsed since meat was eaten. Certain hard cheeses also require a six-hour waiting time before the eating of meat.

For further laws concerning dairy foods and required waiting times, see Kashrut Basics, page 17.

Dairy and Tradition

"A land flowing with milk and honey" is the way the Torah describes the Land of Israel, the land promised to the Jewish people. The Torah itself is compared to milk and honey, which is one of the reasons we eat dairy foods on Shavuot, the holiday that commemorates the giving of the Torah. Cheesecake and blintzes are among the special treats traditionally served on the first day of Shavuot.

Cheese *latkes* on Chanukah recall the deeds of a famous Jewish heroine, Yehudit, in the time of the second *Beit Hamikdash*. Israel was then occupied by the cruel and oppressive Syrian-Greek army. Yehudit helped secure a victory for the Jewish forces by slaying the vicious general of the Greek army, Holofernes. She gave him salty cheese to eat, followed by strong wine to quench his thirst. The wine caused him to fall into a deep slumber. Yehudit then seized his sword and slew him with it. His soldiers fled in fear and confusion. The victory of the Maccabbees followed this brave deed.

Dairy recipes also assume importance during the "Nine Days"-- from the first of Av until the fast day of Tisha B'Av -- a time of mourning for the destroyed *Beit Hamikdash*. Meat is prohibited during this time except on Shabbat or for a *simchah* such as a *brit* or a *siyum*, the completion of a portion of *Talmudic* study.

Chalav Yisrael

Jewish law requires that in the production of dairy products, a *mashgiach* or Jewish supervisor must be present from the beginning of the milking to the end of processing to ensure that only milk from kosher animals is used. Where supervised milk is unavailable, some Rabbinic authorities permit government inspection as sufficient assurance (although not in all countries). All agree, however, that actual supervision is preferable. Milk with such supervision is known as *chalav Yisrael.*

Jewish tradition stresses the importance of using *chalav Yisrael* products exclusively, and emphasizes that using non-*chalav Yisrael* dairy products can have an adverse spiritual effect.

These laws are especially important for children, including infants. Many infant formulas contain milk or dairy ingredients, which are not *chalav Yisrael.* In most cases, a non-dairy formula can be substituted. Even when *chalav Yisrael* is very difficult to obtain, many people, aware of its positive effect on a Jew's spiritual sensitivity, go out of their way to acquire these products. Certainly where it is readily available, one is required by Jewish Law to use these products exclusively.

Breakfast & Light Lunches

CEREAL

Homemade granola is a quick-filling nutritious way for both children and adults to begin the day. The warmth and energy provided by a substantial breakfast are well worth the time and effort. Have a good morning!

GRANOLA

1 cup oil
2 Tbsps. margarine
1 Tbsp. vanilla extract
1 cup dark brown sugar
1 cup honey
2 pounds rolled oats or
1 pound rolled oats and
1 pound wheat flakes
½ cup unhulled
sesame seeds,
slightly crushed in blender
2 cups chopped or
sliced almonds
2 cups wheat germ
1 pound shredded coconut
1 cup sunflower seeds
(optional)
1 cup raisins or
chopped dates (optional)

USE: 4 jelly-roll pans
YIELDS: 5 lbs. granola

Preheat oven to 350°.

In a small mixing bowl, combine oil, margarine, vanilla, brown sugar, and honey. Mix well and set aside. In a large bowl, combine remaining ingredients, except raisins or dates. Stir liquid into dry ingredients until thoroughly mixed.

Pour into four jelly-roll pans and bake for 20 to 25 minutes. Stir every 5 to 7 minutes. Cool, then add dried fruit of your choice.

Store in a covered container; this will keep for weeks in the refrigerator.

VARIATIONS
□ Use maple flavoring instead of vanilla.

□ Add cinnamon and/or other spices to taste.

□ Try other nuts or grains in place of those recommended.

□ Use dried apples or apricots instead of raisins.

1-2-3 GRANOLA

4 cups rolled oats
1 cup wheat germ
½ cup sunflower seeds
¼ cup chopped walnuts
1 cup honey
½ cup oil
½ tsp. vanilla extract

USE: 2-quart saucepan
Jelly-roll pan
YIELDS: 12 servings

Preheat oven to 350°.

In a large mixing bowl, combine first four ingredients. In a 2-quart saucepan, heat honey, oil, and vanilla until syrupy. Add to dry ingredients and mix well. Spread on a jelly-roll pan. Bake for 20 minutes, stirring every 5 minutes.

Store in a covered container; this will keep for weeks in the refrigerator.

Delicious with milk, this granola can also be served plain as a snack.

PANCAKES

As a breakfast or brunch main dish, pancakes make a satisfying meal. Cheese and yogurt pancakes, often known as latkes, *make a delicious side dish for Chanukah, or the Nine Days concluding with Tisha B'Av.*

CHEESE LATKES

3 eggs
1 cup milk
1 cup cottage cheese, drained
1½ cups flour
1 tsp. baking powder
½ tsp. salt
5 Tbsps. sugar
1 tsp. vanilla extract
½ cup oil for frying

USE: 10-inch skillet
YIELDS: 12 pancakes

Place all the ingredients except oil together in a large bowl. Mix until smooth.

Heat ½ cup oil in a skillet. Using a large spoon, drop the batter into hot oil. Fry 2 to 3 minutes on each side, until lightly browned. Continue until batter is used up, adding oil when necessary.

The latkes may be served topped with sour cream, applesauce, or maple syrup.

FARMER CHEESE LATKES

4 eggs
8 ounces farmer cheese
3 Tbsps. sugar
1 tsp. vanilla extract
3 Tbsps. oil or margarine
Dash of salt
½ cup matzoh meal
½ cup oil for frying

USE: 10-inch skillet
YIELDS: 8 pancakes

Beat eggs in a large bowl. Add all remaining ingredients except matzoh meal and frying oil. Mix until well blended. Add matzoh meal and mix until smooth.

Heat ½ cup oil in skillet. Using a large spoon, drop batter into hot oil. Fry 3 to 5 minutes on each side, or until lightly browned. Continue until batter is used up, adding oil when necessary.

VARIATION
□ Raisins or chopped berries may be added.

BASIC PANCAKES

2 cups flour
4 tsps. baking powder
½ tsp. salt
½ cup sugar
2 eggs
2 cups milk
2½ Tbsps. oil
Oil for frying

USE: 10-inch skillet
YIELDS: 24 pancakes

Place flour, baking powder, salt, and sugar in a bowl. In a separate bowl, beat the eggs together lightly. Add milk and oil to the eggs. Add the dry ingredients all at once and mix together with a fork until the batter is slightly lumpy.

Lightly oil a skillet and heat until hot. Using a large spoon, drop batter onto skillet. Fry on one side until bubbles appear. Flip over and fry on the other side. Continue until batter is used up.

The batter may be covered and stored in refrigerator until ready to use.

►

VARIATIONS

□ **Fruit Pancakes:** Add to batter ½ cup thinly sliced apples, blueberries, or 1 diced banana.

□ **Buckwheat Pancakes:** Substitute for flour ⅓ cup buckwheat flour and ⅔ cup unbleached flour to make good old-fashioned buckwheat pancakes.

ORANGE-WALNUT PANCAKES

These delicious pancakes require a little extra effort, but are well worth it!

1 cup flour
½ tsp. baking powder
½ tsp. salt
1 egg
1 cup milk
2 Tbsps. oil for frying

SAUCE
1 Tbsp. margarine
2 cups orange juice
½ cup sugar
½ tsp. cinnamon
¼ cup raisins
½ cup chopped walnuts
¼ cup fine strips orange rind

USE: 10-inch skillet
2-quart saucepan
YIELDS: 8 pancakes

Combine all dry ingredients. Beat egg and milk until thoroughly blended. Add to dry ingredients. Lightly oil a skillet and heat until hot. Using 2 tablespoons of batter, drop onto hot skillet. Brown lightly on both sides. Remove from skillet and fold in quarters. Set aside.

SAUCE: In saucepan over low heat, melt margarine in orange juice, then slowly add remaining ingredients. Remove from heat.

In a large skillet, arrange the pancakes side by side. Pour sauce on top. Reheat before serving.

RYE-OATMEAL PANCAKES

¼ cup rolled oats
¼ cup rye flour
⅔ cup whole-wheat pastry flour
1 tsp. baking powder
2 eggs
1 cup milk
2 Tbsps. oil
3 Tbsps. honey or maple syrup
½ tsp. salt
½ tsp. cinnamon
½ tsp. vanilla extract
2 Tbsps. margarine or butter for frying

USE: 10-inch skillet
YIELDS: 12 pancakes

Mix oats, flours, and baking powder. Mix in eggs, milk, oil, honey, salt, cinnamon, and vanilla.

In a hot skillet, melt the margarine or butter and drop about 2 tablespoons of the batter in the pan for each pancake. When bubbles start to appear on top, flip them over, and fry until golden. Continue until batter is used up.

SWEET FRUIT PANCAKES

The steamed apples and applesauce add a fresh taste to these pancakes. Delicious as either a side dish or dessert!

2 medium apples
2 Tbsps. sugar
¼ tsp. cinnamon
1 egg, beaten
½ cup milk
⅔ cup applesauce
1 cup flour
2 Tbsps. margarine for frying

USE: Vegetable steamer
10-inch skillet
YIELDS: 12 pancakes

Core and slice the apples. Steam them in a vegetable steamer for 5 to 7 minutes. Remove and dice apples. Place in a large bowl.

Combine sugar and cinnamon. Sprinkle over apples. Add egg, milk, and applesauce and beat well. Mix in the flour.

In a hot skillet melt margarine. Using a large spoon, drop batter for each pancake into pan. Fry the pancake batter on a medium flame, about 3 to 5 minutes per side. Continue until batter is used up.

SAUCY BAKED BUBALAS

SAUCE
3 Tbsps. margarine
1 medium onion, diced
½ pound mushrooms, sliced
**3 cups tomatoes,
cut into chunks**
½ tsp. salt
Black pepper to taste
**Fresh sage to taste or
½ tsp. dried basil**
1 clove garlic, crushed

BUBALAS
3 eggs, separated
¾ tsp. salt
½ cup water
1 cup matzoh meal
Oil for frying

TOPPING
**½ cup (2 ounces)
grated mozzarella cheese**

USE: 10-inch skillet
9 x 13-inch baking pan
YIELDS: 4 servings

SAUCE: In a 10-inch skillet saute onions in 3 tablespoons margarine until golden. Add mushrooms, then tomatoes, seasonings and garlic. Simmer covered for about 15 minutes.

Preheat oven to 325°.

BUBALAS: In a large mixer bowl beat egg whites with salt until stiff. In a separate bowl beat egg yolks, water, and half of the matzoh meal with a fork. Fold half of the egg whites into egg-yolk mixture, then fold in second half. Add the remaining matzoh meal.

Heat oil in a skillet. Drop mixture by the tablespoonful into hot oil and fry until golden brown on each side. Drain on paper towels.

TO ASSEMBLE: In the 9 x 13-inch baking pan, spread a thin layer of sauce. Arrange drained bubalas on top and cover with remaining sauce. Top with grated cheese. Bake for 30 minutes or until cheese is golden brown.

YOGURT PANCAKES

1 cup flour
1 Tbsp. sugar
½ tsp. salt
1 tsp. baking powder
1 egg
1 cup plain yogurt
2 Tbsps. oil
2 Tbsps. oil for frying

USE: 10-inch skillet
YIELDS: 12 pancakes

Sift the first four ingredients into a large bowl. Lightly beat the egg. Add the egg and remaining ingredients, except the oil for frying, to the flour mixture. Mix together until well blended.

Heat 2 tablespoons oil in a frying pan. When the oil is very hot, drop large spoon of batter for each pancake into pan. Fry until lightly browned on both sides. Continue until batter is used up.

VARIATION
□ Add raisins to the yogurt mixture, or use 1 cup flavored yogurt instead of plain yogurt.

MUFFINS

Hot from the oven, muffins are a tasty breakfast treat. Perfect muffins are tender inside and rounded on the top. Do not overmix. Batter should be lumpy, not smooth.

BASIC MUFFIN MIX

1¾ cups flour
¾ tsp. salt
⅓ cup sugar
2 tsps. baking powder
2 eggs
4 Tbsps. oil
¾ cup milk or
nondairy creamer or
apple juice

USE: Muffin pan
YIELDS: 12 muffins

Preheat oven to 400°.

Grease muffin pan, or line with paper liners.

Combine flour, salt, sugar, and baking powder in a bowl. In another bowl, beat eggs, adding oil and milk.

Add liquid ingredients to dry ingredients and mix just until moist. Do not overmix.

Fill muffin cups ⅔ full with batter. Lower oven temperature to 375°. Bake 20 to 25 minutes.

VARIATIONS
□ The following can be added to batter before filling cups: ½ cup blueberries, ½ cup chopped walnuts, or ½ cup chopped apples.

□ **Whole-Wheat Muffins:** Substitute ¾ cup whole-wheat flour instead of ¾ cup white flour. Use ¼ cup honey and ¾ cup soy milk instead of sugar and milk. Sprinkle top with cinnamon before baking.

GOLDEN CORN MUFFINS

1¼ cups flour
¾ cup yellow cornmeal
¼ cup sugar
4 tsps. baking powder
1 tsp. salt
1 cup milk
⅓ cup oil
1 egg

USE: Muffin pan
YIELDS: 12 muffins

Preheat oven to 400°.

Grease muffin pan, or line with paper liners.

Mix dry ingredients together in a large bowl until well blended. In a second bowl mix milk, oil, and egg and add to flour mixture. Stir just until blended. Mixture will be lumpy.

Fill muffin cups ⅔ full. Bake for 20 to 25 minutes or until brown.

VARIATION
☐ Half fill lined muffin tins with batter. Add 1 teaspoon raspberry jam to middle of each. Top with batter to fill cups ⅔ full. Bake as directed above.

MAPLE-BRAN MUFFINS

2 eggs
1 cup sour cream,
plain yogurt, or buttermilk
1 tsp. baking soda
1 cup pure maple syrup,
sorgum, rice syrup,
or sugar
1 cup bran
1 cup whole-wheat flour
1 cup raisins or
chopped dates
½ cup chopped nuts or
sunflower seeds

USE: Muffin pan
YIELDS: 12 muffins

Preheat oven to 350°.

Grease muffin pan, or line with paper liners.

In medium mixing bowl, beat eggs. Add remaining ingredients. Mix just until moist. Do not overmix.

Fill muffin cups ⅔ full. Bake for 15 to 20 minutes.

BRAN MUFFINS

¼ cup wheat germ
¼ cup whole-wheat flour
½ cup bran
1½ tsps. baking powder
¼ cup raisins
½ cup milk
1½ Tbsps. corn oil
1 egg, beaten lightly

USE: Muffin pan
YIELDS: 6 muffins

Preheat oven to 400°.

Grease muffin pan or line with paper liners.

Combine first four ingredients until well blended. Add raisins and continue to mix until coated. Add milk, oil, and egg. Mix just until moist. Do not overmix.

Fill muffin cups ⅔ full. Bake for 20 to 30 minutes. Remove from pans quickly to prevent muffins from becoming soggy.

EGGS

High in protein and easy to prepare, eggs are a good choice for breakfast, brunch, or lunch. Serve them scrambled, in French toast with cinnamon and sugar, boiled, poached, or as filled omelets.

EGGS IN JEWISH LAW

☐ Each egg must be opened into a clear dish or glass and checked for blood spots before it is cooked or combined with other food. If a blood spot is found, the whole egg must be discarded, and the cup or dish should be immediately and thoroughly washed with cold water.

☐ An Orthodox Rabbi must be consulted if the blood spot was found after the egg had been combined with other food or placed into a hot utensil. (The food mixture or the pan must be set aside until the Rabbi determines what must be done.)

☐ When boiling eggs, it is customary to boil at least three eggs at a time for *halachic* reasons. Some people have a separate pot just for boiling eggs.

☐ If a blood spot is found in a boiled egg, the whole egg must be discarded.

FRENCH OMELET

6 eggs
⅓ cup milk or water
¾ tsp. salt
⅛ tsp. pepper
2 Tbsps. butter or margarine

CHEESE FILLING
¼ cup grated cheddar cheese

LOX FILLING
2 ounces lox

MUSHROOM FILLING
1 cup sliced mushrooms
1 Tbsp. oil

SPANISH OMELET
1 medium onion, diced
1 small green pepper, diced
1 Tbsp. oil
2 Tbsps. tomato paste
¼ tsp. salt
Dash pepper

VEGETABLE FILLING
1 medium onion, diced
1 Tbsp. oil
1 tomato, chopped

USE: 10-inch skillet
YIELDS: 3 to 4 servings

In a large bowl, mix eggs, milk, salt and pepper with a fork. Heat butter or margarine in a 10-inch skillet over medium heat. Pour in egg mixture. As edges set, carefully push cooked portions at edges toward center so uncooked portions flow to bottom. Tilt as necessary so uncooked eggs can set. While top is still moist, fill if desired. With spatula, fold in half or roll. Turn out onto plate.

CHEESE FILLING: Sprinkle with grated cheese before folding.

LOX FILLING: Cut lox or smoked salmon into 1-inch pieces and add to omelet before folding.

MUSHROOM FILLING: Saute mushrooms in oil until soft. Add to omelet before folding.

SPANISH OMELET: Saute onion and green pepper in oil. Add tomato paste, salt, and pepper. Cook 5 minutes. Add to omelet before folding.

VEGETABLE FILLING: Saute onion in oil. Add chopped tomato and cook 5 minutes. Add to omelet before folding.

CHEESY BAKED FRENCH TOAST

A special dairy oven must be used in baking this dish.

**12 slices white bread,
crusts removed**
**½ pound cheddar or
American cheese, sliced**
4 eggs
2½ cups milk
1 tsp. salt
1 tsp. pepper
½ tsp. vanilla extract
Cinnamon
Brown sugar

USE: 8 x 12-inch baking pan
YIELDS: 6 servings

Butter the bottom of an 8 x 12-inch baking pan. Cover bottom of the pan with 6 slices of bread. Place slices of cheese over bread and cover cheese with remaining 6 slices of bread.

Beat eggs with milk and seasonings in a medium bowl. Pour egg mixture over bread, cover and refrigerate at least 2 hours.

Preheat oven to 325°.

Bake 50 to 60 minutes until French Toast is brown and puffed.

Sprinkle with cinnamon and brown sugar.

LECHO

½ cup margarine
2 to 3 large onions, sliced
6 green peppers, sliced
**1 medium zucchini,
diced (optional)**
½ cup diced mushrooms
6 large tomatoes, cubed
6 eggs
Salt and pepper to taste

USE: 10-inch skillet
YIELDS: 12 servings

In a 10-inch skillet, melt the margarine. Saute onions, green peppers, zucchini, and mushrooms until tender. Add cubed tomatoes and cook 5 minutes more. Lower heat and continue cooking until most of the liquid is reduced.

In a medium bowl beat eggs with salt and pepper and add to vegetables. Stir until done.

Serve over rice or in pita.

SHAKSHOOKA

A creamy Israeli sauce perfect for lunch or a light supper when served over rice or in pita.

3 pounds tomatoes
½ cup margarine
1 medium onion, diced
1 Tbsp. flour
3 eggs
1 tsp. salt
Dash of pepper

USE: 10-inch skillet
YIELDS: 4 to 6 servings

To peel tomatoes, drop them into a saucepan of boiling water for 1 minute. Then plunge into cold water. The skins will slip off easily. Puree the tomatoes in a blender or food processor.

In a large skillet, melt the margarine and saute onion until golden. Add the flour and stir until combined. Stir in the tomatoes and simmer uncovered for 1 hour until thick.

In a medium bowl beat eggs with salt and pepper and add to the tomatoes just before serving. Heat and stir, but do not boil.

LAG B'OMER EGGS

These orange eggs are a special treat for Lag B'Omer.

Eggs
Onion skins
from yellow onions

Allow one egg per person and one whole onion skin per egg. Place eggs and skins into large pot, cover with water, and cook until eggshell turns orange.

MEXICAN SCRAMBLED EGGS

A spicy and exciting breakfast or lunch.

4 Tbsps. margarine
1 small onion, diced
½ green pepper, diced
2 cloves garlic, minced
2 medium tomatoes, diced
8 eggs
2 Tbsps. milk
1 tsp. to 1 Tbsp.
chili powder, to taste
Salt to taste
2 to 3 sprigs parsley, minced
¼ cup Monterey Jack
cheese (optional), grated

USE: 10-inch skillet
YIELDS: 4 servings

Heat 3 tablespoons margarine in a 10-inch skillet. Add onion, pepper, garlic, and tomatoes and saute until soft.

While vegetables are cooking, beat eggs in large bowl with milk. Season with chili powder, salt, and parsley.

Add the remaining 1 tablespoon of margarine to skillet and pour eggs over vegetables. Stir as for scrambled eggs. As eggs begin to become firm, top with cheese.

MEXICAN STYLE EGGS

1 Tbsp. butter or magarine
1 Tbsp. diced onion
4 red chilies, sliced
3 medium tomatoes,
cut into chunks
6 eggs, hard-boiled
and sliced lengthwise
½ cup
Traditional White Sauce
(page 335)
½ cup mashed farmer cheese

USE: 10-inch skillet
1-quart
shallow baking dish
YIELDS: 4 servings

Melt 1 tablespoon butter or margarine in a 10-inch skillet. Saute the onion until soft. Add the sliced chilies and continue cooking over low heat.

Place tomato chunks in a food processor or blender and puree. Add the tomatoes to the frying pan and let stew, covered, for 20 minutes.

Preheat oven to 325°.

Grease a shallow baking dish. Pour in half the sauce to cover the bottom of the dish. Set remaining sauce aside. Place hard-boiled egg halves in a single layer over the sauce and pour remaining sauce over the eggs.

Prepare White Sauce and pour on top of dish. Top with farmer cheese.

Bake for 5 to 10 minutes until cheese melts.

FRITTATA

Frittata is an Italian omelet. It is different from the French in that the French omelet is cooked on one side only and folded so that the inside is moist; the frittata isn't folded, but is placed under the broiler so that the top is golden and puffed.

VEGETABLE FRITTATA

1 medium zucchini, cut into julienne strips

8 medium mushrooms, thinly sliced

1 medium green pepper, sliced

8 cherry tomatoes, quartered

¼ cup olive or vegetable oil

2 cloves garlic, minced

1 tsp. lemon juice

1 tsp. dried rosemary

1 tsp. dried thyme

½ tsp. prepared mustard

8 eggs

½ cup grated Parmesan cheese

1 Tbsp. butter

APPLE FRITTATA

1 apple, peeled and thinly sliced

½ cup chopped walnuts

½ cup raisins

2 tsps. honey

2 tsps. cinnamon

½ tsp. nutmeg

¼ tsp. ground cloves

¼ tsp. coriander

2 Tbsps. butter

8 eggs

2 Tbsps. milk

1 Tbsp. butter

Whipped cream

POTATO FRITTATA

2 cups shredded potatoes

8 scallions, chopped

1 Tbsp. dried dill

¼ cup soy sauce

¼ cup butter or oil

8 eggs

2 Tbsps. water

1 Tbsp. olive or vegetable oil

Scallions

USE: 10-inch skillet
YIELDS: 4 servings

VEGETABLE FRITTATA: In a medium bowl combine zucchini, mushrooms, green pepper, and cherry tomatoes. In a cup combine ¼ cup oil, garlic, lemon juice, rosemary, thyme, and mustard. Pour over vegetables and let marinate 15 minutes. Pour vegetables and marinade into frying pan and saute lightly to evaporate all moisture. Remove from pan and let cool.

In a large bowl, beat eggs with fork or wire whisk; add cheese, and stir in vegetables.

Heat skillet over high heat for 1 minute. Add 1 tablespoon butter and swirl until melted. Add egg mixture. Cook gently over medium heat, lifting sides of frittata to let uncooked eggs flow underneath. Cook 5 to 7 minutes until edges are set. (Top will be soft.) Place pan under broiler flame and broil until top is golden and puffed, 5 to 7 minutes.

APPLE FRITTATA: In a medium bowl, combine apples, walnuts, raisins, honey, cinnamon, nutmeg, cloves, and coriander. Melt 2 tablespoons butter in a skillet. Add fruit and cook over medium-high heat for 7 to 10 minutes until golden. Set aside to cool.

In a large bowl, beat eggs with fork or wire whisk, beating in milk. Stir in apple mixture.

Heat skillet over high heat for 1 minute. Add 1 tablespoon butter and swirl until melted. Add mixture and cook as above.

Garnish with whipped cream.

POTATO FRITTATA: In a medium bowl combine potatoes, scallions, dill, and soy sauce. Melt butter or oil in a 10-inch skillet. Add vegetables and saute, until soft, 5 to 7 minutes. Set aside to cool.

In a large bowl, beat eggs with fork or wire whisk, beating in water. Stir in potato mixture.

Heat skillet over high heat for 1 minute. Add oil and swirl. Add mixture and cook as above.

Garnish with dill or scallions.

EGG SALAD

This is a good sandwich filler or a tasty appetizer served on a bed of lettuce with tomato wedges or olives.

7 eggs, hard-boiled
½ Tbsp. oil (optional)
¼ tsp. salt
1 medium onion, chopped (optional)
1 stalk celery, finely chopped
2 Tbsps. mayonnaise
½ tsp. prepared mustard
⅛ tsp. pepper
2 Tbsps. chopped parsley or chives

YIELDS: 6 servings

Peel eggs. Mash in a medium bowl with oil and salt. Add onion, celery, and mayonnaise. Mix well with mustard and pepper.

Garnish with chopped parsley or chives.

MATZOH BREI

2 matzohs
1 cup water
2 eggs
½ tsp. salt
1 Tbsp. butter or oil

USE: 7-inch skillet
YIELDS: 2 servings

Break matzohs into small pieces and soak in a deep bowl with water for 2 to 3 minutes. Drain and squeeze out water.

In a medium bowl beat the eggs with salt and add softened matzoh. Mix well.

Heat butter or oil in a 7-inch skillet and fry mixture on both sides until crisp.

Sprinkle with cinnamon and sugar or top with sour cream.

Dairy Soups

Soup is an appealing first or second course for any meal. A dollop of sour cream or a layer of bubbly melted cheese add richness. In warm weather try a cold soup served in chilled bowls. In cold weather a hearty, full-bodied soup warms the whole family.

COLD SOUR CREAM—GREEN BEAN SOUP

A refreshing soup to perk up a summer lunch or dinner.

1 pound fresh green beans, cut into 1-inch pieces
1 Tbsp. salt
Water
4 onions, diced
¼ cup margarine or oil
1 pint sour cream
½ tsp. pepper

USE: 6-quart pot
Large skillet
YIELDS: 8 to 10 servings

Place beans in 6-quart pot; add salt and cover with water, leaving approximately 1-inch space from top of pot. Cover and cook beans on high heat until water begins to boil. Lower heat and simmer until beans are tender, approximately 20 minutes. Cool in liquid.

While beans are cooling, saute onions in large skillet in margarine or oil until golden brown. Add the sauteed onions to the beans.

When beans have cooled, remove about 2 cups of reserved liquid from pot and place in separate bowl. Very slowly, using only a small amount at a time, add a little sour cream to the liquid. Mix together, trying not to let the sour cream lump. When the sour cream has dissolved, continue the same procedure until all the sour cream has been used. Pour the sour cream mixture back into the pot of green beans and mix thoroughly.

Add pepper and additional salt if desired. Place in refrigerator and serve cold.

FRESH PEA SOUP WITH DUMPLINGS

4 pounds fresh peas (weight with pods)
4 cups water
1 tsp. brown sugar (optional)
1 tsp. salt
White pepper
½ cup white wine (optional)
2 cups milk
3 scallions, diced

Mini Dumplings (page 139)

USE: 4-quart pot
YIELDS: 6 servings

Shell peas. Cook in a 4-quart pot, in water to cover, about 4 cups, 15 minutes. Puree in blender and put back in pot. Add brown sugar, salt, pepper, wine, and milk. Simmer several minutes until heated through. Serve with dumplings and garnish with scallions.

MINI DUMPLINGS: Prepare dumplings according to directions. Bring to a boil in separate pot of salted water.

FRENCH ONION SOUP

If stoneware soup bowls are available, brown the cheese in the bowls under the broiler for authentic French onion soup!

4 Tbsps. butter
2 Tbsps. oil
7 cups sliced yellow onions
1 tsp. salt
2 tsps. minced garlic
1 tsp. basil
1 tsp. thyme
3 Tbsps. flour
8 cups water
Salt and pepper to taste

CROUTONS
8 1-inch-thick slices French bread
2 tsps. olive oil
1 garlic clove
1 cup grated cheese

USE: 4-quart pot
Baking sheet
YIELDS: 8 servings

In a 4-quart pot melt butter and oil over moderate heat. Add onions and seasonings and cook, stirring occasionally, for 20 to 30 minutes until onions are golden brown. Sprinkle flour over onions and continue stirring 2 to 3 minutes more. While stirring, add water gradually and simmer covered, 40 more minutes. Add salt and pepper to taste.

CROUTONS: Preheat oven to 325°. Brown bread on baking sheet 15 minutes. Lightly brush each slice with olive oil. Turn and brown another 15 minutes or until dry and golden brown. Rub each slice with garlic and set into bowls. Pour soup over bread in bowl and top with grated cheese.

SOUR CREAM—POTATO SOUP

5 cups water
2½ cups peeled and diced potatoes (3 large potatoes)
1 *pareve* bouillon cube or package
½ tsp. black pepper
2 tsps. seasoned salt or 1 tsp. regular salt
1 tsp. ground cumin
1 tsp. arrowroot or ½ Tbsp. cornstarch
¼ cup cold water
1 cup milk or light cream
1 cup sour cream
1 tsp. chervil

USE: 3-quart pot
YIELDS: 4 servings

In a 3-quart pot combine water, potatoes, and bouillon. Simmer until potatoes are tender, about 15 minutes.

Mash potatoes but do not drain. Add pepper, salt, and cumin; simmer 10 minutes. Blend arrowroot into cold water until it is dissolved. Pour into milk and stir slowly into soup. Blend sour cream into soup and heat but do not boil. Sprinkle with chervil and serve immediately.

HEARTY POTATO SOUP

**3 cups peeled and
cubed potatoes**
3 cups water
3 Tbsps. butter
**I cup chopped onions
or leeks**
I carrot, grated
1½ tsps. salt
½ tsp. pepper
2 Tbsps. parsley
3 Tbsps. farina
3 cups milk

USE: 4-quart pot
Small saucepan
YIELDS: 6 servings

In a 4-quart pot, simmer potatoes in water until fork-tender.

In a small pan, heat butter and saute onions until golden brown. Add onions to potatoes. Add grated carrot, salt, pepper, and parsley. Bring to boil and add farina, stirring constantly until thoroughly dissolved. Add milk and heat through until warm. Do not boil.
Serve hot.

CREAMY TOMATO SOUP WITH RICE

Although this creamy, savory soup involves a few simple steps in preparation, the results are sure to please.

2 Tbsps. oil or margarine
2 Tbsps. flour
2 cups hot milk
I onion, finely diced
I carrot, finely diced
I clove garlic, minced

I Tbsp. oil
**I 28-ounce can tomatoes,
chopped, plus liquid**
I bay leaf
½ tsp. basil or parsley flakes
2 tsps. salt
I tsp. sugar (optional)

½ - I cup cooked rice

USE: Small saucepan
4-quart pot
YIELDS: 6 to 8 servings

Heat 2 tablespoons oil in small saucepan and brown flour, stirring constantly. Slowly add hot milk and bring almost to boiling, stirring constantly. Turn off heat and let stand.

In a 4-quart pot, heat I tablespoon oil and saute onion, celery, carrot, and garlic. Add tomatoes and liquid and spices. Add 2 cups water and bring to boil. Simmer covered 15 to 20 minutes and remove bay leaf.

Blend half of soup at a time in blender. Return to pot. Add rice and boiled milk. Reheat but do not boil.

Garnish each bowl with dill.

Entrees and Accompaniments

BLINTZES

The Russians call them blini, *the French call them crepes, and in Jewish cooking, blintz is a household word.*

BLINTZES ILLUSTRATED

1 Prepare batter and filling of your choice. Using a paper towel or basting brush, apply a thin coating of oil to a 7-inch skillet. Place skillet over medium heat until skillet is hot but not smoking.

2 Ladle approximately ⅓ cup of batter into the skillet. Tilt pan to swirl the batter so it covers the bottom of the skillet.

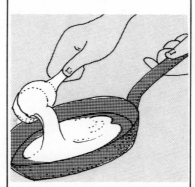

3 Fry on one side until small air bubbles form, and top is set. Bottom should be golden brown. When done, carefully loosen edges of blintz and slip out of skillet onto a plate.

4 Repeat the above procedure until all the batter is used. Grease the skillet as needed.

5 Turn each blintz so that golden brown side is up. Place 3 tablespoons of filling on one edge in a 2½-inch long by 1-inch wide mound.

6 Roll once to cover filling. Fold the sides into the center and continue rolling until completely closed.

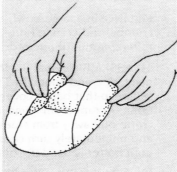

7 Heat 2 tablespoons of oil in the skillet and place each blintz seam side down in the skillet and fry 2 minutes on each side, turning once.

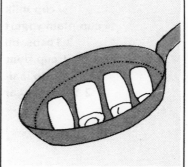

CLASSIC CHEESE BLINTZES

Blintzes are a traditional dish for the holiday of Shavout. Top with sour cream, apple sauce or cinnamon and sugar.

BATTER
4 eggs
½ cup milk
½ cup water
1 cup flour
¼ cup sugar
1 package vanilla sugar
Pinch of salt
1 Tbsp. oil

CHEESE FILLING I
½ pound farmer cheese
4 ounces cream cheese
4 Tbsps. honey or maple syrup
Juice of ½ lemon
1 egg yolk

CHEESE FILLING II
1 pound cottage cheese, strained
2 egg yolks
2 Tbsps. flour
2 Tbsps. sugar
1 tsp. vanilla sugar
¼ cup raisins (optional)

USE: 7-inch skillet
YIELDS: 12 blintzes

BATTER: In a large mixer bowl combine eggs, milk, water and blend well. Gradually add flour, then both sugars, salt and oil. Beat well until there are no lumps in the batter. See Blintzes Illustrated (page 83).

FILLING I: Combine all ingredients in a bowl and beat well. Or combine all the ingredients in a blender container and blend until smooth.

FILLING II: Combine all ingredients, except raisins, in a bowl and beat well. Or all the ingredients can be combined in a blender container and blended until smooth. Then add raisins.

TO ASSEMBLE: Fill and fry according to Blintzes Illustrated.

VARIATION
□ Whole-wheat pastry flour can be used instead of white flour.

ORANGE YOGURT CREPES

BATTER
4 eggs
½ cup orange juice
¼ cup milk
¼ cup plain yogurt
2 Tbsps. oil
1 cup flour
¾ tsp. salt
2 Tbsps. sugar

BATTER: In a large bowl, beat eggs. Add orange juice, milk, yogurt, oil, flour, salt, and sugar. Beat until smooth. Let stand at room temperature for 1 hour.

FILLING: In a large bowl, mix cottage cheese, egg, sugar, crumbs, and orange rind. Beat until smooth and place in refrigerator until needed.

TO ASSEMBLE: Heat a 7-inch skillet. Brush with oil or margarine and spoon in 2 tablespoons of batter. Tilt skillet so that batter covers the bottom of pan evenly. Cook over medium flame 15 to 20 seconds, until edges of crepe pull away from sides of pan; lift crepe with fingers and immediately turn crepe onto waxed paper. Repeat until batter is used up, oiling pan for each crepe.

Place 3 tablespoons of filling on browned side of crepe. Shape filling into 3-inch oblong. Roll once to cover filling.

►

FILLING

1 pound cottage cheese

1 egg

3 Tbsps. sugar

¼ cup fine bread crumbs or cookie crumbs

1 tsp. grated orange rind

2 Tbsps. margarine

USE: 7-inch skillet
YIELDS: 12 servings

Fold the sides to the center and continue rolling until completely closed. Melt 2 tablespoons of margarine in large skillet and fry for 4 to 5 minutes until golden, turning once.

For "how to" diagrams, see Blintzes Illustrated (page 83).

SPINACH BLINTZES

BATTER

4 cups milk

6 eggs

2 Tbsps. margarine or butter, melted

Pinch of salt

4 cups flour

Butter or margarine to coat pan

FILLING

2 pounds spinach or Swiss chard

2 Tbsps. margarine

1 large onion, diced

1 green pepper, diced

1 tsp. salt

Pinch of pepper

Pinch of nutmeg

2 Tbsps. grated mozzarella

TOMATO SAUCE (OPTIONAL)

3 Tbsps. oil

1 large onion, diced

5 plum tomatoes, cut up

1 Tbsp. tomato paste

1 tsp. salt

¼ tsp. pepper

USE: 7-inch skillet
Small saucepan
YIELDS: 3 dozen blintzes

BATTER: Prepare batter in two batches. Place half of the milk, eggs, melted margarine, and salt in a blender. Blend until smooth and light. Continue blending while gradually adding half of the flour. Pour into large bowl. Repeat with other half of the ingredients. Add to large bowl and let rest ½ hour. While batter is resting prepare filling.

FILLING: Soak and carefully check the spinach or Swiss chard. Trim stems. Cook in saucepan with water that clings to leaves for 10 minutes. Drain and set aside. Melt margarine in frying pan and saute diced onion until transparent. Add green pepper and continue cooking 5 minutes more. Next add spinach or chard, salt, pepper, and nutmeg and cook 10 minutes. Remove from flame and stir in grated cheese.

SAUCE: Heat oil in small saucepan and saute onion. Add tomatoes, tomato paste, and seasonings and stir. Lower flame and simmer until heated through.

TO MAKE BLINTZES: Using a basting brush or paper towel apply a thin coating of oil to a 7-inch skillet and heat. Pour a small amount of batter into pan, tilting pan so that batter covers the entire bottom. Brown each crepe lightly on both sides.

TO ASSEMBLE: Place 2 tablespoons of filling on each crepe. Roll once to cover filling. Fold the side to the center and continue rolling until completely closed. Blintzes may be served with Tomato Sauce, and can be eaten either hot or cold.

For "how to" diagrams, see Blintzes Illustrated (page 83).

MUSHROOM-CHEESE BLINTZES

BATTER
1 Recipe Classic
Cheese Blintzes Batter
(page 84)

FILLING
3 Tbsps. margarine
1 large onion, diced
2 cloves garlic, minced
2 pounds mushrooms, sliced
¼ cup diced
green pepper (optional)
3 Tbsps. flour
1 cup milk
½ tsp. salt
⅛ tsp. pepper
½ tsp. basil
1 pound mozzarella or
Monterey Jack cheese, grated

USE: 7-inch skillet
10-inch skillet
YIELDS: 12 blintzes

Prepare batter as directed.

FILLING: Melt margarine in a 10-inch skillet and saute onion, garlic, mushrooms, and green pepper, if used, for 10 to 15 minutes. Add flour and stir. Slowly add milk while stirring; add salt, pepper, and basil. Cook, stirring, over low heat until mixture thickens. Stir in cheese. Once thick, set aside.

TO ASSEMBLE: Fill and fry according to Blintzes Illustrated (page 83).

BAKED BLINTZ LOAF

A delicious variation of classic blintzes, it bakes like a cake, but tastes like real blintzes.

BATTER
½ cup margarine, melted
2 eggs
1 tsp. baking powder
3 Tbsps. sugar
¾ cup milk
1¼ cups flour

CHEESE FILLING
1 pound cottage cheese
2 Tbsps. margarine, softened
1 egg
1 Tbsp. sour cream
1 tsp. salt
1 Tbsp. sugar
4 ounces cream cheese

USE: 9 x 5-inch loaf pan
YIELDS: 4 to 6 servings

Preheat oven to 350°.

Grease 9 x 5-inch loaf pan.

BATTER: Combine all batter ingredients in a large bowl and beat well. Pour half of batter into 9 x 5-inch loaf pan.

CHEESE FILLING: In a bowl, combine all filling ingredients and beat well. Pour filling over batter.

Cover filling with second half of the batter. Bake for 1 hour. Let cool for 10 minutes. Slice and serve with applesauce or sour cream.

CASSEROLES AND VEGETABLES

Vegetables and cheese can be combined for a one-pot meal. Casseroles are a delicious way to present protein, carbohydrates, and vitamins. Simple to make and tasty, these attractive dishes serve as a main or side dish.

BROCCOLI-CHEDDAR CHEESE CASSEROLE

CHEESE SAUCE
1 onion, diced
3 Tbsps. oil
4 Tbsps. butter or margarine
4 Tbsps. flour
2 cups milk
½ tsp. salt or to taste
¼ tsp. pepper
Dash of nutmeg
Pinch of turmeric
¼ tsp. paprika
1 tsp. dry mustard
1½ cups grated cheddar cheese

20 ounces frozen chopped broccoli
½ cup white flour or whole-wheat flour
3 eggs, beaten

¼ cup wheat germ

USE: 7-inch skillet
1½-quart casserole
YIELDS: 6 servings

CHEESE SAUCE: Heat oil in 7-inch skillet; saute onion until golden and set aside.

Preheat oven to 350°.

In a saucepan, melt butter slowly over low heat. Stir in flour, blending until smooth. Slowly stir in milk, then add sauteed onion to flour mixture. Cook mixture, stirring with wooden spoon, until thickened and smooth. Place in oven for 20 minutes. Remove, add seasonings, and stir in cheese until melted. Set aside.

In a separate pot, cook broccoli and drain. In a large bowl combine drained broccoli, flour, and eggs. Add the cheese sauce and pour into a 1½-quart greased casserole.

Sprinkle top with wheat germ. Bake for 35 minutes or until cheese is bubbly.

CLASSIC SCALLOPED POTATOES

6 medium potatoes, thinly sliced
3 Tbsps. chopped onions
3 Tbsps. flour
1 tsp. salt
⅛ tsp. pepper
¼ cup margarine
2½ cups milk, heated

USE: 2-quart casserole
YIELDS: 6 servings

Preheat oven to 350°.

In a greased 2-quart casserole, arrange potatoes in three layers. Between each potato layer, sprinkle one-third of the onion, flour, salt, and pepper, dotting each layer with margarine.

Pour hot milk over the layers.

Bake casserole, covered, for 30 minutes. Uncover and continue baking another 60 minutes or until potatoes are tender.

VEGETARIAN STUFFED EGGPLANT

2 small eggplants
1 tsp. salt
3 Tbsps. oil
1 medium onion, diced
1 green pepper, diced
1 small zucchini, cubed
2 cloves garlic, diced
1 6-ounce can tomato paste
1 tsp. sugar
½ tsp. salt
¼ tsp. pepper
1 tsp. oregano
2 cups cooked kidney beans
8 ounces
Muenster cheese, grated

USE: 10-inch skillet
Baking sheet
YIELDS: 4 servings

Preheat oven to 350°.

Wash eggplant well. Do not peel. Cut each eggplant in half lengthwise. Scoop out centers, leaving 1-inch shell. Dice eggplant pulp and reserve.

Fill 10-inch skillet with ½-inch water and 1 teaspoon salt. Place shells in water, skin side up, and bring to a boil over high flame. Lower flame, cover, and simmer 10 minutes. Drain shells and put them on baking sheet, skin side down.

Heat oil in 10-inch skillet, saute onion, green pepper, zucchini, garlic, and reserved eggplant until tender. Add tomato paste, sugar, seasonings, and cooked kidney beans. Simmer uncovered 10 minutes longer.

Fill shells with vegetable mixture and top with grated cheese. Bake for 10 minutes.

POLENTA WITH TOMATO SAUCE

The heartiness of corn meal, topped with a spiced tomato sauce, makes a delicious side dish.

2 cups milk
1 egg, beaten
¾ cup cornmeal

SAUCE
3 Tbsps. oil
2 medium onions, chopped
½ cup chopped mushrooms
1 15-ounce can tomato puree
¼ tsp. thyme
¼ tsp. sage
¼ tsp. pepper
2 cloves garlic, minced
1 Tbsp. parsley flakes

½ cup grated
mozzarella cheese

USE: Double boiler
9 x 5-inch loaf pan
10-inch skillet
9 x 9-inch baking pan
YIELDS: 6 servings

In the top of a double boiler, over simmering water combine milk and egg. Bring to boil and add cornmeal slowly, stirring constantly to avoid lumps. Cook 10 to 15 minutes or until very thick. Spoon polenta into 9 x 5-inch loaf pan and chill until firm or overnight.

SAUCE: In a 10-inch skillet heat oil and saute onions and mushrooms until tender. Add tomato puree and seasonings and simmer 30 minutes.

Preheat oven to 350°.

When ready to serve, cut polenta into 6 slices and place slices on a 9 x 9-inch baking dish. Top with sauce and grated cheese. Bake uncovered 30 minutes. Let stand 5 minutes before serving.

CAULIFLOWER AND CHEESE PUFF

1 small head of cauliflower
3 ounces cheddar or
Muenster cheese, grated
1 thin slice (½-inch thick)
bread or challah, shredded
2 tsps. prepared mustard
1 Tbsp. mayonnaise
2 eggs, well beaten
Dash of salt
Dash of pepper

USE: 2-quart pot
9 x 5-inch loaf pan
YIELDS: 4 servings

Thoroughly wash cauliflower and break into florets. Place in 2-quart pot with 1-inch of boiling water and cook until soft, about 10 to 15 minutes. Remove cauliflower with a slotted spoon to a large bowl and mash.

Preheat oven to 325°.

Combine 2 ounces cheese, bread, mustard, mayonnaise, eggs, and salt and pepper with cauliflower. Pour into greased 9 x 5-inch loaf pan. Bake for 40 minutes. Top with remaining 1 ounce of grated cheese and place under broiler until browned.

EGGPLANT PARMESAN

2 medium eggplants
Salt

MARINARA SAUCE
2 Tbsps. oil
2 Tbsps. butter or
margarine
2 cloves garlic, minced
4 cups peeled tomatoes
1 6-ounce can tomato paste
8 chopped parsley sprigs
⅛ tsp. black pepper
¼ tsp. salt
1½ tsps. oregano

EGGPLANT COATING
½ cup flour
2 eggs
½ cup bread crumbs or
matzoh meal or
cornflake crumbs
1 tsp. oregano
½ tsp. salt
¼ tsp. black pepper
6 Tbsps. oil
¼ cup butter or
margarine

2 cups grated mozzarella
or cheddar cheese

USE: 10-inch skillet
9 x 13-inch pan
YIELDS: 6 to 8 servings

Slice unpeeled eggplant into ½-inch rounds and sprinkle lightly with salt. Let drain on paper towels for ½ hour.

MARINARA SAUCE: Prepare the Marinara Sauce while the eggplant is draining. Heat the oil and butter in a 10-inch skillet and saute the garlic over a low flame for 5 minutes. Add the tomatoes, tomato paste, and remaining ingredients. Stir well and simmer uncovered for 35 minutes.

Preheat the oven to 350°.

EGGPLANT COATING: Pat the eggplant slices dry and sprinkle lightly with flour. Place the eggs in a bowl and beat lightly. Combine bread crumbs with seasonings in a flat plate. Dip eggplant slices in beaten eggs, then in seasoned bread crumbs. Heat oil and butter or margarine in 10-inch skillet and brown the eggplant slices, cooking for 5 minutes on each side until golden.

TO ASSEMBLE: Cover bottom of pan with a thin layer of sauce. Place eggplant slices on top, spoon half of the sauce over eggplant, and sprinkle with half the cheese. Cover with remaining eggplant. Pour the remaining sauce over the eggplant. Sprinkle with the rest of the cheese. Bake for 20 to 25 minutes.

CREAMY GREEK POTATO SALAD

A new combination of vegetables and dressing gives this potato salad a superb texture and taste.

2 pounds potatoes
1 stalk celery, chopped
½ cup chopped olives
1 Tbsp. grated
American cheese
1 Tbsp. minced parsley
¼ tsp. dill weed
1 tsp. salt
⅛ tsp. black pepper
Juice of 1 lemon
¼ cup mayonnaise
8 ounces cottage cheese
½ cup milk

USE: 3-quart pot
YIELDS: 6 to 8 servings

Boil potatoes in skin until tender, but firm. Cool, peel, and slice the potatoes. Combine remaining ingredients in a large bowl and mix well. Pour over potatoes. Cover and place in refrigerator for a few hours, then mix again. Serve chilled.

LEBANESE PASTRY WITH SPINACH FILLING

DOUGH
1 package dry yeast
1 cup warm water
1 cup milk
5 cups white flour
1½ cups whole-wheat flour
1 Tbsp. salt
¾ cup oil

Oil for brushing on dough

FILLING
2 pounds spinach
2 large onions, chopped
¼ cup oil
1½ cups grated
mild cheddar cheese
¼ tsp. pepper
1 tsp. salt
2 Tbsps. lemon juice
¼ cup chopped
pimiento (optional)

USE: 10-inch skillet
Baking sheet
YIELDS: 24 pastries

DOUGH: In a medium bowl dissolve yeast in water. Add milk, then add dry ingredients and oil. Knead on floured surface until smooth and elastic. Place dough in oiled bowl and brush top with oil. Let dough rise in warm place until double in bulk.

FILLING: Wash spinach and pat dry; chop or tear into small pieces. In a 10-inch skillet saute chopped onion in ¼ cup oil until soft. Combine spinach, onions, cheese, seasonings, lemon juice, and pimiento if desired, and mix well.

Preheat oven to 450°.

TO ASSEMBLE: Punch down dough and roll out in a large square to ¼-inch thickness. Cut into 5-inch squares. Place 1 tablespoon filling on each square and fold over to make a triangle, pinching edges together. Place pastries on greased baking sheet. Brush with oil and bake for 25 minutes or until golden.

BROCCOLI-RICE AND CHEESE CASSEROLE

3 Tbsps. oil
2 medium onions, diced
1 pound broccoli, chopped
4 cloves garlic, minced
1⅓ cups rice
3 cups water
1 tsp. salt
Pepper to taste
½ cup wheat germ
8 ounces mozzarella cheese, coarsely grated
1½ to 2 cups Tomato Sauce (page 336)

USE: 3-quart pot
3-quart casserole
YIELDS: 6 servings

In a 3-quart pot, heat oil and saute onions until golden; add broccoli, garlic, and rice. Cook, stirring, over medium heat for 5 minutes. Add water, salt, and pepper and bring to a boil. Lower heat, cover, and simmer 20 minutes or until all water is absorbed. Add wheat germ and half of the grated cheese.

Transfer mixture to a 3-quart greased casserole. Pour Tomato Sauce over mixture and top with remaining cheese. Place casserole under broiler for approximately 10 minutes or until cheese browns.

SPANAKOPITA

This elegant appetizer or side dish may be prepared in advance and refrigerated, or frozen unbaked until needed. Thaw before baking.

10 ounces fresh spinach
¼ cup butter
1 onion, chopped
2 Tbsps. dill
½ cup grated Parmesan cheese, or hard cheese, grated
1 pound cottage cheese
3 eggs, beaten
Salt to taste
Pepper to taste
8 phyllo sheets
½ cup butter, melted

USE: 10-inch skillet
7 x 11-inch
Pyrex baking dish
YIELDS: 8 servings

Carefully wash spinach, remove stems, and chop. Set spinach aside. In a 10-inch skillet, melt ¼ cup of butter and saute onion until soft. Add the spinach and cook until all the moisture has evaporated.

In a small bowl, combine dill, Parmesan or hard cheese, cottage cheese, and eggs and blend well. Add spinach and season the mixture with salt and pepper to taste.

Preheat oven to 350°.

Line a greased 7 x 11-inch Pyrex baking dish with four phyllo sheets, brushing each piece with melted butter as you layer them. Spread filling evenly over the phyllo sheets, and cover with the remaining four sheets, once again brushing each piece with melted butter. Tuck edges under and brush with butter once more. Bake for 30 minutes until puffed and golden. Serve immediately.

VARIATION
☐ **Whole-Wheat Spinach Pie:** Prepare a double recipe of Whole-Wheat Pie Crust (page 448). Roll out into two pieces. Use the first to line the Pyrex baking dish and the second to cover the filling.

ZUCCHINI AND POTATO CASSEROLE

3 medium potatoes (1 pound),
scrubbed but not peeled
2 Tbsps. butter
2 eggs
8 ounces mozzarella cheese,
finely diced
½ cup grated
Parmesan cheese
1 large zucchini, grated
¼ cup onion, finely diced
¼ tsp. salt
¼ tsp. pepper
2 Tbsps. fine
dry bread crumbs

USE: 3-quart saucepan
9-inch pie plate
YIELDS: 4 servings

In a 3-quart saucepan cook potatoes in boiling salted water 25 to 30 minutes or until tender. Drain and peel them. In a large bowl, mash the potatoes and combine with the rest of the ingredients, except for the bread crumbs and 1 tablespoon of butter.

Preheat oven to 400°.

Generously grease a 9-inch pie plate and coat with half of the bread crumbs. Fill the plate with the potato mixture and smooth top. Sprinkle with the remaining crumbs and dot with the remaining 1 tablespoon of butter. Bake for 30 minutes or until puffed and golden.

TOFU-STUFFED ZUCCHINI

4 zucchini
1 small onion
2 tomatoes, peeled
2 Tbsps. oil
2 Tbsps. flour
8 ounces tofu, blended
2 cloves garlic
Salt to taste
Pepper to taste
6 ounces mozzarella cheese,
grated, for topping

USE: 5-quart Dutch oven
1-quart saucepan
Baking sheet
YIELDS: 8 servings

In 5-quart Dutch oven parboil zucchini for 10 minutes in boiling water. Remove from pot and cool. Cut zucchini in half lengthwise and trim bottoms so they lie flat. Scoop out inside and salt lightly. Chop zucchini pulp, onion, and tomatoes. Set aside.

In a 1-quart saucepan, heat 1 tablespoon oil. Add flour and cook, stirring, for about 5 minutes. Add tofu and cook, stirring until thick.

Preheat oven to 350°.

In a skillet heat 1 tablespoon of oil and saute zucchini, onion, and garlic. Remove from heat. Add chopped tomatoes, season with salt and pepper, and stir in tofu sauce.

Stuff zucchini halves with tofu and vegetable mixtures, then top with mozzarella cheese. Place on greased baking sheet. Bake for 20 to 30 minutes or until cheese melts.

ZUCCHINI PARMESAN

Slices of zucchini layered with tomato sauce and cheese. A delicious vegetarian dish.

6 cups zucchini,
thinly sliced
1 clove garlic,
minced (optional)
3 Tbsps. oil

In a 2-quart saucepan, cook zucchini in small amount of water until crisp and tender. Drain and cool slightly. In small skillet, saute garlic in oil until brown. Stir in tomato sauce, salt, oregano, and basil and heat through.

►

8 ounces tomato sauce
1 tsp. salt
¼ tsp. oregano
¼ tsp. basil
1 cup cottage cheese
1 egg, beaten
1 tsp. parsley flakes
¼ cup bread crumbs
4 ounces mozzarella cheese, shredded

USE: 2-quart saucepan
8 x 8-inch square pan
YIELDS: 4 to 6 servings

Preheat oven to 350°.

In a separate bowl, mix cottage cheese, egg, and parsley flakes. Place half the zucchini in greased 8 x 8-inch pan. Sprinkle with half the bread crumbs, half the sauce mixture, half the cottage cheese mixture and half the mozzarella cheese. Repeat layers, saving enough mozzarella for topping.

Bake for 25 minutes Sprinkle remaining cheese on top and bake 3 more minutes.

Serve immediately.

KUGELS

Jewish cuisine has a wide variety of vegetable and pasta puddings held together with eggs. These dairy kugels are often served as the basis of a weekday meal. Cottage cheese or sour cream gives an added creaminess and flavor, with cinnamon and sugar enhancing the dish.

ALMOND CROWNED KUGEL

KUGEL
8 ounces medium noodles
4 Tbsps. butter, melted
½ cup sugar
1 cup sour cream
2 cups milk
1 pound cottage cheese
½ tsp. salt
1 tsp. vanilla extract
½ pound farmer cheese
½ pound cream cheese
6 eggs, beaten

TOPPING
½ cup brown sugar
½ cup slivered almonds
2 Tbsps. butter, melted

USE: 4-quart pot
9 x 13-inch pan
YIELDS: 9 to 12 servings

Preheat oven to 350°.

KUGEL: In a 4-quart pot cook noodles in boiling salted water for 10 minutes. Drain and rinse with cold water. In a large bowl combine the remaining kugel ingredients and stir in noodles. Pour into a greased 9 x 13-inch pan.

TOPPING: Prepare topping by combining brown sugar, almonds, and melted butter. Sprinkle over noodles. Bake for 1 hour.

CUSTARD KUGEL

8 ounces fine noodles
1 cup butter, softened
1 cup sugar
½ pound cream cheese
8 eggs
1 pint sour cream
2 tsps. vanilla extract

USE: 4-quart pot
12-inch round casserole
YIELDS: 8 servings

Preheat oven to 350°.

In a 4-quart pot cook noodles in boiling salted water for 5 minutes. Drain and rinse in cold water. Turn into a greased 12-inch casserole.

In a separate bowl, beat butter, sugar, cream cheese, eggs, sour cream, and vanilla extract. Pour egg mixture over noodles and mix. Bake for 1 hour or until browned.

Serve chilled.

NOODLE PUDDING WITH CRUMB TOPPING

PUDDING
16 ounces broad noodles
1 pound cottage cheese
1 pint sour cream
1 cup milk
½ cup butter, melted
½ cup sugar
4 eggs, beaten
½ cup raisins or cherries or crushed pineapple, drained

TOPPING
1 cup crushed cornflakes
1 tsp. cinnamon
¼ cup brown sugar

USE: 4-quart pot
9 x 13-inch pan
YIELDS: 9 to 12 servings

Preheat oven to 350°.

PUDDING: In a 4-quart pot cook noodles in boiling salted water for 10 minutes. Drain and rinse with cold water.

In a large bowl mix all pudding ingredients with noodles and pour into a greased 9 x 13-inch pan.

TOPPING: Mix topping ingredients in a separate bowl and sprinkle on top of pudding. Bake for approximately 1 hour or until top is brown.

PINEAPPLE NOODLE PUDDING

PUDDING
8 ounces medium noodles
1 cup fresh pineapple, cut into small cubes
2 Tbsps. sugar
½ pound cottage cheese
4 Tbsps. butter
½ cup brown sugar
3 eggs
1 tsp. vanilla extract
⅓ cup raisins

Preheat oven to 350°.

PUDDING: In a 4-quart pot cook noodles in boiling salt water for 10 minutes. Drain and rinse in cold water. In a small saucepan, place cubed pineapple and add sugar. Cover tightly and cook about 1 minute. Remove from heat.

In a large bowl combine cottage cheese, butter, brown sugar, eggs, vanilla, and raisins. Add pineapple and combine all ingredients with noodles. Place in greased 9 x 13-inch pan.

►

TOPPING
1 Tbsp. butter
¼ cup
graham-cracker crumbs
1 Tbsp. sugar

USE: 4-quart pot
9 x 13-inch pan
YIELDS: 9 to 12 servings

TOPPING: Combine butter, graham cracker crumbs, and sugar. Sprinkle on top of kugel.

Bake for 1 hour.

PASTA AND PIZZA

Bubbly and hot from the oven, pizza and pasta dishes such as lasagna noodles layered with cheese and tomato sauce are delicious alternatives to meat for a main course. Serve them with salad and dessert for a complete meal.

CHEESY LASAGNA IN SPICY SAUCE

8 ounces lasagna noodles

SPICY VEGETABLE SAUCE
2 Tbsps. oil
2 medium onions, minced
4 cloves garlic, minced
2 green peppers,
finely chopped
2 to 4 stalks celery,
finely chopped
½ pound mushrooms, sliced
½ tsp. basil
½ tsp. thyme
½ tsp. oregano
½ tsp. sage
½ tsp. rosemary (optional)
3 dashes curry powder
3 dashes cayenne pepper
Pinch marjoram
2 16-ounce cans
tomato sauce or
5 to 8 fresh tomatoes,
chopped, or 1 20-ounce can
whole tomatoes plus 1
4-ounce can tomato paste
2 bay leaves
½ cup dry red wine

½ pound mozzarella cheese
1 pound cottage cheese

USE: 10-inch skillet
9 x 13-inch pan
YIELDS: 6 servings

Cook lasagna noodles in large pot of boiling salted water until barely tender, 12 to 15 minutes. Drain and rinse with cold water. Lay on linen towel in a single layer and cover with a damp towel.

SAUCE: Heat oil in a 10-inch skillet. Saute onions, garlic, green peppers, celery, mushrooms, and spices. Add in tomato sauce or its equivalent, and bay leaves. Cover and simmer for 1 hour. After 1 hour, stir in the wine and cook for 5 minutes more.

Preheat oven to 350°.

Grate mozzarella cheese and drain excess liquid from cottage cheese through a sieve.

TO ASSEMBLE: Spoon a little sauce into bottom of 9 x 13-inch pan and put a layer of noodles over it. Put more sauce over noodles, dot with spoonfuls of cottage cheese and sprinkle with grated cheese. Continue to make layers until all noodles, sauce, and cheeses are used up, ending with cheese on top.

Bake covered for 45 minutes to 1 hour.

CHEESE-SPINACH LASAGNA ROLLS

A creamy spinach filling rolled up in lasagna noodles and baked in a velvety white sauce.

1 pound lasagna noodles

FILLING
2 bunches fresh spinach or
4 10-ounce packages
frozen chopped spinach
15 ounces ricotta cheese or
small-curd cottage cheese
2 eggs
2 egg yolks
1 cup
grated Parmesan cheese
½ tsp. salt
½ tsp. pepper
¼ tsp. nutmeg

WHITE SAUCE
3 Tbsps. butter
¼ cup flour
1½ cups milk
¼ tsp. salt

USE: 2-quart saucepan
1-quart saucepan
9 x 13-inch baking pan
YIELDS: 8 servings

In large pot, bring water to rapid boil and slip in each lasagna strip. Boil 10 minutes. Drain and rinse in cold water. Lay on linen towel in single layer and cover with damp towel.

FILLING: If using frozen spinach, follow directions on package for cooking and drain well. If using fresh spinach, soak and check leaves. Cook in 2-quart saucepan with water that clings to leaves; drain well. Place spinach in a large bowl with ricotta or cottage cheese, whole eggs, yolks, Parmesan cheese, seasonings, and mix well.

WHITE SAUCE: In a 1-quart saucepan, melt butter and stir in flour. Stir together over heat until blended. Then add milk slowly and stir until sauce thickens. Stir in salt before removing from flame.

Preheat oven to 350°.

TO ASSEMBLE: Cut cooled lasagna in half and spread with 2 teaspoons of filling. Roll up and place seam side down in 9 x 13-inch baking pan. Pour white sauce over all and bake 20 minutes.

MACARONI AND CHEESE CASSEROLE

8 ounces macaroni

SAUCE
2 Tbsps. butter
1 Tbsp. minced onion
(optional)
2 Tbsps. flour
1 tsp. salt
1 tsp. dry mustard
1½ cups milk
2 cups grated Monterey Jack
or cheddar cheese

¼ cup buttered bread crumbs
or 1 sliced tomato
Paprika

USE: 2-quart saucepan
2-quart casserole
YIELDS: 4 servings

Cook macaroni in a large pot of boiling, salted water for 7 to 9 minutes. Drain and rinse in cold water.

SAUCE: Heat butter in a 2-quart saucepan over medium heat and brown onion. Add flour, salt, and mustard and cook until flour stops foaming, stirring continuously. Slowly stir in milk and cook for 2 minutes or until sauce is smooth and thick. Do not overcook. Add 1¼ cups cheese. Heat until melted, stirring occasionally.

Preheat oven to 375°.

Combine macaroni and sauce in a 2-quart greased casserole. Top with remaining cheese, bread crumbs or tomato slices, and paprika. Bake for 20 to 25 minutes or until lightly browned.

TOFU LASAGNA

This protein-rich dish is a complete meal in itself.

**1 8-ounce package
whole-wheat lasagna noodles**

FILLING
2 pounds tofu, mashed
½ cup chopped parsley
1 egg, beaten
1 tsp. onion powder
½ tsp. garlic powder
½ tsp. salt

SAUCE
2 Tbsps. olive oil
1 medium onion, chopped
2 large cloves garlic, minced
**1 medium
green pepper, chopped**
½ pound mushrooms, sliced
1 15-ounce can tomato sauce
2 tsps. oregano
1 tsp. basil
¼ tsp. salt

**1 pound mozzarella
cheese, grated**

USE: 2-quart saucepan
9 x 13-inch pan
YIELDS: 6 servings

In a large pot, bring water to a rapid boil and slip in each lasagna strip. Boil 10 minutes. Drain, rinse, and cool in water. Lay on linen towel in single layer and cover with damp towel.

FILLING: In a separate bowl, mix tofu, parsley, egg, onion powder, garlic powder, and salt.

SAUCE: In a 2-quart saucepan, heat oil and saute onion, garlic, green pepper, and mushrooms for 10 minutes. Add tomato sauce, oregano, basil, and salt and heat through.

Preheat oven to 350°.

TO ASSEMBLE: In the 9 x 13-inch baking dish, layer noodles, filling, sauce, and cheese. Repeat, topping dish with tomato sauce.

Bake for 45 to 50 minutes until bubbly.

NOODLES WITH CREAMED BROCCOLI SAUCE

12 ounces wide noodles
1 medium onion, chopped
¼ cup margarine
2 cups chopped broccoli
1 or 2 cloves garlic, minced
2 Tbsps. chopped parsley
½ tsp. salt
½ tsp. oregano
3 Tbsps. flour
¾ cup milk or water
**2 cups creamed
cottage cheese**
**¼ pound mozzarella
cheese, grated**

USE: 5-quart Dutch oven
or 10-inch skillet
YIELDS: 4 to 6 servings

Cook noodles in large pot of boiling salted water 12 to 15 minutes. Drain and rinse with cold water.

In a 5-quart Dutch oven saute onion in margarine until soft. Add broccoli and cook, stirring until broccoli is tender but still firm. Add garlic, parsley, salt, and oregano. Stir in flour and add milk or water, mixing thoroughly; add cottage cheese and simmer uncovered 5 minutes.

Combine noodles with broccoli sauce and stir in grated cheese. Cook for 2 to 3 minutes to heat through. Serve immediately.

SPAGHETTI AUBERGINE

Eggplant combined with green peppers and mushrooms in a spiced tomato sauce are a tasty complement to spaghetti.

EGGPLANT SAUCE
1 medium eggplant
2 to 3 Tbsps. oil
2 medium onions, diced
1 green pepper, diced
½ pound mushrooms,
cleaned and quartered
2 to 3 cloves garlic, minced
1 16-ounce can tomato sauce

PASTA
1 pound spaghetti
1 tsp. salt
2 Tbsps. oil or margarine
½ pound mozzarella
cheese, grated

USE: 10-inch skillet
5-quart wide pot
YIELDS: 8 servings

EGGPLANT SAUCE: Peel and dice eggplant and sprinkle with salt. Let stand ½ hour, then rinse off salt and pat dry. Pour oil in a 10-inch skillet and heat. Saute onions, pepper, and mushrooms until tender for approximately 15 to 20 minutes. Add garlic, eggplant, and tomato sauce, then simmer uncovered for 20 minutes, stirring occasionally.

PASTA: In large pot, cook spaghetti in boiling salted water 10 minutes. Drain and rinse with cold water. Place spaghetti in a large bowl or serving platter, add oil or margarine, then stir in grated cheese to coat spaghetti.

Pour hot eggplant sauce over spaghetti on serving platter or individual plates.

BAKED STUFFED SHELLS

12 jumbo pasta shells

FILLING
16 ounces cottage cheese
6 ounces mozzarella
cheese, shredded
6 slices
American cheese, diced
1 egg, beaten
¼ cup bread crumbs
1 Tbsp. chopped parsley

8 ounces Marinara Sauce
(page 334)
2 ounces mozzarella
cheese, shredded
2 Tbsps. bread crumbs

USE: 9 x 13-inch baking dish
YIELDS: 6 servings

Cook shells in boiling salted water in wide pot for 12 to 15 minutes. Drain and rinse with cold water. (The shells are easier to handle when well cooled and will not fall apart while being stuffed.) Set aside.

Preheat oven to 350°.

FILLING: In a bowl, combine cottage cheese, mozzarella, and American cheese. Add beaten egg and stir in bread crumbs and parsley. Stuff each cooled shell with cheese mixture.

Spread a thin layer of Marinara Sauce over bottom of a 9 x 13-inch baking dish. Place stuffed shells in pan. Pour remainder of Marinara Sauce over shells. Top with 2 ounces of cheese and 2 tablespoons of bread crumbs. Bake for 45 minutes or until cheese is melted and bubbling and top is golden.

EASY PIZZA

This requires advance preparation, but once dough is prepared, it's quick and simple to assemble.

1 package dry yeast
⅓ cup warm water
1 cup apple juice
3 cups flour
1 tsp. salt
2 8-ounce cans seasoned tomato sauce
8 ounces Muenster cheese, grated
1 tsp. oregano

USE: 2 round pizza pie pans
YIELDS: 16 slices pizza

In a small bowl dissolve yeast in ⅓ cup warm water; let stand 10 minutes. Sift flour and add yeast mixture, salt, and apple juice into a large bowl. Knead and let rise 1½ hours.

Preheat oven to 450°.

Roll out dough and put into greased pans. Spread 1 cup sauce on each. Top with cheese and sprinkle with oregano.

Bake 15 to 20 minutes. Serve hot.

TOFU CRUST PIZZA

CRUST
1 pound tofu
2 eggs
1 Tbsp. oil
½ tsp. salt
2½ to 3 cups whole-wheat flour
3 Tbsps. baking powder

SAUCE
1 14-ounce can tomato sauce or 1 16-ounce can tomato puree or 1 5½-ounce can tomato paste
½ tsp. oregano
¼ tsp. basil (optional)
¼ tsp. thyme (optional)
1 clove garlic, crushed

TOPPING
1 onion
1 green pepper
1 zucchini
15 mushrooms, sliced (1 cup)
1 8-ounce package mozzarella, Muenster, or Edam cheese, sliced or grated

USE: 2 round pizza pie pans
YIELDS: 16 slices

Preheat oven to 350°.

CRUST: In food processor or blender, process tofu, eggs, oil, and salt. Pour into bowl and add flour and baking powder, mixing until dough is sticky but not hard. With wet hands, spread dough in pans.

SAUCE: Pour tomato sauce over dough. (If using tomato paste, mix first with 1 cup water.) Sprinkle on oregano, basil, thyme, and garlic.

TOPPING: Slice onion and pepper into rings. Cut zucchini in rounds. Arrange vegetables on top of sauce. Place cheese slices on top of vegetables.

Bake for 45 minutes. Serve hot.

SAVORY PIZZA

This versatile pizza can be used to create a simple, delicious meal or a more deluxe version of a favorite food.

DOUGH
1 cup apple juice
1 cup warm water
2 packages dry yeast
2 tsps. sugar
5 cups flour
½ tsp. salt
4 Tbsps. oil

SAUCE
2 cups pizza or marinara sauce or
1 can whole tomatoes, blended, plus
2 Tbsps. olive oil and salt, pepper, and oregano to taste

TOPPING
4 cups grated mozzarella cheese (1 lb.)
1 tsp. salt
½ tsp. pepper
1 tsp. oregano
1 tsp. basil
½ tsp. garlic powder
3 Tbsps. olive oil

USE: 2 or 3 pizza pie pans
YIELDS: 3 medium or 2 large pizza pies

Preheat oven to 350° and grease pans.

DOUGH: Dissolve yeast in water. Add sugar. Let bubble for 10 minutes. Add remaining dough ingredients and knead until dough is satiny. Let rest 5 minutes. Divide dough into two or three parts and roll out. Place into pans. Let rise, covered with damp cloth, for 1 hour.

SAUCE: Spread marinara sauce or tomatoes blended with oil and spices onto dough.

TOPPING: Add grated cheese and spices. Drizzle olive oil over pie.

Bake 30 to 35 minutes.

VARIATION
□ **Deluxe Vegetable Pizza:** Before baking, top each pizza pie with 1 cup vegetables. Possibilities include: sauteed mushrooms, onions, peppers or eggplant, or sliced black olives.

QUICHE

Prepare your favorite pie crust for these elegant quiches. If using a packaged frozen pie crust defrost before filling. Vary the vegetable fillings and serve as a main or side dish.

BASIC CHEESE QUICHE

Perhaps the most familiar of all quiches is the cheese quiche. This mouth-watering traditional recipe offers the option of choosing the cheese you prefer — a full-bodied Swiss or cheddar, or a milder mozzarella.

1 unbaked 9-inch pie crust (page 445)
1 cup grated unprocessed cheese (Swiss, cheddar, mozzarella)
1 small onion, chopped
2 Tbsps. margarine

Prepare pie shell according to directions.

Preheat oven to 350°.

Sprinkle grated cheese evenly over the unbaked pie shell. Saute onion with margarine in a 9-inch skillet until transparent. Cool and spoon evenly over cheese in pie shell.

►

4 eggs
¾ cup milk
½ tsp. salt
¼ tsp. pepper
¼ tsp. nutmeg

USE: 9-inch skillet
9-inch deep pie plate
YIELDS: 4 to 6 servings

In a medium bowl, beat eggs lightly; add milk and seasonings. Mix well and gently pour over cheese in pie shell.

Bake for 45 minutes until crust is golden brown.

SPINACH QUICHE

1 prebaked 9-inch pie shell (page 445)
2 Tbsps. butter
1 Tbsp. shallot or onion, chopped
½ pound cooked, well-drained spinach
⅛ tsp. salt
¼ tsp. pepper
⅛ tsp. nutmeg (optional)
3 eggs
¾ cup milk, approximately
¼ cup grated Swiss cheese
1½ Tbsps. cold butter, diced

USE: 10-inch skillet
9-inch pie dish
YIELDS: 4 to 6 servings

Prepare pie shell according to directions and allow to cool.

Preheat oven to 350°.

Melt butter in 10-inch skillet over low heat; add shallot or onion and saute until transparent. Add drained spinach to skillet plus salt, pepper, and nutmeg. Cook 5 minutes. Cool.

In a small bowl, beat eggs lightly, adding milk to equal 1½ cups liquid.

Combine spinach and egg mixtures in a medium bowl, stir well, add grated cheese, and turn into prebaked pie shell. Dot with diced butter and bake until golden, approximately 30 minutes.

TOMATO QUICHE

A "novel" twist in a quiche — all the basic ingredients but with the tang of tomatoes, hinting at an Italian flavor.

1 unbaked 9-inch pie crust (page 445)
1 cup grated Muenster cheese
1 small onion, chopped
2 Tbsps. butter
½ tsp. salt
½ tsp. pepper
3 eggs
¾ cup milk
2 firm tomatoes, thinly sliced

USE: 7-inch skillet
9-inch deep pie dish
YIELDS: 4 to 6 servings

Prepare pie shell according to directions.

Preheat oven to 350°.

Sprinkle grated cheese evenly over the unbaked pie shell. In a 7-inch skillet, saute chopped onion in butter until transparent; add seasoning and cool.

In a medium bowl, beat eggs lightly and add milk, stirring well.

Spoon onions over cheese in pie shell. Place single layer of thinly sliced tomatoes on top of cheese and onions. Carefully pour egg mixture over all.

Bake until crust is golden brown, approximately 40 minutes.

BROCCOLI QUICHE

1 unbaked 9-inch pie crust
(page 445)
½ pound fresh broccoli,
or 1 10-ounce package
frozen broccoli
1 small onion, chopped
2 Tbsps. margarine
¼ tsp. salt
¼ tsp. pepper
¼ tsp. garlic powder
4 eggs
1 cup cold milk
½ cup grated cheese
(Swiss, Monterey Jack,
Muenster, mozzarella)

USE: 2-quart saucepan
7-inch skillet
9-inch deep pie plate
YIELDS: 4 to 6 servings

Prepare pie shell according to directions.

Thoroughly wash fresh broccoli and finely chop. Place in 2-quart saucepan with water to cover. Simmer until tender. Drain well in colander and cool. (If frozen, prepare according to package directions.)

In a 7-inch skillet, saute chopped onion in margarine until transparent, adding salt, pepper, and garlic powder. Cool.

Preheat oven to 350°.

In a medium bowl, beat eggs lightly, add milk, and stir in cooled onions. Spread broccoli in unbaked pie shell, pour egg mixture over it and sprinkle with grated cheese. Bake until crust is golden brown, 35 minutes.

VARIATION
□ This quiche can be adapted to your favorite vegetables: spinach, zucchini, mushrooms, etc.

EGGPLANT AND TOMATO QUICHE

CRUST
1 ¼ cups flour
¼ tsp. salt
½ cup grated cheese
4 Tbsps. butter, softened,
4 to 5 Tbsps. cold water

FILLING
1 medium eggplant,
cut into ½-inch slices
1 Tbsp. salt
2 Tbsps. oil
1 medium onion
1 17-ounce can Italian
plum tomatoes, mashed
½ tsp. salt
½ tsp. pepper
¼ tsp. basil
¼ tsp. oregano
4 eggs

USE: 10-inch skillet
Quiche pan or pie plate
YIELDS: 6 to 8 servings

CRUST: Combine flour, salt, and cheese. Cream in butter, and add enough cold water to make a soft dough. Cover and chill 1 hour.

Preheat oven to 400°.

Roll out into circle large enough to fit quiche pan or pie plate. Fit into pan and pierce with fork in several places.

Bake at 400° for 7 minutes, lower heat and bake at 350° for 5 minutes. Cool.

FILLING: Sprinkle eggplant slices with salt and let stand for 20 minutes. Rinse and pat dry. Heat oil in 10-inch skillet and saute eggplant slices. Remove and drain on paper towels. Saute onion in same pan; add tomatoes. Stir in seasonings and cook 5 minutes. Add eggplant; stir and remove from heat to cool. Beat eggs until light, add to vegetables and mix.

Pour into crust, and bake at 375° for 25 minutes or until set.

GARDEN VEGETABLE QUICHE

These tender spring vegetables nestled in melted cheese are truly a wholesome meal in a pie dish!

CRUST
½ cup butter, diced,
at room temperature
3 ounces unwhipped
cream cheese at
room temperature
1 cup flour

FILLING
2 Tbsps. butter
1 small onion, diced
1 small carrot, diced
½ green pepper, diced
½ cup diced zucchini
4 mushrooms, diced
½ tsp. salt
¼ tsp. pepper
1 tsp. garlic
1 tsp. paprika

1 cup mozzarella
or Muenster cheese
3 eggs
1 cup milk

TOPPING
3 Tbsps. chopped onion
1 Tbsp. butter

USE: 9- or 10-inch deep
pie dish
10-inch skillet
7-inch skillet
YIELDS: 4 to 6 servings

Preheat oven to 350°.

CRUST: In a large bowl, mix butter, cream cheese, and flour by hand. Pat into a ball and chill for 30 minutes.

FILLING: In a 10-inch skillet, melt butter and saute all diced vegetables until tender but crisp. Pour into bowl to cool and toss well with seasonings.

TO ASSEMBLE: Press crust into 9- or 10-inch pie dish and sprinkle with mozzarella. Spoon sauteed vegetables evenly over cheese. Beat eggs lightly with milk and gently pour over vegetables.

TOPPING: In 7-inch skillet, saute 3 tablespoons onion in butter until brown and crisp.

Sprinkle onions over quiche and bake 1 hour. Serve hot.

SOUFFLES

Light and fluffy souffles are stiffly beaten egg whites folded into a base of egg yolks and flavorings. The light texture adds an elegant touch.

EGGPLANT SOUFFLE

1 large eggplant
2 Tbsps. butter or margarine
2 Tbsps. flour
1 cup tomato juice
1 cup cottage cheese
½ cup grated cheddar cheese (optional)
¾ cup day-old bread crumbs or matzoh meal
2 eggs, separated
1 onion, chopped
½ tsp. salt
½ tsp. pepper

USE: 2-quart saucepan
10-inch skillet
2-quart souffle dish
YIELDS: 6 servings

Preheat oven to 350°.

Peel and dice eggplant. Place in 2-quart saucepan, cover with water, and simmer until soft. Drain in colander and mash.

In 10-inch skillet over low heat, melt butter and stir in flour. Slowly add tomato juice, stirring until thick and smooth. Add cooled, mashed eggplant, cottage cheese, cheddar cheese (if desired), crumbs, egg yolks, onion, and seasonings.

Beat egg whites until stiff. Gently fold into mixture. Pour into greased 2-quart souffle dish or casserole.

Bake 45 minutes without opening oven door.

Serve immediately.

CHEESE SOUFFLE I

¼ cup butter
¼ cup flour
1 cup milk
1 cup grated cheddar or Monterey Jack cheese
½ tsp. salt
½ tsp. dry mustard
¼ tsp. white pepper
4 eggs, separated

USE: 2-quart saucepan
2-quart souffle dish
YIELDS: 6 servings

Preheat oven to 325°.

In a 2-quart saucepan, melt butter over low heat. Stir in flour. Add milk slowly and stir constantly until smooth and thick. Add cheese and seasonings. Continue stirring until cheese melts. Remove from heat.

In a large bowl, beat egg yolks. Slowly pour 1 cup of cheese sauce into beaten yolks, then add it to the rest of the cheese sauce.

Beat whites until stiff. Gently pour cheese sauce into center of whites. Fold together with spatula and pour into 2-quart greased souffle dish or casserole.

Bake without opening oven door, uncovered, until golden brown, 35 to 40 minutes.

Serve immediately.

CHEESE SOUFFLE II

1 cup grated cheddar cheese
2¼ cups fresh bread crumbs
½ cup margarine
1¼ cups milk
¾ tsp. salt
¼ tsp. white pepper
5 eggs, separated

USE: Double boiler
2-quart souffle dish
YIELDS: 6 servings

Preheat oven to 325°.

In top of double boiler over simmering water, combine cheese, bread crumbs, margarine, milk, and seasonings. Adjust seasoning, if necessary. While cheese is melting, beat egg yolks well. Cool melted cheese mixture and add yolks.

Beat egg whites until stiff. Gently fold egg whites into the cooled melted cheese mixture. Pour into greased 2-quart souffle dish.

Bake without opening oven door 30 to 35 minutes or until firm.

Serve immediately.

SPECIALTY CHEESE DISHES

These specialty cheese dishes have made their place in Jewish cuisine. They are an elegant addition to a dairy meal.

CHEESE KNAIDLACH

A dairy combination with the look and texture of the traditional soup knaidlach. These cheese knaidlach rolled in flavored bread crumbs are an unusual side dish.

3 eggs, separated
1 pound farmer cheese
⅓ cup sugar
2 Tbsps. farina
1½ tsps. salt
10 cups water
½ to ¾ cup bread crumbs
2 Tbsps. butter for frying
2 tsps. cinnamon
3 Tbsps. sugar

USE: 4-quart pot
7-inch skillet
YIELDS: 6 to 8 servings

In a large bowl beat the egg whites until stiff. Mix in yolks.

In another bowl, beat cheese until smooth, then add to eggs. Add ⅓ cup sugar and farina.

Add salt to water and bring to a boil in a 4-quart pot. Shape cheese mixture into knaidlach. Test one in boiling water to make sure it doesn't fall apart — if it does, add 1 tablespoon farina to mixture. Cover pot and boil knaidlach 20 minutes, then remove with a slotted spoon and cool.

In a 7-inch skillet, brown bread crumbs in butter. Roll each knaidel in hot crumbs, then sprinkle with cinnamon and sugar. Serve hot.

CHEESE KNISHES

Simple Flaky Dough (page 413)

FILLING
1 pound farmer cheese
2 egg yolks
2 Tbsps. sugar
½ tsp. cinnamon
½ cup raisins

Oil
1 egg yolk and 1 tsp. water
Sesame seeds (optional)

USE: Baking sheet
YIELDS: 14 servings

Prepare one recipe Simple Flaky Dough.

FILLING: Combine cheese, 2 egg yolks, sugar, cinnamon, and raisins in a bowl and mix well with a fork. Set aside.

Preheat oven to 425°.

Divide dough into two portions. Roll each half into a 15 x 10-inch rectangle and brush with oil. Place one-half of the cheese mixture along the long edge of each rectangle closest to you and roll like a jelly roll. Place each on a greased baking sheet and, with a sharp knife, cut halfway down at 2-inch intervals. Brush both loaves with egg yolk and water mixture and sprinkle with sesame seeds.

Bake at 425° for 15 minutes. Reduce heat to 375° and continue baking for about 30 minutes longer or until golden.

For "how to" diagrams, see Blintzes Illustrated (page 83).

POTATO VARENIKES

A delicious cooked dough with potato-cheese filling. A special addition to a dairy dinner during the Nine Days.

DOUGH
1 to 1½ cups flour
1 egg, beaten
½ cup milk
½ tsp. salt

FILLING
2 pounds potatoes
3 Tbsps. oil
1 large onion, diced
¾ pound cottage cheese
½ tsp. salt
Dash of pepper (optional)

USE: 4-quart pot
7-inch skillet
6-quart pot
YIELDS: 25 to 30 varenikes

DOUGH: Combine flour, egg, milk, and salt. Divide dough into four pieces and roll each piece out on a floured surface until very thin. Cut out 3-inch circles by flouring the rim of a glass and pressing into dough. Dough will yield approximately 25 to 30 circles.

FILLING: In a 4-quart pot cook unpeeled potatoes in boiling salted water. Let cool. Peel and mash in a large bowl. In a 7-inch skillet saute onion in oil until golden brown. Add the cottage cheese, seasonings and half the sauteed onion to potatoes and mix well.

TO ASSEMBLE: Place 1 teaspoon of filling in center of circles, then fold in half. Wet edges of dough to seal. Press around edges with tines of fork to help keep the dough together.

To cook, bring lightly salted water to a boil in a 6-quart pot. Drop in 6 to 8 varenikes and let cook approximately 5 minutes until they begin to rise to the top. Remove and place in rows on a platter, being careful not to stack them on top of each other. Repeat until all are done. Sprinkle with remaining sauteed onion.

To serve, top with sour cream or yogurt.

Pastries and Desserts

CHEESECAKE

On Shavout, when dairy meals are usually served, cheesecakes are a tradition. Everyone has a favorite recipe for cheesecake. Crusts range from graham cracker to pie shells to cookie-dough pastry. Shaved chocolate, nuts, fresh or canned fruit give a beautiful finish to a simple cheesecake.

CLASSIC CHEESECAKE WITH NUTS

For an elegant presentation, try this custardy cheesecake with the flavor of toasted hazelnuts.

1½ cups hulled hazelnuts or blanched almonds

CRUST
Butter
⅓ cup
graham cracker crumbs

FILLING
2 pounds cream cheese
½ cup heavy cream or sour cream
4 eggs
1¾ cups sugar
1 tsp. vanilla extract

USE: 8-inch round cake pan
YIELDS: 8 servings

TO TOAST NUTS: Preheat oven to 400°. Place nuts on baking sheet and bake until browned, approximately 15 minutes, stirring occasionally to ensure even browning. Remove and cool. Place the nuts in a food processor or blender. For a crunchy texture blend coarsely. For smoother texture blend a little longer until pastelike.

CRUST: Butter the inside of an 8-inch cake pan. Do *not* use a spring-form pan. Sprinkle the inside with graham cracker crumbs and shake the crumbs around the bottom and sides until coated. Shake out remaining crumbs and set aside.

Lower oven to 300°.

FILLING: Place the cream cheese, cream, eggs, sugar, and vanilla in a bowl. Using an electric mixer, blend at low speed. Eventually, as the ingredients blend, increase speed to high. Blend until smooth, then fold in nuts.

TO ASSEMBLE: Pour filling into prepared pan and level the mixture by gently shaking. Insert the pan inside a slightly larger pan and pour boiling hot water into the larger pan to a depth of about ½-inch. Do not let the edge of the cheesecake pan touch the larger pan. Place the pans in preheated oven and bake for 2 hours. Then turn off the oven and let cake sit in oven an hour longer. Lift the cake pan out of the water and place on a rack. Let the cake stand at least 2 hours at room temperature and then refrigerate. Place a round cake plate over the cake and carefully turn upside down to unmold cake.

Serve chilled.

BASIC CHEESECAKE

GRAHAM CRACKER CRUST
18 double graham crackers
⅔ cup margarine, softened
⅓ cup sugar

OR

WHOLE-WHEAT CRUST
½ cup oil
1⅓ cups whole-wheat flour
4 Tbsps. brown sugar
¼ cup shredded coconut (optional)

FILLING
1 pound cream cheese
¾ pound cottage cheese
2 eggs
1½ cups sugar
¼ tsp. salt
2½ Tbsps. cornstarch
1¼ cups sour cream
¾ cup milk
1 tsp. vanilla extract

USE: 9 x 13-inch pan
YIELDS: 20 servings

GRAHAM CRACKER CRUST: Crush graham crackers in blender until finely ground. Place crumbs in a large bowl. Add margarine and sugar and combine well. Press firmly into pan on sides and bottom.

Preheat oven to 350°.

WHOLE-WHEAT CRUST: Mix oil, flour, and sugar together in a medium bowl. Add coconut, if desired. Press mixture into bottom of pan. Bake for 5 to 10 minutes, until lightly browned.

FILLING: Beat cream cheese and cottage cheese together until smooth. Add eggs and beat until blended. Combine sugar, salt, and cornstarch with cheese mixture. Add sour cream, milk, and vanilla. Blend well. Pour filling slowly into crust.

Bake for 1 hour. Turn oven off and allow cake to cool in oven for about 1 hour.

Serve chilled.

TOPPING SUGGESTIONS: Add fresh fruit or berries, shaved almonds, or ½ cup reserved graham cracker crust.

NOTE: Graham crackers can also be crushed by hand. Place in plastic bag and fasten tightly. Crush grahams with rolling pin.

NO-BAKE CHEESE PIE

This delicious creamy cheese pie is easy to prepare. An ideal recipe for those who do not have a dairy oven. However, the graham cracker crust must be baked in a pareve or dairy oven.

GRAHAM CRACKER CRUST
9 double graham crackers
¼ cup margarine, softened
3 Tbsps. brown sugar

FILLING
1 cup cream cheese
½ cup farmer cheese
1 cup sour cream
½ cup honey
1 tsp. vanilla extract

1 pint sliced strawberries or whole blueberries

USE: 9-inch pie pan
YIELDS: 8 servings

Preheat oven to 375°.

GRAHAM CRACKER CRUST: Crush graham crackers in blender until finely ground. Place crumbs in a large bowl. Add margarine and sugar and combine well. Press firmly into pan on sides and bottom. Bake 10 minutes. Remove from oven and cool.

FILLING: In a large bowl combine cheese, sour cream, honey and vanilla. Beat well. Pour filling into cooled crust. Freeze for 8 hours or overnight.

Thaw pie in refrigerator for 1 hour before serving. Garnish generously with fresh strawberries or blueberries.

CREAM CHEESE PIE

GRAHAM CRACKER CRUST
11 double graham crackers
4 Tbsps. sugar
½ cup butter or margarine, softened

FILLING
3 eggs
½ cup sugar
12 ounces cream cheese
1 tsp. vanilla extract

TOPPING
1 cup sour cream
2 Tbsps. sugar
1 tsp. vanilla extract
Reserved crumbs

USE: 9-inch deep-dish pie plate
YIELDS: 8 servings

GRAHAM CRACKER CRUST: Crush graham crackers in blender until finely ground. Reserve ¼ cup crumbs for topping. Place remainder in a large bowl. Add sugar and butter to remaining crumbs and mix well. Line deep dish pie plate and refrigerate.

Preheat oven to 375°.

FILLING: In a large bowl beat eggs well. Add sugar, cream cheese, and vanilla and beat until well blended. Pour into crust. Bake for 20 minutes. Turn off oven and leave pie in oven for 1 hour; remove and cool for 10 minutes.

Raise oven to 450°.

TOPPING: In a small bowl combine topping ingredients and pour over pie. Bake for 5 minutes. Remove and cool. Sprinkle with reserved crumbs and chill for 3 hours before serving.

VARIATION
☐ **Cherry Cheese Tarts:** Reduce amounts of filling ingredients as follows: 2 eggs, ⅓ cup sugar, 8 ounces cream cheese. Using 2 mini-cupcake pans, press a heaping teaspoon of crust mixture in the bottom of each form. Fill each crust with cream-cheese mixture. Bake 10 minutes. Remove and chill thoroughly. When ready to serve top with a teaspoon of canned cherry-pie filling. Yields: 24 tarts.

DELUXE CHERRY CHEESECAKE

GRAHAM CRACKER CRUST
9 double graham crackers
⅓ cup margarine, softened

FILLING
24 ounces cream cheese, softened
1 cup sugar
2 Tbsps. flour
1 Tbsp. lemon juice
2 tsps. grated lemon rind
4 eggs

TOPPING
1 20-ounce can cherry or blueberry pie filling

USE: 9-inch spring-form pan
YIELDS: 10 servings

GRAHAM CRACKER CRUST: Crush graham crackers in blender until finely ground. Place in a large bowl. Add margarine and combine well. Press firmly into pan on sides and bottom.

Preheat oven to 325°.

FILLING: In a large bowl beat softened cream cheese with a hand mixer until smooth. Add remaining ingredients, except eggs. Beat until well blended. Add eggs, one at a time, mixing well after each egg. Pour mixture into crust. Bake for 1¼ hours. Cool and loosen cake from rim of pan.

TOPPING: Spoon pie filling over cheesecake.

Serve chilled.

TOPPING VARIATIONS
☐ Stir 3 tablespoons apricot jam until smooth and spread over cooled cake. Sprinkle top with slivered almonds.

☐ Top with shaved chocolate and walnut halves.

☐ Top with mandarin oranges and crushed pineapple.

CHEESE PIE

CRUST
½ cup sugar
1 cup plus 3 Tbsps. margarine, softened
1 egg
3 Tbsps. orange juice
½ tsp. rum flavoring
2½ cups sifted flour

FILLING
3 eggs, separated
¾ cup sugar
2 cups cottage cheese, sieved
2 Tbsps. flour
¼ tsp. salt
2 Tbsps. sour cream
1 Tbsp. melted margarine
1 tsp. lemon juice

½ cup finely chopped pecans

USE: 2 9-inch pie pans
YIELDS: 2 pies

Grease two 9-inch pie pans.

CRUST: In a large bowl cream sugar and margarine. Add egg and beat until smooth. Stir in juice, rum flavoring, and flour. Mix until dough forms a ball. Wrap in wax paper and refrigerate overnight. Next day, divide dough in half. Roll each half out into a ¼-inch thick circle on a floured board. Fit loosely into two 9-inch pie pans. The crust should be 1-inch wider than the pan so it can be fluted upright.

Preheat oven to 325°.

FILLING: In a small bowl beat whites until stiff. Add ¼ cup sugar and beat until thick and glossy. Set aside. In another bowl beat yolks, add ½ cup sugar, and beat again until thick and smooth. Set aside. Combine cottage cheese, flour, salt, and sour cream and mix in a large bowl. Add yolk mixture. Blend in melted margarine and lemon juice and mix until blended. Fold whites into cottage cheese mixture. Pour into pastry and sprinkle with nuts. Bake for 1 hour and 15 minutes.

Serve chilled.

STRAWBERRY-AMARETTO CHEESECAKE

GRAHAM CRACKER CRUST
9 double graham crackers
3 Tbsps. sugar
⅓ cup butter or margarine, softened

FILLING
2 pounds cream cheese, softened
1½ cups sugar
1 cup heavy cream or milk
6 eggs
3 Tbsps. lemon juice, freshly squeezed
½ tsp. brandy extract
1 cup sour cream
1 Tbsp. vanilla extract
2 Tbsps. flour
1 cup chopped fresh strawberries

GRAHAM CRACKER CRUST: Crush graham crackers in a blender until finely ground. Place in a large mixing bowl, combine with sugar and butter. Press firmly into the bottom of a well-buttered 9- or 10-inch spring-form pan. Chill in the refrigerator for about 30 minutes.

Preheat oven to 425°.

FILLING: In a large bowl, beat the cream cheese, sugar, and cream until smooth. Add the eggs one at a time, making sure that the mixture is smooth after beating in each egg. Add the lemon juice, brandy extract, sour cream, vanilla, and flour; continue to beat until smooth and creamy. Fold in the chopped strawberries. Pour the mixture into the chilled spring-form pan and bake at 425° for 15 minutes, then reduce the temperature to 275° and continue to bake for 1 hour. Transfer to a rack and allow to cool for 3 hours.

TOPPING: In a medium-sized bowl, marinate the strawberries in the Amaretto and sugar for about 3 to 4 hours.

Preheat oven to 350°.

►

TOPPING
**2½ cups sliced
fresh strawberries**
1 cup Amaretto liqueur
½ cup sugar

USE: 9- or 10-inch
spring-form pan
YIELDS: 8 to 10 servings

Drain the strawberries and spread evenly over the top of the cake. Bake for 7 minutes. Transfer to a wire rack and allow to cool completely for 2 hours. Remove the sides of the spring-form pan and refrigerate overnight. Remove cake from refrigerator at least 2 hours before serving. Serve at room temperature.

PINEAPPLE TOPPED CHEESECAKE

GRAHAM CRACKER CRUST
9 double graham crackers
6 Tbsps. sugar
6 Tbsps. ground almonds
**½ cup melted butter or
margarine**
¼ cup sour cream
1 tsp. creme de cacao
¼ to ½ tsp. cinnamon

FILLING
¾ pound cottage cheese
4 ounces cream cheese
1 tsp. vanilla extract
1 cup sugar
2 eggs, beaten

TOPPING
1 cup sour cream
1 tsp. vanilla extract
**1 8-ounce can
crushed pineapple, drained**
½ cup chocolate morsels

USE: 9-inch spring-form pan
YIELDS: 8 servings

GRAHAM CRACKER CRUST: Crush graham crackers in blender until finely ground. Place in a large bowl, add remaining crust ingredients and combine well. Press firmly into sides and bottom of pan. Bake 15 minutes. Cool.

Preheat oven to 350°.

FILLING: In a large bowl, combine filling ingredients and mix well. Pour over crumb crust. Bake for 40 minutes.

TOPPING: In a small bowl, blend sour cream and vanilla and spread over cake. Cover with drained pineapple and sprinkle with chocolate morsels. Bake for an additional 20 minutes. Turn oven off and allow cake to cool in oven for about 1 hour.

Serve chilled.

SUPREME CHEESECAKE

GRAHAM CRACKER CRUST
9 double graham crackers
⅓ cup margarine, softened

FILLING
8 ounces cream cheese
¾ cup sugar
Juice of ½ lemon
8 ounces farmer cheese
2 eggs
3 tsps. vanilla extract

TOPPING
1 cup sour cream
2 tsps. vanilla extract
1 tsp. lemon juice
1 tsp. sugar

USE: 9-inch spring-form pan
YIELDS: 8 servings

GRAHAM CRACKER CRUST: Crush graham crackers in blender until ground fine. Place crumbs in a large bowl. Add margarine and combine well. Press firmly into pie pan on sides and bottom of pan.

Preheat oven to 350°.

FILLING: In medium bowl, beat cream cheese and add the sugar. Add remaining ingredients and beat until smooth and creamy, approximately 2 minutes. Pour into graham cracker crust. Bake for 45 minutes.

TOPPING: In a small bowl, combine topping ingredients and spread on top of baked pie. Bake an additional 15 to 20 minutes.

Serve chilled.

VARIATION
□ **Marble Cheesecake:** Melt 2 ounces baking chocolate with 1 tablespoon of margarine over very low flame. Remove from heat and cool.

Prepare pie filling as directed above. Combine ½ cup cheese mixture with cooled chocolate. Pour remaining filling into prepared pan, then drizzle chocolate-cheese mixture over filling. Cut through filling with knife to marble. Bake and mix topping as directed above.

PASTRY

Nothing adds more to the richness of pastry than fresh cream cheese or butter. A light Babka filled with a smooth creamy filling is the perfect breakfast treat.

HALACHIC NOTE: *Dairy cakes and pastries must be distinguishable as being dairy, and kept separately from pareve baked goods.*

LEMON-CHEESE BABKA

DOUGH
1 tsp. sugar
¾ cup lukewarm water
1 package dry yeast
1 cup milk
6 Tbsps. butter, softened
2 tsps. lemon rind
⅓ cup sugar
1 tsp. salt
2 eggs plus 2 egg yolks
3½ to 4 cups flour
½ cup raisins

DOUGH: In a large bowl, dissolve 1 teaspoon sugar in ¾ cup lukewarm water. Sprinkle yeast on top and let stand for 10 minutes. Stir well. Add milk, butter, lemon rind, sugar, salt, and eggs to yeast mixture. Beat in half of the flour until smooth. Add remaining flour and knead well for 5 minutes. Form into a ball and place in a greased bowl. Cover with a cloth. Let rise in a warm place until double in bulk, about 1 to 1½ hours. Punch down, cover, and let rise again until double in bulk, about 45 minutes. When dough has doubled the second time, punch down and knead in raisins.

►

CHEESE FILLING
8 ounces cream cheese
½ cup cottage cheese
1 egg yolk
½ cup sugar
1 tsp. lemon rind

CRUMB TOPPING
⅓ cup chopped
walnuts or pecans
3 Tbsps. flour
3 Tbsps. butter, softened
3 Tbsps. sugar
¼ tsp. cinnamon

USE: 2 9-inch round layer pans
YIELDS: 2 cakes

CHEESE FILLING: Beat cream cheese and cottage cheese together until smooth. Beat in egg yolk and sugar; stir in lemon rind. Grease two 9-inch round layer pans.

CRUMB TOPPING: Mix all ingredients together well.

Preheat oven to 350°.

TO ASSEMBLE: Divide dough into four equal parts. Press one part into the bottom and sides of each pan. Spread each with about 1 cup cheese filling. Shape remaining dough into 9-inch circles. Place on top of cheese filling and press edges to seal. Sprinkle half of crumb topping over each babka. Let rise in warm place about 1 hour or until dough rises and reaches top of pan (*not* until doubled). Place foil loosely over crumb topping. Bake at 350° for 40 minutes. Invert onto wire rack, then turn right side up. Let cool at least 30 minutes before cutting.

ORANGE CHEESE STRUDEL

DOUGH
1 egg
1 cup butter, melted
¾ cup lukewarm orange juice
3 cups sifted flour
1 tsp. grated orange rind

½ cup ground walnuts
½ cup dry bread crumbs

FILLING
12 ounces cream cheese, softened
¼ cup butter
¼ cup brown sugar
½ tsp. grated orange rind
1 Tbsp. frozen orange juice concentrate
2 Tbsps. flour
2 cups chopped orange segments

USE: Jelly-roll pan
YIELDS: 2 strudels

DOUGH: In a large mixing bowl, beat the egg. Stir in 2 tablespoons butter and half of the orange juice. Stir in half of the flour and the orange rind. Add the remaining flour and juice. Turn dough onto lightly oiled pastry board. Knead 10 minutes. Form into ball, cover for 20 minutes.

Divide dough in half. Spread out a cloth and sprinkle it with flour. Pat half the dough into a 6-inch square. Brush with melted butter. Place hands under middle of dough and pull and stretch in both directions. Move the cloth around until dough becomes tissue-thin and 18-inches square.

Mix walnuts and bread crumbs. Brush the dough with melted butter and sprinkle with half of the walnut-crumb mixture.

Preheat oven to 350°.

FILLING: In a small bowl, beat together all the filling ingredients. Spread 1 cup of filling over one end of the square in an 18 x 3-inch strip. Pick up the opposite end by its corners and fold it over the filled half. Roll tightly like a jelly roll.

Place in pan and repeat with remaining dough and filling. Brush strudel with butter. Bake 1 hour basting every 15 minutes with butter. Cool on rack.

CREAM CHEESE HORN OF PLENTY

DOUGH
8 ounces cream cheese
1 cup butter, softened
2¼ cups flour
⅛ tsp. salt

1 cup confectioners' sugar

Strawberry or raspberry preserves
½ cup chopped walnuts or almonds

USE: Baking sheet
YIELDS: 16 rugelach

DOUGH: Combine cream cheese and butter in a mixing bowl. Add flour and salt. Using a wooden spoon, mix into a smooth ball; avoid overworking the dough. Wrap ball in foil and chill for several hours or overnight, until ball is firm.

Preheat oven to 375°.

Divide dough in half. Place each half on a large board that has been covered with confectioners' sugar. Roll out into a large circle ¼-inch thick. Spread preserves over dough and sprinkle with chopped nuts. Cut like a pie into 3- or 4-inch wedges and roll each wedge, starting at the wide end. Turn ends in toward each other to form a crescent.

Bake for 20 minutes or until golden brown on a greased baking sheet. Let cool before removing from sheet.

ICE CREAMS, CONFECTIONS, AND PUDDINGS

Delight your family and guests with ice cream and other desserts. The addition of fruit, nuts, and spices enhances the flavor.

CHOCOLATE PUDDING

⅔ **cup sugar**
⅓ **cup cocoa**
3 Tbsps. cornstarch
¼ **tsp. salt**
2¼ cups milk
1 tsp. vanilla extract
1 egg (optional; see Note)

USE: 1½-quart saucepan
YIELDS: 6 ½-cup servings

In a 1½-quart saucepan, combine the first four ingredients. Gradually stir in the milk. Cook over medium heat, stirring constantly, until mixture comes to a boil. Boil 1 minute. Add vanilla. Spoon into individual glasses and chill. Serve cold.

NOTE: If using egg, beat egg in a separate bowl with a fork. Add one spoonful of hot pudding at a time to the egg, beating constantly with the fork until the egg mixture is quite warm. Beat this mixture quickly back into the pudding.

VANILLA PUDDING

1 Tbsp. baking powder
4 cups milk
2 cups sugar
2 Tbsps. cornstarch

USE: 3-quart saucepan
YIELDS: 10 servings

Add baking powder to 2 cups of milk and let stand 5 minutes.

Meanwhile, in a saucepan, combine the remaining 2 cups milk with sugar and cornstarch and bring to a boil while stirring continuously until it thickens. Add first 2 cups of milk and continue cooking until it thickens again. It should turn a deep yellow color.

Spoon into individual glasses and chill. Serve cool.

NOTE: Even milk that has turned a bit sour can be used.

BLENDER ICE CREAM

A dairy treat or a tasty pareve substitute made with soy milk.

1 cup milk or soy milk
¼ cup honey or sugar
2 tsps. vanilla extract
1 egg (optional)
4 tsps. cocoa or carob powder
1 cup oil

USE: Blender
YIELDS: 2 cups

Combine all ingredients except oil in blender. Begin to blend at high speed. Remove the top of the blender container and slowly dribble the oil into the center of the milk mixture. Continue until mixture thickens and no more oil can be absorbed. Turn off blender. If a drop of oil remains on top of the mixture turn blender on and off quickly.

Pour mixture into a container and freeze.

VARIATION
□ Instead of cocoa, a ripe banana or ½ cup strawberries may be mashed, or peanut butter or maple flavoring plus walnuts folded in.

NOTE: You can buy a commercial soy milk product or, if it is unavailable, combine 1 part soy flour to 3 parts water in a blender. Blend to eliminate lumps. Simmer on very low flame for 20 minutes, stirring often.

EASY ICE MILK DESSERT

For any age at any time!

2 Tbsps. cocoa or
1 tsp. instant coffee
1 cup sugar
5 large eggs
3 cups milk

USE: 2-quart container
or 16 ice-pop molds
YIELDS: 16 pops

Dissolve cocoa or coffee in a small amount of hot water.

Beat sugar, eggs, and dissolved cocoa or coffee with mixer at high speed until well beaten, about 2 minutes. With mixer still going, gradually add milk. Pour into container or ice-pop molds.

Cover and freeze.

For smoother ice milk, beat again after partially frozen.

Let stand a few minutes before serving in order to scoop easily.

FUDGICLES

A treat that takes only minutes to make.

½ cup margarine, softened
4 eggs
½ cup sugar
1 cup milk
3 Tbsps. cocoa

10 ice cream sticks

USE: Blender
Ice-pop molds
YIELDS: 8 to 10 pops

Place all ingredients into blender container and blend for 8 minutes. Pour mixture into ice-cube trays or small cups with ice cream sticks and freeze. Ice-pop holders may be used.

VARIATION
□ Substitute flavored imitation gel dessert for cocoa to make fruit-flavored variations.

OLD-FASHIONED FRENCH VANILLA ICE CREAM

½ cup sugar
2 Tbsps. cornstarch
¼ tsp. salt
1 egg
2 cups milk
1½ tsps. vanilla extract
1 cup nondairy dessert topping

USE: Double boiler
1-quart container
YIELDS: 1 quart

Mix sugar, cornstarch, and salt in the top of a double boiler. Add egg and stir well. Slowly stir in milk. Place over boiling water and cook, stirring constantly, until mixture is slightly thickened, about 5 to 6 minutes.

Remove from heat, add vanilla and cool. Pour into pan and freeze until just firm. Remove to a chilled bowl. Beat with mixer.

Whip dessert topping. Fold frozen mixture into whipped dessert topping. Refreeze for 2 to 3 hours.

VARIATIONS
☐ **Chocolate:** Omit egg and add 2 ounces unsweetened baking chocolate in its place.

☐ **Coffee:** Substitute 1 cup strong coffee for 1 cup milk.

CREAMY WHITE FUDGE

3 ounces cream cheese
1 tsp. vanilla extract
2¾ cups confectioners' sugar
½ cup chopped walnuts

USE: 9 x 5-inch loaf pan
YIELDS: 16 pieces fudge

Grease a 9 x 5-inch loaf pan.

Beat cream cheese with vanilla until smooth. Continue beating while slowly adding confectioners' sugar. Fold in walnuts.

Spread out in loaf pan and cover with plastic wrap. Refrigerate. This will keep in refrigerator for 2 weeks.

APPLE CRUNCH PUDDING

Apples, cinnamon, and nutmeg make this dessert a real treat.

6 slices white bread or challah
1 cup milk
3 Tbsps. butter
3 eggs
½ cup sugar
1 cup peeled, diced apples
⅔ cup seedless raisins
¼ tsp. nutmeg
¼ tsp. cinnamon
¼ tsp. salt
⅓ cup brown sugar, firmly packed

USE: 6-cup baking dish
2-quart saucepan
YIELDS: 6 servings

Toast bread lightly and cut into ½-inch cubes. Place in a buttered 6-cup baking dish.

Preheat oven to 300°.

In a 2-quart saucepan, heat milk slowly with butter until the butter melts. Pour over bread cubes; let stand ½ hour.

Beat eggs in a large bowl; stir in remaining ingredients except for brown sugar. Fold into bread mixture. Sprinkle brown sugar on top.

Bake for 45 minutes or until apples are tender.

Spoon into dessert dishes. Serve warm, topped with cream or ice cream.

Sidelights

DRINKS

Hot cocoa or old-fashioned milk shakes are delightful and soothing for the whole family.

BASIC MILK SHAKE

2 eggs
3 Tbsps. sugar or honey
5 ice cubes
1½ cups milk

USE: Blender
YIELDS: 2 servings

Place eggs and sugar or honey in blender. Blend until thick. Add ice and milk and blend until frothy.

Serve cold.

VARIATION
□ Omit sugar or honey. Beat eggs in glass and stir in 3 tablespoons fruit juice. Add crushed ice and milk.

BANANA MILK SHAKE

1 cup milk
1 tsp. honey
½ tsp. vanilla extract
1 small ripe banana
1 egg

USE: Blender
YIELDS: 2 servings

Blend all ingredients in blender or food processor for 1 minute, until thick and smooth.

Serve cold.

COCOA DRINK

2 Tbsps. sugar
2 Tbsps. cocoa
Pinch salt
1 cup warm water
3 cups milk

USE: 1½-quart saucepan
YIELDS: 4 servings

In 1½-quart saucepan, combine sugar and cocoa. Add salt and stir in water until well blended. Bring to a boil over low heat and boil 2 minutes, stirring constantly. Add milk slowly, stirring constantly. Heat but do not boil. Serve hot.

VARIATION
□ Add a dash of cinnamon and ¼ teaspoon vanilla extract.

HOT CHOCOLATE DRINK

1½ ounces
semisweet chocolate
¾ cup water
3 Tbsps. sugar
Pinch salt
2¼ cups milk

USE: Double boiler
YIELDS: 4 servings

Combine chocolate and water in top of double boiler. Cook over low flame until chocolate is melted. Add sugar and salt. Pour in milk gradually, stirring constantly. Cook 3 or 4 minutes over low heat. Before serving, beat with wire whisk until frothy.

Serve hot.

DIPS

Decorative platters of cooked and raw vegetables with dips are an elegant way to serve hors d'oeuvres. Serve dips with crackers, cut-up vegetables or fruit.

CHIVE AND CHEESE SPREAD

1 pound pot cheese or
farmer cheese
2 Tbsps. chopped chives
or caraway seeds

USE: Blender
YIELDS: 2 cups

Place cheese in a blender and blend on medium until cheese is a spreadable and creamy consistency.

Place cheese in a bowl and fold in chives or caraway seeds with a rubber spatula. Cover and chill.

CONFETTI DIP

⅔ cup plain yogurt
⅓ cup mayonnaise
2 Tbsps. chopped chives
2 Tbsps. minced onion
2 Tbsps. chopped
green pepper
2 Tbsps. dried parsley
2 Tbsps. chopped pimiento
or red pepper
⅛ tsp. paprika
Dash cayenne pepper
(optional)

USE: 1-quart bowl
YIELDS: 1½ cups

In a small bowl, combine yogurt and mayonnaise. Mix well. Combine remaining ingredients and mix until well blended.

Cover and refrigerate for several hours before serving to allow flavors to blend. Serve chilled.

CREAMY WHITE DIP

1 cup mayonnaise
½ cup fresh parsley sprigs
2 scallions
2 Tbsps. white vinegar
2 tsps. sugar
¼ tsp. salt
¼ tsp. dry mustard
⅛ tsp. garlic powder
⅛ tsp. pepper
½ cup plain yogurt

USE: Blender
YIELDS: 1½ cups

Place all ingredients except yogurt in blender and blend until smooth. Place in a small bowl and fold in yogurt. Cover and chill.

DIET DIP

4 Tbsps. cottage cheese
4 Tbsps. ricotta cheese
2 Tbsps. skim milk
1 tsp. parsley
2 Tbsps. lemon juice
½ tsp. dill
½ small onion
1 Tbsp. soy sauce

USE: Blender
YIELDS: ½ cup

Place all ingredients in blender. Blend well. Pour into a small bowl. Cover and chill.

SPINACH DIP

1 package frozen chopped spinach
½ cup chopped parsley
½ cup chopped scallions
½ tsp. dill seed
½ tsp. oregano
Juice of ½ lemon
1 cup mayonnaise
1 cup sour cream

USE: Blender
YIELDS: 3 cups

Thaw and squeeze out all water from frozen spinach.

Blend spinach, parsley, and scallions in blender or food processor. Remove and add herbs, seasonings, lemon juice. Combine mayonnaise and sour cream in a large bowl. Fold in spinach mixture. Cover and chill.

VEGETABLE-YOGURT DIP

1 medium onion
1 medium cucumber
½ green pepper (optional)
⅔ cup plain yogurt
½ tsp. minced garlic

USE: Blender
YIELDS: 1 cup

Peel and dice onion, cucumber, and green pepper, if desired. Place in blender or food processor and chop. Add yogurt and garlic and blend until creamy.

Place in a small bowl. Cover and chill.

HOMEMADE

Cottage cheese and butter are easy to prepare at home. These recipes are especially helpful to those who pride themselves on making everything "from scratch."

BUTTER

For this recipe you can use either heavy cream or fresh, unhomogenized, whole milk.

1 gallon fresh
whole milk, unhomogenized
or 1 cup heavy cream
Ice water

USE: Wide pot
Blender
YIELDS: ½ cup

If using unhomogenized whole milk begin by placing it in a wide pot. The wider the pot the more cream will accumulate. Bring to a boil and remove from heat. Place the pot in the refrigerator and allow to stand 2 to 3 days. Spoon the cream out of the pot into a container and keep in the freezer. Repeat the process until you have accumulated 1 pint of cream.

Pour cream into blender. Cover and whip at lowest speed until yellow beads about the size of corn kernels form. Pour off the buttermilk. Pour ice water into the blender and blend on low for a few seconds to wash the remaining buttermilk out of the butter. Pour off the cloudy rinse water and repeat three times with more clean ice water or until the rinse water pours off clear.

Put butter into a shallow bowl and work out remaining liquid by pressing butter against the sides of the bowl with a rubber or wooden spatula.

To store butter, cover with plastic wrap or aluminum foil, or press into glass containers. Store in refrigerator for no longer than 2 weeks or freeze no longer than 6 months.

VARIATIONS
□ **Honey Butter:** Work 1 tablespoon honey into the unsalted butter with a wooden spoon.

□ **Salted Butter:** Salt enhances the flavor and lengthens the butter's keeping quality. Add salt, folding butter over salt with a wooden spoon. Repeat process until ½ to ¾ teaspoon salt is worked in and butter is firm and waxy.

COTTAGE CHEESE

½ gallon skim or whole milk
Juice of 2 lemons, strained,
or 4 Tbsps. vinegar

OPTIONAL
Caraway seeds
Paprika
Herbs

USE: 4-quart pot
Colander
YIELDS: 2 cups

In a 4-quart pot bring milk barely to boiling point. Add lemon juice or vinegar and return milk to boiling point. Do not overboil. Remove from fire and let cool, 5 to 10 minutes. Milk should already be separating into curds and whey. (The curds are the white lumps of cheese and the whey is the liquid.) Mix in the caraway seeds, paprika or herbs.

Line a colander with cheesecloth and pour in mixture. Twist the ends of the cheesecloth and hang to drain for 2 to 3 hours.

For a firmer cheese, like farmer or ricotta cheese, squeeze out most of the liquid. If you want it creamier, leave in some liquid. Refrigerate until ready to serve.

For an easy-to-slice cheese, place the cheese, still wrapped in cheesecloth, on a plate. Cover with a brick or a jar filled with water. Refrigerate overnight. Carefully remove cloth and slice.

Soups and Accompaniments

Pareve Soups
Meat Soups
Soup Accompaniments

A rich, hearty broth in autumn, full-bodied bean soup in winter, simmering vegetables fresh from the garden in spring, or chilled fruit soup in summer — soup is the perfect year-round dish. A light soup is a welcome appetizer. Heartier soups make a perfect main dish when accompanied by bread and a salad.

Golden, flavorful chicken soup is traditionally served at the Friday night meal, garnished with egg noodles or feather-light *knaidlach* (matzah balls). Other traditional soups are borscht and thick mushroom-barley soup. Many families serve cold fruit soup on Shabbat afternoon during the hot summer months.

In preparing vegetables and grains for soups, it is necessary to check carefully for small insects, many of which are barely visible. For further information on the checking of vegetables, see page 259.

Pareve Soups

Soups based on vegetables, beans, fruit and the like, containing no meat or dairy products are pareve soups. There are as many variations of these soups as there are cooks. Some feature one or two main vegetables while others are a melange of whatever is in the refrigerator. Dried beans, such as green or yellow split peas, add a fullness and flavor to a soup of garden vegetables. Minestrone, miso, and onion soup illustrate the international appeal of pareve soups.

BARLEY AND MUSHROOM SOUP

Spiked with sherry, this is a perfect soup to begin an elegant meal.

3 Tbsps. oil or margarine
1¼ cups chopped onion
2 cloves garlic, minced
1 pound mushrooms, sliced
1 tsp. salt
Pepper to taste
4 Tbsps. dry sherry
½ cup barley
6 to 7½ cups vegetable stock or water
4 Tbsps. tamari soy sauce

USE: 10-inch skillet
3-quart pot
YIELDS: 6 to 8 servings

In a 10-inch skillet heat oil. Saute onions and garlic. When onions are transparent, add sliced mushrooms, salt, pepper, and sherry, and cook uncovered until mushrooms are soft.

In a 3-quart pot, cook barley in 1½ cups of stock or water until tender. Add sauteed vegetables, tamari, and remaining stock. Cover and bring to a boil. Simmer 20 to 30 minutes.

VARIATION
□ **Barley and Mushroom Meat Soup:** In a 4-quart pot, bring 7½ cups water to a boil. Add salt and pepper, 1 pound beef flanken and 4 to 6 marrow bones. Lower flame and simmer 30 minutes until foam accumulates on top. Skim off foam. Simmer an additional 30 minutes.

Proceed to saute vegetables in skillet as above. Once stock is finished, add barley and cook until tender. Then add sauteed vegetables.

BASIC BEET BORSCHT

Borscht is a classic beet soup eaten hot or chilled, pureed or chunky. Borscht can be used in a dairy meal with a dollop of sour cream added just before serving.

4 pounds beets
8 cups water
2 tsps. salt
2 cloves garlic
Juice of 1 lemon
Pinch of sour salt
1 Tbsp. sugar (optional)

USE: 4-quart pot
YIELDS: 6 to 8 servings

Scrub beets well but do not peel. Place in a 4-quart pot, add 8 cups water and cook 1 to 1½ hours. Remove beets from pot and reserve liquid.

When beets have cooled, peel and grate them on long side of grater. Return grated beets to liquid. Add seasonings and simmer approximately 30 minutes. Garnish with sliced cucumber or scallion.

NOTE: For a thicker and lighter colored beet soup, whip 2 eggs in a bowl. Add a small amount of warm borscht and beat into the eggs. Return mixture to liquid in pot. Stir but do not boil.

BEAN SOUPS can be made of a great variety of beans. To aid digestability it is best to soak the beans for a few hours or overnight and drain before using.

ADUKI-SQUASH SOUP

1 cup aduki beans

4 cups water

1 large onion, chopped

3 cloves garlic, minced

2 tsps. thyme

1 butternut squash

4 stalks celery, sliced

4 carrots, sliced

2 zucchini, sliced

1 tsp. salt

USE: 4-quart pot
YIELDS: 4 to 6 servings

In a 4-quart pot, boil beans in water with onions, garlic, and thyme for 45 minutes to 1 hour. Peel, seed, and chop the squash. Add with remaining ingredients. Cover and simmer for 1 to 1½ hours.

Serve hot and garnish with parsley flakes.

HEARTY BEAN SOUP

4 Tbsps. oil

2 medium onions, diced

4 cloves garlic, minced

1 cup sliced mushrooms

1 cup shredded cabbage

¼ cup barley

1½ cups lentils

½ cup kidney beans

½ cup lima beans

5 carrots, diced

2 stalks celery, diced

1 cup diced zucchini or crookneck squash

2 potatoes, diced

3 tomatoes, diced

1½ tsps. salt

¼ tsp. pepper

1 tsp. thyme

1 tsp. basil

½ tsp. marjoram

½ tsp. cumin

3 to 4 Tbsps. soy sauce

¼ cup fresh parsley

USE: 8-quart pot
YIELDS: 10 to 12 servings

In an 8-quart pot, heat oil and saute onions, garlic, mushrooms, and cabbage. Fill pot halfway with water and add barley, lentils, kidney and lima beans.
Cook 1 hour.

Add vegetables, seasonings, and spices, except parsley. Cook 1 to 1½ hours over medium heat. Stir in parsley last ½ hour. Add more water if necessary.

VARIATION
☐ **Vegetable-Barley Soup:** Omit lentils, kidney and lima beans and increase barley to 1 cup. Add 2 cups cauliflorets.

GOLDEN CARROT SOUP

7 large carrots, grated
1 parsnip, grated
2 scallions
1 potato, grated (optional)
5½ cups water or
vegetable stock
1 onion, finely diced
3 Tbsp. margarine
1 cup nondairy creamer
⅛ tsp. white pepper

USE: 7-inch skillet
6-quart pot
YIELDS: 8 to 10 servings

Place grated carrots, parsnip, white part of scallions, and potato (if used), in a 6-quart pot. Add water or stock and bring to a boil over medium flame. Meanwhile, saute the onion in margarine in a 7-inch skillet on low flame until the onion is translucent but not browned. Add to soup. Cook until vegetables are soft, about 40 minutes.

Remove vegetables, leaving liquid in pot. Blend vegetables in blender until smooth. Return to pot of liquid and add nondairy creamer and pepper.

Garnish individual soup bowls with scallion greens on top.

VARIATION
□ For thicker soup, mix 1 tablespoon cornstarch with ½ cup of water, add to pot of liquid, stir well, and bring to boil *before* adding nondairy creamer.

FRUIT SOUP, *refreshing and chilled is delicious and nutritious. A delightful Shabbat afternoon change of pace on hot summer days. Fruit soups can easily be varied to take advantage of whatever fruits are available.*

PINEAPPLE FRUIT SOUP

6 plums
5 peaches
3 green apples
3 MacIntosh apples
1 16-ounce can
pineapple chunks,
including juice, or
½ fresh pineapple, cubed
½ pint blueberries
¼ pound cherries, pitted
Juice of 1 lemon
4 Tbsps. honey
½ tsp. cinnamon (optional)
¼ tsp. nutmeg (optional)

USE: 4-quart pot
YIELDS: 8 to 10 servings

Cube plums, peaches, and apples. Peel apples only, if desired. Place cut-up fruit in a 4-quart pot. Add pineapple chunks, blueberries, and cherries.

Add water to barely cover fruit. Add lemon juice, honey, and spices, if used. Cook for 1 hour on a very low flame.

Cool and refrigerate. Serve chilled.

NOTE: For dessert, serve cold and top each bowl with a spoonful of whipped dessert topping.

SUMMER FRUIT SOUP

**2 pound peaches,
peeled, pitted, and cubed**

**2 pounds plums,
pitted and cubed**

**1 pound pears,
peeled, cored, and cubed**

**1 pound sour cherries,
pitted or**

**1 16-ounce can
sour cherries, pitted**

**1 pound apricots,
pitted (optional)**

1 cup sugar

1 Tbsp. cornstarch

1 cup cold water

USE: 6-quart pot
YIELDS: 10 to 12 servings

Place all fruit and sugar in a 6-quart pot and cover with water. Cook over medium-low flame until fruit is tender, 30 to 40 minutes.

About 10 minutes before soup is done, mix cornstarch with 1 cup cold water. Add to soup. Bring to boil for remaining 10 minutes.

Cool and refrigerate. Serve chilled.

MINESTRONE SOUP

A full-bodied, well seasoned Italian vegetable soup, wholesome enough to be a meal in itself.

3 Tbsps. oil

1 cup diced onion

½ cup diced celery

¾ cup diced carrots

1 tsp. crushed garlic

**½ cup shredded cabbage,
spinach, or endive**

**1 cup cubed eggplant,
zucchini or string beans**

¾ cup cooked chickpeas

**1 cup chopped
fresh tomatoes**

2 tsps. salt

¼ tsp. black pepper

1 tsp. oregano

1 tsp. basil

¼ cup minced parsley flakes

2 cups tomato sauce

4 cups water or stock

¼ cup wine

½ cup macaroni

USE: 8-quart pot
YIELDS: 12 servings

In an 8-quart pot, heat oil and saute onion, celery, and carrots for 10 minutes. Add all ingredients except macaroni. Bring to a boil, simmer 30 minutes, add macaroni, and cook another 30 minutes. Check water during cooking, and add more if necessary.

Adjust seasonings before serving.

VARIATIONS

☐ **Meat Minestrone:** Add marrow bones for a meaty flavor.

☐ Add 1 cup corn or other vegetable. Do *not* use beets, broccoli, or cauliflower.

☐ Add thyme, sage, or rosemary instead of basil.

☐ Use rice, noodles, or cooked wheat berries instead of macaroni.

VEGETARIAN LENTIL SOUP

Tamari soy sauce and brown rice give this soup a wholesome and tasty twist.

3 Tbsps. oil
1 large onion, diced
3 cloves garlic, minced
4 large carrots, sliced
2 stalks celery, sliced
1 small parsnip, diced
4 potatoes, diced
1½ cups lentils
¼ cup brown rice
½ cup tamari soy sauce
2 tsps. thyme
2 tsps. salt
1 bay leaf
12 cups water

USE: 6-quart pot
YIELDS: 8 to 10 servings

In a 6-quart pot, heat the oil and saute the onion and garlic about 5 minutes until tender. Add remaining ingredients. Bring to a boil and cook over low flame for 1½ hours. Stir occasionally, adding water when necessary.

NOTE: Remove bay leaf before serving.

VARIATION
□ **Vegetarian Pea Soup:** Substitute 1½ cups split peas and ¼ cup barley for lentils, and ¼ cup lima beans for brown rice. Reduce soy sauce to ¼ cup. 1 small sweet potatoe, diced, is optional.

MISO SOUP

Miso is an oriental fermented soy bean paste. It is widely available with Kosher certification in health food stores.

3 Tbsps. miso
½ cup water
3 Tbsps. oil
1 cup thinly sliced carrots, cut diagonally
1 cup shredded cabbage
1 cup celery, thinly sliced
½ cup onion, thinly sliced
1 small clove garlic, crushed
½ tsp. ginger freshly grated, or ¼ tsp. powdered ginger
¼ cup minced parsley
1 cup thinly sliced mushrooms and/or water chestnuts and/or bamboo shoots (optional)
6 cups water
3 Tbsps. tamari soy sauce
½ cup minced scallions
½ pound tofu, cut in 1-inch chunks

USE: 4-quart pot
YIELDS: 6 to 8 servings

In a small bowl mix miso in ½ cup water and set aside.

In a 4-quart pot, heat oil on low flame. Add prepared vegetables and saute for 10 minutes. Add 6 cups water. Bring to a boil and simmer until vegetables are tender, approximately 30 minutes. Add miso mixture and tamari, and stir thoroughly. Do not boil miso.

Serve at once, garnished with scallions and tofu chunks.

GAZPACHO

This zesty tomato vegetable soup of Spanish origin, is usually served chilled. In this version, the vegetables are not cooked and the garlic and vinegar add the characteristic tang. When serving, croutons and chunks of raw vegetables are an attractive garnish.

1 16-ounce can tomato juice
¼ cup vegetable oil
2 Tbsps. wine vinegar or cider vinegar
½ medium green pepper
½ cucumber, peeled
½ onion
1 medium tomato, peeled
1 clove garlic, minced, or ¼ tsp. garlic powder
Salt and pepper to taste

USE: Blender
YIELDS: 4 servings

Pour tomato juice, oil, and vinegar into blender. Cut vegetables into chunks and put into blender. Add garlic, salt and pepper. Blend on medium speed until vegetables are chopped. Chill thoroughly, 1 to 2 hours or longer. Soup can be prepared several days in advance.

The chilled soup may be garnished with cubed avocado, bean sprouts, chopped cucumbers, peppers, tomatoes, hard-boiled eggs, diced scallions, parsley or croutons.

VARIATION
□ **Dairy Gazpacho:** Sprinkle soup with grated cheese or add a tablespoonful of sour cream and chives.

ONION SOUP

4 Tbsps. margarine
10 cups sliced Spanish onions
2 cloves garlic, minced
2 quarts water
¼ cup tamari soy sauce
1½ tsps. salt
1½ tsps. thyme
⅛ tsp. pepper

USE: 4-quart pot
YIELDS: 8 servings

In a 4-quart pot, melt margarine and saute onions and garlic until soft and golden, but not brown. Add water, tamari, and seasonings. Bring to boil, reduce flame and simmer for 40 minutes.

Garnish with toasted croutons and serve hot.

VARIATION
□ **Onion Mushroom Soup:** After onions and garlic have sauteed for 10 minutes, add 1½ cups of thinly sliced mushrooms and 3 stalks thinly sliced celery.

SPLIT PEA SOUP

1 cup split peas
12 cups water
1 onion, diced
1 stalk celery, diced
4 carrots, sliced
1 sweet potato, grated
2 tsps. salt
Dash of pepper
1 clove garlic, minced
1 Tbsp. melted margarine

USE: 6-quart pot
YIELDS: 6 to 8 servings

Soak peas in cold water for 1 hour. Drain and cook peas in 12 cups water for 1 hour, in 6-quart pot. Add vegetables to water with seasonings and garlic.

Cook over low flame for another 30 minutes. Add melted margarine and stir well.

VARIATION
□ Instead of using raw onion and celery, saute them first. Immediately after washing peas, combine all ingredients and cook slowly. Add seasonings only after peas have softened.

POTATO-LEEK SOUP

4 Tbsps. oil
1 large onion, diced
2 large carrots, diced
2 stalks celery, sliced
6 potatoes, diced
4 Tbsps. flour
12 cups water
1 Tbsp. salt
½ tsp. pepper
½ tsp. thyme
2 Tbsps. oil
1 large leek, finely chopped
2 Tbsps. dill

USE: 6-quart pot
7-inch skillet
YIELDS: 10 to 12 servings

Heat oil in 6-quart pot. Saute onion, carrots, and celery in oil for 10 to 15 minutes. Add potatoes to vegetables and stir for ½ minute. Add flour and stir to coat. Quickly add water so flour doesn't stick to pot. Let soup come to a boil and then lower flame.

Simmer uncovered for 40 to 50 minutes. Stir occasionally. Add salt, pepper, and thyme.

In a 7-inch skillet, heat 2 tablespoons of oil and saute leek for 10 to 15 minutes.

At end of cooking add leek and dill to soup and heat through.

CREAMY POTATO SOUP

4 large potatoes, diced
1 large onion, diced
4 cups water
⅓ cup oil
¼ cup minced parsley
2 tsps. salt
½ tsp. pepper

USE: 4-quart pot
YIELDS: 6 servings

Place all ingredients in a 4-quart pot. Cook uncovered over moderate heat 30 to 40 minutes, or until potatoes are soft, stirring occasionally. With wooden spoon, press some potatoes against sides and bottom of pot to break into small pieces.

Serve hot.

SCHAV

1 pound sorrel
(schav or sour grass)
6 cups boiling water
1 egg
1½ tsps. salt
1 hard-boiled egg

USE: 4-quart pot
YIELDS: 4 to 6 servings

Wash sorrel leaves well and pinch off stems. Place leaves in bowl and chop into very small pieces. Tie stems together. Add chopped leaves and bundle of stems to boiling water in 4-quart pot. Cook for 15 minutes. Cool and discard stems.

Beat egg well, and add salt. Gradually add salted egg to the schav, stirring well. Serve cold.

When serving, cut hard-boiled egg into schav.

VARIATION
☐ **Dairy:** Serve topped with sour cream for a dairy soup.

TOMATO SOUP

A recipe especially designed for canning.

1 Tbsp. oil
2 large onions, diced
1 peck ripe tomatoes (8 to 10 large tomatoes), chopped
½ tsp. pepper
4 Tbsps. salt
¾ cup sugar or ½ cup honey
2 tsps. ground cloves
16 cups water
1 Tbsp. cornstarch

USE: 6-quart pot
6 1-pint jars
YIELDS: 6 pints

In a 6-quart pot — enamel or stainless steel — heat 1 tablespoon oil. Saute the onions until soft. Add the remaining ingredients, except cornstarch and boil until tomatoes are soft. Put the soup through a food mill or strainer.

Reheat soup to boiling. Mix cornstarch with a few tablespoons water to make a thin paste and add to soup. Cook soup until slightly thick.

Pack immediately into six clean 1-pint jars which have been previously boiled and drained. Leave ¼-inch head space. Cook in boiling water for 10 minutes. Check seals when jars are cool.

VEGETABLE PUREE SOUP

1 medium zucchini
3 large carrots
1 large onion
1 medium parsnip
1 stalk celery
8 cups water
½ cup barley
Salt and pepper to taste

USE: 3-quart pot
YIELDS: 4 to 6 servings

Peel and dice all the vegetables. Place in a 3-quart pot together with the water, barley, and salt and pepper. Cook ½ to ¾ hour, or until the vegetables are tender and barley is cooked.

Puree the soup in a blender. You may also puree only half the soup, if you prefer. When reheating later, add a little more water.

NOTE: This soup also tastes delicious when served as is, chunky style.

VEGETABLE-SQUASH SOUP

1 large butternut squash
1 large sweet potato, diced
2 stalks celery, diced
3 carrots, diced
1 cup shredded cabbage
2 medium zucchini, diced
2 cups water
1 tsp. marjoram
½ tsp. cumin
½ tsp. salt

USE: 4-quart pot
YIELDS: 4 to 6 servings

Peel, seed, and dice squash.

Place squash and all other vegetables in a 4-quart pot. Add water and seasonings. Bring to a boil and simmer until vegetables are tender, approximately 1 hour.

Puree in food processor or blender. Return to pot, reheat, and serve.

FRENCH TOMATO-ONION SOUP

3 Tbsps. oil
3 large onions, thinly sliced
1 tsp. brown sugar
1 tsp. dried thyme
½ tsp. oregano
1 sprig parsley
1 bay leaf
3 cloves garlic, minced
2 Tbsps. flour
2 Tbsps. tomato paste
1 28-ounce can tomatoes, chopped, plus the liquid, or 3 pounds fresh tomatoes, peeled and chopped
6 cups vegetable stock or water
Salt and pepper to taste
½ cup macaroni or rice

USE: 4-quart pot
YIELDS: 8 servings

In a 4-quart pot, heat the oil and saute onions until golden. Add sugar, herbs, and garlic. Cover pot and simmer 20 to 30 minutes, stirring occasionally. Stir in flour and blend thoroughly.

Stir in tomato paste, tomatoes, and stock. Bring to a boil, lower heat and simmer, covered, ½ hour. Add salt and pepper to taste. Add macaroni or rice and cook until soft.

VARIATION
□ For a meaty soup, use chicken broth instead of vegetable stock.

NOTE: Remove bay leaf before serving.

FESTIVE TOMATO-VEGETABLE SOUP

3 Tbsps. oil
1 large onion, diced
1 cup lentils
1 cup medium barley
2 large stalks celery, with leaves, coarsely chopped
1 large carrot, diced
1 large potato, finely diced
3 Tbsps. minced parsley
1 16-ounce can tomatoes, chopped
2 tsps. salt
¼ tsp. pepper
10 cups water

USE: 6-quart pot
YIELDS: 8 to 10 servings

In a 6-quart pot, heat oil until hot. Add onion and saute about 5 minutes until tender. Place all remaining ingredients in pot with water; bring to boil.

Reduce heat, cover, and simmer for 1 hour, or until lentils and barley are tender. Stir occasionally, adding water if necessary.

Adjust seasonings before serving.

Meat Soups

BEEF SOUPS *are combinations of meat with vegetables, beans, or grains. They make for hearty eating and are an appetizing start to any meal.*

SWEET-AND-SOUR CABBAGE SOUP

The flavor of this sweet-and-sour soup is reminiscent of stuffed cabbage.

**2 pounds flanken,
cut into pieces
1 large onion, sliced
1 large purple or
green cabbage, shredded
⅛ tsp. sour salt or
¼ cup lemon juice
6 medium tomatoes, diced
2 tsps. brown sugar
Salt and pepper to taste
1 cup raisins (optional)**

USE: 6-quart pot
YIELDS: 8 to 10 servings

In a 6-quart pot, place flanken covered with water to about one third the depth of pot. Cook covered over medium heat 1½ hours. Add remaining ingredients and simmer until both cabbage and meat are tender.

Taste and adjust seasonings if necessary. Cook an additional 15 minutes.

Serve hot.

VARIATION
☐ Add 4 medium potatoes, diced, to vegetables.

SPICED CABBAGE SOUP

**3 Tbsps. oil
2 large onions, sliced
1 large clove garlic, minced
2 to 3 marrow bones
1½ pounds stew meat,
cut into 1-inch cubes
½ tsp. caraway seeds
¾ tsp. pepper
8 cups water
1 small head
cabbage, shredded
3 bay leaves (optional)
2 tsps. salt**

USE: 5-quart Dutch oven
YIELDS: 8 to 10 servings

Using a 5-quart Dutch oven, heat oil and saute sliced onions and garlic over medium flame about 5 minutes until tender. Add bones, meat, caraway seeds, pepper, and water. Cook covered over low flame for 1 hour.

Remove bones and add shredded cabbage. Bring to a boil, then lower flame. Add bay leaves, if desired, and salt. Simmer covered, for an additional 30 minutes over a low flame.

Serve hot.

NOTE: If using bay leaves, remove before serving.

HEARTY MEAT AND VEGETABLE SOUP

1 Tbsp. oil
1 onion, diced
2 cloves garlic, minced
1 pound stew meat,
cut into 1-inch cubes
9 cups water
1½ tsps. salt
¼ tsp. pepper
⅓ cup barley
½ cup lima beans
1 cup split peas
1 bay leaf
1 pound marrow bones
1 potato, diced
2 large carrots, sliced
2 stalks celery, diced
1 cup chopped
fresh string beans
1 16-ounce can tomato puree
2 Tbsps. chopped
fresh parsley

USE: 6-quart pot
YIELDS: 8 to 10 servings

Heat oil and saute onion and garlic, in a 6-quart pot, for 2 minutes. Add stew meat, water, salt, pepper, barley, lima beans, split peas, bay leaf, and bones. Bring to a boil. Lower flame and simmer covered for 1 hour.

Add potato, carrots, celery, string beans, tomato puree, and parsley. Cook an additional 1½ hours.

Serve hot.

CHICKEN SOUP *is the classic Jewish dish. Ever popular for Shabbat and Yom Tov, it is perfectly complemented by egg noodles or* knaidlach. *Lovers of chicken soup are quite passionate about the best recipe — each cook has her own favorite.*

CLASSIC CHICKEN SOUP

1 3- to 5-pound
chicken, quartered
12 cups water
3 carrots
1 stalk celery
1 to 2 parsnips
1 onion
1 Tbsp. salt
¼ tsp. pepper

OPTIONAL
1 parsley root
1 clove garlic
Several sprigs of fresh dill
1 sweet potato
1 zucchini

USE: 8-quart pot
YIELDS: 8 to 10 servings

Clean chicken and remove excess fat. Fill an 8-quart pot with the 12 cups of water. Bring to a boil. Place chicken and vegetables in pot. Add salt and pepper. If using optional ingredients, chop parsley root; peel garlic, leaving it whole, pierce with toothpick in order to remove easily. Add both to soup with the dill. Dice the sweet potato, slice zucchini and add to soup.

Simmer covered, for about 2 hours. Remove garlic.

Serve hot.

NOTE: To remove excess fat, prepare soup in advance and refrigerate for several hours or overnight. Fat will congeal on top. Remove, and heat soup before serving.

CHICKEN-BARLEY SOUP

1 3-pound chicken,
cut into eighths
2 Tbsps. oil
11 cups water
3 medium onions, sliced
3 tsps. salt
½ tsp. pepper
1 cup medium barley
2 cups diced celery
¼ cup minced parsley
4 medium carrots, sliced
1 medium parsnip, diced
1 cup sliced fresh mushrooms
1 10-ounce package
frozen peas

USE: 8-quart pot
YIELDS: 8 to 10 servings

Clean chicken and remove excess fat. Pat dry with paper towels. In an 8-quart pot, over medium high heat, brown chicken in oil. Remove chicken and place in a large bowl. Discard fat remaining in pot. Return chicken pieces to pot and add water, onions, salt and pepper.

Rinse barley with running cold water. Add to soup. Bring soup to a boil. Lower flame, cover, and simmer 1½ hours or until chicken is fork-tender, stirring occasionally.

Remove chicken to large bowl and refrigerate 30 minutes or until easy to handle. Remove chicken bones and skin and cut meat into bite-size pieces.

Skim fat from broth. Add chicken, celery, parsley, carrots, parsnip, mushrooms, and peas. Bring soup to a boil. Lower flame, cover, and simmer 40 minutes.

Serve hot.

CREAM OF CHICKEN SOUP

Allow time to prepare Classic Chicken Soup in advance, or simply give a fresh twist to left-over chicken soup.

2 Tbsps. flour
1½ tsps. oil
6 cups Classic Chicken
Soup, strained
1½ cups diced
cooked chicken
Pinch of sugar
1 cup nondairy creamer
1 package frozen peas or
frozen peas and carrots
3 egg yolks, beaten

USE: 4-quart pot
YIELDS: 4 to 6 servings

Over medium heat, blend flour and oil together in a 4-quart pot. Gradually stir in 3 cups of soup until smooth and creamy. Add remaining soup, chicken, and sugar. Simmer 1½ hours.

Add ¾ cup nondairy creamer and frozen peas or peas and carrots.

Beat egg yolks and remaining ¼ cup of creamer together. Add ¼ cup soup to egg mixture, stir well and return to soup. Taste to check seasonings and correct, if necessary.

Soup Accompaniments

Quenelles in France, uszki in Poland, dumplings in America, and knaidlach among Jews — each ethnic group has its way of preparing soup accompaniments. Most soups are enhanced by the addition of noodles, egg drops, croutons, knaidlach, kreplach, or mandlen.

MINI DUMPLINGS

2 eggs
½ cup flour
6 Tbsps. margarine
½ tsp. salt
¼ tsp. nutmeg
Dash white pepper
8 cups water
1 tsp. salt

USE: 4-quart pot
YIELDS: 12 small dumplings

In a small mixing bowl, beat eggs and flour together. Beat in margarine and add seasonings.

In a 4-quart pot bring water and salt to a boil. Drop ½ teaspoonfuls of batter into boiling water, let dumplings rise to the top. Simmer covered an additional 5 minutes.

EGG DROPS

No time to make knaidlach or even boil noodles? Here's a quick alternative.

2 eggs
½ tsp. cornstarch
½ tsp. water

USE: Small bowl
YIELDS: 6 to 8 servings

In a large pot bring 1 quart of soup to a boil.

For each quart of soup, beat 2 eggs in a medium bowl. In a small cup, dissolve ½ teaspoon of cornstarch in ½ teaspoon of water. Add to eggs. When soup comes to a boil, lower flame, add beaten eggs, either ½ teaspoonful at a time or drop by drop from the tines of a fork. Stir while soup continues to boil. When ready, soup should look like clear chicken broth filled with very, very thin noodles. Serve hot.

MANDLEN

2 eggs
1 Tbsp. oil
½ tsp. salt
1¼ cups flour
1 tsp. baking powder

Oil for frying

USE: 10-inch skillet
YIELDS: 4 servings

In a large bowl beat eggs, 1 tablespoon oil, and salt together. Add flour and baking powder to egg mixture and mix to form workable dough. Divide dough into several portions and roll into thin ropes, about ¼-inch in diameter. Cut into ½-inch pieces.

Heat oil several inches deep in pot. Fry until golden. Remove with slotted spoon.

NOTE: May be baked instead of fried. Placed on greased baking sheets and bake at 375° approximately 30 minutes until golden brown. Shake pan occasionally to brown all sides.

PERFECT KNAIDLACH

Fluffy matzoh balls served floating on top of chicken soup are a traditional Jewish food usually served on Shabbat or Yom Tov.

4 eggs, slightly beaten
4 Tbsps. oil
4 Tbsps. ice-cold water
1 cup matzoh meal
1 tsp. salt
½ tsp. pepper
8 cups water
1 tsp. salt

USE: 4-quart pot
YIELDS: 12 knaidlach

In a large bowl mix eggs, oil, and cold water together. Add matzoh meal, salt, and pepper and mix well. Refrigerate for 1 hour.

Bring water and salt to a boil in a 4-quart pot. Lower flame.

Wet palms of hands with cold water and form mixture into balls. Drop into simmering water. Cover pot and cook for 30 minutes. Be sure to keep cover on pot during entire cooking time and 10 minutes after while pot cools.

NOTE: For large, fluffy knaidlach, cook in wide pot, thus allowing lots of room to expand.

KREPLACH ILLUSTRATED

Kreplach are small squares or circles of rolled pasta dough filled with ground beef or chicken and folded into triangles. They can be boiled and served in soup or fried and served as a side dish. They are traditionally served at the Erev Yom Kippur meal as well as on Hoshanah Rabbah and Purim.

1 On a floured board roll dough out as thin as possible without tearing.

2 SQUARES: Cut rolled out dough into 3-inch squares. Place a teaspoon of filling carefully into center.

3 Bring point 1 up to point 4 and seal edges. Moisten edges with tip of finger dipped in water to keep seams closed.

4 ROUNDS: Cut 3-inch circles with round cookie cutter. Place a teaspoon of filling carefully in the center.

5 Lift sides 1-2 and 1-3 to meet in center over filling and press edges together.

6 Fold down top flap of 3-4-2 to middle and pinch edges together forming a triangle. Moisten edges with tip of finger dipped in cold water to keep seams closed.

BASIC KREPLACH

DOUGH
1¾ cups flour
2 eggs
½ tsp. salt
3 Tbsps. oil

FILLING
1 cup ground cooked beef or chicken
1 small onion, grated
1 tsp. salt

USE: 3-quart pot
or 10-inch skillet
YIELDS: 18 kreplach

DOUGH: In a large bowl combine dough ingredients together. Knead and roll out thin on floured board. Cut into 3-inch squares or circles.

FILLING: In a small bowl mix filling ingredients well. See Kreplach Illustrated for filling and folding.

Kreplach can now be either boiled and served in soup or sauteed in oil.

TO BOIL: Place in boiling salted water. Cook approximately 20 minutes until kreplach float to top.

TO SAUTE: Heat oil over medium flame in a 10-inch skillet. Saute boiled kreplach until golden brown on both sides.

NOTE: Dough will roll out more easily after being wrapped in a damp cloth for one hour.

FANCY KREPLACH

DOUGH
2 cups flour
½ tsp. salt
3 Tbsps. oil
2 egg yolks
½ cup water
1½ tsps. baking powder or baking soda

FILLING
1 onion, diced
2 Tbsps. oil
1 cup cooked ground beef or chicken
1 tsp. salt
¼ tsp. pepper
1 egg
1 Tbsp. matzoh meal

USE: 3-quart pot
or 10-inch skillet
YIELDS: 18 kreplach

DOUGH: In a large bowl combine flour, salt, and oil. In a separate bowl, beat egg yolks, water, and baking powder (or soda). Add to flour mixture. Knead and roll out thin on floured board. Cut into 3-inch squares or circles.

FILLING: Saute onion in oil. Add ground beef or chicken and brown for 5 minutes. Remove from heat and cool. Add salt, pepper, egg, and matzoh meal and mix well. See Kreplach Illustrated for filling and folding.

Place in boiling salted water. Cook approximately 20 minutes until kreplach float to top. When ready, remove from pot and serve in soup.

NOTE: This can also be served as a side dish. For crisp kreplach, fry boiled kreplach in heated oil in 10-inch skillet over medium flame until golden brown on both sides.

Pareve Main Dishes

Fish
Vegetarian Dishes

Pareve main dishes, containing neither meat nor dairy ingredients, are a creative and delicious feature of kosher cuisine. These nutritious dishes, consisting of fish, vegetables, tofu, grains, or a combination of these ingredients, are especially appealing in warm weather.

Pareve meat substitutes such as tofu offer new possibilities for the imaginative cook. In Israel, vegetarian main dishes are a feature of everyday life.

During the Nine Days (see page 532) when meat is not eaten except on Shabbat, the kosher cook welcomes suggestions for pareve main dishes.

The pareve main dish recipes that follow, whether in the fish or vegetarian sections, can be combined with either meat or dairy meals.

Light, nutritious and versatile, fish is a pleasant alternative to meat or poultry. Often served as a first course, fish can also be the basis for a meal. The Talmud and mystical tradition emphasize the value of eating fish on Shabbat.

Fish is the perfect food for the health-conscious cook. High in protein, low in calories and quick to prepare, fish is an all-around good choice. Traditional gefilte fish to begin a Shabbat or Yom Tov meal, stuffed white fish to enhance a simchah and a variety of international dishes for delicious dining reflect the great versatility of fish.

Laws Of Kosher Fish

Fish does not have to be slaughtered or salted as do meat and fowl. Only fish that have both *fins* and *scales* are kosher. These include cod, flounder, haddock, halibut, herring, mackerel, pickerel, pike, salmon, trout, and whitefish. Non-kosher fish include swordfish, shark, eel, octopus, and skate, as well as all shellfish, clams, crabs, lobster, oyster and shrimp.

The definition of fins and scales must be as designated by Jewish Law. Not everything commonly called a "scale" meets the Torah's criteria. Therefore, it is best to buy fish from a merchant familiar with kosher fish types.

When buying fish, either buy it whole so that you can see the fins and scales, or, if the fish is sliced, filleted, or ground, buy only from a fish store that sells kosher fish exclusively. This will ensure that knives or other utensils are used only on kosher fish, and that no other mixup can occur.

Packaged and canned fish, such as tuna and sardines, need reliable certification of *kashrut*. Smoked fish must also have a reliable *hechsher* to ensure that it was smoked only with other kosher fish, and that all other *kashrut* criteria have been met.

Combining Fish with Meat or Dairy

Fish and meat may not be cooked or eaten together. However, unlike milk and meat, fish and meat may be eaten at the same meal as separate courses. Silverware and plates which have been used for fish may only be used for meat after they have been washed. Between the fish and meat courses, one should eat something that does not stick to the palate and take a drink (preferably other than water). Some people also rinse their hands slightly between courses.

Customs vary regarding the use of fish and dairy. Most communities permit the combination of fish and butter. In certain communities, fish is not combined with milk or cheese. Fish and dairy may be served at the same meal with separate plates and silverware.

Fish

GEFILTE FISH

Gefilte fish is a delectable mixture of various ground fish especially popular on Shabbat or Yom Tov. Fish is served this way to avoid separating the bones from the fish which is forbidden on Shabbat. Served with horseradish and garnished with carrots from the sauce it may be placed on lettuce leaves with tomato and cucumber slices. On Rosh Hashanah it is a tradition to serve a fish head. The head may be filled with gefilte fish batter and cooked and served like the rest of the fish.

TIPS FOR PERFECT GEFILTE FISH

☐ When buying whole fresh fish, 5 pounds of whole fish will yield 3 pounds of fillets or ground fish.

☐ Use a large pot in order to allow gefilte fish balls room to expand. The more room they have the fluffier they will be. Fill the pot almost ½ full of water and add ingredients for the fish broth.

☐ Prepare all gefilte fish ingredients in a large bowl and work the fish mixture for several minutes with your hands or a very large spoon.

☐ Once fish broth is boiling begin shaping into balls. Wet your hands with cold water. Keep hands constantly wet as you shape the fish. Place between ¼ to ½ cup into palm of your hand and pat into an oval. Using a large spoon, lower the balls gently into the boiling water one at a time; they will remain on top and not sink.

☐ Taste sauce after 1 hour and adjust seasoning if necessary.

JARRING FISH

☐ When preparing large quantities of fish it is possible to keep fish fresh for up to three weeks in the refrigerator.

☐ When the fish has finished cooking, remove the lid but keep the pot on a low flame. (This keeps the water boiling so that fish stays on top, making for easier removal.)

☐ Take some clean, empty glass jars and fill loosely with gefilte fish balls. Add boiling fish sauce.

☐ Close jars very tightly and place them upside down — this vacuum packs the jars. When they cool, place jars of fish right side up in the refrigerator. Not only will they keep well for a few weeks, but the fish tastes fresh when stored in this manner.

PREPARING FROZEN GEFILTE FISH LOAVES

☐ BOILING: Bring Basic Fish Broth to a boil, using fish bones if available as this enhances the flavor (see recipe). Place fish in broth with or without paper, bring to second boil, lower heat and cook 1½ hours.

☐ BAKING WITH SAUCE: Prepare Vegetable Fish Sauce according to recipe. Remove paper from 2 fish loaves and place, frozen, in pan. Cover with sauce and bake at 350° for 2 hours covered or 1 hour covered and 30 to 45 minutes uncovered. Do not use witn sweet gefilte fish loaves.

☐ "HOMEMADE" GEFILTE FISH: Leave two fish loaves in refrigerator overnight to defrost. Blend two eggs, two onions, two carrots and one garlic clove in blender. Place defrosted fish in medium mixing bowl. Add mixture from blender. Add ½-¾ cup matzah meal, 1 tsp. salt and ¼ tsp. pepper. Mix well.

Mixture can then be prepared as gefilte fish balls cooked in Basic Fish Broth (see page 148); shaped into patties and fried on both sides, or placed into greased 9 x 5-inch foil-lined loaf pans and baked at 350°. Yields 15 - 18 portions.

CLASSIC GEFILTE FISH

BASIC FISH BROTH
2 carrots, peeled
3 onions, sliced
6 to 8 cups water
Fish bones and heads, optional
2 tsps. salt
½ tsp. pepper
1 tsp. sugar (optional)

3 pounds ground whitefish, or 2 pounds ground whitefish and 1 pound ground pike
4 medium onions
2 carrots
2 stalks celery
3 to 5 tsps. sugar
5 tsps. salt
1 tsp. pepper
½ cup matzoh meal or 2 slices hard challah
4 eggs, beaten

USE: 8-quart pot
YIELDS: 10 to 12 portions

BASIC FISH BROTH: Slice carrots in half and separate onions into rings. Place in 8-quart pot with water, bones if used, and seasonings. Bring to boil, lower flame, and allow to cook for a few minutes.

While sauce is coming to a boil, prepare fish mixture. Place fish in large mixing bowl. Finely grate onions, carrots, and celery. Add seasonings and matzoh meal. Grate challah to make crumbs. (If using hard challah, remove brown crust and then soak challah in water and squeeze it out before adding it to the mixture.) Mix together. Add the eggs and mix well.

SHAPE: Wet hands and fill palm with fish mixture. Roll in hand until smooth; shape into round or oval balls. Place in pot only when sauce has come to rapid boil. Lower balls gently into pot, leaving a little space between balls. After all balls have been shaped and placed in boiling fish sauce, lower flame and cook covered on medium heat for approximately 1 to 1½ hours. Check water level and seasoning after 1 hour. Adjust if necessary. Allow fish to cool before removing from pot.

NOTE: Eggs can be placed in blender with onions, vegetables, and seasoning, added to ground fish, and mixed together.

GEFILTE FISH

Basic Fish Broth (Classic Gefilte Fish, page 148)
3 pounds ground fish (1 pound pike, 1½ whitefish, ½ pound carp)
3 medium onions, ground
3 eggs, separated
¼ cup matzoh meal (optional)
¼ cup cold water
1 to 2 tsps. salt
½ tsp. pepper

USE: 8-quart pot
YIELDS: 10 to 12 portions

Prepare Basic Fish Broth, as in Classic Gefilte Fish, and bring to boil in an 8-quart pot.

In a large bowl mix ground fish and onions until smooth. Add egg yolks, matzoh meal, cold water, salt and pepper. Beat the egg whites and add to fish mixture.

Wet hands and fill with fish mixture. Roll in hand until smooth; shape into rounds or oval balls. Place in pot only when sauce has come to a rapid boil. Lower balls gently into pot, lower flame and cook uncovered for 1½ hours at slow boil. Liquid will be reduced to one-half. Allow fish to cool before removing from pot.

VARIATION
□ **Sweet Gefilte Fish:** Add 1 teaspoon sugar per pound of fish mixture.

CARP GEFILTE FISH

Basic Fish Broth
(Classic Gefilte Fish,
page 148)
6 pounds ground carp
4 to 5 onions
2 Tbsps. oil
5 eggs
4 tsps. salt
1 tsp. pepper
2 tsps. sugar
¾ cup ground bread crumbs
½ cup water

USE: 7-inch skillet
8-quart pot
YIELDS: 18 to 20 portions

Prepare Basic Fish Broth, as in Classic Gefilte Fish, and bring to boil in 8-quart pot.

Dice onions and saute in a 7-inch skillet in oil over low flame until soft and translucent, approximately 5 to 7 minutes. Place sauteed onions in blender and blend with eggs and seasonings. Adjust seasonings to taste.

Add egg mixture to ground fish in a large bowl. Add bread crumbs and water alternately, a little at a time, mixing well after each addition.

Shape fish by wetting palms of hand and shaping fish into balls. Lower gently one at a time into boiling fish sauce. After all fish balls have been added, lower flame and cook for 1 to 1¼ hours. Allow fish to cool before removing from pot.

GEFILTE FISH PATTIES IN TOMATO SAUCE

FISH MIXTURE
1 onion
1 carrot
2 eggs
2 pounds ground
pike and whitefish
1 Tbsp. salt
2 Tbsps. honey (optional)
1 cup matzoh meal
¼ cup oil for frying

SAUCE
1 onion, diced
2 cloves garlic, minced
1 28-ounce can tomatoes
1 8-ounce can mushrooms
½ tsp. basil
½ tsp. salt
¼ tsp. pepper

USE: 10-inch skillet
YIELDS: 8 patties

FISH MIXTURE: Place onion, carrot, and eggs in food processor or blender and process until smooth. Add to ground fish in a large bowl and mix well. Add salt, honey, and ¼ cup matzoh meal. Mix well until firm. Shape fish mixture into patties. Dredge in remaining ¾ cup matzoh meal and brown in hot oil. Drain on paper toweling.

SAUCE: Add remaining oil to 10-inch skillet and saute onion and garlic until golden. Add canned tomatoes, mushrooms, and seasonings. Cook 15 minutes over low flame. Return fish patties to skillet with sauce and cook an additional ½ hour over low heat. Make sure mixture doesn't burn. Serve cold or hot.

FISH SAUCES

There are a variety of sauces that can be used to enhance the flavor of frozen gefilte fish loaves or any baked sliced fish. The following recipes are the perfect complement to fish. Other sauces can be found on page 331.

FISH SAUCE AUBERGINE

To prepare 2 to 3 pounds of fish or approximately 6 to 8 slices.

2 Tbsps. oil
1 cup water or apple juice
½ tsp. salt
1 onion, diced
1 clove garlic, minced
1 green pepper, diced
1 eggplant, diced
1 8-ounce can tomato sauce
2 to 3 Tbsps. brown sugar
Salt to taste

USE: 2-quart pot
YIELDS: 2 cups sauce

In 2-quart pot, put 2 tablespoons of oil; add liquid, salt, and vegetables, and cook, covered, 1 hour on low flame, stirring occasionally.

Then add 1 can tomato sauce, brown sugar, and salt to taste. Bring to a boil and remove from flame.

Pour over fish and bake in 350° oven for 15 to 30 minutes, depending upon type and size of fish. If baking for longer than ½ hour, cover fish.

VEGETABLE FISH SAUCE

This is an excellent sauce for cooking or baking gefilte fish or loaves. There is enough sauce for 4 pounds of gefilte fish.

2 Tbsps. oil
2 onions, sliced
1 carrot, sliced
2 stalks celery, diced
2 cloves garlic, minced
1 green pepper, diced (optional)
1 8-ounce can tomato sauce
2 cups water
2 bay leaves
½ tsp. salt
¼ tsp. pepper
1 Tbsp. lemon juice
½ Tbsp. sugar

USE: 10-inch skillet
2-quart saucepan
YIELDS: 3 cups sauce

Heat oil in a 10-inch skillet. Saute onions, carrot, celery, garlic, and green pepper until soft. Combine all vegetables, liquid, and spices in 2-quart saucepan. Bring to a boil and cook for 15 to 20 minutes. Adjust seasoning if necessary.

Pour over fish (slices) and bake according to recipe, or use instead of plain tomato sauce when baking fish.

WHOLE AND SLICED FISH

From carp to trout, fresh fish are the picture of versatility. Almost any cooking method, baking, broiling, or steaming, can be used to prepare fish. Fish can be substituted for chicken in many recipes. Serving curried or spicy foods? Try these spices with fish. A stuffed whole fish or tender salmon steak done to perfection provides a light meal fit for a king.

STEAMED GINGER FISH

1 3-pound whole fish;
trout, mullet, or bass
1 tsp. salt
2 Tbsps. oil

SAUCE
1 Tbsp. sherry
2 Tbsps. soy sauce
½ tsp. sugar
½ tsp. salt
1 tsp. peanut oil
2 slices fresh
ginger root, shredded
2 scallions, chopped

USE: Fish steamer
YIELDS: 6 to 8 servings

Leave fish whole. Clean out cavity, removing everything from inside. Rinse in cold water and dry well. Make a few shallow diagonal cuts on top but do not cut through. Rub lightly with salt and oil, then place in shallow dish.

SAUCE: Combine sauce ingredients in small bowl. Spread evenly on fish. Place into steamer. Steam on a low flame until done, approximately 30 to 35 minutes, or a little longer for a larger fish.

WHOLE FISH STUFFED WITH VEGETABLES

3½ to 4 pounds whole fish,
bass, salmon, or trout

STUFFING
½ cup mayonnaise
½ tsp. cayenne pepper
8 large carrots, grated
2 large onions, diced
3 cloves garlic, minced
½ bunch parsley, chopped
4 stalks celery, diced
1 large red pepper, diced

USE: 9 x 13-inch baking pan
YIELDS: 6 to 8 servings

Leave fish whole. Have fish store remove spine and bones. Clean out cavity, removing everything from inside.

STUFFING: Mix mayonnaise and cayenne pepper together in a small bowl and set aside. Prepare all vegetables and toss together in a large bowl with three fourths of mayonnaise mixture. Press stuffing firmly into cavity of fish. Place fish on side in a 9 x 13-inch baking pan. Spread remaining mayonnaise over outside of fish.

Make a tent of aluminum foil over fish. Bake 35 to 45 minutes at 350°. Remove tent for the last 5 minutes of baking.

TASTY BOILED CARP

3 pounds carp, sliced
2 carrots, sliced
1 onion
2 cloves garlic
1 cup water
½ tsp. salt

USE: 2-quart pot
YIELDS: 6 to 8 servings

Wash, scrape, and drain fish.

Place carrots, whole onion, and garlic with 1 cup water in a 2-quart pot. Bring to a rolling boil. When water has boiled, add carp slices and salt. Simmer over medium flame for 40 minutes.

Place fish with sauce in refrigerator and the sauce will gel. Serve cold.

"KNOEBEL" CARP

This fish is marinated overnight in a garlic mixture that gives it a lovely aroma. The taste permeates the fish, which has a beautiful color after it is baked.

5 pounds carp, sliced
5 cloves garlic, crushed
1 Tbsp. coarse salt
1 tsp. pepper
2 Tbsps. paprika

USE: 9 x 13-inch pan
YIELDS: 10 to 12 slices

Wash off carp slices and set aside in bowl, allowing pieces to remain a bit damp.

In the meantime, make a paste with the crushed garlic and seasonings. Rub paste on all sides of carp slices. Lay slices in 9 x 13-inch pan, cover, and place in refrigerator overnight, allowing fish to absorb flavor.

On the following day, bake fish in preheated oven at 350° for ½ hour covered, and another ½ hour uncovered. This dish will also taste excellent if broiled 30 minutes on one side, then turned over and broiled 15 to 20 minutes on other side.

NOTE: This recipe can be prepared in advance in large quantitites. Place prepared unbaked carp in freezer until ready to use; defrost and bake as above.

PICKLED CARP

Prepare this dish the day before to allow time to marinate.

3 pounds carp, sliced
¼ tsp. garlic powder
¼ tsp. black pepper
¼ tsp. crushed red pepper
½ tsp. salt
1 crushed bay leaf
½ cup apple juice
**1 8-ounce can tomato sauce
  or 1 cup ketchup**
1 Tbsp. brown sugar

USE: 3-quart casserole dish
YIELDS: 6 to 8 servings

Wash, scrape, and drain fish.

Place fish slices side by side in a casserole dish. In a separate bowl, mix garlic, black pepper, red pepper, salt, and bay leaf. Add remaining ingredients and mix well. Pour mixture over fish slices, cover dish, and allow to stand overnight in the refrigerator.

Bake covered in preheated oven at 350° for 1 hour. Uncover for last 15 minutes, if desired.

SWEET-AND-SOUR FISH: This popular flavoring lends itself well to many types of fish. Sweet-and-sour fish, prepared one day in advance, is suitable for festive meals and entertaining, and keeps well in the refrigerator for a week.

SWEET-AND-SOUR SALMON OR SALMON TROUT

6 slices salmon or salmon trout
1½ cups reserved fish broth
¼ cup honey
¼ cup lemon juice
⅓ cup white wine
1 onion, diced
1 cinnamon stick

USE: 4-quart pot
1½-quart saucepan
YIELDS: 6 servings

Wash, scrape, and drain fish.

Place fish in 4-quart pot. Cook in salted water for 20 minutes or until tender. Drain, reserving 1½ cups of broth.

In 1½-quart saucepan, combine fish broth with remaining ingredients. Cook over medium heat, stirring constantly, for 5 to 7 minutes. Pour sauce over the fish. Allow to cook for 15 minutes. Refrigerate covered at least 24 hours before serving.

SALMON STEAKS

4 slices salmon
1 Tbsp. oil
1 onion, diced
1 carrot, diced
2 Tbsps. raisins
1 bay leaf
8 peppercorns
Dash salt
1 tsp. sugar
1 Tbsp. lemon juice

USE: Wok or
10-inch skillet
YIELDS: 4 servings

Wash, scrape, and drain fish.

Heat oil in 10-inch skillet or wok on medium flame and saute onion, carrot, and raisins for 5 minutes. Add bay leaf, peppercorns, salt, and sugar. Stir 1 minute. Add salmon and lemon juice. Cover and cook over low flame for 15 to 20 minutes until the fish flakes easily with fork. Serve immediately.

VARIATION
☐ This can be made with a cleaned whole fish.

PICKLED FISH

10 slices salmon, trout, or whitefish
1¼ cups vinegar
2 cups water
3 bay leaves
1 Tbsp. pickling spices
1 Tbsp. black peppercorns
½ cup sugar
1 clove garlic
1 tsp. salt
1 onion
1 lemon, quartered
1 onion, sliced

USE: 4-quart pot
YIELDS: 10 servings

Wash, scrape, and drain fish.

Put vinegar, water, bay leaves, pickling spices, peppercorns, sugar, garlic, salt, and whole onion in a 4-quart pot. Bring to a boil and simmer for 15 minutes. Add the lemon quarters and cook another 5 minutes. Remove the lemon quarters and add the fish slices. Cook for 30 minutes. Remove cooked onion.

Place fish slices in a glass bowl, pour broth over them. Add sliced onion. Cover tightly.

Fish can be kept for up to 2 weeks refrigerated.

MARINATED SWEET-AND-SOUR FISH

In this method of making sweet and sour fish, the fish marinates in spices overnight and is then cooked in mildy spiced vegetable fish stock the next day.

15 slices whitefish, yellow pike, or salmon
Salt to taste
2 Tbsps. pickling spices, bay leaves removed
2 large onions, sliced
2 to 3 carrots, whole or sliced
1 stalk celery (optional)
4 to 5 Tbsps. sugar
½ Tbsp. salt
12 black peppercorns
¼ cup white vinegar
5 to 6 bay leaves

USE: 6-quart pot
YIELDS: 15 servings

Wash, scrape, and drain fish.

If using salmon, handle it very gently so it won't fall apart. Sprinkle every slice, top and bottom, with small amount of salt and pickling spices. Place in a glass dish and cover tightly. Leave fish in refrigerator overnight and wash off salt and spices in the morning.

Place sliced onions, carrots, celery, sugar, salt, and peppercorns in a pot. Put in fish but don't pack too tightly. Add enough water to cover fish. Cook over medium flame for ½ hour. Add vinegar and cook another 15 minutes. Place 5 to 6 bay leaves in pot, removing them after fish has cooled.

Serve warm or cold.

CHOPPED HERRING

Chopped herring is a very tasty and popular dish often served at Melava Malkas. It also makes an excellent spread on bread or challah.

2 salt herrings
Cold water
1 thick slice white bread
2 Tbsps. vinegar
1 Tbsp. chopped onion
1 large tart apple, peeled and chopped
2 tsps. salad oil
⅛ tsp. pepper
Lettuce leaves
1 hard-boiled egg, sliced

USE: Medium bowl
YIELDS: 1 pint

Soak herrings in cold water for 24 hours. Wash well, remove bones, and grind fine.

In a medium bowl soak bread in vinegar. Tear apart and grind with onion, apple, oil, and pepper. Mix together with ground herring. Serve on a bed of lettuce, garnished with slices of hard-boiled egg.

NOTE: Put the egg through a sieve for a perfect garnish.

PESCE AL CARTOCCIO

Fish roasted in aluminum foil has an excellent taste, and is especially good as a diet dish.

1 3- to 4-pound whole fish; trout, mullet, or bass
Salt to taste
Pepper to taste
3 tsps. rosemary
2 cloves garlic, minced

Preheat oven to 375°.

Wash fish in salted water and pat dry inside and out with paper towels.

Sprinkle 12-inch sheet of aluminum foil with salt, pepper, and 1 teaspoon rosemary. Place fish on foil. Put half the minced garlic plus 1 teaspoon rosemary leaves and salt and pepper in the cavity of the fish. ➤

USE: 9 x 9-inch baking pan
YIELDS: 4 to 6 servings

Season the outside of the fish with salt, pepper, and remaining 1 teaspoon of rosemary and garlic.

Wrap the fish tightly in the aluminum foil. Put in a pan and bake for 20 minutes. Turn fish over and bake another 20 minutes. Remove from oven and let cool 10 to 15 minutes. Unwrap and serve immediately.

BATTER FRIED SMELTS

A small lean fish, economical when in season. Deboned smelts can also be baked.

2 pounds smelts

BATTER
1 cup flour
1 Tbsp. baking powder
2 Tbsps. sugar
½ tsp. salt
⅛ tsp. black pepper
2 eggs, beaten
2 Tbsps. oil
1 cup water or nondairy creamer

Oil for deep frying

USE: 10-inch skillet
YIELDS: 6 servings

Wash and clean smelts, and remove heads.

BATTER: In a large bowl combine flour, baking powder, sugar, salt, and pepper. Stir in eggs, oil, and water and blend well. Heat sufficient oil for deep frying in a 10-inch skillet.

Dip smelts, one at a time, into batter. Deep-fry on both sides 8 to 10 minutes, or until golden. Drain on several layers of paper towel.

WHITEFISH

The most commonly served fish on Shabbat is whitefish, whether ground, whole or sliced. A stuffed whole fish has an excellent appearance and is often served on a garnished platter at a brit or other special occasions. Jewish women throughout the generations have developed a repertoire of recipes for whitefish by varying the spices, the vegetables, and the cooking methods. Morroccan Fish features saffron, a Mideastern spice not often found in American cooking.

COATED BAKED WHITEFISH

For a dish that tastes and looks so good, it is surprisingly simple. It may be served on Shabbat instead of gefilte fish.

1 2-pound whitefish, sliced
½ cup matzoh meal
1 tsp. paprika
½ tsp. pepper
¼ tsp. salt

USE: 8 x 8-inch pan
YIELDS: 6 to 8 servings

Preheat oven to 350°.

Rinse and dry fish thoroughly.

Lightly grease 8 x 8-inch pan. Place all ingredients except fish in a bowl and mix. Roll fish in matzoh meal mixture. Place slices in pan and bake 25 to 30 minutes. Do not overbake. This can be served warm but is excellent cold.

SWEET-AND-SOUR WHITEFISH

This fish should be salted and left for a few hours or overnight in the refrigerator. Cook and serve topped with the following sweet-and-sour sauce.

3 pounds whitefish, sliced
1 tsp. salt

SAUCE
1 cup fish stock
½ cup brown sugar
Juice of 1 lemon
1 onion, sliced
1 stick cinnamon
½ cup raisins
2 Tbsps. white wine
Fresh lemon slices,
for garnish

USE: 2½-quart pot
2-quart saucepan
YIELDS: 6 to 8 servings

Rinse fish and dry thoroughly. Sprinkle with salt and refrigerate in a covered glass bowl for a few hours or overnight. Place fish in 2½-quart pot and cover with boiling water. Simmer until tender, 10 to 15 minutes.

Remove fish to clean glass bowl and reserve 1 cup fish stock.

SAUCE: In 2-quart saucepan, simmer fish stock and remaining ingredients about 10 minutes. Strain sauce and pour over fish. Garnish with fresh sliced lemon, if desired. Refrigerate several hours or overnight.

STUFFED WHITEFISH

Ask your fish merchant to remove bones from fish but not to fillet it. Leave the fish whole. It makes an elegant centerpiece and has an unusual smooth taste — without the bones.

1 2-pound whitefish,
split and deboned

STUFFING
3 cups challah cubes
2 Tbsps. parsley flakes
½ cup chopped celery
1 medium onion, diced
3 eggs, beaten
½ cup chopped mushrooms
Salt and pepper
to taste
2 Tbsps. margarine

2 cups marinara or
spaghetti sauce
Lemon slices (optional)
Parsley sprigs (optional)

USE: 9 x 9-inch baking dish
YIELDS: 4 to 6 servings

Preheat oven to 350°.

Rinse fish and dry thoroughly.

STUFFING: Combine challah cubes, parsley flakes, celery, onion, eggs, mushrooms, salt and pepper in a large bowl. Mix well.

Place stuffing in hollow of fish and fasten with skewers. Place in a 9 x 9-inch greased baking dish. Dot fish with margarine. Bake for 30 minutes.

Pour sauce over fish and bake another 15 minutes. Garnish with lemon slices and parsley sprigs, if desired.

STEAMED WHOLE FISH

A lovely way to serve a whole fish. It can easily be garnished with parsley sprigs and lemon slices.

**1 4-pound whitefish,
left whole**
1½ tsps. salt
¾ tsp. pepper
1 onion, sliced
½ tsp. chili powder
½ tsp. thyme
3 cloves garlic
**1 to 2 medium tomatoes,
quartered**
1 tsp. parsley
1 carrot, sliced (optional)
1 small green pepper, sliced
1 cup margarine
1 Tbsp. white wine
Parsley sprigs, for garnish
Lemon slices, for garnish

USE: 6-quart fish steamer
YIELDS: 6 servings

Clean out the cavity of the fish. Rinse and dry fish thoroughly. Sprinkle well with salt and pepper, especially in cavity. Place fish into a 6-quart fish steamer. Put remaining ingredients, except for garnish, over the fish. Steam, covered, for 30 minutes over a low flame. Baste occasionally with the sauce.

Serve hot, garnished with parsley and lemon slices.

VERACRUZ STYLE FISH

The smooth blending of the various vegetables and contrasting spices gives the fish an unusual taste.

2 pounds whitefish, sliced
Juice of 1 lemon
1⅓ pounds tomatoes
**8 small green
frying peppers, sliced**
2 cloves, ground
2 tsps. cinnamon, ground
1 Tbsp. onion, finely diced
4 cloves garlic, minced
¼ cup olive oil
1 Tbsp. minced parsley
Dash salt
2 cups water
2 to 3 hot red peppers, sliced
¼ cup green olives
3 Tbsps. chives

USE: 10-inch skillet
YIELDS: 4 to 6 servings

Rinse fish and dry thoroughly. Place in medium bowl and soak in lemon juice for 10 minutes. Blend the tomatoes, peppers, cloves, and cinnamon in blender.

In 10-inch skillet, saute onion and garlic in olive oil until transparent. Add tomato mixture to skillet and allow to simmer for 8 to 10 minutes. Add parsley, salt, and water to skillet. When water boils, add the lemon-soaked fish, red peppers, olives, and chives. Lower flame and simmer for 15 minutes, until the fish is cooked.

MORROCCAN FISH

The spiced oil, which helps gives this fish its unique taste, is very simple to make but requires preparation at least a week ahead.

1 3-pound whitefish, sliced
1 large green or red pepper
1 to 2 tomatoes
2 to 3 cloves garlic
Water
¾ tsp. salt
2 tsps. saffron
3 Tbsps. spiced oil★

USE: 5-quart Dutch oven
YIELDS: 6 servings

Rinse fish and dry thoroughly. Slice pepper and tomatoes. Peel garlic cloves and cut in half. Line 5-quart Dutch oven with peppers, tomatoes, and garlic and place fish slices on top. Add enough water to cover fish. Bring to a boil, then add salt, saffron, and spiced oil.★ Lower flame and simmer 40 to 50 minutes. This dish may be served hot or cold.

★**Spiced Oil:** Prepare oil at least 1 week ahead. Place 1 tablespoon crushed red pepper into a dish or small jar. Cover with 1 cup olive oil. Let it stand in a cool place or in refrigerator. After a few days, red pepper will settle on the bottom and oil will absorb the color and taste of pepper. This oil can be made in larger quantitites and stored for several months.

CARIBBEAN FISH

4 whitefish fillets
or 4 slices
½ tsp. salt
⅛ tsp. pepper
¼ cup lemon juice
3 Tbsps. peanut oil
1 clove garlic, diced
½ green pepper, diced
½ large onion, diced
½ tsp. curry powder
1 tomato, thinly sliced, or
1 8-ounce can tomato sauce
1 tsp. basil leaves
1 thinly sliced ginger root
1 Tbsp. sugar
½ tsp. thyme

USE: 10-inch skillet
YIELDS: 4 servings

Rinse and dry fish thoroughly. Sprinkle salt, pepper, and lemon juice over fish. In 10-inch skillet, heat oil until hot. Add garlic and saute. When soft, add green pepper and onion and saute until soft. Add curry powder, tomato, and basil. Stir until mixed.

Cook 10 minutes, uncovered. Add ginger, sugar, and thyme and cook an additional 10 minutes. Add the fish fillets or slices.

Cover skillet and cook over low to medium flame for 10 minutes. Serve immediately.

FISH STEW

This is a basic fish stew that can easily be adjusted to your individual taste.

6 slices whitefish
1 tsp. salt
1 tsp. black pepper
¾ tsp. paprika

Rinse and dry fish thoroughly. Sprinkle fish with salt, black pepper, and paprika.

In 10-inch skillet, using 3 tablespoons oil, brown the fish. This should take about 3 to 4 minutes. Remove fish and discard oil.

►

5 Tbsps. oil
1 onion, sliced
1 green pepper, sliced
3 cloves garlic, sliced
1 tomato, cut into eighths
3 Tbsps. margarine
½ tsp. thyme

USE: 10-inch skillet
8 x 8-inch pan
YIELDS: 6 servings

Place remaining 2 tablespoons oil in skillet. Add sliced onion, green pepper, and garlic, and saute on low flame. Add tomato, margarine, and thyme. Saute for 5 minutes. Add fish slices. Cover skillet and cook about 15 minutes or until fish flakes easily with a fork. Serve immediately.

NOTE: If you are using fillets, cook 5 to 10 minutes.

VARIATIONS

□ For a heavier and stronger stew, add 1 diced carrot, 1 small hot pepper, and salt, pepper, paprika, and cumin to taste.

□ Add ginger, basil vegetables, and cooked rice before you add the fish.

FILLETS

Available year round, fillets of cod, sole, trout, and flounder are among the most widely available and can be prepared in a variety of ways. They can be served broiled, baked, fried, or covered with a sauce. Rolling fillets around a stuffing gives an elegant appearance. Try Ceviche, where the fish is marinated by steeping in a lime juice marinade for several hours. A Sweet-and-Sour Sauce or a Ginger Sauce adds a perfect mingling of flavors.

CEVICHE

This deliciously different salad is made of raw fish "cooked" by the lime juice. It must be marinated from 3 to 24 hours before eating.

1 pound firm
white-fleshed fish,
whitefish, haddock, or
red snapper fillets
1 cup freshly squeezed
lime juice

1 cup peeled and
diced tomatoes
1 medium onion, diced
¼ cup oil
1 Tbsp. white wine
1 tsp. oregano
½ tsp. basil
1 tsp. coriander
Salt and pepper to taste
½ tsp. hot pepper sauce

GARNISH
1 avocado or
1 red onion or
2 limes, thinly sliced

USE: Glass bowl
YIELDS: 4 servings

Cut fish fillets into 1-inch cubes.

Place fillets in a glass bowl and pour lime juice over them. Allow to marinate at least 3 to 4 hours in the refrigerator, turning occasionally. (Fish may marinate up to 24 hours.)

After fish has marinated, add remaining ingredients, mixing gently.

Refrigerate several hours before serving. Liquid may be drained off before serving, if desired. Serve as an appetizer in tall stemware or on small plates, garnished with avocado, red onion, or lime slices on top.

BASIC FRIED FLOUNDER

1 pound flounder fillets
1 cup bread crumbs
1 tsp. salt
½ tsp. garlic powder
¾ tsp. onion powder
⅛ tsp. white pepper
2 eggs
½ to ⅔ cup oil

USE: 10-inch skillet
YIELDS: 3 to 4 servings

On a large plate, mix bread crumbs, salt, garlic powder, onion powder, and white pepper. Beat eggs in bowl. Coat fillets with seasoned bread crumbs on both sides. Dip into egg mixture and again into seasoned bread crumbs.

Heat half of oil in 10-inch skillet. When oil is hot, place three or four fillets in skillet and fry over medium flame until golden brown. Turn over with spatula and fry on second side until golden brown. Repeat until all fillets are fried, adding oil as necessary.

HINT: For a spicier fish, lightly salt fillets and let stand for 1 hour. Rinse and pat dry before breading.

CHINESE SWEET-AND-SOUR FRIED FISH

1½ pounds firm-flesh fish,
red snapper, cod, or
halibut fillet

BATTER
1 cup flour
⅓ cup cornstarch
1 tsp. baking powder
1 tsp. salt
1 tsp. vegetable oil
1 egg,
1 cup water

Oil for frying

SAUCE
1 8 oz. can tomato sauce
or 1 cup ketchup
¼ cup cider vinegar
6 Tbsps. white vinegar
1 medium green pepper,
cut into chunks
1 medium onion,
thinly sliced
1 20-ounce can of
pineapple chunks with juice
1 Tbsp. cornstarch
1 Tbsp. cool water

**Chow mein noodles
to garnish**

USE: 10-inch skillet
YIELDS: 4 servings

Cut fish fillets into 1-inch cubes.

BATTER: Combine all batter ingredients in a large bowl. Mix well.

Pour oil 1 inch deep into 10-inch skillet or into deep-fat fryer. Heat oil over medium flame or to 375°. Dip fish in batter and place in a single layer. Fry until golden, 1 to 2 minutes. Drain fish on paper towels and set aside. If there is a good deal of batter remaining, dip some pineapple chunks (from sauce ingredients) in it and fry until golden. Drain.

SAUCE: Combine all sauce ingredients in a 10-inch skillet except for cornstarch and water. Simmer 10 minutes until green pepper is tender-crisp. Mix cornstarch with cool water and add to sauce. Cook 1 to 2 minutes, stirring constantly.

Add fish to sauce and warm through. Serve at once over hot rice, topped with chow mein noodles.

FISH COCKTAIL SALAD

This fish salad makes a beautiful appetizer. Prepare it several hours in advance so that fish will be well chilled before combining it with vegetables and topping with sauce.

4 cod or haddock fillets
1 onion, sliced
2 Tbsps. lemon juice
3 bay leaves
1 green pepper, finely diced
1 stalk celery, finely diced
¼ cup onion, finely diced
Pinch of salt
Dash of black pepper

SAUCE
1 scallion, sliced
1 Tbsp. white horseradish
½ cup mayonnaise
¼ cup chili sauce
Dash cayenne pepper
¼ tsp. salt
1 garlic clove, minced
1 Tbsp. chopped capers (optional)

GARNISH
Lettuce leaves
3 hard-boiled eggs, quartered
3 tomatoes, quartered

USE: 3 quart pot
YIELDS: 6 appetizers

Place fish in a 3-quart pot with water to cover. Add onion, lemon juice and bay leaves. Cook over medium flame until fish flakes easily, about 20 minutes. (Fish may also be steamed.) Drain fish and refrigerate until cold.

Break fish into chunks and place in medium bowl. Add vegetables, salt and pepper and toss lightly.

SAUCE: In a small bowl combine all sauce ingredients and mix well.

Serve on individual plates, lining each plate with lettuce leaves. Arrange fish mixture on lettuce and top with sauce. Garnish with eggs and tomatoes.

NOTE: Make sure fish is cold before serving.

FLOUNDER IN SPICY TOMATO SAUCE

2 pounds flounder fillets
½ cup oil
1 large onion, diced
1 green pepper, diced
3 cloves garlic, minced
1 tsp. chili powder
½ tsp. ground cinnamon
¼ tsp. cumin
½ tsp. salt
2 tsps. sugar
1 14½-ounce can tomato puree
1 cup water

USE: 5-quart Dutch oven
YIELDS: 6 servings

Cut fish into serving portions and set aside.

Heat oil in Dutch oven, and saute onion and pepper until soft. Add garlic, then remaining seasonings and tomato puree. Do not add water yet. Simmer 20 minutes until smooth and thick. Add water and mix well.

Add fish and simmer until it is tender and flakes easily with a fork, about 20 minutes.

Serve with rice and very thinly sliced carrots that have been steamed with margarine, salt, white pepper, and a pinch of sugar.

FLOUNDER WITH CABBAGE, ALSATIAN STYLE

A beautiful dish.

**1½ pounds fresh or
frozen flounder fillets
1 onion, sliced
½ cup boiling water
1 Tbsp. lemon juice
¼ tsp. garlic powder
½ tsp. salt
¼ tsp. pepper
2 Tbsps. margarine
2 quarts (about 2 pounds)
shredded cabbage
¼ cup dry white wine
2 tsps. salt
⅛ tsp. pepper**

**SAUCE
3 Tbsps. margarine
3 Tbsps. flour
1 tsp. salt
⅛ tsp. nutmeg
Pinch white pepper
1½ cups nondairy creamer
¼ cup reserved fish broth,
from poaching liquid**

USE: 2 9 x 13-inch baking pans
10-inch skillet
1½-quart saucepan
YIELDS: 6 servings.

Preheat oven to 350°.

In 9 x 13-inch baking dish, place fish over onion slices. Combine water, lemon juice, garlic powder, salt, and pepper and pour over fish. Top with wax paper, then with aluminum foil. Place in oven to poach for 15 minutes or until fish flakes easily when tested with a fork.

While fish is baking, melt margarine in 10-inch skillet. Add cabbage, wine, salt and pepper. Cover and cook over medium heat, stirring occasionally until tender and crisp, about 10 to 12 minutes.

Place cabbage in a 9 x 13-inch shallow baking dish. Gently remove fish from liquid with slotted spatula and place on cabbage in baking dish. Keep warm. Set aside ¼ cup poaching liquid. Discard remaining liquid.

SAUCE: In 1½-quart saucepan, melt margarine. Stir in flour and seasonings until smooth. Slowly add nondairy creamer and ¼ cup fish broth, stirring constantly. Cook until mixture thickens. Remove from heat and stir until smooth. Spoon sauce evenly over fish.

Bake in oven until lightly browned, about 2 to 3 minutes. Serve immediately.

VARIATION
☐ For Dairy, stir ⅔ cup shredded American cheese into sauce.

TROUT WITH GINGER SAUCE

This is a simple way of cooking sea trout with a different flavor.

4 sea trout fillets

**GINGER SAUCE
3 Tbsps. margarine
1 Tbsp. grated onion
1 clove garlic, minced
2 Tbsps. lemon juice
⅛ tsp. salt
½ tsp. ground ginger**

USE: 9 x 9-inch pan
7-inch skillet
YIELDS: 4 servings

Arrange the fillets in a 9 x 9-inch pan for broiling.

GINGER SAUCE: In a 7-inch skillet, melt the margarine. Add onion, garlic, lemon juice, salt, and ginger, and simmer for 5 minutes. Pour the sauce over the fillets and broil for 10 to 15 minutes, until fish flakes.

TANTALIZING SHABBAT FISH

This dish may be served warm on Friday night or cold on Shabbat day.

3 pounds tile, halibut, or flounder, filleted (reserve bones)
½ cup oil
4 cloves garlic, sliced
2 small tomatoes, diced
1 Tbsp. paprika
1 Tbsp. tomato paste
2 tsps. salt
1 bunch coriander leaves
1 small green pepper, cut into eighths or tenths

FISH ACCOMPANIMENT
1½ pounds carrots, sliced
6 medium potatoes, cubed
2 tsps. paprika
1 cup water
¼ cup oil

USE: 10-inch skillet
4-quart pot
YIELDS: 8 to 10 servings

Cut fish into 8 to 10 equal pieces. Sprinkle with salt.

In 10-inch skillet, heat oil. Add garlic and tomatoes. When tomatoes are simmering, mash with fork; simmer until soft. Add paprika and tomato paste and allow to simmer several more minutes.

When tomato mixture is done, remove sauce to small bowl. Place fish bones on bottom of skillet and place pieces of fish on top of bones. (This prevents the fish from burning.) Spread tomato mixture evenly over pieces of fish. Place coriander leaves and green pepper slices on top of fish and sauce. Simmer for 45 minutes, or until fish is done to your taste.

FISH ACCOMPANIMENT: Prepare carrots and potatoes and place in separate bowls. Sprinkle 1 teaspoon paprika on carrots and potatoes. Mix in well.

Place water and oil in a 4-quart pot. Add carrots, then potatoes. Cook until soft, about 1 hour.

TO SERVE: Place a mixture of potatoes and carrots on dish and top with a piece of fish. (Coriander leaves may be discarded once fish has cooked.)

FLOUNDER-BROCCOLI ROLLS WITH MUSHROOM SAUCE

A delicious and colorful fish dish to serve for a Simchah.

6 large flounder fillets
Salt to taste
10 ounces frozen chopped broccoli, cooked and drained
¼ cup melted margarine
2 Tbsps. lemon juice

SAUCE
¼ cup margarine
1 pound mushrooms, trimmed and sliced
¼ cup flour
1½ cups nondairy creamer
3 Tbsps. lemon juice
Salt to taste

USE: 9 x 9 baking dish
10-inch skillet
YIELDS: 6 servings

Preheat oven to 350°.

Sprinkle flounder lightly with salt. Place one sixth of broccoli on top of each fillet and roll up. Place seam side down in a shallow, greased baking pan. Brush tops with a mixture of melted margarine and lemon juice.

Bake for 30 minutes. Meanwhile prepare sauce.

SAUCE: In a 10-inch skillet, heat margarine until melted and saute mushrooms for 5 minutes. Add flour and nondairy creamer and keep stirring over medium heat until sauce bubbles and thickens. Stir in lemon juice. Simmer, stirring occasionally, for 5 minutes. Season lightly with salt.

When fish is done, remove with spatula onto platter. Top with mushroom sauce.

NEW ENGLAND FISH LOAF

An easy, fluffy fish dish with a taste that is just right.

**3 pounds cod or
haddock fillets**
3 large onions
2 carrots
1 cup bread crumbs
4 eggs
⅓ cup water
¼ cup oil
1 Tbsp. salt
2 Tbsps. sugar
½ tsp. black pepper
½ tsp. paprika (optional)

USE: 9 x 9-inch pan
YIELDS: 8 to 10 servings

Preheat oven to 350°.

Grind fish together with onions, carrots, and bread crumbs into a mixing bowl. Add eggs, water, and oil and mix well. Add seasonings and mix again. Adjust seasonings to taste.

Pour into an oiled 9 x 9-inch pan and sprinkle with paprika. Bake uncovered for 1 hour.

MONDAY NIGHT'S STUFFED FILLETS

A tempting way to use up the leftover challah from Shabbat.

**2 pounds flounder or
sole fillets**

STUFFING
½ pound 3-day-old challah
3 Tbsps. oil
2 onions, diced
1 stalk celery, diced
½ pound mushrooms, sliced
1 egg, beaten

SAUCE
2 Tbsps. oil
1 onion, diced
1 green pepper, diced
2 cups tomato sauce
½ tsp. basil
½ tsp. sugar

USE: 10-inch skillet
2-quart casserole
YIELDS: 6 servings

Wash fillets and pat dry. Set aside.

STUFFING: Slice challah and dampen with water to soften. Squeeze out excess water.

Heat oil in 10-inch skillet and add onions, celery, and mushrooms. Saute until onions are transparent and vegetables are soft. Add the challah and continue to saute about 5 minutes. Remove from heat and cool. Mix in the beaten egg until well blended.

Preheat oven to 350°.

SAUCE: Heat oil in skillet and saute onion and green pepper until onion is transparent. Add tomato sauce, basil and sugar. Simmer for 5 minutes.

TO ASSEMBLE: Divide the stuffing according to number of fillets. Spread one portion of stuffing on each. Roll up fillets and place seam side down in a 2-quart greased casserole dish. Spoon warm sauce over fish. Bake for 30 minutes.

RUSSIAN-DRESSED FLOUNDER

1 pound flounder or
sole fillets
½ cup mayonnaise
½ cup ketchup

USE: 2-quart saucepan
YIELDS: 3 to 4 servings

Roll fish fillets and fasten with a toothpick. In a small bowl mix mayonnaise and ketchup until well blended. Place fish in 2-quart saucepan and pour mayonnaise and ketchup mixture over fish. Cook for approximately 15 to 20 minutes over low flame.

VARIATION
□ Dip fillet slices in mayonnaise and ketchup mixture and bake in 1-quart casserole, covered, at 350° for 20 to 30 minutes.

LEMON FISH

1 large onion, diced
3 pounds flounder fillets,
cut into 6 to 8 pieces
¾ tsp. salt
Water to cover
¼ cup flour
1 tsp. ginger
½ cup dry white wine
Juice from 2 lemons
¼ cup raisins or dates
3 Tbsps. honey (optional)
1 lemon, sliced
6 to 8 parsley sprigs

USE: 10-inch skillet
YIELDS: 6 to 8 servings

Put diced onion in 10-inch skillet. Place fish on top of onions. Sprinkle with salt and cover with water; cover pan and simmer approximately 20 minutes or until fish is done.

Remove fish from pan and place on serving platter. Remove onions with slotted spoon and place on top of fish.

Boil down liquid in pan until there is ½ cup left. Stir in flour, ginger, wine, lemon juice, raisins, and honey. Stir and cook until thick and smooth. Pour over fish. Garnish each piece with lemon slice and parsley sprig.

Serve hot or cold.

CODFISH CREOLE

¼ cup oil
1 cup diced onion
½ cup diced green pepper
1 20-ounce can
peeled tomatoes,
drained and chopped
1 8-ounce can tomato sauce
1 Tbsp. chopped parsley
1 bay leaf
1 clove garlic, minced
½ tsp. salt, or to taste
⅛ tsp. pepper
1 pound cod fillets

USE: 3-quart pot
YIELDS: 3 to 4 servings

Heat oil in a 3-quart pot and saute onion and green pepper. Add remaining ingredients except for cod. Cover and simmer gently for 20 minutes.

Add cod and cook 10 to 15 minutes or until fish flakes easily with a fork.

Serve hot over cooked rice or noodles.

CURRIED COD

A festive way of preparing fried fish — it is marinated afterwards in curry sauce for at least 24 hours.

2½ pounds cod fillets
½ tsp. salt
⅛ tsp. pepper
2 eggs, beaten
2 Tbsps. flour
Oil for frying

SAUCE
½ cup vinegar
1 cup water
1 large onion, sliced
2 bay leaves
6 allspice seeds
1 Tbsp. mild curry powder
2 Tbsps. sugar
½ tsp. salt
⅛ tsp. pepper

USE: 10-inch skillet
2-quart saucepan
9 x 13-inch pan
YIELDS: 6 to 8 servings

Cut fish into single-portion pieces (about 4-inch squares) and sprinkle with salt and pepper. Combine beaten eggs and flour in bowl; mix with a fork until smooth. Dip fish into egg mixture, making sure both sides get coated. Fry on both sides in 10-inch skillet in hot oil until golden. Drain on paper towels.

SAUCE: In a 2-quart saucepan boil vinegar, ½ cup water, onion, bay leaves, and allspice until onion is soft. Add curry powder, sugar, salt, and pepper with the remaining water. Mix well, cover, and simmer for 10 minutes.

Place fish in a 9 x 13-inch pan and pour the hot sauce over it. Cool and refrigerate 1 or 2 days. The flavor improves with time.

NOTE: Fish will keep at least 1 week.

TANGY FLOUNDER

This batter must stand for 6 hours before use.

2½ cups flour
½ tsp. salt
1 cup beer
4 egg whites, stiffly beaten
2 pounds sole or
flounder fillets
Oil for deep frying

USE: 10-inch skillet
YIELDS: 6 servings

Combine flour and salt in a large bowl. Add beer and mix until smooth. Fold in beaten egg whites. Cover and let batter stand for 6 hours. If using frozen fillets, defrost. Dip fish fillets into batter.

Heat oil over medium flame in 10-inch skillet. Deep fry fillets for approximately 15 minutes, or pan-fry for 10 minutes on one side and 5 to 7 minutes on second side. Drain on paper towel.

VEGETABLE-FISH CAKES

2 medium potatoes
2 medium carrots
1 medium onion
1 pound frozen
flounder fillets, defrosted
2 eggs, beaten
1 tsp. salt

Preheat oven to 350°.

In a 3-quart saucepan cook potato, carrot, and onion in moderate amount of water until tender. Add fish the last 10 minutes. Drain liquid and allow to cool for 10 minutes. Mash entire mixture together. Add eggs and seasonings and mix well. Add baking powder and matzoh meal and mix until well blended.

►

¼ tsp. pepper
⅛ tsp. paprika
½ tsp. baking powder
½ cup matzoh meal

USE: 3-quart saucepan
Baking sheet
YIELDS: 12 medium patties

Shape into patties and place on greased baking sheet. Brush tops with a little oil and bake for 20 to 30 minutes.

VARIATION
☐ Fry patties in 10-inch skillet in hot oil. Fry over medium flame until golden-brown and crisp on both sides, approximately 5 to 7 minutes on each side.

SOLE ROLLS WITH POTATO STUFFING

6 sole fillets

STUFFING
1 onion, diced
½ cup diced mushrooms
2 Tbsps. margarine
1½ cups mashed potatoes
or 3 potatoes,
cooked and mashed
½ tsp. salt
Dash of pepper

1 Tbsp. margarine
1 8-ounce can tomato sauce

USE: 10-inch skillet
9 x 9-inch pan
YIELDS: 6 servings

Preheat oven to 350°.

STUFFING: In a 10-inch skillet saute onion and mushrooms in margarine. Add to mashed potatoes with seasonings and mix well. Spread potato mixture over the darker side of the fillets about ¼ inch to ⅓ inch thick. Roll each fillet and secure with toothpick. Place in baking pan and dot with margarine.

Pour tomato sauce over fish and bake for 30 minutes or until fish flakes easily.

SALMON-STUFFED FLOUNDER

This dish is not only delicious, but with its contrasting colors of white and pink, is lovely to look at, too.

1 pound frozen
flounder fillets, defrosted

STUFFING
1 7-ounce can salmon
1 egg
¼ cup matzoh meal
2 tsps. ketchup

1 onion, sliced
1 Tbsp. margarine
1 8-ounce can tomato sauce
or Traditional White Sauce
(page 335)

USE: 8 x 8-inch baking dish
YIELDS: 3 to 4 servings

Preheat oven to 350°.

Combine salmon, egg, matzoh meal, and ketchup in medium bowl. Place 1 or 2 tablespoons of salmon mixture on each fillet, roll up and secure with toothpicks. Line bottom of greased baking dish with onion slices and place fillet rolls on top. Dot rolls with margarine.

Pour tomato sauce or Traditional White Sauce on top. Bake for 30 minutes.

TUNA AND SALMON

Fresh or canned tuna is perfect as a light dinner and very versatile. Low in calories and high in taste, salmon, with its distinctive color and lightness, is both elegant and easy to prepare. Salmon can be substituted for the tuna in many of the recipes.

TUNA SPREAD

An ideal spread to serve on crackers or bread for a buffet luncheon or Simchah.

1 6½-ounce can tuna, drained
3 hard-boiled eggs, peeled
1 carrot, peeled
½ green pepper
small onion
½ tsp. salt
¼ tsp. garlic powder
1½ Tbsps. mayonnaise
½ tsp. lemon juice

USE: 2-quart bowl
YIELDS: 2 cups spread

Put drained tuna, hard-boiled eggs, and vegetables through a food grinder. Then place in 2-quart bowl. Add seasonings, mayonnaise, and lemon juice and mix thoroughly. The spread should be creamy.

VARIATION
☐ Omit green pepper, and add 2 to 3 carrots. Spread will resemble salmon.

TUNA SQUARES

Fluffy, light squares to enhance your buffet luncheon.

2 6½-ounce cans tuna
or 1 15-ounce can
pink salmon, drained
4 eggs, beaten
2 Tbsps. flour
½ cup mayonnaise
1 stalk celery, chopped
1 small onion, diced
¾ cup bread crumbs

SAUCE
1 small onion, diced
1 clove garlic, minced
½ green pepper, diced
1 Tbsp. oil
½ cup tomato sauce
1 tsp. oregano
½ tsp. basil

USE: 7-inch skillet
9 x 9-inch baking dish
YIELDS: 9 servings

In a mixing bowl, combine first 7 ingredients and mix well. Set aside.

SAUCE: In 7-inch skillet, saute onion, garlic, and green pepper in 1 tablespoon oil for 5 minutes. Add tomato sauce, oregano, and basil to mixture in skillet and cook another 10 minutes.

Preheat oven to 350°.

Oil a 9 x 9-inch baking dish and fill with tuna mixture. Pour tomato sauce on top. Bake for 45 to 60 minutes. Cut into nine 3-inch squares and serve hot.

BASIC TUNA SALAD

1 6½-ounce can tuna
1 scallion, finely diced
1 stalk celery, finely diced
2 to 3 Tbsps. mayonnaise
½ tsp. prepared mustard
(optional)
1 Tbsp. ketchup (optional)

USE: Salad bowl
YIELDS: 3 servings

Drain can of tuna. Place tuna in bowl and flake well with fork. Add remaining ingredients and mix together very well.

Ideal to serve in sandwiches either as is, or between lettuce leaves with 2 to 3 tomato slices. Also very tasty served in hollowed-out green pepper cups.

VARIATION
☐ **Vegetable-Tuna Salad:** Combine basic tuna salad with 1 tomato, ½ cucumber, and ½ green pepper, finely diced.

TUNA-TOFU PATTIES

½ pound tofu
1 6½-ounce can tuna
1 egg, beaten
½ medium onion, diced
1 Tbsp. tamari soy sauce
½ cup wheat germ
1 tsp. dried thyme
½ cup flour
½ cup oil for frying

USE: 10-inch skillet
YIELDS: 4 servings

Crumble tofu in medium bowl. Add drained and mashed tuna. Then add egg, onion, tamari, wheat germ, and thyme. Mix well. Form into patties. Dip patties into flour.

Heat 10-inch skillet and add oil to cover bottom of pan. Place patties in hot oil and fry 10 minutes on each side or until brown.

VARIATIONS
☐ Matzoh meal may be used instead of wheat germ.

☐ Instead of frying, patties may be baked in a greased 8-inch square pan at 350° for 45 minutes.

ZUCCHINI-TUNA CAKES

1 medium zucchini
4 slices
white bread, cubed
2 6½-ounce cans tuna, drained
2 eggs, beaten
1 tsp. grated onion
1 tsp. lemon juice
¼ tsp. salt
3 Tbsps. ketchup
(optional)
Oil for frying

USE: 10-inch skillet
YIELDS: 8 cakes

Shred zucchini fine and pat dry until all the juice has drained; set aside.

In a small bowl, soak bread cubes in small amount of water until soft. Squeeze out water.

In mixing bowl, combine zucchini, bread cubes, and remaining ingredients except for oil. Shape into patties.

Heat ¼-inch oil in a 10-inch skillet. When hot add patties. Fry until golden brown on both sides, approximately 5 minutes per side.

VARIATION
☐ **Vegetable-Tuna Cakes:** Omit zucchini and white bread. In blender, blend 2 carrots, 1 medium potato, eggs, and seasoning. Add ⅓ cup wheat germ to mixture. The vegetables can be cooked or raw.

SALAD NICOISE

A decorative way to serve tuna with vegetables.

6 to 8 crisp lettuce leaves
½ pound string beans, blanched
2 hard-boiled eggs, quartered
1 tomato, sliced into 8 wedges
4 cooked potatoes, diced
1 6½-ounce can tuna, drained
8 green olives
8 black olives
1 small red onion, sliced
1 small can anchovies
6 Tbsps. olive oil
2 Tbsps. vinegar

USE: 10-inch platter
YIELDS: 4 servings

Place lettuce on platter. Arrange string beans around outer rim of platter and then alternate in the following order: egg slice, tomato wedge, potatoes. Mound tuna in center and sprinkle with olives, red onions, and anchovies. Serve with dressing of olive oil and vinegar drizzled over vegetables, or favorite dressing.

SUPER SALMON-VEGETABLE PATTIES

A whole meal in one! Great for picnics, yet special enough for company.

1 large potato, cubed
medium zucchini, unpeeled and cubed
2 carrots, sliced into 1-inch slices
2 cups water
2 7¾-ounce cans salmon
4 eggs, beaten
Juice of ½ lemon
¼ cup mayonnaise
1 stalk celery, diced
1 small onion, diced
¾ cup bread crumbs, matzoh meal, or cornflake crumbs
1 tsp. garlic powder
½ tsp. black pepper
½ to 1 tsp. salt
3 to 4 Tbsps. oil

USE: 2-quart saucepan
10-inch skillet
YIELDS: 12 patties

In 2-quart saucepan, boil potato, zucchini, and carrots in 2 cups water until tender.

Drain salmon and remove bones. Using medium-size mixing bowl, combine salmon, eggs, lemon juice, mayonnaise, celery, onion, and bread crumbs. Mix well.

Drain the cooked vegetables and mash well. Add to salmon mixture and mix until well combined, adding seasonings.

Heat oil in 10-inch skillet. Using ¼ cup of fish mixture per patty, form patties and fry in skillet over medium flame, approximately 5 minutes per side, until golden on both sides. Add more oil to skillet if necessary.

TUNA STUFFED POTATOES

Potatoes stuffed with tuna makes for a quick, hot meal.

4 Idaho potatoes
1 6½-ounce can tuna
1 onion, grated
¼ green pepper, grated
1 carrot, grated
½ cup mayonnaise
¼ tsp. salt
⅛ tsp. pepper
⅛ tsp. garlic powder
Paprika

USE: 9 x 9-inch baking pan
YIELDS: 4 servings

Preheat oven to 350°.

Wash potatoes well and pierce each with a fork. Bake whole until soft, about 1 hour. Slice in half lengthwise. Scoop out the inside and set aside.

Drain can of tuna. Place tuna in bowl and flake well with fork. Mash together scooped-out potato with tuna, vegetables, mayonnaise, and seasonings except paprika. Spoon mixture back into potato shells. Sprinkle paprika on top. Place in baking pan. Raise oven temperature to 400° and heat for 10 minutes. Serve hot.

SALMON CELERY LOAF

A loaf is a lovely way to serve fish, and this is a substantial one-dish meal, perfect with a salad.

1 pound or 2 cups
canned salmon, drained
⅔ cup chopped celery
2 Tbsps. vinegar
¾ tsp. salt
¼ tsp. pepper
1 egg
⅔ cup rolled oats,
uncooked
¾ cup nondairy creamer

USE: 9 x 5-inch loaf pan
YIELDS: 4 to 6 servings

Preheat oven to 350°.

Combine all ingredients together in mixing bowl and mix well. Pack into greased 9 x 5-inch loaf pan. Bake for 1 hour.

Allow to stand 5 minutes before removing from pan.

SARDINE SALAD

This unique tasty sandwich spread can be served as an appetizer or on crackers.

1 large can
water-packed sardines
3 to 4 cloves garlic, minced
2 Tbsps. tahini
½ tsp. salt
1 tsp. cumin
2 medium onions, diced
1 pepper, diced
1 Tbsp. oil
Juice of ½ lemon

USE: 7-inch skillet
YIELDS: 2 cups salad

Drain and mash sardines well in a mixing bowl. Add the next 4 ingredients. In an 7-inch skillet, saute onions and pepper in oil until lightly browned. Add sauteed mixture to sardines while still hot. Mix well and add freshly squeezed lemon juice.

Chill and serve.

SALMON OR TUNA KNISHES

DOUGH
2 cups flour
2 tsps. baking powder
½ tsp. salt
¼ cup margarine
¾ cup nondairy creamer or apple juice

FILLING
½ cup celery, finely diced
1 small onion, finely diced
¾ cup sliced mushrooms
2 Tbsps. margarine
1 7-ounce can salmon or 1 6½-ounce can tuna, drained
2 cups cooked green peas
2 Tbsps. chopped pimiento
1 egg, beaten

USE: 10-inch skillet
Baking sheet
YIELDS: 9 main dishes or 18 appetizers

DOUGH: Sift dry ingredients together; cut in margarine with two knives or pastry blender. Add nondairy creamer or juice slowly, just enough to moisten, as when making pie crust. Roll out on floured board into 9 x 18-inch rectangle.

FILLING: In 10-inch skillet saute celery, onion, and mushrooms in margarine until golden brown, about 5 minutes. Add salmon or tuna, green peas, pimiento, and egg. Spread on pastry and roll up jelly-roll style.

For "how-to" illustrations, see Knishes Illustrated, page 308.

Preheat oven to 350°.

Make indentations with a knife for slicing (see Note) and place on greased baking sheet. Bake about 30 minutes or until golden brown.

NOTE: If served as appetizer, slice thin. If served as main dish, slices should be thicker.

Vegetarian Dishes

Vegetarian Main Dishes can be the foundation of healthful eating. We are all concerned with eating a varied and nourishing diet of healthful food, including fresh fruit and vegetables and whole grains. Many of our vegetarian dishes are international in origin. Black beans Cuban-style and rice, together with a green salad, provide a well-balanced meal. Or try Gado-Gado, an Indonesian specialty, proof that kosher cooking is as varied as your taste.

Tofu, squares of processed soy with a creamy taste and texture, is a versatile protein. It combines well with almost anything. Thinly sliced on eggplant, it makes for a "cheesy" topping. Dipped in batter and fried, tofu makes a crisp delicate fritter. It can be curried or stuffed into zucchini, or substituted for hard-boiled eggs in a salad.

Many vegetarian recipes suitable for main dishes are found in the Vegetable Section. Salads such as Tabouli and Chickpea Salad are excellent choices for supper.

VEGETARIAN FOOD IN JEWISH LAW

☐ Grains, vegetables, and tofu are all *pareve* unless combined with either dairy or meat ingredients.

☐ Many of the same laws that apply to vegetables, i.e., washing and checking these foods, using processed vegetables, apply to vegetarian dishes. See Vegetables and Kashrut, page 259, for a discussion on these laws.

☐ It should also be kept in mind when dining out that although a restaurant may call itself vegetarian one cannot assume that the food served there is kosher. Many vegetarian restaurants serve fish and/or dairy foods, both of which require a reliable certification of *kashrut*. For more information, see Food Establishments Requiring Supervision, page 28. It is therefore necessary to ascertain prior to eating in any vegetarian restaurant that it is under Rabbinical supervision.

NUT ROAST

1 onion, diced
1 green pepper, diced
3 Tbsps. margarine or oil
1 cup brown rice, cooked
⅓ cup wheat germ or bread crumbs, matzoh meal, or rolled oats
1 cup diced tomatoes
1 cup ground pecans or walnuts or almonds
1 egg, beaten
2 Tbsps. minced parsley or 1 Tbsp. parsley flakes
¾ tsp. salt
¼ tsp. paprika

USE: 7-inch skillet
9 x 5 inch loaf pan
YIELDS: 6 to 8 servings

Preheat oven to 375°.

In a 7-inch skillet saute onion and green pepper in margarine or oil. Place all remaining ingredients in bowl. Add sauteed vegetables and combine well. Place in greased 9 x 5-inch loaf pan. Bake for 30 minutes.

BLACK BEANS CUBAN STYLE

Serve over rice with a green salad. Hearty appetite!

1 pound black beans
1 onion,
peeled and halved
1 green pepper,
seeded and halved
2 coriander sprigs
(optional)
½ tsp. oregano
1 bay leaf
1 tsp. salt
1 tsp. pepper
1 red pepper, diced
1 onion, diced
1 clove garlic, minced
½ cup olive oil
2 Tbsps. vinegar
1 Tbsp. sugar

USE: 4-quart pot
7-inch skillet
YIELDS: 6 servings

The night before, place beans in a large bowl in water to cover and soak overnight. Drain, rinse, and remove dried beans and stones.

Place beans in 4-quart pot and cover with water to 2 inches above beans. Add halved onion, green pepper, and coriander, if desired. Season with oregano, bay leaf, salt and pepper. Simmer on low flame 1½ to 1¾ hours or until tender, adding water as necessary.

While beans are cooking, in a 7-inch skillet saute red pepper, onion, and garlic in olive oil about 20 minutes or until vegetables are tender.

Once beans are tender add sauteed vegetable mixture, vinegar, and sugar. Crush some beans on side of pot to thicken.

Serve over rice.

VEGETARIAN STUFFED PEPPERS

6 green peppers
Boiling water

STUFFING
½ cup bread crumbs
1 tsp. marjoram
2 cloves garlic, minced
2 Tbsps. minced
fresh parsley
2 eggs, lightly beaten
2 Tbsps. chopped
celery leaves
1 medium onion, diced
½ cup cooked brown rice
2 medium tomatoes, sliced
1 cup tomato sauce or
marinara sauce

USE: 4-quart pot
2-quart casserole
YIELDS: 6 servings

Preheat oven to 350°.

Cut tops off peppers, core, and remove seeds. Parboil peppers by placing them in boiling water in a 4-quart pot to cover for 1 minute. Remove and drain upside down on paper towels.

STUFFING: Combine bread crumbs, marjoram, garlic, parsley, eggs, celery leaves, onion, and brown rice. Mix well and stuff peppers with mixture. Place peppers side by side in a well-oiled casserole. Place a slice of tomato on the top of each stuffed pepper. Cover casserole and bake for 45 minutes. Uncover and bake an additional 15 minutes.

Remove casserole from oven and pour tomato sauce over the peppers. Return peppers to oven and bake another 10 minutes until sauce is hot.

VARIATION
□ **Dairy:** Add ½ pound of mild cheddar or Muenster cheese to the stuffing mixture before baking. (A special dairy oven should be used.)

GADO GADO

An Indonesian specialty of steamed fresh vegetables topped with a hot and spicy peanut sauce.

SAUCE
2 Tbsps. oil
1 onion, diced
2 cloves garlic, minced
1 tsp. minced ginger
½ cup roasted peanuts
¼ cup peanut butter
3 Tbsps. water
¼ tsp. cayenne pepper
1 Tbsp. sugar
1 Tbsp. soy sauce
2 Tbsps. vinegar
1 bay leaf
2 cups water

VEGETABLES
1 pound spinach
1 pound green beans, trimmed
1 pound bean sprouts, minced and drained

GARNISH
2 hard-boiled eggs, sliced
1 cucumber, sliced
½ cup raisins
¼ cup sesame oil

USE: 10-inch skillet
3-quart saucepan
4-quart pot
YIELDS: 4 to 6 servings

SAUCE: In a 10-inch skillet saute onions and garlic in oil for 5 minutes. Add ginger and cook 5 minutes more. Place sauteed vegetables and liquid from skillet into blender container. Add peanuts, peanut butter, 3 tablespoons of water, cayenne pepper and sugar. Blend fine. Return mixture to skillet and add soy sauce, vinegar, bay leaf and 2 cups water. Simmer for 20 minutes.

VEGETABLES: Rinse spinach thoroughly. In a 3-quart saucepan cook in liquid that clings to leaves for 5 minutes. Remove and drain.

Place trimmed string beans into a steamer and place in a 4-quart pot and steam for 10 minutes until bright green in color and still firm.

ASSEMBLE: Spread spinach over plate. Cover with string beans. Scatter bean sprouts over string beans. Pour hot sauce over vegetables. Garnish with hard-boiled egg slices, cucumber slices, and raisins. Drizzle sesame oil over all. Serve hot.

MEATLESS STUFFED CABBAGE

1 large head
of cabbage

FILLING
½ pound mushrooms
1 small onion
1 small carrot
1 stalk celery
2 Tbsps. oil
2 cups brown rice,
cooked
1 egg, lightly beaten
1 tsp. salt
1 tsp. pepper

SAUCE
2 15-ounce cans
tomato sauce
1 cup water
1 green apple,
peeled and diced
¼ cup honey
2 Tbsps. vinegar
¼ cup raisins

USE: 10-inch skillet
9 x 13-inch baking pan
YIELDS: 18 rolls

To prepare cabbage for rolling see Stuffed Cabbage Illustrated (page 217).

FILLING: Once leaves are separated and drained, place mushrooms, onions, carrots, and celery in a food processor. Using steel blade chop vegetables to a fine consistency.

Heat 2 tablespoons oil in a 10-inch skillet and saute vegetables until soft. In a medium bowl combine cooked rice and sauteed vegetables with egg. Season with salt and pepper. Mix well.

Place 1 tablespoon of filling on each leaf and roll according to Stuffed Cabbage Illustrated.

Preheat oven to 350°.

SAUCE: In a large bowl combine all sauce ingredients. Mix well. Spread half of sauce over bottom of a 9 x 13-inch pan and place cabbage rolls in sauce. Pour remaining sauce over rolls.

Cover with foil and bake 1 hour.

TOFU DISHES

Tofu, Oriental bean curd, is fast becoming the wonder food of our time. It is high in protein, low in fat and calories and contains no cholesterol. The following main dish recipes featuring tofu are a satisfying alternative to meat, fish and poultry.

BATTER FRIED TOFU

1 pound firm tofu
½ tsp. salt
1 large egg
2 Tbsps. flour

¼ cup peanut or corn oil
1 tsp. ginger root
1 Tbsp. sliced scallions
½ tsp. salt
½ tsp. sugar
1 Tbsp. soy sauce
½ cup water
1 tsp. cornstarch
combined with
2 Tbsps. water

USE: 10-inch skillet
YIELDS: 4 servings

Cut tofu in half, then cut slices ½ inch thick. Sprinkle with ½ teaspoon salt and set aside for 10 minutes. Lay the tofu on paper towels to absorb excess water. In a small bowl combine egg and flour and mix with a wire whisk into a smooth, thin batter.

Heat 10-inch skillet over a moderate flame until it becomes very hot. Add about 2 tablespoons oil. Dip each tofu slice into the batter and fry eight pieces at a time on both sides until light brown. Add more oil and fry the remaining slices. Set aside.

Heat the same pan with 1 tablespoon oil and stir-fry the ginger root and scallion for 1 minute. Return the fried tofu slices to the pan. Add the salt, sugar, soy sauce, and ½ cup water. Cover and slowly bring to a boil. Cook for about 2 minutes, shaking the pan or gently turning the tofu during the cooking. Mix the cornstarch and water very well, then add to the pan. Gently stir until the tofu is coated with a light glaze. Serve hot.

CURRIED TOFU

3 Tbsps. oil
1 large onion, thinly sliced
2 cloves garlic, minced
3 Tbsps. tamari soy sauce
1 Tbsp. molasses
2 Tbsps. peanut butter
¼ cup raisins
¼ cup cashews
¼ tsp. nutmeg
1 tsp. cumin or curry
1 cup water
1 pound tofu,
cut into ¼-inch cubes

USE: 10-inch skillet
YIELDS: 4 servings

Heat oil in a 10-inch skillet and saute onion and garlic. Add tamari, molasses, peanut butter, raisins, cashews, and spices. Stir while heating over low flame until well blended. Add water and stir until combined well.

Add tofu. Simmer for 5 minutes or more, stirring frequently. Good served with rice or millet.

TOFU "EGG" SALAD

This combination looks and tastes like real egg salad. Use it the same way — as sandwich filler or served on a bed of lettuce and garnished with tomatoes or other vegetables.

½ **pound tofu**
1 **scallion, chopped**
½ **cucumber, diced**
½ **tomato, diced (optional)**
½ **stalk celery,**
diced (optional)
2 **Tbsps. mayonnaise**
1 **Tbsp. tahini**
1 **Tbsp. prepared mustard**
Dash salt
Dash pepper
Dash garlic powder

USE: 1-quart bowl
YIELDS: 2 cups

In a small bowl, mash tofu with fork. Add chopped vegetables, the mayonnaise, tahini, mustard, and seasonings. Mix thoroughly with spoon. Serve cold.

TOFU CACCIATORE

1 **pound tofu**
½ **cup oil for frying**
1 **tsp. olive oil**
1 **large onion**
1 **green pepper, sliced**
1 **small zucchini, sliced**
1 **small yellow squash, sliced**
2 **cloves garlic**
2 **Tbsps. fresh or**
1 **Tbsp. dried basil**
1 **16-ounce can**
tomato sauce
Pinch sea salt

USE: Large skillet
9 x 13-inch baking dish
YIELDS: 8 - 10 servings

Place tofu on plate. Place another plate on top with a weight for 30 minutes.

Saute vegetables and garlic in olive oil 5 to 10 minutes in a large skillet. Add tomato sauce and herbs. Simmer for 10 minutes.

Cut pressed tofu into bite sized pieces, deep fry until golden. Drain on paper towels. Place in 9 x 13-inch baking dish. Cover with sauce. Bake covered at 350° for 15 to 20 minutes. Garnish with parsley.

TOFU BROCCOLI QUICHE WITH MUSHROOMS

CRUST

2 cups flour, either whole-wheat pastry, barley or brown rice, or combination
⅓ cup cold pressed safflower oil
⅓ cup water
¼ tsp. sea salt

FILLING

4 cloves garlic
12 oz. fresh mushrooms
1 Tbsp. extra virgin olive oil
1 tsp. dried basil
1 tsp. dried marjoram
1 cup very small broccoli florets
1½ pounds soft tofu
2 Tbsps. cold pressed sunflower oil
1 Tbsp. apple cider vinegar
½ tsp. sea salt
Fresh ground pepper to taste

USE: 9-inch pie pan
YIELDS: 1 pie

Preheat oven to 350°.

CRUST: Place flour in a large bowl. In a smaller bowl mix together the oil, water and salt, add the flour and blend well. The mixture will be crumbly.

Press the crust into a 9-inch pie pan, ensuring uniform thickness all around, especially where the bottom meets the side. Smooth out the edges to make an even rim.

Bake in preheated oven for 10 minutes, or until crust sounds hollow when tapped with a spoon.

FILLING: Mince garlic. Wipe mushrooms and slice thinly, discarding tough stems. In a large skillet, heat oil over medium heat. Saute garlic for 15 seconds, then add mushrooms and saute over low heat, stirring, for 3 to 4 minutes. Sprinkle on basil and marjoram and saute for 2 minutes more. Remove from heat.

In a medium pot, bring 1 quart of water to a boil, and blanch broccoli for 15 seconds or just until it turns bright green. Remove with a slotted spoon or fine mesh spatula and plunge briefly into a bowl of cold water. Drain and set aside.

Place tofu, vinegar and oil in a blender or food processor and blend until very smooth and creamy. Add salt and freshly ground pepper to taste.

TO ASSEMBLE: Spread mushroom mixture over pre-baked pie crust, top with the broccoli florets, then top with creamed tofu, completely covering the vegetables. Bake for 30 minutes or until tofu ridges take on a faintly beige hue. Good hot or cold.

TOFU-VEGETABLE CASSEROLE

1 medium onion
2 medium carrots
2 medium zucchini
2 pounds tofu
1 clove garlic
2 Tbsps. soy sauce
1 tsp. salt
Paprika for sprinkling on top

USE: 9 x 9-inch baking pan
YIELDS: 9 servings

Preheat oven to 350°.

Grate vegetables. Blend tofu and garlic in food processor or blender along with soy sauce and salt. Combine with grated vegetables. Spread in greased 9 x 9-inch pan and sprinkle paprika on top.

Bake for 45 minutes to an hour, until browned on top and set in center.

VARIATION
□ For extra flavor, add the following seasonings to tofu: 1 tsp. marjoram, ½ tsp. red pepper, and 2 tsps. toasted sesame oil.

TOFU VEGETABLES SAUTE

1 onion
1 carrot
2 stalks celery
1 zucchini
5 mushrooms
1 cup snipped green beans
2 Tbsps. oil
1 pound tofu, cut into pieces
1 Tbsp. tamari soy sauce

USE: 10-inch skillet
YIELDS: 4 to 6 servings

Slice vegetables (except green beans) thin on diagonal slant. Heat oil in 10-inch skillet and saute onion until translucent. Add remaining vegetables and saute 15 to 20 minutes. Add tofu with tamari. Stir into vegetable mixture and saute another 5 minutes.

Serve with cooked rice, barley, or millet.

SPICY GANMO BALLS

2 pounds tofu
3 cloves garlic, minced
4 scallions, sliced
1 Tbsp. parsley
1¼ tsps. salt
3 dashes pepper
1 egg, beaten
½ cup matzoh meal
2 to 3 Tbsps. oil
2 15-ounce-cans tomato sauce

USE: 10-inch skillet
YIELDS: 4 to 6 servings

Squeeze the tofu in a dish towel to remove excess water. In a large bowl, knead the tofu like bread for 5 minutes. Add garlic, scallions, parsley, salt and pepper. Knead 3 more minutes. Add egg, stirring well.

Wet palms of hands. Roll teaspoonful of the mixture between wetted palms. Roll in matzoh meal.

Heat oil in 10-inch skillet. Fry the balls in oil, turning frequently until golden, and then cook in tomato sauce for ½ hour.

VARIATION
☐ Shape into patties and fry.

SPICY TOFU BURGERS WITH RICE

½ pound tofu
1 Tbsp. sesame oil
1 onion
1 carrot
2 celery stalks, diced
2 cups cooked rice
1 Tbsp. mustard
1 Tbsp. miso
½ to 1 cup falafel mix

USE: Large skillet or baking pan
YIELDS: 6 - 8 burgers

Press tofu as described in Tofu Cacciatore while preparing vegetables.

Dice vegetables and saute in oil for 3 to 4 minutes. Place rice in mixing bowl and crumble tofu over rice.

Add sauteed vegetables, mustard, miso and falafel mix, stir to combine all ingredients. Form into burgers or croquettes.

Allow to cool completely before frying. Pan fry or bake at 350° on greased baking pan until golden.

VEGGIE-TOFU PATTIES

1 onion
2 carrots
1 green pepper
1 zucchini
6 to 10 mushrooms
2 cloves garlic
½ pound tofu
1 egg
1 cup bread crumbs or
½ cup wheat germ
and ½ cup bread crumbs
½ cup sunflower seeds
½ tsp. salt
Oil for frying

USE: 10-inch skillet
YIELDS: 12 to 14 patties

Put vegetables and garlic in food processor and blend. Add tofu and egg, then blend again.

Pour into bowl and add bread crumbs, wheat germ, sunflower seeds, and salt. Form into patties. Heat ½ inch of oil in a 10-inch skillet and fry patties 8 to 10 minutes on each side until brown and crisp.

STIR-FRY TOFU AND VEGETABLES

This is good either as a side dish or a main dish.

2 onions or scallions
½ pound mushrooms
1 red or green pepper
2 tomatoes
2 to 3 Tbsps. oil
1 pound tofu,
diced into large chunks
½ tsp. salt
Dash of pepper
¼ tsp. garlic powder
½ tsp. basil

USE: 10-inch skillet
YIELDS: 4 to 6 servings

Dice all vegetables. Heat oil in 10-inch skillet and saute onions. Add mushrooms, tofu, pepper, tomatoes, and seasonings. Stir-fry for 15 minutes until vegetables and tofu are slightly browned and juicy.

Serve hot or at room temperature.

Meat and Poultry Main Dishes

Laws of Kosher Meat and Fowl
Koshering Meat, Fowl and Liver
Kosher Meat Cuts
Meat
Poultry
Stuffings

Meal planning usually begins with the choice of a main dish. For the kosher cook, this choice revolves around the decision to prepare either a meat, dairy, or *pareve* meal. Pots and pans, dishes and tablecloths are chosen accordingly. A large variety of foods find their way to the Jewish table, enhanced by tradition and elevated by the spiritual effect of adherence to the *mitzvah* of *kashrut*.

Long associated with royalty and wealth, meat is traditionally served at Jewish festive occasions. The *Talmud* associates both meat and wine with the idea of *simchah* (joy). Meat or poultry dishes generally provide the centerpiece to a Shabbat or Yom Tov meal to enhance the festivity.

Chicken, with its ability to combine well with any number of vegetables, fruits, and spices, is an international favorite of the Jewish cook. On Friday night it may star in a Moroccan stew spiced with turmeric and served over couscous. Tomato sauce and basil lend a traditionally Italian touch, and Chicken Paprikash is a favorite Eastern European dish. The variety is nearly endless, as you will discover among the many delicious chicken recipes in this section.

Turkey, the New World contribution to tradition, is also quite popular. It is tasty, economical, and easy to prepare. One turkey can serve a large table of Shabbat or Yom Tov guests.

Kosher Meat and Fowl

Kosher meat is unique in all respects, from the types of animals that are permitted to the way they are slaughtered and prepared for consumption. Meat foods are cooked, handled and eaten separately from dairy foods. In addition, a six-hour waiting time is required after eating all types of meat and poultry before any dairy may be eaten. For more information, see Separating Meat and Dairy, page 18.

Only animals that both chew their cud and have split hooves (the two signs mentioned in the Torah) are kosher. Cows, sheep and goats are examples. An animal having only one of the two signs is not kosher.

Interestingly, the Torah enumerates just four animals that either chew their cud or have split hooves, but not both: the pig, the badger, the camel and the hare. Despite the vast increase in scientific knowledge and man's exploration into the furthest corners of the world, not another creature with only one of these signs has been discovered.

Kosher fowl is identified by a tradition handed down

from generation to generation and universally accepted. The Torah names those species of fowl that are forbidden, including all predatory and scavenger birds. Kosher fowl include the domesticated species of chickens, Cornish hens, ducks, geese and turkeys.

A Spiritual Dimension

Our Sages have commented upon the relationship between the type of food we eat and the state of our spiritual refinement. This is particularly true of meat; the care with which we are to approach the eating of animal substances is reflected in the various laws regarding meat, even that of kosher animals.

Meat is not forbidden, but the dietary laws and the prohibition against cruelty to animals prevent us from eating it without forethought and proper preparation. One of the seven Noahide Laws which the Torah gives to all mankind is the prohibition against eating flesh from a living animal. In keeping with the Jews' mission to be a "nation of priests and a holy people," the Torah gives us an even more stringent set of laws regarding the eating of meat.

Our adherence to the laws of *kashrut* does not depend upon our intellectual understanding, but on our desire to fulfill G-d's commands. Nevertheless, according to the Rambam (Maimonides)"...it behooves men to meditate on the laws of our Holy Torah and to know their deeper meaning as much as lies in his power."

Accordingly, our Sages have drawn insights concerning the types of animals we may eat and those we are forbidden to eat. The permitted animals are primarily tame and herbivorous, while we are forbidden to eat beasts or birds of prey, lest we incorporate their fierce and violent nature into our own. The meat of prohibited animals, according to Jewish mysticism, "clogs the heart," or dulls its sensitivity in spiritual matters.

Concerning permitted animals, we have a further restriction against eating the animal's blood. Our language reflects the association of blood with animal passions and instincts, as in "hot-blooded," or "making one's blood boil." The prohibition against the consumption of blood is interpreted to be a precaution against the transference of animalistic tendencies into ourselves.

The laws of *kashrut* are not merely an external discipline; they aim at refining the personality and enhancing spiritual receptivity. The Torah is based upon the relationship between body and spirit. The body is not to be scorned or despised but used as a vehicle in the service of G-d. The detailed physical laws concerning kosher meat are thus directly related to the loftiest spiritual concepts.

Laws of Kosher Meat and Fowl

In the preparation of kosher meat from slaughterhouse to butcher shop to your home, the following procedures must be carefully observed:

Shechitah is the ritual slaughter of a kosher animal, a process governed at each step by a series of complex laws. It is performed by a *shochet*, a Torah-observant and G-d-fearing man who has a high degree of skill and knowledge in the laws and practice of *shechitah*. His speed and precision, together with the perfectly smooth knife required by Jewish Law, protect the animal as much as possible from pain and suffering.

Bedikah is the inspection of the internal organs for potentially fatal diseases or injuries, which would disqualify the animal. Most of the abnormalities that make an animal non-kosher are acceptable under U.S. Government standards, and when the government inspector does condemn an organ, it is almost always that organ alone. In Jewish Law, however, certain diseases or injuries in any part of the body render the entire animal unfit.

Nikur, more commonly referred to as *treibering*, involves removing certain forbidden veins and fats from the meat. They are extremely prevalent in the hindquarter, and due to the complexity involved in their removal, this part of the animal is generally not sold as kosher. See Kosher Meat Cuts, page 194.

Melichah, also known as *koshering*, is the salting and soaking of the meat after all the non-permissible veins and fats have been removed. The salting process consists of the following steps: rinsing, soaking, salting, and triple rinsing. The meat is salted within 72 hours of slaughter. Liver is not *koshered* in the usual manner but is broiled separately over an open fire. Both of these procedures serve to remove every last trace of blood from the meat. For more information, see Koshering Meat, Fowl, and Liver, page 189.

Although the salting board and basin that were a standard feature of our grandmothers' kosher kitchens have largely given way to reliance on the butcher to fulfill the laws of soaking and salting, this should not be a substitute for our careful study of these laws.

Those on a salt-free diet should consult an Orthodox Rabbi as to how to prepare their meat.

Laws of Kosher Chicken

The laws concerning the slaughtering and *koshering* process for chicken and other fowl are nearly identical to the laws that apply to meat. Special care is taken when salting chicken to ensure that the inside of the chicken is thoroughly cleaned out and that the salt reaches well into the cavities of the chicken and between flaps.

Whole chickens, even if *koshered*, are often sold with a bag of giblets and liver inside the body cavity. This bag *must* be removed prior to cooking because contact with the raw liver could make the chicken "*traif*." If the chicken has been immersed in hot water or cooked without removing the liver, an Orthodox Rabbi must be consulted.

Although kosher chickens are carefully checked by the processors to ensure that the animal is free of diseases or major wounds, occasionally there is an oversight. If one notices a broken or dislocated bone; or blood, pus, or discoloration around the end of the drumstick or around a wound, an Orthodox Rabbi should be consulted. These problems might make the entire chicken non-kosher.

If buying packaged chicken, it must bear a reliable seal of *kashrut*. Look for a *plumba*, a small metal tag on the wing or bag indicating the *hechsher*.

SELECTING YOUR BUTCHER

Today's kosher consumer is usually not directly involved in the preparation of kosher meat. Nevertheless, through her careful decisions concerning where to shop, she is ultimately responsible for the *kashrut* of the meat and poultry she serves.

The butcher plays a crucial role in the *kashrut* process. He must be thoroughly knowledgeable in the many laws relating to kosher meat, and be a person of unquestioned integrity and personal Torah observance. Because adherence to every detail of *halachah* may sometimes mean loss of money for the seller, the butcher's own commitment to Torah Law must be of the highest order. Even if the store is closed on Shabbat, if the butcher is not Shabbat-observant at home, he cannot be trusted in the matter of *kashrut*. A reliable butcher always allows a *mashgiach*, *kashrut* supervisor, to inspect his plant to see that all laws are properly observed and that the highest standard of *kashrut* is maintained.

The Hebrew sign, בשר כשר (*Basar Kasher* — "kosher meat"), is not sufficient assurance of *kashrut*. The presence of non-kosher meat on the same premises can easily lead to mixups. Many butchers do not salt their meat but rather depend on the consumer to request that it be salted. Sometimes only a tiny, hidden sign notifies the buyer of this fact. One must ask to make sure the meat has been salted. If one has used unsalted meat, an Orthodox Rabbi must be consulted regarding the status of the pots and dishes.

The term *Glatt Kosher* refers to meat which comes from a kosher, properly slaughtered animal which, upon its examination after the slaughtering, has been found completely free of any imperfections in the lungs. Simply "kosher" is when some of these imperfections are found but were declared permissible.

The term *Glatt Kosher* is also often commonly used to declare certain foods, restaurants, etc., completely kosher with strict supervision. Just as with establishments bearing the sign (*Basar Kasher* — "kosher meat"), the term *Glatt Kosher* alone is not a sufficient guarantee of proper supervision.

If you plan to *kosher* the meat or chicken in your home, your butcher must tell you the exact time of slaughtering so that you will be able to *kosher* the meat within 72 hours of that time.

Buying Packaged Meat

Meat advertised or labeled as kosher in a supermarket requires careful scrutiny. On chickens, a small metal tag called a *plumba*, bearing the name of the poultry supplier, is generally attached to the wing of the chicken. The *plumba* bears the seal of *kashrut* ensuring that the chicken has been properly *koshered*. If the chicken is cut into parts, the *plumba* should be attached to the bag in which the chicken is packaged.

Many self-service meat markets sell packaged kosher meat prepared under strict supervision. Be sure the package also states that the meat has been *koshered*.

Liver included with packaged or other chicken must be removed before the chicken is thawed or cooked. The liver must be *koshered* separately by being broiled over an open flame. See Koshering Liver, page 192.

Only meat cuts from the front half of the animal are kosher. However, some of these kosher meat cuts are often labeled with the standard names for non-kosher meat cuts, such as "London Broil" or "spare ribs." These cuts are somewhat similar to the non-kosher ones, and are labeled in this way for the convenience of consumers. Before buying these cuts of meat, make sure the cut comes only from the front part of the animal and has been prepared by a reliable butcher under competent *kashrut* supervision.

NOTE: The same care one uses in selecting a butcher should be exercised in choosing a restaurant or hotel. It should be under Rabbinic supervision and there should be a Torah observant Jew who supervises the kitchen regarding *kashrut*. For more information, see Food Establishments Requiring Supervision, page 28.

For more on the laws of kosher meat, see Kashrut Basics, page 17.

Koshering Meat, Fowl and Liver

"And you shall not eat any blood, whether that of fowl or of beast, in any of your dwellings." (Leviticus 7:26)

For generations, the process of *koshering* (removing the blood from) meat was the domain of the Jewish homemaker, often involving all the family members in the various steps. Today, rather than being a familiar aspect of the Jewish home, *koshering* is usually done at the butcher shop beyond sight of the consumer. However, many families do *kosher* their meat, and it is important for every kosher homemaker to develop an appreciation and working knowledge of the step-by-step process by which kosher meat reaches the table.

For meat to be fit for Jewish consumption, several steps are required. The first step is *shechitah* (ritual slaughter), followed by *bedikah* (inspection for disease), and *nikur* or *treibering* (removal of forbidden fats and veins). The last step is *koshering*. For more information on the *kashrut* of meat, see page 187.

Koshering is the process by which the blood is removed from the flesh of meat and fowl before it is prepared for eating. Only meat from kosher animals, properly slaughtered and with the forbidden parts already removed, may be koshered. The *koshering* process, known as *melichah* (salting), entails the following steps: washing or rinsing off the meat; soaking it in water; salting it; and rinsing it very well three times.

The complete *koshering* process should take place within 72 hours of the *shechitah*; therefore, before *koshering*, it is imperative to know exactly when the *shechitah* took place. For further information, see Koshering Within 72 Hours, below.

The *koshering* process can be performed by the butcher or at home. Whether you entrust the *koshering* of your meat to a qualified butcher or choose to do it yourself, a working knowledge of the process is an important aspect of our understanding of *kashrut*.

Following is a step-by-step guide to *koshering*. If you are *koshering* meat for the first time, it is advisable to observe the process being done by an experienced, knowledgeable person.

People on strictly salt-free diets should consult an Orthodox Rabbi as to how to *kosher* their meat.

BEFORE KOSHERING

The following guidelines apply to both meat and fowl. There are extensive preparations for *koshering* fowl which are described after the section on *koshering* meat.

Handling The Meat Or Fowl: After receiving meat or fowl from the butcher, it must be handled properly until after it is *koshered*. Meat and blood drippings should not come into contact with any other food. However, the meat may be put into the refrigerator if it is covered well on all sides so that it doesn't leak.

Meat or fowl must be fully defrosted, and if very cold it should be allowed to stand a while at room temperature. It should not be placed near a fire or come into contact with hot water since this cooks the blood in and the salt will not be effective in drawing it out. In addition, it should not come into contact with any salt before the process begins.

If the meat is to be ground, *koshering* must take place before grinding. The head and internal organs of the animal must be removed before *koshering*. To determine which parts can be used and how to prepare them, consult an Orthodox Rabbi.

The complete *koshering* process should take place within 72 hours of *shechitah*. If this is not possible, the soaking of the meat must begin before the 72 hours elapses. It should soak for thirty minutes.

If the soaking was done within 72 hours, but it was not possible to continue to the next step, salting, until a later time, then the *koshering* process must be done again from the beginning, starting with soaking. This must be begun within 72 hours of the completion of the first soaking.

If 72 hours have elapsed and the soaking

Koshering Within 72 Hours

process was not begun, the meat or fowl can only be *koshered* by broiling it over a fire, because the pores become impenetrable and the salt can no longer draw out the blood. See Koshering Liver, page 192. It may not be reheated in a way that it sits in its own juices; for example, fried in oil.

made into a pot roast, or heated in the oven on foil.

If the 72 hours ends on Shabbat and the meat was not soaked before Shabbat, it is necessary to consult an Orthodox Rabbi.

Equipment Needed

The following items should be used exclusively for *unkoshered* meat. One should take into consideration the amount of meat to be *koshered* when determining whether the room one is working in has ample space and proper facilities. If extra counter space is needed, cover all counters so that no blood can drip through.

Knife - to cut out blood clots or to cut large pieces of meat into pieces small enough to handle easily.

Water - to soak, rinse and wash off the meat. Water used in the *koshering* process should be at room temperature.

Pail or Basin - in which to soak the meat.

Course Salt - to draw out the blood. Thin table salt is not good because it melts into the meat

and does not draw the blood out. Neither should the crystals be so large that they roll off the meat.

Board or Rack - to place salted meat on. This can be made of any material, such as wood or formica. A perforated board with many holes, or a rack with slats, is excellent so that the blood can flow out. If the board has grooves or is flat, it should be placed on a slant to enable the blood to flow down. The board should not have bumps or cracks that would allow blood to collect.

Basin, Sink or Tub - for the board to be placed on so that the blood can drip into it. Drippings make a sink non-kosher, therefore, a kosher sink should not be used. Consult an Orthodox Rabbi if no other sink or basin is available.

Lighting - During the complete *koshering* process, be sure the room is well lit.

THE KOSHERING PROCESS FOR MEAT AND FOWL

It is important to follow each step in the process carefully, bearing in mind the various time factors. The *koshering* process requires one's undivided attention, so distractions should be eliminated as much as possible. If any questions or problems arise along the way, do not hesitate to seek Rabbinic guidance.

Step 1 - Preliminary Washing: The meat must be washed very well to remove all visible blood. All blood clots or discolorations, (black, dark, red,

etc.) should be cut out before washing.

Step 2 - Soaking: The meat should be immersed in room temperature water for at least 1/2 hour. If the meat was accidently left soaking for 24 consecutive hours, this meat becomes unkosher and cannot be used, because it is considered as having been cooked without prior *koshering*.

After the meat has been soaked, it may be cut into smaller pieces if desired. It then would be necessary to rinse each cut piece very well, especially the newly cut ends. The meat does not have to be soaked again.

Step 3 - Salting: Before salting, the meat must be washed off. (One may use the same water in which it was soaked.) Then, inspect the meat to be sure that there is no visible blood. Shake off excess water and allow the meat to sit for a short period of time so that the salt does not dissolve too easily. However, the meat should remain damp enough for the salt to stick to it.

Salt the meat thoroughly on all sides, but not so thickly that the blood would be prevented from flowing out. The salted meat should remain on the board for a minimum of one hour. If it remained in salt for twelve hours or more, consult an Orthodox Rabbi.

If a piece of meat falls off the board (while the salt was still on), it should be returned immediately, preferably to a separate board. It must be kept apart from the rest of the meat throughout the remaining process, and Rabbinic guidance is necessary.

Bones are *koshered* just like meat and together with the rest of the meat. However, if the bones have no meat on them, they should be kept on top or on the side of the board during the *koshering* process so that no blood from the other pieces of meat reaches them.

In placing the salted pieces of meat on the salting board, one should be sure that nothing blocks or interferes with the free draining of the blood, since this would defeat the whole purpose of salting. If there is insufficient room on the board, the pieces may be placed on top of each other, as long as there is no place for blood to collect. Since the blood content varies according to the type of meat (e.g., chicken contains less blood than beef), consult an Orthodox Rabbi as to how to place the meat on the board when *koshering* different types of meat simultaneously.

Step 4 - Triple Rinsing: After the meat has lain in salt the required period of time, rinse it well. Rub off and remove the salt from all sides. This is done three separate times.

The first time, the meat should be rinsed under running water, and rubbed while under the water. Turn it constantly so that all sides come into contact with the water.

The second and third times, the meat may either be rinsed again under running water, or soaked in a clean basin of fresh water. The basin must be rinsed out separately each time, and fresh water used for both the second and third rinsing. If using a basin, pour the water into it before placing the meat in it.

KOSHERING FOWL

The *koshering* process for fowl is the same as for meat — rinsing, soaking, salting, and triple-rinsing. In addition, there are extensive preparations of the fowl which are often left to be done at home. It is therefore important to know and recognize the parts of the fowl which must be removed.

It is preferable to cut the fowl in half for the *koshering* process. If one wishes to roast or broil it whole, the opening should be wide enough to remove all the insides. Special care should be taken to see that all blood clots and internal organs are completely removed. When salting, be sure that the inside surfaces are covered with salt.

The following steps are taken before *koshering*:

Feathers: The feathers are removed from the fowl before the *koshering* process. The fowl may not be soaked in warm water to soften the feathers nor held over a large fire. However, one may pass the fowl lightly over a small flame to remove the pinfeathers, moving it continuously so that the fowl will not become heated.

Head and Neck: The complete head is removed. The complete foodpipe (gullet), and windpipe are removed before salting thus allowing better salting of the rest of the neck. As mentioned above, all blood clots and discolorations must be removed. These are extremely common at the top of the neck (close to where the *shechitah* took place), and it is therefore necessary to cut off the top of the neck.

Veins: The two thin white veins inside the neck must be removed. They can be exposed by cutting into the bottom of the neck and then pulled out, or by cutting down the length of the neck.

If it is too difficult to remove them, at least cut several slits into the neck so that the blood will flow out of the veins.

Wings: The ends of the wings are removed.

Legs: The tips of the toes including the nails from the toes of the fowl are removed. The leg is cut into at the joint which joins the foot to the drumstick.

Insides: All internal organs must be removed before *koshering*.

☐ The stomach must be opened, the inner membrane and all waste products removed, then the stomach wall checked to make sure it has not been punctured by a stone or nail which would create a *sha'alah*.

☐ The intestines should be checked for punctures.

□ The liver is set aside for broiling (see Koshering Liver, below).

□ One must be careful to remove the kidneys. They are located in the cavity on the inside of the back (thigh), and are sometimes a little difficult to remove. Occasionally, they may be discovered inside a fowl even after it has been *koshered*, in which case they should be removed.

□ If one wishes to eat any of the internal organs, consult an Orthodox Rabbi as to their preparation.

Handling the Fowl During the Koshering Process

Before preparing fowl for *koshering*, be sure to read the preceding instructions for *koshering* meat. All of the steps outlined in the previous section on *koshering* meat apply when *koshering* fowl. However, due to the many crevices and folds of skin, the additional precautions for *koshering* fowl are listed below.

Rinsing: The fowl must be rinsed off very well, especially in the following places:

□ the hole of the neck (the head and skin of the neck must have already been removed),

□ all the folds, e.g. near the wings,

□ between the skin and meat in the places they have separated,

□ all around the fat.

Salting: The fowl should be salted all over very well, and especially in all the crevices mentioned above.

If the fowl is still whole, be sure the entire inside is covered with salt.

Placing On The Board: When the fowl is to be placed on the board after it is salted it should be placed so that the blood can flow out. If it has been cut in half, then the cavity should be placed facing downward. If it is whole, it should be placed with the larger hole downward.

Eggs Found In Fowl

Eggs which are found in a freshly slaughtered fowl and have not yet developed a shell should be *koshered* according to the regular *koshering* process and are considered *fleishig*. However, they should be placed on the top of the board so that no blood from the other pieces of meat can flow on them. The skin of the eggs must be removed before soaking. These eggs should be prepared in meat utensils.

Regarding the *koshering* and use of eggs which have already begun to develop a shell, and their status as to *fleishig* or *pareve*, an Orthodox Rabbi must be consulted.

KOSHERING LIVER -
A SPECIAL BROILING PROCESS

Liver of beef and poultry may not be *koshered* by soaking and salting. Due to liver's high blood content, salting is not sufficient to draw out the blood. Therefore, liver can be *koshered* only by a special broiling process. Under some circumstances, other meat and fowl are *koshered* by this method. Liver should be broiled within the first 72 hours after *shechitah*. If not, it still may be *koshered* by broiling, but afterwards it may not be reheated in a way that it sits in its own juices; for example, fried in oil, made into a pot roast, or heated in the oven on foil. Therefore, when buying liver, one should inquire as to the time of *shechitah* to determine whether or not it can be re-cooked after broiling. Even if the butcher himself broiled the liver, one must inquire as to whether it was *koshered* within 72 hours after *shechitah*.

One should be careful about buying packaged liver, for many *sha'alot* can be involved.

If liver is found wrapped inside a chicken, it *must* be removed before cooking the chicken or placing the chicken under hot water. The liver can then be *koshered* separately. Consult an Orthodox Rabbi if the chicken was cooked with the liver inside, or if any liver was in a bag containing liquid.

Procedure For Koshering Liver

Washing: Thoroughly wash off all outside blood and remove all visible blood clots.

Broiling: When broiling a whole calf or beef liver, cut into it across its length and width before broiling. Then the liver should be placed with the cut side down on the rack for broiling. Immediately before broiling, salt all sides of the liver lightly with coarse salt.

Broil over an open fire with nothing between the fire and the liver so that the blood can flow out freely. A thin wire net with large holes may be used to hold the liver over the fire. The liver should be rotated over the fire a few times so that all sides are exposed to the fire. The meat is to be broiled until the entire piece is at least half-done, not just the crust. The pieces of liver should not be too large for the heat to penetrate.

When broiling liver using an open flame from a

gas range, stove top or under flame in broiler, cover all sides around the flame very well with foil so that no blood splashes onto the stove and renders it unkosher.

For the same reason, liver should not come into contact with kosher utensils such as plates, bowls, and knives, until it is completely *koshered*. The drippings and pan used to catch the drippings are non-kosher, and care should therefore be taken that kosher food does not come in contact with the non-kosher drippings or pan. For use of an electric broiler or other method, consult an Orthodox Rabbi.

Rinsing: After broiling, the liver should be rinsed three times, as is explained above for *koshering* meat.

WHEN TO CONSULT A RABBI

When *koshering* meat, fowl, or liver, a *sha'alah* (question of Torah Law) should be asked of an Orthodox Rabbi if any irregularity in the meat or fowl is noticed or if there has been a deviation in the usual *koshering* process. Never hesitate to ask a *sha'alah* even if somewhat similar situations have occurred previously, for each case is judged according to its own circumstances.

Consult the Rabbi as soon as possible after first noticing the problem. If possible, bring the piece of meat or fowl to him. If one notices an irregularity on the fowl while it is whole, then it is preferable that the whole fowl should be brought to the Rabbi.

Even if the irregularity is discovered after the meat or fowl has been *koshered*, whether by the butcher or at home, do not hesitate to consult a Rabbi. An oversight may have occured. Ask the *sha'alah* before cooking the meat or fowl, in order to prevent complications.

As a general guideline, consult an Orthodox Rabbi on any apparent abnormality in the meat or fowl. Some particular abnormalities include:

☐ an unusual growth in the animal, or an extra, missing or deformed organ;

☐ any broken or dislocated bones, or an unusual collection of blood in any organ, which may indicate some damage to the animal;

☐ any blood, pus, or discoloration around the end of the drumstick or around a wound;

☐ any unusual coloring of any organ;

☐ unusual softness of the tissues of any organ;

☐ any foreign material (such as a stone or pin) found inside the animal.

Checklist for Abnormalities

Kosher Meat Cuts

COOKING MEAT *can be enhanced by a good understanding of the various meat cuts and how they are best prepared. When purchasing kosher meat, the priority must be that of reliable* kashrut. See Selecting Your Butcher, page 187.

☐ If quality kosher meat is unavailable in your area, it can be ordered from a butcher in a nearby large Jewish community. Butchers in large cities will often ship frozen meat.

☐ The preparation of meat is an art, and butchers can prepare different cuts of meat on request if they do not have them on hand. Discuss with your butcher the types of cuts, how they are best cooked, and whether they are boned or boneless. The following pages are a general guide to various cooking methods for various cuts. Although any piece of meat can be corned or pickled, brisket is a popular choice for this method.

☐ Kosher meat cuts are obtained from the permissible part of a kosher animal, which consists of the front section until the 12th rib. Even the front part of the animal contains certain veins and fat which must be cut off. *Treibering* is the removal of these veins and fats from the animal. After the 12th rib it becomes exceedingly difficult to remove them. Therefore the common practice is that the second half is not *treibered* or sold as kosher.

☐ The following illustrations show the major parts of a kosher animal. The dividing line at the 12th rib is clearly indicated. The most common cuts from the permissible section are listed. A variety of cuts can be obtained from each part of the animal, depending upon how the butcher prepares it. Some cuts are referred to by different names, and are indicated in brackets. Remember that these illustrations represent cuts of meat which in actuality are three-dimensional. Therefore, what appears to be a matter of simple sub-division depends greatly upon the butcher's choice. Some cuts of meat may overlap sections, comprised of meat coming from both the Neck and Shoulder, for example. The butcher may choose to slice a section into steaks, leave it whole as a roast, or lift the meat off the bone for a boneless roast or a rolled roast.

☐ Parts such as the tongue, liver and sweetbreads need special preparation, such as *treibering* for the tongue. When ordering lamb, bear in mind that it is a small animal and if quantities will be needed for a special occasion, it is necessary to order well in advance.

NOTE: Some kosher cuts are labeled with the names of non-permissible cuts that they resemble. Two such examples of this are the Club Steak and the T-Bone steak, which usually come from the non-kosher Short Loin section of the animal. In kosher cuts, they come from the Chuck. When buying meat labeled in this way, make sure the cuts are only from the front part of the animal and have been prepared by a reliable kosher butcher.

Acknowledgements to Mr. J. Kreitenberg and Mr. A. Tzivin for their assistance in preparing this section.

BEEF

Neck

Braise or cook in liquid.
Boneless Neck or Rolled Neck
Brick Roast
Ground Beef
Stew Beef

Chuck

Braise or cook in liquid.
Boneless Chuck Pot Roast
Boneless Chuck Roll
Chuck Short Ribs or Flanken
Club Steak
Eye Chuck Roast
French Roast
Ground Beef
Middle Chuck Steak |California Steak|
Single Chuck Steak
Stew Beef
T-Bone Steak

Rib

Panbroil, panfry or roast.
Barbeque Ribs
Boneless Rib Roast or Steak
Chateaubriand Steak (for Beef Wellington)
Rib Eye Roast
Rib Eye |Delmonico| Steak
Rib Flanken
Rib Roast or Steak
Spare Ribs
Standing Rib Roast
Top of the Rib Roast
Triangle Pot Roast

Shoulder

Braise or cook in liquid.
Beef Kalechel
Beef Shishkabob
Blade Steaks |Minute Steak|
Boneless Shoulder Pot Roast or Steak
End Roast or Steak
London-Broil
Pepper Steak
Short |Minute| Roast or Steak
Shoulder Steak |Fillet Steak|
Silver Tip Roast

Foreshank

Braise or cook in liquid.
Ground Beef
Round Kalechel
Shank Cross Cuts |Kalechel Steaks|
Shank Knuckle |Kalechel Roast|
Stew Beef

Brisket

Braise or cook in liquid.
First Cut Brisket
Fresh Brisket
Second Cut Brisket

Plate

Braise or cook in liquid.
Beef Flank Steak, Cubed
Ground Beef
Plate Flanken
Plate Steak Rolls
Rolled Plate
Short Ribs
Skirt Steak
Stew Beef

Other Kosher Parts
Liver
Tongue
Sweetbreads

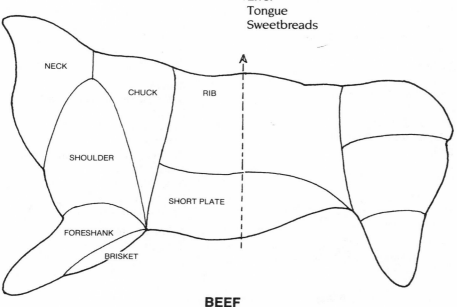

BEEF

VEAL

Neck
Braise or cook in liquid.
Boneless Neck or Rolled Neck
Ground Veal
Stew Veal

Shoulder
Braise, cook in liquid, panfry or roast.
Blade Roast or Steak
Boneless Shoulder Roast or
Ground Veal
Rolled Shoulder Roast
Stew Veal
Veal Cutlet

Rib
Braise, panfry or broil.
Arm Roast or Steak
Boneless |French| Rib Chop
Rib Chop |First Cut Veal Chops|
Rib Chop |Second Cut Veal Chops|
Rib Roast
Second Cut Veal Chops
Stew Veal

Foreshank
Braise or cook in liquid.
Foreshank |Veal Kalachel|
Ground Veal
Stew Veal

Breast
Braise, cook in liquid, panfry or roast.
Breast
Boneless Riblets
Spareribs
Stuffed Breast of Veal
Veal Flanken

Other Kosher Parts
Liver
Tongue
Sweetbreads

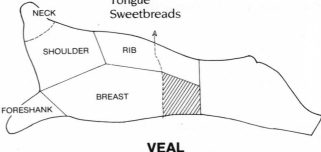

VEAL

LAMB

Neck
Braise or cook in liquid.
Lamb Shishkabob
Neck Slice
Stew Lamb

Shoulder
Braise, cook in liquid, panbroil, panfry or Roast.
Arm Chop
Blade Chop
Boneless Shoulder Roast or Steak
Cushion Shoulder
Ground Lamb
Lamb Chop
Round Bone Shoulder Steak
Shoulder Roast
Shoulder Shishkabob
Square Cut Shoulder Roast
Stew Lamb

Rib
Panbroil, panfry or roast.
Crown Roast |Crown of Lamb|
Frenched Rib Chop |French Lamb|
Ground Lamb
Rack of Lamb
Rib Chop |Baby Lamb Chops|
Roast
Stew Lamb

Shank
Braise or cook in liquid.
Shank of Lamb

Breast
Braise, panbroil, panfry or roast.
Breast
Ground Lamb
Lamb Skirt
Riblets |Lamb Barbeque Ribs|
Rolled Breast
Spareribs
Stew Lamb
Stuffed Lamb Breast

Other Kosher Parts
Tongue

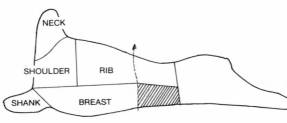

LAMB

Meat

ROASTS

Roast beef will always create a festive meal. There are two general methods for cooking a roast. The first is a long, slow oven method that results in less shrinkage and produces a more tender meat. The second method for pot roast is to sear or brown the meat quickly over a high flame and then slowly simmer it in a bed of root vegetables — carrots, onion, and potatoes. A marinade will enhance the flavor and further tenderize the meat. Roasts can be served hot or at room temperature, thus lending themselves easily to Shabbat and Yom Tov meals.

BEEF WELLINGTON

This is a special dish, well worth the extra preparation time!
HALACHIC NOTE: *In order to fry, cook, or bake liver, it must already have been broiled within 72 hours after the time of slaughtering. See Koshering Liver, page 192.*

**3-pound boneless
rib eye roast, trimmed**
1 pound mushrooms, minced
6 scallions, minced
4 Tbsps. margarine
2 Tbsps. chopped parsley
6 chicken livers, broiled
2 Tbsps. brandy
**Simple Flaky Dough
(page 413)**
**1 egg yolk beaten
with 1 Tbsp. water**

USE: Large baking sheet
Roasting pan
YIELDS: 6 to 8 servings

Place meat on rack in roasting pan and roast in a 400° oven until done, about 1½ hours. Set aside to cool. Saute mushrooms and scallions in margarine. Add parsley and cook an additional 2 minutes. Set aside to cool. Prepare liver by blending chicken livers in a food processor. Add brandy to a smooth paste. Set aside.

On a floured board roll pastry dough ⅛-inch thick to a rectangle a little more than double the size of the roast. Spread the liver over the dough to within 1 inch of the edges. Spread mushroom mixture over liver. Place beef in the center of the dough. Bring one long side of dough up over the roast, brush edge of dough with some beaten egg. Bring other long side of dough up, overlapping egg-brushed dough. Press to seal. Fold up both ends of dough and brush with beaten egg and press to seal. Place seam side down on large baking sheet. Brush top and sides with remaining egg. Make two to three slashes to create a vent.

Preheat oven to 450°. Bake for 20 minutes or until pastry is golden brown. Slice and serve.

POT ROAST IN WINE SAUCE

1 large onion, sliced
2 Tbsps. oil or margarine
1 4-ounce can tomato sauce
1 Tbsp. coarse salt
**1 clove garlic, minced,
or ½ tsp. garlic powder**
3- to 4-pound end of steak
1 cup dry red wine

USE: 6-quart Dutch oven
YIELDS: 6 to 8 servings

Using a 6-quart Dutch oven, saute onion in oil or margarine until golden brown. Add tomato sauce, salt, and garlic. Mix well.

Place roast on top of onion. Pour wine over meat. Cover tightly and cook on low flame 1½ to 2 hours. Turn once.

When cool, slice and reheat slices 5 to 10 minutes in gravy. Center slices may be rare.

CRANBERRY POT ROAST

3-pound brisket or
top of rib
2 stalks celery, sliced
1 medium onion, diced
1 medium
green pepper, diced
½ cup water
1 16-ounce can
cranberry sauce
1 16-ounce can
marinara sauce
1 clove garlic, diced

USE: 3-quart saucepan
YIELDS: 6 to 8 servings

In a 3-quart saucepan, brown meat 5 minutes on each side. Remove from saucepan. Place prepared vegetables in saucepan with ½ cup water and simmer over low flame until soft. Add cranberry and marinara sauces to vegetables and heat until bubbly. Add garlic.

Place meat in pot. Simmer over low flame for 1½ to 2 hours. Allow meat to cool; slice. Return slices to pot and warm. Serve with sauce.

NOTE: Browning meat for a longer amount of time adds extra flavor.

FESTIVE VEGETABLE ROAST

With the addition of a variety of vegetables that blend perfectly when cooked for the proper amount of time, this roast has taste and color when served.

5-pound rolled roast
2 Tbsps. flour
¼ cup oil
1 large onion, diced
2 stalks celery, sliced
3 cups soup stock or water
1 6-ounce can tomato paste
2 tsps. salt
⅛ tsp. pepper
1 bay leaf
½ tsp. garlic
3 medium potatoes, sliced
6 carrots, sliced
8 ounces frozen string beans
8 ounces frozen green peas

USE: 6-quart Dutch oven
YIELDS: 10 to 12 servings

Coat roast with flour. Heat oil in 6-quart Dutch oven, and place roast in heated oil. Add onion, celery, soup stock, tomato paste, and seasonings. Bring to a boil, then cook over low flame for 2 hours.

Arrange potatoes and carrots around the meat. Allow to cook an additional half hour. Add string beans and peas and cook another 20 minutes. Add salt if necessary.

Serve meat on a large platter surrounded with vegetables.

HOMEMADE CORNED BEEF

Begin the preparation for this dish two weeks in advance.

5-pound brisket
1⅓ cups coarse salt
3 Tbsps. sugar
1 Tbsp. cracked peppercorns
2 tsps. allspice
2 tsps. thyme
1 tsp. paprika
1 tsp. sage
1 tsp. ground bay leaf
1 Tbsp. pickling spices
1 tsp. saltpeter
for coloring (optional)

USE: 5-quart Dutch oven
YIELDS: 24 slices

Combine salt, sugar, and spices in a small bowl. Put the meat in a sturdy plastic bag and rub with the spiced salt. Press out as much air as possible and tie off bag. Place in a large bowl or roaster. Cover meat with a pan containing a 5-pound weight for the first 2 days. Keep refrigerated.

Within a few hours, red liquid will exude from the meat. Massage the meat and turn the bag over once a day for 2 weeks.

Once cured, the meat will keep several months in the refrigerator, but turn it every few days. Part of the meat may be cooked and the rest kept.

Before cooking, wash off the salt and soak the meat in a large bowl of cold water for about 24 hours, changing the water occasionally. The meat should soften and will eventually feel like fresh meat. If the meat has been cured for a number of weeks, let it soak longer. Place in a 5-quart Dutch oven and cover halfway up with water. Cook for 2 hours or until soft.

Remove from water, cool, and slice very thin.

SWEET-AND-SOUR POT ROAST

3-pound rolled roast
or brisket
½ tsp. salt
¼ tsp. pepper
Pinch nutmeg
2 Tbsps. flour
2 Tbsps. oil
4 large onions, sliced
1 clove garlic, minced
1 cup dry red wine
2 Tbsps. tomato paste
2 Tbsps. honey
1 Tbsp. vinegar
1 tsp. thyme
4 sprigs parsley
2 celery tops
1 bay leaf

USE: 5-quart Dutch oven
YIELDS: 6 servings

Preheat oven to 325°.

Dust roast with salt, pepper, nutmeg, and flour. In 5-quart Dutch oven, heat oil, brown roast, and remove.

Brown onions and garlic in remaining oil. Return meat to pot and add remaining ingredients. Cover, place in oven and bake for approximately 2 hours.

NOTE: Remove bay leaf before serving.

SLICED ROAST IN APRICOT MUSHROOM SAUCE

The addition of apricot preserves to this wine and mushroom sauce gives the meat an unusual tart flavor and a beautiful glaze. Excellent for that special occasion.

5-pound end of steak roast
2 onions, diced
**3 cloves garlic,
whole or diced**
1 pound mushrooms, sliced
⅔ cup apricot preserves
1 cup dry red wine
½ cup water
¼ tsp. pepper
2 bay leaves

USE: 1 covered roasting pan
YIELDS: 10 to 12 servings

Begin preparation at least 6 hours before serving.

Preheat oven to 350°.

Trim roast. Place vegetables, apricot preserves, liquid, and seasoning into a medium bowl. Mix until combined. Place meat in roasting pan and pour apricot mixture over it. Bake covered for 2 to 2½ hours.

Check roast during baking. You may want to turn it over so that flavor of juice gets well absorbed. When done, remove from oven and allow to cool. Refrigerate for a few hours or overnight.

One hour before serving, slice meat into ¼-inch slices. Preheat oven to 300°. Return meat to sauce and reheat for 30 minutes. Serve warm.

SPICED APPLE-BUTTER BRISKET

4- to 4½-pound brisket
1 small onion, quartered
1 clove garlic, halved
10 whole cloves
Water

SAUCE
10 ounces apple butter
½ cup dry white wine
2 Tbsps. scallions, minced
3 Tbsps. prepared mustard
1½ tsps. salt
¾ tsp. curry powder
½ tsp. pepper

USE: 8-quart pot
YIELDS: 8 to 10 servings

In an 8-quart pot, combine brisket, onion, garlic, and cloves. Add enough water to cover meat. Bring to a boil and simmer until meat is tender, about 2½ hours. Remove brisket from pot.

SAUCE: While meat is cooking, combine apple butter, white wine, scallions, mustard, salt, curry powder, and pepper in a 2-quart saucepan. Heat until apple butter melts, stirring occasionally.

Preheat oven to 325°.

Place brisket in a roasting pan and brush with apple butter sauce. Roast uncovered 30 minutes until meat is heated through. Baste 2 or 3 times during roasting.

STEWS AND MEAT DINNERS

Stew is basically a long-simmering combination of meat, vegetables, and liquid providing a substantial one-pot meal. Other meat dinner dishes, such as Stir Fry Beef and Scallions or Shish Kabob provide taste and novelty to your every day meal plan or Yom Tov menu.

CHUNKY BEEF AND BEAN STEW

The addition of beans to this stew requires some advance preparation.

8 ounces pinto beans
4 cups water
2 Tbsps. vegetable oil
¾ pound stew meat,
cut into 1-inch cubes
1 medium onion, diced
2 stalks celery,
cut into 1-inch slices
2 medium turnips,
cut into 1-inch chunks
2 tsps. salt
½ tsp. thyme
½ tsp. pepper
3 carrots, thinly sliced
3 cups water

USE: 5-quart pot
YIELDS: 2 to 4 servings

Rinse beans in running cold water and discard any stones or shriveled beans. In a 5-quart pot over high heat, bring 4 cups water to a boil and add beans. Boil 3 minutes. Remove pot from heat; cover, and allow to stand 1 hour. Drain and rinse beans; set aside.

Using the same pot and making sure it is dried well, heat oil and cook beef chunks over medium-high heat until well browned. With a slotted spoon remove meat to small bowl. Set aside. In remaining oil in pot, over medium heat, saute onion until tender, stirring occasionally.

Add meat, beans, and remaining ingredients with 3 cups water. Heat to boiling. Reduce heat to low, cover, and simmer 1½ hours.

CITRUS-SURPRISE STEAK

This steak has a chutney-like Oriental flavor.

2 pounds skirt steak
cut into 1-inch cubes
¼ cup flour
1 tsp. salt
¼ tsp. pepper
3 Tbsps. oil
1 medium onion,
thinly sliced
1 cup ketchup
½ cup water
1 orange, unpeeled,
thinly sliced
1 lemon, unpeeled,
thinly sliced

USE: 10-inch skillet
Casserole dish
YIELDS: 4 to 6 servings

Preheat oven to 350°.

In a small bowl mix flour, salt, and pepper. Dredge meat in seasoned flour. In 10-inch skillet, using 3 tablespoons oil, brown meat evenly.

Put onion slices in casserole dish. Place meat over onions. Combine ketchup and water and pour over meat. Arrange orange and lemon slices in a pattern over steak. Bake in oven for 1 hour or until steak is tender.

PEPPER STEAK WITH RICE

**1 pound shoulder steak,
cut ½-inch thick**
1 Tbsp. paprika
2 Tbsps. margarine
2 cloves garlic, minced
1½ cups beef broth
1 cup sliced scallions
**2 green peppers,
cut into strips**
2 Tbsps. cornstarch
¼ cup water
¼ cup soy sauce
2 tomatoes, cut into eighths

3 cups cooked rice

USE: 10-inch skillet
YIELDS: 2 to 4 servings

Soften steak by pounding until thin. Cut into ¼-inch-wide strips. Sprinkle meat with paprika and allow to stand while preparing other ingredients.

In a 10-inch skillet, brown meat in margarine. Add garlic and broth, cover, and simmer 30 minutes. Stir in scallions and green peppers. Cook, covered, for an additional 15 minutes.

In a small bowl blend cornstarch, water, and soy sauce. Pour into meat mixture, stirring constantly until clear and thickened, about 2 minutes. Add tomatoes and stir gently. Serve over bed of warm fluffy rice.

VARIATION
☐ For more tender meat, cook 15 minutes longer.

SHISH KABOB

For the best taste, begin preparation the evening before.

**2 pounds shoulder, skirt,
or chuck steak,
cut into 1-inch cubes**

MARINADE
1 cup oil
¼ tsp. pepper
½ cup water
1 tsp. sugar
1 onion, sliced
2 cloves garlic, minced
1 lemon, sliced
2 bay leaves
½ cup dry red wine

1 pint cherry tomatoes
**2 green peppers,
cut into 1-inch pieces**
1 pound mushroom caps
**½ pound pearl onions, or
regular onions, quartered**

USE: 8 skewers
YIELDS: 8 servings

MARINADE: Combine marinade ingredients in a large bowl. Place meat cubes in marinade. Cover and leave 2 to 3 hours or overnight in refrigerator. Turn meat several times so that flavors are absorbed.

Place meat cubes on skewers, alternating different vegetables between meat cubes.

Place over hot coals or in oven broiler, 3 to 4 inches under flame, turning as necessary to cook until meat is evenly done, approximately 10 to 15 minutes and basting several times with leftover marinade. Serve over plain cooked rice with basting marinade poured over it.

NOTE: If skewers have wooden handles, be sure to cover with tin foil so they don't burn.

STIR-FRY BEEF WITH SCALLIONS

The unusual taste of this beef dish is well worth the extra effort needed for its preparation.

1½ pounds round steak

MARINADE
2 Tbsps. soy sauce
2 Tbsps. cornstarch
2 Tbsps. cold water

4 Tbsps. peanut or corn oil
1 bunch scallions,
cut into 2-inch lengths
4 cloves garlic

SAUCE
2 Tbsps. soy sauce
1 tsp. sugar
2 tsps. vinegar
4 tsps. sesame oil
2 Tbsps. white wine

USE: 10-inch skillet
or wok
YIELDS: 4 to 6 servings

Slice beef very thin.

MARINADE: In a large bowl mix all marinade ingredients together. Add beef to marinade and set aside for 20 minutes.

Heat a wok or 10-inch skillet and add 1 tablespoon oil. Add scallions and stir-fry a few seconds. Remove to a warm serving dish. Heat the same wok again and add 2 tablespoons oil. When the oil is hot, add the beef. Stir-fry quickly over high heat until the beef just changes color. Do not overcook. Place on warm serving dish.

SAUCE: Add remaining tablespoon of oil to hot wok. Add the sauce ingredients and stir sauce mixture for a second. Return the scallions and beef to wok. Stir to mix with sauce.

Serve immediately over rice.

IRANIAN STEW WITH EGGPLANT

Persian flair is evident in this combination of lemon, cinnamon, and nutmeg with eggplant.

1 large eggplant
Salt
1 pound stew meat,
cut into 1-inch cubes
1 medium onion, sliced
9 Tbsps. oil
3 medium tomatoes,
cut into eighths
½ cup water
Pinch of nutmeg
¼ tsp. cinnamon
¼ tsp. pepper
½ cup tomato juice
1 Tbsp. tomato paste
1 Tbsp. lemon juice

USE: 2 10-inch skillets
YIELDS: 3 to 4 servings

Peel eggplant and cut into 1-inch cubes. Sprinkle with salt and let stand. Saute cubed stew meat and onion in 3 tablespoons oil, in 10-inch skillet. Add tomatoes, water, and seasonings and simmer covered 30 minutes.

Rinse eggplant and pat dry. In a second 10-inch skillet saute eggplant in remaining 6 tablespoons oil, then add to meat, along with tomato juice, tomato paste, and lemon juice. Continue cooking until flavors are well mixed and meat is soft, another 45 minutes to 1 hour.

Serve over rice.

VARIATION
☐ **Italian Stew With Eggplant:** Add a little basil or oregano and garlic. Omit nutmeg, cinnamon, and lemon juice. Serve over pasta.

OVEN STEW

2 tsps. flour plus
¼ cup flour
¼ tsp. paprika
¼ tsp. pepper
2 pounds stew meat,
cut into 1-inch cubes
2 Tbsps. oil
4 small onions, quartered
1 cup whole,
small mushrooms
4 small carrots, sliced
3 potatoes, cubed
1 cup celery, sliced
1 cup water
16 ounces tomato sauce

USE: 5-quart Dutch oven
YIELDS: 4 to 6 servings

Preheat oven to 400°.

Combine flour and seasonings in bag. Drop in meat cubes and shake until coated. Mix meat with oil and place in 5-quart Dutch oven. Bake uncovered for 30 minutes. Stir once.

Add vegetables, 1 cup water, and tomato sauce. Lower oven to 350° and bake, covered, for 1½ hours.

SWEET-AND-PUNGENT CHINESE RIBS

2 Tbsps. oil
3 pounds beef spareribs,
separated
1 medium onion, diced
1 green pepper, diced
1 clove garlic, minced
1 cup pineapple juice
¾ cup cider vinegar
¾ cup water
2 Tbsps. ketchup
1 Tbsp. soy sauce
2 Tbsps. cornstarch
2 Tbsps. water
½ cup brown sugar

USE: 10-inch skillet
YIELDS: 4 servings

Heat oil in 10-inch skillet and brown ribs over medium flame. When done, remove ribs from skillet and set aside.

In oil remaining in skillet, saute onion, green pepper, and garlic. Add pineapple juice, vinegar, water, ketchup, and soy sauce, stirring until smooth. Combine cornstarch and water and add to sauce with brown sugar. Bring to a boil, stirring constantly. Reduce heat and add ribs.

Simmer, uncovered, 1 hour or until tender, stirring occasionally. Serve hot.

SWISS STEAK

1½ pounds London broil
2 Tbsps. flour
1½ tsps. salt
¼ tsp. pepper
1 medium onion, diced
3 Tbsps. oil

Cut London broil into four pieces. In a small bowl combine flour, salt, and pepper. Coat pieces well with seasoned flour.

►

1 8-ounce can tomato sauce

1 cup water

3 medium potatoes, quartered

1½ cups frozen or canned peas

USE: 10-inch skillet
YIELDS: 4 to 6 servings

In 10-inch skillet, over medium heat, saute onion in oil until golden. Add meat and brown slowly on both sides. Add tomato sauce and water to meat and bring to a boil. Add potatoes. Cover skillet tightly and simmer 1 to 1½ hours or until meat is tender. Add peas 10 to 15 minutes before serving.

VARIATION
☐ String beans may be used instead of peas.

HUNGARIAN GOULASH

3 Tbsps. oil

1½ cups chopped onion

1 small green pepper, finely diced

1 large clove garlic, minced

2 pounds stew meat, cut into ¾-inch cubes

6 cups water

2 Tbsps. paprika

4 tsps. salt

¼ tsp. cayenne pepper

1½ pounds potatoes, diced

1 16-ounce can tomatoes, sliced, with liquid

USE: 5-quart Dutch oven
YIELDS: 4 to 6 servings

Using a 5-quart Dutch oven, heat oil and over low heat saute onion, green pepper, and garlic for 10 minutes or until tender. Add meat and brown. Add water and seasonings. Bring to boil. Lower flame, cover, and simmer for 1½ hours.

Add potatoes and cook covered 15 minutes, or until potatoes are tender. Stir in tomatoes with liquid. Heat for another few minutes.

CURRIED PEPPER STEAK

2 cloves garlic, minced

2 Tbsps. oil

2 pounds shoulder steak, thinly sliced across the grain

2 green peppers, cut into strips

2 onions, sliced

1 cup mushrooms, sliced

½ tsp. salt

½ tsp. pepper

¾ cup dry red wine

¾ tsp. curry powder

USE: 10-inch skillet
YIELDS: 4 to 6 servings

In a 10-inch skillet saute 1 clove garlic in oil for 2 minutes. Discard. Add meat and brown. Remove meat. Saute peppers, onions, and remaining garlic until tender. Add mushrooms, salt, and pepper and cook until mushrooms begin to soften.

Add meat and wine. Cover and simmer 30 minutes. Stir in curry powder and simmer 20 to 30 minutes, until tender.

Serve over rice.

MEAT TZIMMES

Carrot tzimmes is traditionally served on Rosh Hashanah. This meat variation, baked as a casserole after it is initially stewed, becomes a meal in itself. It can be served at a Yom Tov meal.

1 pound stew meat, cut into 1-inch cubes
¼ cup chicken fat
1 onion, sliced
2 sweet potatoes, peeled and quartered
4 thick carrots, cut into 2-inch slices
Salt and pepper to taste
¼ tsp. cinnamon (optional)
Dash nutmeg (optional)
¼ cup water
½ pound prunes (optional)

USE: 2-quart saucepan
2-quart casserole
YIELDS: 4 servings

In a 2-quart saucepan, sear meat in chicken fat over medium flame. Add onion slices, then all remaining ingredients except prunes. Cover and simmer 30 minutes. Pour into 2-quart casserole. Add prunes.

Preheat oven to 350°.

Place in oven and bake until sweet potatoes become a little crusty and beef is done, about 45 minutes longer.

ROPA VIEJA

In this Spanish recipe, the meat is cut into thin strips and sauteed in a mild sauce.

2 cups water
2 pounds shoulder steak
2 onions
2 cloves garlic
1 large green pepper
⅓ cup oil
1 8-ounce can tomato sauce
1 tsp. salt
2 to 3 bay leaves
½ cup dry wine
1 small can pimientos

USE: 5-quart Dutch oven
YIELDS: 4 servings

In 5-quart Dutch oven, bring 2 cups of water to boil. Add meat to blanch. Drain. With meat still in pot, make a stock by adding 1 onion, 2 garlic cloves, and enough water to cover half the meat. Bring to a boil.

Remove from fire. Pour meat and stock into a large bowl. Let meat marinate in stock for 1 hour.

Cutting with the grain, separate meat into thin strips to make thin, stringy pieces. Slice second onion into thin rings. Slice pepper into thin strips. Remove garlic from marinade and saute in ⅓ cup oil in 5-quart Dutch oven. Mash garlic. Add onion rings and pepper slices and fry until onion is translucent. Add remaining ingredients, except for pimientos. Cook 15 to 20 minutes, stirring occasionally. Chop pimientos and add.

Serve with white rice and green salad.

NOTE: Remove bay leaves before serving.

CHOLENT: MEAT AND PAREVE

Cholent *is a tasty stew or soup that includes meat, potatoes, beans, and/or rice or barley in a variety of combinations. It is served on Shabbat day during the noon meal. Because of the custom of eating a hot, cooked meal on Shabbat, many people place special emphasis on the importance of eating* cholent. *Every culture has its own version and we have included several classic ones. The preparation of* cholent *is simple, and the method by which it is kept warm for the Shabbat meal is unique.*

PREPARATION OF CHOLENT

- ☐ The *cholent* should be at least half cooked on Friday and then a short while before Shabbat it is placed on top of a *blech*, a metal sheet which covers the burners and knobs

- ☐ Leave a low flame on under the *blech* so the *cholent* can continue to cook throughout the night.

- ☐ It is then served warm at noon on Shabbat. For further information see Food Preparation on Shabbat, page 496.

USING A CROCKPOT

When an overnight flame heats up the kitchen too much, especially in the summer, we can often turn to the crockpot or slow-cooker.

- ☐ Any *cholent* recipe may be used in a crockpot. It can either be started on top of the stove and cooked for 1½ hours, then placed in the crockpot and set on "low" before Shabbat, or it can be put up earlier in the day and cooked on "high" for 6 hours, and set on "low" for Shabbat.

- ☐ NOTE: Jewish Law requires that the temperature knob be covered with aluminum foil and that the food be at least half cooked before Shabbat begins. In addition, if the crockpot has a removeable serving bowl, there must be foil or some other material intervening between the bowl and the heating element (to serve as a *blech*).

CLASSIC CHOLENT WITH MEAT

Cholent is the traditional hot dish served Shabbat day for lunch. A hearty, flavorful "stew," its heady aroma fills the house.

½ **cup kidney beans**
½ **cup lima beans**
½ **cup navy beans**
6 small potatoes
**1 pound stew meat,
cut into cubes**
½ **cup fine or
medium barley**
1 onion
1½ **tsps. salt**
½ **tsp. pepper**
**1 tsp. garlic powder or
3 cloves garlic, minced**

USE: 6-quart pot
YIELDS: 4 to 6 servings

The night before you prepare this dish, put all the beans in a large bowl and cover with cold water. Allow to soak overnight. Before cooking, drain beans and discard any stones and dried-out beans.

Peel potatoes, and cut into desired size and add to pot. Rinse meat and barley. Peel onion. Place in a 6-quart pot. Add drained beans and water until pot is three-quarters full. Add salt, pepper, and garlic. Cover and bring to a boil, then reduce heat. Let simmer at least 1 hour and add water when necessary. Place on *blech* before Shabbat, making sure water is 1-inch above ingredients. Keep pot tightly covered.

VARIATION
- ☐ Add 2 ounces ketchup or 2 tablespoons paprika.

CHICKEN CHOLENT

½ to ¾ cup aduki beans
½ cup baby lima beans
4 to 6 chicken quarters
(legs and thighs)
Salt and pepper, to taste
Garlic, to taste
Paprika, to taste
2 potatoes, quartered
1 sweet potato,
cut into thick slices
1 onion, quartered
1 carrot,
peeled and quartered
½ cup barley
¼ to ⅓ cup wheat berries
3 to 5 Tbsps.
tamari soy sauce
1 bay leaf

USE: 6-quart pot
YIELDS: 6 to 8 servings

The night before you prepare this dish, put all the beans in a large bowl and cover with cold water. Allow to soak overnight. Before cooking, drain beans and discard any stones and dried-out beans.

Season chicken with salt, pepper, garlic, and paprika (if desired, cumin and coriander can also be used). Place chicken on bottom of pot. Add potatoes, sweet potato, onion, carrot, and drained beans. Add water to cover. Add barley and wheat berries.

Bring *cholent* to boil. Add tamari and bay leaf and simmer for at least 1½ hours. Add water when necessary, making sure water is 1 inch above ingredients. Place on *blech* before Shabbat. Keep pot tightly covered.

VARIATION
☐ Substitute 1 pound veal kolechal and 1 pound flanken for the chicken.

HUNGARIAN POTATO CHOLENT

This recipe should be started at least 2 hours before Shabbat. It requires a little extra care and effort but its excellent flavor is well worth it.

4 Tbsps. oil
2 large onions, diced
10 large potatoes,
quartered
2 Tbsps. paprika
2 Tbsps. pareve
beef-flavored soup mix
1 Tbsp. salt
1 cup presoaked red or
white beans and/or
1½ pounds cubed beef

USE: 6-quart pot
YIELDS: 8 to 10 servings

Heat oil in a 6-quart pot. Add diced onions and saute until onions are transparent, about 5 minutes. Add half the potatoes to the pot and season with paprika, soup mix, and salt. Coat well with oil and spices and cook over low heat about 15 minutes. Add the rest of the potatoes and gently mix until they are coated with oil and spices. Continue cooking on a low flame at least a half hour, turning every few minutes.

Add the beans and or meat. Cook stirring another 15 minutes. Add water to cover. Cook for 1 hour. Adjust seasoning to taste. Place on *blech* before Shabbat.

SEPHARDIC CHOLENT

The combination of special seasonings, plus the addition of hard-boiled eggs and chickpeas to the classic cholent, gives this dish a unique taste and reputation.

1½ cups chickpeas
2 pounds flanken, cut up
Bones for extra taste (optional)
8 medium potatoes, peeled
2 Tbsps. salt
¼ tsp. nutmeg
¼ tsp. curry
½ tsp. sugar
8 hard-boiled eggs, peeled

USE: 6-quart pot
YIELDS: 8 servings

The night before you prepare this dish put chickpeas in a large bowl and cover with cold water. Allow to soak overnight. Before cooking drain beans and discard stones and dried-out beans.

Place chickpeas in a 6-quart pot. Add meat and bones. Add whole potatoes and seasonings and cover completely with water. Cook over low flame for 2 hours, add eggs and place on *blech* before Shabbat.

Serve in soup bowls, ladling broth into bowl with 1 potato, 1 egg, and a piece of meat per person.

TEBEET

Another version of a classical Sephardic cholent with the addition of brown rice and flavorful seasoning.

1 large chicken, with fat
½ tsp. pepper
¼ tsp. turmeric
8 to 10 cups water
2 Tbsps. tomato paste or 2 tomatoes, diced
4 tsps. salt
¾ tsp. cardamom
¼ tsp. cinnamon
¼ tsp. cloves
¼ tsp. nutmeg
4 cups white or brown rice

USE: 8-quart pot
YIELDS: 8 to 10 servings

Clean chicken and remove pieces of fat. Set chicken aside and put fat into heavy 8-quart pot. Add pepper and turmeric and cook over high flame for 5 minutes until fat melts. Place chicken in fat and brown on all sides.

In a large bowl mix water and tomato paste; add salt and remaining spices. Pour mixture over the chicken bring to a boil, and cook 10 minutes.

Remove chicken and set aside.

Add rice to boiling sauce in pot, and cover. Lower flame and cook 15 minutes. Replace chicken in pot — add more water if too dry. Cover and place on *blech* before Shabbat.

PAREVE BEAN CHOLENT

The hearty flavor of beans, free of meat or fat, makes this cholent a little lighter than its meaty cousin.

½ cup pinto beans
½ cup kidney beans
½ cup baby lima beans
½ cup barley
2 Tbsps. oil
2 large onions, diced
3 to 4 potatoes,
peeled and sliced
1 package onion soup mix
1 15-ounce can tomato sauce

USE: 4-quart pot
YIELDS: 6 to 8 servings

The night before you prepare this dish, put all the beans in a large bowl and cover with cold water. Allow to soak overnight. Before cooking, drain beans and discard stones and dried-out beans.

Heat oil in a 4-quart pot, and saute onions until translucent, 5 to 7 minutes. Add barley and beans to onions. Cover with water, bring to a boil and cook 30 minutes over low flame, making sure there is enough water in the pot. Add potatoes and cook 30 minutes more.

Once beans are soft, carefully stir in onion soup mix and tomato sauce. Let cook 15 minutes more. Before Shabbat, place on *blech*. Keep pot tightly covered on low flame all night.

NOTE: Instead of soaking overnight, beans may be placed in a pot with water to cover. Bring to a boil, remove from heat, and allow to stand 1 hour. Drain and rinse and proceed as though beans had been soaked overnight.

CHALLAH CHOLENT KUGEL

A wonderful addition to any cholent. It resembles a "super-knaidel" in look and taste.

1-pound challah
2 cups hot water
3 eggs, beaten
1 onion, diced
1 tsp. salt
½ tsp. pepper

YIELDS: 6 servings

Shred or tear challah and place in a large bowl. Pour hot water over it and soak for several minutes. Squeeze out excess water. Mix with remaining ingredients. Form into roll and place on square of aluminum foil. Roll foil around challah mixture and seal.

Place on top of *cholent*, cover with water.

When serving, remove from aluminum foil, slice into 6 to 8 slices, and serve in *cholent* or as side dish to meat.

CHOLENT KUGEL

Once this cholent kugel absorbs the flavor of the cholent, it looks and tastes like real kishke.

2 medium onions, diced
2 cups flour
2 tsps. salt
¼ tsp. pepper
1 Tbsp. paprika (optional)
1 cup oil

YIELDS: 8 servings

In a large bowl combine onion, flour, and seasonings. Then add oil until the kugel holds together enough to be shaped and hold firm. Shape into oval loaf. It can then be placed on top of the cooked *cholent* before it is placed on *blech*. Make sure the *cholent* is covered with sufficient amount of water and that the water is boiling when the kugel is placed in it.

The kugel can also be wrapped in aluminum foil and placed on top of the *cholent*.

GROUND BEEF

MEAT LOAF, HAMBURGERS, or MEATBALLS *are all variations on a theme with infinite possibilities. Meatballs in Cabbage Sauce, Meat Knishes, juicy Dutch Meat Loaf, are just a few of the many dishes plain or fancy, traditional or modern that call for ground beef.*

CHICKEN-BEEF ROLL

Ground beef and chicken combine to make an interesting two-tone effect. An attractive and economical alternative for company dinner.

MEAT
1½ pounds ground beef
1 onion, grated
1 egg, beaten
3 Tbsps. matzoh meal
2 cloves garlic, minced

CHICKEN
4 chicken breasts, ground
1 onion, grated
1 egg, beaten
3 Tbsps. matzoh meal
2 cloves garlic, minced

BROTH
Water
1 onion, sliced
Dash paprika
½ tsp. salt

USE: Roasting pan
YIELDS: 8 to 12 servings

MEAT: In a large bowl mix ground beef with onion, egg, matzoh meal, and garlic. Don't overhandle. Set aside.

CHICKEN: In a separate large bowl mix ground chicken with onion, egg, matzoh meal, and garlic. Set aside.

Preheat oven to 350°.

TO ASSEMBLE: Cut two pieces of aluminum foil 12 x 16-inches. Spread the ground chicken on one and the ground beef on the other. Meat mixture should cover piece of aluminum foil entirely.

Place foil with chicken mixture chicken side down over beef mixture. Remove top foil. Roll like a jelly roll from the wide side and wrap tightly in aluminum foil.

Place in a roasting pan with 1-inch of water, onion, paprika, and salt. Bake for 1 hour.

HINT: For smooth slices, freeze before slicing. Defrost and rewarm.

VARIATION
☐ Aluminum-foil-wrapped roll can be boiled in a large pot with water to cover, onion, salt, and paprika for 1½ hours, covered, over a medium flame.

DUTCH MEAT LOAF

1½ pounds ground beef
1 cup soft bread crumbs
1 onion, diced
1 15-ounce can tomato sauce
1 egg, beaten
1½ tsps. salt
¼ cup water
2 Tbsps. sugar
2 Tbsps. prepared mustard

USE: 9 x 5-inch loaf pan
YIELDS: 4 to 6 servings

Preheat oven to 350°.

In a large bowl combine ground beef, bread crumbs, onion, ¾ cup tomato sauce, egg, and salt. Mix well and shape into loaf. Place in loaf pan. Combine remaining tomato sauce with water, sugar, and mustard. Pour over loaf.

Bake 1½ hours. Remove from oven and let stand a few minutes before slicing.

BATTER-DIPPED MEATBALLS WITH SAUCE

1½ pounds ground beef
½ cup dried bread crumbs
2 Tbsps. grated onion
¼ cup beer
1 egg
1 tsp. salt
¼ tsp. pepper

BATTER
⅔ cup beer
2 eggs, beaten
4 Tbsps. oil
1½ cups flour
1 tsp. baking powder
1½ tsps. salt
¼ tsp. pepper

Oil for frying

MUSTARD SAUCE
1 cup mayonnaise
½ cup prepared mustard
½ tsp. sugar
¼ tsp. salt
¼ tsp. paprika
⅛ tsp. cayenne pepper

USE: 10-inch skillet
YIELDS: 4 to 6 servings

In a large bowl mix first 7 ingredients well. Shape into ½-inch balls.

BATTER: Mix all ingredients together in a small bowl. Dip each meatball in batter and coat well.

In a 10-inch skillet, heat oil approximately 1-inch deep. Fry meatballs about 3 minutes in hot oil. Remove from pan and drain on paper towel.

MUSTARD SAUCE: Prepare sauce by mixing all ingredients together in a small bowl.

To serve as an hors d'oeuvre place sauce in small bowl in the center of large plate and place meatballs around it.

MEATBALLS IN CABBAGE SAUCE

2 pounds ground beef
½ cup uncooked rice
2 eggs, beaten
Salt
Pepper

CABBAGE SAUCE
1 32-ounce jar sauerkraut, undrained
2 onions, chopped
1 cabbage, shredded
1 16-ounce can cranberry sauce
½ cup sugar
1 cup water

USE: 5-quart Dutch oven
YIELDS: 8 to 10 servings

In a large bowl combine ground beef, rice, eggs, salt, and pepper. Form into small balls.

CABBAGE SAUCE: In 5-quart Dutch oven combine sauerkraut, onions, cabbage, cranberry sauce, and sugar. Add water and bring to a boil. Add meatballs, cover, and simmer 1 hour.

Serve with baked or mashed potatoes.

STUFFED MEAT LOAF SPIRAL

This meat loaf rolled as a jelly roll adds an elegant touch to any meal.

2 pounds ground beef
2 cloves garlic, minced
2 eggs, beaten
¼ tsp. oregano
¼ tsp. thyme
½ cup wheat germ
2 cups Challah-Mushroom Poultry Stuffing (page 254)

USE: 9 x 13-inch baking pan
YIELDS: 8 servings

Preheat oven to 350°.

In a medium-size bowl, combine ground beef, garlic, beaten eggs, oregano, thyme, and wheat germ. Roll or pat meat mixture onto 12 x 12 piece of waxed paper. Spread stuffing mixture on top of meat. Carefully roll as for a jelly roll.

Place roll in a greased 9 x 13-inch baking pan. Bake 1½ hours. Remove from oven and let stand a few minutes before slicing.

MEATBALLS IN CARAWAY SAUCE

1 cup coarsely grated raw potato
1 pound lean ground beef
1 tsp. seasoned salt or ½ tsp. regular salt
¼ tsp. black pepper
1 Tbsp. chopped dried parsley
½ tsp. onion powder
1 tsp. grated lemon peel
1 egg, beaten
3 Tbsps. flour
2½ cups hot water
4 tsps. beef-stock base

CARAWAY SAUCE
Stock from meatballs
¼ tsp. black pepper
1 tsp. caraway seeds
1 Tbsp. cornstarch
1 Tbsp. cold water

USE: 3-quart saucepan
YIELDS: 4 servings

Drain excess liquid from potatoes. In a large bowl combine potatoes, ground beef, salt, pepper, parsley, onion powder, lemon peel, and egg. Mix thoroughly and form into 1½-inch balls.

Place flour on a plate and roll each meatball in it.

Combine hot water and beef-stock base in 3-quart saucepan with tight cover. Bring to a boil. Drop each meatball into boiling stock, cover, and simmer 30 minutes. When done, remove meatballs with slotted spoon. Reserve liquid for sauce. Keep meatballs warm while preparing sauce.

CARAWAY SAUCE: Add pepper and caraway seeds to stock. Simmer 10 minutes. Mix cornstarch with cold water and stir into stock, stirring constantly until thickened. Pour sauce over meatballs. Serve hot.

Serve with baked or mashed potatoes.

MEATBALLS IN SWEET-AND-SOUR SAUCE

This is ideal as an appetizer, but it can also be used for a main course.

1 pound ground beef
1 egg, beaten
½ cup bread crumbs
½ onion, grated
¾ tsp. salt
¾ tsp. pepper
½ tsp. oregano

SAUCE
1 cup jellied cranberry sauce
¾ cup ketchup
¼ cup brown sugar
2 tsps. lemon juice

USE: 3-quart saucepan
YIELDS: 24 meatballs

In a large bowl combine ground beef, egg, bread crumbs, onion, and seasonings. Form into 1-inch balls.

SAUCE: In a 3-quart saucepan, combine cranberry sauce, ketchup, brown sugar, and lemon juice. Cook over low flame 25 to 30 minutes. Stir often to keep smooth.

Add meatballs and simmer for 1 hour. Serve hot.

NOTE: This can be used for a main course by making the meatballs larger.

SWEET-AND-SOUR MEATBALL DINNER

1 pound ground beef
1 tsp. salt
½ tsp. pepper

SAUCE
1 1-pound can pineapple chunks in heavy syrup
½ cup cider vinegar
2 Tbsps. soy sauce
½ cup light brown sugar
2 tsps. ground ginger
2 Tbsps. cornstarch
½ tsp. salt

1 Tbsp. oil
¼ cup diced onion
1 cup diced celery
1½ cups diced green pepper
1 14½-ounce can stewed tomatoes, drained

Hot, cooked rice

USE: 10-inch skillet
YIELDS: 4 to 6 servings

In a bowl, mix ground beef with salt and pepper. Shape into small meatballs, using 1 heaping teaspoon for each.

SAUCE: About 2 hours before serving, drain syrup from pineapple into a 1-pint measuring cup. Reserve chunks. Fill to the 1-cup mark with water. Pour into a bowl. Stir in vinegar, soy sauce, brown sugar, ginger, cornstarch, and ½ teaspoon salt.

In a 10-inch skillet, heat oil over moderately high heat. Add meatballs and brown quickly. Add diced vegetables and pineapple chunks.

Pour sauce over meatballs and vegetables; add stewed tomatoes. Cover and cook over low flame 45 minutes to an hour.

Serve with hot rice.

ITALIAN MEATBALLS SPAGHETTI

A hearty, flavorful sauce enhances the flavor of these meatballs.

SAUCE
2 Tbsps. oil
2 onions, sliced
½ pound mushrooms, sliced
3 stalks celery, diced
2 green peppers, diced
½ tsp. salt
½ tsp. pepper
¼ tsp. chili powder
¼ tsp. paprika
1 to 2 cloves garlic, minced
1 tsp. sugar
1 6-ounce can tomato paste
1 20-ounce can tomato juice

1¼ pounds ground beef
1 egg, beaten
¼ cup bread crumbs
¼ cup water
2 Tbsps. ketchup
Salt and pepper to taste

½ pound spaghetti, cooked and drained

USE: 4-quart pot
7-inch skillet
YIELDS: 4 to 5 servings

SAUCE: Heat 2 tablespoons oil in 4-quart pot. Add onions, mushrooms, celery, and green peppers, and saute until soft. Add salt, pepper, chili powder, paprika, garlic, and sugar.

Add tomato paste and tomato juice; allow to simmer covered. Sear about ¼ pound meat in a 7-inch skillet and add to sauce. Continue to simmer.

In a large bowl mix remaining 1 pound of meat with egg, bread crumbs, water, and ketchup. Season with salt and pepper. Form into small balls and drop into sauce.

Simmer about 1 hour. Serve with cooked and drained spaghetti.

JUICY BROILED HAMBURGERS

2 pounds ground beef
3 eggs, beaten
¼ cup matzoh meal or wheat germ
1 tsp. salt
½ tsp. pepper
1 Tbsp. onion powder or chopped fresh onion
2 Tbsps. ketchup
2 Tbsps. prepared mustard
¼ cup water

USE: Broiler pan
YIELDS: 8 to 10 hamburgers

Combine all ingredients in a large bowl and mix well. Shape into hamburger patties and place on broiler pan spaced well apart.

Broil 3 to 4 inches below flame on both sides until golden brown and slightly crisp, 15 minutes on first side and 5 minutes on other side.

VEGETABLE MEAT LOAF

2 pounds ground beef
1 zucchini, peeled
4 carrots
1 potato
4 stalks celery
1 large onion
3 cloves garlic
1 tsp. salt
½ tsp. pepper
4 eggs, beaten
Oil

USE: 9 x 9-inch baking pan
YIELDS: 9 servings

Preheat oven to 350°.

Place meat in large bowl. Peel and cut vegetables into medium-sized pieces. Place in blender. Add garlic, salt, pepper, and eggs. Puree in blender and add to meat.

Combine vegetables thoroughly with meat, and mix until meat does not feel too loose.

Pat meat mixture into a greased 9 x 9-inch pan. Bake for 1 hour. Remove from oven and let stand a few minutes before cutting into squares.

MEAT KNISHES

MEAT MIXTURE
1 large onion, diced
2 stalks celery, diced
½ cup diced green pepper
3 Tbsps. oil
1¼ pounds ground beef
½ to ¾ tsp. salt
¼ tsp. pepper
2 Tbsps. tomato sauce

DOUGH
1¾ cups flour
2 tsps. baking powder
½ tsp. salt
5 Tbsps. margarine
⅔ cup nondairy creamer

Mustard to taste

USE: 10-inch skillet
9 x 13-inch baking pan
YIELDS: 6 servings

MEAT MIXTURE: In a 10-inch skillet fry onion, celery, and green pepper in oil until soft, but not brown. Add meat and saute until brown. Add salt and pepper. Stir in 2 tablespoons of tomato sauce. Remove from heat and cool.

DOUGH: Combine flour, baking powder, and salt in a small bowl. Cut margarine into dry ingredients with two knives until mixture reaches consistency of corn meal. Add nondairy creamer, a few drops at a time, mashing with fork after each addition, until dough holds together in a ball.

TO ASSEMBLE: Roll out dough on floured board into a rectangle, about ¼-inch to ½-inch thick. Spread dough with mustard, then spread meat mixture on dough. Roll up, jelly-roll fashion. Place roll on ungreased pan, seam side down. Prick dough in several places with fork to allow steam to escape.

Bake until brown, about 45 minutes. Remove from oven and let stand a few minutes before slicing.

STUFFED VEGETABLES *make an elegant presentation. Traditional Stuffed Cabbage or more trendy Stuffed Onions are but two of the many variations of this type of dish. Pasta is also a perfect complement to ground beef. Puffed little pillows of homemade ravioli or a steaming lasagna are good for both family or entertaining.*

STUFFED CABBAGE ILLUSTRATED

This favorite Hungarian gourmet dish, also known as holiptches, *is sure to win lots of compliments. It can serve as an appetizer or main course.*

PREPARING CABBAGE LEAVES

☐ METHOD 1 - BOILING: Use a 4-quart pot or larger. Fill more than halfway with water and bring to a boil. Add whole cabbage, stem down. If it seems the cabbage might tip, hold it at the top with a fork. Cook over a small flame for approximately 15 minutes, until leaves soften. Remove from pot, and while cabbage is still hot, cut out inside core and remove outer leaves one by one until you reach leaves which are too small for rolling. (The top layer may have to be thrown out.) Fill while leaves are still hot.

☐ METHOD 2 -FREEZING: Place cabbage in the freezer and leave there for 2 to 3 days. Remove and allow to defrost overnight. Cabbage rolls can be made in the morning. When cabbage has defrosted, cabbage leaves are limp. Remove leaves carefully, lifting each one separately and tearing off at the bottom. Leaves come out very large this way. Fill according to instructions below.

☐ CHECKING CABBAGE LEAVES: Once the cabbage has been separated into individual leaves, then the leaves should be rinsed well to remove any insects.

☐ NOTE: To enhance the flavor of the sauce, shred remaining cabbage and saute with a diced onion in 2 tablespoons of oil. Add sauce and place cabbage rolls on top.

1 Place a tablespoon of filling mixture on the rib of leaf, near the base.

2 Fold base of leaf over filling and roll once. Fold sides toward center to enclose and make straight edges.

3 Continue rolling until completed and gently place seam side down into pot.

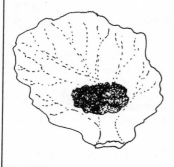

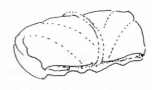

BASIC STUFFED CABBAGE

1 large cabbage

FILLING
1½ pounds ground beef
½ cup uncooked rice
3 tsps. oil
1 medium onion, minced
2 cloves garlic, minced
1 egg, beaten

SAUCE
3 Tbsps. oil
2 Tbsps. flour
1 46-ounce can tomato juice
3 to 4 Tbsps. tomato paste
½ cup sugar or
¼ cup honey
1½ cups water
2 bay leaves or
juice of 1 lemon
Salt to taste
1 large apple,
peeled and diced
¼ cup raisins

USE: 8-quart pot
YIELDS: 18 cabbage rolls

Prepare cabbage by either boiling or freezing method. See Stuffed Cabbage Illustrated. Remove and check leaves.

FILLING: Combine all ingredients for meat mixture in a bowl and mix well. Roll cabbage leaves according to illustrations.

SAUCE: Heat oil in 8-quart pot, stir in flour, and cook until brown. Add rest of ingredients in order listed. Bring to boil and cook for 5 minutes. Add cabbage rolls carefully, placing them in sauce one by one. The rolls may be piled in layers if necessary.

Cook on low flame for 2 hours, adding more water if necessary.

VARIATIONS

□ **Stuffed Green Peppers:** Prepare above meat mixture and fill eight green peppers that have been washed and cored.

Prepare half of sauce mixture. Bring to boil in 5-quart Dutch oven. Add stuffed green peppers and cook covered on medium flame for 1½ to 2 hours.

□ **Vegetarian Stuffed Cabbage:** Instead of meat mixture prepare **Rice Stuffing** (page 255) and place into cabbage leaves.

□ **Quick-and-Easy Sweet-and-Sour Sauce:** Use 2 large cans whole cranberry sauce and 2 large cans tomato sauce. Prepare cabbage as above. Combine all ingredients for meat mixture and roll cabbage leaves as described above. Combine cranberry sauce and tomato sauce in a 6- to 8-quart pot. Place cabbage rolls in the sauce. Cover and simmer 1 hour.

SWEET-AND-SOUR STUFFED CABBAGE

1 medium cabbage

SAUCE
2 Tbsps. margarine
2 onions, sliced
3 cups canned tomatoes,
with juice
1½ tsps. salt
½ tsp. pepper
Beef bones (optional)

FILLING
1 pound ground beef
4 Tbsps. uncooked rice
4 Tbsps. grated onion

Prepare cabbage by either boiling or freezing method. See Stuffed Cabbage Illustrated. Remove and check leaves.

SAUCE: Heat margarine in 6-quart pot and saute onions. Add tomatoes, salt, pepper, and bones. Cover and cook for 30 minutes.

FILLING: In a bowl combine meat, rice, onion, egg and water. Place 1 large tablespoon of mixture onto each leaf and roll according to illustrations.

Place cabbage rolls in sauce. Cover and cook for 1½ hours over low heat. Sauce should cover at least half the rolls. If more sauce is necessary, add 1 cup tomato juice.

After 1½ hours, add honey, lemon juice, and raisins and cook 15 minutes more.

►

1 egg, beaten
3 Tbsps. cold water

SEASONING
3 Tbsps. honey
¼ cup lemon juice
¼ cup seedless raisins

USE: 6-quart pot
YIELDS: 14 to 16 cabbage rolls

NOTE: Stuffed cabbage freezes well. When reheating defrosted stuffed cabbage, 6 potatoes cut in quarters may be added. Cook until potatoes are tender.

STUFFED EGGPLANT

2 small eggplants
3 Tbsps. oil
2 medium onions, diced
1 green pepper, diced
2 cloves garlic, minced
1½ pounds ground beef
6 ounces tomato paste
1 tsp. salt
¼ tsp. pepper

USE: 10-inch skillet
9 x 13 inch baking pan
YIELDS: 4 servings

Wash eggplants well. Do not peel. Cut in half, lengthwise. Scoop out eggplant centers, leaving 1 inch of pulp as a shell.

Dice scooped-out eggplant. In a 10-inch skillet, saute diced eggplant in oil with onions, green pepper, and garlic until tender and well cooked. Add ground beef to sauteed vegetables. Break up with fork and saute until well done. Combine meat and vegetable mixture with tomato paste, salt, and pepper.

Preheat oven to 325°.

Fill eggplant shells with meat mixture. Place on greased baking pan and bake, covered, until shells are soft, approximately 1 hour.

STUFFED MUSHROOMS

An elegant appetizer.

20 medium to large
whole fresh mushrooms

FILLING
¾ pound ground meat
1 egg, beaten
4 Tbsps. matzoh meal
¼ tsp. garlic powder
¼ tsp. onion powder

SAUCE
2 Tbsps. margarine
1 medium onion, chopped
1 Tbsp. soy sauce
1 Tbsp. onion soup mix
1½ cups water

USE: 10-inch skillet
YIELDS: 20 stuffed mushrooms

Rinse and wipe mushroom caps and carefully remove stems. Dice stems; save caps.

FILLING: In a medium bowl combine meat, egg, matzoh meal, garlic and onion powders and mix well.

SAUCE: In 10-inch skillet, melt margarine and saute onion until transparent. Add soy sauce, onion soup mix, and sliced stems. Saute for 2 minutes.

Fill each mushroom cap with a spoonful of ground meat mixture. Place stuffed caps in skillet with sauce. Cover and simmer for 30 to 45 minutes. Serve warm.

PASTA and GROUND BEEF are a classic combination that is found in almost every cuisine.

LASAGNA

SAUCE
1 Tbsp. oil
1 medium onion, diced
1 clove garlic, minced,
or 1 tsp. garlic powder
1 green pepper, diced
1 pound ground beef
1 16-ounce can whole
tomatoes, with liquid
1 15-ounce can tomato sauce
2 Tbsps. chopped
fresh parsley or
dried parsley flakes
1 tsp. sugar
1 tsp. basil
½ tsp. salt
½ tsp. pepper

8 ounces lasagna noodles
½ tsp. oil

USE: 10-inch skillet
6-quart pot
9 x 13-inch baking dish
YIELDS: 6 to 8 servings

SAUCE: In 10-inch skillet, heat oil and saute onion, garlic, and green pepper until soft. Add ground beef, stirring until meat browns. Add tomatoes with liquid, tomato sauce, parsley, sugar, basil, salt and pepper. Heat to boiling, stirring occasionally. Simmer uncovered 30 minutes.

Fill a 6-quart pot half full of water. Bring to a boil. Boil lasagna noodles until tender. Add ½ teaspoon oil to prevent sticking. Rinse in colander with cold water and drain.

Preheat oven to 350°.

Cover bottom of a 9 x 13-inch baking dish with sauce mixture. Line with noodles, and spoon sauce over noodles. Add another layer of noodles and top with remaining sauce. Bake covered for 45 minutes.

EGGPLANT LASAGNA

SAUCE
2 medium onions, diced
1 green pepper, diced
2 Tbsps. oil
1½ pounds ground beef
1 15-ounce can
tomato sauce
6 ounces tomato paste
1 tsp. garlic powder
½ tsp. basil
½ tsp. oregano
1 tsp. salt
¼ tsp. pepper
1 Tbsp. brown sugar

SAUCE: Saute onions and pepper in oil in 10-inch skillet until soft. Add ground beef and brown, stirring to break up lumps. Add tomato sauce, tomato paste, garlic powder, herbs, salt, pepper, and sugar. Reduce heat and simmer, covered, 20 minutes.

Fill a 6-quart pot half full of water. Bring to a boil. Boil lasagna noodles until tender. Add ½ teaspoon oil to prevent sticking. Rinse noodles in a colander with cold water, and drain.

Peel and slice eggplants. Add salt and pepper to matzoh meal. Dip eggplant slices first in egg and then in matzoh meal. Heat oil in 10-inch skillet at least ¼ inch deep and fry eggplant until nicely browned.

Preheat oven to 350°.

►

8 ounces lasagna noodles
½ tsp. oil

2 large eggplants
1 tsp. salt
¼ tsp. pepper
Matzoh meal
2 eggs, beaten
Oil for frying

USE: 10-inch skillet
6-quart pot
9 x 13-inch baking dish
YIELDS: 8 servings

Layer ingredients in a 9 x 13-inch baking dish as follows: sauce, noodles, eggplant, sauce, repeating layers and ending with sauce on top. Bake for 1½ hours.

LASAGNA IN VEGETABLE SAUCE

SAUCE
1 large onion, diced
2 Tbsps. oil
4 cloves garlic, minced,
or ½ tsp. garlic powder
¼ tsp. basil
¼ tsp. thyme
¼ tsp. oregano
¼ tsp. curry (optional)
2 green peppers, diced
2 stalks celery, diced
½ pound mushrooms, sliced
1 cup pitted
black olives, chopped
1 15-ounce can tomato sauce
or 6 chopped fresh tomatoes
and 6 ounces tomato paste
2 bay leaves
¾ to 1 cup dry red wine
1 pound ground beef

8 ounces lasagna noodles
½ tsp. oil

USE: 10-inch skillet
6-quart pot
9 x 13-inch baking dish
YIELDS: 6 to 8 servings

SAUCE: In 10-inch skillet, saute onion in oil. Add garlic, basil, thyme, oregano, and curry and saute together until onions are soft. Add diced peppers, celery, and mushrooms. Cover and simmer 5 to 10 minutes. Add chopped olives and stir in tomato sauce or fresh tomatoes and tomato paste. Add bay leaves. Cover and simmer 1 hour (1½ hours for fresh tomatoes). Stir in wine and cook an additional 5 minutes. Add ground beef to mixture, and simmer until meat is browned, another 20 minutes.

While the meat is browning, fill a 6-quart pot half full of water. Bring to a boil. Boil lasagna noodles until tender. Add ½ teaspoon oil to prevent sticking. Rinse in a colander with cold water and drain.

Preheat oven to 350°.

Cover bottom of a 9 x 13-inch baking dish with sauce. Line with noodles, and spoon one-half of the sauce over the noodles. Cover sauce with noodles and use remaining sauce on top.

Bake at 350° for 30 minutes.

VARIATIONS
☐ Crumble 1 pound of tofu into a small bowl. Combine with 1 beaten egg, salt, pepper, onion powder, garlic powder, and ¼ cup chopped fresh parsley. Layer in order; sauce, noodles, sauce, tofu, noodles, sauce.

☐ Combine thawed frozen spinach and 1 beaten egg. Layer in order: sauce, noodles, sauce, spinach, noodles, sauce.

GROUND BEEF SPECIALTIES, *international or traditional, are always a treat. Lightly spiced* Empanadas *or a mild chili, all enhance your reputation as a versatile cook.*

CHILI CON CARNE

This chili is tasty and not too hot — just right for the whole family.

1 cup dried kidney beans
1 pound ground beef
3 Tbsps. oil
1 onion, diced
1 clove garlic, minced
½ green pepper, diced
1 tsp. to 1 Tbsp.
chili powder (to taste)
½ tsp. cumin
1 tsp. paprika
⅛ tsp. cloves
1 bay leaf
Salt to taste
4 cups water
1 1-pound can peeled
tomatoes, cut up

USE: 3-quart saucepan
YIELDS: 4 to 6 servings

The night before you prepare this dish, put beans in a large bowl and cover with cold water. Allow to soak overnight. Before cooking, drain beans and discard any stones and dried-out beans.

In 3-quart saucepan, brown beef in oil with onion, garlic, and green pepper. Add all seasonings, beans, and water. Cover and cook on low to medium flame for 1 hour.

Add tomatoes and cook until beans are done, about 30 minutes more. Correct seasoning to taste and serve hot.

STUFFED ONIONS

6 medium Spanish onions
2 Tbsps. oil
1 green pepper, diced
½ pound ground beef
½ tsp. salt
¼ tsp. pepper
1 tsp. sugar
⅓ cup raisins,
soaked in boiling water
1 cup chicken stock
1 Tbsp. oil

USE: 4-quart pot
10-inch skillet
1-quart saucepan
6 x 10-inch
glass baking pan
YIELDS: 6 stuffed onions

Peel onions. Remove centers with a grapefruit knife, being careful not to cut through bottom. Reserve center portion. Place onions in a 4-quart pot, adding enough boiling water to cover. Cook on a low flame until soft, approximately 20 minutes. Remove from water, draining carefully, and dry with cut portion face down.

Preheat oven to 350°.

Chop reserved onion centers. In a 10-inch skillet saute in oil with green pepper. Add meat, salt, pepper, and sugar, stirring constantly to remove lumps. Continue until meat browns. Remove from flame and add raisins.

In a 1-quart saucepan heat stock. While it is heating, fill onions with meat mixture and place in 6 x 10-inch baking pan. Add stock to pan.

Bake approximately 40 minutes, or until golden, basting occasionally with stock and oil to prevent dryness.

MOUSSAKA

A Greek specialty that combines eggplant with a hearty meat and tomato sauce, and a delicate white sauce.

1 large eggplant
4 to 5 Tbsps. oil

MEAT SAUCE
2 pounds ground beef
1 onion, peeled and diced
2 cloves garlic, minced
1 tsp. oregano
1 tsp. thyme
Dash cinnamon
Dash salt
Dash pepper
1½ cups tomato sauce

WHITE SAUCE
3 Tbsps. margarine, melted
3 Tbsps. flour
1 cup nondairy creamer or water
Dash salt
Dash nutmeg

USE: 10-inch skillet
7 x 11-inch Pyrex dish
1-quart saucepan
YIELDS: 4 to 6 servings

Slice eggplant into ½-inch slices. Heat oil in a 10-inch skillet and fry eggplant lightly on both sides, approximately 3 minutes. Remove and place in 7 x 11-inch dish.

MEAT SAUCE: Combine ground beef with onion, garlic, spices, salt and pepper, and tomato sauce in 10-inch skillet. Simmer on low flame until meat is cooked. Spoon meat sauce over eggplant in casserole dish.

Preheat oven to 350°.

WHITE SAUCE: Melt margarine in small 1-quart saucepan and add flour. Stir together, then add nondairy creamer or water and cook until thickened.

Add salt and nutmeg. Heat through but do not boil. Pour sauce over meat mixture in baking dish and bake for 40 minutes.

MEAT-FILLED PIROGEN

An excellent appetizer, especially when topped with mushroom sauce.

All-purpose Dough (page 414) or
½ Simple Flaky Dough (page 413)
3 Tbsps. oil
1 onion, diced
1 pound ground beef or chicken
2 eggs, beaten
½ cup mushrooms, diced (optional)
1 garlic clove, minced
1 tsp. prepared mustard
Salt and pepper, to taste
1 egg yolk
1 tsp. water

USE: 7-inch skillet
Baking sheet
YIELDS: 10 to 12 pirogen

Prepare dough of your choice.

Heat oil in a 7-inch skillet and saute onion, garlic, and mushrooms. Let cool and place in bowl.

Combine with ground meat. Add eggs and spices.

Preheat oven to 350°

TO FILL: Roll out the dough to a ¼-inch thickness and cut into 3-4 -inch rounds or squares. Put teaspoonful of filling in the center and fold edges over. Moisten finger with water and run over inner edge of circle. Pinch to close securely, shaping into triangles or crescents.

Brush with egg yolk beaten with water. Put on ungreased baking sheet and bake for 20 minutes or until golden.

EMPANADAS

Lightly seasoned beef fills these South American turnovers.

DOUGH
4 cups flour
1 Tbsp. salt
½ cup oil
1 cup water

FILLING
2 to 3 Tbsps. oil
1 onion, diced
1 pound ground beef
1 Tbsp. salt
1 tsp. pepper
2 eggs, hard-boiled (optional)
20 green olives, pitted and sliced
Oil
1 egg yolk (optional)

USE: 10-inch skillet
YIELDS: 2 to 3 dozen

DOUGH: In a large bowl mix flour, salt, oil, and water very well. Form ball and leave for 15 minutes in cool place covered with a cloth.

FILLING: In a 10-inch skillet heat oil and brown diced onion. Add ground beef and season with salt and pepper. Stir frequently, and remove from flame once meat is browned. Mash eggs and add if desired.

TO ASSEMBLE: Roll out dough approximately ¼ inch thick. Cut out circles 4 inches in diameter. Place 1 to 2 tablespoons filling on one half of each circle, adding pitted sliced olive. Fold dough over filling, wet inside edge with finger dipped in water, press together, and seal. Make sure dough is closed well so meat won't fall out. Press ends together with a fork or for a decorative design flute edges with fingertips.

BAKE OR FRY: Preheat oven to 350°. Brush with egg yolk and bake on greased baking sheets for 30 minutes. Or fry in 10-inch skillet in heated oil 10 minutes on first side and 5 minutes on second side until golden brown.

QUASAT "SCOTCHED EGGS"

For a different taste and texture, delight your guests with this unusual dish.

1 pound ground beef
1 egg, beaten
¼ cup matzoh meal
¾ tsp. salt
½ tsp. pepper
½ tsp. allspice
4 hard-boiled eggs, shelled
1 egg, beaten
Oil for deep frying
2 tsps. oil
¾ cup vinegar
¾ cup water

USE: 1½ to 2-quart saucepan
YIELDS: 4 "Scotched Eggs"

In a small bowl mix together ground beef, 1 egg, matzoh meal, salt, pepper, and allspice until well blended.

Divide mixture into four portions. In the palm of your hand, flatten one portion into a patty.

Put 1 hard-boiled egg in the middle of the patty and close meat around it. This is done by pinching meat at the seam and patting well between both palms. Smooth ball by glazing with the remaining beaten egg.

Repeat with remaining portions. In a 1½- to 2-quart saucepan, deep-fry each ball, one at a time; keep turning it so it will not open.

In another pot (large enough for all four to fit in the bottom), place 2 teaspoons of oil, then four balls, vinegar, and water. Bring to a boil. Simmer over medium flame until water has boiled out and only 2 tablespoons of liquid remain in pot.

Cool; refrigerate overnight. Next day, cut into slices. Serve cold.

SHEPHERD'S PIE

3 Tbsps. oil
2 medium onions, diced
1 green pepper, diced
1 stalk celery, diced
1 pound ground beef
½ cup chicken soup or gravy
4 large potatoes
2 eggs, beaten
1 tsp. salt
¼ tsp. pepper
Margarine (optional)
Paprika (optional)

USE: 10-inch skillet
4-quart saucepan
8 x 8 inch baking dish
YIELDS: 4 servings

In a 10-inch skillet heat oil and saute onions. When translucent, remove one-half of the onion and set aside. Add pepper and celery to remaining onion and saute until soft. Add meat, stirring until brown. When browned, add stock or gravy.

Boil potatoes in a 4-quart pot of boiling salted water. Peel and mash with beaten eggs, salt, pepper, and reserved sauteed onion.

Preheat oven to 350°.

Layer a greased 8 x 8-inch baking dish, beginning with a layer of mashed potatoes, then a layer of meat, and finally a layer of potatoes. Dot with margarine and paprika, if desired. Bake for 30 minutes until potatoes begin to brown.

VEAL AND LAMB

Veal and lamb have a versatility and distinctive flavor, lending an elegance to any meal. Their beauty is in their natural taste and tenderness. As they are lower in fat content than other cuts of meat, they are often cooked in a casserole with vegetables, which enhances their flavor and retains their juices. Many kosher cuts are available and various ways of preparing them include roasting, broiling, or stewing.

VEAL MARENGO

4 veal chops
½ cup flour
2 tsps. paprika
¼ cup olive oil
1 cup white rice
1 onion, diced
1 clove garlic, minced
¼ tsp. tarragon
2 cups chicken stock
1 cup sliced mushrooms
1 green pepper, diced
1 onion, diced
1 carrot, sliced
2 cups plum tomatoes
¼ cup white wine

USE: 5-quart Dutch oven
YIELDS: 4 servings

Preheat oven to 350°.

Dredge veal chops in flour seasoned with 1 teaspoon paprika and set aside. In a 5-quart Dutch oven heat oil and toast rice until golden. Remove from pot and set aside. To remaining oil add: 1 teaspoon paprika for color, onion, garlic, and tarragon. Add veal chops, making sure they are covered with seasoned oil on both sides. Saute until browned. Set aside.

Return rice to Dutch oven and combine with remaining ingredients. Cover with veal and sauteed onion and garlic. Cover and bake for 45 to 60 minutes.

VARIATION
□ **Chicken Marengo:** Use chicken instead of veal. Substitute rose wine for white wine. Omit rice and chicken stock and serve over spaghetti.

CROWN OF LAMB STUFFED WITH RICE AND VEGETABLES

**4- to 5-pound
crown rib of lamb**

BROWN RICE STUFFING
1 cup brown rice
2 cups water
¼ tsp. salt
1 Tbsp. oil
2 onions, diced
1 green pepper, diced
2 carrots, thinly sliced
½ cup water
3 Tbsps. tamari soy sauce
1 cup halved mushrooms
**½ bunch parsley,
finely chopped**

USE: Large roasting pan
3-quart saucepan
10-inch skillet
YIELDS: 8 servings

Preheat oven to 350°.

Stand up crown rib of lamb (attached lamb chops) and lightly sprinkle with salt. Tie the two ends together or join with skewers to make a circle. Cover exposed bones on the top with aluminum foil so they don't burn. Roast in large open roasting pan for 2 hours.

After lamb is placed in oven begin preparing the stuffing.

Wash and drain rice. Place in 3-quart saucepan with water and bring to a boil. Add salt, cover, and simmer for 45 minutes.

Heat oil in 10-inch skillet and saute onions. Add green pepper and carrots and saute over high flame for 3 minutes. Lower flame, and add ½ cup water and 3 tablespoons tamari, and cook for 5 more minutes. Then add mushrooms and cook for another 5 minutes. When done, combine vegetables and their juices with rice and parsley. Add more tamari to taste if necessary. Let stand covered until ready to use.

Place stuffing in center of crown of lamb and roast for another 30 minutes.

SWEET-AND-SOUR LAMB

**3 pounds lamb stew meat,
cut into 1½-inch cubes**
2 onions, diced
3 Tbsps. margarine
¼ cup flour
2 Tbsps. brown sugar
⅓ cup cider vinegar
1 32-ounce can tomatoes
2 Tbsps. tomato paste
½ tsp. salt
1 tsp. pepper
1 bay leaf
1 stalk celery
2 sprigs parsley
2 cloves garlic, minced
1 tsp. thyme
1½ cups chicken stock
1 Tbsp. cornstarch
1 Tbsp. water

USE: 5-quart Dutch oven
YIELDS: 6 servings

In a 5-quart Dutch oven saute lamb and onions in margarine, browning well on all sides. Sprinkle lamb with flour, stir well, and cook an additional 5 to 10 minutes.

Combine brown sugar, vinegar, tomatoes, tomato paste, salt, and pepper and add to the lamb. Cook, uncovered, 10 to 15 minutes. Add bay leaf, celery, parsley, garlic, thyme, and stock. Bring to a boil, cover, and simmer 1½ hours or until tender. Remove bay leaf and celery. Return to a boil. Combine cornstarch and water to form a paste and stir into the liquid. Cook an additional 5 minutes.

MEDITERRANEAN LAMB STEWED IN WINE

4 pounds lamb stew meat,
cut into 1½-inch cubes
3 Tbsps. margarine
3 onions, sliced
1 stalk celery, sliced
2 carrots, sliced
4 tomatoes,
peeled and diced
1 cup beef or
chicken stock
1 cup dry red wine
1 tsp. sugar
3 cloves garlic, minced
2 bay leaves
Salt and pepper to taste
1½ tsps. dried thyme
2 Tbsps. cornstarch
2 Tbsps. cold water
½ cup chopped black olives

USE: 5-quart Dutch oven
YIELDS: 8 to 10 servings

Saute meat in margarine in a 5-quart Dutch oven until well browned. Remove meat and saute onions in remaining margarine. When onions are soft, add celery, carrots, and tomatoes, cooking an additional 5 to 10 minutes and stirring frequently. Pour off excess fat and return meat to pan. Add stock, wine, and seasonings. Cover and simmer 1½ hours. When tender, remove bay leaves.

In a small bowl dissolve cornstarch in 2 tablespoons cold water to form a paste and stir into stew. Bring to a boil. Add black olives. Continue cooking another few minutes and adjust seasonings to taste.

GLAZED VEAL POT ROAST

4 to 5 pound rolled,
boneless veal shoulder roast
3 Tbsps. oil
2 tsps. salt
½ tsp. pepper
¼ tsp. thyme
2 cups water
4 medium carrots,
halved crosswise
½ pound small white onions
½ pound medium mushrooms

GLAZE
2 Tbsps. cornstarch
2 Tbsps. cold water
1 10-ounce package
frozen peas
2 egg yolks
Chopped fresh dill

USE: 8-quart pot
YIELDS: 8 to 10 servings

In 8-quart pot, over medium to high heat, braise veal roast on all sides in oil. Add salt, pepper, thyme, 2 cups water, bring to a boil. Reduce heat to low; cover and simmer 1¼ hours. Add carrots and onions. Cover and simmer 30 minutes. Add mushrooms, cover and simmer 15 minutes longer or until vegetables and veal are tender. When veal is done, place on platter with vegetables. Keep warm.

GLAZE: In a cup, stir cornstarch and 2 tablespoons cold water until blended. Gradually stir into liquid in 8-quart pot. Cook, stirring, until gravy is slightly thickened. Add peas; heat through. In a separate bowl, beat egg yolks. Stir in small amount of hot gravy. Slowly pour egg mixture back into gravy, stirring rapidly to prevent lumping. Cook, stirring, until thickened. *Do not boil.*

To serve, pour some gravy over sliced veal and vegetables. Garnish vegetables with dill.

SWEET-AND-SOUR VEAL RIBS

3 pounds veal cut as ribs
1 cup sweet red wine
2 Tbsps. sugar
¾-inch slice ginger root, diced
3 large cloves garlic
¼ cup soy sauce
Water

USE: 5-quart Dutch oven
YIELDS: 6 to 8 servings

Preheat oven to 300°.

Cut veal through to the bones. Place veal in 5-quart Dutch oven. In a bowl, combine remaining ingredients. Pour over veal. Add water until half the veal is covered.

Bake in oven, covered, until veal is soft, 2 hours. Uncover and cook for 1 more hour. Turn veal a few times during the cooking.

VEAL STEW

½ cup flour
1 tsp. onion powder
1 tsp. garlic powder
1 tsp. salt
1 tsp. paprika
2 pounds veal stew meat, cut into 1½-inch chunks
3 Tbsps. oil
1 large onion, sliced
2 cloves garlic, minced
1 cup sliced mushrooms
3 potatoes, cubed
2 carrots, sliced
½ small green pepper, diced
2 tomatoes, diced
1 stalk celery, diced
2 cups dry red wine
1 tsp. thyme
⅛ tsp. curry powder
2 Tbsps. soy sauce
1 tsp. salt
½ tsp. pepper

USE: 4-quart pot
YIELDS: 4 to 6 servings

Mix flour, onion powder, garlic powder, salt, and paprika in bowl. Toss veal in the flour mixture until coated. In a 4-quart pot brown the pieces in oil and remove from pot. Add onion, garlic, and mushrooms to oil and saute for 10 minutes. Return veal to pot and add the potatoes, carrots, green pepper, tomatoes, and celery. Add wine and seasonings. Bring to a boil, lower heat, and simmer for 2 hours, until meat is tender.

STUFFED BREAST OF VEAL

A traditional dish with a delicious mashed-potato stuffing.

3- to 4-pound breast of veal with pocket

2 onions, sliced in rings
2 Tbsps. margarine

Rinse veal and pat dry.

In a 10-inch skillet saute onions in margarine until lightly browned. Put in roasting pan.

►

STUFFING

3 Tbsps. oil
¼ cup minced onion
¼ cup diced celery
2 cups hot mashed potatoes
1 cup bread crumbs
1 tsp. salt
1 tsp. poultry seasoning
2 eggs, beaten

Salt, to taste
Pepper, to taste
Paprika, to taste
**Celery leaves from
several stalks**
½ cup water
1 bay leaf

USE: 10-inch skillet
Large roasting pan
YIELDS: 6 to 8 servings

Preheat oven to 325°.

STUFFING: Heat oil in 10-inch skillet and saute onion and celery over low flame. Then add potatoes, crumbs, salt, poultry seasoning, and eggs to mixture. Set aside.

Stuff veal pocket and sew up. Season outside of veal with salt, pepper, and paprika. Place celery leaves in roasting pan on top of sauteed onions, place seasoned veal on top, and add ½ cup water and bay leaf. Roast, covered, for 2½ hours until tender.

VARIATION
☐ For added taste, glaze with a mixture of 4 tablespoons ketchup and 4 tablespoons mustard, brushed over veal during the last 30 minutes of roasting.

SPECIALTY CUTS

Liver and tongue offer good nutritional value. Platters of molded chopped liver are the legendary choice at Bar Mitzvah and wedding buffets, along with tongue and P'tchah.

PICKLED TONGUE IN APRICOT SAUCE

This dish makes an elegant entree for a festive meal.

**1 tongue
(pickled or plain)**

APRICOT SAUCE
1½ cups apricot nectar
⅓ cup raisins
2 to 3 Tbsps. brown sugar
1 Tbsp. flour
1 Tbsp. lemon juice

USE: 4-quart pot
10-inch skillet
YIELDS: 6 to 8 servings

TONGUE: Fill 4-quart pot three-quarters full of water. Add tongue. When water boils and darkens, change water and continue cooking in fresh water. If tongue is pickled, repeat the process, changing the water a second time. This time, bring to a boil on a high flame and then lower flame to cook over medium flame for 2 to 3 hours until tender. After tongue has cooked, and while it is still warm, hold with fork and peel off skin. When cooled, cut into ¼-inch slices.

APRICOT SAUCE: Approximately 30 minutes before serving, mix sauce ingredients in a 10-inch skillet and bring to a boil. Add in as many of slices of tongue as will be served. Shut off flame and allow tongue to warm in the sauce for several minutes.

VARIATION
☐ Warm tongue in **Tomato-Mushroom Sauce** (page 336).

MARINATED TONGUE

1 onion, diced
1 Tbsp. parsley
1 to 2 cloves garlic, minced
4 to 5 Tbsps. vinegar or
2 Tbsps. lemon juice
and 2 Tbsps. water
Salt and pepper to taste
1 tongue,
precooked and sliced

USE: 1-quart jar
YIELDS: 6 to 8 servings

Place all ingredients except tongue in large glass jar. Cover and shake well. Add tongue slices and shake well. Refrigerate for a day. Turn upside down for several hours to assure that marinade is completely absorbed.

Serve chilled.

FRANKS IN BLANKETS

This popular appetizer is often served at cocktail parties.

Double Recipe
Simple Flaky Dough
(page 413)
20 frankfurters
Mustard to taste
1 egg, lightly beaten
Sesame seeds

YIELDS: 5 dozen

Prepare dough according to instructions. Divide into 4 balls and refrigerate for 2 hours.

Roll dough out to ⅛-inch thickness. Cut dough into rectangles the length of the frankfurter and wide enough to wrap around the frankfurter. Spread a coating of mustard down the middle of the rectangle. Place frankfurter on mustard, lift sides, and roll around frankfurter. Press edges together to seal. Brush dough with beaten egg and sprinkle with sesame seeds. Cut into three or four sections and place on lightly oiled baking pan. Bake at 400° for 20 minutes or until golden brown.

P'TCHAH

An original Eastern European delicacy, p'tchah is popular as an appetizer for meat meals on special occasions. It is a jelled dish, grayish-yellow in color, and is garnished with sliced egg. The minced garlic adds a sharp taste.

1 calf's foot or
2 dozen chicken feet
and necks
Water to cover
1 large onion
Salt
1 to 2 cloves garlic, minced
Pepper
3 to 4 hard-boiled eggs

USE: 6-quart pot
9 x 13-inch pan
YIELDS: 16 to 20 servings

Wash calf's foot or chicken feet very well. (If using chicken feet, soak for a few minutes in very hot water, and peel skin from legs.) Place in 6-quart pot, with water to cover. Add large onion and small amount of salt. Bring to boil, then cook on a very low flame for 3 to 3½ hours, until meat is very tender. Reserve stock. (Calf's foot may take a bit longer.) Pick meat from bones and grind fine.

Spread ground meat on the bottom of a 9 x 13-inch pan, and slowly pour on the stock. Add minced garlic and season with salt and pepper to taste. For an attractive garnish, use hard-boiled sliced eggs, placed on top of stock.

When cooled, place in refrigerator. Once it jells, skim fats. Cut into cake-size pieces and serve cold.

TONGUE IN ONION SAUCE

**1 large or
2 small tongues, plain
(3 to 4 pounds)
4 Tbsps. oil
3 large onions, sliced
1 tsp. salt
Dash pepper**

USE: 4-quart pot
10-inch skillet
YIELDS: 8 to 10 servings

Place tongue in 4-quart pot and cover with water. When water boils and darkens, change water and continue cooking in fresh water until tender, approximately 1½ hours. Test with a fork to see if it is tender. After tongue has cooked and while it is still warm, hold with fork and peel off skin. When cooled cut into slices.

In a 10-inch skillet, heat oil, then add onions and saute until golden. Sprinkle with salt and pepper, then add the sliced tongue and warm over very low flame until just heated through.

ITALIAN-STYLE CHICKEN LIVERS

HALACHIC NOTE: *In order to fry, cook, or bake liver, it must already have been broiled within 72 hours after the time of slaughtering. See Koshering Liver (page 192).*

**4 Tbsps. oil
1 small onion, diced
1 small clove garlic, minced
1 26- to 30-ounce
can tomatoes, diced
6 ounces tomato paste
½ cup sliced mushrooms
1½ tsps. sugar
½ tsp. oregano
1 bay leaf
2 pounds small
chicken livers, broiled**

USE: 3-quart saucepan
10-inch skillet
YIELDS: 6 to 8 servings

In 3-quart saucepan, heat 2 tablespoons of oil and saute onion and garlic until tender. Drain off oil. Stir in remaining ingredients, except liver and remaining 2 tablespoons oil. Simmer the sauce, uncovered, for 45 minutes, stirring occasionally.

Meanwhile, in a 10-inch skillet, cook liver in remaining oil for about 5 minutes, stirring gently. Pour sauce over liver and bring to a boil.

Serve over spaghetti or noodles.

CHOPPED LIVER

A *famous Jewish dish, often served on Shabbat afternoon as an appetizer. It is often prepared in different molded shapes at a Kiddush or buffet.*

HALACHIC NOTE: *In order to fry, cook or bake liver, it must already have been broiled within 72 hours of slaughtering. See Koshering Liver (page 192).*

**1 pound broiled liver
3 eggs, hard-boiled
1 large onion, diced
4 Tbsps. oil
½ tsp. salt
¼ tsp. pepper**

USE: 7-inch skillet
YIELDS: 4 servings

Grind liver and eggs. Saute onion in oil in a 7-inch skillet and add to liver mixture. Add salt and pepper and mix well.

Place on bed of lettuce with tomato wedges. Garnish with grated hard-boiled egg white.

LIVER BLINTZES AND SAUCE

HALACHIC NOTE: *In order to fry, cook, or bake liver, it must already have been broiled within 72 hours of slaughtering. See Koshering Liver (page 192).*

CREPES
4 eggs
1 cup flour
1 tsp. salt
1 cup water

1 Tbsp. oil

FILLING
1 pound Chopped Liver
(page 231)

SAUCE
1 onion, diced
2 Tbsps. oil
1 to 2 stalks celery, diced
1 8-ounce can mushrooms
2 meat bones
1 cup water

USE: 7-inch skillet
3-quart saucepan
YIELDS: 12 blintzes

CREPES: In a large bowl beat eggs. Add flour, salt, and water and beat until well blended. Heat 1 tablespoon of oil in a 7-inch frying pan. When oil is hot, add about 2 tablespoons batter, tilting pan to all sides. When surface begins to blister, turn over and fry 30 seconds longer. Remove with spatula and place on paper towel to drain excess oil.

Repeat above procedure until all the batter is used.

FILLING: Prepare chopped liver. Put a tablespoon of liver mixture on each crepe. Then fold the crepe according to Blintzes Illustrated (page 83).

SAUCE: To make sauce, saute diced onion in oil until golden brown in 3-quart saucepan. Then add diced celery and saute 10 minutes over low flame. Add mushrooms, meat bones, and water. Cook for ½ hour. Remove bones from pot and spoon sauce over crepes. Serve warm.

If crepes were prepared a long time in advance, they can be rewarmed in oven before adding sauce.

VARIATION
☐ For thicker sauce, add 3 tablespoons flour. Stir well.

Poultry

Chicken and other poultry lend themselves to a wide variety of traditional and gourmet dishes. Try some of our delicious international recipes for a welcome change for weekday or Shabbat meals.

KOSHER POULTRY

- ☐ Kosher poultry includes the domesticated species of chicken, turkey, duck, Cornish hen and goose.

- ☐ Chicken, like meat, should be bought from a reliable kosher butcher. Packaged chicken in a supermarket, must bear a reliable seal of *kashrut*. Look for a *plumba*, a small metal tag on the wing or bag indicating the *hechsher*.

- ☐ Whole poultry is often sold with giblets packed in the cavity. These must be removed before cooking so that the raw liver does not come in contact with the bird.

- ☐ The laws concerning the *koshering*, salting and rinsing process for poultry are similar to those of *koshering* meat. See Koshering Fowl, page 191.

CHICKEN

Fried, baked, or stewed chicken, whole or cut up, is an integral part of almost every cuisine. Plentiful and inexpensive, low in cholesterol too, chicken can be the backbone of your meat main dishes.

ARROZ CON POLLO

The classic Mexican chicken with rice.

1 **3-pound chicken, cut into eighths**
3 **Tbsps. oil**
2 **medium onions, diced**
2 **cloves garlic, minced**
1½ **cups uncooked rice**
1 **15-ounce can tomatoes, cut up**
2½ **to 3 cups chicken stock**
¼ **tsp. powdered saffron**
1 **tsp. salt**
⅛ **tsp. pepper**
1 **large or 2 medium fresh tomatoes, cut up**
1 **cup fresh peas**
2 **pimientos, cut into strips**

USE: 6-quart Dutch oven
YIELDS: 4 to 6 servings

Rinse chicken, remove excess fat, and pat dry.

In Dutch oven, heat oil and brown chicken well for 15 minutes. Remove chicken from pan and saute onions in remaining oil. Add garlic and rice and stir over low heat several minutes, until rice is golden. Return chicken to pot and add all remaining ingredients, except peas and pimientos, using only 2½ cups of chicken stock. Cover and simmer 35 to 45 minutes or bake 1½ hours in preheated 350° oven.

Add peas and pimientos. Add extra stock only if rice is dry. Simmer 5 more minutes or bake another 15 minutes.

VARIATIONS
☐ Leftover chicken may be substituted.

☐ Use brown rice, but be sure rice is tender enough before serving; start with 3 cups stock.

BASIC BAKED CHICKEN

Choose one of the three methods below for a simple and delicious Shabbat tradition. Your favorite seasoning sprinkled or spread on quartered chicken and baked make a classic Friday night meal and is simple enough for an everyday supper.

2 3-pound chickens, quartered

SEASONING
1 large onion, sliced into rings
Salt
Garlic powder
Pepper
Paprika
Matzoh meal (optional)

GLAZE
⅓ cup oil
1 tsp. salt
1 Tbsp. garlic powder
1 Tbsp. onion powder
2 Tbsps. paprika

HONEY-SOY SAUCE
⅓ cup honey
3 Tbsps. prepared mustard
3 Tbsps. soy sauce

USE: 1 large roasting pan
YIELDS: 8 servings

Rinse chickens, remove excess fat, and pat dry. Prepare one of the three variations below.

Preheat oven to 350°.

SEASONING: Place onion slices on the bottom of baking pan or roaster large enough to hold chicken in one layer. Fit pieces into pan. Mix seasonings together and sprinkle over chicken. Bake covered for 1 hour and uncovered for ½ hour.

GLAZE: Prepare chicken as above and place in a large roasting pan.

Combine oil and seasonings in a cup and brush on chicken quarters with a pastry brush. Bake covered for 1 hour and uncovered for ½ hour.

HONEY-SOY SAUCE: Prepare chicken as above and place in a large roasting pan.

Combine all ingredients in a cup and brush on chicken quarters. Bake uncovered for 1¼ to 1½ hours.

CHICKEN IN MUSHROOM SAUCE

This flavorful sauce gives the chicken a light, smooth taste, adding a touch of elegance with little effort.

2 3-pound chickens, quartered
2 to 3 Tbsps. oil
1 large onion, diced
4 sprigs parsley, chopped
1 cup sliced mushrooms
¼ tsp. salt
¼ tsp. white pepper
2 cloves garlic, minced
2 Tbsps. flour
2 cups Tokay wine
2 lemons

USE: 2-quart saucepan
Roasting pan
YIELDS: 8 servings

Rinse chickens, remove excess fat, and pat dry.

In a 2-quart saucepan, heat oil over medium flame and saute onions, then add parsley, mushrooms, salt, pepper, and garlic. Simmer over low flame for 10 to 15 minutes. Stir in flour and mix well. Add the wine. Cook and stir until mixture has thickened (approximately 5 to 10 minutes).

Preheat oven to 350°.

Place chicken pieces in roasting pan and pour sauce over chicken. Bake covered 1 hour and then remove cover and bake for another ½ hour.

Squeeze lemon juice on the chicken while it is still warm.

BREADED BAKED CHICKEN I

1 3 pound
chicken, quartered
1 tsp. salt
⅛ tsp. pepper
½ tsp. garlic powder
1 tsp. paprika
½ cup mayonnaise
1 cup bread (challah)
crumbs or cornflake crumbs
or matzoh meal

USE: 9 x 9-inch baking pan
YIELDS: 4 servings

Rinse chicken, remove excess fat, and pat dry.

Preheat oven to 350°.

In a small bowl combine salt, pepper, garlic powder, and paprika with mayonnaise. Smear all over both sides of chicken, then dip into bread crumbs. Place skin side up in lightly greased 9 x 9-inch baking pan.

Bake covered for 45 minutes. Uncover and bake for an additional 15 to 20 minutes.

BREADED BAKED CHICKEN II

1 3-pound chicken
cut into eighths
1 cup flour
2 eggs, beaten
1 tsp. salt
⅛ tsp. pepper
½ tsp. garlic powder
1 cup matzoh meal
½ tsp. salt
3 Tbsps. margarine

USE: 9 x 9-inch baking pan
YIELDS: 4 servings

Rinse chicken, remove excess fat, and pat dry.

Preheat oven to 350°.

Put flour in one shallow bowl; put eggs with 1 teaspoon salt, pepper, and garlic powder in a second shallow bowl; and matzoh meal with ½ teaspoon salt in third shallow bowl.

Heat margarine in 9 x 9-inch baking pan in oven until it melts. While it is melting, dredge both sides of chicken in flour, then dip in egg mixture, and then in matzoh meal.

Place chicken skin side down in heated margarine. Bake for 40 minutes. Turn chicken over and bake an additional 20 to 25 minutes.

HONEY BREADED CHICKEN

2 3-pound chickens,
cut into eighths
2 eggs, beaten
2 Tbsps. water
1 cup matzoh meal
1 tsp. salt
⅛ tsp. pepper
½ cup oil
½ cup hot water
¼ cup honey
1 cup orange juice

USE: 10-inch skillet
Dutch oven or roasting pan
YIELDS: 6 to 8 servings

Rinse chickens and remove excess fat, and pat dry.

In a shallow bowl combine eggs and water and beat well. In another shallow bowl, combine matzoh meal, salt, and pepper. Dip chicken in egg mixture, then roll in matzoh meal.

Heat oil in 10-inch skillet over medium flame. Place coated chicken in hot oil and brown on both sides, approximately 5 minutes per side. Remove chicken to a Dutch oven or covered roasting pan.

In a small bowl combine hot water, honey, and orange juice. Pour over chicken and cover. Simmer slowly on stove top or place in preheated 325° oven for 45 minutes, or until tender. Baste occasionally.

CHICKEN RATATOUILLE

**2 2-pound chickens,
cut into eighths
2 large onions, sliced
1 clove garlic, minced
¼ cup olive or salad oil
2 Tbsps. flour
½ cup water
1 28-ounce can tomatoes
3 medium potatoes,
cut into 1-inch chunks
2½ tsps. salt
½ tsp. basil
½ tsp. oregano
½ tsp. sugar
¼ tsp. pepper
1 medium eggplant,
cut into 1½-inch chunks
2 medium zucchini,
cut into ½-inch slices
1 green pepper,
cut into ¼-inch slices**

USE: 5-quart Dutch oven
YIELDS: 6 servings

Rinse chicken, remove excess fat, and pat dry.

In 5-quart Dutch oven, over medium to high heat, cook onions and garlic in hot oil, stirring occasionally until golden brown, about 5 minutes. With slotted spoon, remove onion mixture to plate; set aside. In remaining oil, saute chicken several pieces at a time, until well browned on all sides.

Remove Dutch oven from heat; stir in flour until well blended. Gradually stir in water and tomatoes with their liquid; add onion mixture, potatoes, salt, basil, oregano, sugar, and pepper. Place chicken pieces over the vegetables. Heat to boiling over high heat. Reduce heat to low and simmer 45 minutes, stirring occasionally. Add eggplant, zucchini, and green pepper. Cover and cook 15 minutes longer or until vegetables and chicken are fork-tender, stirring occasionally. Skim off fat from liquid.

BAKED SWEET-AND-SOUR CHICKEN

**2 3-pound chickens,
quartered or cut
into eighths
1 large onion,
sliced into rings
2 stalks celery, sliced
1 green pepper, sliced
1 yellow squash,
sliced (optional)
12 mushrooms (optional)
4 to 5 potatoes (optional)
Paprika (optional)**

**SAUCE
4 Tbsps. oil
2 Tbsps. vinegar
⅓ cup ketchup
⅓ to ½ cup honey**

USE: Roasting pan
YIELDS: 8 to 10 servings

Rinse chickens, remove excess fat, and pat dry.

Preheat oven to 300°.

Line bottom of baking pan with onion rings, celery, green pepper, yellow squash, and mushrooms.

Combine sauce ingredients in a small bowl, mixing by hand until smooth. Cover both sides of each piece of chicken with sauce. Place chicken skin side up on top of vegetables. Pour any remaining sauce over chicken. Bake covered for 2 hours.

After chicken has baked for 1 hour, peel and slice potatoes. Cook in a 2-quart saucepan in small amount of water for 15 minutes. Drain and cool. When chicken has 15 minutes left in oven, sprinkle potatoes with paprika and place under chicken.

NOTE: During last 30 to 45 minutes of baking, it may be necessary to add a small amount of hot water to bottom of pan if no sauce is left.

MOROCCAN CHICKEN

1 3-pound chicken,
quartered
2 Tbsps. oil
3 cloves garlic, halved
⅛ tsp. black pepper
3 Tbsps. cider vinegar
1 cup ripe olives,
pitted and chopped
2 tomatoes, diced (optional)
½ cup dry white wine

USE: 10-inch skillet
YIELDS: 4 servings

Rinse chicken, remove excess fat, and pat dry.

In 10-inch skillet, heat oil over medium flame. Saute garlic, being careful not to scorch it. Remove garlic and add chicken pieces; braise on all sides until golden brown.

Add pepper, vinegar, olives, and tomatoes to pan and simmer 30 minutes. Add wine, cover, and simmer until chicken is tender, approximately 30 minutes longer.

PUFFY DEEP-FRIED CHICKEN

1 2½-pound chicken,
cut into eighths
1½ cups boiling water
Oil for deep-frying

BATTER
1 cup flour
¼ tsp. salt
2 tsps. baking powder
1 egg
1 cup water

VEGETABLES
1 bok choy, washed and cut
into 2-inch lengths
½ cup mushrooms, fresh,
dried, or canned
½ cup canned
Chinese baby corn
½ cup canned
water chestnuts
¼ pound fresh snow peas
or frozen peas

SAUCE
2 Tbsps. cornstarch
3 Tbsps. soy sauce
1 tsp. sugar
2 tsps. ginger

USE: 4-quart pot
10-inch skillet
YIELDS: 4 to 6 servings

Rinse chicken, remove excess fat, and pat dry.

Cook chicken for 30 minutes in 4-quart pot containing 1½ cups boiling water. Set broth aside.

BATTER: In a medium bowl combine flour, salt, and baking powder. Beat the egg with water and add to dry ingredients, mixing until batter is smooth.

Pour 1-inch of oil into a 10-inch skillet and heat until very hot. Dip chicken in batter, then place in skillet and fry on both sides until browned. Lower flame and continue cooking approximately 20 to 30 minutes. Drain on paper towels.

Remove oil except for 2 tablespoons. Stir-fry bok choy, then add rest of vegetables and fry for a few minutes. Add broth and bring to a boil.

SAUCE: Combine sauce ingredients in a small bowl and add to vegetables. Continue stirring until mixture thickens.

Serve chicken on a bed of vegetables over rice.

INDIAN CHICKEN CURRY

1 3-pound chicken,
cut into eighths
6 Tbsps. margarine
2 small onions, diced
1 clove garlic, minced
2 Tbsps. flour
2 Tbsps. curry powder
2 tsps. ground ginger
2 tsps. ground cardamon
1 tsp. salt
2 medium tomatoes, diced
1 cup peeled,
chopped apples
1 cup chicken broth
⅓ cup raisins (optional)

USE: 10-inch skillet
YIELDS: 4 to 6 servings

Rinse chicken, remove skin and excess fat.

In a 10-inch skillet, melt 3 tablespoons margarine and brown chicken until golden brown. Remove chicken and set aside.

Add remaining 3 tablespoons margarine and saute onions and garlic until tender. Mix flour and seasonings and stir into pan. Add tomatoes, apples, broth, and raisins, if used, and simmer 5 minutes.

Return chicken to pan and simmer for 40 minutes. Serve over rice.

POULET CHASSEUR

1 3-pound chicken,
quartered
¼ tsp. salt
¼ tsp. pepper
½ tsp. seasoned salt
¼ tsp. paprika
2 Tbsps. flour
2 Tbsps. margarine
2 shallots, minced
½ onion, diced
1 cup mushrooms, diced
1 Tbsp. flour
1 tsp. salt
⅛ tsp. pepper
½ tsp. garlic powder
½ tsp. chopped parsley
¾ cup tomato sauce
½ cup sparkling or
dry white wine

USE: 10-inch skillet
YIELDS: 4 servings

Rinse chicken, remove excess fat, and pat dry.

Combine seasonings and flour in a bag and shake well. Add dried chicken pieces and shake to coat. Heat margarine in 10-inch skillet. Brown chicken on both sides.

Remove chicken. Add shallots, onion, and mushrooms and saute. Sprinkle in 1 tablespoon flour and stir. Add remaining seasonings, parsley, tomato sauce, and wine. Bring to a boil. Lower flame and replace chicken in sauce.

Cover and simmer for 1 hour, or until tender.

VARIATION
☐ Instead of tomato sauce, use ¼ teaspoon tarragon or chervil and ¾ cup canned tomatoes.

ITALIAN CHICKEN

1 3½-pound chicken, cut into eighths
½ cup flour
½ to ¾ cup oil
1 stalk celery, diced
¼ pound fresh mushrooms, sliced
1 medium onion, sliced
1 green pepper, diced
1 15-ounce can tomato sauce
1 tsp. oregano
1 tsp. basil
½ tsp. salt
2 cloves garlic, minced
1 6-ounce can tomato paste

USE: 10-inch skillet
Roasting pan
YIELDS: 4 to 6 servings

Rinse chicken, remove excess fat, and pat dry.

Coat chicken in flour. In 10-inch skillet, heat oil and brown chicken on all sides. Remove chicken and place in roasting pan.

Preheat oven to 350°.

Saute vegetables in remaining oil until tender-crisp. Add tomato sauce, seasonings, garlic, and tomato paste. Pour over chicken. Bake covered for 1 to 1½ hours.

JUICY PINEAPPLE CHICKEN

1 3-pound chicken, quartered
3 Tbsps. oil
1 15-ounce can pineapple chunks
1 large onion, sliced
1 28-ounce can tomatoes
1 green pepper, diced
1 4-ounce can mushrooms
2 scallions (optional)

SAUCE
1 cup pineapple juice
½ cup sugar
½ cup vinegar
1 Tbsp. cornstarch
Dash salt

USE: 10-inch skillet
1½-quart saucepan
Roasting pan
YIELDS: 4 servings

Rinse chicken, remove excess fat and pat dry.

Heat oil in 10-inch skillet and brown chicken.

Preheat oven to 350°.

Drain pineapple chunks, and reserve liquid for sauce.

Layer sliced onion in roasting pan and add browned chicken, vegetables, and drained pineapple chunks. Bake, covered, for 30 minutes.

While chicken is baking, stir ¾ cup reserved pineapple juice, sugar, and vinegar together in 1½-quart saucepan. Simmer over low flame. Make a paste of cornstarch, salt and remaining juice, and add to hot mixture, beating briskly. Cook, stirring constantly, until thickened. Pour sauce over chicken and vegetables and bake 30 minutes covered, then 30 minutes uncovered.

APRICOT CHICKEN

This glaze is exceptionally easy and produces a beautiful chicken with extra moistness and flavor.

1 3-pound chicken, quartered
3 Tbsps. apricot jam
3 Tbsps. lemon juice
3 Tbsps. ketchup
3 Tbsps. mayonnaise
1 envelope, 1⅜ ounces, onion soup mix

USE: 1½-quart saucepan
Roasting pan
YIELDS: 4 servings

Rinse chicken, remove excess fat, and pat dry.

Preheat oven to 350°.

Place chicken skin side up in roasting pan.

In 1½-quart saucepan, bring remaining ingredients to a slow boil, stirring constantly. Remove from heat immediately and pour over chicken.

Bake for 1¼ hours, uncovered.

SOUTHERN FRIED CHICKEN

1 3-pound chicken, cut into eighths
½ cup nondairy creamer
1 egg
1 cup flour
2 tsps. garlic salt
2 tsps. paprika
1 tsp. pepper
1 tsp. onion powder
2 heaping Tbsps. solid shortening

USE: 10-inch skillet
YIELDS: 4 servings

Rinse chicken, remove excess fat, and pat dry.

Combine nondairy creamer and egg in a shallow bowl.

Put flour and seasonings into a bag and shake well. Add chicken pieces to flour mixture and shake to coat. Dip chicken in egg mixture. Shake chicken a second time in flour until evenly coated.

Melt shortening in a 10-inch skillet until hot. Fry chicken until golden brown on both sides over low flame, about 30 minutes on each side. Drain on paper towels, and serve hot.

ZUCCHINI-STUFFED CHICKEN

1 3½-pound chicken, quartered
2 medium zucchini
3 Tbsps. margarine
3 slices day-old bread
1 egg, slightly beaten
⅛ tsp. pepper
½ tsp. salt
½ cup honey

USE: 1½-quart saucepan
Roasting pan
YIELDS: 4 servings

Rinse chicken, remove excess fat, and pat dry.

Shred unpeeled zucchini in food processor or grate on large holes of a hand grater. In a 1½-quart saucepan, melt margarine and add zucchini. Cook, stirring, about 3 minutes. Remove from heat. Grate or shred bread into crumbs and add to zucchini. Stir in egg and seasonings, mixing well.

Preheat oven to 400°.

Carefully loosen skin on each chicken quarter to form a pocket and spoon one fourth of the stuffing into each. Brush each quarter with honey and bake for 50 minutes until tender.

STUFFED CHICKEN AND RICE

1 4-pound chicken
1 small onion, finely diced
2 Tbsps. olive oil
¾ cup uncooked long-grain white rice
3 Tbsps. pine nuts or slivered almonds
1 lemon
1¼ cups chicken broth
1 clove garlic, minced
2 Tbsps. dried currants
½ tsp. salt
¼ tsp. cinnamon
¼ pound mushrooms, sliced
¼ tsp. rosemary leaves

USE: 10-inch skillet
Roasting pan
YIELDS: 4 to 6 servings

Rinse chicken, remove excess fat, and pat dry.

In medium skillet, saute onion in oil until transparent. Stir in rice and pine nuts. Cook until light brown.

Squeeze and reserve juice of lemon and grate lemon rind.

Stir chicken broth, garlic, currants, salt, cinnamon, and lemon rind into rice. Cook, uncovered, over low heat for 20 minutes (rice will be slightly chewy).

Preheat oven to 350°.

Fill cavity of the chicken with rice mixture. Place chicken, breast side up, in roasting pan. Arrange mushrooms around chicken. Drizzle reserved lemon juice over chicken and mushrooms, then sprinkle with rosemary. Make a "tent" of aluminum foil to loosely cover roasting pan. Roast for about 1½ hours.

SPANISH POTTED CHICKEN

1 3½-pound chicken, quartered
2 Tbsps. oil
½ cup flour
2 onions, sliced
¼ cup dry white wine
1 pound tomatoes, canned or fresh, peeled and cut up
6 cloves garlic, minced
1 stalk celery, finely diced
3 sprigs parsley, finely chopped
1 bay leaf
½ tsp. dried thyme
⅛ tsp. pepper
1 Tbsp. cornstarch

USE: 10-inch skillet
YIELDS: 4 servings

Rinse chicken, remove excess fat and pat dry.

Heat oil in 10-inch skillet and brown chicken. Sprinkle chicken with flour. Turn to coat evenly on all sides. Add onions, wine, tomatoes, and all other ingredients except cornstarch. Cover and simmer on medium to low flame, about 45 minutes.

Uncover. Dissolve cornstarch in a little cold water and stir into gravy. Bring to boil and cook an additional 15 minutes.

CHICKEN FILLETS

Cut-up or ground chicken fillets represent the best in versatility. From India, China, or Russia, the variety is as wide as the world. Leftover chicken as well, from soup or oven, cut up and used to fill a pot pie, a flaky dough or knish, certainly adds flair to your main dish repertoire.

NOTE: *Chicken breasts in recipes are whole. If using chicken cutlets or fillets, each fillet is usually one half of the breast.*

CHICKEN BURGERS

1 pound ground raw chicken
1 medium onion, finely grated
1 stalk celery, finely grated
2 slices challah
1 egg, beaten
½ tsp. salt
⅛ tsp. pepper
2 Tbsps. matzoh meal
½ cup matzoh meal or cornflake crumbs
2 Tbsps. oil

USE: 10-inch skillet
YIELDS: 6 servings

Put ground chicken, grated onion, and celery in a medium bowl. In another bowl, soak challah thoroughly in hot water. Then squeeze out water and mix challah into chicken mixture. Add egg, salt, and pepper, and matzoh meal. Mix well.

Shape into patties and dip each patty into matzoh meal or cornflake crumbs. In a 10-inch skillet, heat oil. Place burgers in skillet and fry evenly on both sides until golden brown, approximately 5 to 7 minutes per side.

CHICKEN DUMPLINGS

An unusual ground chicken variation. Excellent as an appetizer or served in soup.

2 whole chicken breasts, ground
1 onion, grated
¼ cup bread crumbs or matzoh meal
Pinch of salt
Pinch of pepper
1 egg, beaten

STOCK
8 cups water
1 carrot, sliced
1 onion, sliced
1 parsley root
Dash salt
Dash pepper
Dash sugar

USE: 3-quart pot
YIELDS: 4 servings

In a medium bowl, combine ground chicken with onion, bread crumbs, salt, pepper, and egg. Mix together and form into small balls.

STOCK: In 3-quart pot, boil water with carrot, onion, parsley root, salt, pepper, and sugar. Bring to a rapid boil and add the chicken balls. Simmer, covered, on low flame for 1½ hours.

CHICKEN KIWI SAUTE

The special way the vegetables and fruit are sliced make this a beautiful dish.

2 whole chicken breasts, skinned and boned, sliced into strips
3 Tbsps. oil
1 medium onion, sliced lengthwise
1 cup diagonally sliced celery
1 cup thinly sliced carrots
1¾ cups cold chicken broth
4 tsps. cornstarch
½ tsp. grated lemon or lime peel
½ tsp. salt
Dash pepper
2 to 3 kiwis, peeled and sliced

USE: 10-inch skillet
YIELDS: 4 servings

Heat oil in a 10-inch skillet. Saute chicken in 1 tablespoon oil until cooked. Remove from skillet. Add remaining 2 tablespoons oil and vegetables. Saute until tender but still crisp. Return chicken to skillet.

In a small bowl, combine broth, cornstarch, peel and seasonings. Pour over chicken, then cook and stir until thickened, approximately 10 to 15 minutes. Gently stir kiwi into mixture.

Serve immediately over rice.

CHICKEN POT PIE

Prepare this in a foil pan and keep it in the freezer for a convenient supper.

CRUST
1 cup flour
⅓ cup shortening
½ tsp. salt
2 Tbsps. cold water

FILLING
6 Tbsps. chicken fat or other oil
1 medium onion, diced
1 potato, diced
½ cup thinly sliced carrots
6 Tbsps. flour
½ tsp. salt
⅛ tsp. pepper
2½ cups chicken stock
2 cups diced cooked chicken
½ cup canned peas
2 Tbsps. chopped pimientos (optional)

USE: 2-quart saucepan
2-quart casserole
YIELDS: 4 to 6 servings

CRUST: Sift flour into medium bowl. Cut shortening and salt into flour and mix with fork until pieces are about the size of a pea. Sprinkle water over mixture and blend with fork. Shape into a ball; wrap with plastic wrap and chill well.

FILLING: In 2-quart saucepan, heat chicken fat until it melts. Add onion, potato, and carrots and saute until tender. Stir in flour, salt, and pepper and mix quickly and well. Over medium heat, gradually stir in chicken stock, stirring constantly to make a thick, creamy sauce. Add diced chicken, peas, and pimientos. Pour chicken mixture into a 2-quart casserole.

Preheat oven to 400°.

Roll out dough on floured surface to size of casserole. Place crust over the casserole, piercing with fork near the center. Bake for 30 minutes, or until crust is browned.

CHICKEN AND PEPPERS

2 medium green or
red peppers
½ pound mushrooms
5 Tbsps. oil
2 whole chicken breasts,
skinned and boned
3 Tbsps. soy sauce
1 Tbsp. dry sherry
2 tsps. cornstarch
⅛ tsp. garlic powder
⅛ tsp. sugar
½ cup water

USE: 10-inch skillet
YIELDS: 4 servings

Slice peppers and mushrooms thin and saute in 2 tablespoons hot oil in a 10-inch skillet. Reserve vegetables. Cut chicken into 2-inch chunks.

In a small bowl, combine chicken, soy sauce, sherry, cornstarch, garlic powder, and sugar. Fry chicken in an additional 3 tablespoons oil in 10-inch skillet until tender-crisp, about 5 minutes. Add vegetables and water and heat to boiling. Serve immediately.

LEMON CHICKEN

2 whole chicken breasts,
skinned and boned
Oil for frying

MARINADE
1 tsp. salt
1 Tbsp. soy sauce
1 tsp. sesame oil

BATTER
1 cup flour
¼ cup cornstarch
2 tsps. baking powder
¼ tsp. sugar
¾ cup water

LEMON SAUCE
4 Tbsps. fresh lemon juice
4 Tbsps. sugar
3 Tbsps. white vinegar
¾ cup chicken broth
2 tsps. cornstarch
Salt to taste

1 cup shredded lettuce
½ cup thinly sliced lemon

USE: Deep skillet
Wok or 1½-quart saucepan
YIELDS: 4 servings

Cut chicken breasts into bite-size pieces. In a small bowl mix marinade ingredients, combine with chicken, and set aside for 20 minutes. In another bowl combine batter ingredients and mix until smooth.

Heat 3 tablespoons oil in wok. As the oil is heating, add 1 tablespoon warm oil to batter and stir to blend. Dip chicken into batter and deep-fry until golden brown and crispy. Fry one-fourth of the pieces at a time and keep warm on a rack in oven.

LEMON SAUCE: Combine ingredients for sauce in a small bowl. Heat 2 tablespoons of oil in wok or small saucepan. Stir the lemon sauce to be sure the cornstarch is in suspension and add to the warm oil. Cook and stir until the sauce thickens, plus 1 minute more to avoid starchy taste.

Arrange chicken pieces on a platter over the shredded lettuce. Pour the lemon sauce over the chicken and garnish with lemon slices. Serve immediately.

NOTE: For crispier chicken, the sauce can be served on the side.

SZECHUAN CHICKEN

This recipe is perfectly adaptable for use with beef as well as chicken.

2 whole chicken breasts, skinned and boned
2 Tbsps. oil
3 cloves garlic, minced
1 onion, sliced
1 carrot, julienned
1 medium zucchini, sliced
¼ bunch broccoli florets
¼ head cauliflower florets
2 cups mung bean sprouts

SAUCE
¼ cup water
⅓ cup tamari soy sauce
⅓ cup corn syrup
¼ to ½ tsp. crushed red pepper
2 Tbsps. cornstarch

USE: 10-inch skillet
or wok
YIELDS: 4 servings

Slice chicken breasts against the grain into ¼-inch slices. Set aside.

Heat oil in 10-inch skillet or wok and stir-fry garlic, onion, and carrot 5 minutes. Add chicken and cook 10 minutes more. Add remaining vegetables, saute, and continue cooking 5 to 10 minutes.

SAUCE: To chicken-vegetable mixture, add water, soy sauce, corn syrup, crushed red pepper, and 2 tablespoons of cornstarch. Stir, heating through, until sauce thickens.

Serve over rice.

NOTE: 3 cups of diced leftover chicken can be used in place of chicken breast; it should be added with vegetables.

CHINESE STIR-FRIED CHICKEN

2 whole chicken breasts, skinned and boned
¼ cup soy sauce
2 Tbsps. dry sherry
2 Tbsps. orange marmalade
2 tsps. cornstarch
2 tsps. peeled, minced ginger root or
½ tsp. ground ginger
½ tsp. crushed red pepper
1 small orange
2 6-ounce packages frozen Chinese pea pods, thawed
Oil
Salt
1 4½-ounce can blanched whole almonds or
1 3-ounce can walnuts
1 medium bunch scallions, minced

USE: Wok
or 5-quart Dutch oven
YIELDS: 4 servings

Cut each breast in half, and each half into six chunks. In a medium bowl, combine chicken, soy sauce, sherry, marmalade, cornstarch, ginger, and red pepper. Set aside. Cut orange into thin slices; cut each slice in half. Set aside. Drain pea pods; pat dry with paper towels.

Place 2 tablespoons oil in wok or 5-quart Dutch oven over high heat and cook pea pods with ½ teaspoon salt, stirring quickly and frequently (stir-frying), until pea pods are tender-crisp, about 2 minutes. Spoon pea pods onto plate. Keep warm.

In same wok, heat an additional ½ cup salad oil and cook almonds until lightly browned, stirring frequently with slotted spoon. Spoon almonds onto paper towels to drain, leaving the oil in the wok. In remaining oil over medium heat, cook scallions, stirring frequently until browned but not burned, about 5 minutes. With slotted spoon, remove scallions; discard. In same wok over high heat, in remaining oil, stir-fry marinated chicken pieces with marinade until chicken is tender, stirring frequently about 5 minutes. Remove wok from heat.

To serve, spoon chicken mixture into center of large, warm platter. Arrange pea pods around chicken, place orange slices around pea pods. Sprinkle almonds over chicken.

ORIENTAL CELERY AND CHICKEN

A fresh way of serving leftover chicken.

**2 cups boiled chicken,
cut into bite-sized pieces**
1 cup chicken broth
4 Tbsps. soy sauce
3 tsps. sugar
1½ cups sliced celery
1 small onion, sliced
2 Tbsps. oil
**¼ cup toasted
almonds (optional)**

USE: 10-inch skillet
YIELDS: 2 servings

In a small bowl, combine chicken, chicken broth, soy sauce, and sugar. Set aside.

Heat oil in a 10-inch skillet and saute celery and onion until lightly browned. Add chicken and sauce mixture to the sauteed ingredients. Cook for 3 to 5 minutes, stirring constantly. Sprinkle with chopped almonds.

EGG FOO YOUNG

Egg Foo Young is an Oriental omelet filled with chicken or meat and vegetables.

2 Tbsps. oil
1 medium onion, diced
1 stalk celery, diced
**1 Tbsp. finely chopped
green pepper or parsley**
**1 can bean sprouts,
drained (reserve liquid)**
**1 cup coarsely chopped
cooked chicken**
6 eggs, slightly beaten
½ tsp. salt
Oil for frying

SAUCE
**Juice from above
vegetables**
**1 cup reserved liquid
from bean sprouts**
1 Tbsp. cornstarch
1 tsp. sugar
2 Tbsps. soy sauce

USE: 8-inch frying pan
1-quart saucepan
YIELDS: 4 servings

Heat oil in 8-inch frying pan. Saute onion, celery, green pepper, and bean sprouts until soft. Add the chicken and cook a few minutes longer. Set pan aside and cool.

Add salt to beaten eggs. Using a slotted spoon, remove vegetable and chicken mixture, reserving liquid in bottom of pan for sauce. Combine vegetable and chicken mixture with eggs and mix well.

Rinse out frying pan. Heat 1 tablespoon oil in skillet and pour in one fourth of the mixture at a time, about ½ inch deep. Cook until brown, turn and brown on other side. Serve with hot sauce.

SAUCE: In a 1-quart saucepan, combine the juice from the cooked vegetables with 1 cup of the reserved liquid from the bean sprouts. Set aside ¼ cup of this mixture and heat the remaining liquid to boiling. Blend 1 tablespoon cornstarch, 1 teaspoon sugar, and ¼ cup reserved liquid. Add to boiling mixture. Cook, stirring until thick. Add soy sauce. Spoon a few tablespoons sauce on top of each omelet.

SCHNITZEL

The basic method of breading and frying boned chicken breasts make this an old-time favorite in Jewish cooking.

2 eggs, beaten
2 whole chicken breasts, skinned, boned and halved
1 cup matzoh meal
1 tsp. salt
½ tsp. garlic powder
Oil for frying

USE: 10-inch skillet
YIELDS: 4 servings

Beat eggs in a shallow bowl.

Dip chicken breasts into beaten eggs. Combine matzoh-meal with salt and garlic powder in another flat bowl. Dredge chicken breasts in mixture.

Heat oil in 10-inch skillet and fry coated chicken breasts over medium flame, approximately 10 to 12 minutes on one side and 7 minutes on other side, until golden brown. Test doneness by piercing meat with fork to see if chicken is tender.

VARIATION
☐ **Mustard Schnitzel:** Coat chicken with 2 tablespoons prepared mustard. Dip in bread-crumb mixture. Fry as above or broil for 15 minutes on each side.

LEMONY CHICKEN KABOBS

The chicken must be marinated at least 2 hours to make a flavorful kabob.

2 whole chicken breasts, skinned and boned
3 medium lemons
¼ cup olive or vegetable oil
1 Tbsp. sugar
1 Tbsp. cider vinegar
2 tsps. salt
¼ tsp. cayenne pepper
1 clove garlic, minced
3 small zucchini
½ pound medium mushrooms

SAUCE
¼ cup margarine
1 Tbsp. lemon juice
1 Tbsp. chopped parsley
½ tsp. salt
Dash cayenne pepper

USE: Four 14-inch metal skewers
1½ quart saucepan
YIELDS: 4 servings

Cut each chicken breast in half and each half into six pieces.

Grate 1 tablespoon lemon peel from lemon; squeeze juice from lemons to make ⅓ cup. In a bowl, mix lemon peel, lemon juice, oil, sugar, vinegar, salt, cayenne pepper, and garlic; set aside.

Cut each zucchini crosswise into four chunks. Trim tough stem ends from mushrooms. Add chicken, zucchini, and mushrooms to lemon mixture. Toss lightly to coat well. Cover and refrigerate at least 2 hours, stirring occasionally.

About 30 minutes before serving, on four 14-inch metal skewers, alternately thread chicken, zucchini, and mushrooms, reserving marinade. Place skewers on rack in broiling pan and broil 15 minutes or until chicken is fork tender, brushing occasionally with lemon marinade and turning kabobs occasionally.

SAUCE: Meanwhile, prepare sauce by melting margarine in 1½-quart saucepan over medium heat. Stir in lemon juice, parsley, salt, and cayenne pepper. Stir until well blended. Do not boil. To serve, arrange kabobs on platter. Place sauce in bowl to serve with kabobs.

CHICKEN KIEV

4 Tbsps. margarine

2 Tbsps. chives

2 whole chicken breasts, skinned and boned

¼ to ½ cup bread crumbs

½ tsp. salt

½ tsp. paprika

⅔ cup flour

1 egg, beaten

4 Tbsps. oil

USE: 10-inch skillet
YIELDS: 4 servings

Cream margarine with chives. With fingers form into a rectangular block about 3 inches long. Wrap in plastic wrap and put in freezer until firm.

Cut chicken breasts in half and lay between sheets of waxed paper and pound flat.

Once margarine is firm cut into four 3-inch pieces. Place each piece on one chicken breast. Fold over edges and roll so that margarine is completely enclosed.

Combine breadcrumbs, salt and paprika. Dredge chicken rolls with flour, dip in egg and then seasoned bread crumbs.

Heat 4 tablespoons of oil in a 10-inch skillet and fry chicken until evenly browned, approximately 20 minutes on one side, 15 minutes on the other side.

CHINESE CHICKEN WITH CASHEWS

3 whole chicken breasts, skinned, boned and diced

1 egg white

Dash salt

Dash pepper

2 Tbsps. cornstarch

⅓ cup oil

1 slice ginger, shredded

1 clove garlic

1 cup chopped mushrooms

½ cup chopped bamboo shoots

½ cup chopped water chestnuts

1 10-ounce package frozen or fresh peas

3 tsps. sugar

1 Tbsp. cornstarch

¼ cup soy sauce

¼ cup water

¼ cup cashews

USE: 10-inch skillet
YIELDS: 4 to 6 servings

Combine first five ingredients in a large bowl and mix together. Heat oil in a 10-inch skillet and add chicken mixture. Let mixture fry slowly until just cooked, approximately 20 minutes. Remove chicken mixture from skillet and set aside.

Remove all oil from skillet except for 2 tablespoons. Turn heat to high, add ginger, garlic, and then all the vegetables and fry for 2 minutes.

Return chicken to skillet. Combine sugar, cornstarch, soy sauce, and water in a bowl and add slowly to the chicken and vegetables.

Add cashews and let simmer for 3 minutes.

Serve over rice.

HUNGARIAN CHICKEN PAPRIKASH

3 large onions, diced
2 heaping Tbsps. chicken fat
or 3 Tbsps. oil
1 tsp. salt
¼ tsp. pepper
2 stalks celery, diced
1 tomato, diced, or
⅓ cup ketchup
¼ green pepper, diced
1 heaping tsp. paprika
2 whole chicken breasts,
skinned and boned
1½ cups water
1¼ cups raw rice

USE: 10-inch skillet
YIELDS: 4 servings

Place onions, chicken fat, salt and pepper in 10-inch skillet. Saute over low heat until brown, about 10 to 15 minutes. Add diced celery, tomato, and green pepper to skillet and continue cooking. Sprinkle paprika over mixture and stir occasionally. While vegetables are stewing, cut up chicken into 1-inch cubes and add to skillet. Cover and keep simmering slowly until chicken is tender, about 15 minutes. Add a little water to prevent burning.

When chicken is tender, add 1½ cups water and 1¼ cups rice. Continue to simmer on top of stove for 10 to 15 minutes.

Preheat oven to 350°.

Place covered skillet in oven for about 30 minutes more, until rice is tender.

CURRIED CHICKEN

The right combination of spices makes for an intriguing taste.

3 whole chicken breasts,
skinned and boned
3 Tbsps. oil
1½ cups chopped onions
2 cloves garlic, minced
3 Tbsps. lemon juice
3 tsps. curry powder
1½ tsps. salt
¾ tsp. cumin
¾ tsp. turmeric
¾ tsp. paprika
¼ tsp. white pepper
1 bay leaf
¼ cup water

USE: 3-quart saucepan
YIELDS: 6 servings

Cut chicken into 1-inch cubes. Heat oil in 3-quart saucepan and stir-fry chicken cubes several minutes until golden. Stir in onions and garlic and saute 3 minutes. Stir in remaining ingredients. Heat to boiling and simmer uncovered 15 minutes. Add more water if necessary.

Serve with rice.

VARIATION
☐ Sauteed vegetables and/or walnuts may be added the last few minutes of cooking.

CHICKEN APPETIZERS

Giblets, liver, and wings are all used for traditional Jewish dishes. Chopped chicken liver is a hallmark of Jewish cuisine, surpassed in popularity only by the bagel.

SAUTEED CHICKEN LIVERS

Halachic Note: In order to fry, boil, or bake liver, it must already have been broiled within 72 hours after the time of slaughtering. See Koshering Liver, (page 192).

¼ cup margarine
¼ cup oil
1 large onion, thinly sliced
1 pound koshered chicken livers
1 clove garlic, minced
⅛ tsp. allspice
1 bay leaf
⅛ tsp. black pepper
⅔ cup wine, preferably white
Juice of 1 lemon
2 Tbsps. minced fresh parsley

12 ounces broad noodles, cooked and drained
4 Tbsps. margarine

USE: 10-inch skillet
YIELDS: 4 servings

In 10-inch skillet, heat margarine and oil. Add onions and saute until golden. Add livers and saute 2 to 3 minutes. Add garlic, allspice, bay leaf, pepper, and wine. Stir. Cover and simmer 5 minutes. Add lemon juice and parsley and simmer 5 more minutes.

Stir margarine into warm, drained noodles.

Serve livers and sauce over noodles.

"BUFFALO" WINGS

18 chicken wings (about 3 pounds)
½ cup soy sauce
¼ cup ketchup
¼ cup hot pepper sauce
1 stick margarine

USE: Small saucepan
Broiling pan
YIELDS: 8 to 10 appetizer servings

Place wings in broiling pan.

Combine other ingredients in small saucepan over low heat until margarine is melted. Brush wings with part of mixture and broil for 10 minutes. Turn wings; brush with remaining sauce and broil for 10 to 15 minutes longer.

SWEET-AND-SOUR CHICKEN FRICASSEE

2 large onions, sliced
1 Tbsp. chicken fat or oil
2 pounds chicken
necks and gizzards
1 28-ounce can
peeled tomatoes
Juice of 1 large lemon,
approximately 3 Tbsps.
1 tsp. salt
¼ tsp. pepper
2 Tbsps. sugar
1 pound ground beef
2 eggs, beaten
½ cup bread crumbs
or matzoh meal
¼ cup water
½ tsp. salt
⅛ tsp. pepper

USE: 10-inch skillet
3-quart saucepan
YIELDS: 6 to 8 servings

In a 10-inch skillet, saute onions in chicken fat. Remove onions and place in 3-quart saucepan. In remaining fat, sear chicken parts until browned. Place in pot with onions. Add tomatoes, lemon juice, salt, pepper, and sugar. Bring to a boil, lower flame and simmer.

While gizzards are simmering, put ground beef in medium bowl. Add eggs, bread crumbs, water, salt, and pepper. Mix well. Form into small balls and drop into chicken-tomato mixture. Cover and simmer over low flame for 2 hours. Add more water if necessary to prevent burning.

VEGETABLE FRICASSEE

Serve this fricassee as either an appetizer or a hearty entree.

4 Tbsps. oil or margarine
½ green pepper, diced
2 stalks celery, diced
1 clove garlic, minced
2 medium onions, diced
1 tsp. salt
⅛ tsp. pepper
¾ tsp. paprika
2 pounds chicken
necks and gizzards
Water
1½ pounds ground beef
1 egg, beaten
2 Tbsps. matzoh meal
¼ tsp. salt
Dash pepper
2 Tbsps. oil
1 heaping tsp. flour
¾ cup cold water

USE: 4-quart pot
10-inch skillet
YIELDS: 6 to 8 servings

In a 4-quart pot, heat oil. Add green pepper, celery, garlic, and onions and saute until tender. Add salt, pepper, and paprika. Cut chicken parts into three to four pieces each and brown separately in 10-inch skillet. When vegetables are soft, add chicken. Add enough water to cover and bring to a boil, then lower flame and simmer for ¾ hour.

While chicken parts are simmering, put ground beef in medium bowl. Add egg, matzoh meal, salt, and pepper. Shape into 1-inch balls and sear in 2 tablespoons of oil in a 10-inch skillet. Then add to chicken and cook together for 30 minutes. Mix flour with water and add to pot; stir until smooth and thick. Bring to a boil, then turn off flame. Serve over toast, rice, or noodles.

POULTRY SPECIALTIES

Provide a change of pace for your Yom Tov meal or simchah with turkey, duck, or Cornish hen. A turkey stuffed with kasha to feed a crowd combines Jewish and American traditions.

To retain the flavor of roast poultry and to prevent it from drying out, wrap turkey with a cheese cloth dipped in oil and spices before roasting, or place poultry in an oven roasting bag together with vegetables and spices. Don't hesitate to make a whole turkey; leftover turkey meat can be used interchangeably with chicken in various salads, chow meins, or stir-fry recipes.

ROAST DUCK

1 5-pound duck

Poultry Stuffing
of your choice
(pages 254-255)

Salt

Pepper

1 cup flour

1 clove garlic, cut up

1 sliced onion

1 cup orange juice

USE: Roasting pan
YIELDS: 4 servings

Clean duck, removing excess fat; stuff with desired stuffing and sew up. Season, and rub all over with flour. Make slits in skin; insert pieces of garlic. Place on a roasting rack so that the fat can drain off. Place onion rings on bottom of roasting pan.

Roast covered at 350° for about 2½ to 3 hours, until tender. Baste with 2 to 3 Tbsps. orange juice every 20 minutes. Uncover during last half hour to brown.

BRAISED DUCK IN ORANGE SAUCE

4 Tbsps. oil

2 3-lb. ducks,
cut into quarters

1 onion, sliced

4 large tomatoes, chopped

2 cloves garlic, minced

2 bay leaves

1 tsp. cinnamon

2 tsps. salt

2 cloves

1 tsp. thyme

1 tsp. black pepper

2 cups orange juice

1 cup water

USE: 5-quart Dutch oven
YIELDS: 6 to 8 servings

Heat oil over medium flame in 5-quart Dutch oven. Brown duck with onions for 10 minutes. Turn duck over and brown on second side.

Add tomatoes, garlic and spices, and cook for 10 more minutes. Add orange juice and water, and bring to a boil. Reduce heat and simmer for 30 minutes. Turn pieces. Continue cooking another 45 minutes or until tender.

SERVING SUGGESTION: Place duck on rice and cover with sauce.

TURKEY AND STUFFING

1 10- to 12-pound turkey
2 large onions, sliced
2 stalks celery, sliced
1 cup water
½ tsp. salt

KASHA STUFFING
2 cups kasha
1 egg, beaten
1½ tsps. salt
¼ cup oil or margarine
1 large onion, diced
½ cup diced celery
½ cup diced carrots
½ cup mushrooms
4 cups chicken broth
¼ tsp. parsley
⅛ tsp. tarragon (optional)
⅛ tsp. nutmeg (optional)

BASTING
¾ cup oil or
melted margarine
1 Tbsp. paprika
Salt and pepper
to taste

USE: 10-inch skillet
Large roasting pan
YIELDS: 10 to 12 servings

Rinse turkey and pat dry.

Place sliced onions and celery on bottom of roasting pan. Add water and salt, then place a rack over the vegetables.

STUFFING: Place kasha in medium bowl and add the beaten egg and salt. Set aside. Heat oil or margarine in 10-inch skillet until hot and add onion, celery, carrots and mushrooms. Saute lightly. Add the kasha mixture and broth. Cover and cook over low flame for 15 minutes. At the end of cooking time, add the parsley and seasonings. Fill cavity of turkey with stuffing. Stuff loosely. Sew up cavity. Wrap any extra stuffing in foil and bake with turkey for 1 hour.

Place turkey, breast side down, on rack in roasting pan. Bake in a 325° oven for about 30 minutes per pound. Turn over approximately every 45 minutes, basting each time. For an evenly browned turkey, baste the skin on all sides with oil or melted margarine, paprika, and salt and pepper.

NOTE: When freezing turkey, remove stuffing first.

ROCK CORNISH HENS WITH STUFFING

4 Rock Cornish hens
2 cloves garlic, minced
2 tsps. salt
½ tsp. pepper

STUFFING
4 Tbsps. margarine
1 medium onion, diced
½ pound mushrooms
1½ cups cooked rice
Salt to taste
Pepper to taste

USE: 10-inch skillet
Roasting pan
YIELDS: 4 servings

The night before roasting the hens, combine garlic, salt, and pepper. Rub hens inside and out with seasoning. Cover and refrigerate overnight.

STUFFING: Melt margarine in a 10-inch skillet and saute onion until soft; add mushrooms and cook another few minutes. Combine vegetables with cooked rice and season with salt and pepper.

Loosely fill cavities of hens with stuffing. Truss and sew closed. Place the hens breast side down in a roasting pan and roast at 350° for 1 hour, basting frequently. Turn breast side up and roast 15 minutes longer.

Stuffings

Steaming mixtures of sauteed vegetables combined with chunks of challah, potatoes, rice, or kasha, make for wonderful stuffing or dressing. Packed lightly into a chicken, ready for roasting, it provides that something extra-special for dinner. Leftover homemade challah should never be thrown out but is perfect to use as stuffing.

Traditionally, the large cavity of a chicken, duck, or turkey is stuffed. But the skin of the neck, the helzel, can also be stuffed. Stuffing may also be slipped under the skin of the chicken breast.

Making a stuffing is a simple process. Once it is prepared it is packed lightly into the cavity to be stuffed. Often the opening needs to be sewn with a large needle and strong thread to secure the stuffing well. Remember to remove the thread before serving. Poultry is stuffed most often, but breast of veal and fish can also be used. See meat and fish sections for tempting recipes.

CELERY AND MUSHROOM STUFFING

4 cups cubed day-old white bread or challah
¼ cup oil or chicken fat
½ cup onion, finely diced
¾ cup diced celery
1 cup canned mushrooms, drained
2 eggs, beaten
1 tsp. salt
⅛ tsp. pepper
1 tsp. poultry seasoning (optional)

USE: 7-inch skillet
YIELDS: Stuffing for
5 to 6-pound duck
or chicken

Measure bread into a large bowl. Soak in hot water until soft, squeeze out water. Heat oil or fat in 7-inch skillet. Add onion, celery, and mushrooms; cook about 5 minutes. Pour over bread and mix well. Add eggs and seasonings to bread mixture.

Stuff duck or chicken. Roast as directed.

NOTE: If any extra stuffing remains after filling the duck, place it in a greased ovenproof dish or greased hand-fashioned foil cup and bake with the duck, basting with the drippings.

CHALLAH-MUSHROOM POULTRY STUFFING

¼ cup margarine
2 stalks celery, finely diced
1 medium onion, finely diced
3 cups fresh mushrooms, finely diced
2 cloves garlic, minced
2 slices challah
Salt and pepper to taste

USE: 10-inch skillet
YIELDS: Stuffing for 1 chicken

Heat margarine in a 10-inch skillet. Saute vegetables and garlic.

Crumb the bread, 1 slice at a time, in a blender or food processor, and add to the vegetables. Add salt and pepper and mix well.

Stuff into large chicken. Roast as directed.

CRACKER STUFFING

1 box salted crackers
2 cups hot water
3 eggs, beaten
1 cup canned mushrooms, sliced and drained
1 large onion, diced
½ tsp. salt
¼ tsp. pepper

USE: Mixing bowl
YIELDS: Stuffing for 2 chickens

Soak crackers in hot water for 2 to 3 minutes. Squeeze out excess water.

Add remaining ingredients and mix well. Stuff chickens. Roast as directed.

RICE STUFFING

Use this stuffing for either breast of lamb or veal.

2 Tbsps. oil
1 onion, diced
1 stalk celery, diced
2 Tbsps. green pepper, diced
¼ tsp salt
¼ tsp. paprika
¼ tsp. curry powder (optional)
1½ to 2 cups cooked rice

USE: 7-inch skillet
YIELDS: Stuffing for a 3- to 4-pound breast of lamb or veal

In a 7-inch skillet, heat the oil and saute onion, celery, and green pepper. Mix in seasonings. Add vegetables to rice and mix well. Proceed according to lamb or veal recipe.

VARIATION
☐ **Brown Rice and Vegetable Stuffing:** See Crown of Lamb Stuffed with Rice and Vegetables (page 226).

ZUCCHINI STUFFING

3 medium zucchini
2 carrots
2 Tbsps. oil
1 medium onion, diced
2 cloves garlic, chopped
3 eggs, beaten
½ tsp. salt
¼ tsp. pepper
½ cup matzoh meal

USE: 7-inch skillet
YIELDS: Stuffing for 1 chicken

Grate zucchini and carrots on large holes of grater and put in bowl.

Heat oil in 7-inch skillet and saute onion and garlic about 3 minutes until translucent. Remove from flame. Add to vegetables with eggs, seasoning, and matzoh meal.

Stuff chicken. Roast as directed.

Side Dishes

Vegetables, Side Dishes and Salads
Kugels and Traditional Specialties
Grains and Pastas
Dips and Dressings

Vegetables and grains, a vital part of every diet, also provide variety in taste, color, and texture. They complement and enhance the main dish while adding valuable nutrients to the meal.

Latkes, kugel, tzimmes and fresh and cooked cold salads often serve as side dishes at Shabbat and Yom Tov meals. Marinated salads or salads with a mayonnaise-based dressing, such as coleslaw or potato salad, are popular because they can be prepared in advance for a large crowd. Many of these dishes may be served hot, cold, or at room temperature.

Some vegetables traditionally served on various occasions are chickpeas at a *Shalom Zachar*, carrot dishes and *tzimmes* on Rosh Hashanah, and potato *latkes* on Chanukah. On Passover, bitter vegetables known as *maror* as well as other vegetables play an essential role in the *seder*.

Vegetables and Kashrut

Fresh fruits, vegetables and grains are, in their natural unprocessed state, kosher and *pareve*. They do not need a *hechsher* and can be used with either dairy or meat. However, once a vegetable is combined with a dairy or meat product, it remains dairy or meat respectively.

Processed vegetables such as those canned or frozen, may pose a problem. They are sometimes creamed and may contain non-kosher, dairy or meat ingredients; or they may have been processed in vessels used for meat, dairy, or even non-kosher products.

A more common problem with vegetables involves possible insect infestation. The prohibition against consuming insects, even very tiny ones, is quite strict. In recent years, due to Federal regulations restricting insecticide spraying and genetic changes causing some insects to become more resistant to the insecticides, there are increasing amounts of insects such as thrips and aphids infesting some vegetables, especially green and leafy varieties. Although quite small, they are visible to the naked eye and must be removed. Aphids range in size from 2 -5 millimeters (1/16 - 1/8 of an inch).

Many vegetables, fruits, nuts, and grains must be checked before cooking or eating for the presence of small insects. Packages of pasta are also occasionally infested. Some particularly severe problem vegetables are artichokes, asparagus, brussels sprouts, cauliflower, and leafy vegetables.

The method of checking depends on the vegetables. Leafy vegetables such as cabbage and lettuce should be checked leaf by leaf. Washing under running water or soaking in salt water is helpful, but the vegetables must also be inspected under a bright light, either daylight or artificial light. Certain vegetables, such as celery, and zucchini may be used after they are washed under running water and scrubbed with a vegetable brush.

The degree to which insects are present varies according to the region, season, and origin of the produce. An Orthodox Rabbi in your community should be consulted for his recommendations for checking and using these vegetables.

Vegetables, Side Dishes and Salads

AVOCADO SALAD

2 to 3 small avocados
4 eggs, hard-boiled
1 large onion, chopped
2 tsps. salt
½ tsp. ground chili powder
¼ cup minced parsley
2 Tbsps. vinegar or lemon or lime juice
½ tsp. coriander seed (optional)
Lettuce leaves

USE: Small bowl
YIELDS: 6 servings

Peel avocados and eggs; mash together well. Combine with chopped onion. Add remaining ingredients and mix well.

Serve scoops on bed of lettuce, or as a dip.

NOTE: To prevent avocado from turning brown, save pit and replace in salad. Remove just before serving.

MIMOSA ASPARAGUS VINAIGRETTE

2½ pounds fresh asparagus

DRESSING
2 tsps. vinegar
Juice of one lemon
Salt and pepper to taste
½ cup oil
1 Tbsp. parsley

2 eggs, hard-boiled, for garnish

USE: 10-inch skillet
YIELDS: 8 to 10 servings

Soak and thoroughly wash asparagus, breaking off hard portion at base of stem. Lay asparagus down in a 10-inch skillet. Add 1 inch of water and bring to a boil. Simmer until tender but still bright green. Place on a round serving dish, side by side, in a circle, with tips pointed to center. Allow to cool.

DRESSING: Mix vinegar, lemon juice, salt, and pepper. Add oil, mixing continuously. Pour onto asparagus tips and sprinkle with parsley.

MIMOSA TOPPING: Separate the egg whites and yolks. Separately, push them through a strainer (egg yolk may be mashed). Sprinkle the yolks over the asparagus tips in the center, and the whites around the yolks. These colors, green, yellow, and white, are the colors of the mimosa plant.

BEANS, *whether green or yellow, combine well with tomatoes or tomato sauces. The Spiced String Beans have a delicate taste, while the Four Bean Salad is a filling and robust addition to a meal. There is a large variety of dried beans available in every supermarket. They serve as a staple in many cuisines. From Chilean Lentils to Pasta E Fagioli, beans are truly international.*

Whether using beans in salad, soup, or stew it is best to presoak beans several hours in advance. They require less cooking time and absorb less water.

HOMEMADE BAKED BEANS

**1 pound Great
Northern white beans
2 tsps. salt
1 15-ounce can tomato sauce
½ cup brown sugar
1 medium onion, peeled
2 whole cloves**

USE: 3-quart saucepan
2-quart casserole
YIELDS: 6 servings

The night before, put beans in a large bowl with water to cover. Let stand overnight. In the morning, drain beans. Place in a 3-quart saucepan with fresh water to cover. Bring to a boil and cook until beans are just soft, about 1 hour. Add salt after 45 minutes. Drain liquid from beans and reserve.

Preheat oven to 325°.

Combine tomato sauce and brown sugar. Add 1 cup of reserved cooking liquid.

Place beans in a casserole and cover with sauce mixture. Stick the two cloves into the onion and put into the beans. Cover.

Bake for 5 to 6 hours until sauce is thick and syrupy and beans are soft.

EASY FOUR-BEAN SALAD

Use all four beans or any combination. If using less, reduce dressing.

**1 16-ounce can chickpeas
1 16-ounce can kidney beans
1 16-ounce can green beans
1 16-ounce can wax beans
1 16-ounce can corn
1 onion, chopped
1 green or red pepper, diced**

**DRESSING
½ cup vegetable oil
½ cup vinegar or lemon juice
1 tsp. oregano
1 tsp. garlic
½ Tbsp. salt
Pepper to taste**

USE: 3-quart bowl
YIELDS: 8 to 10 servings

Drain beans and corn; mix together in a large bowl. Add the onion and pepper. Combine dressing ingredients and toss with salad, gently but thoroughly. Chill and serve. Keeps up to 2 weeks refrigerated in closed container.

VARIATION
□ Add 2 tablespoons soy sauce to dressing and omit salt.

SPANISH BEANS

2 to 3 Tbsps. oil
1 medium onion, diced
2 to 3 cloves garlic, minced
Salt and pepper to taste
½ tsp. paprika
⅛ tsp. cumin
**⅛ tsp. crushed
red pepper (optional)**
**3 Tbsps. snipped
fresh parsley**
**½ tsp. shredded
fresh coriander**
1 green or red pepper, diced
**⅓ cup tomato sauce or
1 fresh tomato, quartered**
1 tsp. crushed basil leaves
**1 16-ounce can pink or
black beans or
2 cups cooked and
drained, dried beans**
1 Tbsp. white vinegar
**1 Tbsp. dry red wine
(optional)**

USE: 3-quart saucepan
YIELDS: 4 servings

In a 3-quart saucepan, heat oil to very hot. Add onion and saute until transparent. Add minced garlic and saute 1 minute. Add seasonings and spices as listed, through coriander, stirring quickly after each addition.

Add diced green or red pepper and saute until tender. Add tomato sauce or fresh tomato and crushed basil. Cover and simmer for 10 to 15 minutes until tomato is cooked.

Add beans and vinegar. Cook covered, over low heat, for about ½ hour, allowing beans to absorb flavors.

Add wine and boil 1 minute more before serving to evaporate alcohol.

VARIATION
☐ Use different beans, i.e., chickpeas or kidney beans.

PASTA E FAGIOLI

½ pound macaroni
**2 cups cooked navy beans
(or beans of your choice)**
3 carrots, diced
2 stalks celery, diced
1 onion, diced
**1 16-ounce can
peeled tomatoes, cut up**
2 cloves garlic, minced
1 bay leaf
1 tsp. oregano
½ tsp. basil
Salt to taste
⅓ cup oil
Parsley for garnish

USE: 3-quart saucepan
YIELDS: 6 servings

Cook macaroni, drain, and set aside.

In a 3-quart saucepan, mix beans with vegetables, seasonings, spices, and oil; cook together for 15 minutes. Add macaroni and cook on medium heat an additional 15 minutes. Garnish with parsley.

NOTE: Remove bay leaf before serving.

VARIATION
☐ **Dairy:** Add grated mozzarella cheese.

CHILEAN STYLE LENTILS

1 cup lentils
1 stalk celery
3 Tbsps. oil
1 large onion, diced
3 cloves garlic, diced
1 green pepper, diced
1 large tomato, chopped
3 Tbsps. chopped
fresh parsley or
1 Tbsp. dried parsley
1 tsp. oregano
1 tsp. paprika
½ tsp. cumin

USE: 10-inch skillet
2-quart saucepan
YIELDS: 4 servings

Place lentils in pot. Cover with water. Add 1 stalk celery*
bring to a boil, turn flame down, and simmer about 30
minutes.

In a 10-inch skillet, in 3 tablespoons oil, saute for
5 minutes, onion, garlic, green pepper, tomato, parsley,
and oregano. Add the paprika and cumin. Saute and stir
occasionally until soft and lightly browned.

Drain lentils. Add the sauteed mixture to the lentils. Stir
until well mixed, then serve.

VARIATION
□ **Dairy:** Sprinkle top with grated cheese.

*NOTE: Celery nullifies the gaseous reaction to beans
and aids digestion.

GREEN BEAN AND CARROT SALAD

1 pound fresh green beans
4 carrots, cut
into julienne strips
2 Tbsps. oil
2 Tbsps. wine vinegar
½ tsp. salt
Pepper to taste
½ red onion

USE: 3-quart saucepan
YIELDS: 4 to 6 servings

Wash and trim ends of green beans and prepare carrots.

In a 3-quart saucepan cook together in small amount
water until tender, but still crisp, about 15 to 20 minutes.
Drain and place vegetables in bowl.

Mix oil, vinegar, salt, and pepper. Slice onion wafer-thin.
Add dressing to vegetables. Toss all ingredients and
chill.

VARIATION
□ Instead of carrots, cook 10 whole medium mushrooms
with beans.

SPICED STRING BEANS

Mildly spiced with unusual flavor, this makes a very special side dish.

3 pounds fresh string beans
2 tsps. salt
¼ cup oil
¼ tsp. turmeric
½ tsp. cumin
¼ cup water

USE: 3-quart saucepan
YIELDS: 8 to 10 servings

Wash and trim beans. Put all the ingredients into a 3-quart
saucepan and mix well. Cook, covered on a small flame for
30 minutes. Serve warm or cold.

NOTE: Do not substitute or omit spices.

GREEN BEAN ALMANDINE

2 pounds green beans, trimmed and rinsed
2 tsps. salt
½ cup margarine
1 cup slivered almonds
½ tsp. salt
½ tsp. pepper

USE: 6-quart pot
7-inch skillet
YIELDS: 6 to 8 servings

Fill 6-quart pot half full of water. Add salt and bring to a rapid boil. Drop in green beans, bring back to a boil and cook uncovered for 10 to 12 minutes or until tender but still crisp.

Place in a colander and rinse with cold water. Drain and reserve.

In a 7-inch skillet melt margarine and add almonds. Saute about 5 minutes until lightly browned.

Return beans to 6-quart pot and turn heat to medium to evaporate all moisture from beans.

Pour almonds and margarine over beans. Add additional salt and pepper, and toss gently to coat all beans.

Serve at once.

VARIATION
□ Substitute ½ pound mushrooms for almonds and proceed as above.

STIR-FRY BEAN SPROUTS WITH GINGER

¾ pound bean sprouts
3 Tbsps. corn oil
1 clove garlic, slightly crushed
¼-inch slice of ginger, shredded or
1 tsp. ground ginger
1 large scallion, shredded
1 tsp. salt
½ tsp. sugar
Dash of white pepper
1 tsp. cornstarch dissolved in 2 Tbsps. chicken broth or soy sauce
1 tsp. sesame oil

USE: Wok
YIELDS: 4 to 6 servings

Wash and drain bean sprouts. Put sprouts in a colander and pour boiling water over them.

Heat a wok and add oil. When oil is very hot, add garlic and ginger. (If using ground ginger, add with sugar, salt, and pepper.) Press garlic down into oil, then remove and discard. Add the scallions and stir. Add bean sprouts, salt, sugar, and pepper. Stir quickly for a few seconds.

Stir the cornstarch mixture and pour into wok. Stir until a glaze forms over bean sprouts. Add the sesame oil. Stir once more and serve immediately.

NOTE: Sesame oil can be obtained from the top of tahini or sesame butter.

BEETS *produce a bright-red color in a borscht or a beet salad. They combine well in a salad with fruit or other vegetables such as carrots and potatoes. Cook them in orange juice to retain their sweetness.*

BEET AND WHEAT SALAD

½ cup whole-wheat berries
1 bunch fresh
beets and greens
4 to 5 scallions
Handful curly parsley
1 Tbsp. oil
1 Tbsp. tamari soy sauce

USE: 2-quart saucepan
3-quart saucepan
YIELDS: 4 to 6 servings

In a 2-quart saucepan cook whole-wheat berries in 2 cups water. If using pressure cooker, cook for 40 to 50 minutes; otherwise, cook for 1½ to 2½ hours. Drain.

In a 3-quart saucepan cook unpeeled beets in water to cover until tender. Cut up beet leaves and stems; add to beets. Continue cooking until leaves wilt, drain and cool. Peel beets and cut into julienne strips. Slice scallions and chop parsley. Combine wheat berries and vegetables, including beet leaves and stems. Add oil and tamari soy sauce. Toss and chill. Adjust tamari soy sauce to taste.

BEET WALDORF SALAD

A salad made with raw beets — crunchy, colorful, and with the tang of fresh fruit.

2 large raw beets
1 medium green apple
1 large carrot
1 stalk celery
½ cup fresh pineapple,
cut into bite-sized chunks
¼ cup mayonnaise, diluted
with 1 Tbsp. pineapple juice
½ cup chopped walnuts
Juice of 1 lemon
2 Tbsps. sugar (optional)

USE: Large bowl
YIELDS: 4 servings

Peel beets, apple and carrot.

Coarsely grate beets and carrot into a large bowl. Chop apple and celery. Combine all ingredients and toss well.

Chill at least 20 minutes before serving.

HARVARD BEETS

3 medium beets
⅓ cup sugar
½ Tbsp. cornstarch
¼ cup lemon juice
6 Tbsps. beet liquid
2 Tbsps. margarine

USE: 3-quart saucepan
1½-quart saucepan
YIELDS: 4 servings

Place scrubbed whole, raw beets in 3-quart saucepan, cover with water and cook until tender. Slip skins off and slice. Reserve liquid.

In 1½ quart saucepan mix sugar and cornstarch well. Stir in lemon juice and beet liquid. Boil this mixture for 5 minutes.

Add sliced beets and stir until coated. Allow to stand for at least 30 minutes.

Before serving, add margarine and reheat.

CLASSIC BEET VINAIGRETTE

A Russian potato and beet salad with vinaigrette dressing is often served as a side dish at a Kiddush.

8 medium potatoes
3 carrots
6 medium beets
4 scallions
3 sour pickles

DRESSING
1 Tbsp. salt
3 Tbsps. sugar
**⅓ cup vinegar
or lemon juice**
¼ cup oil
¼ tsp. pepper

USE: 4-quart pot
YIELDS: 12 servings

Scrub potatoes, carrots, and beets and place in a 4-quart pot. Cover vegetables with water and cook until soft. Potatoes and carrots will become tender before the beets. Remove them and continue to cook beets.

Let vegetables cool, and peel; cut potatoes and beets into cubes. Peel and dice carrots, scallions, and pickles and then mix all vegetables together in a large mixing bowl.

Mix together dressing ingredients, add to vegetables and toss well. Potatoes will take on a red appearance. Chill and serve.

STEAMED VEGETABLES VINAIGRETTE

Broccoli, green beans, and chickpeas are original additions to the traditional Russian beet and potato salad.

2 medium beets
1 large broccoli
3 medium carrots
1 cup green beans
½ cup water
1 16-ounce can chickpeas
**1 cup diced
cooked potatoes**
1 green pepper, diced
1 red pepper, diced
½ bunch scallions, diced

DRESSING
1 cup vegetable oil
½ cup cider vinegar
1 to 2 cloves garlic, minced
¼ tsp. thyme
¼ tsp. oregano
¼ tsp. rosemary
⅛ tsp. white pepper
⅛ cup soy sauce

USE: Vegetable steamer
YIELDS: 10 servings

Prepare the first 4 ingredients in the following way: Peel beets and cut into thin julienne strips. Thoroughly wash broccoli and cut into 1-inch pieces. Peel carrots and slice thin. Wash and trim ends of green beans; slice diagonally into ½-inch pieces.

Using a vegetable steamer lightly steam beets, broccoli, carrots, and green beans.

In a large bowl, combine steamed vegetables with chickpeas, potatoes, and raw vegetables.

In a shaker bottle or blender, combine dressing ingredients. Toss vegetables with dressing while still warm.

Chill before serving.

BROCCOLI *is served raw or cooked. It adds distinction to a salad and lends itself to any number of sauces, including vinaigrette. Peel the stalk for more tenderness. In Broccoli and Cauliflower Salad the contrast of colors and textures is appealing to the eye and the palate. For information on checking broccoli see page 259.*

BROCCOLI AND CAULIFLOWER SALAD

A crisp, colorful raw vegetable salad.

**1 large broccoli
1 medium cauliflower
2 to 3 medium carrots
2 zucchini
4 scallions**

**DRESSING
¼ cup oil
⅓ to ½ cup vinegar
1 tsp. salt
1 Tbsp. sugar
2 cloves garlic, minced
⅓ tsp. pepper**

USE: Large mixing bowl
YIELDS: 8 to 10 servings

Thoroughly wash broccoli and cauliflower; cut into florets, then place in a large bowl.

Peel and slice carrots; add to bowl. Dice zucchini and scallions and add to vegetables.

Mix dressing ingredients. Pour over vegetables in bowl and toss.

Serve chilled.

BROCCOLI AND OLIVE SALAD

**1 large broccoli
½ cup diced black olives
6 radishes**

**DRESSING
9 Tbsps. olive oil
3 Tbsps. wine vinegar
1 tsp. salt
¾ tsp. pepper
¼ tsp. dry mustard**

**2 tomatoes,
sliced into wedges
½ cup Spanish nuts or
peanuts**

USE: Large mixing bowl
YIELDS: 6 servings

Thoroughly wash and cut broccoli into florets, then place in large mixing bowl. Add olives and radishes.

Mix dressing ingredients together and add to vegetables.

Garnish with tomato wedges and Spanish nuts.

CABBAGE *can serve as the base of a raw salad or may be sauteed with a sweet-and-sour sauce. It is also a good addition to a variety of stir-fried vegetables served over rice. Red Cabbage has a similar texture to its green ''cousin.'' Its color adds a nice contrast in raw salads or coleslaw. Cook it also with a sweet-and-sour sauce for variety. For information on checking cabbage see page 259.*

SAUTEED CABBAGE

2 large onions, diced
2 Tbsps. oil
1 head green cabbage
1 tsp. salt
½ tsp. pepper

USE: 10-inch skillet
YIELDS: 8 servings

In a 10-inch skillet saute onions in oil until golden brown. Cut cabbage in large slices and stir-fry for 15 minutes over medium flame. Add salt and pepper.

Serve either warm or cold as a side dish.

VARIATIONS
□ **Dairy:** Top with sour cream.

□ **Cabbage Strudel:** Shred cabbage finely and saute 1 hour on small flame, stirring occasionally. Fill strudel leaves and bake at 350° until golden brown, about 45 minutes.

SWEET-AND-SOUR-CABBAGE, PEKING STYLE

1 small head green cabbage
1 tsp. salt
2 Tbsps. sugar
½ tsp. cornstarch
2 Tbsps. soy sauce
2 Tbsps. vinegar
3 Tbsps. corn oil
1 clove garlic

USE: Wok
YIELDS: 4 to 6 servings

Cut cabbage into quarters, and remove core. Cut each quarter into 1-inch chunks; separate leaves. Combine salt, sugar, cornstarch, soy sauce, and vinegar.

Heat wok and add oil. Add garlic and brown slightly. Remove garlic and discard. Add cabbage to hot oil, and stir-fry over high heat for a few seconds. Lower heat slightly and continue to stir-fry for a few minutes. Add soy-sauce mixture to cabbage. Cook, stirring, until sauce is thickened well and blended with cabbage.

Serve immediately.

CRUNCHY CABBAGE AND RICE SALAD

1 large head of cabbage
(green or a combination
of green and purple)
2 large MacIntosh apples
¾ cup chopped walnuts
2 cups cooked brown rice
¾ cup raisins

DRESSING
¾ cup mayonnaise
⅓ cup honey

USE: Large salad bowl
YIELDS: 8 servings

Shred or grate cabbage as desired and place in a large bowl. Peel and finely dice apples; add. Add walnuts, rice and raisins. Combine well.

Make dressing by mixing mayonnaise and honey. Pour over vegetables and toss lightly.

Serve chilled.

BASIC COLESLAW

This classic dish is popular as either a relish or a side dish. It is commonly served at simchot, such as a Kiddush. The following recipe is for the basic coleslaw with two different dressings to choose from.

**1 medium head
green cabbage**

2 large carrots, grated

1 green pepper, slivered

1 onion, minced (optional)

DRESSING

¾ cup mayonnaise

**⅓ cup vinegar or
lemon juice**

1 tsp. salt

2 Tbsps. sugar

4 Tbsps. warm water

COLESLAW MARINADE

2 Tbsps. coarse salt

1 cup vinegar

2 cups water

½ cup sugar

1 tsp. black pepper

2 Tbsps. mayonnaise

USE: Large salad bowl
YIELDS: 10 to 12 servings

Shred or grate cabbage as desired. Combine vegetables in a large bowl.

In a separate smaller bowl combine ingredients of preferred dressing and mix well. Add dressing to vegetables and toss until coated. Cover and refrigerate until ready to serve. The taste improves if coleslaw stands in dressing for a few hours prior to serving.

COLESLAW MARINADE: Combine above vegetables in a large bowl and sprinkle with salt. Pour vinegar, water, and seasonings over vegetables. Add mayonnaise and mix well. Allow to marinate covered at least 1 hour in the refrigerator. Before serving remove coleslaw to serving bowl or container and drain off excess marinade.

NOTE: If onion is used, the coleslaw should be eaten within 2 to 3 days.

VARIATION
□ **Kohlrabi Salad:** Substitute 1 large bunch of kohlrabi for cabbage. Peel and grate. Dress and serve like cabbage.

CABBAGE WITH SPICY VINAIGRETTE

½ large head green cabbage

**2 medium green peppers,
thinly sliced**

1 small onion, grated

**1 6-ounce package radishes,
thinly sliced**

DRESSING

½ cup cider vinegar

**½ cup salad or
olive oil**

2 Tbsps. brown sugar

2 tsps. salt

1 tsp. dry mustard

1 tsp. ground cinnamon

½ tsp. ground allspice

¼ tsp. ground ginger

USE: Large salad bowl
YIELDS: 16 servings

Shred or grate cabbage as desired. Place in a large bowl. Add green peppers, onions, and radishes. Combine well.

Mix all dressing ingredients and pour over vegetables. Toss lightly.

Cover and refrigerate at least 2 hours to blend flavors.

SWEET-AND-SOUR PURPLE CABBAGE

Nutmeg is a natural complement to this unusual dish.

1 large purple cabbage
½ cup margarine
Salt to taste
Pepper to taste
1 tsp. nutmeg
3 Tbsps. white vinegar
3 Tbsps. brown sugar, or more to taste
1 cup raisins
2 cooking apples, cored, peeled, and cut into small pieces (about 2 cups)

USE: 5-quart Dutch oven
YIELDS: 6 to 8 servings

Preheat oven to 400°.

Cut away and discard the core of the cabbage; shred fine.

Heat margarine in a 5-quart Dutch oven. Add cabbage. Sprinkle with salt, pepper, and nutmeg. Add the vinegar, brown sugar, raisins, and diced apples. (Do not add any more liquid.) Cover pot, bring to a boil, and cook about 10 minutes, stirring occasionally. Remove from heat and place in the oven; bake, covered, 1½ hours, stirring occasionally.

If desired, add more nutmeg and brown sugar to taste.

CARROTS *are a staple ingredient in many cuisines. Their color, texture, and flavor enhance many dishes and they are available year round. Whether grated, marinated, or cooked in a traditional tzimmes, carrots will appeal to a variety of tastes. The Pareve Tzimmes has the unusual addition of cinnamon and orange juice to accent the taste of the carrots and sweet potato.*

PAREVE TZIMMES WITH KNAIDEL

3 Tbsps. oil
2 onions, diced
3 to 4 cloves garlic, sliced
2 pounds carrots, sliced diagonally
3 sweet potatoes, diced
1 stick cinnamon
½ to 1 cup orange juice

KNAIDEL
4 eggs
¼ cup oil
¾ cup boiled water
Salt to taste
Pepper to taste
1 tsp. baking powder
1 to 1½ cups matzoh meal

USE: 4-quart pot
YIELDS: 8 servings

In a 4-quart pot, heat oil, then add onions and saute. Add garlic and saute until soft and slightly browned.

Add carrots, sweet potatoes, and cinnamon stick. Add orange juice.

KNAIDEL: Mix all ingredients together except matzoh meal. Mix until well blended. Then gradually add the matzoh meal until thick. Form into a loaf, and place in pot over vegetables.

Cook, covered, over a very low flame for 1 hour. Stir occasionally to make sure it does not stick.

Serve hot.

BABY CARROTS IN HAWAIIAN CHERRY SAUCE

An excellent tzimmes *for Rosh Hoshanah or an ideal side dish for a* simchah.

3 16-ounce cans small, whole baby carrots, with liquid
1 10-ounce can maraschino cherries, well drained
1 16-ounce can unsweetened pineapple chunks or tidbits, with juice
3 cinnamon sticks
½ tsp. lemon juice
¼ cup sugar
2-3 Tbsps. cornstarch
¾ cup cold water

USE: 4-quart pot
YIELDS: 8 to 10 servings

Combine all ingredients except cornstarch and water in a 4-quart pot. Bring to a boil.

In a separate bowl combine cornstarch gradually with cold water. Mix well to make sure there are no lumps; it should be very smooth. Pour into boiling carrots, stirring gently. Cook about 3 minutes or until just slightly thickened.

STIR-FRIED CARROTS AND CELERY

4 carrots
4 stalks celery
2 to 3 Tbsps. margarine
Dash salt
½ Tbsp. ground ginger or ½-inch piece of fresh ginger, diced
1 Tbsp. sugar

USE: 10-inch skillet
YIELDS: 4 servings

Peel carrots and trim ends. Cut into julienne strips. Wash and trim ends of celery. Cut into julienne strips. Heat margarine in 10-inch skillet. Add carrots, celery, seasonings and sugar.

Stir-fry 10 to 15 minutes or more, over a low to medium flame. Cook until lightly tender.

Serve hot.

CARROT WALNUT SALAD

5 to 6 carrots
3 Tbsps. mayonnaise
1 tsp. sugar
1 tsp. cinnamon
1 tsp. vanilla extract (optional)
2 Tbsps. freshly squeezed lemon juice
¼ cup chopped walnuts
¼ cup raisins

USE: Medium bowl
YIELDS: 4 to 6 servings

Peel carrots and trim ends. Grate or shred carrots. Add remaining ingredients and toss very well. Serve cold.

VARIATIONS
□ Add 2 diced apples or 1 cup crushed pineapple. Omit lemon juice.

□ **Dairy:** Substitute sour cream for mayonnaise. Omit lemon juice.

EASY YOM TOV TZIMMES

1 tsp. oil
4 to 6 carrots, sliced
1 large sweet potato, cubed
2 to 3 tsps. honey or
4 Tbsps. sugar
¼ cup orange juice
Dash of salt
2 slices pineapple,
cut into pieces
½ tsp. nutmeg (optional)

USE: 2-quart saucepan
YIELDS: 4 servings

Coat bottom of 2-quart saucepan with oil and heat. Add carrots and cook on low heat for about 10 to 15 minutes. Add sweet potato, honey, orange juice, and dash of salt. Cook over low flame for 30 minutes.

Add pineapple and nutmeg, if desired. After 5 minutes, remove from heat. Serve warm.

SWEET POTATO AND CARROT TZIMMES

1 pound carrots
6 sweet potatoes
½ cup pitted prunes
(optional)
1 cup orange juice
½ cup honey or brown sugar
½ tsp. salt
¼ tsp. cinnamon
2 Tbsps. margarine
1 20-ounce can pineapple
chunks, drained
1 11-ounce can mandarin
oranges, drained

USE: 3-quart saucepan
3-quart casserole
YIELDS: 8 servings

Peel carrots and cut into 1-inch slices. Peel and slice sweet potatoes into ½-inch slices. In a 3-quart saucepan cook carrots and sweet potatoes in boiling, salted water to cover, until tender but firm. Drain carrots and sweet potatoes and place in 3-quart casserole with prunes. Combine gently.

Preheat oven to 350°.

Mix orange juice, honey, salt, and cinnamon. Pour evenly over casserole. Dot top with margarine. Bake, covered, for 30 minutes. Uncover, stir gently, add pineapple chunks and mandarin oranges and bake another 10 minutes.

VARIATION
□ Cook ingredients listed, in pot, using juice from pineapple and mandarin oranges in place of water.

STEAMED CARROT AND ZUCCHINI SALAD

2 large carrots
2 medium zucchini

DRESSING
½ cup corn oil
¼ cup cider vinegar
¾ tsp. salt
¼ tsp. pepper
¼ tsp. dried tarragon
¼ tsp. dried basil
⅛ to ¼ tsp. oregano

USE: 2-quart saucepan
YIELDS: 4 servings

Peel and slice carrots diagonally into ¼-inch slices. Slice zucchini into ¼-inch slices. Cook carrots in 1 cup boiling water 3 minutes. Add zucchini and cook 2 more minutes. Drain vegetables well.

In small bowl, combine oil, vinegar, seasonings, and spices. Mix well. Pour over hot vegetables, cover and chill. Serve as side dish as is, or over lettuce leaves.

CAULIFLOWER's *shape and color provide interesting variety. Broken into florets they can be marinated, dipped into a tempura batter and fried, or added to a salad. In the Cauliflower Salad, the red pimientos, black olives, and white cauliflower offer a stark contrast of colors and textures. For information on checking cauliflower see page 259.*

MARINATED CAULIFLOWER

1 medium cauliflower
¾ cup oil
2 Tbsps. fresh lemon juice
1 clove garlic, minced
3 Tbsps. chopped shallots
1 tsp. salt
¼ tsp. sugar
⅛ tsp. pepper
1 tsp. parsley flakes
6 Tbsps. red wine vinegar
1 Tbsp. white vinegar

USE: 1½-quart saucepan
YIELDS: 6 servings

Thoroughly wash cauliflower and cut into florets.

Boil florets in 1 inch of water for 7 minutes, or until tender. Allow to cool. Combine remaining ingredients in large jar and shake well. Pour over cauliflower and toss well.

Refrigerate overnight. Stir occasionally.

Serve in relish dish.

CAULIFLOWER SALAD

An excellent side dish for all meat dishes.

1½ to 2 cups thinly sliced cauliflower
½ cup coarsely chopped ripe black olives
¼ cup drained and chopped pimientos
¼ cup minced green onions
4 Tbsps. oil
2 to 3 Tbsps. vinegar
1 tsp. salt
½ tsp. pepper
Pinch of marjoram
Pinch of oregano
5 cups shredded salad greens

USE: Salad bowl
YIELDS: 6 servings

Put cauliflower, olives, pimientos, and green onions in a large salad bowl. Add oil and vinegar.

Add salt, pepper, marjoram, and oregano. Toss. Add greens and toss again.

CHICKPEAS, *of Middle Eastern origin, have found their way into Jewish cuisine through Israeli cooking. Hoummous and Falafel are the best known Israeli versions. Hoummous is a thick dip of pureed cooked chickpeas with tahini, lemon juice, garlic, and water. Falafel are deep-fried balls of ground chickpeas, usually eaten with pita, the round Israeli bread. Chickpeas are also especially tasty in cold salads with a variety of spices. Soaking the chickpeas first will shorten the cooking time.*

CHICKPEA SALAD

½ pound dried chickpeas,
cooked, or 2 16-ounce
cans chickpeas
1 medium onion, chopped
½ cup chopped
sweet red pepper
½ cup chopped green pepper

DRESSING
1 cup cider vinegar
½ cup olive or
vegetable oil
1 tsp. oregano
1 tsp. salt
¼ tsp. pepper
½ tsp. garlic powder

USE: Large salad bowl
YIELDS: 4 servings

Combine all vegetables in a large bowl, mix well.

Mix dressing ingredients, pour over vegetables. Toss lightly and serve.

SAVORY BAKED CHICKPEAS

1 cup dried or
2 cups cooked chickpeas
2 to 3 Tbsps. oil
1 onion, diced
2 cloves garlic, minced
1 green pepper, diced
1 16-ounce can
peeled tomatoes, chopped,
or 4 diced tomatoes
plus ¼ cup tomato juice
½ tsp. salt
Dash of pepper
Basil to taste
Tarragon to taste
Parsley to taste

USE: 3-quart saucepan
10-inch skillet
2 quart-casserole
YIELDS: 4 to 6 servings

Soak dried chickpeas overnight in water. Drain, add fresh water to cover and cook in a 3-quart saucepan for 1 hour or until soft but firm. Drain again.

Preheat oven to 325°.

In heated oil, saute onion and garlic in 10-inch skillet. Add other ingredients and drained chickpeas. Mix well.

Place in 2-quart casserole and bake, covered, for 1 hour.

Serve either warm or cold.

NOTE: This dish can also be cooked over a low flame for 1 hour. Use 5-quart Dutch oven instead of skillet.

VARIATION
☐ Add 1 cup cooked wheat berries or bulgur wheat.

ARBIS

This basic chickpea dish is traditionally served at a Shalom Zachar.

4 pounds dried chickpeas
4 Tbsps. salt
2 tsps. white pepper

USE: 8-quart pot
YIELDS: 6 to 8 quarts

Begin a day in advance, if possible. Rinse the chickpeas thoroughly to remove any dirt or foreign particles. In a large bowl, cover with a liberal quantity of water and soak uncovered a minimum of 2 hours. This serves to soften and enlarge the chickpeas.

Drain chickpeas in a colander. Put into an 8-quart pot, filling with water to cover. Add salt and pepper; cook for about 3 hours or until skins begin to peel. Do not overcook.

While still warm, drain thoroughly in a colander. Place in a large bowl until ready to serve. Adjust seasoning to taste.

Refrigerate as soon as cooled and keep in refrigerator until immediately before serving. Serve in round bowls.

VARIATION
□ **Super-Quick Pressure-Cooker Method:** Soak chickpeas in a large pot of water for 2 hours. Then place 2 pounds of chickpeas and one-half of the seasoning into a 6-quart pressure cooker. Cover with just enough water to barely cover. Cook for 10 minutes after pressure goes up. Then run pressure cooker under cold water until pot cools down. Drain chickpeas. Repeat with remaining 2 pounds chickpeas and seasonings. This method will prevent skin of chickpeas from falling off due to overcooking.

GARDEN CHICKPEA SALAD

A new twist to the classic vegetable salad ingredients, tossed with chickpeas instead of lettuce. Result: crunchy taste and good eye appeal. Begin at least 4 hours before serving.

1½ cups dried chickpeas,
cooked
1 to 2 tomatoes, diced
1 cucumber, diced
4 radishes, finely diced
2 scallions, minced or
2 Tbsps. red onion, minced
1 Tbsp. cider vinegar
1 Tbsp. lemon juice
8 Tbsps. vegetable oil
¼ tsp. dry mustard
1 to 2 cloves garlic, minced
2 Tbsps. fresh parsley,
minced
Salt and pepper to taste

USE: Large salad bowl
YIELDS: 4 to 6 servings

In large bowl, place chickpeas and remaining ingredients. Mix well.

Chill at least 2 hours before serving.

FALAFEL

An Israeli fast food specialty. High in protein and very tasty.

2 cups dried or 4 cups cooked and drained chickpeas
3 cloves garlic, minced
2 Tbsps. parsley
2 Tbsps. lemon juice
3 Tbsps. tahini
½ tsp. turmeric
½ tsp. cumin
1 tsp. black pepper
1½ tsps. salt
2 eggs
4 Tbsps. bread crumbs

USE: 4-quart pot
10-inch skillet
YIELDS: 40 balls

Soak dried chickpeas overnight. Rinse and drain. Cook in a 4-quart pot 1½ to 2 hours until very soft. Drain chickpeas in a colander.

Place chickpeas in a food processor. Add all ingredients except bread crumbs and process. Or grind chickpeas through a meat grinder with garlic and parsley. Place in a large bowl and add other ingredients except bread crumbs.

Add bread crumbs to make mixture stiff enough to form into balls. Cover bowl and chill mixture for at least 1 hour.

Form falafel balls with wet hands using 1 tablespoon of mixture. Heat about 1½ inches of oil in a 10-inch skillet to hot. Fry balls until golden about a dozen at a time. Drain on absorbent paper.

Serving Suggestion: Serve in pita bread pockets with diced vegetable salad, and tahini sauce mixed with lemon juice and garlic powder. Sauerkraut and hot sauce are optional.

EGGPLANT *has been introduced to America from European and Mideastern cuisines. Its bland taste and soft, smooth texture are an excellent base in casseroles, dips, and side dishes. A firm, unblemished skin indicates a fresh, white interior. Before frying eggplant, slice and salt it to draw out the bitter taste; rinse well and pat dry. Eggplant can be served in a variety of ways in salads and cold side dishes, which are popular on Shabbat and Yom Tov. It also combines well with other sauteed vegetables. Ratatouille is a lovely blend of vegetables which are seasoned, sauteed, and simmered in a tomato sauce.*

EGGPLANT SALAD

3 medium eggplants, unpeeled
1 cup salt
4 cups water
¼ cup vinegar

DRESSING
¾ cup olive oil
2 cloves garlic, minced
Dash of pepper

USE: 3-quart saucepan
YIELDS: 8 to 10 servings

Wash the unpeeled eggplants and cut into match-stick size pieces. Put in a plastic colander and sprinkle with 1 cup salt. Let drain for 5 to 6 hours, pressing occasionally to help drain out the liquid.

In a 3-quart saucepan combine water with vinegar and bring to a boil. Add drained eggplant and cook 1 minute. Eggplant should be completely covered. Add more water if necessary. Remove from fire and let eggplant steep in water for 5 minutes. Drain eggplant in colander again.

Combine ingredients for dressing in a glass or plastic container. Add drained eggplant and mix well. Chill and serve.

VARIATION
☐ **Eggplant Pate:** Combine cooked eggplant with ¼ cup mayonnaise and run through the blender until thick.

EGGPLANT-TOMATO SALAD

1 medium ripe eggplant
1 small onion, minced
¼ cup olive or vegetable oil
1 large clove garlic, minced
3 canned tomatoes, pureed,
or 3 fresh peeled and
cooked tomatoes, pureed, or
3 to 4 Tbsps. tomato puree
Salt to taste
Pepper to taste
Lemon juice to taste

GARNISHES
Fresh parley
Cherry tomatoes
Black olives

USE: 10-inch skillet
YIELDS: 4 servings

Cook eggplant over an open medium to low flame, turning it every few minutes with a fork until the outside is evenly charred and the inside is tender, from 20 to 30 minutes. Remove from fire and cool. Peel eggplant and either chop fine or grind.

In a 10-inch skillet saute minced onion in olive or vegetable oil until soft. Add garlic. Stir in eggplant and tomato puree. Simmer over very low flame for 30 minutes, adding more oil if necessary to prevent scorching. Stir frequently. Season to taste with salt, pepper, and lemon juice. Put into bowl and cover. Chill in refrigerator.

Decorate with garnishes and serve with pita bread.

VARIATION
□ Remove stem from eggplant and cut in half vertically. Brush cut sides of eggplant with oil and place cut side down on aluminum foil. Broil about 4 inches below heating element until skin is charred and flesh is tender.

MARINATED EGGPLANT

1 eggplant
Salt
½ to ¾ cup oil
Approximately ¾ cup vinegar
Approximately ¾ cup water
½ bulb garlic
½ tsp. salt

USE: 10-inch skillet
YIELDS: 4 servings

Wash eggplant. Slice crosswise about ¼ inch thick or less. Sprinkle salt over slices and let stand for about 15 minutes. Rinse off salt with cold water and pat dry. Heat oil in 10-inch skillet and saute eggplant on both sides until soft. Drain on paper towels and place in bowl. Mix equal parts vinegar to water until mixture covers eggplant.

Mince garlic and put into liquid. Add ½ teaspoon salt. Cover and let marinate for 24 hours.

SZECHUAN EGGPLANT

1 pound eggplant,
firm and shiny
1 tsp. toasted sesame oil
½ cup corn oil
1 large clove garlic, minced
1 Tbsp. minced
fresh ginger root

Wash and remove stem of eggplant. Cut eggplant into 2-inch fingerlike strips. Heat a wok until hot. Add oils. When oil is hot, add eggplant. Stir-fry for about 15 to 20 minutes or until eggplant is soft. Remove eggplant.

Reheat wok. Add garlic and ginger. Stir and add sauce ingredients. Bring sauce to a boil. When sauce has come to a boil, add eggplant; cook and stir until thick. Serve hot or at room temperature.

►

SAUCE

2 tsps. vinegar
½ tsp. salt
2 tsps. sugar
1 Tbsp. soy sauce
1 cup water
1 Tbsp. corn starch

USE: Wok or 10-inch skillet
YIELDS: 4 to 6 servings

VARIATION
□ For spicier eggplant, hot pepper sesame oil can be used in place of toasted sesame oil.

RATATOUILLE

Sauteed eggplant cubes with vegetables. For best flavor, do not overcook.

1 large eggplant
2 medium zucchini
1 large onion
1 large green pepper
¼ cup olive oil
2 cloves garlic, minced
3 tomatoes, chopped, or
5 Tbsps. tomato paste
plus 3 Tbsps. water
1 tsp. salt
⅛ tsp. pepper
½ tsp. basil
½ tsp. oregano

USE: 3-quart saucepan
YIELDS: 6 to 8 servings

Cut the eggplant into 1-inch cubes. Slice the zucchini into 1-inch rounds. Chop onion coarsely and cut green pepper into small squares. Heat the olive oil and saute the onion, green pepper, and garlic in a 3-quart saucepan with a lid. Stir in eggplant and zucchini and saute a few additional minutes. Add tomato and seasonings.

Cover and simmer gently for 30 minutes or until all vegetables are well cooked. Uncover and turn up heat to evaporate excess liquid.

VARIATIONS
□ **Kabatchki:** Omit zucchini, basil, oregano, and garlic. Add ¼ cup granulated or brown sugar. Omit tomatoes. Use only tomato sauce or ketchup.

□ When serving cold, sprinkle with additional basil or minced parsley.

□ Add 2 sliced carrots with green pepper and allow to saute 10 minutes. Add 6 sliced mushrooms together with tomatoes at end. Add juice of 1 lemon and 2 tablespoons water. Can be baked in covered dish for 45 minutes.

OLIVE AND EGGPLANT SALAD

1 medium eggplant
4 Tbsps. olive oil
1 medium tomato
4 black olives
4 green olives
1 sour pickle
½ tsp. red cayenne pepper
1 Tbsp. dried parsley
2 cloves garlic, minced
3 Tbsps. lemon juice
1 tsp. salt

USE: 10-inch skillet
YIELDS: 4 servings

Peel eggplant; trim ends. Slice and cut into cubes. Sprinkle eggplant with salt and allow to stand 30 minutes. Drain, rinse, and pat dry. Heat oil in 10-inch skillet and saute eggplant until browned. Allow to cool.

Dice tomato, olives, and pickle. Place in large bowl and add fried eggplant. Add cayenne pepper, parsley, and garlic. Mix well. Sprinkle with lemon juice and salt.

Serve cold.

MARINATED MUSHROOMS

These slightly pink mushrooms add an elegant accent to any main course.

**1 pound fresh mushrooms,
whole**

MARINADE
¾ cup salad oil
¾ cup red wine vinegar
¼ cup finely chopped onion
¼ cup finely chopped parsley
1 tsp. salt
1 tsp. sugar

USE: 2-quart covered bowl
YIELDS: 6 servings

Peel mushrooms or wash well.

Place mushrooms in large mixing bowl. Combine marinade ingredients and pour over mushrooms. Refrigerate covered for 1 hour.

If desired, mushrooms can be sliced.

ORIENTAL MUSHROOMS

Oriental Mushrooms make a fine side dish to complement any meat or chicken dish.

**1 pound whole,
fresh mushrooms**
3 Tbsps. oil
1 medium onion, diced
3 tsps. flour
½ cup water
**3 tsps. brown gravy mix
or 1 bouillon cube**
1½ Tbsps. soy sauce

USE: 10-inch skillet
YIELDS: 4 to 6 servings

Peel mushrooms or wash well; slice and set aside. Heat oil in 10-inch skillet and saute onion until transparent. Add mushrooms and saute while stirring. Sprinkle flour over the mushrooms and stir well. Add water and stir in gravy mix and soy sauce.

Simmer over medium heat for 5 minutes.

NOTE: If using bouillon cubes, add 2 extra teaspoons flour.

SIMPLE REFRIGERATOR PICKLES

Prepare these delicious pickles at least 5 days in advance.

4 cups sugar
4 cups vinegar
½ cup salt
1⅓ tsps. turmeric
1⅓ tsps. celery seed
1⅓ tsps. mustard seed
**3 medium onions,
thinly sliced**
10 pounds kirbys, unpeeled

USE: 3 1-quart jars
YIELDS: 3 1-quart jars

Mix sugar, vinegar, salt, and spices together. Place 1 sliced onion in each of three sterilized jars. Wash the kirbys well, slice thin, and fill the three jars with the slices. Pour the sugar-vinegar syrup over the kirbys. Screw on lids.

Store in refrigerator at least 5 days before using. These pickles will keep 2 to 3 months in the refrigerator.

DILL PICKLES

10 small kirbys, unpeeled
½ bunch fresh dill
4 to 5 garlic cloves,
cut in half
1 Tbsp. pickling spices
⅓ cup salt
1 Tbsp. vinegar
Water to cover

USE: 1 2-quart canning jar
YIELDS: 1 2-quart jar

Wash kirbys very well. They should be approximately 1 inch in diameter; if larger, cut them in half. Cut stems. Place dill, garlic, pickling spices, salt, and vinegar into sterilized jar. Then, put kirbys into jar and fill jar with boiling water. Cover tightly.

Place jar in a dark room or closet. Pickles will be half sour in 1 week, completely sour in 2 weeks.

PEARL ONIONS

3 Tbsps. oil
1 pound frozen pearl onions
2 Tbsps. vinegar
2 Tbsps. brown sugar

USE: 10-inch skillet
YIELDS: 4 servings

Place 3 tablespoons oil in 10-inch skillet and simmer onions on a low flame for 7 to 10 minutes. Meanwhile, combine vinegar and brown sugar in a small bowl.

When onions are done, turn off flame and pour vinegar and sugar mixture over onions. Stir until just coated. Serve immediately.

DEEP-FRIED ONION RINGS

The delicious flavor and aroma of crunchy onion rings!

6 medium (2½ pounds)
Bermuda onions
Ice water

BATTER
1 egg, lightly beaten
1 cup nondairy creamer
¼ tsp. salt
3 Tbsps. oil
1 cup plus 2 Tbsps.
all-purpose flour
Cooking oil
for deep-fat frying

USE: 2 to 3-quart saucepan
YIELDS: 6 to 8 servings

Peel and cut onions into ¼-inch-thick slices. Separate into rings. Soak in ice water for at least 2 hours, then drain and dry thoroughly.

In a medium bowl, combine beaten egg, creamer, salt, and 3 tablespoons oil. Blend in flour, stirring just until moistened.

Fill deep fryer or saucepan one third to one half full with oil. Heat to 375°. Using a fork, dip onion rings one at a time in batter to cover; remove and let excess batter drip back into bowl. Working quickly, place each ring in the hot oil. Fry rings, a few at a time, on both sides, about 2 to 3 minutes, or until golden brown. Make sure rings remain separate. Remove from oil with slotted spoon. Drain on paper towels.

Repeat with remaining batter and onions. Keep cooked onion rings warm on a paper towel-lined baking sheet in a 250° oven. Sprinkle with salt before serving.

CAUTION: Keep oil temperature at 375°. Wait a few seconds between batches.

PINEAPPLE FRITTERS

Pineapple dipped in a smooth batter and lightly fried will complement any main course.

**10 slices freshly cored
pineapple or
1 16-ounce can
pineapple rings**

**BATTER
2 eggs
3-4 Tbsps. water
½ cup flour
1 tsp. baking powder
Pinch of salt
1 Tbsp. sugar
Oil for frying**

USE: 10-inch skillet
YIELDS: 10 fritters

Pat pineapple slices dry.

BATTER: In a large bowl mix liquid ingredients and flour with baking powder, salt, and sugar until smooth and creamy. Add 3 to 4 tablespoons of water.

In a 10-inch skillet heat oil ⅛-inch deep until hot.

Dip fruit into batter to coat both sides. Fry over medium flame approximately 1 minute on each side.

VARIATION
□ This batter is excellent for apple fritters (apples should be peeled, cored, and sliced) and also for zucchini fritters. Cut unpeeled zucchini into ¼-inch-wide slices. Fry two to three minutes per side. When using vegetables, omit sugar and add ½ teaspoon salt, and pepper to taste.

PICKLED GREEN PEPPERS

**8 small,
firm green peppers
1½ cups vinegar
1½ cups water
⅓ to ½ cup sugar
4 Tbsps. oil
Dash salt
2 bay leaves**

USE: 1-quart jar
YIELDS: 8 servings

Wash green peppers and place on baking sheet in 350° oven until skin wrinkles. Remove from oven and submerge in cold water. Peel the peppers.

Mix the remaining ingredients together and put in a glass jar. Add the green peppers and let marinate at least 24 hours before serving.

SWEET RED PEPPERS

**15 red peppers
1 cup oil
2 tsps. salt
1 cup vinegar
½ cup sugar**

USE: 6-quart pot
YIELDS: 25 to 30 servings

Cut the peppers into thin, round slices.

In a 6-quart pot, heat the oil. Add the peppers, salt, vinegar, and sugar. Stir well. Let simmer over low flame for 30 minutes or until peppers are soft. Stir once while cooking.

Put peppers into a glass jar. If kept tightly covered in refrigerator, peppers can be stored for up to 1 month.

POTATOES *are probably the most versatile of all vegetables. They are filling, nutritious, and inexpensive. Potato Salad is a popular side dish with several variations offered here. The Potato Zucchini Salad is a colorful, novel salad with a sharp and tangy taste. The sweet potato, a close relative of its plainer cousin, has a sweet flavor and bright orange hue. Whether baked or combined with fruits, vegetables, and spices, it perks up any meal.*

SPECIAL POTATO SALAD

A potato salad with an original flavor.

3 pounds potatoes, unpeeled
3 scallions
4 pickles

DRESSING
2 Tbsps. mayonnaise
2 Tbsps. olive oil
2 Tbsps. apple cider vinegar
Juice of ½ lemon
2 Tbsps. pickle juice

USE: 4-quart pot
YIELDS: 10 servings

Place unpeeled potatoes in 4-quart pot filled with water and cook until soft for approximately 40 minutes. Do not overcook. Rinse, peel and dice while still warm. Place in a large bowl.

In a small bowl, mix mayonnaise, oil, vinegar, lemon juice, and pickle juice. Chop scallions and pickles; add to mixture.

Pour dressing over diced potatoes. Mix well. Place in refrigerator and chill overnight.

SIMCHAH POTATO SALAD

This is a decorative potato salad to please a crowd.

10 pounds baking potatoes, preferably California or Idaho, unpeeled
1 bunch scallions, chopped, or 2 medium onions, finely chopped
1 or 2 carrots, grated
1 green pepper, chopped
10 black olives, chopped
6 to 8 eggs, hard-boiled and chopped
2 stalks celery, chopped (optional)

DRESSING
2 Tbsps. vinegar
3 tsps. salt
1 tsp. pepper
1 tsp. dry mustard
2 tsps. sugar
2 cups mayonnaise
1 Tbsp. dry white wine (optional)

USE: 10-quart pot
YIELDS: 30 servings

Place unpeeled potatoes in 10-quart pot. Fill with water to cover and cook until soft, about 1 hour. Do not overcook. Rinse, peel, and dice while still warm into 1-inch cubes. Place in a large bowl.

Combine vegetables with potatoes; add olives and chopped eggs and celery if desired.

In a separate bowl, mix dressing ingredients until well blended. Seasoning may be adjusted according to your personal taste. Pour dressing over potato salad and mix gently until coated.

Chill until ready to serve.

Garnish with red or green pepper rings, carrot curls, or tomato wedges.

CLASSIC POTATO SALAD

3 pounds potatoes, unpeeled
1 large green pepper, finely diced
1 large carrot, finely grated
2 pickles, finely diced
2 scallions

DRESSING
6 heaping Tbsps. mayonnaise
1 tsp. salt
½ tsp. garlic powder
¼ tsp. pepper
2 Tbsps. lemon juice
½ tsp. dry mustard (optional)

USE: 4-quart pot
YIELDS: 8 servings

Place unpeeled potatoes in 4 quart pot. Cover and cook for approximately 40 minutes. Rinse in cold water.

While potatoes are still warm, peel and cube. Combine with other vegetables in a large bowl.

In a small bowl, combine dressing ingredients. Mix until smooth. Pour dressing over potato mixture and mix until thoroughly coated.

May be served warm or cold.

VARIATION
□ Add 1 cup cooked peas and carrots to above, or substitute for pickles and scallions.

POTATO-ZUCCHINI SALAD

Potato salad with a new twist.

8 medium potatoes, unpeeled
4 medium zucchini
1 pound string beans (optional)

DRESSING
1 small red onion, chopped
2 cloves garlic, minced
½ cup olive oil
⅓ cup red wine vinegar
Salt and pepper to taste

USE: 2 4-quart pots
YIELDS: 12 servings

Place unpeeled potatoes into pot with cold water. Cover, bring to a boil and cook until just tender, about 40 minutes. Remove skins and cut into large cubes.

Wash zucchini and cube. When using string beans, trim ends, and cut into ½-inch slices. Place in another pot, add 1-inch water, and bring to a boil. Simmer 5 minutes until tender-crisp. Drain immediately. Combine potatoes, zucchini, and string beans.

Combine salad dressing ingredients and pour over into salad. Toss.

Serve warm or cold.

VARIATION
□ Add olives and red peppers; top with cherry tomatoes.

FRENCH FRIES

4 to 5 large potatoes
Ice water
Oil for frying
Salt to taste

USE: 10-inch skillet
YIELDS: 4 servings

Peel potatoes, rinse off, and dry well. Cut into thin, round slices or into long julienne strips. Place in ice water for 30 minutes. Drain and dry well.

Heat generous amount of oil in 10-inch skillet. Gently add potatoes to hot oil, and fry over medium flame, for 7 to 10 minutes. With spatula, turn potatoes to other side and fry until crisp, another 5 to 10 minutes. Remove potatoes onto plate covered with paper towels to drain off excess oil. Sprinkle with salt. Serve warm.

POTATO LATKES

By the light of the Chanukah menorah, young and old enjoy this crisp, holiday treat.

5 large potatoes, peeled
1 large onion
3 eggs
⅓ cup flour
1 tsp. salt
¼ tsp. pepper
¾ cup oil for frying

USE: 10-inch skillet
YIELDS: 4 to 6 servings

Grate potatoes and onion on the fine side of a grater, or in a food processor; or put in a blender with a little water.

Strain grated potatoes and onion through a colander, pressing out excess water. Add eggs, flour, and seasoning. Mix well.

Heat ½ cup oil in skillet. Lower flame and place 1 large tablespoonful batter at a time into hot sizzling oil and fry on one side for approximately 5 minutes until golden brown. Turn over and fry on other side 2 to 3 minutes.

Remove from pan and place on paper towels to drain excess oil. Continue with remaining batter until used up, adding more oil when necessary.

Serve with applesauce on the side.

VARIATION
☐ **Zucchini or Carrot Latkes:** Substitute 5 medium zucchini or 5 medium carrots for potatoes.

SPICY BAKED POTATOES

6 medium potatoes
3 Tbsps. oil
1½ Tbsps. paprika
1 Tbsp. salt
Dash black pepper

USE: 9 x 13-inch baking pan
YIELDS: 6 servings

Preheat oven to 350°.

Scrub potatoes well and cut into halves. In a small dish, combine oil and seasonings. Line a 9 x 13-inch baking pan with aluminum foil (to avoid a messy clean-up job later). Place potato halves on pan and drizzle tops with oil mixture. Bake for 1½ to 2 hours. Serve hot.

VARIATION
☐ Using ¼ cup margarine, dot potatoes generously. Sprinkle with paprika, salt, and pepper. Place cut side down to bake for 1 hour. Turn over, and bake another ½ hour.

CRISPY BAKED POTATO SLICES

4 large potatoes
4 Tbsps. margarine
1 tsp. salt

USE: 9 x 9-inch pan
1-quart saucepan
YIELDS: 2 to 4 servings

Preheat oven to 425°.

In a small saucepan, melt margarine. Add salt and turn off flame.

Slice potatoes crosswise into medium-thin slices. In an oiled baking pan, arrange potato slices one layer deep, overlapping edges slightly. Dribble half the margarine on top of the potatoes. Cover with foil and bake 30 minutes.

After 30 minutes, uncover pan and pour remaining margarine over potatoes. Bake uncovered for 45 minutes longer, until tender inside and golden crispy outside.

GOURMET SWEET POTATOES

**4 medium sweet potatoes
or 1 20-ounce can
½ tsp. salt
½ cup brown sugar
1 Tbsp. cornstarch
1 cup orange juice
¼ cup raisins
¼ cup margarine
3 Tbsps. sherry
2 Tbsps. chopped walnuts
½ tsp. grated orange peel**

USE: 3-quart saucepan
9 x 9-inch baking pan
1-quart saucepan
YIELDS: 8 servings

Cook sweet potatoes in boiling salted water in 3-quart saucepan until tender. Drain, peel, and halve potatoes lengthwise. Arrange in shallow dish or pan. Sprinkle lightly with ¼ teaspoon salt.

Preheat oven to 350°.

Mix brown sugar, cornstarch, and ¼ teaspoon salt in 1-quart saucepan. Blend in orange juice and raisins. Stir while quickly bringing to a boil. Add remaining ingredients and pour over potatoes. Bake uncovered for 20 minutes or until potatoes are well glazed.

STUFFED SWEET POTATOES

**3 large sweet potatoes
2 Tbsps. margarine
¼ cup crushed pineapple
½ cup brown sugar
Dash of lemon juice**

USE: 9 x 9-inch baking pan
YIELDS: 6 servings

Preheat oven to 350°.

Cut potatoes lengthwise and place in 9 x 9-inch baking pan. Bake until soft, about 1 hour.

Scrape out pulp into small bowl, leaving shells. Add remaining ingredients to pulp and beat until fluffy. Fill shells with mixture and bake until browned, about 10 minutes.

SWEET POTATO PUFFS ON PINEAPPLE

**3 large sweet potatoes
or yams
½ cup sugar
1 Tbsp. cinnamon
2 eggs
½ cup matzoh meal or
bread crumbs
½ cup shredded coconut
12 slices canned
pineapple rings
2 Tbsps. red currant jelly**

USE: 3-quart pan
9 x 13-inch baking pan
YIELDS: 12 servings

Peel sweet potatoes and cut into large cubes. Place in pot and cover with water. Cook for 30 minutes until soft and allow to cool. Mash sweet potatoes and combine with sugar, cinnamon, eggs, matzoh meal, and ¼ cup coconut (save remaining ¼ cup for topping).

Preheat oven to 350°.

Arrange pineapple slices in a greased 9 x 13-inch pan. Mound sweet potato mixture onto each pineapple slice. Sprinkle with remaining coconut. Make an indentation in center of each puff and fill with ½ teaspoon jelly.

Bake uncovered for 30 minutes.

VARIATION
□ Make kugel instead of patties: Spread sweet potato mixture evenly in pan. Top with pineapple slices and make indentations in center of each slice and fill with jelly.

CANDIED SWEET POTATOES

3 large sweet potatoes or yams
4 Tbsps. margarine, melted
½ cup brown sugar
½ Tbsp. cinnamon

USE: 3-quart saucepan
9 x 9-inch baking pan
YIELDS: 6 servings

In a 3-quart covered saucepan cook sweet potatoes covered with water and boil until soft, about 40 minutes. Cool, peel, and cut in quarters. Roll in margarine, then in sugar and cinnamon mixture.

Preheat oven to 375°.

Place on greased 9 x 9-inch baking pan and bake uncovered for 45 minutes. Rotate pan every 10 minutes.

TWO-TONE POTATO ROLL

This two-tone white-potato and sweet-potato roll adds color to any meal.

10 large white potatoes, cubed
2 large onions, minced
5 Tbsps. oil
7 to 8 sweet potatoes, cubed
¾ tsp. salt
6 Tbsps. margarine

USE: 2 4-quart pots
7-inch skillet
10 x 15-inch baking sheet
YIELDS: 10 servings

In 4-quart pot boil white potatoes in salted water for 45 minutes or until soft; drain.

While potatoes are boiling, saute onions in a 7-inch skillet in oil until transparent; do not burn.

Cook sweet potatoes in separate 4-quart pot for 45 minutes or until soft; drain. Mash sweet potatoes until smooth. Set aside. In a separate bowl, mash white potatoes very well until smooth. Add salt, margarine, and onions. Mix well. Spread white potatoes over aluminum foil to ½-inch thickness. Spread sweet potatoes over white potatoes. Roll up jelly-roll fashion, pulling the foil away as you roll. Freeze 5 to 6 hours until semifrozen.

Preheat oven to 400°.

When ready to use, slice with very sharp knife. Place slices on greased baking sheet and bake for about 15 minutes.

NOTE: The rolls may be kept in freezer for longer periods of time. When ready to use, defrost slightly and proceed as above.

SALADS *made with a variety of vegetables and a freshly made dressing are the perfect accompaniment to any dinner.*

CUCUMBER SALAD

3 to 4 cucumbers
1 Tbsp. salt
1 medium onion
½ cup vinegar
¼ cup water
½ Tbsp. sugar
Dash pepper

USE: 2-quart covered bowl
YIELDS: 8 to 10 servings

Peel cucumbers and slice very thin. Place slices in bowl and sprinkle with salt. Allow to stand for 30 minutes or longer. Squeeze water out of cucumber slices and put in a bowl.

Slice onion into thin rings and put in bowl with cucumbers. Add remaining ingredients, mix well, and refrigerate several hours before serving.

Serve cold with meat or poultry.

VARIATION
☐ Substitute juice of 2 lemons for vinegar, and omit water. Additional salt may be required.

LEAFY GREEN SALAD WITH FRENCH DRESSING

1 clove garlic
1 head lettuce
1 bunch watercress
1 head endive
1 head escarole
2 tomatoes
6 radishes

FRENCH DRESSING
2 Tbsps. sugar
2 Tbsps. vinegar
⅓ tsp. crushed
hot red pepper
1 tsp. paprika
¾ cup olive oil
1 clove garlic, minced
½ tsp. salt

**FRENCH TOMATO
DRESSING**
¾ cup olive oil
¼ cup vinegar
1 Tbsp. sugar
2 Tbsps. catsup
¼ cup dry mustard
½ tsp. salt
Dash black pepper

USE: Large wooden
salad bowl
YIELDS: 12 servings

Rub salad bowl with clove of garlic. Discard garlic. Thoroughly wash and pat dry lettuce, watercress, endive and escarole. Cut up heart leaves of lettuce, sprays of watercress, stalks of endive, and several escarole leaves. Cut tomatoes into wedges of eighths.

DRESSING: Choose one of the dressings. Place all dressing ingredients in a jar and shake well. Pour over vegetables and garnish with radish roses.

Serve cold.

WALDORF SALAD

5 green and/or
red apples
2 stalks celery
1 cup chopped walnuts
1 cup raisins
¼ cup mayonnaise

USE: Salad bowl
YIELDS: 5 to 6 servings

Core apples. Chop apples and celery into small pieces; add walnuts and raisins. Mix in enough mayonnaise to coat all pieces, approximately ¼ cup.

ISRAELI SALAD

Israeli salad is distinguished by the tiny diced tomatoes and cucumber and the light, fresh oil and lemon dressing. It can be varied by the addition of croutons, parsley, scallions, and garlic.

2 large tomatoes
2 cucumbers
1 red or green pepper
1 scallion
2 cloves garlic, minced
1 Tbsp. minced fresh parsley
½ tsp. salt
Pepper to taste
1 tsp. minced fresh mint (optional)
¼ cup oil
2 to 3 Tbsps. lemon juice

USE: Salad bowl
YIELDS: 6 servings

Wash tomatoes and cut into ⅓-inch cubes. Peel cucumbers and dice into ⅓-inch cubes. Dice pepper into cubes. Chop scallions fine.

Place all vegetables in salad bowl. Add remaining ingredients and mix well. Refrigerate until ready to serve.

WINTER GARDEN SALAD

½ head lettuce
1 large cucumber, peeled
1 medium green pepper
½ cup diced celery
½ cup sliced scallions
4 radishes
3 medium tomatoes
3 shredded spinach or red cabbage leaves (optional)

DRESSING
⅓ cup oil
⅛ cup vinegar
1 tsp. salt
Pinch sugar
⅛ tsp. pepper
1 clove garlic, minced

USE: Salad bowl
YIELDS: 4 servings

Prepare vegetables to desired size, and combine in salad bowl.

Combine dressing ingredients in jar. Shake well. Add dressing to salad and toss.

VARIATIONS

□ Garnish with 2 hard-boiled eggs, cut into quarters.

□ A good salad in falafel.

□ **Dairy:** Garnish with mozzarella cheese sticks.

□ **Greek Salad (Dairy):** Add black olives and chunks of cheese, such as Monterey Jack, and also oregano and mint, to taste.

SPINACH *has a distinctive dark-green color and tangy taste. When cooked in a cream sauce, it takes on a smooth velvety appearance. One very popular and tasty salad includes spinach, hard-boiled eggs, mushrooms, and a vinaigrette dressing. For information on checking spinach see page 259.*

SPINACH, EGG, AND ONION SALAD

½ pound fresh spinach
1 Tbsp. prepared mustard
1 Tbsp. vinegar
Salt and pepper to taste
5 Tbsps. corn or vegetable oil
2 hard-boiled eggs, peeled and diced or chopped
1 Tbsp. finely chopped onion or scallion

USE: Salad bowl
YIELDS: 6 servings

Soak, thoroughly wash, and dry spinach. Trim stems. Tear into small pieces and set aside. In salad bowl, combine mustard, vinegar, and salt and pepper. Blend with a wire whisk or fork. Add oil and continue beating until smooth. Add eggs, spinach and onion. Toss well.

VARIATION
☐ Two bunches watercress may be substituted for spinach. One-half dozen fresh mushrooms, thinly sliced, may be added before onion.

CREAMED SPINACH

1 pound spinach
1 medium onion, diced
3 Tbsps. margarine
2 Tbsps. flour
¼ cup nondairy creamer
Salt and pepper to taste

USE: 10-inch skillet
YIELDS: 4 servings

Thoroughly wash and dry spinach; carefully tear into small pieces. In 10-inch skillet, saute onion in margarine. Stir in flour and gradually stir in creamer. Add spinach, salt, and pepper and simmer 5 minutes.

VARIATIONS
☐ When serving with meat, use chicken soup or meat gravy in place of nondairy creamer.

☐ Add diced tomato and 1 minced garlic clove when onion is golden.

TOASTED ALMOND BUTTERNUT SQUASH

1 medium butternut squash
Salt
3 Tbsps. margarine
½ cup maple syrup
Dash of nutmeg
⅓ cup sliced toasted almonds

USE: 3-quart saucepan
1-quart casserole
YIELDS: 4 servings

Preheat oven to 350°.

Cut squash in half and remove seeds. Place squash in 3-quart saucepan, and cook in boiling salted water until tender, approximately 30 minutes. Scoop out pulp and mash well. Add margarine, maple syrup, and nutmeg, mixing well.

Place squash mixture in an oiled casserole and top with toasted sliced almonds. Bake for 8 to 10 minutes until just heated through. Serve warm.

SPAGHETTI SQUASH SLAW

1 spaghetti squash
3 carrots, shredded
1 medium
green pepper, diced
2 scallions, diced
½ cup mayonnaise
4 Tbsps. lemon juice
½ tsp. salt
¼ tsp. pepper
1 Tbsp. sugar

USE: Baking sheet
YIELDS: 4 cups

Preheat oven to 350°.

Cut spaghetti squash in half, lengthwise. Place on baking sheet and bake for approximately 45 minutes or until tender.

Remove from oven, allow to cool, and scrape the strands out with a fork, into mixing bowl.

Add the remaining vegetables to squash. Mix together and add mayonnaise and seasonings. Toss together until colors and seasonings are well blended.

TEMPURA BATTER

Vegetables coated in this light tempura batter and then fried enhance any main dish. Also perfect for pineapple fritters and even for frying small fish fillets.

3 egg yolks
2 cups ice water
2 cups flour
Dash of salt
Oil or shortening

USE: Medium bowl
Deep-fryer or
10-inch skillet
YIELDS: 12 to 16 servings

In a medium bowl, combine egg yolks and ice water. Stir in flour gradually, add salt, and stir with wire whisk or wooden spoon until batter is combined. Do not overmix.

Dip vegetables in batter. Fry in hot oil or shortening until golden.

Use batter as soon as it is mixed as the ice water helps create a lacy effect when coated foods are fried.

Serve warm.

Serving Suggestion: Use for broccoli, cauliflower florets or thinly sliced zucchini rings.

MARINATED TOMATOES

6 to 8 tomatoes
½ cup oil
⅓ cup wine vinegar
½ tsp. salt
2 tsps. oregano
½ tsp. black pepper
½ tsp. dry mustard
2 cloves garlic, minced
1 to 2 Tbsps. minced onion
Parsley (optional)

USE: Covered bowl
YIELDS: 6 servings

Slice tomatoes crosswise and arrange in deep dish or bowl. Mix remaining ingredients well. Pour over tomatoes and let marinate, covered, in refrigerator overnight.

VARIATION
☐ Use basil in place of oregano and omit the mustard. Tomatoes and basil grow well and taste delicious together — they're a traditional twosome.

SPAGHETTI SQUASH SAUTE

2 medium spaghetti squash
(about 2½ pounds total)
¼ cup margarine
1 small onion, diced
1 small eggplant (about
¾ cup diced ½-inch cubes)
¾ cup sliced mushrooms
2 medium tomatoes, diced
2 tsps. parsley flakes or
¼ cup minced fresh parsley
2 Tbsps. wine
2 cloves garlic, minced
1½ tsps. paprika

USE: 6-quart pot
10-inch skillet
YIELDS: 6 servings

Pierce squash with fork in several places and boil for 30 minutes in 6-quart pot, or bake in preheated oven at 350° for 45 minutes until tender.

While squash is cooking, heat the margarine in the 10-inch skillet and saute the onion until soft. Add the eggplant, mushrooms, and tomatoes and cook, stirring occasionally, until vegetables are tender. Add seasonings.

When squash is tender, cut in half lengthwise, remove the seeds, and scrape out the strands with a fork. Add "spaghetti" strands to sauteed vegetables and cook 4 to 5 minutes to mingle flavors.

STIR-FRIED VEGETABLES

2 Tbsps. olive, peanut
or safflower oil
½ inch fresh ginger
1 medium onion
2 medium carrots
1 stalk celery
1 head broccoli (optional)
1 medium zucchini
1 medium yellow squash
1 pound tofu (optional)
2½ cups mushrooms
1 cup bean sprouts (optional)
1 Tbsp. tamari soy sauce
½ tsp. rosemary
½ tsp. thyme

USE: Wok or 10-inch skillet
YIELDS: 6-10 servings

Slice all vegetables finely before cooking. Keep vegetables separate, as they are added to wok according to cooking time needed. Onion, ginger and garlic, when used, are added first, to bring out flavor, then longer-cooking vegetables such as carrots are added. Quick-cooking vegetables are added last.

Peel and dice ginger. Thinly dice onion. Peel and slice carrot and celery diagonally. Cut broccoli into small florets. Slice zucchini and squash twice lengthwise and then cross-wise into small slices. Drain and cube tofu. Wash, trim and slice mushrooms lengthwise. Wash sprouts.

Heat wok for 30 seconds over high flame. Add oil, stirring with slotted spoon to cover pan. Heat 30 seconds. Add ginger and turn flame to low or medium-low. After 15 seconds add onion, stir to coat with oil. Cook 1 minute. Add carrots, celery, and broccoli (if used). Cook 5 minutes, stirring frequently. Add zucchini and squash. Cook 5 minutes, stirring frequently. Add tofu (if used) and mushrooms, still stirring. Cook 5 more minutes. Add sprouts and spices. Stir and toss for 3 minutes. Serve warm.

SWEET-AND-SOUR SPINACH SALAD

1 pound fresh spinach
12 ounces fresh mushrooms
6 radishes
½ cup slivered almonds

DRESSING
1 cup oil
¼ cup lemon juice
2 Tbsps. vinegar
Dash salt
Dash pepper
Dash garlic powder
3 coddled eggs
(boiled 1 minute), cooled
1 tsp. dry mustard
⅓ cup honey

USE: Salad bowl
YIELDS: 12 servings

Soak, thoroughly wash, and dry spinach. Strip off leaves and tear into small pieces. Discard stems. Peel and slice mushrooms thin. Wash radishes and slice thin. Combine vegetables with almonds and toss.

Combine ingredients for dressing in jar and shake well. Pour dressing over salad immediately before serving.

VARIATION
□ **Caesar Salad (Dairy):** Instead of spinach, use regular lettuce leaves; add garlic croutons and grated hard cheese. Use same dressing, substituting 1 teaspoon sugar for honey.

TURNIP RELISH

1 medium turnip
1 medium scallion, finely diced
1 very small red onion, finely diced
⅛ to ¼ tsp. salt
4 Tbsps. oil

USE: Small bowl
YIELDS: 3 to 4 servings

Peel turnip and grate on medium grater holes. Add scallion, onion, salt and oil; mix together.

Use relish to accompany meal.

VARIATION
□ In a 7-inch skillet saute diced small white onion in oil with ½ tsp. minced garlic and 2 small diced red onions. Stir until golden brown. Add to grated turnip.

STEAMED VEGETABLE MEDLEY

2 medium carrots
2 stalks celery
1 medium onion
1 bunch broccoli
½ pound mushrooms
¼ cup oil
¼ cup water
1¼ tsps. salt
½ tsp. sugar

USE: 4-quart pot
YIELDS: 8 servings

Cut each carrot in half, then lengthwise into matchstick strips. Cut each celery stalk crosswise into thirds, then lengthwise into matchstick strips. Slice onion thin. Thoroughly wash and cut broccoli into florets and slice stalk into ½-inch pieces. Cut mushrooms in half.

In a 4-quart pot, heat oil and saute mushrooms. Add onion and saute 2 minutes longer. Add remainder of vegetables, water, salt, and sugar. Stir. Cover pot and cook, stirring occasionally, 10 to 12 minutes until vegetables are just tender.

MARINATED VEGETABLES

MARINADE
¼ cup olive oil
3 Tbsps. apple cider vinegar
Juice of 2 lemons
½ tsp. oregano
½ tsp. basil
½ tsp. salt
2 Tbsps. white wine
½ tsp. pepper
2 cloves garlic, crushed

1 bunch broccoli
1 head cauliflower
3 stalks celery,
cut into 1-inch slices
5 to 6 dill pickles
1 green or red pepper
12 green or black olives

USE: 4-quart pot
YIELDS: 12 servings

Mix marinade ingredients in a large bowl. Set aside

Thoroughly wash broccoli and cauliflower. Cut cauliflower into florets.

Fill a 4-quart pot with about 2 inches of water. Place metal steamer basket in the pot and fill with cauliflower, broccoli, and celery. Steam until cooked but still very crisp.

Slice pickles and add to marinade. Dice pepper and olives; add to marinade. Cut stems of broccoli into ½-inch pieces and cut tops into florets. Add cauliflower florets.

Mix vegetables and marinate covered overnight in refrigerator.

VARIATION
□ Add sliced hard-boiled eggs.

VEGETABLES FOR THE DISCRIMINATING

1 to 1½ pounds each
of assorted vegetables,
not exceeding a total
of 5 pounds

MARINADE
3 *pareve* chicken-flavored
bouillon cubes
3 cups water
1 cup white wine
1 cup oil
½ cup fresh lemon juice
1 tsp. thyme
2 cloves garlic
10 peppercorns
1 tsp. chopped
fresh coriander or
10 coriander seeds
¼ bunch parsley
½ tsp. salt

USE: 3-quart pot
YIELDS: 10 servings

Combine all marinade ingredients in 3-quart pot. Bring marinade to boil and let simmer, partially covered, for 45 minutes. Strain, and return to pot. Simmer.

Cook each vegetable separately over low flame in simmering marinade until tender-crisp. When vegetable is done, remove with slotted spoon. Serve hot or cold, each vegetable separately or combined with other marinated vegetables.

SUGGESTED COOKING TIMES:

Carrots, julienned . . . . 7 to 8 minutes
Cauliflower florets . . . . 6 to 8 minutes
Eggplant, julienned or cubed . . . . 6 to 8 minutes
Green beans, whole . . . . 4 to 5 minutes
Mushroom caps, whole . . . . 1 minute
Peppers, julienned . . . . 6 to 8 minutes
Zucchini, julienned or
cut into thin rounds . . . . 4 minutes

HEARTY VEGETARIAN CHOPPED LIVER

1 pound lentils
4 cups chopped onion
6 Tbsps. oil
12 to 16 hard-boiled eggs
2 Tbsps. peanut butter
½ tsp. white pepper
2 tsps. salt

GARNISH
Lettuce
Horseradish
Tomato slices

USE: 3-quart saucepan
10-inch skillet
YIELDS: 12 servings

In a 3-quart saucepan cook lentils according to the package directions. Drain. (The longer you cook them, the softer they get.) Saute onion in a 10-inch skillet, in 3 tablespoons oil until brown. Peel the eggs. Chop lentils and eggs fine.

Mix the lentil mixture with sauteed onions and remaining oil. Add peanut butter, pepper and salt.

Serve scoops on lettuce cups with white or red horseradish and sliced tomatoes.

VEGETABLE CURRY

2 cups green or wax beans
3 medium potatoes, diced
3 medium carrots, diced
¼ cup oil
2 tomatoes, diced
¼ cup raisins
1 cup peas
1 tsp. cumin
1 tsp. salt
½ tsp. dry mustard
1 tsp. turmeric
½ tsp. ground coriander
Dash pepper

USE: 3-quart pot
YIELDS: 6 servings

Wash and trim ends of string beans. Cut into 1-inch pieces. In 3-quart pot, place beans, potatoes, and carrots. Cover with ½ to 1 cup water. Cook until crisp and tender, about 5 to 10 minutes. Add oil, tomatoes, raisins, peas, and seasonings. Simmer 20 minutes.

Serve warm with rice.

VARIATION
☐ Replace water with tomato juice.

CLASSIC VEGETARIAN CHOPPED LIVER

Tasty as a spread for crackers or as an appetizer served on a bed of lettuce.

1 pound fresh string beans
(or equivalent frozen)
1 pound fresh peas
(or equivalent frozen)
2 medium onions, diced
2 Tbsps. oil
4 hard-boiled eggs
1 cup shelled walnuts
1 tsp. salt

USE: 2-quart saucepan
YIELDS: 6 to 8 servings

Wash and trim string beans. Shell peas. Cook or steam beans and peas until tender.

Saute onions in oil until golden brown. Place peas, beans, and onions in food processor. Peel eggs. Add the eggs, walnuts, and salt.

Using shredder, process until chunky, not smooth. (Coarse blade of grinder may be used.)

QUICK VEGETARIAN CHOPPED LIVER

An excellent alternative to the real chopped liver — creamy and delicious.

6 to 8 hard-boiled eggs
1 16-ounce can peas
1 8-ounce can mushrooms
1 16-ounce can green beans
½ cup chopped walnuts
¼ cup mayonnaise
Scant 1 tsp. salt
¼ tsp. pepper

USE: Small bowl
YIELDS: 6 to 8 servings

Grind eggs, vegetables, and nuts together. Add mayonnaise, salt and pepper; mix together.

Serve on a bed of lettuce as an appetizer.

ZUCCHINI *has a crisp texture and is equally tasty raw or cooked. It combines well with other vegetables and serves as a casing for a variety of stuffings.*

MEDITERRANEAN STUFFED ZUCCHINI

3 medium zucchini
2 Tbsps. oil
1 cup uncooked rice
1 large onion, diced
½ cup chopped dried apricots
½ cup raisins
Dash salt
Dash pepper
1 tsp. curry powder
Dash garlic powder (optional)
2 to 2½ cups water

USE: 3-quart pot
10-inch skillet
9 x 13-inch baking pan
YIELDS: 6 servings

Wash and trim ends of zucchini. Parboil 5 minutes in 3-quart pot and drain. Slice lengthwise. Scoop out center, leaving shells intact. Chop and reserve the pulp. Drain.

In a 10-inch skillet, with 1 tablespoon oil, brown the rice, stirring constantly so it will not stick. Put in bowl and set aside. In same skillet, in remaining tablespoon oil, saute onion and chopped-up zucchini pulp for about 5 minutes. Return browned rice to skillet. Add chopped apricots, raisins, and seasonings along with 2 cups water. Boil until rice is just tender, about 15 minutes.*

Preheat oven to 350°.

In greased 9 x 13-inch baking pan, place zucchini shells, fill with rice mixture and bake for 15 minutes. Serve warm.

*NOTE: If covering skillet, an additional ½ cup water may be needed. Keep flame at medium while cooking rice to make sure it doesn't burn.

STUFFED ZUCCHINI

6 medium zucchini
2 Tbsps. oil
1 cup chopped mushrooms
½ cup grated carrots
1 onion, diced
⅛ tsp. pepper

Preheat oven to 350°.

Wash zucchini and trim ends. Place into 6-quart pot. Cover with water, bring to boil, and cook on medium flame for 5 to 10 minutes. Remove from pot. Cut zucchini in half lengthwise and scoop out the pulp. Chop and reserve the pulp.

1 tsp. salt
⅛ tsp. garlic powder
2 Tbsps. parsley
2 eggs, beaten
Reserved zucchini pulp
2 Tbsps. margarine

USE: 6-quart saucepan
10-inch skillet
2 9 x 13-inch baking pans
YIELDS: 12 servings

Heat oil in 10-inch skillet. Saute mushrooms, carrots, and onion. Add seasonings, parsley, eggs, and reserved pulp. Mix well.

Fill the zucchini shells and place in greased pans. Dot with margarine. Bake for 30 minutes.

VARIATION
☐ Use ½ cup cooked rice or ½ cup bread crumbs instead of carrots.

ZUCCHINI AND CARROT JULIENNE

Colorful and crunchy, this is an interesting combination of vegetables.

3 small zucchini
3 carrots
1 green pepper
1 red onion
6 radishes
6 scallions
½ pound mushrooms

DRESSING
½ cup oil
½ cup vinegar
½ tsp. salt
½ tsp. pepper
½ tsp. turmeric
½ tsp. dry mustard

YIELDS: 4 to 6 servings

Leave zucchini unpeeled and cut in ½-inch slices. Place in a large salad bowl. Cut carrots and green pepper into julienne strips and add. Cut onion into slices and separate into rings and add. Slice radishes, scallions and mushrooms and combine with other salad ingredients.

Combine dressing ingredients in a jar and shake well. Pour over salad and toss to coat vegetables.

Serve chilled.

NOTE: This salad keeps for a day or two covered in the refrigerator.

ZUCCHINI-STUFFED TOMATOES

2 large firm tomatoes
1 tsp. margarine
1 medium zucchini, sliced
½ cup sliced mushrooms
¼ cup chopped onion
¼ tsp. sugar
½ tsp. basil
½ tsp. garlic
½ tsp. salt
⅛ tsp. pepper
½ cup croutons or
½ cup cooked rice

USE: 10-inch skillet
8 x 8-inch baking pan
YIELDS: 2 servings

Preheat oven to 350°.

Cut ½-inch slice from tomato tops. Scoop out and reserve pulp. Sprinkle shells with salt and turn upside down to drain. Chop pulp.

In 10-inch skillet, melt margarine. Add tomato pulp, zucchini, mushrooms, onions, sugar, basil, garlic, and salt and pepper. Cook 5 minutes, uncovered, until liquid is evaporated. Add croutons or rice. Mix well and spoon into tomato shells. Place shells in 8 x 8-inch baking pan. Cover and bake for 15 minutes. Uncover and bake for an additional 10 minutes.

NOTE: If doubling recipe, tomatoes need to be baked longer than 15 minutes.

VARIATION:
☐ **Dairy:** Sprinkle with grated mozzarella cheese before baking.

Kugels and Traditional Specialties

KUGELS

Kugel or pudding? Lokshen or noodles? Whether you call it lokshen kugel or noodle pudding, it is a delicious combination of noodles, eggs and oil. This is a traditional dish for Shabbat and Yom Tov.

Though potatoes and noodles have long been standard, the basis of a kugel may now be broccoli, carrots, or fruit, while the substitution of whole-wheat noodles provides added nutrition. A salt and pepper kugel is a must in any Jewish cook's list of basic recipes. Sweet potatoes are a welcome and colorful alternative to white potatoes, while a challah kugel is the best way to use up last week's challah.

NOTE: Jewish law requires that all leafy vegetables should be checked for insects before using in any recipe (page 259).

BAKED BROCCOLI KUGEL

1 bunch broccoli
3 eggs
3 Tbsps. flour
1½ cups reserved stock
1½ tsps. salt
¼ to ½ tsp. pepper
2 Tbsps. chopped parsley
¼ tsp. grated lemon rind
1 tsp. lemon juice
⅛ tsp. nutmeg
⅛ tsp. dill

USE: 3-quart saucepan
9-inch square pan
YIELDS: 9 servings

Thoroughly wash broccoli and trim off tough ends.

Cook in 3-quart saucepan, in 2 cups of boiling salted water until tender. Drain and reserve 1½ cups liquid. Chop broccoli and set aside.

Preheat oven to 350°.

Break eggs into a 2-quart bowl and beat with flour, reserved liquid and seasonings. Add chopped broccoli and mix again. Pour mixture into a greased 9-inch square pan. Place baking dish into a larger baking pan filled with 1 inch warm water. Bake for 45 minutes.

CREAMY BROCCOLI KUGEL

1 large bunch broccoli
1 cube vegetable bouillon
1½ Tbsps. margarine
1½ Tbsps. flour
½ cup nondairy creamer
½ cup mayonnaise
1 Tbsp. onion soup mix
3 eggs, beaten
½ cup corn flake crumbs

Thoroughly wash broccoli and trim off tough ends.

Cook in a 3-quart saucepan with water to cover until tender but not too soft. Add vegetable bouillon to water and continue to cook. Drain water and mash broccoli.

Preheat oven to 350°.

Combine margarine, flour, and nondairy creamer in a 1½-quart saucepan. Simmer over a low flame until thickened. Remove from flame and allow to cool 5 minutes.

Add mayonnaise, onion soup mix, and eggs and mix well. Add cooled mixture to broccoli and mix until well combined.

►

USE: 3-quart saucepan
1½-quart saucepan
8-inch square pan
YIELDS: 9 servings

Grease 8-inch square pan. Pour ¼ cup crumbs on the bottom of pan and pour broccoli mixture on top. Sprinkle top with remaining ¼ cup corn flake crumbs. Bake for 30 minutes.

CARROT LOAF

This is an appealing carrot kugel that tastes like cake.

½ cup margarine, softened
½ cup brown sugar
1 egg, beaten
3 Tbsps. orange juice
1½ cups flour
1 tsp. baking powder
½ tsp. baking soda
1 tsp. salt
½ tsp. cinnamon
½ cup chopped walnuts
(optional)
2 cups grated carrots

USE: 9½ x 5½ inch loaf pan
YIELDS: 8 servings

Preheat oven to 350°.

Cream softened margarine with sugar in a large bowl. Add egg, juice, dry ingredients and nuts. Add grated carrots and mix well. Place in a 9½ x 5½-inch greased loaf pan. Bake for 30 minutes.

Serve warm or at room temperature.

CARROT RING

1 pound carrots, sliced
1 bay leaf
1 medium onion, peeled
Salt
3 tsps. cinnamon
1 tsp. ground ginger
Pepper to taste
5 eggs, separated
1 cup sugar
½ cup matzoh meal
1 cup ground walnuts

USE: 3-quart saucepan
2½ to 3-quart ring mold
YIELDS: 10 to 12 servings

In a 3-quart saucepan, place carrots, bay leaf, onion, and salt. Cover with water and cook 20 minutes or until soft. Discard bay leaf and onion, drain carrots and mash in a large bowl. Stir in seasonings. Beat egg yolks with sugar until thick and add to seasoned carrots. Mix well.

Preheat oven to 350°.

In a medium bowl, beat egg whites until stiff. Mix matzoh meal and walnuts into carrots. Fold in egg whites.

Turn into a greased 2½- to 3-quart ring mold or bundt pan. Set pan in a larger baking pan of hot water.

Bake for 40 minutes.

VARIATION
☐ For Rosh Hashanah, use equal amount of raisins in place of walnuts.

CAULIFLOWER KUGEL

1 large head cauliflower
2 large onions, diced
4 Tbsps. oil
¼ tsp. pepper
2 eggs, beaten
2 Tbsps. matzoh meal or wheat germ
1 Tbsp. corn flake crumbs

USE: 3-quart saucepan
7-inch skillet
9-inch square pan
YIELDS: 9 servings

Thoroughly wash cauliflower. Separate into large florets. Cook cauliflower in 3-quart saucepan with small amount of water for 20 minutes, until tender.

Preheat oven to 350°.

While cauliflower is cooking, saute onions in oil, in a 7-inch skillet. Cook until soft and very lightly browned. When cauliflower is tender, drain and mash. Add sauteed onions and remaining ingredients, except corn flake crumbs. Mix well.

Place cauliflower mixture in a greased 9-inch square pan. Sprinkle top with corn flake crumbs. Bake for 45 to 60 minutes.

CHALLAH KUGELS *are creamy and sweet. They are perfect for using up last Shabbat's challah. The challah should be somewhat dry.*

CLASSIC CHALLAH KUGEL

12 ounces challah
1½ cups water
1½ cups nondairy creamer
3 eggs, beaten
½ cup sugar
1 tsp. vanilla extract
1 tsp. cinnamon
½ to 1 cup raisins
2 Tbsps. margarine, melted

USE: Bundt pan
9 x 13-inch baking pan
YIELDS: 12 to 16 servings

Preheat oven to 375°.

Crumble or grate challah into medium bowl. Combine water and nondairy creamer; pour over challah and soak for 10 minutes. Add remaining ingredients and mix well.

Pour into well-greased bundt pan and place bundt pan in a 9 x 13-inch baking pan containing 1 inch of water.

Bake for 1 hour.

SWEET CHALLAH KUGEL

1 pound challah
1 cup orange or apple juice
⅓ cup raisins or
2 large apples, sliced
4 eggs, beaten
½ cup honey or
1 cup sugar
3 Tbsps. oil

Preheat oven to 350°.

Remove crust from the challah and break into chunks into a large bowl. Pour juice over challah and soak until soft. Meanwhile soak raisins in hot water to soften.

Add eggs, honey, oil, vanilla, salt, and cinnamon to challah. Add raisins or apples to mixture. Combine well.

Bake in greased 9½ x 5½-inch loaf pan for 45 to 50 minutes. Crust should be brown when done. ►

2 tsps. vanilla extract
½ tsp. salt
2 tsps. cinnamon

USE: 9½ x 5½-inch loaf pan
YIELDS: 8 to 10 servings

NOTE: For a fluffier kugel separate egg whites from yolks and beat whites until stiff, then add to other ingredients.

CLASSIC SALT-AND-PEPPER LOKSHEN KUGEL

12 ounces fine noodles
4 Tbsps. oil or margarine
4 eggs, beaten
1 tsp. salt
1 tsp. pepper
Oil for frying

USE: 4-quart pot
10-inch skillet
YIELDS: 8 to 10 servings

In a 4-quart pot of boiling salted water, cook noodles until soft, about 5 minutes. Rinse and drain. Put noodles in a bowl and add oil. Set aside to cool, 15 minutes. Add beaten eggs, salt, and pepper.

Heat oil in 10-inch frying pan until very hot. Pour in noodle mixture and fry on medium to low flame, covered, for 15 minutes. Lift kugel with spatula and slide onto a large plate. Add more oil to the pan if necessary, then using another large flat plate flip kugel over onto uncooked side and slide back into pan and fry for another 10 to 15 minutes.

VARIATIONS
□ **Favorite Onion Lokshen Kugel:** For richer flavor, omit ½ teaspoon salt and pepper and substitute a package of dry onion soup mix boiled in 1 cup water, or saute 1 large onion and 1 cup mushrooms in 4 tablespoons margarine, and add to noodle mixture.

□ Instead of frying, pour mixture into a greased 9 x 9-inch baking dish and bake at 375° for approximately 45 to 50 minutes, or until top is brown and crisp.

□ For fluffier kugel, double the amount of eggs.

PINEAPPLE WHOLE-WHEAT NOODLE KUGEL

So tasty they'll never know it's good for them!

12 ounces
whole-wheat noodles
4 eggs, beaten
¼ cup oil
1 16-ounce can
crushed pineapple
½ cup raisins
3 cooking apples,
finely sliced
¼ cup honey
¼ tsp. cinnamon
½ tsp. salt

USE: 4-quart pot
9 x 13-inch pan
YIELDS: 12 to 16 servings

In a 4-quart pot of boiling salted water cook noodles until soft. Drain, rinse, and set aside to cool for 15 minutes.

Preheat oven to 350°.

In a large bowl, combine all ingredients and mix well. Add noodles and stir. Pour mixture into a greased 9 x 13-inch pan and bake for 45 minutes.

PINEAPPLE UPSIDE-DOWN NOODLE KUGEL

8 ounces medium noodles
3 Tbsps. margarine, melted
6 eggs, beaten
¾ cup sugar
1 tsp. lemon juice
¼ tsp. salt
1 can pineapple slices
1 cup pineapple juice, drained from can
Maraschino cherries
½ cup brown sugar

USE: 4-quart pot
9 x 9-inch baking pan
YIELDS: 9 servings

In a 4-quart pot of boiling water cook noodles until soft, 12 to 15 minutes. Rinse and drain. Set aside to cool, 15 minutes.

In a large bowl combine noodles, margarine, eggs, sugar, lemon juice, salt, and pineapple juice.

Preheat oven to 350°.

In a well-greased 9-inch square pan, place three rows of three pineapple slices each. Put a maraschino cherry in the center of each slice and sprinkle with brown sugar. Pour noodle mixture over pineapples and bake for 40 minutes. Cool in pan.

Turn out onto plate to serve.

PLUM NOODLE KUGEL

6 ounces medium noodles
1½ pounds fresh plums or 1½ pounds plums and nectarines, mixed
3 eggs, beaten
¾ cup sugar
1 tsp. cinnamon
1 cup applesauce
2 Tbsps. margarine, melted
1 cup soft bread crumbs
½ cup chopped almonds (optional)

USE: 4-quart pot
9-inch round baking pan
YIELDS: 9 servings

In a 4-quart pot of boiling salted water cook noodles until soft. Rinse and drain and set aside to cool for 15 minutes.

Preheat oven to 350°.

Remove pits from unpeeled plums and cut into large chunks. In a large bowl mix fruit with noodles, eggs, sugar, cinnamon, applesauce, margarine, and ¾ cup bread crumbs. Pour into greased 9-inch round pan and sprinkle top with remaining ¼ cup bread crumbs and nuts, if used.

Bake for 50 minutes or until golden brown.

SPINACH LOKSHEN KUGEL

16 ounces fine noodles
1 pound fresh spinach
2 onions, diced
2 Tbsps. oil
6 eggs, beaten
½ cup oil
Salt to taste

In a 4-quart pot of boiling salted water, cook noodles until barely soft, 5 minutes; rinse, drain, and set aside in a large bowl.

Thoroughly wash spinach and remove stems, place in a 4-quart saucepan and cook in a small amount of water. Remove spinach from the pot, drain, chop and add to the noodles. In a 7-inch skillet saute diced onion in 2 tablespoons of oil until golden and add to the spinach-noodle mixture.

Preheat oven to 350°.

►

USE: 4-quart saucepan
7-inch skillet
9 x 13-inch baking pan
YIELDS: 12 to 16 servings

Stir in eggs and ½ cup of oil. Add salt to taste and mix well. Pour mixture into greased 9 x 13-inch pan. Bake for approximately 40 minutes.

VARIATIONS
☐ Saute ¾ cup sliced mushrooms and ½ cup sliced celery and add to spinach-noodle mixture.

☐ For softer kugel, add 2 additional eggs.

SWEET NOODLE KUGEL

8 ounces medium noodles
¼ cup margarine,
cut into small pieces
4 eggs, beaten
½ cup sugar
½ cup raisins
4 apples, grated
1 tsp. cinnamon
1 tsp. salt

TOPPING
1 tsp. cinnamon
¼ cup sugar
¼ cup corn flake crumbs

USE: 4-quart pot
8 x 8-inch baking pan
YIELDS: 9 servings

Cook noodles in 4-quart pot of boiling salted water for 10 minutes. Rinse. Drain and put into large bowl. While noodles are still hot, add margarine and mix until all the margarine is melted. Allow to cool 5 minutes.

Preheat oven to 350°.

Add eggs, sugar, raisins, apples, cinnamon, and salt to noodles and mix well. Pour into a greased 8 x 8-inch baking pan.

TOPPING: Combine cinnamon, sugar, and corn flake crumbs. Sprinkle over top of kugel, cover, and bake for 50 minutes. Uncover and bake 10 minutes longer until golden brown.

Serve warm or cold.

VARIATION
☐ Substitute wheat germ for cornflake crumbs.

YERUSHALAYIM KUGEL

A noodle kugel specialty from Israel. The unique flavor of carmelized sugar creates this special effect.

12 ounces thin noodles
½ cup oil
1½ cups sugar
6 eggs, lightly beaten
Salt and pepper to taste

USE: 4-quart saucepan
1-quart saucepan
9 x 13 inch baking pan
YIELDS: 16 servings

In a 4-quart pot of boiling water, cook noodles 5 to 7 minutes, drain and rinse, place in a large bowl and set aside.

In a 1-quart saucepan, combine oil and sugar; cook over low flame until sugar is liquid and brown, about 20 minutes. Pour carmelized sugar over noodles and set aside to cool.

Preheat oven to 350°. Place greased 9 x 13-inch baking pan to preheat as well.

Add eggs to cooled mixture and season with salt and pepper. Mix well. Pour into preheated pan and bake for 1 hour.

TOFU NOODLE KUGEL

8 ounce package flat artichoke noodles
½ pound soft tofu
½ cup water
2 Tbsps. tahini
1 Tbsp. miso or pinch sea salt
Pinch of nutmeg and cinnamon
1 tsp. vanilla extract
½ cup raisins
½ cup roasted, chopped walnuts
½ tsp. grated lemon or orange rind

USE: 3-quart pot
9 x 9 inch baking dish
YIELDS: 10-12 servings

Boil noodles in water in 3-quart pot until al dente and drain. Blend tofu and other ingredients except raisins and nuts in blender. Mix noodles with sauce. Add raisins and nuts. Place in baking dish and cover with foil. Bake at 350° for 15 minutes. Remove foil, bake 5 to 10 minutes.

GOLDEN POTATO KUGEL

A delicious classic. This fail-proof kugel is most successful when prepared with a food processor.

6 eggs
¼ cup margarine
2 medium onions
12 medium potatoes
⅔ cup flour
½ tsp. baking powder
2½ tsps. salt
½ tsp. pepper

USE: 9 x 13-inch baking pan
YIELDS: 12-16 servings

Preheat oven to 350°

Blend eggs, onions and margarine. Grate potatoes to a medium consistency. Rinse and drain in large colander. Mix all ingredients in large bowl. Coat 9 x 13-inch pan with 3 Tbsps. oil and place in heated oven for 5 minutes.

Bake 1½ to 2 hours until golden brown.

TRADITIONAL POTATO KUGEL

6 medium potatoes
1 onion
3 eggs, beaten
⅓ cup flour, wheat germ, or matzoh meal
1½ tsps. salt
¼ tsp. pepper
4 Tbsps. oil
¼ tsp. baking powder

USE: 9 x 9-inch baking pan
YIELDS: 9 servings

Preheat oven to 350°.

Peel potatoes and place in a large bowl of cold water. Peel onion. Grate on small holes of grater into a clean bowl. Add eggs to potato-onion mixture. Stir in remaining ingredients and mix well with a fork.

Place in greased 9 x 9-inch baking pan. Bake for at least 1 hour or until light brown and crisp.

VARIATIONS

□ Grate 3 potatoes and a small head of cauliflower.

□ Add 2 medium carrots, grated, to potato mixture.

□ All ingredients except flour can be blended in blender. Then stir in flour, mix, and place in greased pan. Bake until top is browned; the inside will remain very soft.

POTATO ZUCCHINI KUGEL

A modern variation of the traditional favorite potato kugel.

6 medium potatoes
1 medium onion
3 medium zucchini
6 eggs, beaten
2 Tbsps. oil
1 tsp. salt
⅛ tsp. pepper
½ cup flour (optional)

USE: 9 x 13-inch baking pan
YIELDS: 12 to 16 servings

Preheat oven to 350°. Place greased 9 x 13-inch pan into oven to preheat as well.

Peel potatoes and place in a large bowl of cold water. Peel onion and zucchini. If vegetables are to be grated by hand, leave vegetables whole. If food processor is used, cut into large chunks. Pour grated vegetables into a large bowl. Add eggs, oil, salt, and pepper and mix well.

Pour into heated pan and bake until golden brown, about 1 to 1¼ hours.

VARIATION
☐ Reverse the proportions of potatoes and zucchini and use 1 more egg.

SOUTHERN SWEET POTATO PONE

¾ cup molasses
½ cup dark brown sugar
¾ cup nondairy creamer
½ to ¾ tsp. cinnamon
½ to ¾ tsp. nutmeg
½ tsp. salt
3 eggs, lightly beaten
5 to 6 sweet potatoes
(4 cups grated)

USE: 1½-quart casserole
YIELDS: 6 to 8 servings

Combine all ingredients except sweet potatoes in large mixing bowl. Peel sweet potatoes and grate 1 cup at a time, adding each cup to mixture as it is grated to keep sweet potato from darkening.

Preheat oven to 350°.

Mix all ingredients well and pour into a greased 1½-quart casserole. Bake for 20 minutes. Stir once and continue baking an additional 40 minutes or until top is browned and pone pulls away from the sides of the casserole.

HONEYED SWEET POTATO CASSEROLE

An excellent side dish for Rosh Hashanah or Sukkot. Try it as a dessert topped with orange slices or dessert whip.

4 medium sweet potatoes
½ cup honey or sugar
½ tsp. cinnamon
¼ tsp. salt
2 eggs, lightly beaten
2 Tbsps. margarine
½ cup orange marmalade
or pineapple jam

USE: 3-quart saucepan
1-quart casserole
YIELDS: 6 servings

Peel and slice sweet potatoes and cook in a 3-quart saucepan in salted water until tender, then drain. Mash in a large bowl.

Preheat oven to 350°.

Combine potatoes with all ingredients and mix well. Spread into 1-quart greased casserole.

Bake for 30 to 40 minutes. The top should be lightly browned and a cake tester should come out clean.

VEGETABLE KUGEL

2 medium zucchini
2 sweet potatoes
3 white potatoes
1 medium yellow squash
or butternut squash
1 large onion,
diced and sauteed
in ½ cup margarine, or
1 package onion soup mix
and ½ cup margarine
2 eggs, beaten
1 tsp. salt

USE: 3-quart saucepan
9 x 13-inch baking pan
YIELDS: 12 to 16 servings

Peel and cut vegetables into 1½-inch cubes. In a 3-quart saucepan cook in water until soft. Drain excess water and mash vegetables well.

Preheat oven to 350°.

Add sauteed onions or onion soup and margarine. Add eggs and salt and mix well.

Pour into greased 9 x 13-inch baking pan. Bake for 30 to 40 minutes.

ZUCCHINI KUGEL

3 pounds zucchini,
peeled and sliced
½ cup chopped onions
½ cup bread crumbs
2 eggs, beaten
½ cup margarine
1 tsp. salt
½ tsp. pepper
1 Tbsp. sugar

USE: 4-quart pot,
9 x 9-inch baking pan
YIELDS: 9 servings

In a 4-quart pot boil zucchini in salted water to cover until tender, about 15 minutes. Drain.

Preheat oven to 350°.

Mash the zucchini in a large bowl. Add all the remaining ingredients except for ¼ cup of margarine and mix well.

Pour into greased 9 x 9-inch baking pan and dot with the rest of the margarine. Bake for 1 hour.

RICE KUGEL

1 cup uncooked white rice
2 cups water
⅓ cup raisins
4 eggs, lightly beaten
1 cup orange juice
¾ cup sugar
⅓ cup oil
2 tsps. vanilla extract
¼ tsp. cinnamon
½ tsp. nutmeg

USE: 2-quart saucepan
9 x 9-inch baking pan
YIELDS: 9 servings

In a covered 2-quart saucepan, cook rice in water until soft but not mushy. While rice is cooking, soak the raisins to soften.

Preheat oven to 350°.

Combine eggs, orange juice, sugar, oil, vanilla, and remaining spices in a bowl. When rice is cooked, combine with other ingredients and add drained raisins.

Pour into 9 x 9-inch greased baking pan. Bake for 1 hour.

VARIATION
□ **Pineapple Rice Kugel:** Omit orange juice and raisins and substitute 1 cup crushed pineapple.

NOTE: Brown rice can be used instead of white. Use 1 cup brown rice and 2½ cups of water. Cook rice covered, over low flame for 45 minutes.

WHOLESOME RICE PUDDING

1 cup cooked brown rice
6 ounces tofu, blended
¼ tsp. vanilla extract
¼ cup honey
3 Tbsps. rolled oats
¼ cup raisins
¼ tsp. cinnamon
Pinch of powdered ginger
2 eggs, beaten
1 Tbsp. oil
3 tsps. chopped almonds

USE: 8 x 8-inch baking pan
YIELDS: 4 servings

Preheat oven to 350°.

Combine rice and tofu into a bowl and add vanilla, honey, oats, raisins, seasonings and eggs. Mix well. Pour mixture into a well greased 8 x 8-inch baking pan. Dribble oil over top and sprinkle with almonds.

Bake for 25 minutes or until set.

DELUXE FRUITY RICE KUGEL

2 cups uncooked white rice
4 cups water
½ cup raisins
4 eggs, beaten
⅓ cup nondairy creamer
⅓ cup oil
¾ cup flour
2 heaping Tbsps. orange marmalade
2 heaping Tbsps. apricot jam
¼ tsp. salt
Dash of pepper
1 tsp. sugar
1 tsp. cinnamon

USE: 2-quart saucepan
9 x 13-inch baking pan
YIELDS: 12 to 16 servings

In a covered 2-quart saucepan, cook rice in water until soft, but not mushy. Cover raisins with warm water and soak to soften while rice is cooking. Combine eggs, creamer, and oil in bowl; slowly add flour, stirring to avoid lumps.

Preheat oven to 350°.

Add marmalade, jam, salt and pepper. When rice is soft, add to other ingredients and finally add raisins.

Pour into a greased 9 x 13-inch baking pan. Sprinkle sugar and cinnamon on top. Bake for 1 hour or until set and top is golden brown.

KNISHES AND KISHKE

Knishes and Kishke are a mainstay at Bar Mitzvah and wedding buffets. There is nothing so delicious as a hot knish filled with potatoes and fried onions. Knishes may be prepared in tiny portions, to serve as hors d'oeuvres; medium size, to serve as a snack or side dish; or large enough to serve as an entree. Cabbage, kasha, and potato are all common fillings. They can be prepared with a minimum of fuss. Kishke is a mixture of flour, oil, and vegetables cooked alone or with a cholent, tzimmes, *or chicken. The taste of the main dish then permeates the kishke with its flavors and aromas.*

KNISHES ILLUSTRATED

1 Prepare the knish dough of your choice, using the All-Purpose Pastry Crust or Simple Flaky Dough. (See page 413). While it is chilling in the refrigerator prepare your favorite filling. Once it is ready, set it aside to cool.

2 Divide dough in half and roll each half into a 10 x 15-inch rectangle.

3 KNISH ROLL: Place half of the filling 1-inch from edge in a 3 x 12-inch strip.

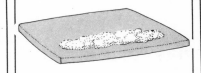

4 Roll filled side over (two times) like a jelly roll and tuck ends under. Carefully place on greased cookie sheet. Brush glaze over roll and slice through the crust at 2-inch intervals.
Repeat with second half of dough and filling, and bake as instructed.

5 INDIVIDUAL KNISHES: With a sharp knife cut six 5 x 4-inch rectangles. Place filling in center of each small rectangle.

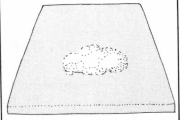

6 Fold one half over other half. Press to seal sides. Place on a greased baking sheet and brush with glaze. Repeat with second half of dough and filling, and bake as instructed.

CLASSIC POTATO KNISH

The dough for this knish is also ideal rolled out to cover a pot pie.

ALL-PURPOSE CRUST
2 cups flour
2 tsps. baking powder
1 tsp. salt
¼ cup margarine
¾ cup apple juice
1 egg, beaten, for glaze

POTATO FILLING
6 medium potatoes
¼ cup oil
2 large onions, diced
3 tsps. salt
1½ tsps. pepper
2 eggs, beaten

USE: 4-quart pot
7-inch skillet
YIELDS: 2 rolls or
1 dozen knishes

CRUST: In a large bowl sift flour with baking powder and salt. Cut margarine in with pastry blender or fingertips until dough is the consistency of coarse crumbs. Add ½ cup of apple juice and mix. Add the rest of the apple juice, 1 tablespoon at a time, until dough can be gathered into a ball. Knead 1 minute. Cover and refrigerate 30 minutes.

POTATO FILLING: Boil unpeeled potatoes in 4-quart pot in salted water. Cook until tender. While still warm, peel and mash. Heat oil in 7-inch skillet and saute onions until golden and soft. Add onions to mashed potatoes. Add seasonings and beaten eggs.

Preheat oven to 350°.

TO ASSEMBLE: Divide dough in half. Roll each half into a 10 x 14-inch rectangle. To fill, see Knishes Illustrated. Glaze each loaf with beaten egg.

Bake for 35 to 40 minutes or until golden for rolls, and 20 to 35 minutes for individual knishes.

VARIATION
□ **Kasha Knishes:** Mix 2 cups mashed potatoes with 2 cups cooked kasha and combine with sauteed onions, eggs, and seasoning. Proceed as above.

FLAKY CABBAGE KNISH

This dough should be refrigerated for at least 2 hours before rolling.

SIMPLE FLAKY DOUGH
1 cup margarine
2 cups flour
½ tsp. salt
⅓ cup ice water
2 Tbsps. vinegar
2 egg yolks
1 tsp. water
Sesame seeds, optional

CABBAGE FILLING
4 Tbsps. oil
4 cups shredded cabbage
1 large onion, diced
1 tsp. salt
⅛ tsp. pepper

USE: 2-quart saucepan
Baking sheet
YIELDS: 2 rolls or
1 dozen knishes

DOUGH: Cut margarine into flour and salt with a pastry cutter or two knives. In a separate bowl, mix cold water, vinegar, and one egg yolk. Add a little at a time to flour mixture, working in until thoroughly combined. Do not overmix — dough should be soft, not sticky. Place dough in plastic bag and refrigerate for 2 hours or more before rolling.

CABBAGE FILLING: In a 2-quart saucepan, heat oil. Saute cabbage and onion until tender. Remove from heat. Add salt and pepper and mix well. Cool.

Preheat oven to 425°.

TO ASSEMBLE: Divide dough in half. Roll each half into a 10 x 14-inch rectangle. To fill, see Knishes Illustrated. Beat egg yolk with 1 teaspoon of water and glaze each loaf. Sprinkle with sesame seeds if desired. Bake for 15 minutes at 425°. Reduce heat to 375° and continue baking for approximately 30 minutes or longer until golden brown.

VEGETABLE KISHKE

This looks and tastes like the real thing.

½ cup oil
2 stalks celery, sliced
2 carrots, sliced
1 onion, quartered
1½ cups flour
1½ tsps. salt
1 tsp. paprika
Pepper to taste

USE: Baking sheet
YIELDS: 6 to 8 slices kishke

Place ½ cup oil and cut-up vegetables in blender and blend until a thick paste is formed. Empty into bowl, add flour and seasonings, and mix well.

Shape into roll on a large piece of greased aluminum foil. Roll tightly in foil. Bake on baking sheet for 1 to 1½ hours at 350°. Slice and serve.

VARIATION
☐ For cholent, follow above directions, but bake only ½ hour; then place kishke wrapped in foil on top of food in cholent pot just before Shabbat. Leave it inside until cholent is served.

CRACKER KISHKE

1 box salted crackers
2 stalks celery, sliced
2 carrots, sliced
1 onion, quartered
½ cup margarine, melted
Salt and pepper to taste

USE: Small bowl
YIELDS: 6 to 8 slices kishke

Place all ingredients in blender or food processor and process.

Remove from blender into bowl. Shape into roll on a large piece of greased aluminum foil. Roll tightly in foil. Place in freezer overnight.

Bake at 375° for 40 minutes.

VEGETABLE SPECIALTIES AND PIES

When the occasion calls for that extra touch of elegance, here's a variety of specialties to choose from.

MUSHROOM TURNOVERS

Simple Flaky Dough
(Flaky Cabbage Knish,
page 309)
1 large onion, diced
½ cup margarine
½ pound mushrooms, diced
½ tsp. salt
Pepper to taste
2 Tbsps. flour
¼ cup water

USE: 10-inch skillet
Baking sheet
YIELDS: 12 turnovers

Prepare 1 recipe of Simple Flaky Dough and refrigerate for 2 hours.

Heat margarine in a 10-inch skillet and saute onion until tender. Add diced mushrooms and cook an additional 5 to 10 minutes; add salt, pepper, and flour and stir until smooth. Stir in water gradually and cook over low heat, stirring continuously, until thickened. Set aside to cool.

Preheat oven to 425°.

FLAKY DOUGH: Roll to ⅛-inch thickness. Cut into 3-inch rounds. Place a teaspoon of mushroom filling in the center of each round. Fold the dough over the filling, and press edges together with the tines of a fork. Place on ungreased baking sheet. Prick tops of turnovers with fork to allow steam to escape. Bake at 425° for 15 minutes; reduce heat to 375° and bake 15 minutes or until golden.

ONION SOUFFLE TART

DOUGH
2 cups flour
I tsp. baking powder
½ tsp. salt
2 Tbsps. margarine
at room temperature
¼ cup oil
2 egg yolks
½ cup water

FILLING
I pound onions
2 Tbsps. oil
2 eggs, separated
I Tbsp. chopped parsley
½ tsp. oregano
2 Tbsps. margarine
¼ tsp. salt
Pinch of white pepper

USE: 10-inch skillet
9 x 9-inch baking pan
YIELDS: 9 servings

DOUGH: Place dry ingredients in medium bowl; add margarine, oil, and egg yolks. Mix with wooden spoon, adding water slowly. Finish mixing by hand and chill in refrigerator 30 minutes.

FILLING: Dice onions. In a 10-inch skillet, saute onions in oil until transparent. Cool. In bowl, mix egg yolks, parsley, oregano, and margarine. Add onions, salt and pepper. Set aside to cool.

When onion mixture has cooled to room temperature, beat egg whites until stiff in a small bowl.

Gently fold into onion mixture, one third at a time.

Preheat oven to 350°.

Spread dough onto the greased 9 x 9-inch baking pan, pushing up against the sides to form a rim, and cover with onion mixture. Bake for 20 to 25 minutes.

SPINACH SOUFFLE

The fine soft consistency of this souffle is produced by first putting spinach leaves through a blender or food processor.

I pound fresh spinach or
2 10-ounce packages
frozen spinach
2 large cloves garlic
2 Tbsps. margarine
2 Tbsps. flour
2 eggs, separated
½ tsp. salt

USE: 10-inch skillet
8-inch round
or square pan
YIELDS: 8 servings

If fresh spinach is used, wash well and trim the stems. Cook in water that clings to the leaves until tender and drain. If frozen is used, cook in small amount of boiling salted water until tender and drain. Place spinach and garlic into the container of a blender or food processor and blend until smooth.

In a 10-inch skillet melt the 2 tablespoons of margarine and add the 2 tablespoons of flour. When this bubbles, pour in spinach and stir well. Pour into a large bowl and cool. Add the 2 egg yolks and mix well.

Preheat oven to 350°.

In a small bowl, beat the egg whites with ½ teaspoon of salt until stiff. Gently fold egg whites into spinach mixture, one third at a time. Pour into greased 8-inch round or square baking pan and bake for 45 minutes. Serve immediately.

CHINESE EGG ROLLS

A delicious, thin, flaky dough.

WRAPPERS
2 cups flour
½ tsp. salt
½ cup ice water
1 egg, beaten

FILLING
2 cups thinly sliced cabbage
2 Tbsps. oil
½ cup bean sprouts
½ cup chopped scallions
½ cup chopped
water chestnuts or
bamboo shoots
1 tsp. salt
1 tsp. sugar
1 Tbsp. sherry
Cornstarch

SAUCE 1
1 Tbsp. soy sauce
2 tsps. sugar
1 tsp. salt
1 egg, beaten
¼ cup melted margarine
or shortening

TANGY APRICOT SAUCE 2
3 Tbsps. cider vinegar
3 Tbsps. brown sugar
5 Tbsps. apricot
or peach preserves
¼ cup ground ginger
1 clove garlic, minced
Dash red pepper

USE: 10-inch skillet
YIELDS 12 egg rolls

WRAPPERS: In a large bowl, combine flour and salt. Add water and egg. Mix with a spoon until a soft ball is formed. On a lightly floured surface, knead dough about 2 minutes or until smooth and elastic. Cover with a damp towel and refrigerate 30 minutes.

Divide into six equal pieces. Cover the dough that is not being worked on with the damp towel to prevent it from drying out. On a lightly floured surface, roll one piece at a time into a 14 x 7-inch paper-thin rectangle. Cut in half into a 7-inch square for egg rolls and fill.

FILLING: In a 10-inch skillet saute cabbage in oil for 5 minutes. Add remaining filling ingredients, except for cornstarch, and mix. Cook uncovered another 5 minutes. Pour mixture into a colander and drain and cool 30 minutes.

TO ASSEMBLE: Place an egg roll wrapper like a diamond with point facing you. Dust cornstarch lightly over wrapper. Place 3 to 4 tablespoons of filling on lower section (nearest you). Fold bottom point over filling then fold in two side points to make an envelope. Continue to roll. Sprinkle top point with water and press to seal. Continue with all filling and wrappers until all are finished.

Deep fry in hot fat 360° for 4 to 8 minutes on each side turning only once. Drain well.

SAUCE: Prepare either sauce to serve with the egg rolls. Mix all ingredients in small bowl.

Serve egg rolls hot with sauce and hot Chinese mustard.

NOTE: When preparing egg-roll wrappers in advance, dust corn starch over each piece before stacking. Wrap securely with plastic wrap or foil if not using immediately. Can be kept in the refrigerator for up to 1 week or frozen up to 3 months.

VEGETABLE PIES *made with savory vegetables are a lovely side dish with a gourmet look and the appeal of a dessert. Try a Sweet Potato Pie to brighten a Yom Tov meal.*

SQUASH PIE

1 large butternut squash
2 eggs
1 Tbsp. margarine
⅓ cup honey
¼ tsp. salt
½ tsp. cinnamon
¼ tsp. nutmeg
1 prebaked 9-inch pie shell, frozen or homemade (page 445)

USE: 3-quart saucepan
9-inch pie plate
YIELDS: 8 servings

Cut squash into big chunky pieces. Cook in 3-quart saucepan in simmering water until soft. Peel and put into blender.

Preheat oven to 375°.

Add all remaining ingredients to blender in order listed. Blend.

Pour into pie crust. Bake for 45 minutes to 1 hour.

This pie is best served warm but may be served cold.

TZIMMES BARS

An interesting variation to the traditional tzimmes *served on Rosh Hashanah.*

¼ cup margarine, softened, or ¼ cup solid shortening
¼ cup sugar
6 Tbsps. cherry liqueur
1 cup peeled, grated apples
1 cup grated sweet potatoes
¾ cup matzoh meal
½ cup pitted, chopped prunes
1 Tbsp. lemon juice
½ tsp. cinnamon
½ tsp. salt

USE: 9 x 9-inch baking pan
YIELDS: 9 servings

Preheat oven to 350°.

Cream margarine and sugar in a large bowl. Add remaining ingredients and stir until well blended. Spoon into a well-greased 9 x 9-inch baking pan.

Bake for 45 minutes or until firm and lightly browned. Cool on rack before cutting into squares.

SWEET POTATO PIE

**2 cups cooked,
mashed sweet potatoes**
1 tsp. cinnamon
½ tsp. powdered ginger
½ tsp. salt
½ cup light brown sugar
¾ cup nondairy creamer
2 Tbsps. margarine, melted
3 eggs, beaten
**2 9-inch prebaked pie shells,
frozen or homemade
(page 445)**

USE: 2 9-inch pie plates
YIELDS: 16 servings

Preheat oven to 450°.

Mix sweet potatoes with spices and sugar. Add creamer, melted margarine, and eggs. Mix well and pour into pie shells.

Bake at 450° for 10 minutes, then reduce to 350° for 45 minutes.

DELUXE VEGETABLE PIE

1 medium onion, diced
1 cup chopped cabbage or
1 cup diced zucchini
1 cup diced fresh carrots
½ cup mushrooms
½ cup water
1 Tbsp. oil
1 Tbsp. flour
½ cup nondairy creamer
1 cup fresh or frozen peas
1 egg, beaten
¼ tsp. thyme
⅛ tsp. salt
⅛ tsp. pepper
1 clove garlic, minced
**1 unbaked deep-dish 9-inch
pie shell**

USE: 3-quart saucepan
9-inch deep-dish pie plate
YIELDS: 8 servings

Place onion, cabbage, and carrots in 3-quart saucepan with ½ cup water and steam until tender, about 5 minutes. Set vegetables aside.

Preheat oven to 350°.

In 3-quart saucepan heat oil and stir in flour over medium heat until four is golden brown. Add creamer slowly, stirring constantly to prevent lumping until thickened. Remove from fire. Add cooked vegetables and peas. Beat the egg in quickly and thoroughly. Add seasonings.

Mix well and pour filling into pie shell. Bake for 20 to 25 minutes. Be careful not to overfill pie shell.

VARIATIONS
☐ **Dairy:** Top with grated cheese during last 10 to 15 minutes of baking.

☐ **Individual Tarts:** Substitute 8 tart shells for piecrust; fill and bake as directed.

Grains and Pasta

WHITE AND BROWN RICE

Rice is a food staple around the world. It can be prepared simply for a weekday supper or served as the basis for a complex combination of flavors and textures. We have adapted the recipes of many countries to our own palate. Spanish rice simmers in a fragrant tomato sauce; Chinese rice dishes perfectly combine rice, stir-fried vegetables, and a light sauce. Brown rice with its added nutrition and nutty flavor can be substituted for white rice in many of these recipes. Crunchy toppings accent the bland smoothness of rice; sesame seeds, sunflower seeds, nuts, or lightly steamed vegetables are good accompaniments. Instead of water for cooking try chicken stock or liquid from cooked vegetables for additional flavor.

TIPS FOR PERFECT RICE

☐ WHITE RICE: Combine 1 cup of rice with 2 cups salted water and 1 tablespoon of oil in a 3 quart pot. Bring to boil and simmer covered 12 to 14 minutes, or until all water is absorbed. Makes 3 cups of rice.

☐ BROWN RICE: Combine 1 cup brown rice with 2½ to 3 cups salted water and 1 tablespoon of oil in a 3 quart pot. Bring to boil and simmer covered 40 to 45 minutes.

NOTE: For alternative method to prepare either white or brown rice, follow procedure above but instead of simmering, once rice begins to boil turn off flame and let pot stand covered; 15 minutes for white rice and 40 minutes for brown rice.

DELUXE BROWN RICE

1 small onion
1 clove garlic (optional)
2 scallions
¼ green pepper (or a red one, if available, for color)
2 to 3 Tbsps. oil
1 cup chopped broccoli florets (optional)
¼ cup shredded cabbage
2 cups cooked brown rice
2 tsps. soy sauce
Salt
Dash pepper
2 tsps. toasted sesame or sunflower seeds

USE: Heavy 10-inch skillet
YIELDS: 4 to 6 servings

Dice the onion, garlic, scallions, and pepper into very small pieces. Heat the oil in a heavy 10-inch skillet, and saute onion and garlic in oil over a medium flame until golden. Add scallions, pepper, broccoli, and then cabbage, stirring until vegetables are tender.

Add the rice, breaking up any lumps with a wooden spoon. (If using leftover rice that seems very lumpy, steam it slightly first.) Mix rice well. Add soy sauce and cook for a few minutes while continuing to stir. Season to taste.

Serve immediately. Top each portion with sesame or sunflower seeds.

CLASSIC DINNER RICE

2 Tbsps. oil
2 Tbsps. margarine
1 onion, diced
½ pound mushrooms, diced
2 carrots, diced
1 green pepper, diced
2 cups white rice
2 tsps. salt
1 tsp. pepper
1 tsp. saffron
4 cups water

USE: 10-inch skillet
YIELDS: 8 to 10 servings

In a heavy 10-inch skillet with a tight-fitting lid, heat oil and margarine. Add diced vegetables and saute until soft, 5 to 8 minutes. Add rice and stir to coat grains with oil. Stir in seasoning and add water. Bring water to a boil and cover. Simmer 20 to 30 minutes or until all liquid is absorbed.

Fluff rice with fork and serve hot.

CANTONESE FRIED RICE

4 Tbsps. oil
1 medium onion, diced
2 eggs, beaten
1 Tbsp. soy sauce
2½ cups cooked rice
Dash of pepper

USE: 10-inch skillet
YIELDS: 4 servings

In 10-inch skillet, heat oil on medium flame. Add diced onion and saute until translucent. Add eggs and fry, stirring constantly to break eggs into tiny pieces. Add soy sauce and stir.

Add cooked rice. Sprinkle with dash of pepper. Combine well, stirring over heat, about 2 minutes. Add a little more soy sauce if necessary.

SAVORY PECAN RICE

½ cup margarine
½ cup chopped onion
1 pound mushrooms, chopped
1 cup diced celery and celery leaves (optional)
1 Tbsp. salt
½ tsp. pepper
½ tsp. marjoram
⅛ tsp. sage
⅛ tsp. thyme
4 cups cooked rice
⅔ cup finely chopped pecans
Water to moisten

USE: 10-inch skillet
3-quart casserole
YIELDS: 8 to 10 servings

Preheat oven to 350°.

In a 10-inch skillet, melt margarine and saute vegetables. Stir in seasonings. Remove from fire and stir in rice, nuts, and water.

Turn into a greased casserole and bake for 30 minutes covered, then bake uncovered for another 30 minutes, adding water if rice gets too dry.

VARIATION
□ **Chicken Pecan Rice:** Place four uncooked chicken pieces on top of rice mixture in casserole and bake covered 30 minutes and uncovered 30 minutes.

MUSHROOM AND RICE CASSEROLE

2 cups white rice
5 cups water
1 tsp. salt
½ cup margarine, melted
1 package onion soup mix
1 pound mushrooms, diced

USE: 3-quart casserole
YIELDS: 8 servings

Preheat oven to 350°.

Combine all ingredients in large casserole dish. Mix well and bake approximately 40 minutes until done.

VARIATION
□ **Top-of-the-stove method:** Bring salted water to boil in 3-quart pot. Add margarine and onion soup mix. Stir until it dissolves in water. Add rice and mushrooms. Lower flame and cover pot. Simmer for 20 minutes, stirring occasionally.

SPANISH RICE

¼ cup corn or olive oil
2 cups white rice
1 large onion, diced
1 medium
green pepper, diced
2 to 3 medium cloves
garlic, chopped
¼ cup tomato puree
2 medium tomatoes, diced
4 cups water
2 tsps. salt
1 tsp. pepper
1 Tbsp. brown sugar

USE: 4-quart pot
YIELDS: 8 servings

Heat ¼ cup oil in 4-quart pot. Add 2 cups rice. Reduce heat and saute rice until golden and toasted. While heat is on medium, add diced onion and green pepper. When soft, add garlic and continue to stir. Add tomato puree to mixture. Stir continuously so that liquid is absorbed and ingredients are evenly mixed. Add water and stir. Add salt, pepper, and brown sugar. Cook covered on low to medium flame 15 to 20 minutes until rice absorbs all the liquid.

PERSIAN RICE

Begin by soaking the rice the night before. This exotic dish can be placed on the blech for Friday night or Shabbat lunch as the Persians do.

2 cups white rice
2 cups boiling water
1 medium onion
1 pound carrots
2 Tbsps. oil
1 cup raisins
2 medium potatoes
4 Tbsps. oil

USE: 4-quart pot
10-inch skillet
YIELDS: 8 servings

Soak 2 cups of rice overnight in enough water to cover. Drain rice, put into a 4-quart pot, cover with 2 cups boiling water. Simmer about 5 minutes until rice is just soft. Set rice aside.

Chop onion. Peel carrots and cut into matchstick-size pieces. In a 10-inch skillet saute onions and carrots in 2 tablespoons of oil until soft. Add raisins and cook 2 minutes more. Set aside.

Peel and slice the potatoes thin. Put 2 tablespoons oil in the bottom of a heavy 4-quart pot. Place potato slices in a single layer in the oil. Spoon half the rice over the potatoes. Spread the sauteed vegetables over the rice and top with remaining rice. Sprinkle last 2 tablespoons of oil over the rice. Cover the pot with a paper towel and put on a tight-fitting cover. Cook over very low heat at least 45 minutes.

RICE SALADS *made with fluffy and firm rice make a colorful addition to a buffet table or an interesting change for a Shabbat salad.*

CHILLED RICE SALAD

**2 cups cooked brown rice
(grains should be separate)**

**1 cup chopped fresh
parsley, loosely packed**

**1 cup chopped scallions,
loosely packed**

**¼ cup chopped
fresh mint (optional)**

¼ cup olive or vegetable oil

¼ cup lemon juice

¼ tsp. cumin

½ garlic clove, crushed

Salt to taste

Pepper to taste

4 medium tomatoes, chopped

8 radishes, thinly sliced

USE: 2-quart bowl
YIELDS: 4 to 6 servings

In a 2-quart bowl combine rice, parsley, scallions, mint, oil, lemon juice, and seasonings. Toss well and chill. Before serving, add tomatoes and radishes, then toss again.

ROSY RICE SALAD

2 cups water

1 cup red wine

1 cup brown rice

2 medium zucchini, diced

1 cup diced mushrooms

1 large red onion, diced

1 clove garlic, diced

⅓ cup oil

⅓ cup lemon juice

1 tsp. salt

2 Tbsps. sugar

2 medium tomatoes, diced

USE: 3-quart pot
Large salad bowl
YIELDS: 8 to 10 servings

To prepare rice, combine water and wine in a 3-quart pot and bring to a boil. Add rice, cover, and cook 45 minutes until tender. Set rice aside and cool.

In a large bowl, combine rice with diced vegetables (except tomatoes) and garlic. In a separate bowl combine oil, lemon juice, and salt and sugar. Mix well and toss the rice and vegetables with the dressing. Just before serving, add diced tomatoes. Serve warm or cold.

WHOLESOME GRAINS

Kasha and Barley are delicious served plain as side dishes or substituted for other grains in a main dish. Kasha has a tasty full flavor. A famous traditional version, Kasha Varnishkas, is a blend of kasha and noodles.

KASHA VARNISHKAS

This old-fashioned heimishe dish is not only tasty, but nutritious as well.

2 Tbsps. oil
1 onion, diced
1 cup diced mushrooms (optional)
1 cup whole kasha
1 egg, beaten
2 cups boiling soup stock or water
1 tsp. salt
¼ tsp. pepper
1½ cups bowtie noodles, cooked and drained
2 Tbsps. margarine

USE: 2-quart saucepan
1-quart saucepan
YIELDS: 4 to 6 servings

Heat oil in a 2-quart saucepan over medium flame. Saute onion and mushrooms until golden brown, about 5 minutes. Add kasha. Stir in beaten egg. Saute for 2 minutes, stirring with fork or wooden spoon until grains are separate.

At the same time, in a 1-quart saucepan bring liquid to a boil. Pour boiling liquid over kasha, add seasonings, and simmer covered for 10 to 15 minutes, until kasha has absorbed all the liquid and is dry and fluffy.

In serving bowl, combine drained noodles with kasha, while both are still warm. Melt in 2 tablespoons margarine, and mix until everything is well combined.

Serve warm.

TABOULI

Bulgur or cracked wheat is a nutritious whole grain rich in fiber and B vitamins. This salad is flavorful and easy to prepare.

1 cup bulgur
1 cup boiling water
1 cup chopped parsley
1 medium onion, diced
2 cups chopped tomatoes
¼ cup chopped coriander (optional)
sprig fresh mint, chopped
¾ cup lemon juice
½ cup oil
Salt to taste
Pepper to taste

USE: Large mixing bowl
YIELDS: 8 servings

Place bulgur in a large mixing bowl. Pour 1 cup boiling water over the bulgur and let stand 30 minutes, or until all water is absorbed. Combine bulgur with vegetables, lemon juice, oil, salt, and pepper.

Refrigerate, covered, a few hours or overnight. Serve cold.

SHLISHKAS

A delicious alternative to pasta — with real Old-World flavor.

4 large potatoes
3 cups flour
1 egg
1 Tbsp. oil
1 Tbsp. salt
1 cup bread crumbs
1 Tbsp. oil

USE: 4-quart pot
10-inch skillet
YIELDS: 6 servings

Peel potatoes and boil in 4-quart pot in salted water until tender. Drain and put in a large bowl. Add flour, egg, 1 tablespoon oil, and salt; mash together. Roll out into long ropes, ½ inch wide, on a floured board.

Cut into 1½-inch pieces. Drop into 4-quart pot of boiling water. Boil for 10 minutes until they float to the top. Continue to cook 5 minutes longer. Drain in a colander.

Add 1 tablespoon oil to bread crumbs in a large bowl, add shlishkas and toss to coat. In a 10-inch skillet, in 1 tablespoon oil, fry shlishkas until bread crumbs are browned.

Serve hot.

TOASTED BARLEY AND MUSHROOMS

⅔ cup barley
4 cups boiling water
2 beef bouillon cubes
3 Tbsps. margarine
¼ pound fresh mushrooms, sliced
⅛ cup scallions, sliced
1 clove garlic, minced
½ tsp. salt
¼ tsp. thyme, crushed
Dash of pepper

USE: 10-inch skillet
2-quart saucepan
YIELDS: 4 servings

Preheat oven to 350°.

Place barley on ungreased baking sheet and bake for 20 minutes until light golden brown, shaking pan occasionally.

Stir toasted barley into 4 cups boiling water. Add bouillon cubes. Reduce heat, cover, and simmer 1 hour until tender, stirring occasionally. Drain and set aside.

In a 10-inch skillet, melt margarine and cook mushrooms, scallions, and garlic until tender, about 3 to 5 minutes.

Add drained barley, salt, thyme, and pepper. Continue cooking over medium heat 2 to 3 minutes until heated through. Serve hot.

PASTA

PASTA *is so well known in America that its Italian origin is often forgotten. Now widely available in a variety of shapes and flavors, one often sees whole-wheat or spinach pasta in stores next to the white version. For an effective balance of color and tastes, combine white and whole-wheat spaghetti. Pasta adapts well to a variety of sauces. Whether complemented by a fragrant sauce, or nestled under a pile of lightly steamed vegetables with a bit of cream or cheese, pasta is a perfect dish.*

Though usually eaten hot, pasta retains its taste when served cold. Macaroni Salad is brightened by the addition of several kinds of raw vegetables. Homemade noodles have a special appeal; the difference between fresh homemade noodles and the store-bought variety is unmistakeable.

HOMEMADE HAND-ROLLED PASTA

The amount of this recipe may be increased. It is an excellent dough for lasagna and kreplach. If possible, avoid making the dough in damp weather.

1¾ cups flour or
1⅔ cups whole-wheat flour
2 extra-large eggs, beaten
2 tsps. oil
Pinch of salt

YIELDS: 4 servings
or 1 pound noodles

Place flour in a mound on a board and make a well in the center. Add eggs, oil, and salt. Mix together with a fork and incorporate flour from inner rim of well. When half the flour has been incorporated, start to knead, using the palms of the hand and not the fingers. Use most of the flour, then sift remaining flour and set aside. Knead dough for 10 minutes. Divide in two portions.

TO ROLL: Dust board with remaining sifted flour. Roll out each ball of dough as thin as possible, rotating the round of dough, while rolling. When the round becomes too large to move by hand, lightly drape the sheet of dough on the rolling pin, then, holding other end of sheet, reverse direction of rolling pin.

Cut into ½-inch to ¾-inch-wide strips. If pasta is not to be used immediately, dry for several hours. Place strips on a clean cloth and allow to dry 30 minutes. Store in a brown paperbag in refrigerator. Dough can be stored up to 2 weeks.

Fresh pasta cooks more quickly than commercial. Place in boiling water and begin checking after 5 minutes. Whole-wheat pasta needs more cooking time.

VARIATION
☐ This recipe is also ideal for preparation in pasta machine. Prepare dough and follow manufacturer's directions.

PASTA SHELLS WITH SWEET-AND-SOUR SAUCE

An elegant accompaniment to a festive meal.

1 medium zucchini, finely diced
1 large onion, finely diced
4 Tbsps. margarine
1 Tbsp. olive oil
1 cup mushrooms, finely diced
(optional)
¾ tsp. salt
1 to 2 cloves garlic, minced
4 large tomatoes, diced
½ cup white wine
¼ tsp. basil
¼ tsp. rosemary
½ small bay leaf
Dash pepper
1 tsp. sugar
1 tsp. white vinegar
16 ounces shells

USE: 10-inch skillet
4-quart saucepan
YIELDS: 4 to 6 servings

In a 10-inch skillet, saute zucchini and onion in margarine and oil until slightly tender.

Add remaining ingredients, except the shells, to sauteed vegetables and simmer covered about 1½ hours or until thick.

In a 4-quart pot cook shells in boiling salted water until soft, about 10 minutes. Rinse, drain, and combine with sauce.

Serve hot.

SPAGHETTI WITH WHITE TUNA SAUCE

This wine-flavored sauce offers a sophisticated change of pace.

**8 ounces spaghetti
or linguine**

4 Tbsps. margarine

2 cloves garlic, minced

2 Tbsps. flour

**2 cups dry white wine,
water, or fish stock**

**¼ cup chopped
fresh parsley**

¼ tsp. salt

Dash of pepper

**1½ tsps. crushed
thyme leaves**

**2 7-ounce cans tuna,
drained and chopped**

USE: 2 3-quart saucepans
YIELDS: 4 servings

In a 3-quart saucepan cook spaghetti in boiling, salted water. When done, rinse, drain, and set aside.

While spaghetti is cooking, melt margarine in a 3-quart saucepan. Add garlic and stir-fry 1 minute over moderate heat. With a wire whisk, stir in flour, making sure there are no lumps; add the liquid while stirring. Add the chopped parsley, salt, pepper, and thyme; simmer gently 10 minutes. Add tuna and heat through.

Serve warm over spaghetti or linguine.

FRIED CABBAGE AND NOODLES

½ head cabbage

1 large onion, diced

4 Tbsps. oil

1 tsp. salt

½ tsp. pepper

½ tsp. paprika

8 ounces medium noodles

USE: 10-inch skillet
3-quart saucepan
YIELDS: 4 to 6 servings

Grate cabbage on large holes of grater. Heat oil in 10-inch skillet. Add onion, cabbage, and seasonings. Saute on low flame uncovered until soft and lightly browned, approximately 45 minutes, stirring occasionally.

In a 3-quart saucepan, cook noodles in boiling salted water until tender. Rinse, drain and combine with sauteed cabbage. Mix gently and serve hot.

PASTA SALADS *are a stylish change from potato salad. Served cold they add color and texture to a luncheon meal or buffet table.*

MACARONI-TUNA SALAD

8 ounces elbow macaroni

**1 7-ounce can tuna,
drained and flaked**

2 sour pickles

2 scallions

In a 3-quart saucepan cook macaroni in boiling water. When done, rinse and drain. Combine with tuna in a large bowl.

Chop pickles, scallions and celery if used. Add vegetables with mayonnaise and seasoning to tuna and macaroni and mix well.

►

1 stalk celery (optional)
¼ to ⅓ cup mayonnaise
¼ tsp. white pepper
Salt

USE: 3-quart saucepan
Large mixing bowl
YIELDS: 6 servings

Cover and chill.

MULTI-COLOR NOODLE SALAD

8 ounces
white spiral noodles
8 ounces spinach
spiral noodles
1 10-ounce package frozen
cauliflower, partially thawed
2 10-ounce packages frozen
broccoli, partially thawed
4 Tbsps. oil
3 carrots, slivered
Garlic powder to taste
Salt to taste

USE: 4-quart pot
10-inch skillet
Large salad bowl
YIELDS: 10 to 12 servings

In a 4-quart pot cook noodles in boiling salted water. When done, rinse, drain, and set aside.

Chop cauliflower and broccoli. In a 10-inch skillet heat 2 tablespoons of oil. Add cauliflower, broccoli, and carrots. Saute until soft. Combine sauteed vegetables with noodles. Add 2 tablespoons of oil, garlic powder, and salt. Mix well.

NOTE: If using fresh broccoli and cauliflower, they should first be steamed until slightly tender. Then break into florets and saute in heated oil along with slivered carrots.

SWEET-AND-SOUR PASTA SALAD

You may want to make this unusual salad a day in advance in order to bring out the flavor.

8 ounces elbow macaroni
2 carrots, shredded
2 green peppers, shredded
1 onion, diced
2 Tbsps. olive oil
2 Tbsps. apple cider vinegar
Juice from ½ lemon
3 Tbsps. mayonnaise
½ tsp. salt
1 tsp. honey

USE: 4-quart pot
Large salad bowl
YIELDS: 6 to 8 servings

In a 4-quart pot cook macaroni in boiling salted water. When done rinse, drain, and set aside.

In a large bowl combine vegetables. Add oil, vinegar, lemon juice, mayonnaise, salt, and honey. Add cooked macaroni and toss. Let salad marinate several hours or overnight.

Serve cold.

PASTA SPECIALTIES *feature a combination of pasta with fresh vegetables and spices for authentic Italian flavor.*

SPAGHETTI WITH EGGPLANT ITALIENNE

16 ounces spaghetti
1 large eggplant
1 small onion, diced
5 Tbsps. oil
2 cloves garlic, minced
2 pounds tomatoes, peeled and diced
1 6-ounce can tomato paste
⅓ cup water
2 tsps. salt
¼ tsp. red pepper
½ tsp. dried basil
¼ tsp. dried oregano
¼ cup chopped fresh or 2 Tbsps. dried parsley

USE: 4-quart pot
10-inch skillet
YIELDS: 6 to 8 servings

In a 4-quart pot cook spaghetti in boiling salted water. When done, rinse, drain, and set aside.

Peel and cube eggplant; salt cubes and let sit 30 minutes. Then rinse, drain, and pat dry.

In a 10-inch skillet saute onion in 2 tablespoons lightly heated oil for 2 to 3 minutes until tender and golden. Add minced garlic and tomatoes. Stir in tomato paste, water, and seasonings. Cover and simmer 5 minutes.

Saute eggplant in 10-inch skillet in remaining 3 tablespoons oil until light brown and soft. Stir often. Add to tomato sauce along with parsley. Cook over low heat for 30 minutes. Add additional water if necessary.

Pour sauce over cooked spaghetti. Serve hot.

VARIATION
□ **Dairy:** Grate 6 ounces mozzarella cheese and sprinkle a little bit over each serving while sauce is hot, so that cheese melts slightly.

PASTA PRIMAVERA

16 ounces spaghetti
1 10-ounce package frozen peas
1 bunch broccoli florets, cut into small pieces
2 zucchini, cubed
2 Tbsps. margarine
1 onion, chopped
3 cloves garlic, minced
2 tomatoes, peeled and chopped
½ cup dry white wine
½ tsp. dried basil
½ cup nondairy creamer
½ tsp. salt
¼ tsp. pepper

USE: 4-quart pot
3-quart saucepan
YIELDS: 4 to 6 servings

In a 4-quart pot cook spaghetti in boiling salted water. When done, rinse, drain and set aside.

In a 3-quart saucepan, cook peas in boiling water for 5 minutes, then add broccoli and cook for 5 more minutes. Add zucchini and cook for 1 minute. Drain vegetables and run under cold water.

In a 3-quart saucepan, heat margarine, add onion and garlic, then saute until translucent. Add tomatoes, wine, basil, and nondairy creamer. Cook for several minutes until slightly thickened. Season with salt and pepper; pour sauce over spaghetti and top with cooked vegetables.

Toss and serve hot.

Dips and Dressings

DIPS

Dips and spreads served with crackers, bite-size raw vegetables or potato chips are delightful as snacks, appetizers or light meals. Garnish with bits of olives, chopped parsley, pimiento, or any contrasting vegetables. Baba Ganoush, with its smoky eggplant taste, is delicious and the Yemenite Zchug has a spiciness that is particularly Mideastern in flavor.

CURRIED MAYONNAISE DIP

A good accompaniment to cold meat and poultry.

2 cups mayonnaise
1 Tbsp. curry powder
1 clove garlic, minced
¼ tsp. turmeric
¼ tsp. salt
⅛ tsp. pepper
Dash ginger

YIELDS: 2 cups

Combine all ingredients in a bowl and mix well.

Refrigerate in closed container until ready to serve.

GREEN MAYONNAISE DIP

1 bunch scallions
¾ cup mayonnaise
1 Tbsp. lemon juice

YIELDS: 1 cup

Remove white part of scallions. Wash and cut green portion into medium-size pieces and place in blender. Add mayonnaise and lemon juice and blend until creamy.

Refrigerate in closed container until ready to serve.

CHATZILIM

A favorite Israeli eggplant appetizer. The distinctive charred flavor comes from cooking the eggplant over an open flame.

2 large eggplants
5 cloves garlic
1 onion, diced, (optional)
3 Tbsps. mayonnaise
Dash of pepper
¼ tsp. salt (optional)
1 tsp. sugar (optional)

YIELDS: 2-3 cups

Cook eggplant over an open medium to low flame, turning it every few minutes with a fork until the outside is even charred and the inside is tender, from 20 to 30 minutes.

Remove from fire and cool. Peel eggplant. Place eggplant, diced garlic, and all other ingredients in food processor.

Serve as a dip with pita or challah.

PARSLEY DIP

This parsley dip is good and hot.

2 cloves garlic, minced
¼ cup olive oil
Pinch salt
Juice of 1 lemon
1 bunch parsley

YIELDS: 1 cup

Place garlic, olive oil, salt, and lemon juice in food processor. Add parsley and process until smooth.

Delicious spread on challah.

AVOCADO DIP

1 ripe avocado
1 Tbsp. lemon juice or
juice of ½ lemon
¼ cup mayonnaise
1 small onion, diced
½ tsp. salt
Dash pepper
½ tsp. garlic powder

YIELDS: 1½ cups

Peel avocado. Remove pit and reserve. Cut avocado into chunks.

Place avocado with remaining ingredients in blender and blend until smooth.

Refrigerate if not using immmediately. Be sure to place avocado pit in the spread and cover tightly with plastic wrap until ready to serve. This keeps the avocado from turning brown.

BABA GANOUSH

A delicious Middle Eastern eggplant salad or dip. Be sure eggplant is thoroughly baked before you begin.

1 large eggplant
1 onion, diced
1 green pepper, diced
6 Tbsps. olive oil
Juice of 1 large lemon
3 cloves garlic, minced
1 tsp. salt
¼ tsp. pepper
3 to 4 Tbsps. tahini
(optional)
2 to 3 Tbsps. mayonnaise

USE: 7-inch skillet
YIELDS: 1½ cups

Prick eggplant on all sides with fork. Wrap in aluminum foil, place in oven at 400° and bake for 45 minutes to 1 hour or until soft. Split the baked eggplant and allow to drain. Scoop out the pulp and mash fine or process in food processor.

In a 7-inch skillet saute onion and green pepper in 6 tablespoons of oil.

Mix lemon juice and garlic into eggplant. Add sauteed onion, green pepper, and excess olive oil. Mix well or process. Add salt, green pepper, and tahini. Add enough mayonnaise to lighten the color. Add more lemon juice or vinegar if you prefer a tangier taste.

Refrigerate in a closed container until ready to serve.

Arrange on a platter garnished with cut-up fresh vegetables.

GUACAMOLE

2 ripe avocados 2 medium tomatoes, finely diced 1 small onion, grated or diced 2 tsps. lemon or lime juice 1 tsp. salt 2 cloves garlic, minced Chili powder to taste Cumin or coriander, to taste (optional) YIELDS: 3 cups	Peel avocado. Remove pit and reserve. In a medium bowl mash avocado well. Add diced tomatoes, grated onion, and remaining ingredients. Add more salt and lemon juice if desired. Mix well. Refrigerate if not using immediately. Be sure to place avocado pit in the spread and cover tightly with plastic wrap until ready to serve. This keeps the avocado from turning brown. Serve with corn chips or tacos.

HOUMMOUS WITH TAHINI

A tasty Israeli dip served with fresh vegetables and pita.

2 cups dried chickpeas 1½ tsps. baking soda 5 cloves garlic, minced 4 tsps. salt 1 cup lemon juice 1 cup tahini 2 Tbsps. olive oil ¼ cup chopped fresh parsley Lemon slices Paprika USE: 6-quart pot YIELDS: 6 cups	Place chickpeas in a large bowl. Add baking soda and cover with water. Keep refrigerated overnight. Drain and rinse. Cover chickpeas with water in 6-quart pot and simmer 1 to 1½ hours or until tender. Drain. Grind chickpeas in a grinder. Place in large bowl. Add garlic, salt, lemon juice, tahini, and olive oil. Blend thoroughly. Refrigerate in closed container until ready to serve. May be kept in refrigerator up to 2 weeks. Arrange on a platter garnished with parsley, lemon slices and paprika. VARIATION □ Substitute two cans drained chickpeas.

VEGETABLE EGGPLANT SALAD

3 Tbsps. olive oil 1 onion, finely diced 2 cloves garlic, minced 1 green pepper, diced 1 zucchini, cubed 1 eggplant, peeled and cubed 6 to 7 fresh tomatoes, cut into pieces ½ tsp. basil ½ tsp. salt USE: 10-inch skillet YIELDS: 3 to 4 cups	In a 10-inch skillet heat 3 tablespoons of oil. Saute onion and garlic for 5 minutes. Add remaining vegetables and seasonings. Cook until all vegetables are very soft, about 1 hour. Mash well or blend in blender. Refrigerate in closed container until ready to serve. Serve as dip or spread directly on crackers and garnish with olive rounds or bits of pimiento.

ANCHOVY DIP

½ tube anchovy paste
2 cups mayonnaise
1 onion
2 cloves garlic
4 to 6 Tbsps. lemon juice

YIELDS: 3 cups

Place all ingredients in blender, adding enough lemon juice to make a creamy consistency.

Refrigerate in closed container until ready to serve.

TAHINI-SESAME DIP SUPREME

Serve with fish, falafel, or vegetables.

1 cup sesame tahini
½ cup fresh lemon juice
(3 to 4 lemons)
3 cloves garlic, minced
1 tsp. salt
¼ to ½ cup cold water

YIELDS: 2 cups

Place first four ingredients in blender. As they whip, slowly add water. Color will begin to change from tan to white and will have a thin consistency.

Pour in bowl and garnish with fresh parsley or paprika.

TOFU TAHINI DIP

1 pound tofu
1 cup tahini
¾ cup lemon juice
2 tsps. salt
2 cloves garlic

YIELDS: 3 cups

Blend or process all ingredients until smooth.

Refrigerate in closed container until ready to serve.

YEMENITE ZCHUG

This is a very hot Yemenite dip. Use as you would mustard with fish, meat, or chicken.

2 bunches coriander
(cilantro)
3 small, hot green peppers
4 to 5 cloves garlic
1 large lemon, peeled
½ tsp. salt or to taste

YIELDS: 2 to 3 cups

Wash and cut the stems off the coriander. Rinse well in clear water, and squeeze out all the excess water.

Cut up peppers, mince garlic, and dice lemon. Place all ingredients in blender at high speed until just blended. Do not let it get watery — keep it thick.

Add salt to taste. Refrigerate in closed container until ready to serve.

NOTE: When working with hot peppers, avoid touching face and eyes. It's best to wear rubber gloves.

SALAD DRESSINGS

Dressings are exactly what the word implies. They "dress up" a salad, and homemade dressings have added zest and appeal. Pick a dressing that will complement your salad; vary ingredients and seasonings to suit the salad. Olive oil, corn oil, and vegetable oil each impart a different taste, as does lemon juice or vinegar. Fresh herbs are always best. Most salads are tastiest when the dressing is added just before serving so the vegetables retain their crispness, while other dressings are added in advance to allow the flavor to develop. Remember to add just enough dressing to coat the vegetables; don't drown the salad. Homemade dressings can be kept refrigerated for at least one week.

ITALIAN DRESSING

1 clove garlic
½ tsp. dry mustard
½ tsp. basil
½ tsp. salt
4 Tbsps. wine vinegar
½ cup olive oil

YIELDS: ¾ cup

Put garlic in garlic press and put in small bowl. Add mustard, basil, salt, and vinegar. Stir in oil and mix until blended. Store in covered jar. Refrigerate until ready to use. Shake well before using.

ROSEMARY MUSTARD DRESSING

4 Tbsps. prepared mustard
4 Tbsps. flour
2 tsps. salt
4½ tsps. sugar
¾ cup white vinegar
1½ tsps. rosemary

YIELDS: 1 cup

In a small bowl mix mustard with flour, salt, and sugar until thoroughly blended. Slowly add vinegar while constantly stirring.

Beat into a smooth, thick sauce. Season with 1½ teaspoons rosemary. Store in covered jar and refrigerate until ready to use.

VARIATION
□ Substitute 1½ teaspoons of sage or tarragon for rosemary.

VINAIGRETTE DRESSING

½ cup oil
¼ cup vinegar
3 Tbsps. prepared mustard
1 Tbsp. chopped scallions
1 tsp. garlic powder
Salt and pepper to taste
Dash of oregano, basil, tarragon, dill

YIELDS: 1 cup

In a small bowl combine oil and vinegar. Stir in mustard and scallions. Season with garlic powder, salt, pepper, and other spices of your choice. Store in covered jar and refrigerate until ready to use.

VARIATION
□ **Lemon-Herb:** Substitute ¼ cup lemon juice and 2 teaspoons of grated lemon peel for vinegar. Omit mustard.

CLASSIC FRENCH DRESSING

¾ cup oil
1 tsp. salt
1 tsp. sugar
¼ cup vinegar or
lemon juice
¼ tsp. pepper

YIELDS: 1 cup

In a small bowl combine all ingredients and beat well with a wire whisk or fork until smooth.

Store in a covered jar and refrigerate until ready to use.

GARLIC-PARSLEY DRESSING

1 bunch fresh parsley
1 cup olive oil
½ cup cider vinegar
1 to 2 cloves garlic, minced
2 Tbsps. soy sauce

YIELDS: 2 cups

Trim stems from parsley and discard. In small bowl, soak parsley in salted water. Drain.

In blender or processor, combine oil, vinegar, parsley, garlic, and soy sauce. Blend until parsley is chopped fine. Store in covered jar. Refrigerate until ready to use. Shake well before using.

MAYONNAISE-BASED DRESSINGS *are best on very crisp greens, cabbage, iceberg, and Romaine lettuce.*

CREAMY WHITE DRESSING

6 heaping Tbsps. mayonnaise
6 Tbsps. lemon juice
2 tsps. sugar
1 tsp. salt
1 tsp. garlic powder
1 tsp. pepper
1 tsp. paprika
1 tsp. dried parsley flakes
(optional)

YIELDS: 1 cup

Mix mayonnaise and lemon juice together until very smooth. Add seasonings and stir until well blended.

Keep refrigerated until served.

TIGER DRESSING

½ cup mayonnaise
¼ cup prepared horseradish

YIELDS: ¾ cup

Combine mayonnaise and horseradish and mix well.

Keep refrigerated until served.

VARIATION
□ Substitute 1 tablespoon prepared mustard and
1 teaspoon lemon juice for horseradish.

CREAMY PARSLEY DRESSING

A versatile dressing, this can be used as a dip, a salad dressing, or over chilled fish.

1 clove garlic
1 medium onion
¼ cup fresh parsley
1 cup mayonnaise
1 Tbsp. lemon juice
1 Tbsp. vinegar
½ tsp. salt
Fresh-ground black pepper,
to taste
¾ tsp. tarragon

YIELDS: 2 cups

Grind garlic, onion, and parsley in food processor. Scrape into large bowl. Blend in, by hand, mayonnaise, lemon juice, vinegar, salt, pepper, and tarragon. Chill at least 1 hour before serving.

VARIATION
☐ **Dairy:** To use as a dip for dairy meals, add ½ cup sour cream.

RUSSIAN DRESSING

½ cup mayonnaise
3 Tbsps. chili sauce
or ketchup
1 tsp. sweet
pickle relish

YIELDS: 1 cup

In a small bowl combine all ingredients. Stir well. Keep refrigerated until served.

SAUCES

Sauces are flavorful and colorful complements to fish, vegetables, poultry, and meat. They are the hallmark of a good cook. As well as imparting their own unique flavor, they enhance the dish for which they are prepared. Sauces should be used sparingly and should not mask the taste of the main food. Barbecue Sauce, with its tangy taste, gives a picnic atmosphere to any meal. The sweetness of Fruit Sauce studded with pineapple chunks and cherries is a perfect complement to meat. The Traditional White Sauce or bechamel sauce with its creamy texture and delicate taste goes well with broccoli or cauliflower.

HOLLANDAISE

½ cup margarine
3 egg yolks
1 Tbsp. lemon juice
1 Tbsp. water
½ tsp. prepared mustard
½ tsp. salt

USE: 2-quart saucepan
YIELDS: 1 cup

In a 2-quart saucepan melt margarine until foamy.

Pour hot water into blender container to heat it. Discard water. Put in egg yolks, lemon juice, water, and seasonings. Cover container and blend until smooth. Turn blender to high; remove center cover and very, very slowly pour margarine in a stream into the egg yolk mixture until mixture is like thick cream.

Serve over poached eggs or broccoli, green beans, or asparagus.

SIMPLE MOCK HOLLANDAISE

4 Tbsps. mayonnaise
1 tsp. prepared mustard

YIELDS: ¼ cup

In a small bowl, mix together well.

Serve over steamed vegetables.

"BEEF" GRAVY

A *beef-flavored gravy that contains no meat products.*

¼ cup margarine
¼ cup flour
1⅓ cups water
1 *pareve* beef-flavored
bouillon cube
Salt to taste
Garlic powder to taste
1 5-ounce bottle
soy sauce
2 Tbsps. cornstarch
¼ cup cold water

USE: 2-quart saucepan
YIELDS: 2 cups

In a 2-quart saucepan, melt margarine and stir in flour. Brown flour over medium heat. Pour in water and stir until smooth. Add beef-flavored cube, salt, and garlic. Cook, stirring, until thickened. Pour in soy sauce.

Combine cornstarch with ¼ cup cold water. Stir to dissolve all the lumps and pour into the gravy. Stirring constantly, bring back to a boil over medium heat and boil 1 minute.

FRUIT SAUCE

Use this spicy sweet sauce to glaze roast meat or poultry.

1 cup canned apricots or
peaches, plus syrup
1 cup maraschino cherries
plus syrup
1 cup pitted prunes
1½ cups pineapple chunks,
plus syrup
¼ cup cornstarch
⅔ cup brown sugar
½ tsp. cinnamon
½ tsp. allspice
½ tsp. dry mustard
1 tsp. salt
½ cup water
2 Tbsps. margarine, melted
2 Tbsps. vinegar

USE: 2½-quart saucepan
YIELDS: Fruit sauce for
8 pieces of chicken
or 1 large roast

In a large bowl, combine apricots or peaches, cherries, prunes, and pineapple chunks, with their liquid, to measure 4 cups.

Place fruits and liquids in 2½-quart saucepan. Heat to boiling.

Mix cornstarch, sugar, spices, and salt with ½ cup water. Add to hot liquid, stir, and cook until thickened. Add margarine and vinegar.

Spread sauce over chicken or meat after it is halfway done, and continue broiling or baking until done.

SPECIAL BARBECUE SAUCE

½ cup ketchup
½ cup honey
¼ cup apple cider vinegar
1 large clove
garlic, minced
1½ tsps. basil
Salt to taste
Pepper to taste
1½ Tbsps. maple syrup
1 Tbsp. soy sauce
½ tsp. oregano
Dash dry mustard
½ cup water

YIELDS: 2 cups

In a screwtop jar or bowl mix all ingredients together. Refrigerate for at least 1 hour before using.

□ **Barbecued Chicken:** Brown the chicken pieces in hot oil or, even better, brown them under a broiler. Place the chicken in a casserole and cover with the barbecue sauce. Bake covered at 350° for about ½ hour or until chicken is tender. Uncover and bake 10 minutes more to concentrate sauce.

BARBECUE SAUCE

½ cup white vinegar
⅓ cup water
¼ cup sugar
¼ cup corn syrup
1 6-ounce can
tomato paste
2 tsps. oil
½ tsp. salt
½ tsp. pepper
2 cloves garlic, minced
1 Tbsp. chopped onion
½ tsp. oregano
½ tsp. red pepper (optional)

YIELDS: 2 cups

In a screwtop jar or bowl, mix first six ingredients together. Add seasonings. Shake or mix well.

Pour over food to be baked or roasted and proceed as usual.

CHILI-HORSERADISH SAUCE

⅔ cup chili sauce
2 Tbsps. horseradish
3 Tbsps. lemon juice
2 to 3 drops
Tabasco sauce (optional)

YIELDS: 1 cup

In a small bowl, combine all ingredients. Chill until ready to use.

Serve with cooked fish.

VARIATION
□ Instead of chili sauce, use ½ cup mayonnaise plus 1 Tbsp. chili powder. Use white horseradish. Add 1 diced scallion and 1 minced garlic clove.

ORANGE SAUCE

1 cup orange juice
1 Tbsp. orange rind
1 tsp. lemon rind
½ cup confectioners' sugar
1 Tbsp. cornstarch
2 Tbsps. margarine
¼ cup raisins
1 Tbsp. lemon juice

USE: 1½-quart saucepan
YIELDS: 2 cups

Combine orange juice, rinds, sugar, and cornstarch in 1½-quart saucepan. Bring to boil. Add margarine and raisins. Simmer for 5 minutes and remove from heat. Stir in lemon juice.

Serve over tongue, duck, or crepes; or slice tongue and heat in sauce.

ANCHOVY-TOMATO SAUCE

This is a fish-based sauce, and should not be served with meat.

¼ cup olive oil
3 onions, diced
2 garlic cloves, diced
3 pounds fresh tomatoes, peeled, seeded and diced
3 anchovies
1 Tbsp. basil
3 sprigs parsley
Salt to taste
Pepper to taste

USE: 3-quart saucepan
YIELDS: 4 to 6 servings

In a 3-quart saucepan, heat oil and saute onions and garlic until soft. Remove from heat. Add remaining ingredients, return to heat and cook slowly until the tomatoes are cooked down and thickened.

Push through a strainer or puree in a blender. Return to pot and simmer an additional hour.

Serve over hot pasta.

MARINARA SAUCE

3 Tbsps. salad or olive oil
¾ cup chopped onion
1 clove garlic, minced
2 16-ounce cans tomatoes
6 ounces tomato paste
1 cup water
1 Tbsp. sugar
1½ tsps. salt
1½ tsps. oregano
½ tsp. pepper
1 bay leaf

USE: 12-inch skillet
YIELDS: 6 to 8 servings

In a 12-inch heavy skillet, heat the oil and saute onion and garlic until soft.

Puree tomatoes in blender or cut with edge of spoon. Add puree and remaining ingredients to onion and garlic. Simmer uncovered, stirring occasionally, for 1 hour. Remove bay leaf.

VARIATION
□ **Meat Sauce:** Brown 1 pound ground beef with onion and garlic. Puree tomato in blender. Then proceed with the remaining ingredients and directions as given above.

Serve over hot pasta.

SWEET-AND-SOUR SAUCE

Sweet-and-sour sauce is traditional for chicken or meat.

2 Tbsps. oil
1 large onion, diced
¼ cup vinegar
½ cup ketchup
¼ cup brown sugar

USE: 1½-quart saucepan
YIELDS: 1 cup

In a 1½-quart saucepan, heat oil and lightly saute onion. Add vinegar and ketchup and mix well. Add brown sugar and stir.

TRADITIONAL WHITE SAUCE — BECHAMEL

White Sauce is the most popular sauce for vegetables, and Bechamel is the most popular version of White Sauce.

2 Tbsps. margarine
2 Tbsps. flour
1 cup hot liquid
¼ tsp. salt
Dash pepper

USE: 1-quart saucepan
YIELDS: 1½ to 2 cups

Melt margarine in 1-quart saucepan. When bubbling, stir in flour to make a smooth paste. Add the liquid all at once, stir in one direction only; the liquid is traditionally milk, but water, clear broth, nondairy creamer, or liquid from cooked mild-flavored vegetables can be used as well. Cook until sauce begins to boil and thickens. Lower flame and simmer 2 to 3 minutes. Season with salt and pepper.

VARIATIONS

☐ **Thin Sauce:** Reduce margarine and flour to 1 tablespoon each and proceed as above.

☐ **Curry Sauce:** Add 1 to 2 teaspoons or curry powder and ⅛ teaspoon powdered ginger.

☐ **Mock Hollandaise Sauce:** After basic sauce has thickened, beat 2 egg yolks into the sauce and add 6 tablespoons of margarine, 1 tablespoon at a time. Last, add 1 tablespoon of lemon juice and mix well.

☐ **Cheese Sauce:** When basic sauce comes to a boil, stir in ¾ cup grated cheddar cheese, ⅛ teaspoon dry mustard and a dash of red pepper. Cook, stirring, 2 to 3 minutes.

☐ **Mushroom Sauce:** Increase margarine to 5 tablespoons. Melt in 10-inch skillet and saute ½ pound of sliced mushrooms and a small onion, diced. Add 5 tablespoons of flour and continue as in basic sauce above.

☐ **Never-Fail White Sauce:** Melt margarine and add flour as above. Cook until flour is golden brown. Remove from heat and set aside. Heat liquid in a separate saucepan until almost boiling. Remove from heat. Return margarine-flour mixture to fire and pour all liquid in at once. Stir in one direction only. Once it comes to a boil, add salt, lower flame, and cook, stirring, for 12 to 14 minutes.

TOMATO SAUCE

Especially good with pasta.

2 Tbsps. margarine
1 clove garlic, minced
¼ cup chopped onion
¼ cup chopped
green pepper
1 carrot, diced (optional)
2 Tbsps. chopped
fresh parsley
2 cups peeled and
chopped tomatoes
Dash salt
Freshly ground pepper,
to taste
½ tsp. dried basil
Dash hot pepper sauce
or cayenne

USE: 10-inch skillet
YIELDS: 4 servings

In 10-inch skillet, melt margarine and saute garlic, onion, green pepper, and carrot until almost tender. Add parsley, tomatoes, salt and pepper. Cook until tomatoes are cooked down and only ¼ cup of liquid remains.

Add basil and pepper sauce and cook a few minutes more to blend the flavors.

NOTE: It will take longer to cook down fresh tomatoes than canned.

Serve over hot pasta.

VARIATION
☐ **Tomato-Mushroom Sauce:** Substitute ½ cup sliced mushrooms for carrots.

RELISHES

Sweet or savory relishes are tasty accompaniments to meat and poultry. Usually mixtures of spiced simmered fruits, they dress up the Shabbat or Yom Tov table.

CRANBERRY RELISH

1 pound fresh cranberries
2 apples, unpeeled
2 oranges, unpeeled
½ cup orange juice
2 cups sugar
1 cup water

USE: 2½-quart saucepan
YIELDS: 4 to 5 cups

Rinse cranberries and drain.

Slice apples and oranges, keeping skins on. Place in food processor or blender along with orange juice and cranberries. Blend until smooth.

Place mixture in 2½-quart saucepan. Add sugar and water and simmer 10 minutes.

Cool before serving.

HOT CRANBERRY-RAISIN SAUCE

1 pound fresh cranberries
1 cup raisins
1 cup water
1 12-ounce jar
cherry preserves
¼ cup sugar
1 Tbsp. grated orange peel
½ tsp. salt

USE: 3-quart pot
YIELDS: 4 cups

Rinse cranberries and drain.

In blender, blend cranberries, raisins, and water until cranberries are finely chopped. Do half at a time, pouring mixture into 3-quart pot. Then add remaining ingredients to pot. Heat mixture to boiling over a high flame. Reduce heat and simmer 5 minutes, stirring frequently. Serve hot.

This sauce will keep for two weeks in a refrigerator. Reheat just before serving.

CRANBERRY CHUTNEY

Serve this unusual chutney as a meat accompaniment.

1 pound fresh cranberries
2 cups sugar
1 cup water
1 Tbsp. grated orange peel
1 cup orange juice
1 cup raisins
1 cup chopped walnuts
1 cup chopped celery
1 medium apple,
cored and diced
1 tsp. ground ginger

USE: 3-quart saucepan
YIELDS: 7 cups

Rinse cranberries and drain.

In a 3-quart saucepan over medium heat, place cranberries, sugar, and water and bring to boil, stirring mixture frequently. Reduce heat to low and simmer 5 minutes.

Remove from heat and stir in remaining ingredients. Cover and refrigerate chutney until ready to serve. Serve with hot curries.

TURKISH TOMATO RELISH

3 Tbsps. oil
1 medium onion, diced
1 green or
red pepper, diced
2 Tbsps. flour
2 cups diced tomatoes
1 Tbsp. minced fresh parsley
2 Tbsps. water
or tomato sauce
Dash chili powder
Salt and cayenne pepper
to taste

USE: 2-quart saucepan
YIELDS: 6 servings

Heat oil in 2-quart saucepan. Add onion and pepper and saute until onion is golden and pepper is tender. Stir in flour. Add remaining ingredients, stirring constantly. Simmer 10 minutes.

Serve with meat, fish, pasta, or rice.

CONDIMENTS

Homemade condiments have a refreshing color and taste. Mayonnaise, mustard, and chraine *(horseradish) complement fish and chicken. They are especially welcome to a cook who takes pride in using her own ingredients.*

MUSTARD

4 ounces dry mustard
3 Tbsps. cold water
2 cups boiling water
½ cup sugar
3 to 4 Tbsps. vinegar

YIELDS: 1 cup

In a medium bowl combine mustard powder and just enough cold water to make a thick paste. Pour boiling water over it. Let sit 15 to 20 minutes until cool. Carefully drain off water.

Add ½ cup sugar and mix to make creamy. Add vinegar until preferred taste and consistency are achieved.

HOMEMADE BERRY JAM

**4 cups strawberries,
blueberries, or raspberries**
1 cup water
2 cups sugar

USE: 3-quart saucepan
YIELDS: 8 to 10 ounces jam

Soak any of the fruits listed in water for several hours. Hull or remove stems. Then rinse and drain.

Place berries, sugar, and water in a 3-quart saucepan. Bring to a boil on medium flame, then let simmer on a low flame for about 1 hour or more if necessary. Stir frequently to avoid scorching as mixture thickens. When thick, pour into a glass container, keeping a metal spoon upright in glass to prevent it from cracking.

Let cool, then refrigerate. The berries condense greatly during thickening process.

HOMEMADE HORSERADISH

The "bite" of this homemade chraine *reminds us of the Pesach seder.*

1 pound horseradish root
2 medium beets
**¼ cup sugar,
or to taste**
**5 tsps. salt,
or to taste**
1 cup white vinegar

YIELDS: 1½ to 2 cups

Peel horseradish root and beets and cut into 1-inch chunks. Grind fine in electric grinder, blender, food processor, grater, or juicer. The juicer produces the least amount of tears. If using a juicer, the pulp will be fine, almost powdery — simply mix it back into the juice.

Combine sugar, salt, and vinegar and add to combined horseradish-beet mixture. Refrigerate in tightly covered glass containers.

NOTE: If root is not crisp, refresh it by soaking in cold water overnight in the refrigerator.

MARINARA SAUCE FOR CANNING

This is the ideal recipe to "put up" the surplus tomato crop from your garden.

1 cup olive oil
**6 onions, grated
or finely chopped**
**20 to 24 cloves
garlic, minced**
**12 pounds plum tomatoes,
quartered**
6 Tbsps. parsley flakes
3 Tbsps. oregano
1 Tbsp. basil
10 bay leaves
2 Tbsps. salt
Red pepper to taste
⅓ cup red wine

USE: 6- to 8-quart
stainless-steel or enamel pot
8 1-pint canning jars
YIELDS: 7½ pints

Place oil in a 6- to 8-quart pot and heat until hot. Add onions and saute. Turn off heat and add garlic. Add tomatoes to onions, put back on heat, and simmer several minutes. Puree mixture in a food mill or blender. Return to pot.

Add remaining ingredients to tomato mixture and simmer covered about 1 hour, or until thickened.

TO CAN: Pour hot sauce into clean and hot sterilized jars, leaving ½ inch headspace. Cook in a boiling water bath for 45 minutes. Check that seals are down when cool.

TUNISIAN TOMATO PASTE

This Tomato Paste makes an excellent spread on bread or crackers.

20 large tomatoes
½ cup olive oil
5 green peppers, diced
1 bay leaf
8 to 10 cloves garlic
½ tsp. salt

USE: 5-quart Dutch oven
YIELDS: 4 cups

Blanch tomatoes by placing them in a large bowl of hot water for approximately 5 minutes. Lift out each tomato with a fork and run it under cold water. Peel tomatoes, cut in half, squeeze out juice and seeds. Cut into pieces.

Heat oil in 5-quart Dutch oven and add tomatoes, peppers, bay leaf, garlic, and salt. Simmer covered for 2 hours, stirring frequently to prevent sticking. The consistency should be pasty.

NOTE: If you prefer a spicier taste, add more garlic and chili pepper.

EASY BLENDER MAYONNAISE

1 egg
2 Tbsps. vinegar
½ to 1 tsp. dry mustard
1 tsp. sugar
½ tsp. salt
Dash white or black pepper
Dash paprika
1 cup oil

YIELDS: 1¼ cups

Place all ingredients, except oil, in blender. Blend on high speed. Pour oil into center in a very slow, steady stream until thick.

NOTE: Chill blender container first.

CATSUP

A perfect recipe for canning.

18 medium tomatoes, quartered
2 medium onions, diced
1 cinnamon stick (3 inches) or 1½ tsps. ground cinnamon
2 cloves garlic, minced
1 cup cider vinegar
1¼ tsps. salt
1 tsp. paprika
3 Tbsps. sugar (optional)

USE: 6-quart pot
YIELDS: 1½ pints

In 6-quart pot, simmer tomatoes and onion for ½ hour. Puree tomato and onion mixture in a food mill or blender. Add remaining ingredients to tomato mixture and simmer 45 to 60 minutes, or until thickened, stirring occasionally. Remove cinnamon stick.

Pour into clean, hot ½-pint or pint jars. Cook in a boiling water bath for 10 minutes. Check seals when cool.

Cake and Pastry

Cakes
Frostings and Fillings
Cookies
Pastries
Bars

Elegant and delicious cakes enhance any good cook's reputation. A tray of varied cakes and pastries is a good way to lend a festive touch when entertaining, or for a *simchah*. Home-baked cakes and bread have always been a sign of hospitality, going back to the time of Avraham and Sarah, when Sarah baked "hearthcakes" for the three angels who came to their tent (Genesis 18:6).

Some traditional cakes are honey cake for Rosh Hashanah, *hamantashen* for Purim, and dairy cheesecake for Shavuot. Enjoy our recipes for luscious chocolate cakes, fluffy chiffon and sponge cakes, fragrant coffee cakes and more.

Cakes and Kashrut

A number of *kashrut* factors enter into the baking of cakes, pies and cookies. These apply equally to commercially-prepared baked goods and should be kept in mind when choosing a bakery or a brand-name product.

The cakes in this section are all *pareve*. However, if they are baked in a meat or dairy oven, their *pareve* status may be affected. Therefore, one should preferably bake cakes in a *pareve* oven. See The Oven, page 21.

Cakes containing dairy ingredients must be prepared with separate utensils, including blender, mixer, spoons, bowls, and pans. Dairy cakes and other baked goods should preferably be baked in an oven designated for dairy use exclusively.

Most baking ingredients require *kashrut* certification. Among them are oil, shortening, margarine, fillings, spices and flavorings, and chocolate products. They must also be certified as *pareve* when used in *pareve* cake. This is especially true of chocolate because even dark chocolate often contains milk powder, or is processed on equipment also used for dairy products. Some cake mixes are dairy, so examine the label carefully when using a commercial mix.

Eggs must be examined for the presence of blood spots *before* they are combined with other eggs or ingredients to prevent the other items from becoming non-kosher. Open each egg individually into a clear cup. If an egg has a blood spot, the egg must be discarded. Rinse the cup thoroughly with cold water before using it again. Brown eggs, prevalent in some parts of the country, are much more likely to contain blood spots. If you can't find white eggs, ask your grocer about the possibility of carrying them, or try one of the larger supermarkets. Organic eggs, too, frequently have blood spots. An

Orthodox Rabbi must be consulted if the blood spot was found after the egg had been added to a mixture or after it was placed into a hot utensil. The mixture or the pan must be set aside until the Rabbi states what must be done.

When baking many cakes, cookies, or pastries, the laws of separating *challah* may apply. See The Mitzvah of Separating Challah, page 47.

For further information concerning the categories of *pareve*, dairy, bakeries, *pat Yisrael*, blessings, and *hechsher*, consult the index for relevant pages.

SUCCESSFUL BAKING

Every type of cooking is an art, but baking requires special skill. With care and attention, home bakers can achieve a professional look for their baked goods. A prime factor in achieving this technique is proper baking equipment.

Before beginning a new recipe, give yourself enough time to check the recipe and your supplies. Be sure you have the correct ingredients available. For best results, be precise. Does the recipe call for baking chocolate or cocoa powder? Jam or preserves? Confectioners' or brown sugar? A well-stocked pantry precludes the need for last minute substitutions.

We have provided, for your convenience, a list of baking equipment, and a list of baking substitutions for those times when the proper ingredients are not available (page 539).

BAKING EQUIPMENT

Mixers
Portable electric hand mixer
Standard all-purpose mixer

Baking Pans
Use correct size pan for best results
9 or 10-inch round tube pan
    (*with removable center*)
9 or 10-inch spring form pan
9 x 13-inch pan
10 x 15-inch jelly roll pan
11 x 16-inch baking pan
8 x 8-inch square pan
9-inch round pie plate
9½ x 5½-inch loaf pan
Cookie sheets, at least 2
Cupcake pan

Utensils
Mixing bowls, large and small
Nest of metal or plastic dry measure cups
    (1 cup, ½ cup, ⅓ cup, ¼ cup)
Glass liquid measuring cup
    (1 to 4 cup sizes)
Set of measuring spoons
Rubber Spatula
Pastry Blender
Pastry Brush
Rolling Pin
Cookie Cutters
Cookie Press
Cooling Racks
Pastry Tube

Cakes

The highest acclaim comes to a good homemaker for her freshly baked cakes. Adorning the table for Shabbat, Yom Tov, and simchahs or a snack for the family, homebaked cakes are always served with pride.

ALMOND CROWN CAKE

This cake glazes itself with a delicious almond-sugar coating.

2 to 3 Tbsps. margarine, softened
¾ cup sliced almonds
1⅓ cups sugar
¾ cup margarine, softened
1 tsp. vanilla extract
¼ tsp. almond extract
1 tsp. grated lemon peel
3 eggs, separated
2½ cups sifted flour
3 tsps. baking powder
1 tsp. salt
½ cup nondairy creamer
½ cup water

USE: 10-inch tube pan
YIELDS: 1 cake

Preheat oven to 325°.

Generously grease bottom and sides of a 10-inch tube pan with 2 to 3 tablespoons margarine. Press in almonds. Sprinkle with 1 tablespoon of sugar.

In a large mixer bowl cream ¾ cup margarine with remaining sugar. Add vanilla, almond extract, and lemon peel. Beat in egg yolks until light and fluffy.

In a separate bowl, sift together flour, baking powder, and salt. Combine nondairy creamer and water. Add dry ingredients to creamed mixture alternately with liquid, beating after each addition. Beat egg whites until stiff but not dry. Gently fold into batter. Carefully turn into prepared pan.

Bake for approximately 1 hour and 10 minutes. Let cake stand in pan about 10 minutes. Invert onto wire rack and let cool at least 2 hours before removing from pan.

CLASSIC APPLE CAKE

1 cup oil
2 cups sugar
3 eggs
3 cups flour
1 tsp. salt
1 tsp. baking soda
1 tsp. vanilla extract
3 cups peeled, cored, and cubed apples
1 cup raisins
1 tsp. cinnamon

USE: 9-inch tube or bundt pan
YIELDS: 1 cake

Preheat oven to 350°.

Grease and flour a 9-inch tube or bundt pan.

In a large mixer bowl, beat oil with sugar. Add eggs, then flour, salt, baking soda, and vanilla. Set aside.

In a separate bowl, toss cubed apples, raisins, and cinnamon until apples are coated. Stir apple mixture into batter. Batter will be very stiff.

Spoon into the greased tube or bundt pan and bake for 1 hour. Cool completely before cutting.

APPLE FILLED CAKE

5 cups flour
1 cup sugar
2 eggs
1½ cups margarine, softened
1 tsp. baking powder
1 cup apple juice or orange juice
1 cup matzoh meal
3 pounds apples, peeled and sliced
5 Tbsps. sugar
1 tsp. cinnamon

USE: 11 x 16-inch cake pan
YIELDS: 20 squares

Preheat oven to 350°.

Grease an 11 x 16-inch pan.

Beat first six ingredients in large mixer bowl until a soft dough is formed.

Divide dough into two equal parts. On floured board, roll out one-half of the dough to fit baking pan. Place rolled-out dough on the greased pan.

Pour three fourths of the matzoh meal over dough, then spread sliced apples over matzoh meal. Combine sugar and cinnamon and sprinkle over apples. Pour remaining matzoh meal over apple mixture. Roll out second half of dough and place on top of apples.

Bake for 1½ hours. When cool, cut into 3-inch squares with a sharp knife.

ROYAL APPLE CAKE

CRUST
½ cup margarine, softened
2 egg yolks
4 Tbsps. sugar
2 cups flour
1½ tsps. baking powder
2 Tbsps. brandy

FILLING
6 apples, peeled and diced
1 egg
2 Tbsps. sugar
1 Tbsp. cornstarch
½ cup nondairy creamer
2 Tbsps. lemon juice

CRUMB TOPPING
1⅓ cups flour
½ cup margarine
½ cup sugar
Confectioners' sugar

USE: 9 x 13-inch cake pan
YIELDS: 1 cake

Preheat oven to 350°.

Grease and flour a 9 x 13-inch pan.

CRUST: In a mixer bowl, combine all ingredients for crust and mix well. Pat onto the bottom of the greased and floured cake pan.

FILLING: Spread layer of apples over crust. In a small bowl, mix egg, sugar, and cornstarch until there are no lumps. Then slowly, while mixing, add nondairy creamer and lemon juice. Pour over apples.

CRUMB TOPPING: Mix flour, margarine, and sugar to a crumbly consistency. Sprinkle over filling. Bake for 45 minutes to 1 hour. When cool, top with confectioners' sugar.

APPLESAUCE CAKE

This cake is so moist it makes an extra-special dessert.

1 cup margarine, softened
2 cups sugar
2 eggs
1 32-ounce jar applesauce
4 cups flour
3 tsps. baking soda
2 tsps. cinnamon
1 tsp. ground cloves
½ tsp. salt
1 cup raisins

USE: 9 x 13-inch cake pan
YIELDS: 1 cake

Preheat oven to 325°.

In a large mixer bowl, cream margarine and sugar. Add eggs and mix well. Pour in applesauce, beating well, then add dry ingredients. Fold in raisins and mix until combined well.

Pour batter into an ungreased 9 x 13-inch cake pan and bake for 1 hour. Cool completely before cutting.

ANGEL SQUARES

A great recipe for people on a low-cholesterol diet. An angel-light cake without egg yolks or oil.

7 egg whites
Dash salt
2 cups sugar
2 cups flour
2 tsps. baking powder
1 tsp. vanilla extract
1 cup hot nondairy creamer
½ cup chopped cashews or
salted peanuts,
for decoration

"BUTTER" FROSTING
2 cups confectioners' sugar
¼ cup margarine, softened
½ tsp. vanilla extract
2 to 3 Tbsps.
nondairy creamer

CHOCOLATE DRIZZLE
2 ounces sweet chocolate
2 Tbsps. nondairy creamer
1 Tbsp. margarine

USE: 9 x 13-inch cake pan
Double boiler
YIELDS: 24 squares

Preheat oven to 350°.

Generously grease bottom only of 9 x 13-inch cake pan.

In large mixer bowl, beat egg whites and salt until soft mounds form. Gradually add 1 cup sugar, beating until stiff peaks form. Set aside.

In medium mixer bowl, combine remaining sugar, flour, and baking powder and mix well. Add vanilla and hot nondairy creamer. Blend at low speed until moistened, scraping bowl occasionally. Gently fold egg whites into batter by hand until well mixed. Pour into prepared pan; spread to cover bottom of the pan.

Bake for 30 to 35 minutes or until top springs back when touched lightly in center.

Cool cake completely, then frost with "Butter" Frosting. Sprinkle with chopped nuts. Drizzle with Chocolate Drizzle. Cut into 2-inch squares.

"BUTTER" FROSTING: In a small mixer bowl, combine all ingredients, using just enough nondairy creamer so that the mixture is thin enough to spread. Beat at medium speed until creamy.

CHOCOLATE DRIZZLE: In double boiler, combine all ingredients. Heat over low flame until just melted. Mix well and drizzle with a spoon over the "Butter" Frosting.

TASTY BANANA CAKE

3 cups flour
1⅔ cups sugar
1 tsp. salt
3 tsps. baking powder
3 tsps. instant coffee
½ tsp. maple flavoring
¾ cup shortening
¾ cup nondairy creamer
¾ cup water
3 eggs
½ medium-size
ripe banana, mashed

BANANA FROSTING
½ ripe banana, sliced
½ cup margarine, softened
1 tsp. lemon juice
2 cups confectioners' sugar

½ cup chopped nuts

USE: 9 x 13-inch cake pan
YIELDS: 1 cake

Preheat oven to 350°.

Grease and flour bottom only of 9 x 13-inch cake pan.

In a large mixer bowl, combine all cake ingredients and blend at low speed until moistened. Then beat for 3 minutes at medium speed, scraping bowl occasionally.

Pour batter into prepared pan, spreading to edges. Bake for 25 to 30 minutes until top springs back when touched lightly in center.

Cool completely, remove from pan, and frost with banana frosting. Sprinkle frosting with nuts.

BANANA FROSTING: In a small bowl, cream banana, margarine, and lemon juice. (Mixture may look curdled.) Blend in confectioners' sugar. Beat until creamy.

BEST-EVER BANANA CAKE

¾ cup margarine, softened
1½ cups sugar
2 eggs
1 cup mashed ripe bananas
1 tsp. baking soda
1 tsp. baking powder
1 tsp. vanilla extract
2 cups flour
½ cup apple juice or
orange juice
½ cup chopped pecans
1 cup shredded coconut

CREAMY FROSTING
1 egg yolk
½ cup margarine, softened
½ tsp. coconut extract
½ tsp. vanilla extract
2 cups confectioners' sugar

USE: 9 x 13-inch cake pan
or 2 9-inch cake pans
YIELDS: 1 sheet or layer cake

Preheat oven to 350°.

Grease and flour one 9 x 13-inch or two 9-inch cake pans.

In a large mixer bowl, cream margarine and sugar. Add eggs one at a time, beating after each addition until light and fluffy. Add mashed bananas and beat 2 minutes, then add baking soda, baking powder, and vanilla. Add flour alternately with liquid, beginning and ending with flour. Fold in pecans and coconut and mix well.

Pour into greased and floured pan or pans. Bake for 25 to 30 minutes for 9-inch cake pans, or 1 hour for 9 x 13-inch cake pan. Cool and frost, if desired.

CREAMY FROSTING: Combine all ingredients in mixing bowl and beat until light and fluffy.

In order to frost and fill two-layer cake, frosting recipe should be doubled.

BANANA PEANUT BUTTER BREAD

2 large ripe bananas, mashed
1 egg
1 tsp. vanilla extract
⅓ cup oil
½ cup honey
1½ cups whole-wheat flour
1 tsp. baking soda
½ tsp. salt
½ tsp. cloves
½ cup chunky peanut butter
¼ to ½ cup sunflower seeds
¼ to ½ cup sesame seeds
Whole walnuts or slivered almonds (optional)

USE: 9½ x 5½-inch loaf pan
YIELDS: 1 loaf cake

Preheat oven to 350°.

Grease and flour a loaf pan.

In a large mixer bowl, beat bananas, egg, vanilla, oil and honey, for 1 minute on low speed. Mix together flour, baking soda, salt, and cloves and blend into banana mixture. Stir in peanut butter and seeds.

Pour mixture into the greased and floured loaf pan. Bake for 1 hour until done. Cool completely before cutting.

Decorate top with walnuts or slivered almonds, if desired.

BANANA BREAD

2 cups flour
1 cup brown sugar
1 tsp. baking powder
1 tsp. salt
½ tsp. baking soda
2 eggs
½ cup margarine, softened
1 cup mashed ripe bananas (2 medium-size bananas)
½ cup chopped walnuts
¼ cup wheat germ

USE: 9½ x 5½-inch loaf pan
YIELDS: 1 loaf cake

Preheat oven to 350°.

Grease and flour loaf pan.

Sift together dry ingredients into a large bowl. Add eggs, margarine, and bananas, and mix well. Fold in nuts and wheat germ. Mixture will be thick.

Pour into loaf pan. Bake for 65 to 75 minutes, or until toothpick inserted in center comes out clean. Cool completely before cutting.

If desired cake can be sprinkled with confectioners' sugar when cooled.

FLUFFY CARROT CAKE

2 cups sugar
4 eggs
1½ cups grated raw carrots
1 cup raisins (optional)
2 cups flour
1 tsp. baking soda
1 tsp. baking powder
Pinch of salt
¾ cup oil

USE: 9-inch square cake pan
YIELDS: 1 cake

Preheat oven to 350°.

Grease and flour a 9-inch square cake pan.

In a large mixer bowl beat sugar and eggs. Stir in carrots and raisins. Sift flour with baking soda, baking powder, and salt. Alternating oil and flour mixture, add to carrot mixture and mix well.

Pour into greased and floured cake pan. Bake for 55 to 60 minutes or until toothpick inserted in center comes out clean. Cool completely before cutting.

CARROT-PINEAPPLE CAKE

3 cups flour
1 tsp. baking soda
2 tsps. cinnamon
½ tsp. salt
½ cup oil
2 cups sugar
2 tsps. vanilla extract
2 cups grated raw carrots
1 cup drained
crushed pineapple
1½ cups chopped walnuts
3 eggs

USE: 10-inch tube pan
YIELDS: 1 cake

Preheat oven to 350°.

Grease and flour a 10-inch tube pan.

In a small bowl, sift together flour, baking soda, cinnamon, and salt. In a separate large mixer bowl, beat together oil, sugar, and 1 teaspoon vanilla. Add half the flour mixture and mix well. Beat in carrots, pineapple, remaining teaspoon vanilla, and nuts. Add remaining flour mixture and beat well. Beat in eggs, one at a time.

Pour batter into greased tube pan. Bake for 70 minutes. Cool completely before cutting.

SPICY CARROT CAKE

2 cups grated raw carrots
⅓ cup boiling water
½ cup oil
3 eggs
1¼ cups sugar
2 cups flour
1¼ tsps. baking soda
1 tsp. cinnamon
1 tsp. nutmeg
1 tsp. salt
1 tsp. cloves
1 tsp. vanilla extract
1 cup chopped walnuts

Orange Cream Frosting
(page 392)

USE: 9 x 13-inch cake pan
YIELDS: 1 cake

Preheat oven to 350°.

Grease and flour a 9 x 13-inch cake pan.

In a large bowl beat all cake ingredients except nuts at low speed for 1 minute, scraping sides of bowl constantly. Then beat at medium speed for 2 minutes. Add nuts and mix well.

Pour into greased cake pan. Bake for 45 to 50 minutes. Frost with Orange Cream Frosting.

CHIFFON and SPONGE *cakes are perfect plain cakes; the volume of the egg whites gives the cake a light airiness. The basic difference between the two is that chiffon cake is made with oil; sponge is not. A true sponge cake may be made without baking powder, for the air and steam are what cause the cake to rise (instead of a leavening agent). A sponge cake is the basis for the most elegant and elaborate iced layer cakes.*

TIPS FOR PERFECT CHIFFON AND SPONGE CAKE

☐ In these cakes, the egg yolk and white are always separated. Beat the egg yolks until light and foamy. Add sugar gradually to the egg yolks to achieve a thick texture and pale yellow color.

☐ Whites should be beaten to stiff peaks. Do not scrape the sides of the bowl during beating. Don't overbeat or whites will become dry and separate.

☐ Gently fold egg whites with a rubber spatula into other ingredients. Cut down through the center and up the sides. Repeat until whites are broken into the size of small peas. Push batter gently into the pan, leveling lightly. Cut with a knife to break any large air bubbles.

☐ Bake in an ungreased pan, because the egg whites tend to pull away from sides of pan.

☐ To check if done, press top lightly with a finger; it should spring back. If baked in a tube pan, cracks in the top (which are typical) should feel dry.

☐ To cool a tube cake, invert the cake over a bottle at least 1½ hours. Let it cool completely before removing from pan.

☐ To remove from pan, cut gently around the side and tube of pan with a knife. Invert the cake gently onto a plate. A tube pan with a removable rim makes the process easier.

☐ To cut a chiffon cake into layers — measure and use wooden toothpicks to mark the cutting line. Cut a notch into side of cake so that layers can be aligned, after middle is filled. Use a serrated long-bladed knife and cut with a sawing motion.

PERFECT CHIFFON CAKE

7 eggs, separated
Pinch salt
1½ cups sugar
2¼ cups flour
3 tsps. baking powder
¾ cup apple juice or orange juice or water
2 tsps. vanilla extract
½ cup oil
½ tsp. almond extract (optional)

USE: 10-inch tube pan
YIELDS: 1 cake

Preheat oven to 350°.

Beat egg whites and salt in large mixing bowl on high speed until peaks form. Gradually add ½ cup sugar, 1 tablespoon at a time, beating until stiff but not dry. Set aside.

In a separate bowl, beat egg yolks, remaining sugar, and other ingredients well. Fold whites into egg yolk mixture with a rubber spatula and gently combine well.

Pour into an ungreased 10-inch tube pan and bake for 1 hour. When done, immediately invert pan on top of soda bottle. Cool at least 3 hours before removing so that it will not fall. When cool, loosen edges and remove cake from pan.

VARIATIONS
☐ **Almond Chiffon Cake:** Use apple juice for liquid and add ¾ cup ground almonds to sugar-yolk mixture. Do not omit almond extract.

☐ **Chiffon Cake With Sprinkles:** Add 6 tablespoons chocolate sprinkles to batter.

MAPLE-NUT CHIFFON CAKE

2 cups flour
¾ cup sugar
¾ cup dark brown sugar, firmly packed
1 Tbsp. baking powder
¾ cup water
2 tsps. maple extract
½ cup oil
7 eggs, separated
1 cup finely ground walnuts

USE: 10-inch tube pan
YIELDS: 1 cake

Preheat oven to 350°.

Combine flour, sugar, brown sugar, and baking powder in a large mixer bowl. Make a well in the center. Add water, maple extract, oil, and egg yolks. Beat until fluffy and smooth. Fold in nuts. In a medium mixer bowl beat the egg whites until stiff but not dry. Fold egg whites into batter gently with spatula.

Pour mixture into ungreased 10-inch tube pan. Bake 50 to 60 minutes. Cake is ready when it springs back to the touch. When done, immediately invert on a soda bottle. Cool at least 3 hours before removing so that it will not fall. When cool, loosen edges and remove cake from pan.

VARIATION
☐ **Coffee-Nut Chiffon Cake:** Add to recipe 1 egg, ½ cup oil, ½ tsp. salt, and substitute ¾ cup hot black coffee for water. Beat salt into egg whites. Follow directions above.

NEVER-FAIL SPONGE CAKE

5 eggs, separated
⅛ tsp. salt
1 cup sugar
2 Tbsps. lemon juice
1 tsp. grated lemon rind
1 cup flour

USE: 10-inch tube pan
YIELDS: 1 cake

Preheat oven to 350°.

In a medium mixer bowl, beat egg whites with salt until foamy. Add ½ cup sugar and continue beating gradually until stiff. Set aside.

In another bowl, beat yolks until light yellow in color. Add remaining ½ cup sugar, continuing to beat. Add lemon juice and rind. Gradually add flour. Gently fold in whites until completely blended. Pour into ungreased 10-inch tube pan.

Bake for 50 minutes or until top springs back when touched lightly in center. When done, immediately invert on top of soda bottle. Cool at least 3 hours so that it will not fall. When cool, loosen edges and remove cake from pan.

COCOA CHIFFON CAKE

⅔ cup cocoa
¾ cup boiling water
7 eggs, separated
1¾ cups sugar
1½ cups flour
1½ tsps. baking soda
1 tsp. salt
½ cup oil
2 tsps. vanilla extract

Preheat oven to 325°.

In a small bowl stir together cocoa and water until smooth; set aside. In a large mixer bowl beat egg whites until foamy. Gradually add ¼ cup sugar and continue beating until stiff but not dry.

In a medium mixer bowl, combine flour, remaining sugar, baking soda, and salt. Blend in egg yolks, oil, vanilla, and cocoa mixture. Beat at low speed until smooth. Carefully fold in egg whites until thoroughly blended. ➤

COCOA GLAZE

3 Tbsps. melted margarine
2 Tbsps. light corn syrup
⅓ cup cocoa powder
1 tsp. vanilla extract
2 cups confectioners' sugar
4 to 5 Tbsps. hot water

USE: 10-inch tube pan
YIELDS: 1 cake

Pour batter into ungreased 10-inch tube pan. Bake for 1 hour and 10 minutes. When done, immediately invert on a soda bottle. Cool at least 3 hours before removing so that it will not fall. When cool, loosen edges and remove cake from pan.

COCOA GLAZE: In a small mixer bowl, combine margarine, corn syrup, and cocoa, and beat well. Beat in vanilla and confectioners' sugar. Add hot water, 1 tablespoon at a time until glaze is smooth and of pouring consistency. Pour over cooled cake.

COFFEE SPONGE CAKE

6 eggs, separated
Dash salt
2 cups sugar
2 cups flour
3 tsps. baking powder
Dash salt
1 Tbsp. instant coffee
1 tsp. vanilla extract
1 cup water
1 cup chopped walnuts or pecans (optional)

USE: 10-inch tube pan
YIELDS: 1 cake

Preheat oven to 350°.

In medium mixer bowl, beat egg whites and salt at high speed until foamy. Gradually add ½ cup sugar, continuing to beat until stiff peaks form. Set aside.

In medium mixer bowl, add egg yolks and remaining ingredients, except nuts. Blend at low speed until moistened, then beat 1 minute at medium speed, scraping bowl occasionally. Fold egg whites into mixture until well combined. Fold in nuts. Pour batter into ungreased 10-inch tube pan.

Bake for 55 to 60 minutes or until top springs back when touched lightly in center. When done, immediately invert pan on soda bottle. Cool at least 3 hours. When cool, loosen edges and remove cake from pan.

CLASSIC SPONGE CAKE

5 eggs, separated
1½ cups sugar
½ cup orange juice
½ cup oil
Rind of 1 lemon
1 tsp. vanilla extract
1½ cups flour
1 tsp. baking powder

USE: 9-inch tube pan
YIELDS: 1 cake

Preheat oven to 350°.

In a medium mixer bowl, beat egg whites, gradually adding ¾ cup sugar. Beat until stiff but not dry. Set aside in refrigerator.

In large mixer bowl, beat egg yolks, remaining ¾ cup sugar, orange juice, oil, lemon rind, and vanilla until thick and light yellow. Beat in flour and baking powder.

Gently fold in egg whites with spatula. Pour into ungreased 9-inch tube pan.

Bake for 40 to 45 minutes. When done, immediately invert on soda bottle. Cool at least 3 hours. When cool, loosen edges and remove cake from pan.

MAPLENUT-SPRINKLE SPONGE CAKE

4 eggs, separated
Dash salt
½ cup maple-flavored syrup
¾ cup sugar
1½ cups flour
1 tsp. baking powder
½ cup cold water
2 ounces (5 Tbsps.)
chocolate sprinkles
Chopped walnuts (optional)

MAPLE-CHOCOLATE GLAZE
1 Tbsp. margarine
1-ounce square
unsweetened chocolate
1 cup confectioners' sugar
4 to 6 Tbsps.
maple-flavored syrup
¼ tsp. maple extract

USE: 10-inch tube pan
Small saucepan
YIELDS: 1 cake

Preheat oven to 350°.

Beat egg whites and salt in mixer bowl at high speed until foamy. Gradually add maple syrup, continuing to beat until stiff peaks form. Set aside.

Put egg yolks in large mixer bowl and add remaining ingredients except for nuts and glaze. Blend at low speed until moistened. Beat for 1 minute at medium speed, scraping bowl occasionally. Fold egg whites carefully and mix by hand until well combined. Pour into an ungreased 10-inch tube pan.

Bake for 45 to 50 minutes or until top springs back when touched lightly in center. When done, immediately invert pan on soda bottle. Cool at least 3 hours. When cool, loosen edges, remove from pan, and drizzle with Maple-Chocolate Glaze. Sprinkle with nuts if desired.

MAPLE-CHOCOLATE GLAZE: In a small saucepan, melt margarine and chocolate on low heat. Remove from fire and add remaining ingredients. Stir until smooth.

BERRY-SAUCED SPONGE CAKE DESSERT

6 eggs, separated
1 cup sugar
1 tsp. grated lemon rind
¼ cup boiling water
1 Tbsp. lemon juice
1 cup flour
1½ tsps. baking powder
¼ tsp. salt

BERRY SAUCE
2 cups unsweetened
frozen strawberries
2 cups frozen raspberries
½ cup sugar
¼ cup corn syrup
1 stick cinnamon
1 Tbsp. lemon juice

USE: 10-inch tube pan
Small saucepan
YIELDS: 1 cake

Preheat oven to 350°.

In large mixer bowl, beat egg yolks with sugar, lemon rind, and boiling water. When cool, beat in lemon juice. Add dry ingredients and stir until blended.

In a separate bowl, beat egg whites until stiff, then fold into batter. Pour into an ungreased 10-inch tube pan.

Bake for 45 minutes. When done, invert pan on soda bottle. Cool at least 3 hours. When cool, loosen edges and remove from pan.

BERRY SAUCE: Combine all ingredients in a saucepan and stir over medium flame until sugar dissolves. This makes approximately 5 cups. Allow to cool. Before serving, cut cake into 1-inch slices and arrange on cake plate. Spoon 1 cup of sauce over cake and serve remainder of sauce on the side.

CHOCOLATE CAKE *enthusiasts say that everyone is a chocolate lover. How could anyone resist the rich chewy moistness of brownies, the buttery creaminess of chocolate icing, and the flavorful goodness of a chocolate cake studded with chocolate sprinkles?*

CLASSIC CHOCOLATE CAKE

4 eggs
1⅓ cups oil
2¼ cups sugar
1½ tsps. vanilla extract
2¾ cups flour
3 tsps. baking powder
1½ tsps. baking soda
½ tsp. salt
1 cup cocoa
1¾ cups strong hot coffee

USE: 9 x 13-inch baking pan
or 9-inch tube pan
YIELDS: 1 cake

Preheat oven to 350°.

Grease bottom of 9 x 13-inch pan, or 9-inch tube pan.

In large mixer bowl, cream eggs, oil, sugar, and vanilla. In small bowl combine all dry ingredients except cocoa. Mix cocoa together with hot coffee. Add dry ingredients alternately with liquid to mixer bowl, ending with dry ingredients.

Bake for 1 hour or until toothpick inserted in center comes out clean. Allow to cool on cake rack and frost with frosting or glaze of your choice.

CHOCOLATE LAYER CAKE

When making this cake dairy, it should be mixed with dairy utensils and baked in a dairy oven.

6 ounces
semisweet chocolate
¼ cup water or coffee
2¼ cups flour
1 tsp. baking soda
Dash of salt
¾ cup margarine, softened
1¾ cups sugar
1 tsp. vanilla extract
3 eggs
1 cup buttermilk or
1 cup nondairy creamer
mixed with 1 tsp. vinegar

CHOCOLATE-HONEY CREAM
6 ounces
semisweet chocolate
¼ cup honey
2 Tbsps. water
Dash of salt
2 cups nondairy
dessert topping, defrosted
1½ tsps. instant coffee

USE: 3 9-inch round cake pans
Small saucepan
YIELDS: 1 3-layer cake

Preheat oven to 375°.

Grease three 9-inch round cake pans.

Place chocolate and water in small saucepan and heat over low flame until mixed. Set aside and let cool.

Mix together dry ingredients in a small bowl and set aside.

In large mixer bowl, cream margarine, sugar, vanilla, and eggs. Add dry ingredients alternately with buttermilk to creamed mixture. Add melted chocolate to batter and mix well. Pour into greased cake pans.

Bake for 25 to 30 minutes or until toothpick inserted in center comes out clean. Be careful not to overbake.

Allow to cool completely before putting on cream.

CHOCOLATE-HONEY CREAM: Melt chocolate, honey, water, and salt over low flame and set aside. In a large bowl, whip topping and coffee powder until stiff. Add chocolate mixture and mix until combined.

Place first cake layer on dish and spread with cream. Add second layer and spread with cream. Add third layer and frost the entire cake — on top and sides — with remaining cream.

Refrigerate frosted cake until ready to serve.

BLACK DEVIL'S FOOD CAKE

1 cup cocoa

2 cups strong, hot coffee

3 cups flour

2 tsps. baking soda

½ tsp. baking powder

Pinch of salt

4 eggs

1 cup margarine, softened

2¼ cups sugar

2 tsps. vanilla extract

½ tsp. almond extract

6 to 8 maraschino cherries, diced (optional)

USE: 9 x 13-inch cake pan
YIELDS: 1 cake

Preheat oven to 325°.

Grease a 9 x 13-inch cake pan.

Mix cocoa and coffee together in a small bowl until there are no lumps. In a separate bowl combine dry ingredients. Beat together eggs, margarine, sugar, and vanilla and almond extracts in a large mixer bowl.

Add flour mixture alternately with the cocoa-coffee mixture, beginning and ending with dry ingredients. Fold in cherries.

Pour batter into prepared pan and bake for 45 minutes to an hour, or until toothpick inserted in center comes out clean.

When cooled, cake can be frosted with either Chocolate Swirl Frosting (page 391), or Easy Marshmallow Frosting (page 392).

CHOCOLATE FUDGE CAKE

½ cup cocoa

1 tsp. instant coffee

1 cup boiling water

2½ cups flour

3½ tsps. baking powder

½ cup margarine, softened

2 cups brown sugar

4 eggs, well beaten

1 tsp. vanilla extract

½ cup orange juice

USE: 9 x 13-inch cake pan
YIELDS: 1 cake

Preheat oven to 350°.

Grease a 9 x 13-inch cake pan.

Measure cocoa and coffee powder into a small bowl; add boiling water gradually, and stir continuously until well blended. Set aside to cool.

Sift together flour and baking powder. Set aside.

Cream margarine and sugar in a large bowl; add eggs and vanilla and beat well. Add dry ingredients alternately with orange juice. Lastly, add cooled cocoa mixture and stir well.

Pour into greased cake pan and bake for 40 to 45 minutes.

COCONUT CAKES *have a distinctively sweet flavor especially loved by children.*

CHOCOLATE MACAROON CAKE

FILLING

1 egg white

¼ cup sugar

1 cup shredded coconut

1 Tbsp. flour

1 tsp. vanilla extract

CAKE

½ cup shortening

1¾ cups sugar

3 eggs and 1 egg yolk

2 cups flour

Preheat oven to 350°.

Grease a 10-inch tube pan.

FILLING: In a small bowl beat egg white until soft peaks form. Gradually add in sugar, beating until stiff. By hand, stir in coconut, flour, and vanilla and mix. Set aside.

CAKE: Cream shortening, sugar, and eggs in a large bowl. Sift together dry ingredients and add alternately with water and vanilla.

Pour half of batter into greased tube pan. Drop filling evenly over batter and then cover with remaining batter. Bake for 1 hour. Allow cake to cool 1 hour before removing from pan.

➤

½ cup cocoa
Pinch of salt
1 tsp. baking soda
2 tsps. vanilla extract
1¼ cups water

USE: 10-inch tube pan
YIELDS: 1 cake

If desired, cake can be covered with a chocolate or vanilla glaze.

COCONUT CAKE

½ cup margarine, softened
1½ cups sugar
3 eggs
1½ tsps. vanilla extract
2¼ cups flour
2 tsps. baking powder
Pinch salt
1¼ cups nondairy creamer
1 Tbsp. lemon juice
1 cup shredded coconut

Easy Marshmallow Frosting
(page 392)

USE: 2 8-inch round cake pans
YIELDS: 1 layer cake

Preheat oven to 350°.

Generously grease and lightly flour two 8-inch round layer-cake pans.

In a large mixer bowl, cream margarine. Gradually add sugar, beating until light and fluffy. Add eggs, one at a time, beating well after each. Add vanilla, flour, baking powder, salt, creamer, and lemon juice. Blend at low speed until moistened, then turn to medium speed, scraping bowl occasionally. Stir in ½ cup coconut.

Pour batter into pans, spreading to the edges. Bake for 30 to 35 minutes until top springs back when touched lightly in center. Cool 10 minutes and remove from pans.

Prepare Easy Marshmallow Frosting. Frost one layer with Marshmallow Frosting, top with second layer, and frost entire cake. Sprinkle with remaining coconut.

CRANBERRY FRUIT BREAD

2 cups sifted flour
1 cup sugar
1½ tsps. baking powder
½ tsp. baking soda
Pinch of salt
¼ cup solid shortening
¾ cup orange juice
1 Tbsp. grated orange rind
1 egg, well beaten
½ cup chopped walnuts
½ cup golden raisins
1½ cups fresh
chopped cranberries

USE: 9½ x 5½-inch loaf pan
YIELDS: 1 loaf cake

Preheat oven to 350°.

Grease a loaf pan.

In a large mixer bowl sift together dry ingredients. Cut in shortening until mixture resembles coarse cornmeal. Combine orange juice, rind, and egg; add to dry ingredients. Mix until batter is moist. Fold in nuts, raisins, and cranberries.

Spoon into greased loaf pan. Bake for 55 to 60 minutes. Let cool and remove from pan.

Refrigerate for a few days to allow flavor to permeate the cake.

POUND CAKES *are deliciously rich and moist. Because of their density, one cake will yield many servings.*

358

CAKE AND PASTRY

Cakes

MARBLE-SWIRL POUND CAKE

2 cups sugar
1 cup margarine, softened
3½ cups flour
3 tsps. baking powder
1 cup orange juice
2 tsps. vanilla extract
4 eggs
¼ cup cocoa

USE: 10-inch tube pan
YIELDS: 1 cake

Preheat oven to 350°.

Grease a 10-inch tube pan and set aside.

In a large mixer bowl, beat sugar and margarine at low speed until blended. Increase speed to high and beat until light and fluffy.

Add remaining ingredients except cocoa and beat at low speed until well mixed, constantly scraping bowl with rubber spatula. Increase speed to high and beat 4 minutes longer, occasionally scraping bowl.

Pour half of batter into tube pan. Add cocoa to remaining batter and mix well. Pour over white batter and swirl with large spoon to obtain marbled effect.

Bake for 1 hour, or until toothpick inserted in center comes out clean.

HAWAIIAN POUND CAKE

1 cup margarine, softened
1½ cups sugar
6 eggs
2½ cups flour
½ tsp. baking powder
½ tsp. ground ginger
1 8½-ounce can crushed
pineapple, drained
1 cup grated or
flaked coconut

USE: 10-inch bundt pan
YIELDS: 1 cake

Preheat oven to 350°.

Generously grease and flour a 10-inch bundt pan.

In large mixer bowl, cream margarine and sugar until light. Add eggs one at a time, beating well after each addition. Add remaining ingredients. Blend at low speed until thoroughly combined, scraping bowl occasionally.

Pour batter into prepared pan, making sure it reaches edges all around. Bake for 55 to 60 minutes or until a toothpick inserted in center comes out clean.

Cool for 30 minutes before removing from pan.

COCOA POUND CAKE

1 cup margarine, softened
½ cup solid shortening
2¼ cups sugar
5 eggs
3 cups flour
½ cup cocoa
½ tsp. baking powder
1 tsp. vanilla extract
½ cup nondairy creamer
½ cup water

USE: 10-inch tube pan
YIELDS: 1 cake

Preheat oven to 325°.

Generously grease and flour a 10-inch tube pan.

In large mixer bowl, cream margarine and shortening. Gradually add sugar, creaming until light and fluffy. Add eggs, one at a time, beating well after each one. Add remaining ingredients and blend at low speed until thoroughly combined, scraping bowl occasionally.

Pour batter into prepared tube pan. Bake until toothpick inserted in center comes out clean, approximately 75 to 80 minutes.

Cool for 30 minutes before removing from pan.

COFFEE CAKE *is a fairly dry, not-too-sweet cake, so named because it is often served for breakfast with a cup of coffee. These cakes may have fruit fillings or toppings, or most commonly a streusel topping. Other traditional coffee cakes may be found under Yeast Cakes.*

CHERRY-ALMOND COFFEE CAKE

1½ cups flour
¼ cup sugar
Pinch of salt
¾ cup nondairy creamer
1 egg
2½ tsps. baking powder
¼ cup solid shortening

TOPPING
⅔ cup cherry jam
¼ cup brown sugar
½ cup sliced almonds
2 tsps. cinnamon

VANILLA GLAZE
1 cup confectioners' sugar
½ tsp. vanilla extract
3 Tbsps. water

USE: 9 x 13-inch cake pan
YIELDS: 1 cake

Preheat oven to 375°.

Grease a 9 x 13-inch cake pan.

Measure all cake ingredients into a large mixer bowl. Blend thoroughly and beat vigorously for 1 minute. Pat dough into pan with wet hand.

TOPPING: Mix jam thoroughly to soften it. Drizzle over the cake. Mix brown sugar, sliced almonds, and cinnamon and sprinkle over jam.

Bake for 25 to 30 minutes.

VANILLA GLAZE: While cake is baking, prepare glaze by mixing all ingredients thoroughly. Glaze while still warm.

COFFEE CAKE

1 cup margarine, softened
1 cup sugar
3 eggs
2½ cups flour
1 tsp. baking soda
2 tsps. baking powder
1 cup less 1 Tbsp. nondairy dessert topping
1 tsp. lemon juice
1 tsp. vanilla extract

FILLING
1 cup chopped walnuts
½ cup sugar
1 tsp. cinnamon

USE: 9 x 13-inch cake pan
YIELDS: 1 cake

Preheat oven to 350°.

Grease a 9 x 13-inch cake pan.

In a large mixer bowl, cream margarine and sugar. Add eggs, and set mixture aside. Combine flour, baking soda, and baking powder in a medium bowl and set aside.

In a separate bowl, whip dessert topping, then add lemon juice and vanilla. Alternately add flour and whipped topping to creamed margarine mixture.

FILLING: Mix nuts, sugar, and cinnamon in a separate bowl.

Pour half the batter into the greased cake pan and sprinkle half of nut mixture over batter; then pour in remaining batter and top with remaining nut mixture. Bake for 30 to 35 minutes.

COFFEE CRUNCH CAKE

2 cups flour
1¼ cups sugar
2 tsps. baking powder
2 tsps. instant coffee
1 tsp. vanilla extract
½ cup solid shortening
½ cup nondairy creamer
and ½ cup water
2 eggs
2 Tbsps. molasses

MOCHA FROSTING
2 Tbsps. margarine, softened
1½ cups confectioners' sugar
1 tsp. instant coffee
½ tsp. vanilla extract
2 to 3 Tbsps.
nondairy creamer

CRUNCHY TOPPING
¼ cup flour
2 Tbsps. brown sugar
2 Tbsps. margarine
½ cup chopped pecans

USE: 9 x 13-inch cake pan
Shallow baking pan
YIELDS: 1 cake

Preheat oven to 350°.

Generously grease bottom only of 9 x 13-inch cake pan.

In a large mixer bowl, combine all cake ingredients. Blend at low speed until moistened, then beat 3 minutes at low speed, scraping bowl occasionally. Pour batter into prepared pan and spread to corners of pan.

Bake for 30 to 35 minutes, or until top springs back when touched lightly in center.

Let cake cool completely before frosting it with Mocha Frosting. Sprinkle top of cake with Crunchy Topping.

MOCHA FROSTING: In a small bowl, beat all ingredients with nondairy creamer until thin enough to spread.

CRUNCHY TOPPING: In a small bowl, combine flour and brown sugar. Cut in margarine until mixture is crumbly. Stir in pecans. Pour into shallow baking pan and bake at 350° for 12 minutes or until lightly browned. Cool and break into small pieces.

QUICK STREUSEL KUCHEN

2 cups flour
2 tsps. baking powder
¾ cup sugar
Pinch of salt
2 eggs, beaten
½ cup apple juice or
any other liquid
½ cup oil

STREUSEL TOPPING
½ cup brown sugar
2 Tbsps. flour
¾ tsp. cinnamon
2 Tbsps. margarine
½ cup chopped nuts
(optional)

USE: 9-inch square cake pan
YIELDS: 1 cake

Preheat oven to 350°.

Grease a 9-inch square cake pan.

In a large mixer bowl, sift together all dry ingredients. Add eggs, juice, and oil, and mix well.

STREUSEL TOPPING: Combine brown sugar, flour, and cinnamon. Work in margarine with fingers until the mixture is like crumbs. Add nuts if desired.

Pour cake batter into greased cake pan, then sprinkle on topping. Bake for 30 to 35 minutes.

CHOCOLATE NUT-FILLED CRUMB CAKE

1 cup margarine, softened
¾ cup sugar
3 cups flour
1 tsp. baking powder
Pinch of salt
7 egg yolks
1 tsp. vanilla extract

FILLING
7 egg whites
Pinch of salt
1 cup sugar
Rind of 1 orange, grated
Rind of 1 lemon, grated
½ pound walnuts, chopped
2 ounces semisweet chocolate, melted

3 Tbsps. strawberry jam
¼ cup flour

USE: 9 x 13-inch cake pan
YIELDS: 1 cake

Preheat oven to 350°.

Grease a 9 x 13-inch cake pan.

In a large mixer bowl, cream margarine with sugar. In a small bowl sift together flour, baking powder, and salt. By hand, beat in egg yolks, vanilla, and dry ingredients into creamed margarine and sugar. Divide dough into two parts — one-third and two-thirds.

FILLING: In a separate mixer bowl, beat egg whites with a pinch of salt until stiff. Beat in sugar, grated orange and lemon rinds, walnuts, and melted chocolate.

Place larger portion of dough in bottom of pan and pat down. Spread a thin layer of jam over the dough, then the filling.

Add the ¼ cup flour to the remaining one-third portion of dough and mix well. Crumble the dough over the filling.

Bake for 50 minutes. While warm, cut into diamond-shaped pieces. Cool and serve in individual cupcake holders.

FRUIT CRUMB CAKE

½ cup and 2 Tbsps. margarine, softened
2 cups flour
1¼ cups sugar
2 tsps. baking powder
1 tsp. grated lemon rind
1 tsp. vanilla extract
3 egg yolks

FILLING
3 Tbsps. apricot or strawberry jam
1 20-ounce can lemon-pie filling
½ cup raisins
2 apples, peeled and grated
3 egg whites

USE: 9 x 13-inch cake pan
YIELDS: 1 cake

Preheat oven to 350°.

Grease a 9 x 13-inch cake pan.

In a large mixer bowl, combine first six ingredients, using only 1 cup of the sugar, and mix together with two forks or a pastry blender. Add egg yolks one at a time and mix until consistency is like cornmeal. Remove 1 cup for topping. Pat dough into greased cake pan.

FILLING: Dot or cover lightly with jam. Add pie filling and top with raisins and grated apples.

Beat the 3 egg whites with ¼ cup of sugar until stiff and spread over apples. Sprinkle top of cake with reserved cup of dough.

Bake for approximately 45 to 50 minutes.

EASY MIX-BY-HAND CRUMB CAKE

2 eggs
1 cup sugar
1 cup oil
1 Tbsp. lemon juice
4 Tbsps. orange juice
1 tsp. vanilla extract
Pinch of salt
6 cups flour
2 tsps. baking powder
2 tsps. cinnamon

FILLING
16 ounces jam
3 Tbsps. orange juice
4 grated apples
1 Tbsp. cinnamon
2 Tbsps. sugar
2 Tbsps. lemon juice
or
1 20-ounce can cherry or blueberry pie filling

USE: 11 x 16-inch baking pan
YIELDS: 20 squares

Preheat oven to 350°.

Grease 11 x 16-inch baking pan.

Mix eggs, sugar, oil, lemon juice, orange juice, and vanilla in large mixer bowl. Then add dry ingredients. Mix together for 2 minutes — dough should feel crumbly. Take half the dough and crumble by hand into greased baking pan.

FILLING: Mix jam and orange juice together until smooth. Spread over crumbs. Combine grated apple with cinnamon, sugar and lemon juice. Spread over jam. Or fill with favorite pie filling. Crumble remaining dough over filling.

Bake for about 45 minutes until lightly browned.

Remove from oven. Allow to cool slightly; while still warm cut into 3-inch squares. Cool in pan.

Dust with confectioners' sugar.

NOTE: This cake freezes well after it has been cut into squares. The squares should be slightly separated for freezing so they can be removed from freezer as needed.

FRUIT SWIRL CAKE

5 eggs
1½ cups sugar
½ cup margarine, softened
½ cup solid shortening
3 cups flour
1½ tsps. baking powder
1 tsp. vanilla extract
1 tsp. almond extract

1 20-ounce can cherry pie filling

GLAZE
1 cup confectioners' sugar
4 tsps. nondairy creamer

USE: 9 x 13-inch cake pan
YIELDS: 1 cake

Preheat oven to 350°.

Grease a 9 x 13-inch cake pan.

In a large mixer bowl, place first eight ingredients and mix well at low speed. Spread three fourths of the batter into the greased cake pan. Spoon pie filling over batter and then with a tablespoon drop remaining batter over filling.

Bake for 50 minutes. While still warm, drizzle glaze over cake.

GLAZE: Combine sugar and nondairy creamer and mix well until a smooth consistency is reached.

HONEY CAKE, *also known as* lekach, *is traditionally served on Rosh Hashanah to symbolize our prayers for a good and sweet year. A common custom on Erev Yom Kippur is to request a piece of honey cake from another person, often the sexton of the synagogue. This transaction symbolizes a substitute for any charity a person might have been destined to receive in the coming year; it also represents the giver's wish that the recipient should have a good year. In Chassidic communities the Rebbe distributes* lekach *to his followers, and many bake some of it into their own honey cake, to share the Rebbe's blessing with all who eat at their table. It is also the custom of many people not to eat nuts on Rosh Hashanah. For this reason we have made the nuts optional in many of our honey cake recipes.*

SPICED HONEY CHIFFON CAKE

3 Tbsps. oil
1 cup sugar
3 eggs, separated
1 cup honey
½ tsp. salt
1 tsp. baking powder
1 tsp. baking soda
2¾ cups flour
½ tsp. ginger
½ tsp. anise
1 tsp. cinnamon
½ tsp. nutmeg
½ tsp. cloves
1 cup orange juice
2 tsps. instant coffee
1 cup raisins (optional)
**1 cup chopped walnuts
    (optional)**

USE: 9 x 13-inch cake pan
YIELDS: 1 cake

Preheat oven to 325°.

In a large mixer bowl, cream oil and sugar. Add egg yolks and honey. Beat well.

In a small mixer bowl sift together salt, baking powder, and baking soda, flour and spices. Mix the orange juice with the coffee. Add alternately with the dry ingredients to batter, beating well after each addition. Fold in raisins and/or nuts.

Beat egg whites in a separate bowl until stiff, then fold into batter. Pour into ungreased pan.

Bake for 45 to 50 minutes.

VARIATIONS
☐ Additional cinnamon may be substituted for anise, nutmeg, and cloves.

☐ Omit nuts for Rosh Hashanah.

HONEY SPONGE CAKE

6 eggs, separated
1 cup sugar
3 Tbsps. honey
3 Tbsps. strong black coffee
2 Tbsps. oil
1 tsp. cinnamon
3 cloves, crushed (optional)
1 Tbsp. brandy
1¼ cups flour
1½ tsps. baking powder

USE: 10-inch tube pan
YIELDS: 1 cake

Preheat oven to 350°.

In a small mixer bowl beat egg whites with ½ cup sugar until stiff but not dry and set aside.

In a separate bowl, cream egg yolks and ½ cup sugar. Add honey, coffee, oil, cinnamon, cloves, and brandy. Beat until thick and light in color.

With a spatula, fold in flour and baking powder until well blended. Then fold in egg whites gently and carefully until well blended. Pour into ungreased tube pan. Bake for 1 hour. When done immediately invert on soda bottle. Cool at least 3 hours before removing so that cake will not fall. When cool, loosen edges and remove cake from pan.

CLASSIC HONEY CAKE

3 eggs
1⅓ cups honey
1½ cups sugar
1 cup strong black coffee
2 tsps. baking powder
3 Tbsps. margarine,
softened
1 tsp. baking soda
4 cups flour
1 tsp. cinnamon

USE: 9 x 13-inch cake pan
YIELDS: 1 cake

Preheat oven to 325°.

Grease and flour a 9 x 13-inch cake pan.

In a large mixer bowl, beat eggs and honey together. Add sugar and mix again. Mix coffee with baking powder, and then add with margarine to the egg mixture. Add baking soda, flour, and cinnamon and beat together well.

Pour into greased cake pan. Bake for 55 minutes to an hour.

OLD-FASHIONED LEKACH

1 cup honey
1 cup oil
1 cup brown sugar
3 eggs
1 cup strong hot
black coffee
2 tsps. baking powder
1 tsp. baking soda
3½ cups flour
¼ tsp. salt
1 tsp. cinnamon
1 tsp. nutmeg
½ tsp. cloves
¼ tsp. ginger
¾ cup chopped walnuts
(optional)

USE: 9 x 13-inch cake pan
YIELDS: 1 cake

Preheat oven to 325°.

Line a 9 x 13-inch cake pan with wax paper; grease the paper.

In a large mixer bowl, cream honey, oil, and sugar. Add eggs one at a time, beating after each addition. Combine coffee, baking powder, and baking soda; mixture will bubble.

Combine flour with salt and spices and add alternately with the coffee to the creamed mixture. Dust nuts with flour and drop into batter.

Pour the batter into the wax-papered and greased pan. Bake for 1 hour.

VARIATION
□ Omit nuts for Rosh Hashanah; ½ cup raisins may be substituted.

A JELLY ROLL *is a rolled cake, usually white sponge. A thin layer of cake is baked, then covered with a filling, such as jelly, mocha, or ice cream and rolled to create a spiral. Two different fillings may be used; one to fill the inside and one to frost the outside.*

TIPS FOR PERFECT JELLY ROLLS

□ Bake the cake on a 10 x 15-inch jelly-roll pan lined with wax paper. Bake at 350° for 12-15 minutes unless otherwise specified in recipe.

□ Dust a dish towel with confectioners' sugar. After the cake is baked, turn it onto the towel.

□ Remove the wax paper immediately and trim any crusty edges.

□ While still hot, carefully roll the towel and cake along the long side. This keeps cake from cracking.

□ When cool, unroll towel and fill cake with jelly, frosting, or ice cream. Reroll and place seam side down on plate.

□ The outside may also be frosted or simply dusted with confectioners' sugar.

□ Yeast cakes may also be made jelly-roll style.

BASIC JELLY ROLL

6 eggs
¾ cup sugar
1 cup flour
1 tsp. vanilla extract
Pinch of salt

FILLING
¾ cup jam or
Chocolate "Butter" Cream
(page 391)
Confectioners' sugar

USE: Jelly-roll pan
YIELDS: 1 jelly roll

Preheat oven to 350°.

Line a jelly-roll pan with a piece of greased wax paper.

In a medium mixer bowl cream eggs and sugar until light lemon color. Sift in flour, ⅓ at a time. Add vanilla and salt, and beat well. Pour into prepared jelly-roll pan.

Proceed according to Tips for Perfect Jelly Rolls. Bake 15 to 20 minutes or until top springs back when touched lightly.

FILLING: After cake has cooled unroll and spread with jam or Chocolate Butter Cream. Reroll. Dust lightly with confectioners' sugar.

VARIATION
□ **Chocolate Roll:** Substitute ⅔ cup flour and ⅓ cup cocoa for 1 cup of flour.

CHIFFON JELLY ROLL

3 eggs, separated
1 cup sugar
2 Tbsps. lemon juice
½ cup water
Dash of salt
1 cup flour
1 tsp. baking powder

FILLING
¾ cup raspberry jam or
Chocolate Cream
(page 396)
Confectioners' sugar

USE: Jelly-roll pan
YIELDS: 1 jelly roll

Preheat oven to 350°.

Line a jelly-roll pan with a piece of greased wax paper.

In a medium mixer bowl beat egg yolks until thick. Add ½ cup sugar and lemon juice; beat until thick and add water. In a separate mixer bowl, beat egg whites, salt, and remaining sugar. Fold whites into yolks. Fold flour and baking powder into mixture. Pour into prepared jelly-roll pan.

Proceed according to Tips for Perfect Jelly Rolls.

FILLING: After cake has cooled unroll and spread raspberry jam or Chocolate Cream. Reroll. Dust lightly with confectioners' sugar.

CHOCOLATE NUT ROLL

I cup ground walnuts
¼ cup sifted flour
¼ cup cocoa
5 eggs, separated
Pinch of salt
⅔ cup sugar
½ tsp. vanilla extract

WALNUT CREAM
Confectioners' sugar
1 10-ounce container
nondairy dessert topping
½ cup chopped walnuts

VANILLA CREAM
1 10-ounce container
nondairy dessert topping
1 package
instant vanilla pudding

USE: Jelly-roll pan
YIELDS: 1 jelly roll

Preheat oven to 350°.

Line the bottom of a jelly-roll pan with a piece of greased wax paper.

In a small bowl mix walnuts with flour and cocoa; set aside. In a large mixer bowl beat egg whites and salt until barely stiff, then gradually beat in ⅓ cup sugar. With same beater, beat yolks with remaining sugar and vanilla extract until thick. Pour yolks over egg whites, gently fold together. Gradually fold in walnut mixture. Pour into prepared jelly-roll pan.

Bake for 20 minutes until top springs back when touched lightly. Proceed according to Tips for Perfect Jelly Rolls.

After cake has cooled unroll and fill with one of the fillings below. Dust with confectioners' sugar.

WALNUT CREAM FILLING: Whip dessert topping. Add nuts and whip until blended. Spread over cake and reroll.

VANILLA CREAM FILLING: In a bowl, whip dessert topping. Add instant vanilla pudding and beat. Spread over cake and reroll.

VARIATION
□ **Lemony Chocolate Nut Roll:** Fill with Lemon Custard Filling (page 396). Reroll and dust with confectioners' sugar.

MARBLE CAKES *are light and festive, yet easy to make. A few unusual varieties are included.*

DRIZZLED MARBLE CAKE

⅔ cup solid shortening
1½ cups sugar
1 tsp. vanilla extract
4 eggs
2⅓ cups flour
3 tsps. baking powder
¼ tsp. salt
1 cup water or apple juice

MARBLE
4 Tbsps. cocoa
3 Tbsps. sugar
5 Tbsps. hot water

USE: 9 x 13-inch cake pan
YIELDS: 1 cake

Preheat oven to 350°.

Grease and flour the bottom of a 9 x 13-inch cake pan.

In a large mixer bowl, cream shortening with sugar. Add vanilla and eggs one at a time, beating after each addition. In a small bowl combine flour, baking powder, and salt.

Add the liquid and dry ingredients alternately to the egg mixture. Pour into greased and floured pan.

MARBLE: Combine cocoa and sugar with enough hot water to make a paste. Drizzle onto batter and cut through batter with knife to marble.

Bake for 45 to 60 minutes or until a toothpick inserted in center comes out clean.

CHERRY MARBLE CAKE

2 eggs
1¼ cups sugar
¾ cup solid shortening
1 cup unwhipped
nondairy dessert topping
2½ cups flour
1½ tsps. baking powder
⅓ cup maraschino
cherry juice
¼ cup cold water
2 ounces unsweetened
melted chocolate
½ cup chopped walnuts
½ cup drained, chopped
maraschino cherries

USE: 10-inch bundt pan
YIELDS: 1 cake

Preheat oven to 350°.

Generously grease a 10-inch bundt pan and set aside.

In a large mixer bowl, combine first eight ingredients. Blend at low speed until moistened, then beat 3 minutes at medium speed, scraping bowl occasionally.

Divide batter in half. To one half add the melted chocolate and blend well. To the other half stir in nuts and cherries until well mixed.

Spoon chocolate and cherry batters alternately into prepared pan. Bake for 45 to 55 minutes or until a toothpick inserted in center comes out clean.

Cool for 30 minutes before removing from pan.

MARBLE CHIFFON CAKE

8 eggs, separated
Pinch of salt
2 cups sugar
¾ cup oil
1 tsp. vanilla extract
2 cups flour
1½ tsps. baking powder
¾ cup orange juice
2 Tbsps. cocoa

USE: 10-inch tube pan
YIELDS: 1 cake

Preheat oven to 350°.

In a large mixer bowl, beat whites with salt until foamy. Gradually add 1 cup sugar, constantly beating until stiff. Set aside.

In a separate mixer bowl, beat egg yolks with remaining sugar, then add oil and vanilla. Add flour and baking powder alternately with juice. Mix well and gently fold beaten egg whites into mixture. See Tips for Perfect Chiffon Cakes (page 351).

Pour half of batter into ungreased tube pan and add cocoa to remaining batter. Mix very well. Spoon cocoa mixture over white mixture and swirl to obtain marbled effect.

Bake for 45 minutes. When done immediately invert on soda bottle. Cool at least 3 hours so cake will not fall. When cool loosen edges and remove cake from pan.

OCASIONAL CAKES *lend a memorable touch to any happy event, whether a birthday, anniversary, sheva brachot or the like.*

LEMON BUNDT CAKE

**5 Tbsps.
graham cracker crumbs**

CAKE
1⅓ cups sugar
⅔ cup solid shortening
3 eggs
1 Tbsp. grated lemon rind
2 cups flour
Dash salt
1 tsp. baking powder
**⅔ cup nondairy creamer
with 1 Tbsp. lemon juice
or white vinegar**

**Lemon Custard Filling
(page 396)**

USE: 10-inch bundt pan
YIELDS: 1 cake

Preheat oven to 375°.

Prepare Lemon Custard Filling and let cool while preparing cake.

Generously grease a 10-inch bundt pan; sprinkle with 2 tablespoons graham cracker crumbs.

In a large mixer bowl, cream sugar and shortening until light and fluffy. Add eggs one at a time, beating well after each addition. Add lemon rind, flour, salt, baking powder, and nondairy creamer and blend at low speed just until thoroughly combined, scraping bowl occasionally. Pour batter into prepared pan, spreading to edges. Sprinkle 2 tablespoons graham cracker crumbs over batter.

Carefully pour Lemon Custard Filling over graham cracker crumbs, forming ring in center of batter. Sprinkle with remaining 1 tablespoon graham cracker crumbs.

Bake for 45 to 50 minutes or until top springs back when touched lightly in center. Cool for 1 hour before removing from pan.

CHOCOLATE-NUT FILLED CAKE

3 cups flour
½ cup sugar
⅜ cup apple juice
1 cup margarine, softened
4 egg yolks
2 tsps. baking powder

**CHOCOLATE MERINGUE
FILLING**
4 egg whites
1 cup sugar
1 tsp. vanilla extract
2 apples, grated
½ cup chopped almonds
**2 ounces semisweet
chocolate, melted**
Juice and rind of 1 lemon

Confectioners' sugar

USE: 9 x 13-inch cake pan
YIELDS: 1 cake

Preheat oven to 350°.

In a medium mixer bowl mix together flour, sugar, and juice. In a large mixer bowl cream margarine and egg yolks, and add flour mixture. Add baking powder and mix well. Set aside.

CHOCOLATE MERINGUE FILLING: In a medium mixer bowl beat egg whites until soft peaks form. Gradually add sugar, beating until stiff. Stir in vanilla, apples, almonds, chocolate, juice and rind.

TO ASSEMBLE: Pat two thirds of dough into ungreased 9 x 13-inch pan. Pour filling over dough. Roll out remaining dough on aluminum foil. Gently place foil side up on top of filling and remove foil.

Bake for 45 minutes. Sprinkle with confectioners' sugar while hot. Cool completely before cutting.

MOCHA-OATMEAL CAKE

The glaze is an important part of this unusual cake.

2 Tbsps. instant coffee
1 cup oatmeal
1⅓ cups boiling water
¾ cup solid shortening
1 cup sugar
1 cup brown sugar
2 eggs
1½ tsps. vanilla extract
2 cups flour
1¼ tsps. baking soda
¾ tsp. salt
3 Tbsps. cocoa

COFFEE GLAZE

1½ Tbsps. margarine, softened
1 cup confectioners' sugar
½ tsp. vanilla extract
1½ Tbsps. instant coffee
1 to 2 Tbsps. warm water

USE: 9- or 10-inch tube pan
YIELDS: 1 cake

Preheat oven to 350°.

Grease and flour a 9- or 10-inch tube pan.

In a small bowl, combine coffee and oatmeal. Pour the boiling water over the mixture and mix well. Cover and let stand 20 minutes.

In a large mixer bowl cream shortening with both sugars. Add eggs and vanilla and beat well. Sift together flour, baking soda, salt, and cocoa. Add oatmeal mixture to batter, then add dry ingredients, mixing very well.

Pour batter into prepared pan. Bake for 50 to 55 minutes. Cool 30 minutes before removing from pan.

COFFEE GLAZE: In a small bowl beat ingredients for glaze together until smooth. Drizzle over cooled cake.

NOTE: Do not substitute oil for shortening.

ORANGE DRIZZLE CAKE

1 cup solid shortening
2 cups sugar
1 tsp. orange extract
2 Tbsps. grated orange rind
5 eggs
3 cups flour
1 Tbsp. baking powder
¾ cup orange juice

DRIZZLE

⅔ cup sugar
¼ cup margarine
⅓ cup orange juice

USE: 9 x 13-inch cake pan
Small saucepan
YIELDS: 1 cake

Preheat oven to 350°.

Grease and flour a 9 x 13-inch cake pan.

In a large mixer bowl cream shortening, sugar, orange, and rind together until well blended. Beat in eggs one at a time. Add flour, baking powder, and juice.

Pour batter into greased cake pan. Bake for 50 minutes. Cool for 30 minutes before removing from pan.

DRIZZLE: Combine sugar, margarine, and orange juice in small saucepan. Cook over low heat until margarine is melted. Pour over warm cake and let it soak in.

RUM CAKE

If using buttermilk, use dairy utensils and bake in a dairy oven.

1 cup margarine, softened
2 cups sugar
4 eggs
1 tsp. vanilla extract
1 tsp. lemon extract
4 cups flour
½ tsp. baking soda
½ tsp. baking powder
1 tsp. salt
1 cup buttermilk or
1 cup less 1 Tbsp.
nondairy creamer with
1 Tbsp. white vinegar

SAUCE
½ cup sugar
⅛ cup water
¼ cup margarine
1½ tsps. rum flavoring

USE: 9-inch tube pan
YIELDS: 1 cake

Preheat oven to 350°.

Grease and flour a 9-inch tube pan.

In large mixer bowl, beat together margarine, sugar, eggs, vanilla and lemon extracts.

Sift together dry ingredients and add to bowl alternately with buttermilk or nondairy creamer with vinegar.

Pour into greased tube pan and bake for 1 hour.

SAUCE: Place sugar, water, and margarine in a 1 quart saucepan. Heat until mixture bubbles, then simmer for another 5 minutes. Remove from heat and stir in rum extract. Pour over hot cake and let cool in pan at least 30 minutes. When cool, loosen edges and remove from cake pan.

STRAWBERRY SHORTCAKE SUPREME

CRUST
½ cup margarine
4 Tbsps. oil
3 cups flour
Rind of 1 lemon or orange, grated
1 egg plus 2 egg yolks
½ cup sugar

ITALIAN PASTRY CREAM
(page 396)

FRESH FRUIT TOPPING
1½ pounds strawberries, peaches or apricots
Juice of 1 lemon
2 Tbsps. sugar

USE: 12-inch round pan
YIELDS: 1 cake

Preheat oven to 375°.

Grease a 12-inch round cake pan.

CRUST: Melt margarine and oil in a saucepan and let stand until cool. Pour flour into a mixer bowl and make a well in center. Pour in margarine-oil mixture, grated rind, egg, and egg yolks. Mix well. Add sugar and mix again. Knead dough just until it forms a ball. Wrap dough in a damp dish towel and set aside in cool place (not in refrigerator) for 30 minutes.

With a rolling pin, roll out dough into a circle. Put pan over circle and cut the dough to fit pan. Place circle of dough in pan and bake for 30 minutes. Remove from oven and let cool.

ITALIAN PASTRY CREAM: Prepare according to directions and cool.

FRESH FRUIT TOPPING: Wash fruit and remove pits or stems. If using large strawberries, cut in half. Sprinkle lemon juice and sugar over the fruit. Set aside.

Remove baked pastry from pan and put on serving dish. Spread pastry cream on evenly and arrange fruit in a design.

SPICE CAKE

½ cup margarine, softened
½ cup sugar
½ cup brown sugar
2 eggs
1¾ cups flour
1½ tsps. baking powder
1 tsp. salt
½ tsp. cinnamon
½ tsp. cloves
½ tsp. nutmeg
½ cup strong coffee, cooled
½ cup raisins

USE: 9 x 13-inch cake pan
YIELDS: 1 cake

Preheat oven to 350°.

Grease 9 x 13-inch cake pan.

In a large bowl cream together margarine, and both sugars. Beat in eggs, one at a time. Add flour, baking powder, salt, cinnamon, cloves, nutmeg, and coffee. Dust raisins lightly with flour, then add to rest of mixture. Pour into prepared pan.

Bake for 20 - 25 minutes until done.

Cool for 30 minutes before removing from pan.

TORTA

A torte is a special cake often made without flour, using a combination of nuts, sugar, and eggs.

5 eggs, separated
1¾ cups sugar
4 cups ground nuts★

FROSTING
¾ cup cocoa
¼ cup solid shortening
2 tsps. vanilla extract
3 Tbsps. water
1 cup confectioners' sugar

USE: 2 9-inch round pans
Double boiler
YIELDS: 1 torte

Preheat oven to 350°.

In a large mixer bowl beat egg whites until fluffy, gradually adding sugar; then beat until stiff. In a small bowl beat egg yolks and fold into egg whites. Fold in nuts until just combined.

Spread batter on ungreased wax paper in two 9-inch round cake pans. Bake for 15 to 20 minutes, or when toothpick inserted in center comes out clean. Cool cake for 1 hour before removing from pan.

FROSTING: When cake is cool, combine all frosting ingredients in the top of a double boiler and cook over simmering water until of spreadable consistency.

Spread frosting on top of first layer. Top with second layer and frost top of torte.

★NOTE: Use filberts, almonds, peanuts, either alone or in combination.

TURKISH COFFEE TORTE

6 eggs, separated
Pinch of salt
1 cup sugar
1 Tbsp. coffee liqueur
½ cup instant coffee
8 ounces walnuts, ground

BUTTERCREAM FILLING
½ cup margarine, softened
4 ounces semisweet chocolate, melted and cooled
¼ cup confectioners' sugar
1 egg yolk
1 Tbsp. coffee liqueur
1 tsp. instant coffee
4 Tbsps. coffee liqueur

½ cup apricot or raspberry jam

GLAZE
½ cup plus 3 Tbsps. sugar
½ cup cocoa
½ cup nondairy creamer
¼ cup margarine
1 tsp. instant coffee

TOPPING
Sliced almonds (optional)

USE: 2 9-inch springform pans
1-quart saucepan
YIELDS: 1 torte

Preheat oven to 325°.

Grease two 9-inch springform pans.

In a medium mixer bowl beat 6 egg whites until foamy. Add pinch of salt and beat until soft peaks form. Gradually add ⅓ cup sugar and beat until stiff but not dry. Set aside.

In a large mixer bowl, using same beaters, beat egg yolks with remaining ⅔ cup of sugar. Blend in liqueur, coffee powder, and nuts. Carefully fold this mixture into the beaten egg whites.

Pour mixture into the two greased pans and bake for 20 to 25 minutes. When done, cool cake for 1 hour before removing from pan.

BUTTERCREAM FILLING: Combine margarine, melted chocolate, confectioners' sugar, egg yolk, 1 tablespoon coffee liqueur, and coffee powder in large mixer bowl and beat until fluffy.

GLAZE: To make glaze, combine all ingredients in a 1-quart saucepan and heat over low heat, stirring constantly until smooth and slightly thickened, about 5 minutes. Let cool.

TO ASSEMBLE: Unmold cakes from pan sides, leaving bottoms on. Brush the top of each layer with the 4 tablespoons of coffee liqueur from the filling. Spread the jam over the top of one layer. Spread the buttercream over the top of the other layer. It should be about ¼ inch thick. Invert one layer over the other and remove metal base from the top. Spread buttercream over the top and sides of the cake and place cake in the freezer for at least 2 hours.

After a minimum of 2 hours, place cake on rack. Work over waxed paper. Pour glaze over cake, carefully smoothing it with a knife in order to completely cover the cake. Decorate cake with sliced almonds on the tops and sides of the cake.

WHITE CAKE *is the "basic" cake. It lends itself easily to many variations, with all types of fillings, frostings, and flavors. It serves as the base for the most complex decorated cakes and also for the simplest everyday cake.*

BASIC WHITE CAKE

1 cup margarine, softened
2 cups sugar
4 eggs
3½ cups flour
½ tsp. salt

Preheat oven to 350°.

Grease and flour a 9 x 13-inch cake pan.

In a large mixer bowl, cream margarine well. Gradually add sugar, then one egg at a time, beating well after each addition. ▶

4 tsps. baking powder
1⅓ cups nondairy creamer
or pineapple juice
2 tsps. vanilla extract

USE: 9 x 13-inch cake pan
YIELDS: 1 cake

In a separate bowl, combine flour, salt, and baking powder. Add dry ingredients to creamed shortening alternately with liquid, using mixer on low speed. Add vanilla and mix well.

Pour into prepared pan. Bake for 45 to 55 minutes, or until toothpick inserted in cake comes out clean. Cool completely before cutting.

VARIATIONS

□ **Apple Cake:** Peel and thinly slice 3 apples. Combine 1 teaspoon cinnamon with 3 tablespoons sugar and coat apples with mixture. Pour two thirds of batter into pan, make a layer of apples over batter, then pour remaining batter over apples.

□ **Blueberry Cake:** Sprinkle *top* of batter with 2 cups washed and dried blueberries; they will blend nicely into batter during baking. To prevent blueberries from settling to the bottom of cake, do not mix blueberries into the batter before baking.

□ **Chocolate Chip Cake:** Mix 1 cup chocolate chips into batter before pouring into pan.

□ **Chocolate Marble Cake:** Melt 4 ounces semisweet chocolate together with 2 tablespoons margarine. Once mixture has melted, combine with 2 tablespoons of Basic White Cake batter, then drizzle combination across top of batter in pan and fold lightly into rest of batter.

□ **Coconut Cake:** Mix 1 cup shredded coconut into batter and sprinkle ½ cup on top of batter.

WHITE CAKE WITH COCONUT FROSTING

7 egg whites
½ tsp. white vinegar
2 cups sugar
1 cup margarine, softened
1 tsp. vanilla extract
3 cups flour, sifted
3 tsps. baking powder
1 cup nondairy creamer

FROSTING
Boiled White Frosting
(page 393)
1 cup flaked coconut

USE: 2 9-inch cake pans
YIELDS: 1 layer cake

Preheat oven to 350°.

Grease the bottoms of two 9-inch round cake pans and line with wax paper.

In a large mixer bowl, beat egg whites until foamy. Beat in vinegar, then gradually add 1 cup of sugar, 1 tablespoon at a time, until egg whites form soft peaks. Set aside.

In a separate mixer bowl, beat margarine until creamy; add remaining sugar and vanilla. Sift dry ingredients together, and add to margarine-sugar mixture alternately with nondairy creamer, stirring between each addition until batter is smooth. Gently fold in egg whites and mix well.

Pour batter into prepared pans and bake for 30 minutes or until center springs back when lightly pressed with fingertips.

Cool 10 minutes before removing from pans, and peel off wax paper. Let cake cool completely before frosting.

FROSTING: Spread Boiled White Frosting between layers and on top and sides of cake. Sprinkle generously with coconut.

LEMON-FILLED WHITE LAYER CAKE

2¼ cups flour
1⅔ cups sugar
3½ tsps. baking powder
Pinch of salt
1¼ cups nondairy creamer
⅔ cup shortening
1 tsp. vanilla extract
5 egg whites

FILLING
Lemon Custard Filling
(page 396)

WHITE MOUNTAIN
FROSTING
½ cup sugar
¼ cup light corn syrup
2 Tbsps. water
2 egg whites
1 tsp. vanilla extract

USE: 2 9-inch
round cake pans
1-quart saucepan
YIELDS: 1 layer cake

Preheat oven to 350°.

Grease and flour two 9-inch round cake pans.

In a large mixer bowl, combine the first seven ingredients and beat on low speed for 30 seconds, scraping bowl constantly. Beat on high speed for another 2 minutes. Beat in egg whites on high speed, scraping bowl every 2 minutes.

Pour into prepared pans and bake for 30 to 35 minutes, or until a toothpick inserted in center comes out clean.

Cool 10 minutes before removing from pans.

FILLING: Prepare Lemon Custard Filling. Spread over top of one layer and place second layer on top. If filling is too soft, refrigerate until set.

WHITE MOUNTAIN FROSTING: Mix sugar, corn syrup, water in 1-quart saucepan. Cover and heat to rapid boil over medium heat. Remove cover and boil rapidly to 242° on candy thermometer, or until a very small amount of mixture dropped into very cold water forms a firm ball that holds its shape when pressed. As mixture boils, beat egg whites in small mixer bowl until stiff peaks form. Pour hot syrup very slowly in a thin stream into egg whites, beating constantly on medium speed. Add vanilla, and beat on high speed until stiff peaks form.

Spread on top and sides of cake.

WONDER CAKE

1 cup margarine, softened
1½ cups flour
5 eggs
1½ cups sugar
1 tsp. baking powder
1 tsp. vanilla extract

MOCHA FILLING
1 cup sugar
⅓ cup flour
1 Tbsp. instant coffee
1 cup nondairy creamer
1-ounce square
unsweetened chocolate
½ cup margarine, softened
1 tsp. vanilla extract

1 cup nondairy
dessert topping, whipped

Preheat oven to 350°.

Generously grease and lightly flour two 8-inch round layer-cake pans.

In a large mixer bowl, cream margarine at high speed until light and fluffy. Add flour and blend at low speed, just until thoroughly combined. Set aside.

In small mixer bowl, beat eggs at high speed until foamy. Gradually add sugar, continuing to beat until thick and lemon colored. Blend in baking powder and vanilla. Pour over butter-flour mixture. Blend together at low speed until throughly combined, scraping bowl occasionally. Pour batter into prepared pans.

Bake for 25 to 30 minutes or until top springs back when touched lightly in center.

Cool 10 minutes before removing from pan. Remove and cool completely. Cut layers in half across the middle to make four round, equally thin layers.

Spread Mocha Filling on top of layers to within ½-inch of edge on top layer. Place layers one on top of the other. Frost sides and around top edge with whipped topping. Chill for at least 1 hour before serving. ▶

USE: 2 8-inch round
cake pans
2-quart saucepan
YIELDS: 1 layer cake

MOCHA FILLING: In a 2-quart saucepan, combine ½ cup sugar with flour and coffee. Gradually stir in nondairy creamer until smooth. Add chocolate. Cook over low heat, stirring constantly, until mixture thickens and chocolate melts completely. Remove from heat, cool to room temperature. Set aside.

In small mixer bowl, cream margarine, remaining ½ cup sugar, and vanilla until light and fluffy. Add cooled chocolate mixture and blend at low speed until thoroughly combined.

CHOCOLATE CHIP CAKE

1½ cups sugar
½ cup solid shortening
2 Tbsps. margarine
4 eggs, separated
3 cups flour
3 tsps. baking powder
½ cup water
½ cup orange juice

FILLING
1 12-ounce package
chocolate chips
3 Tbsps. sugar
1 Tbsp. cocoa
1 tsp. cinnamon

USE: 11 x 14-inch cake pan
YIELDS: 1 cake

Preheat oven to 350°.

Grease and flour an 11 x 14-inch cake pan.

In large mixer bowl, beat together sugar, shortening, and margarine until creamy. Add egg yolks, one at a time. Sift together flour and baking powder in a small bowl and add to mixture alternately with water and juice. Mix thoroughly. In a medium mixer bowl beat whites until light and fluffy; fold into batter.

FILLING: Combine all filling ingredients together and mix well.

Pour one half of the batter into the prepared pan. Sprinkle one half the filling mixture over batter in pan. Pour remainder of batter over the filling. Sprinkle the top with the remaining filling mixture. Bake 40 to 45 minutes, or until a toothpick inserted in center comes out clean. Cool completely before cutting.

NUT-AND-JELLY LAYER CAKE

1 cup margarine, softened
2 cups sugar
4 eggs
4 cups flour
2 tsps. baking powder
2 tsps. baking soda
Pinch salt
1 cup orange juice
2 tsps. vanilla extract

FILLING
4 tsps. cinnamon
½ cup sugar
1½ cups chopped walnuts
1½ cups strawberry preserves

USE: 9 x 13-inch cake pan
YIELDS: 1 cake

Preheat oven to 350°.

Grease and flour a 9 x 13-inch cake pan.

In a large mixer bowl cream margarine and sugar until light lemon colored. Beat in eggs, one at a time. In a separate bowl, mix together flour, baking powder, baking soda, and salt. Combine with margarine mixture, ½ cup at a time, alternating with juice and vanilla. Set aside.

FILLING: Combine cinnamon, sugar, and nuts.

Layer ingredients in prepared pan in the following order: half of the batter, jelly, and nut mixture, remaining batter, jelly, and nut mixture.

Bake for 45 minutes. Cool completely before cutting.

SPECIALTY CAKES *are the perfect addition to any festive occasion. With some extra effort you can produce these bakery classics and be rewarded with professional quality and superb taste.*

TRI-COLOR COOKIE SQUARES

Important — The recipe for batter must be divided in three and mixed separately. Do not mix entire recipe at once.

6 eggs
1½ cups sugar
3 cups flour
3 tsps. almond extract
Food coloring,
yellow, red, and green
1½ cups margarine (each
½ cup melted, cooled
and reserved separately)
1 32 ounce jar raspberry jam

GLAZE
⅓ cup margarine
½ cup cocoa
⅓ cup nondairy creamer
1 tsp. vanilla extract
2½ cups confectioners' sugar

USE: 3 10 x 15-inch
jelly-roll pans
1-quart saucepan
YIELDS: 75 cookies

Preheat oven to 350°.

Grease three 10 x 15-inch jelly-roll pans and line with wax paper.

Layer 1: In a mixer bowl, combine 2 eggs and ½ cup sugar, and beat well. Add 1 cup of flour, 1 teaspoon of almond extract and a few drops of yellow food color. Continue beating for 2 minutes. Fold in ½ cup (1 stick) of melted and cooled margarine. Pour into prepared jelly-roll pan, spreading batter to all the corners. Bake for 12 minutes. Cool cake on rack.

Layer 2: Repeat above but instead add a few drops of red food color.

Layer 3: Repeat above but instead add a few drops of green food color.

TO ASSEMBLE: Turn first layer out, upside down on clean aluminum foil. Spread well with ½ cup raspberry jam. Turn second layer over first and press gently, making sure layers are completely joined. Spread with raspberry jam and press third layer over.

GLAZE: In a 1-quart saucepan melt margarine, stir in cocoa. Cook 1 minute. Remove from heat. Stir in remaining ingredients and mix until smooth. Spread on cake while hot. Let cool and harden.

Once cool cut into 2 x 1-inch cookies.

MOCHA CREAM ROLL

This "melt in the mouth" cake is made without flour.
HALACHIC NOTE: *The blessing* shehakol, *rather than* mezonot, *is said before eating this cake.*

5 eggs at room
temperature, separated
1 cup confectioners' sugar
Dash salt
3 Tbsps. cocoa

MOCHA CREAM FILLING
1½ cups nondairy
dessert topping
½ cup cocoa
¼ cup confectioners' sugar
2 Tbsps.
coffee-flavored liqueur

Preheat oven to 400°.

Line a jelly-roll pan with a piece of greased wax paper.

In a large mixer bowl, beat egg whites until soft peaks form. Beating at high speed, sprinkle in ½ cup of the confectioners' sugar until glossy peaks form. Set aside.

In a medium mixer bowl, beat egg yolks at high speed until thick and lemony. Reduce speed to low and add salt, ½ cup of confectioners' sugar, and 3 tablespoons of cocoa. Beat until well blended.

With rubber spatula, carefully fold egg-yolk mixture into egg whites until blended. Pour mixture into prepared pan and bake for 15 minutes or until top springs back. Proceed according to Tips for Perfect Jelly Rolls.

While jelly roll is cooling, prepare filling, frosting, and glaze. ►

CHOCOLATE FROSTING
1 6-ounce package
semisweet chocolate pieces
2 Tbsps. margarine
2 Tbsps. white corn syrup
3 Tbsps. nondairy creamer

WHITE GLAZE
¾ cup confectioners' sugar
4 tsps. water

USE: Jelly-roll pan
Double boiler
YIELDS: 1 jelly roll

MOCHA CREAM FILLING: With mixer at medium speed, beat all ingredients until stiff peaks form.

CHOCOLATE FROSTING: Melt chocolate pieces and margarine over hot water in a double boiler. Remove from heat and beat in corn syrup and nondairy creamer until smooth.

WHITE GLAZE: Beat sugar with water until smooth in a small bowl.

TO ASSEMBLE: Unroll cake in towel. Spread Mocha Filling. Reroll. Spread Chocolate Frosting over top and sides of roll. Drizzle glaze over frosting in a decorative design. Keep refrigerated.

CHOCO-FILLED 8-LAYER CAKE

6 eggs, separated
1¼ cups sugar
2 Tbsps. lemon juice
¼ cup cornstarch
¾ cup flour
½ tsp. salt

CHOCO FROSTING
6 ounces semisweet
baking chocolate
6 egg yolks
1 cup sugar
¾ cup nondairy
dessert topping
1¾ cups margarine, softened

Chopped pistachio nuts

USE: 4 15 x 10-inch
jelly-roll pans
Double boiler
YIELDS: 1 layer cake

Preheat oven to 375°.

Line four 15 x 10-inch jelly-roll pans with wax paper.

Prepare cake recipe twice — do *not* attempt to double recipe.

In a large mixer bowl, beat egg yolks until thick; gradually beat in sugar and 1 tablespoon lemon juice. Sift together cornstarch and flour and add to batter, then add remaining lemon juice. Beat until smooth.

In a separate bowl, beat egg whites with salt until stiff and fold into mixture. Set batter aside. Prepare cake batter a second time. Pour half of each recipe on one jelly-roll pan.

Bake for 10 to 15 minutes. When done, turn jelly-roll pans over and peel off paper. Cool and cut cakes in half lengthwise. There should be 8 layers, 5 inches wide and 15 inches long.

CHOCO FROSTING: In top of double boiler, melt chocolate.

In a separate bowl, beat egg yolks and sugar and stir in nondairy dessert topping. Add to melted chocolate and cook on low flame, stirring until thick. Let cool.

In another bowl, cream margarine and beat in chocolate mixture, 1 tablespoon at a time, until of a smooth, spreading consistency.

TO ASSEMBLE: Spread frosting between layers, on the tops and on the sides. Decorate with chopped nuts and refrigerate.

CHECKERBOARD CAKE

CHOCOLATE CAKE
7 eggs, separated
1 cup sugar
¼ cup oil
½ cup flour
½ cup cocoa
1 tsp. baking powder
1 tsp. baking soda

WHITE CAKE
7 eggs, separated
1 cup sugar
¼ cup oil
1 cup flour
1 tsp. baking powder
1 Tbsp. lemon juice

FILLING
¼ cup margarine, softened
2 Tbsps. cocoa
2 Tbsps. instant coffee
Pinch salt
3 cups confectioners' sugar
3 Tbsps. nondairy whipped topping
1½ tsps. vanilla extract

CHOCOLATE ICING
5 ounces semisweet baking chocolate
1½ Tbsps. margarine
2 tsps. water
2 Tbsps. corn syrup

USE: 2 15 x 10-inch jelly-roll pans
Double boiler
YIELDS: 2 7½-inch cakes

Preheat oven to 350°.

Line two 15 x 10-inch jelly-roll pans with ungreased wax paper.

CHOCOLATE CAKE: In a large mixer bowl, beat egg whites, gradually adding ¼ cup of sugar until stiff but not dry. Set aside. In a separate mixer bowl, combine egg yolks and remaining ¾ cup of sugar. Beat until light lemon colored. Add oil and continue beating. Sift dry ingredients together and add to egg yolk mixture. Mix well. Gently fold in egg whites with rubber spatula until well combined. Pour onto wax paper in pan.

Bake for 20 minutes. Cool cake in pan on rack. When cool, turn over and peel off wax paper.

WHITE CAKE: Using white cake ingredients prepare as Chocolate Cake. Pour into wax paper in pan.

Bake for 20 minutes. When cool, turn over and peel off wax paper.

FILLING: Cream margarine in a large mixer bowl. Add all remaining ingredients. Beat to a spreadable consistency.

CHOCOLATE ICING: Cook all ingredients together in the top of a double boiler. Keep warm while assembling the cake.

TO ASSEMBLE: Cut each cake into quarters, cutting in half lengthwise and across the width. Each quarter is 5-inches wide by 7½-inches long. Cut each quarter into three strips about 1½-inches wide by 7½-inches long.

Layer 1: On a clean piece of wax paper or foil place a white strip, spread one side with filling, then place a chocolate strip next to it. Spread filling on one side of this strip and place a white strip next to it. Spread filling on top of all three strips.

Layer 2: Place a chocolate strip on top of filling and spread one side with filling. Place a white strip next to it. Spread filling on one side of it and place a chocolate strip next to it. Spread top with filling.

Layers 3 & 4: Repeat layers 1 and 2. Do not spread filling over fourth layer but pour icing over entire cake and smooth with a metal spatula.

Repeat layering process above to make a second cake.

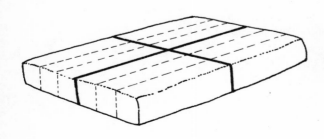

RAINBOW CAKE

This superb frosted white cake is combined with fruit rinds and food colorings to create a beautiful rainbow effect. It is exceptional, even when made as a simple white cake, yielding 1 large 11 x 14-inch cake.

CAKE
3½ cups flour
2½ cups sugar
5 tsps. baking powder
1 tsp. salt
¾ cup solid shortening
1½ cups nondairy creamer
4 eggs
2 tsps. vanilla extract
2 tsps. each lemon, orange, and lime rind
Food coloring, yellow, red, and green

LEMON CUSTARD FILLING
½ cup sugar
¼ cup cornstarch
¼ tsp. salt
2 egg yolks
¾ cup cold water
⅓ cup lemon juice
2 Tbsps. margarine

ORANGE CREAM FROSTING
½ cup margarine, softened
1 pound confectioners' sugar
2 Tbsps. orange juice
2 Tbsps. corn syrup
2 tsps. vanilla extract
Food coloring, yellow and red
Orange slices with peel removed
Pecans
Lime slices with peel removed

USE: 3 9-inch round cake pans
2-quart saucepan
YIELDS: 1 9-inch layer cake

Preheat oven to 350°.

Grease and flour three 9-inch round cake pans.

CAKE: Sift flour, sugar, baking powder, and salt into a mixer bowl. Add shortening, nondairy creamer, eggs, and vanilla. Beat at low speed for 1 minute, then increase to high speed. Beat for 3 minutes longer, scraping bowl with rubber spatula. Divide batter into 3 different bowls.

To the first bowl add lemon rind and yellow food coloring; stir just to blend, then pour into one of the prepared pans.

To the second bowl, add orange rind and red and yellow food coloring; stir just to blend, then pour into second prepared pan.

To the batter in the third bowl, add rind of lime and green food coloring; mix to blend, then pour into third prepared pan.

Bake for 30 minutes or until top springs back when touched lightly.

Cool cake for 5 minutes. Loosen cakes around edges with spatula, then invert on wire racks and let cool completely.

LEMON CUSTARD FILLING: Combine sugar, cornstarch, and salt in 2-quart saucepan. Beat in egg yolks and ¾ cup water with a wire whisk until smooth.

Bring to a boil over medium flame, stirring constantly with a wooden spoon. Boil for 1 minute until it thickens and bubbles. Remove from heat and stir in lemon juice and margarine. Pour into glass bowl and cover surface with plastic wrap. Cool completely.

ORANGE CREAM FROSTING: In a small bowl, cream margarine.

Beat in confectioners' sugar ½ cup at a time. Add orange juice, corn syrup, and vanilla. Beat until mixture is of spreading consistency. Tint a rich orange color with yellow and red food coloring.

TO ASSEMBLE: Put layers together with Lemon Custard Filling. Frost sides and top of cake with Orange Cream Frosting.

Arrange orange slices in a swirling pattern on top; insert a pecan between each orange slice, and place lime slices in center.

Refrigerate until serving time.

YEAST CAKES

A *yeast cake in the oven fills the house with its tantalizing aroma. Kuchens, babkas, cocosh; yeast cakes have many names but their taste and texture is unmistakeable. Usually a yeast cake is kneaded and must rise twice, so be sure to allow enough time; its lightness is worth the extra effort.*

HALACHIC NOTE: *When baking large quantities of yeast cake, it may be necessary to separate the challah portion. See Flour and Liquid Requirements for Separating Challah, page 47.*

BASIC SWEET DOUGH

This basic sweet dough can be filled with a variety of fillings to produce tasty coffee cakes or buns.

½ **cup sugar**
2 **packages dry yeast**
1½ **tsps. salt**
6½ to 7 **cups flour**
1¼ **cups apple juice**
1 **cup margarine**
3 **eggs, at room temperature**
½ **tsp. vanilla extract**

USE 1-quart saucepan
YIELDS: 2 loaves or
2 10-inch round cake

In a large mixer bowl, combine sugar, yeast, salt, and 2 cups of flour. In a 1-quart saucepan, heat apple juice and margarine until warm. Margarine doesn't have to melt.

Gradually add warm liquid to dry ingredients, beating with mixer at low speed. Increase speed to medium and beat 2 minutes. Add eggs and vanilla and 2½ cups of flour. Beat 2 more minutes. By hand, stir in enough additional flour to make a stiff dough, about 2 cups.

Turn dough onto a lightly floured board and knead 8 to 10 minutes until smooth and elastic, adding more flour if necessary.

Place dough in a well-oiled bowl and turn to oil the top. Cover and let rise in warm place about 1 hour until doubled in bulk. Punch down, turn onto floured board, cover with bowl and allow to rest 15 minutes for easier shaping.

See Classic Cocosh Yeast Cake for filling and baking instructions.

CHOCOLATE CHIP COFFEE RING

½ **Basic Sweet Dough**
(above)
1 **cup chocolate chips**

TOPPING
½ **cup flour**
½ **cup chopped walnuts**
1 **tsp. vanilla extract**
½ **cup sugar**
½ **cup margarine**
⅓ **cup chocolate chips**
1 **tsp. instant coffee**

USE: 10-inch tube pan
YIELDS: 1 cake

Grease 10-inch tube pan.

Prepare Basic Sweet Dough. Knead chocolate chips into dough. Roll into a 10-inch-long roll. Lay roll in a greased 10-inch tube pan.

TOPPING: In a small bowl combine ingredients for topping so that they form coarse crumbs. Sprinkle over dough in tube pan. Let rise 15 minutes.

Preheat oven to 350°.

Bake for 45 to 50 minutes. Cool in pan on wire rack for 20 minutes. Carefully remove from pan and cool completely on a wire rack.

CLASSIC COCOSH YEAST CAKE AND FILLINGS

This is a very versatile dough, also good to fill and shape as rugelach, buns, or Danish pastry.

DOUGH
2 ounces fresh yeast
1¼ cups lukewarm water
5 eggs
1 cup sugar
1 cup oil
2 tsps. baking powder
8 cups flour
8 Tbsps. margarine, melted
2 egg yolks

RICH COCOSH FILLING
¼ cup sugar
2 Tbsps. confectioners' sugar
2 Tbsps. cocoa
¼ cup ground walnuts
(optional)

JAM FILLING
¾ cup raspberry jam
3 Tbsps. sugar
1 Tbsp. cinnamon

FRUIT FILLING
½ cup strawberry jam
⅓ cup ground almonds
¼ cup coconut
¼ cup raisins

MOHN FILLING
1 cup poppy seeds

USE: 2 baking sheets
YIELDS: 4 loaves

Dissolve yeast in 1 cup lukewarm water in a large bowl. Let stand 5 minutes. When it bubbles add eggs, sugar, oil, and baking powder. Gradually add flour. Knead dough until smooth, about 5 minutes. Place in a greased bowl; turn to oil top. Cover and let rise in a warm place until doubled in bulk, about 1½ hours. Punch down.

Divide dough into four equal portions.

Grease two baking sheets.

On a floured board, roll out each piece of dough to an 18 x 12-inch rectangle. Brush with 2 tablespoons melted margarine and cover each roll with filling. Fillings are given in amounts for 1 roll each.

Roll up on the long side like a jelly roll. Place seam side down on a well-greased pan. Make slits halfway through the dough, about 2 inches apart. Repeat process with other three portions of dough. Cover and let rise about 1½ hours.

Preheat oven to 350°. Brush with beaten egg yolk and bake for 45 minutes or until brown.

RICH COCOSH FILLING: In a small bowl, combine granulated sugar, confectioners' sugar, cocoa, and nuts. Sprinkle generously over melted margarine on the dough.

JAM FILLING: Mix jam, sugar, and cinnamon and spread on dough.

FRUIT FILLING: Mix jam and nuts. Spread over the dough. Sprinkle coconut and raisins over the jam.

MOHN FILLING: Spread poppy seeds over melted margarine on the dough.

VARIATION
□ **Cinnamon Flower Ring:** Using ¼ of recipe, roll out to 18 x 12-inch rectangle. Brush with three tablespoons oil. In small dish combine ½ cup sugar, 2 tablespoons cinnamon, and ¼ cup ground walnuts. Spread over entire rectangle. Roll tightly like jelly roll.

Beginning one inch from the end slit dough lengthwise through all layers to the end. Gently separate two halves so that you have two long strands made up of several layers each. Beginning from top of roll, gently expose layers and twine strands across one another, crossing over approximately five times. Bring both ends of coil together, shaping into a circle. Trim a short 1-inch off each end and join by pinching layers together. Bake in greased 9-inch round pan for 50 to 60 minutes. Cool on rack.

BABKA

1 cup apple juice
½ cup honey
1 tsp. salt
2 ounces fresh yeast
½ cup oil
2 eggs, at room temperature, well beaten
7 cups flour

FILLING
½ cup oil or
¼ cup margarine, softened
¾ cup honey
Cinnamon
¾ cup raisins

TOPPING
1 Tbsp. margarine, softened
¼ cup flour
3 Tbsps. sugar

USE: 3 9 x 5-inch loaf pans
YIELDS: 3 loaves

Pour apple juice and honey into a small saucepan and heat until just warm. Stir in the salt and yeast. Let stand for 5 to 10 minutes until bubbly.

Pour ½ cup of oil into a large bowl and stir in eggs. Add yeast mixture. Stir in 7 cups of flour. Turn dough onto well-floured board and knead 5 minutes until glossy.

Place dough into a well-oiled bowl and turn to oil the top. Cover and let stand in a warm place until doubled in bulk, about 1 hour. Punch down dough and divide into thirds. Roll a third of the dough into a 10 x 8-inch rectangle.

FILLING: Spread a light coating of oil or margarine over the dough. Drizzle ¼ cup honey over the oil. Combine cinnamon and ¼ cup raisins and scatter over the honey. Roll up on the 10-inch side as for a jelly roll.

TOPPING: Combine topping ingredients until they have the consistency of coarse crumbs. Twist the rolled dough several turns and place in a well-greased pan. Sprinkle top with one third of the crumb topping.

Repeat rolling, filling, and shaping procedure with each remaining part of the dough. Sprinkle tops with remaining crumb topping. Cover loaves and let stand in a warm place for 30 minutes.

Preheat oven to 350°. Bake for 35 to 40 minutes.

VARIATION
☐ Combine ¾ cup brown sugar with ¾ cup of cocoa. Omit the honey and sprinkle over the dough in place of the cinnamon-raisin filling.

CINNAMON-ORANGE BUNS

These orange spiced buns bake together to form a beautiful round flower-like coffee cake.

¾ cup orange juice
½ cup margarine
½ cup sugar
1 tsp. salt
½ cup warm orange juice
2 packages dry yeast
5 to 6 cups flour
2 eggs
2 Tbsps. grated orange rind

½ cup margarine, melted

In a 2-quart saucepan, combine ¾ cup orange juice, margarine, sugar, and salt. Stir over medium heat until sugar melts. Remove from heat and let cool to lukewarm. Meanwhile, pour ½ cup warm orange juice into a small bowl and sprinkle yeast over it. Let stand 5 minutes until bubbly.

In a large bowl beat 2 cups of the flour into the orange juice and margarine mixture. Beat in eggs and orange rind. Stir in the dissolved yeast. Gradually beat in enough of the remaining flour to make a soft dough. Turn out onto a lightly floured board and knead 10 to 15 minutes until dough is satiny and smooth. Place dough into a well-oiled bowl and turn to oil the top. Cover and put in a warm place and let rise until doubled in bulk, 2 to 2½ hours.

►

FILLING
⅔ cup brown sugar
2 tsps. cinnamon
2 tsps. grated orange rind
1 cup raisins

GLAZE
1½ cups confectioners' sugar
1 Tbsp. margarine, softened
¼ cup orange juice

USE: 2-quart saucepan
2 8-inch round
cake pans
YIELDS: 24 buns

FILLING: In a small bowl, combine filling ingredients.

After dough has risen, punch down and divide in half. Roll half of the dough into an 8 x 16-inch rectangle on a floured board. Spread ¼ cup of melted margarine over the dough and sprinkle half of the cinnamon and orange filling over the margarine.

Roll up like a jelly roll on the 16-inch side. Cut into twelve 1¼- to 1½-inch slices and place each slice cut side down in a greased 8-inch round layer-cake pan. Place nine slices side by side around pan and three slices in the center.

Repeat rolling, filling, and shaping procedure with second half of the dough and filling. Place in a second greased 8-inch round layer-cake pan. Cover pans and put in a warm place to rise for 1½ hours.

Preheat oven to 375°.

Bake for 35 to 40 minutes. Remove from oven and cool.

GLAZE: In a small bowl, beat sugar and margarine until light. Add orange juice and beat until the glaze is smooth. Drizzle lightly over the warm buns.

SPICY EUROPEAN COFFEE CAKE

2 envelopes dry yeast
1½ cups warm water
¾ cup sugar
½ cup oil
4 eggs
1 cup apple juice
1 Tbsp. salt
8 cups flour
½ tsp. nutmeg
½ tsp. cinnamon
1 cup margarine, softened

FILLING
¾ cup sugar
½ tsp. nutmeg
½ tsp. cinnamon
1½ cups raisins
1½ cups chopped almonds

GLAZE
1 egg yolk, beaten

USE: 1 baking sheet
or 3 9 x 5-inch loaf pans
YIELDS: 3 loaves

Sprinkle yeast over warm water in a large bowl. Add 2 tablespoons of sugar and wait 5 minutes until bubbly. Add rest of sugar, oil, eggs, apple juice, salt, and 3 cups of flour. Beat with a wooden spoon. Add nutmeg and cinnamon and remaining flour, 1 cup at a time, until dough is of the consistency to be kneaded.

Knead dough on floured surface until smooth and elastic. Cover and let rise in oiled bowl until doubled in bulk.

Divide dough into three portions and roll first portion into a rectangle. Spread two-thirds of rectangle with one-sixth of softened margarine, then fold one-third over, then fold again. Chill about 1 hour and roll out. Repeat margarine and folding. Chill again.

FILLING: Combine sugar, nutmeg, cinnamon, raisins, and nuts.

Grease three 9 x 5-inch loaf pans.

Roll out chilled dough into a rectangle and spread with one-third of sugar-raisin mixture. Roll up like a jelly roll. Seal seam tightly and place seam side down in a loaf pan.

Prepare other portions of dough in same manner. Let rise until doubled in bulk, 30 minutes.

Preheat oven to 350°.

GLAZE: Brush tops of loaves with egg yolk. Bake for 35 minutes until golden.

CHERRY TOPPED YEAST CAKE

2 ounces fresh yeast
¼ cup lukewarm water
½ cup margarine, softened
½ cup sugar
3 eggs
¼ cup nondairy creamer
½ tsp. salt
¼ tsp. lemon flavoring
3 cups flour, sifted
2 Tbsps. sugar
¼ tsp. cinnamon

CHERRY TOPPING
3 Tbsps. cornstarch
½ cup sugar
¼ tsp. salt
**1 16-ounce can
tart red cherries,
drained (reserve juice)**
**Juice from cherries
plus water to make 1 cup**
**Several drops
red food coloring**
or
**1 20-ounce can
cherry pie filling**

GLAZE
¼ cup confectioners' sugar
1 Tbsp. nondairy creamer

USE: 9 x 13-inch pan
2-quart saucepan
YIELDS: 1 cake

Grease 9 x 13-inch cake pan.

In a small bowl dissolve yeast in lukewarm water. Let stand 5 minutes until bubbly. Cream margarine and sugar together in a large bowl. Beat in eggs, nondairy creamer, salt, lemon flavoring, and yeast. Stir in flour and mix well. Spread evenly in pan. Combine sugar and cinnamon and sprinkle over the dough.

CHERRY TOPPING: Combine cornstarch, sugar, and salt in a 2-quart saucepan; add the cherry juice and water mixture. Cook over low heat, stirring, until mixture comes to a boil and thickens. Stir in cherries and food coloring. Cool.

Spread the cherry topping or the cherry pie filling evenly over the sugar and cinnamon. Cover the pan and let rise in a warm place for 1 hour.

Preheat oven to 375°. Bake for 35 to 40 minutes.

GLAZE: In a small bowl while cake is baking, combine confectioners' sugar with the nondairy creamer. While cake is still warm, drizzle the glaze over the cake. Allow cake to cool from 1½ to 2 hours before cutting and serving.

CHOCOLATE-MERINGUE COFFEE CAKE

**½ Basic Sweet Dough
(page 380)**
½ cup chopped walnuts
¼ cup raisins
1 tsp. cinnamon
1 cup sugar
**3 egg whites,
at room temperature**
1 cup chocolate chips
Confectioners' sugar

USE: 10-inch tube pan
YIELDS: 1 cake

Grease 10-inch tube pan.

Prepare Basic Sweet Dough.

In a small bowl combine walnuts, raisins, cinnamon, and ½ cup sugar. Set aside.

In another small bowl, beat egg whites until foamy. Gradually add ½ cup sugar, 2 tablespoons at a time, beating until egg whites are stiff but not dry. Set meringue aside.

Roll out dough on a lightly floured board and into a 10 x 16-inch rectangle. Spread meringue over the dough, leaving a ½-inch border. Sprinkle walnuts and sugar mixture evenly over the meringue. Then sprinkle with chocolate chips. Beginning at 16-inch side, roll dough like a jelly roll. Pinch seam to seal. Lay seam side down in a greased 10-inch tube pan. Cover and let rise about 45 minutes in a warm place.

►

Continued

Preheat oven to 350°.

Bake for 45 to 50 minutes or until golden. Cool in pan on a wire rack for 20 minutes. Carefully remove from pan and cool completely on a wire rack. Sprinkle with confectioners' sugar before serving.

PEACH KUCHEN

2 to 2½ cups flour
¼ cup sugar
¼ tsp. salt
1 package dry yeast
½ cup nondairy creamer
¼ cup water
½ cup margarine
2 egg yolks

1-pound, 14-ounce can sliced peaches, well drained

CRUMB TOPPING
5 Tbsps. margarine, softened
⅓ cup brown sugar
1 egg yolk
1 cup flour
2 tsps. cinnamon

USE: 1-quart saucepan
9 x 9-inch pan
YIELDS: 1 cake

Grease a 9 x 9-inch square pan.

In a large mixer bowl, combine ½ cup of flour, ¼ cup sugar, ¼ teaspoon salt, and dry yeast. In a 1-quart saucepan heat nondairy creamer, water, and margarine. Heat until very warm (120°F) and gradually add to dry ingredients. Beat 2 minutes at medium speed. Add 2 egg yolks and 1 more cup of flour; beat 2 more minutes at high speed. Add enough additional flour to make a stiff batter. Spread in pan. Arrange peaches on top of the batter.

CRUMB TOPPING: Cream margarine with brown sugar, egg yolk, 1 cup flour, and cinnamon. Mix well and sprinkle over the peaches.

Cover and let rise 1 hour.

Preheat oven to 350°. Bake for 45 minutes or until done. Cool in pan.

VARIATION
☐ **Apple Kuchen:** Peel and core 2 large baking apples. Thinly slice and arrange on batter instead of peaches. Sprinkle with crumb topping as above.

GOLDEN CROWN

2 packages dry yeast
¼ cup warm water
½ cup sugar
¾ cup lemon juice, room temperature
½ cup solid shortening
1 tsp. salt
2 eggs
4½ cups flour
1½ cups brown sugar
2 tsps. cinnamon
1 cup chopped walnuts
½ to ⅔ cup oil

USE: 9- or 10-inch tube pan with unremovable center
YIELDS: 1 cake

Dissolve yeast in ¼ cup warm water and stir in 1 tablespoon of sugar. Let stand until bubbly.

In mixer bowl, cream the remainder of the sugar with the lemon juice, shortening, and salt. Beat in the 2 eggs, and bubbly yeast. Add flour until dough can be kneaded and knead 5 minutes. Cover and let rise 1½ hours. Punch down. Cover and let rest 10 minutes more.

Shape dough into golf-ball-size balls. In a small bowl combine brown sugar, cinnamon, and nuts. Roll balls in oil, then roll in cinnamon-sugar mixture to coat. Arrange balls in a 9- or 10-inch tube pan. Sprinkle with remaining cinnamon-sugar mixture. Cover and let rise 1 hour.

Preheat oven to 350°. Bake for 40 minutes.

YEASTED SWEET ROLLS spiced with cinnamon or nuts are tasty for breakfast or snacks.

OLD-FASHIONED CINNAMON BUNS

½ **Basic Sweet Dough**
(page 380)

FILLING
½ **cup light brown sugar,**
firmly packed
½ **cup chopped walnuts**
½ **cup raisins**
1½ **tsps. cinnamon**
¼ **cup margarine**

GLAZE
1 **cup confectioners' sugar**
4 **tsps. water**

USE: 1-quart saucepan
Baking sheet
YIELDS: 18 buns

Prepare Basic Sweet Dough recipe.

Grease baking sheet.

FILLING: Combine brown sugar, walnuts, raisins, and cinnamon in a small bowl. Melt the margarine in a 1-quart saucepan.

Place dough on floured board. Roll dough into 18 x 12-inch rectangle. Brush with melted margarine and sprinkle with sugar mixture. Starting with 18-inch side, roll dough jelly-roll fashion; pinch seam to close. With seam side down, cut roll crosswise into 18 slices. Pinch outer sides together on the bottom of each bun — the center will puff up and filling won't run out. Place on a baking sheet. Cover and let rise about 40 minutes until doubled in bulk.

Preheat the oven to 400°. Bake for 20 minutes.

GLAZE: While buns are baking, combine sugar and water to make glaze. While buns are warm, brush with glaze.

HAZELNUT SWEET ROLLS

2 **packages dry yeast**
¼ **cup warm water**
⅓ **cup sugar**
⅓ **cup margarine, softened**
¾ **cup nondairy creamer**
2 **tsps. salt**
2 **tsps. grated orange rind**
2 **eggs**
4 **to** 4½ **cups flour**

NUT FILLING
⅓ **cup margarine, softened**
1 **cup confectioners' sugar,**
sifted
1 **cup ground or**
finely chopped hazelnuts

GLAZE
¼ **cup orange juice**
3 **Tbsps. sugar**

USE: 1-quart saucepan
Cookie sheets
YIELDS: 1½ to 2 dozen rolls

In a small bowl dissolve yeast in ¼ cup warm water. Stir in 1 tablespoon of sugar taken from the ⅓ cup. Let stand 5 minutes until bubbly.

In a 1-quart saucepan combine margarine and nondairy creamer and heat until margarine melts. Cool to lukewarm.

In a large bowl combine remaining sugar, salt, and orange rind. Beat in eggs and yeast mixture. Slowly beat in flour until a stiff dough is formed. Mix well. Cover and let stand 30 minutes.

NUT FILLING: In a medium bowl cream ⅓ cup margarine. Blend in sifted confectioners' sugar. Add nuts and mix.

Grease baking sheets.

TO ASSEMBLE: On a floured board, roll dough to a 22 x 12-inch rectangle. Spread filling along one half of dough along 22-inch side of dough. Fold uncovered dough over filling.

Cut crosswise into 1-inch strips. Twist each strip four or five turns. Hold one end down on a baking sheet to make center of roll and curl strip around center, tucking other end under.

►

Once all rolls are formed, cover with a towel and let rise until doubled in bulk, 45 to 60 minutes.

Preheat oven to 375°. Bake rolls for 15 minutes until golden.

GLAZE: While rolls are baking combine orange juice and sugar in a small bowl. Brush onto top of rolls and bake 5 minutes longer. Remove from baking sheet and cool on rack.

VARIATION
☐ Substitute walnuts or almonds for the hazelnuts.

CINNAMON-NUT CRISPS

2 ounces fresh yeast
½ cup lukewarm water
2 eggs, well beaten
1 cup lukewarm nondairy creamer
3 Tbsps. sugar
1½ tsps. salt
1 tsp. vanilla extract
4½ to 5 cups flour
4 Tbsps. margarine, melted
1 cup brown sugar, firmly packed
1 tsp. cinnamon
¾ cup finely chopped almonds
⅓ cup chopped raisins

USE: 2 baking sheets
YIELDS: 2 dozen buns

In a small bowl soften yeast in ½ cup lukewarm water. Let stand 5 minutes until bubbly.

Meanwhile, in a large bowl, combine eggs, nondairy creamer, sugar, salt, vanilla, and softened yeast. Gradually add 4¼ to 5 cups flour, mixing until dough is stiff. Knead until smooth, 4 to 5 minutes on a well-floured board. Place in a greased bowl and oil the top. Cover tightly. Let rise in a warm place until doubled in bulk, about 1½ hours.

Grease two baking sheets.

Roll out to a 26 x 20-inch rectangle about ¼-inch thick. Brush with 2 tablespoons melted margarine. Combine the brown sugar and cinnamon. Sprinkle one half of this mixture over the dough.

Fold long sides into center, so that rectangle is 26 x 10 inches. Then fold in half lengthwise so that rectangle is 26 x 5 inches, making four layers. Press firmly to seal. Now roll out to a 26 x 12-inch rectangle. Brush with 2 tablespoons melted margarine.

Combine almonds, raisins, remaining brown sugar, and cinnamon mixture. Sprinkle mixture over the dough. Roll as for a jelly roll, starting with the 26-inch side. Cut into 1-inch slices.

Dip one cut side of each roll into flour and place floured side up on a board which has been sprinkled with sugar. Roll out to ¼-inch thickness. Place on baking sheet sugar side up and let rise 15 minutes. While first pan is rising, place the rest of the rolls on second baking sheet sugar side up, and let rise. Rolls may rise longer than 15 minutes.

Preheat oven to 375°. Bake for 15 to 18 minutes until golden brown.

CINNAMON FINGERS

2 packages dry yeast
½ cup warm water
½ cup sugar
½ cup boiling apple juice
½ cup margarine
½ tsp. salt
1 tsp. vanilla extract
1 egg
3½ cups flour
Oil
½ cup cinnamon
½ cup sugar

USE: 8 x 8-inch cake pan
YIELDS: 12 fingers

In a small bowl, sprinkle yeast over ½ cup of warm water. Stir in 1 tablespoon of sugar taken from the ½ cup. Let stand 5 minutes until bubbly.

Meanwhile, pour ½ cup boiling apple juice into a large bowl over rest of sugar, margarine, salt, and vanilla. Mix with fork and allow to cool.

When cooled, pour yeast into shortening mixture, then add the egg. Mix well. Stir in 3½ cups of flour with a wooden spoon. Once dough is formed, cover with aluminum foil and chill for 4 hours.

Preheat oven to 350°.

Grease an 8 x 8-inch cake pan.

Pinch off pieces of dough and roll into frankfurter-shaped pieces 1 to 1½ inches wide and 2 inches long. Combine cinnamon and sugar in a small bowl. Dip in oil and roll in cinnamon-and-sugar mixture. Place close together in cake pan. Bake for 20 minutes or until done.

Frostings and Fillings

Frostings may be boiled, hand-or machine-mixed, quick or time-consuming. They are thick or thin, creamy or glazed. There are almost as many ways to make frostings as there are frostings themselves. Frostings may be drizzled, spread on with a spatula, swirled, dripped from a spoon, or pressed from a pastry bag. Be sure that your frosting complements the cake in texture and color.

FROSTING A CAKE

☐ Before frosting, be sure the cake is cool. Brush off all crumbs.

☐ Turning the cake as you work makes frosting it easier. Put the cake plate on top of a large bowl or on a lazy Susan.

FROSTING A LAYER CAKE

☐ Place the first layer top side down on a cake plate and frost it almost to the edge. Press a plastic spatula into the frosting at the center and turn it in one direction, slowly moving the spatula toward the cake edge.

☐ Place the second layer top side up on the frosted layer so that the flat bottoms face each other; the cake will now be even.

☐ Frost sides twice; first a thin coat to set the crumbs. Let it set about 20 minutes to keep the crumbs from mixing with the final frosting. Then frost the top, swirling the frosting or leaving it smooth.

FINAL TOUCHES

After frosting your cake, here are some easy creative final touches.

☐ Use the back of a spoon or spatula to swirl S's or circles into the frosting.

☐ Make a spiral design: Hold the spatula at the center of the cake, turning the cake and drawing the spatula outward.

☐ Using a knife or spatula, draw parallel lines in the frosting, about 1 inch apart. Turn the cake and draw lines at 45 or 90-degree angles.

☐ Use a table fork to make a plaid effect on the frosting. Draw the fork lightly across the frosting. Repeat at right angles.

DECORATING WITH MELTED CHOCOLATE

The following two patterns require melted chocolate — melt 2 ounces of chocolate with ½ teaspoon solid shortening:

☐ Drizzle melted chocolate across the frosting in lines 1-inch apart. Then draw the edge of the knife or a toothpick across the lines.

☐ Drip melted chocolate from a teaspoon around the edge of a frosted cake. Let the chocolate run down the sides.

CHOCOLATE DECORATING

☐ Cutouts:
*1 cup chocolate chips
2 Tbsps. solid shortening*
Bring water to boil in the bottom of a double boiler. Place chocolate chips and shortening into the top half and put over boiling water. Heat until chocolate and shortening are melted. Place a large sheet of aluminum foil flat on a counter top or

table and pour melted chocolate onto it. Spread with a spatula to ⅛-inch thickness and allow to cool. Using cookie cutters, cut out shapes. To make your own shapes, use the serrated metal edge of the aluminum foil box and make your own cutters.

☐ Leaves

3 ounces sweet chocolate
1 tsp. margarine

Pick several dozen leaves (be careful that they are from nonpoisonous plants; unsprayed rose leaves are excellent). Wash and dry leaves. Bring water to boil in bottom of double boiler and place chocolate and margarine in top half over boiling water and melt. Brush chocolate onto underside of leaves, about ⅛-inch thick, being careful not to cover the edges. Refrigerate to harden. When hard, carefully peel off the leaves. Store in refrigerator until ready to use.

☐ Chocolate Horns

3 ounces sweet chocolate
1 tsp. margarine

Melt chocolate as above. Mark 3-inch squares on aluminum foil. Use 1 teaspoon of melted chocolate to cover each 3-inch square. Harden in refrigerator. Loosen from foil and allow chocolate to soften at room temperature. Then roll foil and chocolate together. Return to refrigerator to harden. Peel off aluminum foil when ready to use. Dust with confectioners' sugar and use on top of cakes or other desserts.

☐ Chocolate Curls

1 bar sweet or semisweet chocolate

Have chocolate at room temperature. Use a vegetable parer dipped in hot water to run along the edge of the bar, producing a curl of chocolate.

ALTERNATIVES TO FROSTING

☐ Sift confectioners' sugar lightly over the cake.

☐ Place a doily over the cake and sift confectioners' sugar over the entire doily. Remove doily by lifting straight up.

CHOCOLATE-MINT FROSTING

3 ounces semisweet baking chocolate
4 Tbsps. margarine
3 Tbsps. water
1½ cups confectioners' sugar
Pinch salt
1 tsp. vanilla extract
3 drops oil of peppermint
3 egg yolks

YIELDS: Frosts 1 8-inch layer cake or 1 9-inch tube cake

In a small saucepan melt chocolate, margarine, with water over very low flame. Remove from heat. Combine sugar, salt, vanilla, and oil of peppermint in a mixer bowl. Add melted chocolate mixture and beat at low speed until fluffy. Add the egg yolks one at a time and beat at high speed until light and fluffy.

CHOCOLATE SWIRL FROSTING

¼ cup margarine or
solid shortening, melted, or
¼ cup oil
½ cup cocoa
¼ tsp. salt
⅓ cup nondairy creamer
1½ tsps. vanilla extract
1 pound confectioners' sugar

YIELDS: Frosts 1 9-inch
layer cake

Combine melted margarine with cocoa and salt in a mixer bowl. Beat in nondairy creamer and vanilla. Beat in confectioners' sugar a cup at a time until smooth. Add more nondairy creamer, 1 tablespoon at a time, to achieve desired spreading consistency.

SATINY CHOCOLATE FROSTING

½ cup solid shortening
1½ cups confectioners' sugar
½ cup cocoa
1 egg
1 tsp. vanilla extract
½ tsp. rum flavoring or
Cognac
¼ cup nondairy
dessert topping

YIELDS: Frosts 1 9 x 13-inch
cake or 1 9-inch
tube cake

Cream shortening in a mixer bowl. Add all ingredients and beat at high speed until smooth, at least 2 minutes.

CHOCOLATE "BUTTER" CREAM

1 cup margarine, softened
1 pound confectioners'
sugar, sifted
2 tsps. instant coffee
2 tsps. hot water
4 ounces semisweet
chocolate, melted
2 Tbsps. rum
2 eggs

YIELDS: Frosts
1 9 x 13 inch cake

Cream margarine and sugar in a mixer bowl. Dissolve coffee in hot water and add to margarine-sugar mixture. Add chocolate and rum and beat well. Beat in eggs, one at a time, until frosting is smooth and fluffy. If not using immediately, store in covered container. Beat again when ready to spread.

COCOA FLUFF FROSTING

**8 ounces
nondairy dessert topping
4 Tbsps. cocoa
4 Tbsps. sugar**

YIELDS: Frosts 1 9-inch
tube cake

In a mixer bowl beat dessert topping at high speed until stiff peaks form. Beat in cocoa and sugar.

Frost cake and keep refrigerated.

COCOA-MOCHA FROSTING

**½ cup margarine or
½ cup solid shortening,
softened
1 tsp. vanilla extract
2 cups confectioners' sugar
½ cup cocoa
¼ tsp. salt
1 tsp. instant coffee
1 to 2 Tbsps. cold water**

YIELDS: Frosts 1 9-inch
layer cake

In a mixer bowl cream margarine or shortening and vanilla. Sift sugar, cocoa, and salt together and add to creamed margarine. Dissolve instant coffee in water and add, a tablespoon at a time, beating until smooth and creamy.

ORANGE CREAM FROSTING

**½ cup margarine, softened
1 pound confectioners' sugar
2 Tbsps. orange juice
2 Tbsps. corn syrup
2 tsps. vanilla extract
Yellow and red food coloring**

YIELDS: Frosts 1 9-inch
round cake

In a mixer bowl, cream margarine. Add confectioners' sugar, ½ cup at a time, until it has all been beaten into the margarine. Beat in orange juice, corn syrup, and vanilla until a spreadable consistency is reached. Tint frosting a rich orange color with yellow and red food coloring.

EASY MARSHMALLOW FROSTING

**2 egg whites
¼ tsp. salt
¼ cup sugar
¾ cup light corn syrup
1 tsp. vanilla extract**

YIELDS: Frosts 1 9 x 13-inch
cake, or frosts and fills
1 9-inch layer cake

In a mixer bowl, beat egg whites with salt until foamy. Gradually add sugar, continuing to beat until stiff peaks form. Pour corn syrup into egg whites, beating constantly. Add vanilla and continue beating until thick enough to spread.

BASIC CREAMY WHITE FROSTING

¼ cup margarine, softened
3 cups confectioners' sugar
1 tsp. vanilla extract
Dash of salt
3 to 5 Tbsps.
nondairy creamer

YIELDS: Frosts 1 9 x 13-inch
cake

In a mixer bowl, cream margarine. Add confectioners' sugar, vanilla, salt, and enough nondairy creamer to achieve a spreadable consistency. Beat until smooth and creamy.

VARIATIONS
□ **Creamy Coffee Frosting:** Dissolve 1 teaspoon instant coffee in 1 tablespoon of hot water. Add with nondairy creamer to Basic Creamy Frosting, using 1 tablespoon less nondairy creamer.

□ **Creamy Lemon Frosting:** Use 3 to 5 tablespoons lemon juice in place of nondairy creamer in Basic Creamy Frosting and omit vanilla. Stir in 1 teaspoon grated lemon peel.

BOILED WHITE FROSTING

2 cups sugar
½ cup water
2 Tbsps. light corn syrup
Pinch salt
4 egg whites
½ tsp. vinegar
1 tsp. vanilla extract

USE: 2-quart saucepan
YIELDS: Frosts 1 9-inch
layer cake

Combine sugar, water, corn syrup, and salt in 2-quart saucepan. Boil over medium heat, stirring until sugar is dissolved. Wash sugar crystals from side of pan with a pastry brush dipped in water. Clip candy thermometer to side of pan. Boil syrup to the soft-ball stage (240° on candy thermometer) or until a fork, when dipped into the syrup and held above pan, will form a thread.

While syrup is cooking, beat the egg whites in mixer bowl with electric mixer until foamy. Add vinegar and vanilla and continue to beat until whites form stiff peaks. Pour the hot syrup very slowly in a thin stream into the egg whites while continuing to beat the mixture. Beat until thick.

WHITE FROSTING

1¾ cups solid shortening
2 pounds confectioners' sugar
2 egg whites
4 Tbsps. hot water
1 tsp. almond, rum or
lemon extract (optional)

YIELDS: Frosts and decorates
2 9-inch layer cakes

Combine all the ingredients in a large mixer bowl and beat for 10 minutes. Keep refrigerated until ready to use.

Using half of frosting to frost top and sides of cakes. Place remaining half into a pastry tube and proceed with your favorite decorations.

GLAZES

A glaze is simple to make and will dress up any cake. Generally it is made immediately before use.

BASIC WHITE GLAZE

The perfect glaze for many different cakes because it is adaptable to so many different flavors.

1 cup confectioners' sugar
1 Tbsp. margarine, softened
1 tsp. vanilla extract
1 to 2 Tbsps. nondairy creamer or water

YIELDS: Glazes
1 9 x 13-inch cake

In a small mixer bowl, beat all ingredients with enough nondairy creamer until thin enough to drizzle.

VARIATION
☐ In place of vanilla, substitute an equal amount of almond extract, ¼ teaspoon lemon, or ¼ teaspoon cinnamon with a dash of nutmeg.

CARAMEL GLAZE

6 Tbsps. margarine
⅔ cup brown sugar
4 Tbsps. nondairy creamer
1½ cups confectioners' sugar
1 tsp. vanilla extract
3 to 4 Tbsps. nondairy creamer or water

USE: 2-quart saucepan
YIELDS: Glazes
1 9 x 13-inch cake

Melt margarine in 2-quart saucepan. Stir in brown sugar and 4 tablespoons of nondairy creamer. Bring to a boil, lower flame, and continue cooking for 1 minute, stirring constantly. Remove from heat and cool to lukewarm.

Pour into mixer bowl and beat in confectioners' sugar. Add vanilla and enough nondairy creamer or water until spreadable consistency is reached.

CHOCOLATE GLAZE

2 ounces unsweetened chocolate
1 cup confectioners' sugar
½ tsp. vanilla extract
1 to 2 Tbsps. warm water

USE: Double boiler
YIELDS: Glazes
1 9 x 13-inch cake

In the top of a double boiler melt chocolate over hot but not boiling water. Place chocolate in a mixer bowl. Beat all ingredients with enough water until thin enough to drizzle.

CHOCOLATE CREAMY GLAZE

6 Tbsps. cocoa
1 cup sugar
⅓ cup solid shortening
1 egg yolk

USE: 1½-quart saucepan
YIELDS: Glazes
1 9 x 13-inch cake

Combine cocoa and sugar in a 1½-quart saucepan and cook gently until sugar melts and begins to boil. Remove from heat and cool until lukewarm. In a mixer bowl beat shortening with egg yolk. Add in melted sugar/cocoa mixture and beat well.

HAND MIXED GLAZES *are great for cupcakes and cookies and for times when you don't want to take out the mixer.*

COCOA GLAZE

1¼ cups confectioners' sugar
3 Tbsps. cocoa
1 Tbsp. instant coffee
3 Tbsps. oil
4 to 6 Tbsps. water

YIELDS: Frosts
1 9 x 13-inch cake
or 1 dozen cupcakes

In small bowl combine dry ingredients. Add oil. Mix. Gradually add water, 1 tablespoon at a time until spreadable consistency is reached.

WHITE GLAZE

1½ cups confectioners' sugar
1 tsp. vanilla extract
1 tsp. lemon juice
3 Tbsps. oil
4 to 6 Tbsps. water

YIELDS: Frosts
1 9 x 13-inch cake
or 1 dozen cupcakes

Place confectioners' sugar in small bowl. Add flavoring and oil. Mix. Gradually add water, 1 tablespoon at a time until spreadable consistency is reached.

FILLINGS & CREAMS

The perfect filling will enhance your cream puffs, jelly rolls, or layer cakes. An excellent way to transform your plain cakes.

BASIC ALMOND PASTE

This almond paste can be rolled out and placed between layers of a cake, or shaped into marzipan fruits or decoration.

2¼ cups almonds
1 pound confectioners'
sugar, sifted
2 egg whites
1 tsp. almond extract

YIELDS: Filling for
1 9-inch layer cake

To blanch almonds, put in pot of boiling water and remove from heat. Let stand 5 minutes; slip skins off. Spread almonds on cookie sheet and place in a low oven (250°) to dry.

Once almonds are dry, grind in food processor or blender to a fine, mealy texture. Combine ground almonds and confectioners' sugar in a large bowl. Work together with fingers until well blended.

Beat the egg whites with a fork until frothy. Add one half of the beaten egg whites to the almond mixture and mix to a paste. Add almond extract and mix thoroughly. Slowly add enough of the remaining egg white to make mixture the consistency of pie pastry.

Place on cold surface and knead paste like a yeast dough until smooth.

CHOCOLATE CREAM

6 ounces chocolate chips
½ cup margarine, softened
¼ cup hot water
4 egg yolks, lightly beaten
2 Tbsps. confectioners' sugar
1 tsp. vanilla extract
YIELDS: Filling for
1 9-inch layer cake

Combine all ingredients in a blender container. Blend on high speed until mixture is smooth. Chill several hours.

ITALIAN PASTRY CREAM

This is an excellent filling for cream puffs and doughnuts. Most important: Do not allow cream to boil.

4 egg yolks
6 Tbsps. sugar
2 tsps. flour
1 cup nondairy creamer, chilled
½ tsp. vanilla or orange extract or small piece of lemon rind

CHOCOLATE PASTRY CREAM
Italian Pastry Cream (see above)
2 Tbsps. nondairy creamer
2 Tbsps. cocoa
1 Tbsp. sugar

USE: Double boiler
YIELDS: 1½ cups pastry cream

In bottom part of double boiler, bring water to a boil and let simmer. Put egg yolks into a bowl. Add sugar and flour. Stir mixture with a wooden spoon, always in the same direction, until flour and sugar are completely incorporated into yolks and the color is a light yellow. Slowly add cold nondairy creamer, mixing steadily. Pour mixture into top of double boiler. Add vanilla extract.

Place top of double boiler over the simmering water. (If making Chocolate Pastry Cream, see variation below and combine added ingredients here.) Stir constantly with wooden spoon until mixture is thick and coats the spoon. Do not allow the cream to boil. Once thickened, remove top of double boiler from hot water and continue stirring another 2 to 3 minutes. Transfer cream to a bowl and cool.

CHOCOLATE PASTRY CREAM: Prepare white pastry cream. In a separate saucepan, heat 2 tablespoons of nondairy creamer until lukewarm. Add 2 tablespoons of cocoa and 1 tablespoon of sugar. Stir until dissolved. Add this mixture to the white pastry cream in the top of the double boiler once it has become warm. Stir with wooden spoon until cream is thick and coats the spoon. Do not boil. Once thickened, remove top of double boiler from hot water and continue stirring 2 to 3 minutes. Transfer cream to a bowl and cool.

LEMON CUSTARD FILLING

½ cup sugar
¼ cup cornstarch
¼ tsp. salt
2 egg yolks
¾ cup cold water
⅓ cup lemon juice
2 Tbsps. margarine
USE: 2-quart saucepan
YIELDS: Filling for
1 9-inch layer cake

Combine sugar, cornstarch, and salt in a 2-quart saucepan. Beat in egg yolks and ¾ cup water with wire whisk until smooth. Bring to a boil over medium flame, stirring constantly with a wooden spoon. Boil for 1 minute, until it thickens and bubbles. Remove from heat and stir in lemon juice and margarine. Pour into a glass bowl and cover surface with plastic wrap. Cool completely.

Cookies

Hurray for crunchy munchies! Cookies just the size to pop into a child's mouth seem to satisfy the child that is within each of us. Choose dense, chewy oatmeal cookies, crisp, light sugar cookies, or rich chocolate chip cookies. What a variety!

Cookies can be as fancy or elaborate as any other dessert. They can be made from two doughs, rolled up jelly-roll fashion, and sliced into beautiful pinwheel cookies. Sugar them, ice them, fill them, shape them any way you please. Cookie-cutters with Jewish and Holiday motifs are now widely available. For a special educational treat for children, shape cookies into letters of the Hebrew alphabet.

TIPS FOR MIXING AND BAKING

- ☐ Mix cookie dough quickly, as overhandling may cause toughness.
- ☐ Chill the cookie dough well before shaping, both to help the cookies hold their shape while baking and for easier handling.
- ☐ Cookies should be baked on a cookie sheet. Dark cookie sheets absorb heat and cookies may brown too much.
- ☐ Always fill the cookie sheet putting cookies of even size and thickness usually one inch apart. On a partially filled sheet, the heat will be drawn to the cookies and they may burn.
- ☐ Always preheat the oven.
- ☐ Use only one oven rack so the heat will circulate evenly.
- ☐ When done, remove cookies from the sheet immediately and place on wire rack to stop the cooking process.
- ☐ Cookies are usually baked on greased cookie sheets, depending on the amount of fat in the dough.
- ☐ If not enough cookie sheets are available, use heavy duty foil. Cut to fit the cookie sheet. While cookies are baking, place more dough on the sheet of foil. This way one sheet of foil can be removed and the second sheet placed on the cookie sheet immediately.

COOLING AND STORING

- ☐ Never overlap warm cookies on cooling rack.
- ☐ If dipping cookies in confectioners' sugar, dip twice — once while warm and again when cooled.
- ☐ Store in a container with a tight-fitting cover.
- ☐ To crisp, reheat cookies in the oven for 5 minutes.
- ☐ If cookies dry out, add a piece of apple to the container.
- ☐ A large cookie sheet holds approximately 16 cookies.
- ☐ When freezing cookies, place them back to back in pairs and put in even rows in plastic bags.
- ☐ Unbaked cookie dough may be frozen for several months.

DROP COOKIES

Drop Cookies are made of soft dough which is dropped from a spoon onto the cookie sheet which is usually greased. These cookies flatten as they bake. Leave about 1½ inches between cookies. Place approximately 16 cookies per sheet.

CHOCOLATE CHIP COOKIES

These are also wonderful baked in a 9 x 13-inch pan and cut into squares.

1 cup margarine, softened
¾ cup sugar
¾ cup brown sugar
1 tsp. vanilla extract
2 eggs
2½ cups flour
1 tsp. baking powder
6 ounces chocolate chips

USE: Cookie sheets
YIELDS: 4 dozen cookies

Preheat oven to 350°.

In a large mixer bowl cream margarine and sugars. Add vanilla and eggs, one at a time, mixing well. Combine flour and baking powder and add to mixture. Mix until dough is formed, then add chocolate chips and mix until they are evenly distributed in dough.

Drop dough onto cookie sheet by teaspoonfuls, leaving approximately 2 inches between each.

Bake for 13 to 15 minutes, until bottoms are just slightly brown and top is still a little soft. Cookies will harden a bit after they are removed from the oven.

GINGER SNAPS

¼ cup margarine
¼ cup light brown sugar
1 Tbsp. light corn syrup
2 Tbsps. molasses
1½ tsps. ginger
¼ tsp. baking powder
½ tsp. lemon juice
⅔ cup flour

USE: 2-quart saucepan
Cookie sheet
YIELDS: 1 dozen cookies

Preheat oven to 350°.

In a 2-quart saucepan, combine margarine, brown sugar, corn syrup, molasses, and ginger. Cook on small flame until syrupy. Allow to cool 5 minutes. In a large mixer bowl dissolve baking powder in lemon juice. Add the flour and cooled syrup. Beat well.

Spoon level teaspoonfuls onto a cookie sheet, spacing 3 inches apart.

Bake for 8 to 10 minutes. Remove from cookie sheet and cool.

LADY FINGERS

4 eggs, separated
Pinch salt
¾ cup sugar
1 tsp. vanilla extract
¾ cup flour
Confectioners' sugar

Preheat oven to 350°.

In large mixer bowl, beat egg whites and salt until soft peaks form. Gradually add ¼ cup sugar and beat until whites are stiff and glossy. Set aside.

In a small mixer bowl, mix egg yolks, vanilla, and ½ cup sugar on medium speed until thick and pale yellow. With rubber spatula, fold flour into egg whites; then fold into

►

USE: Cookie sheets
YIELDS: 4 dozen lady fingers

egg-yolk mixture. Spoon mixture in elongated shapes, 3 inches long, onto ungreased cookie sheets 1 inch apart (or use pastry bag for easier handling.) Sprinkle lightly with confectioners' sugar.

Bake for 15 minutes until light brown. Remove from cookie sheet and cool.

CRUNCHY CHIP COOKIES

1 cup margarine, softened
½ cup sugar
1½ cups brown sugar
2 eggs
1½ tsps. vanilla extract
2 cups flour
1 tsp. baking soda
½ tsp. salt
2 cups rolled oats, uncooked
12 ounces chocolate chips
3 ounces chow-mein noodles, chopped

USE: Cookie sheets
YIELDS: 7 to 8 dozen cookies

Preheat oven to 350°.

In a large mixer bowl, cream margarine and sugars. Add eggs and vanilla and beat well. Beat in flour, baking soda, and salt. Mix well. Fold in the rolled oats, chocolate bits, and chow-mein noodles. Blend well.

Drop onto cookie sheet by teaspoonfuls, leaving 1 inch space between cookies.

Bake for 15 minutes. Remove from cookie sheet and cool.

ORANGE DROP COOKIES

⅔ cup solid shortening
¾ cup sugar
1 egg
½ cup orange juice
2 Tbsps. grated orange peel
2 cups flour
½ tsp. baking powder
½ tsp. baking soda

ORANGE FROSTING
2½ Tbsps. margarine, softened
1½ Tbsps. orange juice
2 Tbsps. grated orange peel
1½ cups confectioners' sugar

USE: Cookie sheets
YIELDS: 3 dozen cookies

Preheat oven to 375°.

Grease cookie sheets.

In a large mixer bowl cream shortening, sugar, and egg at medium speed, and beat until light and fluffy, scraping sides of bowl occasionally. Add orange juice and peel. Combine flour, baking powder, and baking soda. Add to mixture and continue mixing just until combined.

Drop batter by rounded teaspoonfuls two inches apart onto cookie sheets.

Bake 10 to 12 minutes. Remove from cookie sheets to cool. Then frost.

ORANGE FROSTING: In small bowl, combine frosting ingredients until of spreading consistency.

PEANUTTY-SESAME COOKIES

¼ cup sesame seeds
¼ cup margarine, softened
¼ cup peanut butter
½ cup sugar
½ cup brown sugar
½ tsp. baking soda
⅓ tsp. salt
1½ cups flour
2 eggs
1 tsp. vanilla extract

USE: Cookie sheets
YIELDS: 3 dozen cookies

Preheat oven to 375°.

Grease cookie sheet.

In a small pan, toast sesame seeds for 5 minutes, stirring occasionally. Remove from oven.

In a large mixer bowl cream together margarine, peanut butter, and sugars. Stir in baking soda, salt, and flour. Add eggs, vanilla, and toasted sesame seeds and mix until blended. Drop by rounded teaspoonfuls on cookie sheet.

Bake for 10 to 12 minutes. Remove from cookie sheet and cool.

RAISIN-COCONUT COOKIES

4 egg whites
¾ cup flour
½ tsp. baking powder
¼ tsp. cinnamon
2 cups confectioners' sugar
1 cup shredded coconut
½ cup raisins
½ cup chopped walnuts

USE: Cookie sheets
YIELDS: 2 dozen cookies

Preheat oven to 325°.

Grease cookie sheet.

In a large mixer bowl beat egg whites until stiff. Add flour, baking powder, cinnamon, and sugar, and mix well. Add coconut, raisins, and walnuts, and mix well.

Drop dough by teaspoonfuls on cookie sheet, about 2 inches apart. Bake for 15 minutes. Remove from cookie sheet and cool.

STIR 'N DROP COOKIES

2 eggs
⅔ cup oil
2 tsps. vanilla extract
1 tsp. grated lemon rind
¾ cup sugar
2 cups flour
2 tsps. baking powder
½ tsp. salt

USE: Cookie sheets
YIELDS: 3 dozen cookies

Preheat oven to 400°.

Beat eggs with a fork. Stir in oil, vanilla, and lemon rind. Blend in sugar. Sift together flour, baking powder, and salt. Add to egg mixture.

Drop by teaspoonfuls about 2 inches apart on ungreased cookie sheet. Stamp each cookie flat with bottom of a glass dipped in sugar. (Lightly oil bottom of glass, then dip in sugar.)

Bake for 8 to 10 minutes. Remove from cookie sheet and cool.

VARIATION
□ Decorate cookies with nuts or chocolate bits prior to baking.

EGG KICHLACH

A dry cookie popular at a buffet Kiddush — it's so light and airy!

6 eggs
1 cup oil
1¾ cups flour
2 Tbsps. sugar
1 Tbsp. cinnamon
½ cup sugar

USE: Cookie sheets
YIELDS: 3 dozen cookies

Preheat oven to 300°.

Combine all ingredients except cinnamon and sugar together in large bowl of mixer. Mix at medium speed for 20 minutes.

Drop on ungreased cookie sheet by teaspoonfuls, placing 2 inches apart. Combine cinnamon and sugar and sprinkle over cookies.

Bake for 30 to 40 minutes until golden brown. Remove from cookie sheet and cool.

CHEWY MERINGUES

2 egg whites
1 cup confectioners' sugar
½ tsp. vanilla extract
Pinch salt
1 cup shredded coconut
2 cups cornflakes
6 ounces chocolate chips
Maraschino cherries (optional)

USE: Cookie sheets
YIELDS: 2 dozen meringues

Preheat oven to 250°.

Lightly grease cookie sheet.

In a large mixer bowl, beat egg whites until stiff. Add sugar gradually, beating until peaks form. Add vanilla and salt. Sprinkle coconut, cornflakes, and chocolate chips over egg-white mixture and fold in.

Drop by tablespoonfuls on cookie sheet. Place ½ maraschino cherry in center, if desired.

Bake for 30 minutes. Remove from cookie sheet and cool.

MOLDED COOKIES

Molded Cookies are made from a stiff dough that is shaped by hand into balls or other design. They may be rolled in egg white, sugar, shredded coconut, or ground nuts, before or after baking.

BON BON SURPRISES

1 cup solid shortening
½ cup confectioners' sugar
1 tsp. vanilla extract
2¼ cups sifted flour
¼ tsp. salt
Colored sprinkles
Chocolate chips (optional)

USE: Cookie sheets
YIELDS: 3½ dozen cookies

Preheat oven to 375°.

Grease cookie sheets.

In a large mixer bowl cream shortening and sugar and blend in vanilla. Add flour and salt.

Pinch off enough dough to form 1-inch balls and dip into colored sprinkles, or wrap dough around chocolate chips.

Bake for 10 to 12 minutes until golden. Remove from cookie sheets to cool.

ALMOND CONFECTIONERY BALLS

A hostess favorite and easy enough for your children to make.

1 cup margarine, softened
¼ cup confectioners' sugar
1 tsp. vanilla extract
⅛ tsp. almond extract
2 cups flour
1 cup ground almonds
Confectioners' sugar

USE: Cookie sheets
YIELDS: 6 dozen cookies

Preheat oven to 350°.

In a large mixer bowl cream margarine and confectioners sugar until light and fluffy. Add vanilla and almond extract. Beat again. Add flour and almonds and combine well.

Form into ¾-inch balls. Place 1 inch apart on ungreased cookie sheet. Bake for 20 minutes.

When cookies are done, only the bottoms will be brown. Roll cookies in confectioners' sugar while still warm. Cool.

VARIATION
☐ **Walnut Balls:** Substitute 1 cup of ground walnuts for 1 cup ground almonds.

CHINESE ALMOND COOKIES

2¾ cups flour
1 cup sugar
½ tsp. salt
½ tsp. baking soda
1 cup margarine, softened
1 egg
1 tsp. almond extract
⅓ cup whole almonds

USE: Cookie sheets
YIELDS: 4½ dozen cookies

Preheat oven to 325°.

Grease cookie sheet.

In a large mixer bowl sift together flour, sugar, salt, and baking soda. Cut in margarine. Add egg and almond extract and mix into smooth dough.

Shape dough into 1-inch balls. Place almond in center of ball and flatten slightly.

Bake for 15 to 18 minutes. Remove from cookie sheet to cool.

OATMEAL AND RAISIN COOKIES

2 cups flour
1 cup sugar
1 cup dark brown sugar
1 tsp. baking powder
1 tsp. baking soda
½ tsp. salt
½ tsp. cinnamon
1 cup solid shortening
2 eggs
½ tsp. vanilla extract
1½ cups rolled oats
1 cup raisins
½ cup chopped almonds

USE: Cookie sheets
YIELDS: 4 dozen cookies

Preheat oven to 375°.

Mix dry ingredients in mixer until well combined. Add shortening, eggs, and vanilla, and mix well. Add oats, raisins, and nuts, and mix well.

Form into 1-inch balls and place on ungreased cookie sheet 3 inches apart.

Bake for 10 to 12 minutes until tops are browned. Remove from cookie sheets to cool.

VARIATION
☐ Dip unbaked cookies into sugar before baking.

CHOCOLATE SNOWBALLS

½ cup solid shortening
2 cups sugar
4 eggs
2 tsps. baking powder
2 tsps. vanilla extract
½ tsp. salt
4 cups flour
4 ounces bittersweet chocolate, melted
Confectioners' sugar

USE: Cookie sheets
YIELDS: 5 dozen cookies

In a large mixer bowl, cream shortening and sugar. Add eggs, one at a time, and beat well. Add baking powder, vanilla, and salt. Mix well. Beat in flour and chocolate. Cover and refrigerate dough for 2 hours.

Preheat oven to 375°.

Grease cookie sheet.

Form dough into balls, using 1 teaspoon of dough for each. Pour confectioners' sugar into a bowl and roll balls in sugar, coating well. Place on cookie sheet 3 inches apart.

Bake for 10 to 12 minutes. Remove from cookie sheet to cool.

CHOCOLATE THUMBPRINTS

1 ounce bittersweet chocolate
½ cup margarine
1 cup sugar
1 egg, separated
¼ tsp. vanilla extract
1 cup flour
¼ tsp. salt
¾ cup chopped walnuts
1 6-ounce package chocolate chips or jam

USE: Double boiler
Cookie sheets
YIELDS: 2 dozen cookies

Preheat oven to 350°.

Grease cookie sheet.

Melt chocolate over simmering water in top of a double boiler. Pour into large bowl and add margarine, sugar, egg yolk, and vanilla; mix until creamy. Add flour and salt and mix. Shape into balls the size of large marbles.

In a small bowl beat egg white until foamy. Dip each dough ball in egg white and then roll in nuts. Place on cookie sheet, 1 inch apart. Make a thumbprint in center of each.

Bake for 10 minutes. Remove from oven. While cookies are still warm, place a few chocolate chips or a drop of your favorite jam in each thumbprint. Cool before serving.

CHOCOLATE CRISPY COOKIES

1½ cups flour
½ tsp. baking soda
¼ tsp. salt
½ cup margarine, softened
1 cup sugar
1 egg
1 tsp. vanilla extract
2 cups crisped rice cereal
6 ounces chocolate chips

USE: Cookie sheets
YIELDS: 2 dozen cookies

Preheat oven to 350°.

Grease cookie sheet.

In a large mixer bowl mix together flour, baking soda, and salt. Add margarine and sugar and beat until smooth. Beat in egg and vanilla. Mix in cereal and chocolate.

Shape into balls and place 2 inches apart on cookie sheet. Bake for 12 minutes until golden brown. Remove from cookie sheet to cool.

HONEY COOKIES

3 eggs	In a large mixer bowl beat eggs, sugar, oil, and honey together for 5 to 7 minutes. Gradually sift in flour and baking soda. Refrigerate overnight.
½ cup sugar	
½ cup oil	
8 ounces honey	Preheat oven to 350°.
3½ cups flour	Working with floured hands, shape dough into 1-inch balls. Flatten with fingers. Place on floured baking sheet.
1 tsp. baking soda	
USE: Cookie sheets	Bake for 12 to 15 minutes until golden brown. Remove from cookie sheet to cool.
YIELDS: 5 dozen cookies	

JAM DIAGONALS

½ cup margarine, softened
¼ cup sugar
1 tsp. vanilla extract
⅛ tsp. salt
1¼ cups flour
¼ cup seedless raspberry jam

GLAZE
¾ cup confectioners' sugar
4 tsps. lemon juice

USE: Cookie sheets
YIELDS: 2 dozen bars

Preheat oven to 350°.

Grease cookie sheets.

In large mixer bowl cream margarine, sugar, vanilla, and salt until fluffy. Gradually stir in flour until blended. Divide dough into thirds.

On a lightly floured surface, using your hands, roll each piece of dough into a 9-inch rope. Place 3 inches apart on a cookie sheet.

With your finger, make ½-inch hollow down the center of each rope. (Rope will flatten.) Fill hollows with jam.

Bake for 15 to 20 minutes until golden brown. Cool on cookie sheet.

GLAZE: Blend confectioners' sugar and lemon juice until smooth. Drizzle over jam. When glaze is set, cut diagonally into 1-inch bars.

LEMON SNOWBALLS

½ cup margarine, softened
⅔ cup sugar
2 tsps. grated lemon rind
1 egg
3 Tbsps. lemon juice
1 Tbsp. water
1¾ cups flour
¼ tsp. baking soda
½ tsp. salt
½ cup ground walnuts
Confectioners' sugar

USE: Cookie sheets
YIELDS: 3 to 4 dozen cookies

Preheat oven to 350°.

Beat first six ingredients together in a large mixer bowl until blended. Sift together flour, baking soda, salt, and nuts. Add to mixer bowl and beat well.

Flour hands and form dough into 1-inch balls. Place about one inch apart on ungreased cookie sheets.

Bake for 10 to 15 minutes. Cookies will only brown on the bottom. Remove cookies from cookie sheet immediately and roll in confectioners' sugar while still warm.

NO-EGG COOKIES

1 cup cornstarch
1 cup confectioners' sugar
2 cups flour
1½ cups margarine, softened

USE: Cookie sheets
YIELDS: 5 dozen cookies

Preheat oven to 300°.

Place all ingredients together in bowl. Using mixer, beat until ingredients form a smooth dough. If mixture is too dry, add a drop of apple juice. Form dough into little balls. Place on ungreased cookie sheets and press down with a fork.

Bake for 30 minutes. Only bottom of cookies will be browned. Remove from cookie sheet to cool.

PEANUT BUTTER AND JELLY COOKIES

A peanut butter lover's special!

½ cup margarine, softened
½ cup peanut butter
½ cup sugar
½ cup brown sugar
1 egg
1¼ cups flour
½ tsp. baking powder
¼ tsp. salt
¼ tsp. baking soda

Strawberry, raspberry, or your favorite jam

USE: Cookie sheets
YIELDS: 2 dozen cookies

In a large mixer bowl beat softened margarine, peanut butter, and sugars together well. Add egg and blend together. Add flour, baking powder, salt, and baking soda, and mix well. Wrap dough in plastic wrap or wax paper and chill at least 1 hour.

Preheat oven to 325°.

Grease cookie sheets.

Pinch off pieces of dough and roll into small balls. (If larger cookies are desired, shape larger balls.) Place balls on cookie sheet about 2 inches apart. Press down cookie with back of a teaspoon. Make an impression with your thumb in the center of each cookie. Place enough jam (about ½ teaspoon) to fill depression.

Bake 7 to 10 minutes and remove when edges are lightly browned. Remove from cookie sheet to cool.

VARIATION
☐ Substitute ½ cup wheat germ for ½ cup flour.

RUM BALLS

These cookies are really a no-bake confection. A snap to make. Have the children try their hand.

8 ounces tea biscuits
½ cup sugar
2 Tbsps. cocoa
½ cup water
2 Tbsps. rum
2 Tbsps. margarine
½ cup coconut
Sprinkles (optional)

YIELDS: 2 dozen rum balls

Crush biscuits into small crumbs. Place in bowl.

Mix sugar, cocoa, and water in a small pot. Bring to a boil, stirring constantly. Remove from flame, add rum and margarine. Mix until margarine is melted. Pour mixture onto biscuits and mix well until biscuits are coated. Form into small balls. Roll the balls in coconut and sprinkles. Store in refrigerator.

BLACK-AND-WHITE COOKIES

1 cup margarine, softened
⅔ cup sugar
2 tsps. vanilla extract
½ tsp. salt
2 eggs
2 cups flour

WHITE ICING
1 cup confectioners' sugar
¼ tsp. vanilla extract
2 Tbsps. hot water
1 Tbsp. oil
1 drop lemon juice

CHOCOLATE ICING
¾ cup confectioners' sugar
4 tsps. cocoa
2 Tbsps. hot water
½ to 1 Tbsp. oil

USE: Cookie sheets
YIELDS: 2 dozen medium
or 1 dozen large cookies

Preheat oven to 375°.

In a large mixer bowl cream margarine and sugar together. Add remaining dough ingredients, adding eggs one at a time. Shape into medium-sized (2½-inch) balls and place on ungreased cookie sheet. Space 2 inches apart to allow for spreading.

Bake for 15 minutes. Remove from cookie sheet to cool.

While cookies are baking, prepare frostings in two separate bowls.

When cookies are slightly cooled, turn over and frost each cookie on flat side — one-half with white icing and one-half with chocolate icing.

WHITE ICING: In a small bowl combine all white icing ingredients until of spreading consistency.

CHOCOLATE ICING: In a small bowl combine all chocolate icing ingredients until of spreading consistency.

BROWN SUGAR SANDWICH COOKIES

1 cup margarine, softened
¾ cup brown sugar, firmly packed
1 egg yolk
2¼ cups flour

ORANGE "BUTTER" CREAM FILLING
2 Tbsps. margarine, softened
1¼ cups confectioners' sugar
½ tsp. vanilla extract
1 tsp. grated orange rind
1 Tbsp. nondairy creamer or orange juice
1 egg yolk

USE: Cookie sheets
YIELDS: 2 dozen
sandwich cookies

Preheat oven to 325°.

In a large mixer bowl cream margarine and brown sugar. Blend in egg yolk and flour to form a dough. Shape into marble-sized balls. Place on ungreased cookie sheet and flatten to ⅓-inch thick with palm of hand. Press design on cookies with a fork (going only in one direction).

Bake for 8 to 10 minutes.

ORANGE "BUTTER" CREAM FILLING: Combine margarine and confectioners' sugar. Add liquid ingredients and flavoring and mix until filling is smooth.

Remove cookies from cookie sheet while still warm. Form sandwiches by spreading filling on the bottom of one cookie and covering filling with the bottom of another cookie.

ROLLED COOKIES

Rolled Cookies are made of a stiff dough which is rolled out and cut into shapes. Shaping the cookies is a lot of fun! It is a favorite activity for children.

BASIC COOKIE DOUGH

3 eggs
1 cup margarine, softened
½ tsp. vanilla extract
4 cups flour
2 cups confectioners' sugar
3 tsps. baking powder

USE: Cookie sheets
YIELDS: 7 to 8 dozen cookies

Preheat oven to 350°.

Grease cookie sheets lightly.

In a large mixer bowl, beat eggs. Add margarine and vanilla. Add flour, sugar, and baking powder, and mix until well blended.

Roll out dough on a floured board to ¼-inch thickness and cut into desired shapes. Place on cookie sheet.

Bake for 10 to 12 minutes or until slightly browned. Remove from cookie sheet to cool.

VARIATION
☐ This is also good as a pie crust.

DATE COOKIES

1 cup sugar
1 cup brown sugar
1 cup margarine, softened
3 eggs
1 tsp. vanilla extract
4 cups flour
1 tsp. salt
1 tsp. baking soda

FILLING
1 pound dates, chopped
½ cup sugar
½ cup currants or raisins

USE: 1½-quart saucepan
Cookie sheets
YIELDS: 5 to 6 dozen cookies

In a large mixer bowl, combine sugars and margarine and blend well. Add eggs and vanilla and mix well. Add flour, salt, and baking soda, and mix until dough is smooth. Cover dough and chill for 1 hour.

FILLING: Place dates, sugar, and currants or raisins in 1½-quart saucepan. Cook over low heat until sugar melts and comes to a boil.

Roll out dough on a floured board to ¼-inch thickness. Spread filling on dough. Roll dough like a jelly roll and refrigerate another hour.

Preheat oven to 375°.

Grease cookie sheets.

Slice dough and place on cookie sheet. Bake for 10 to 12 minutes. Remove from cookie sheet to cool.

GINGERBREAD BOYS

5 cups flour
1½ tsps. baking soda
2 to 3 tsps. ground ginger
1 tsp. ground cinnamon
1 tsp. ground cloves
½ tsp. salt
1 cup solid shortening
1 cup sugar
1 large egg
1 cup light molasses
2 Tbsps. white vinegar
Red cinnamon candies

USE: Cookie sheets
YIELDS: 3 dozen
gingerbread boys

In a large bowl, sift flour, baking soda, ginger, cinnamon, cloves, and salt. Set aside.

In a large mixer bowl, cream shortening and sugar together. When creamy, beat in egg, molasses, and vinegar. Stir in flour mixture one-quarter at a time. Mix well after each addition, using your hands if necessary. Cover dough and chill 3 hours or longer.

Preheat oven to 375°.

Grease cookie sheets.

Divide dough in half. On a lightly floured board, roll one piece of dough ⅛-inch thick. Dip a 5 x 3-inch gingerbread-boy cutter in flour and cut dough. Place cookies on cookie sheets and use cinnamon candies to make buttons. Proceed with second half of dough.

Bake 5 minutes. Remove from cookie sheet to cool.

HAMANTASHEN, *the classic Purim cookies, are eagerly awaited by everyone young and old. They are versatile and can be made from a good sweet yeast dough, flaky dough, or, as presented below, traditional cookie dough. The fillings as well can be mixed and matched. Prune butter (lekvar) and poppy seeds (mohn) are traditional but one can use any kind of jam or preserves or apple butter.*

HAMANTASHEN ILLUSTRATED

1 Prepare dough of your choice. Divide dough into four portions.

2 On a floured board roll out each portion to about ⅛-inch thick. Using a round biscuit or cookie cutter cut 3-inch circles.

3 Place ½ to ⅔ teaspoon of desired filling in the middle of each circle.

4 To shape into triangle, lift up right and left sides, leaving the bottom down, and bring both sides to meet at the center above the filling.

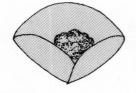

5 Bring top flap down to the center to meet the two sides. Pinch edges together.

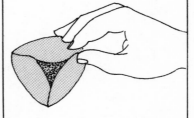

6 Place on greased cookie sheets 1 inch apart and bake in a 350° preheated oven for 20 minutes.

TRADITIONAL HAMANTASHEN

Hamantashen, a traditional Purim delight, is a three-cornered pastry filled with mohn *(poppy seeds) or other sweet filling.*

4 eggs
1 cup sugar
½ cup oil
Juice of 1 lemon
Rind of 1 lemon, grated
1 tsp. vanilla extract
5 cups flour
2 tsps. baking powder

FILLINGS
1 pound prepared mohn filling (poppy seed)
or 1 pound lekvar (apple or prune butter)
or see Poppy Bars, page 438, for Poppy Seed Filling

USE: Cookie sheets
YIELDS: 4 dozen hamantashen

Preheat oven to 350°.

Grease cookie sheet.

Beat eggs and sugar. Add remaining ingredients, and mix well. Divide into four parts.

Proceed to assemble and bake according to Hamantashen Illustrated.

NOTE: If glaze is desired, brush with beaten egg.

HAMANTASHEN

4 cups flour
4 eggs
¾ cup sugar
1 cup margarine, softened
1 Tbsp. orange juice
2 tsps. baking powder
1 tsp. vanilla extract
Pinch of salt
1 tsp. orange rind

FILLINGS
1 pound lekvar (apple or prune butter) or
1 pound strawberry or apricot preserves

USE: Cookie sheets
YIELDS: 4 dozen hamantashen

Preheat oven to 350°.

Grease cookie sheets.

Place all ingredients in a large mixer bowl and beat together. You may add a drop more juice or flour, depending on consistency of dough. Roll dough into a ball. Divide into four parts.

Proceed to assemble and bake according to Hamantashen Illustrated.

VARIATION
□ Substitute ½ cup of oil for 1 cup margarine and juice of 1 lemon for 1 tablespoon orange juice and 1 teaspoon orange rind.

ONION COOKIES

These savory cookies are excellent for a Kiddush.

3 eggs
½ cup oil
1 level tsp. kosher salt
1 tsp. baking powder
2 large onions, grated
3 to 4 cups flour

USE: Cookie sheets
YIELDS: 4 to 6 dozen cookies

Preheat oven to 425°.

Grease cookie sheets.

In a medium mixer bowl combine all ingredients, adding flour ½ cup at a time, and mixing until a soft dough is formed.

Roll out dough thin and cut shapes with a small cookie cutter or small whiskey glass.

Bake on cookie sheets for 8 to 10 minutes until lightly browned. Remove from cookie sheets to cool.

PINWHEEL COOKIES

These festive cookies dress up any pastry tray. They have good eye appeal and taste great too.

4 eggs
1 cup margarine, softened
1 tsp. vanilla extract
Rind of 1 lemon
Juice of 1 lemon
4 cups flour
1 Tbsp. baking powder
Pinch salt
2 cups confectioners' sugar
½ to ⅓ cup cocoa

USE: Cookie sheets
YIELDS: 8 dozen cookies

In a large mixer bowl, combine all ingredients except cocoa. Mix until smooth dough is formed. Divide dough in half. Add cocoa one half a tablespoon at a time and knead in until desired color is obtained.

Divide white dough into two equal parts and divide chocolate dough into two equal parts. Roll out first half of white dough on floured aluminum foil. Also roll out one half of chocolate dough onto floured aluminum foil. Place cookie dough together with aluminum foil on the top and bottom. Peel off top sheet of foil and roll up cookie doughs jelly-roll fashion. Wrap in wax paper and refrigerate several hours. Repeat above procedure with second half of dough.

Lightly grease cookie sheets.

Preheat oven to 350°.

Slice cookies ¼-inch thick and place slices on cookie sheet. Bake for 10 to 15 minutes. Remove from cookie sheet to cool.

REFRIGERATOR COOKIES

Refrigerator Cookies are made from a stiff rich dough which is shaped into a long roll, chilled well, sliced, and baked. Keep a few rolls in your freezer for unexpected company.

BUTTERSCOTCH REFRIGERATOR COOKIES

1¾ cups sifted flour
1 tsp. baking powder
½ tsp. salt
½ cup margarine, softened
1 cup dark brown sugar

In a small bowl, sift flour, baking powder, and salt together and set aside. In a large mixer bowl cream margarine and brown sugar. Add egg, vanilla, and walnuts. Beat in flour until dough is smooth. Chill 30 minutes.

▶

1 egg
½ tsp. vanilla extract
½ cup chopped walnuts

USE: Cookie sheets
YIELDS: 4 to 5 dozen cookies

Shape into two rolls, 1½ inches in diameter, and wrap in wax paper. Chill several hours until firm.

Preheat oven to 350°.

Cut into ⅛-inch slices. Place on ungreased cookie sheet. Bake for 10 to 12 minutes. Remove from cookie sheet to cool.

CHERRY-WALNUT REFRIGERATOR COOKIES

1 cup margarine, softened
1 cup sugar
1 tsp. vanilla extract
⅓ tsp. salt
2½ cups flour
2 dozen maraschino cherries, drained and chopped
1 cup coarsely chopped walnuts

USE: Cookie sheets
YIELDS: 4 to 5 dozen cookies

In a large mixer bowl, cream margarine and sugar. Add remaining ingredients and mix well. Form dough into two 12-inch rolls. Wrap in wax paper or aluminum foil and chill 4 hours or overnight.

Preheat oven to 350°.

Grease cookie sheets.

Slice into ⅛- to ¼-inch slices and place on cookie sheet. Bake for 13 to 15 minutes. Remove from cookie sheet to cool.

PRETZELS

These hard pretzels are better than the commercial variety.

1 package dry yeast
½ cup warm water
¼ cup oil
1 tsp. salt
1 Tbsp. sugar
¾ cup nondairy creamer
4 cups flour
1 large egg, beaten
Coarse salt

USE: Cookie sheets
YIELDS: 4 dozen pretzels

Preheat oven to 425°.

In a large mixer bowl, dissolve yeast in warm water. Add oil, salt, sugar, nondairy creamer, and flour, and knead until smooth. Pull off small pieces of dough and form into ropes by rolling between palms of hands.

Form "pretzel" shapes, thin rods, nuggets, or long, thick, pretzels. Place on cookie sheets lined with brown paper. Brush pretzels with beaten egg and sprinkle with coarse salt.

Bake immediately for 12 to 15 minutes or until brown.

WALNUT CRESCENTS

½ cup margarine, softened
¼ cup sugar
1 tsp. vanilla extract
⅛ tsp. salt
⅓ cup ground walnuts
1¼ cups flour
Confectioners' sugar

USE: Cookie sheets
YIELDS: 2 dozen cookies

In large bowl of mixer, cream margarine, sugar, vanilla, and salt until fluffy. Stir in nuts. Gradually stir in flour until well blended. Wrap airtight and chill 1 hour (or longer).

Preheat oven to 350°.

Pinch off walnut-size pieces. Roll into 4-inch fingers. Shape in crescents and place 1 inch apart on an ungreased cookie sheets.

Bake for 12 to 14 minutes or until golden. Cool. Sprinkle with confectioners' sugar sifted through a small strainer.

PRESS COOKIES

Press Cookies offer a larger variety of shapes and sizes. Each press comes with instructions for use. Follow them carefully for best results. Decorate with sprinkles, candied cherries, and chocolate chips.

CHOCOLATE PRESS COOKIES

½ cup solid shortening
1 cup sugar
½ tsp. vanilla extract
1 egg
2 ounces unsweetened chocolate, melted
2 cups flour
½ tsp. salt
2 Tbsps. nondairy creamer

USE: Cookie sheets
YIELDS: 6 dozen cookies

Preheat oven to 350°.

In a large mixer bowl, cream shortening, sugar, and vanilla extract. Add egg and beat until fluffy. Blend in melted chocolate. Sift flour and salt together and stir into creamed mixture alternately with nondairy creamer.

Follow manufacturer's directions for cookie press and shape directly onto ungreased cookie sheets.

Bake about 13 minutes. Remove from cookie sheet to cool.

CINNAMON PRESS COOKIES

½ cup margarine, softened
1 cup sugar
1 tsp. vanilla extract
2 eggs
2 cups flour
½ tsp. salt
2 tsps. baking powder
2 tsps. cinnamon

USE: Cookie sheets
YIELDS: 5 dozen cookies

In a large mixer bowl, cream margarine, sugar, and vanilla. Add eggs one at a time and beat until fluffy. Sift together flour, salt, baking powder, and cinnamon and stir into creamed mixture. Mix well. Cover and chill at least 1 hour.

Preheat oven to 425°.

Follow manufacturer's directions for cookie press and shape dough directly onto ungreased cookie sheets.

Bake for 7 to 9 minutes. Remove from cookie sheet to cool.

SPRITZ COOKIES

1 cup margarine, softened
¾ cup sugar
1 egg
1 tsp. vanilla extract
2½ cups flour
¼ tsp. salt
1 tsp. baking powder

USE: Cookie sheets
YIELDS: 5 dozen cookies

Preheat oven to 350°.

In a large mixer bowl, cream margarine and sugar until light and fluffy. Beat in egg and vanilla. Combine flour, salt, and baking powder, and add to creamed margarine and sugar mixture. Mix well.

Follow manufacturer's directions for cookie press and press directly onto ungreased cookie sheets.

Bake for about 13 minutes. Remove from cookie sheet to cool.

Pastries

"Good things come in small packages." Any abundant Viennese table will testify to the pleasures of pastry. This category encompasses so many mouth-watering yummies — cream puffs, strudels, tarts, and the like. These small delicacies lend themselves well to decorations.

PASTRY DOUGHS, *relatively simple to prepare, bring an elegance to appetizers, side dishes, and desserts.*

SIMPLE FLAKY DOUGH

1 cup margarine
2 cups flour
½ tsp. salt
⅓ cup ice water
2 Tbps. vinegar
2 egg yolks
1 tsp. water
Sesame seeds (optional)

YIELDS: 1 dozen knishes or turnovers

Cut margarine into flour and salt with a pastry cuttter or two knives. In a separate bowl, mix cold water, vinegar, and one egg yolk. Add a little at a time to flour mixture, working in until thoroughly combined. Do not overmix — dough should be soft, not sticky. Place dough in plastic bag and refrigerate for 2 hours or more before rolling.

CLASSIC FLAKY DOUGH

An authentic flaky dough well worth the effort. Use this dough for rugelach, turnovers, and knishes.

3½ cups flour
2 Tbsps. oil
2 tsps. sugar
½ tsp. salt
¾ to 1 cup ice water
1¾ cups margarine, softened

YIELDS: 3 dozen knishes or turnovers

Place 2½ cups of the flour in a large bowl. Add oil, sugar, and salt, and mix. Knead while slowly adding water — dough should not be too wet or sticky. Shape into a square. Cover with plastic wrap and refrigerate for at least 1 hour.

Cut margarine into reamining cup of flour using pastry knife or fork, then mix in with hands. Set margarine mixture aside. Roll dough on floured surface into a 10 x 16-inch rectangle. Spread margarine mixture on half of the dough, leaving a ½-inch border. Fold dough in half over margarine and seal edges all around.

Once again roll dough into a 10 x 16-inch rectangle. Fold dough over from each side to meet in the middle. Then fold in half. Rectangle should measure 4 x 10 inches. Cover with plastic and refrigerate for 1 hour.

Place again on floured surface and roll out to 10 x 16 inches. Fold dough over from each side to meet in the middle. Reroll into 10 x 16-inch rectangle.

Repeat, folding the dough as above, with one third of each side of dough folded toward the middle. Cover and refrigerate for 2 hours before using.

BASIC PASTRY DOUGH

This dough may be kept several days in the refrigerator. It also freezes well once it's baked.

**1 cup cold margarine
or solid shortening
2 cups flour
1 Tbsp. cold water
1 Tbsp. vinegar
1 egg yolk
Pinch salt**

YIELDS: 2 9-inch crusts
or 1 dozen knishes
or turnovers

In a large bowl, cut cold margarine into flour with two knives or pastry blender until mixture is like coarse meal. Combine water, vinegar, egg yolk, and salt. Mixing by hand, gradually work liquid into mixture until evenly blended.

Shape dough into a ball, cover, and refrigerate at least 2 hours. Work dough in small portions. Avoid overhandling. Keep dough cold.

Roll for knishes, rugelach, or as a pot pie crust.

ALL-PURPOSE DOUGH

Ideal for pirogen. Also suitable for rugelach and piecrusts with addition of ¼ cup sugar to dough.

**1½ cups flour
¼ tsp. baking powder
½ cup margarine
1 egg
3-4 Tbsps. cold water**

YIELDS: 1 piecrust or
10-12 portions

Mix dry ingredients. Cut in margarine. Add egg. Gradually add enough water to hold dough together, but do not overhandle.

Wrap in wax paper or damp towel and refrigerate for ½ hour.

APPLE TURNOVERS

**1 Double Recipe
Simple Flaky Dough
(page 413)**

**FILLING
6 apples, peeled and diced
1½ tsps. cinnamon
6 Tbsps. flour
¾ cup sugar**

**GLAZE
1½ cups confectioners' sugar
4 to 6 Tbsps. water**

USE: Cookie sheet
YIELDS: 2 dozen turnovers

Defrost dough if frozen.

Preheat oven to 350°.

Grease cookie sheet.

Roll out dough and cut into 4-inch squares, one sheet at a time.

FILLING: Mix filling ingredients together in a medium bowl until well combined. Place 1 teaspoon of filling into the center of each square. Fold square over into a triangle and carefully seal edges with the tines of a fork, pressing the edges together.

Make five little slits on the top of each pastry with the tip of a knife. Place on cookie sheet. Bake for 15 to 20 minutes.

GLAZE: Beat confectioners' sugar with water until spreadable. While turnovers are still hot, drizzle the glaze over the pastries.

VARIATION
□ Use packaged frozen flaky dough and canned apple pie filling for a quick dessert.

BAKLAVA

A traditional Middle Eastern dessert. A layered pastry of phyllo dough, walnuts, and honey syrup. Work quickly, for the phyllo dough becomes brittle when exposed to air too long.

1 pound walnuts, finely chopped
3 Tbsps. sugar
1 tsp. cinnamon
1 pound phyllo dough
1 cup melted shortening

HONEY SYRUP
¾ cup sugar
¾ cup water
¼ cup lemon juice
½ cup honey

USE: 10 x 15-inch baking pan
2-quart saucepan
YIELDS: 24 pieces

Grease a 10 x 15-inch baking pan.

In a bowl, combine nuts, sugar, and cinnamon. Set aside.

In 10 x 15-inch baking pan, begin layering phyllo sheets by folding sheets to fit pan. Brush each sheet generously with melted shortening. Use half the sheets, and brush shortening on each one.

Spread nut mixture on top of phyllo sheets. Spread remaining phyllo sheets on top of nut mixture, using the same method as above — brushing each layer with melted shortening. When completed, run knife around edges of pan and spread remaining shortening on top. Refrigerate at least 1 hour.

Preheat oven to 350°.

After refrigerating the baklava, cut through top layer only, without cutting through the bottom layer, with parallel diagonal lines and then cross them to form the traditional diamond shapes. Bake until golden brown, about 25 to 30 minutes.

HONEY SYRUP: Prepare syrup by heating sugar, water, lemon juice, and honey in a 2-quart saucepan to boiling. Simmer uncovered 10 minutes.

When baklava has finished baking, remove from oven and finish cutting through all the layers. Pour cooled syrup over warm baklava.

NOTE: Phyllo sheets dry very quickly. Use only a few sheets at a time, keeping the rest covered with a damp towel or return to plastic bag.

ALMOND TART SHELLS

½ cup margarine, softened
¼ cup sugar
¼ tsp. almond flavoring
⅛ tsp. salt
1 egg white
½ cup ground or grated blanched almonds
1½ cups flour

USE: Mini-muffin pans
Cookie sheet
YIELDS: 2 dozen

In a large mixer bowl, cream margarine, sugar, almond flavoring, and salt until fluffy. Add egg white and beat well. Stir in ground almonds and flour until well blended. Wrap dough airtight and chill 1 hour or longer.

Preheat oven to 350°.

Pinch off a tablespoonful of dough at a time and press into mini-muffin pans. With lightly floured thumb press dough into mold, forming a shell about ⅛ inch thick. Place pans on cookie sheet and bake until golden, 10 to 12 minutes. While still warm, turn muffin pans upside down, tap gently with a spoon to loosen, and cool on rack.

Fill with desired pie filling, jam, fruits, or pudding.

BEER KICHEL

1 cup beer
½ cup oil
2 to 3 cups flour
Confectioners' sugar

USE: Pot for deep-frying
YIELDS: 7 to 8 dozen cookies

In a large mixer bowl mix beer, oil, and enough flour to make a fairly stiff dough. Mix by hand.

Roll out dough on a floured surface. Cut into rectangular shapes and make a lengthwise slit in center of rectangle. Put one end through the slit and pull all the way out. This twists the sides of the rectangle.

Deep-fry in hot oil. Remove when brown with a slotted spoon. Sprinkle with confectioners' sugar.

CREAM PUFFS

These feather-light cream puffs can be filled as below with Italian Pastry Cream or whipped cream or pudding of your choice.

1 cup water
½ cup margarine
1 cup flour
4 eggs

FILLING
Italian Pastry Cream
(page 396)

USE: 1½-quart saucepan
Baking sheet
YIELDS: 1 dozen cream puffs

Preheat oven to 400°.

In 1½-quart saucepan, heat water and margarine and bring to a rolling boil. Stir in flour all at once. Stir vigorously over low heat until mixture forms a ball, about 1 minute.

Remove from heat and beat in eggs one at a time, using a wooden spoon. Continue beating until mixture is smooth.

Drop by teaspoonfuls on ungreased baking sheet about 2 inches apart. Bake 35 to 40 minutes or until puffed and golden. Allow to cool in oven.

FILLING: Prepare one recipe of Italian Pastry Cream and set aside to cool.

Fill pastry tube with filling, cream, or pudding. Pierce the side of each puff with a skewer. Squeeze filling into puffs. Dust with confectioners' sugar.

VARIATION
□ **Chocolate Glazed Eclairs:** Drop full tablespoons of batter, 3 inches apart, on ungreased baking sheet. Using a spatula, shape into strips 4 inches long and 1¼ inches wide. Bake as for puffs.

After eclairs are baked, press in filling through a small hole pierced in the side of the eclairs with a skewer.

To glaze, melt 1 cup of semisweet chocolate pieces with 2 tablespoons margarine in the top of a double boiler. When chocolate melts, add 2 teaspoons honey or corn syrup, 1½ tablespoons nondairy creamer or orange juice, and 1½ tablespoons water. Stir ingredients together. Melt over low flame a few minutes and spread immediately over eclairs. Glaze will harden in minutes.

CUPCAKES *are great for children's parties. Decorate them with frosting and sprinkles or candies. Perfect as an after-school snack as well.*

BASIC CUPCAKES

⅓ cup solid shortening
1¾ cups flour
¾ cup sugar
2½ tsps. baking powder
½ tsp. salt
1 egg
¾ cup nondairy creamer or orange juice
½ tsp. vanilla extract

USE: Cupcake pan
YIELDS: 1 dozen cupcakes

Preheat oven to 375°.

In a large mixer bowl cream shortening, then sift in dry ingredients. Add egg and ½ cup nondairy creamer or juice and mix until flour is moist. Beat 2 minutes. Add remaining liquid and vanilla. Mix well.

Line cupcake pan with paper liners and fill one-half to two-thirds full. Bake for 20 to 25 minutes. Cool on rack and frost with frosting of your choice.

VARIATIONS

□ **Favorite Party Cupcakes:** Place flat-bottomed ice-cream cones in cupcake tin. Fill cones halfway with batter. Bake as usual. Cook on rack and frost with favorite frosting.

□ **Candy Cupcakes:** Crush peppermint candy until very fine. Use approximately ½ cup crushed candy and decrease sugar to ½ cup.

CHOCOLATE CUPCAKES

1½ cups flour
1½ tsps. baking powder
½ tsp. salt
¾ tsp. baking soda
1 tsp. vanilla extract
½ cup cocoa
1½ cups sugar
⅔ cup oil
¾ cup coffee (made with 1 Tbsp. instant coffee and ¾ cup hot water)
2 eggs

USE: Cupcake pan
YIELDS: 1 dozen cupcakes

Preheat oven to 350°.

In a large mixer bowl mix ingredients together in order given and beat thoroughly.

Line cupcake pan with paper liners and fill one-half to two-thirds full. Bake for 35 minutes. Cool on rack and frost with frosting of your choice.

NOTE: If you don't have a cupcake pan, use a 9 x 13-inch baking pan and foil cupcake holders. Fill foil no more than halfway, otherwise cupcakes will be too large and unappetizing.

BLUEBERRY CUPCAKES

2½ cups sifted cake flour
2½ tsps. baking powder
1 tsp. salt
1¼ cups sugar
⅔ cup margarine, softened
1 tsp. vanilla extract
1 cup nondairy creamer
2 eggs
1 pint blueberries
1 Tbsp. flour

USE: Cupcake pan
YIELDS: 2 dozen cupcakes

Preheat oven to 375°.

In a large mixer bowl combine flour, baking powder, salt, and sugar. Add margarine, vanilla, nondairy creamer, and eggs. Mix until well combined. Rinse blueberries and dust with flour. Fold berries into batter.

Line cupcake pan with paper liners and fill one-half to two-thirds full. Bake for 25 to 30 minutes. (Test after 25 minutes.) Cool on rack.

DOUGHNUTS, *an old-fashioned treat, are never quite as good when store-bought. Try homemade! The procedure is to roll them, cut into shapes, and fry in hot oil until golden brown. A special doughnut cutter will cut uniform rings. Doughnuts are a traditional food on Chanukah, like potato latkes, because they are fried in oil.*

DOUGHNUTS

2 ounces fresh yeast
¼ cup warm water
2 tsps. sugar
1 egg
½ cup water
½ cup orange juice
Pinch salt
3 Tbsps. margarine
1 Tbsp. oil
4 ¼ cups flour
⅓ cup sugar

Oil for frying
Confectioners' sugar

USE: 4-quart pot
YIELDS: 4 dozen doughnuts

In a large bowl dissolve yeast in water and sugar. Allow to stand for several minutes until bubbly. Add remaining ingredients and knead until smooth, about 15 to 20 minutes. Cover dough and allow to rise until doubled in bulk — about 1 hour.

Roll out dough ½-inch thick on a floured surface. Cut into circles with doughnut cutter. Allow to rise again until doubled in bulk, about 30 minutes.

Heat 3 to 4 inches of oil in a 4-quart pot until hot. Deep-fry doughnuts in hot oil with cover on pot (it makes doughnuts expand). When golden brown, remove cover, turn doughnuts over, and brown on second side. Remove with slotted spoon. Drain and cool on paper towels. Sprinkle with confectioners' sugar.

SUFGANIOT

Traditional Chanukah doughnuts.

1¾ ounces fresh yeast
1½ cups warm water

Place yeast, water, and sugar in a small bowl. Allow to stand several minutes until bubbly. ➤

1 Tbsp. sugar
3 eggs
½ cup oil
½ cup sugar
½ cup nondairy creamer
1 tsp. vanilla extract
1 tsp. grated lemon peel
6 to 7 cups flour

Oil for frying
Confectioners' sugar

USE: 2-quart pot
YIELDS: 5 to 6
dozen doughnuts

In a large mixer bowl place eggs, oil, sugar, nondairy creamer, vanilla, and grated lemon peel. Add yeast mixture. Add flour until soft dough is formed. (Dough need not be dry; it should be softer than challah dough.) Knead for a few minutes. Cover and allow to rise until doubled in bulk, about 1 to 1½ hours.

Roll out dough ½-inch thick on floured surface. Cut out circles with a doughnut cutter.

Place 2 or 3 inches oil in a 2-quart saucepan and heat over a medium flame until hot. Place four doughnuts at a time in the oil. Brown on one side and then on the other. Remove with slotted spoon. Drain and cool on paper towels. Dust with confectioners' sugar.

NOTE: To test if dough is ready for rolling, place a small piece in a glass of water — if the dough floats to the top, it is ready.

JELLY DOUGHNUTS

Making these feather-light doughnuts is quite a job. But the compliments you receive make them well worth the effort. Eat them while piping hot.

1 ounce fresh yeast
½ cup lukewarm
nondairy creamer
½ cup flour
Pinch of salt
½ cup margarine
3 egg yolks
1½ Tbsps. sugar
½ cup lukewarm
nondairy creamer
2¾ cups flour

FILLING
Jam or
Italian Pastry Cream
(page 396)
1 pound solid shortening
½ cup confectioners' sugar

USE: Double boiler
4-quart pot
YIELDS: 18 to 24 doughnuts

In a small bowl, dissolve yeast in ½ cup lukewarm nondairy creamer. Pour ½ cup flour in a large bowl. Make a well in the flour and pour in dissolved yeast and a pinch of salt; mix well. Cover bowl with a towel and let stand in a warm place until sponge is double in bulk, about 1 hour.

While dough is rising, melt margarine in top of double boiler over boiling water. Remove from flame and pour margarine into a large bowl and allow to cool 15 to 20 minutes. When cool, add egg yolks one at a time and mix. Add sponge to egg yolk mixture and beat well for 10 to 15 minutes.

Add sugar and ½ cup of lukewarm nondairy creamer, stirring continuously. When completely mixed, add 2½ cups of flour a little at a time, continuing to stir mixture. Once all the flour has been added, continue kneading until dough detaches from sides of the bowl. Cover bowl with a towel and let rise in a warm place until double in bulk, about 1½ hours.

Sprinkle remaining ¼ cup of flour over board and place dough on it. Gently roll out with a rolling pin to ¼-inch thickness. With 2-inch cookie cutter cut out twenty-eight circles.

On fourteen circles, place 1 teaspoon of jam or pastry cream. Moisten edges with finger dipped in a glass of water. Cover pastry with remaining fourteen circles. Press edges together tightly. Cover doughnuts and let rise 1 hour.

In a 4-quart pot, melt 1 pound solid shortening. Deep-fry each doughnut ½ minute on each side. Remove with slotted spoon and drain on paper towels. Once cool sprinkle with confectioners' sugar.

SEPHARDIC "KICHEL"

3 cups flour
2 tsps. baking powder
½ tsp. salt
½ cup margarine
½ cup sugar
¾ cup nondairy creamer
2 eggs
1 tsp. vanilla extract
Oil for frying
Confectioners' sugar

USE: 3-quart saucepan
YIELDS: 7 to 8 dozen kichel

Combine flour, baking powder, and salt in large bowl. Beat in margarine, sugar, nondairy creamer, eggs, and vanilla. Mix until smooth dough is formed.

Roll out a handful of dough ¼-inch thick on a floured board. Cut into strips 4-inches long and 1½-inches wide. Cut slit in center of each strip and pull the other end through.

In a 3-quart saucepan, heat oil to 375°. Drop dough into hot oil and fry 1 to 2 minutes until light brown. Remove with slotted spoon. Drain on paper towels and sprinkle with confectioners' sugar.

NAPOLEONS

These elegant pastries are made of delicious vanilla custard sandwiched between two sheets of light flaky dough.

Simple Flaky Dough
(page 413)

FILLING
1 10-ounce container
nondairy dessert topping
1 package instant
vanilla pudding

USE: 2 jelly-roll pans
YIELDS: 2 dozen Napoleons

Prepare Simple Flaky Dough according to instructions. After refrigerating for 2 hours remove from refrigerator. Lightly grease 2 jelly roll pans.

Preheat oven to 350°.

Divide dough into two equal portions. Roll out each piece a little larger than pan and place one on each, making sure that dough is folded over rim of pan to prevent dough from shrinking while baking. Bake until lightly browned. Allow to cool completely.

FILLING: In a mixer, mix filling until stiff. Spread on one portion baked pastry. Cover with second baked pastry. Top with confectioner's sugar or Chocolate Glaze (page 394).

FLAKY RUGELACH

Begin this recipe early enough to allow the dough to rest.

2 cups margarine, softened
1 10-ounce container
nondairy dessert topping
5½ to 6½ cups flour

FILLING
2 cups apricot jam

USE: Cookie sheet
YIELDS: 6 dozen small rugelach

In a large mixer bowl cream margarine. Add dessert topping and then flour. Mix until dough is formed. Cover and refrigerate 4 hours or overnight.

Divide dough into six portions. To fill and shape see Rugelach Illustrated.

Preheat oven to 350°.

Bake for 25 to 35 minutes, until lightly browned.

NOTE: This dough is not sweet so a sweeter filling may be desired.

VARIATION
□ This is excellent as pie crust.

RUGELACH ILLUSTRATED

These crisp, light crescents are a popular traditional treat. The dough is chilled, then rolled into large circles and cut into triangles and filled.

1 On a lightly floured board roll out dough approximately ⅛-inch thick. Brush a light coating of oil over circle. Spread filling over oil allowing a ½-inch margin around the end, and in the center of dough. Cut into 12 to 18 triangles, depending on desired size.

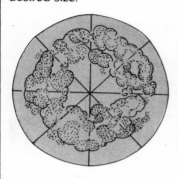

2 Work each triangle individually, rolling from wide outer edge inward to form a roll. Gently bend both ends toward center to form a crescent .

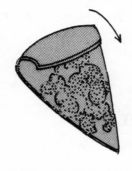

3 Brush each cookie with beaten egg or oil to glaze. Place on lightly greased cookie sheet and bake according to recipe.

CLASSIC RUGELACH

Begin this recipe the day before in order to allow the dough to rest overnight.

1 package dry yeast
¼ cup lukewarm water
1 cup margarine
2 eggs
3 cups flour
3 Tbsps. sugar

FILLING
1 cup apricot jam
¾ cup cinnamon
and ¾ cup sugar

USE: 1½-quart saucepan
Cookie sheet
YIELDS: 4 dozen rugelach

In a small bowl dissolve yeast in warm water, let stand until bubbly.

In 1½-quart saucepan, melt margarine. In a separate bowl, beat eggs. Stir in flour and sugar. Add melted margarine and yeast and mix until dough is formed. Cover bowl and refrigerate overnight.

Remove dough from refrigerator and divide into four equal parts. To fill and shape see Rugelach Illustrated.

Preheat oven to 350°.

Bake for 15 minutes, until lightly browned.

HONEY RUGELACH

2 packages dry yeast
½ cup warm water
1 tsp. sugar
½ cup margarine
½ cup honey
3 eggs
5½ cups flour
½ cup nondairy creamer or
orange juice

FILLING
¾ cup cocoa
and ¾ cup sugar

USE: 1½-quart saucepan
Cookie sheet
YIELDS: 6 dozen rugelach

In a small bowl dissolve yeast in water and add sugar; let stand until bubbly.

In 1½-quart saucepan, melt margarine. Pour into a large bowl. Add remaining ingredients, including yeast, and mix until well combined. Form dough into ball and cover with wax paper. Freeze for 1 hour or refrigerate overnight.

Remove dough from freezer or refrigerator and divide into six equal parts.

Preheat oven to 350°.

To fill and shape see Rugelach Illustrated. Bake for 30 minutes or until browned.

VARIATION
□ An excellent dough for Hamantashen (page 409).

COOKIE RUGELACH

This is an excellent and versatile dough. It can also be used for strudel.

4 eggs
1 cup oil
½ to ¾ cup sugar
5 to 6 cups flour
4 tsps. baking powder
Pinch salt
1 cup orange juice
2 tsps. vanilla extract

FILLINGS
1 Tbsp. cinnamon
and 1 cup sugar
or ½ cup cocoa
and 1 cup sugar
or 1½ cups ground nuts

USE: Cookie sheet
YIELDS: 6 dozen small rugelach

In a large mixer bowl combine eggs, oil, and sugar, and mix until creamy. Combine dry ingredients and add alternately with juice and vanilla, mixing until smooth. Chill dough for 1 hour or leave in refrigerator overnight. Divide into six equal parts. To fill and shape see Rugelach Illustrated.

Preheat oven to 350°.

Bake until slightly browned, approximately 30 to 45 minutes.

VARIATION
□ **Strudelettes:** Prepare dough and refrigerate overnight. Divide into six equal parts. Roll out each piece into a rectangle on a floured board. Brush with oil, spread filling over oil. Roll like a jelly roll and place seam side down on board. Cut into 2-inch pieces and place 1 inch apart on greased cookie sheet.

STRUDEL *baking is a real craft. The paper-thin strudel dough is filled, rolled jellyroll style, and baked. Before baking, brush the top with melted margarine.*

APPLE STRUDEL

The dough for real Viennese Strudel should be stretched thin enough to "read a newspaper through." Patience is required but the end product is worth the effort.

DOUGH
7 Tbsps. oil
¾ to 1 cup warm water
2 cups flour
½ cup margarine, melted

FILLING
½ cup margarine
3 Tbsps. soft breadcrumbs
¾ cup chopped walnuts
2 pounds Cortland apples, peeled and diced
2 tsps. cinnamon
½ cup sugar
½ cup seedless raisins

USE: Baking sheet
YIELDS: 2 strudel rolls

DOUGH: Combine oil and 6 tablespoons of warm water. Sift flour into a heated bowl. Make a well in the flour and pour in oil and water mixture. Work into a soft dough, adding more warm water by tablespoons as necessary. Knead the dough on a lightly floured board at least 10 minutes. Knead into a ball and place in a heated bowl, cover with a towel and let stand at least 30 minutes.

FILLING: Melt margarine in a large frying pan and gently saute breadcrumbs until lightly brown. In a large bowl combine nuts, apples, cinnamon, sugar and raisins. Set aside.

TO STRETCH DOUGH: Spread a large clean tablecloth over the countertop or table. Sprinkle the cloth lightly with flour. Separate dough into two portions. Roll out into a rectangle the first as thin as possible, being careful not to tear it. Brush the dough with a little warm oil. Flour knuckles and place hands under the dough and stretch it over the back of the hands by pulling the hands away from each other until the dough is paper thin. Move around the work space so that the dough is stretched in all directions without strain. Cut away any thick edges. Brush dough with melted margarine.

TO FILL AND ROLL: Spread one half of the bread crumbs and apple mixture over the dough in a 4-inch wide strip to within 2 inches of the edge. Fold the long edge of the dough over the filling. Then lift the edge of the cloth and carefully roll the strudel like a jelly roll. Gently push the roll off the sheet so it is seam side down on a well-greased baking sheet. Brush roll with melted margarine.

Repeat stretching, filling, and rolling with remaining half of dough and filling as above.

Preheat oven to 425°.

Place baking sheet with both rolls in the center of oven. Bake 10 minutes, lower temperature to 400° and bake another 30 minutes or until strudels are browned and crisp.

FLAKY STRUDEL

DOUGH
3 cups flour
1 egg
¾ cup lukewarm water
¼ cup white vinegar
Pinch salt (optional)
1 Tbsp. sugar
2 cups shortening

FILLING
½ pound walnuts, ground
2 egg whites, beaten
¾ cup sugar
¼ cup raisins
1 tsp. vanilla extract
1 tsp. lemon juice
1 Tbsp. strawberry jam

1 egg yolk, beaten

USE: Baking sheet
YIELDS: 4 rolls

DOUGH: Put flour in a large bowl and make a well in the center. Break egg into well. Mix water with vinegar and pour into well. Add salt and sugar and mix together until dough is formed. Divide dough into four pieces.

Roll out each piece of dough into a rectangle on floured board ⅛-inch thick. Spread half of shortening on top of all four pieces. Fold dough in thirds and place in freezer overnight. Next day remove from freezer and roll out again ⅛-inch thick. Spread remaining shortening on all four pieces of dough and fold each in thirds lengthwise.

Preheat oven to 400°.

FILLING: Combine all ingredients until well mixed.

Roll out each piece of dough ⅛-inch thick and spread filling over center. Fold each side over center so that dough is folded into thirds.

Place strudel on greased baking sheet and brush with egg yolk. Bake for 30 minutes. When done, slice into 3-inch pieces.

WINE STRUDEL

DOUGH
4 cups flour
1 cup red wine
1 cup oil

FILLINGS
1 tsp. cinnamon
and ¾ cup sugar, or
½ cup raisins and
½ cup ground nuts, or
½ cup coconut and
½ cup jelly

½ cup apple or
orange juice
¼ cup sugar
and 1 tsp. cinnamon

USE: Baking sheet
YIELDS: 5 to 6 rolls

DOUGH: In a large bowl combine flour, wine, and oil, and mix well. Cover and refrigerate dough for 6 hours or overnight.

Preheat oven to 350°.

Divide dough into five or six pieces. Roll out one piece of dough into a rectangle on floured board ⅛-inch thick. Spread dough with a portion of desired filling. Roll up jelly-roll fashion, stretching dough if necessary. Place on greased baking sheet and brush top with apple or orange juice. Sprinkle top with cinnamon and sugar. Cut into slices 1½ inches apart, but do not slice all the way through. Repeat with remaining pieces of dough.

Bake for 30 to 50 minutes.

Bars

Crunchy, chewy, layered bars are perfect for a snack or dessert. They are excellent to serve a crowd. Rich with spices, plump with fruits and nuts, they are a dainty, delicious finger food.

Brownies, often studded with raisins and nuts, are the most famous bar cookie. Butterscotch, banana, and date-nut bars are also popular favorites.

When serving bar cookies they should be uniform, with well-cut shape, rich and appealing flavor, and moist texture. They are often thin and delicate. Cut them in squares, diamonds, or rectangles and serve in individual paper cups.

TIPS FOR BAKING BARS

- ☐ Cool bars in the pan. They crumble if cut while warm.

- ☐ Frosting will give the bars a tasty finish.

- ☐ Wrap in foil after cooling. Freeze quickly — once the kids come home the bars won't make it to the freezer.

- ☐ Bars may be stored in the baking pan, tightly wrapped. But for extra freshness, wrap individually.

SPICY BANANA BARS

These bar cookies are soft, delicate little cakes. A perfect complement to any platter.

**1 cup mashed bananas
(2 large bananas)**
¾ cup solid shortening
3 eggs
3 cups flour
2¼ cups sugar
1½ tsps. baking powder
¾ tsp. baking soda
¾ tsp. salt
2¼ tsps. cinnamon
¾ tsp. ground cloves
1 cup walnuts (optional)
¾ cup nondairy creamer

WHITE FROSTING
3 Tbsps. hot water
3 cups confectioners' sugar
6 Tbsps. melted margarine

USE: 9 x 13-inch baking pan
YIELDS: 2 dozen squares

Preheat oven to 350°.

Grease 9 x 13-inch baking pan.

Combine bananas, shortening, and eggs in large mixer bowl. Mix dry ingredients and nuts together in separate bowl. Add dry ingredients to banana mixture alternately with the nondairy creamer.

Place dough into a prepared baking pan. Bake for 40 minutes. Cover with frosting while warm. Cool in pan, then cut into 2-inch squares when cool.

WHITE FROSTING: Combine all ingredients in a small mixer bowl and mix until smooth.

APRICOT WALNUT SQUARES

⅔ **cup dried apricots**
½ **cup margarine, softened**
¼ **cup sugar**
1⅓ **cups flour**
1 **cup light brown sugar**
2 **eggs**
½ **cup chopped walnuts**
½ **tsp. baking powder**
½ **tsp. vanilla extract**
Pinch salt
Confectioners' sugar

USE: 8-inch square pan
1½-quart saucepan
YIELDS: 16 squares

Preheat oven to 350°.

Grease 8-inch square pan.

Place apricots in 1½-quart saucepan with water to cover and cook, covered, for 15 minutes. Drain and chop.

In small mixer bowl, beat butter or margarine, sugar, and 1 cup flour until crumbly. Pat dough into pan. Bake 25 minutes.

In same bowl, mix apricots, brown sugar, eggs, walnuts, baking powder, vanilla, salt, and remaining ⅓ cup flour. Pour over baked pastry and bake an additional 25 minutes.

Cool in pan, then cut into 2-inch squares. Sprinkle with confectioners' sugar.

BROWNIES, *moist and rich, live in everyone's childhood memory. Dense and chewy, there is a wide range of flavors to be found in different types of brownies.*

CHOCOLATE-MINT BROWNIES

A moist, rich brownie with a creamy mint-flavored frosting. It will melt in your mouth with each bite.

4 **ounces semisweet baking chocolate**
1 **cup margarine, softened**
4 **eggs**
2 **cups sugar**
2 **tsps. vanilla extract**
1¼ **cups flour**
½ **tsp. salt**
1 **cup chopped walnuts**

MINT FROSTING
1 **pound confectioners' sugar**
½ **cup margarine, softened**
3 **to 4 Tbsps. nondairy creamer**
1 **tsp. peppermint flavor**
Green food coloring

CHOCOLATE GLAZE
1 **4-ounce sweet chocolate bar or**
⅔ **cup chocolate chips or**
2 **ounces semisweet baking chocolate and**
2 **Tbsps. margarine**

9 x 13-inch baking pan
YIELDS: 2 dozen brownies

Preheat oven to 325°.

Grease 9 x 13-inch baking pan.

Melt chocolate and margarine over boiling water on very low flame. Set aside to cool

In a large mixer bowl, beat eggs until light. Beat in sugar and vanilla. Add melted chocolate and margarine and mix well. Fold in flour, salt, and nuts.

Pour into baking pan. Bake for 30 to 35 minutes or until barely set. Set aside to cool. Frost and glaze once cooled, then cut into 2-inch squares.

MINT FROSTING: Beat all frosting ingredients together in a small bowl. Spread on cooled brownies.

CHOCOLATE GLAZE: In the top of double boiler melt chocolate and margarine over boiling water. Drizzle over the frosting.

BUTTERSCOTCH BROWNIES

Margarine and light brown sugar create the butterscotch goodness of these brownies.

¼ cup margarine, softened
½ cup nondairy creamer
2 cups light brown sugar
2 eggs
½ tsp. salt
1½ cups flour
2 tsps. baking powder
1 tsp. vanilla extract
1 cup chopped pecans

USE: 9 x 13-inch baking pan
YIELDS: 2 dozen brownies

Preheat oven to 350°.

Grease a 9 x 13-inch baking pan.

In a large mixer bowl, cream margarine. Add remaining ingredients and mix until thoroughly combined. Spread into pan and bake for 30 to 35 minutes.

Cool in pan, then cut into 2-inch squares.

CAROB NUT BROWNIES

⅔ cup margarine, softened
⅔ cup honey
2 eggs
1 tsp. vanilla extract
1 cup carob powder
1 cup unbleached flour
2 tsps. baking powder
½ tsp. salt
⅓ cup hot water
1 cup chopped walnuts

USE: 8-inch square baking pan
YIELDS: 16 brownies

Preheat oven to 350°.

Lightly grease 8-inch square pan.

In a large mixer bowl, cream margarine and honey and beat in eggs and vanilla. Combine carob powder, flour, baking powder, and salt, and stir into first mixture, adding hot water and nuts. Stir well.

Spread into square baking pan. Bake for 20 to 25 minutes. Cool in pan, then cut into 2-inch squares.

CLASSIC CHOCOLATE BROWNIES

2 cups sugar
4 eggs
⅔ cup margarine, softened
4 ounces semisweet chocolate, melted
2 tsps. vanilla extract
1⅓ cups flour
1 tsp. baking powder
½ tsp. salt
1½ cups chopped walnuts

USE: 9 x 13-inch baking pan
YIELDS: 2 dozen brownies

Preheat oven to 350°.

Grease a 9 x 13-inch baking pan.

In a large bowl combine sugar, eggs, margarine, melted chocolate, and vanilla, and beat until creamy. Add flour, baking powder, and salt, and mix well. Stir in nuts.

Pour into baking pan. Bake for 30 to 35 minutes. Cool in pan, then cut into 2-inch squares.

MARBLED CHOCOLATE-NUT BROWNIES

CHOCOLATE BATTER
½ cup flour
½ tsp. baking powder
¼ tsp. salt
2 squares semisweet
baking chocolate, melted
¾ cup sugar
2 eggs, beaten
2 tsps. apple juice
1 tsp. vanilla extract

WHITE BATTER
½ cup flour
½ tsp. baking powder
¼ tsp. salt
⅓ cup margarine
¾ cup sugar
2 eggs, beaten
2 tsps. apple juice
1 tsp. almond extract
½ cup finely ground walnuts
or almonds
¼ cup wheat germ (optional)

USE: 2 8-inch square
baking pans
YIELDS: 32 brownies

Preheat oven to 300°.

Grease two 8-inch square baking pans.

CHOCOLATE BATTER: In a large mixer bowl, combine flour, baking powder, and salt. Add melted chocolate. Add sugar, eggs, juice, and vanilla, and mix until well combined and smooth.

WHITE BATTER: In a large mixer bowl, sift flour, baking powder, and salt. Add margarine, sugar, eggs, juice, and almond extract. Mix until well combined and smooth. Add ground nuts and wheat germ until well mixed.

Spoon chocolate batter into both pans and then spoon white batter on top of it. Zigzag spoon back and forth across the pan — this will give a marble effect.

Bake about 50 minutes or until sides pull away slightly from pan.

Cool in pan, then cut into 2-inch squares.

PINEAPPLE BROWNIES

¾ cup margarine, softened
1½ cups sugar
3 eggs
1 tsp. vanilla extract
1½ cups flour
1 tsp. baking powder
½ tsp. salt
½ tsp. cinnamon (optional)
1 cup crushed pineapple,
well drained
2 ounces unsweetened
baking chocolate, melted
½ cup chopped walnuts

USE: 9 x 13-inch baking pan
YIELDS: 2 dozen brownies

Preheat oven to 375°.

Grease and flour a 9 x 13-inch pan.

In a large mixer bowl, cream margarine and sugar. Add eggs one at a time, beating well after each addition. Add vanilla, then dry ingredients, mixing thoroughly.

Remove half of batter to a separate bowl and stir in pineapple. Add chocolate and nuts to remaining batter and mix well.

Spread half of chocolate-nut mixture in baking pan. Spread all of the pineapple mixture over the chocolate layer. Drop spoonfuls of remaining chocolate mixture over pineapple layer and spread carefully to cover.

Bake for 35 to 40 minutes. Cool in pan, then cut into 2-inch squares.

CHOCOLATE BROWNIE CAKE

1 cup cocoa
3 cups sugar
2 cups flour
1 tsp. vanilla extract
8 eggs
1 cup oil
2 tsps. baking powder
Pinch of salt
1 cup chopped
walnuts (optional)

USE: 11 x 14-inch baking pan
YIELDS: 3 dozen brownies

Preheat oven to 350°.

Grease and flour an 11 x 14-inch baking pan.

In a large mixer bowl, mix first four ingredients well. Add eggs and oil and mix on low speed. Then add baking powder, salt, and nuts, and mix again.

Pour into pan. Bake for 35 to 45 minutes until cake is set. Cool in pan, then cut into 2-inch squares.

WHOLE-WHEAT BROWNIES

½ cup margarine, softened
1 cup sugar
2 eggs
1 tsp. vanilla extract
¾ cup whole-wheat flour
½ tsp. baking powder
Pinch salt
3 ounces unsweetened
baking chocolate, melted
1 cup
coarsely chopped walnuts

USE: 8-inch square baking pan
YIELDS: 16 brownies

Preheat oven to 350°.

Grease an 8-inch square baking pan.

In a large mixer bowl, cream margarine and sugar well. Beat in eggs and then vanilla. Add dry ingredients separately, then chocolate and nuts. Mix the liquid and dry ingredients together well.

Spread in pan and bake for 20 minutes. Cool in pan then cut into 2-inch squares.

CARAMEL SQUARES

12 ounces chocolate chips
⅓ cup nondairy creamer
2 Tbsps. plus
1 cup margarine, softened
2¼ cups brown sugar
2 eggs
Pinch salt
1 tsp. vanilla extract
2 cups flour

USE: 1½-quart saucepan
9 x 13-inch baking pan
YIELDS: 2 dozen squares

Preheat oven to 350°.

Grease a 9 x 13-inch pan.

In a 1½-quart saucepan melt chocolate chips, nondairy creamer, and 2 tablespoons margarine over a low flame. Set aside.

In a 1½-quart saucepan melt 1 cup margarine and brown sugar. Allow to cool. Combine eggs, salt, vanilla, and flour in a bowl. Add cooled margarine-sugar mixture and beat well.

Pour half of caramel batter into 9 x 13-inch baking pan. Slowly pour chocolate mixture over the batter by making lines. Take a knife and run chocolate through batter to make a marble design. Pour remaining half of batter over the cake.

Bake for 45 minutes or until cake is set and done. Cool in pan and cut into 2-inch squares.

LIGHT 'N DARK WALNUT BROWNIE BARS

CRUST
⅓ cup margarine, softened
⅓ cup light brown sugar
⅞ cup flour
⅔ cup ground walnuts

BATTER
1 cup granulated sugar
½ cup margarine, softened
1 tsp. vanilla extract
2 eggs
1 cup flour
1½ tsps. instant coffee
½ tsp. baking powder
½ tsp. salt
⅔ cup chopped walnuts
1 ounce unsweetened baking chocolate, melted

USE: 9-inch square baking pan
YIELDS: 16 brownies

Preheat oven to 350°.

Grease a 9-inch square baking pan.

CRUST: Mix together crust ingredients in a small bowl and pat into pan.

BATTER: In a large mixer bowl, cream granulated sugar, margarine, and vanilla. Beat in eggs, one at a time. Stir in flour, instant coffee, baking powder, and salt. Stir in walnuts, making sure all ingredients are well combined. Remove half of batter to a separate bowl and stir in melted chocolate, leaving other half of batter plain.

Alternate spoonfuls of light and dark batter over crust dough in pan, and cut with a knife to marble it. Bake for 35 minutes. Cool in pan, then cut into 2-inch squares.

CHERRY-NUT SQUARES

1 cup margarine, softened
1 cup brown sugar
1 egg
1 tsp. vanilla extract
¼ tsp. salt
½ tsp. baking powder
2 cups flour

TOPPING
12 ounces chocolate chips
⅓ cup chopped or diced maraschino cherries
¾ cup sliced almonds

USE: 9 x 13-inch baking pan
YIELDS: 3 dozen squares

Preheat oven to 350°.

Grease 9 x 13-inch baking pan.

In a large mixer bowl, cream margarine and brown sugar thoroughly. Beat in egg, vanilla, salt, and baking powder. Stir in flour, blending thoroughly. Spread in pan.
Bake for 20 minutes or until golden brown.

TOPPING: Immediately upon removing from oven, sprinkle with chocolate chips, spreading with spatula as the chocolate melts.

Pat cherries dry and combine with nuts in a separate bowl and sprinkle evenly over the chocolate. When cool, cut into 3-inch squares or bars.

VARIATION
☐ Instead of almonds, substitute ¾ cup toasted, grated coconut, or chopped brazil nuts or pistachio nuts.

CHOCOLATE CHIP-APRICOT BARS

This bar can be frozen for later use. It is a standout on a platter with other cakes.

1 cup margarine, softened
1½ cups sugar
2 egg yolks
2½ cups flour
1 tsp. vanilla extract
10 ounces apricot jam
1 cup chocolate chips
4 egg whites
½ tsp. salt
2 cups chopped walnuts

USE: 11 x 14-inch baking pan
YIELDS: 3 dozen squares

Preheat oven to 350°.

Grease 11 x 14-inch baking pan.

In a large mixer bowl, cream margarine, ½ cup sugar, and egg yolks. Add flour and vanilla and knead with fingers.

Pat dough onto pan. Bake 15 to 20 minutes until browned.

Remove from oven and spread jam on top. Then sprinkle with chocolate chips.

In a large bowl, beat egg whites and salt until stiff. Gradually add remaining cup sugar. Gently fold in nuts. Carefully spread mixture on top of jam and chocolate chips.

Bake for 25 minutes. Cool in pan, then cut into 2-inch squares.

CHOCOLATE CHIP-PEANUT BARS

2 cups flour
½ cup sugar
½ cup brown sugar
1½ tsps. baking powder
Pinch salt
½ cup solid shortening
1 tsp. vanilla extract
¾ cup nondairy creamer
2 eggs
6 ounces chocolate chips
1 cup diced maraschino cherries
1 cup chopped salted peanuts

FROSTING
2 cups confectioners' sugar
2 Tbsps. margarine
2 to 3 Tbsps. nondairy creamer
½ tsp. vanilla extract

GLAZE
4 ounces semisweet chocolate, melted

USE: 10 x 15-inch jelly-roll pan
Double boiler
YIELDS: 3 dozen squares

Preheat oven to 350°.

Grease a 10 x 15-inch jelly-roll pan.

In a large mixer bowl, mix all batter ingredients except chocolate chips, cherries, and nuts. Blend in mixer at medium speed for 2 minutes. Stir in chocolate chips, cherries, and nuts.

Spread batter on greased jelly-roll pan. Bake for 25 to 30 minutes until lightly browned.

FROSTING: In a small bowl, mix frosting ingredients. Spread over bars while still warm.

GLAZE: Melt chocolate in a double boiler over a low flame. If necessary, add a tablespoon of water to the chocolate. Drizzle over frosting. Cool in pan and cut into 2-inch squares.

CHERRY MACAROON BARS

1 cup flour
½ cup margarine, softened
3 Tbsps. sugar
2 eggs
1 cup sugar
½ cup flour
½ tsp. baking powder
¼ tsp. salt
1 tsp. vanilla extract
¾ cup chopped walnuts
½ cup grated coconut
½ cup maraschino cherries, drained and quartered

USE: 9-inch square baking pan
YIELDS: 9 squares

Preheat oven to 350°.

Grease an 9-inch square pan.

In a large bowl mix flour, margarine, and 3 tablespoons sugar by hand and spread thinly in greased baking pan. Bake for 25 minutes.

Beat eggs. Stir in remaining ingredients and mix well. Spread mixture over hot baked pastry.

Bake for 20 to 25 minutes more. Cool on rack and cut into 3-inch squares.

TU B'SHVAT FRUIT BARS

On Tu B'Shvat we celebrate the birthday of the trees (page 531). It is a custom to eat the fruits ot the land of Israel. This bar is a delightful combination of some of these fruits.

1¾ cups oil
1¾ cups honey
5 eggs
1 Tbsp. cinnamon
4 cups flour
2 cups raisins
2 cups chopped dates
2 cups chopped figs
2 cups chopped walnuts

USE: 2 10 x 15-inch jelly-roll pans
YIELDS: 5 dozen squares

Preheat oven to 350°.

Grease two 10 x 15-inch jelly-roll pans.

In a large mixer bowl, combine all ingredients and mix well. Divide batter in half and spread each half on two jelly-roll pans.

Bake for 20 minutes. Cool in pan, then cut into 2-inch squares.

DATE-NUT BARS

A wholesome bar with an incredibly moist texture.

8 ounces dates, finely chopped
1 cup walnuts, chopped medium fine
1 cup raisins
1 orange rind, grated
1 tsp. cinnamon
1 cup sugar

Preheat oven to 350°.

Place dates and walnuts in medium bowl. Add raisins, grated orange rind, cinnamon, and sugar. Mix in bowl and set aside while preparing batter. This will soften dried fruit.

➤

½ cup margarine, softened
2 eggs
2 cups flour
2 tsps. baking powder
2 Tbsps. orange juice
1 tsp. vanilla extract

USE: 2 baking sheets
YIELDS: 4 loaves

In large mixer bowl, cream margarine and eggs. Add flour and baking powder and combine well. Batter will be stiff. Add orange juice and vanilla and mix again. Then fold chopped date-and-nut mixture into batter.

Divide batter into four portions. Form into four oblong loaves, approximately 10-inches long by 1½ inches wide by ½-inch high. Form loaves directly onto ungreased baking sheet, placing them 3 inches apart.

Bake for 15 to 20 minutes. Cool and cut across the length into 1-inch by 1½-inch bars.

MANDELBROIT FOR A CROWD

Mandelbroit tastes even better aged. Excellent when prepared one week in advance; wrap unsliced cooled loaves in aluminum foil for one week.

1 8-ounce can almond paste, crumbled, or Basic Almond Paste (page 395)
3 cups sugar
1½ tsps. salt
1 cup margarine, softened
1 cup solid shortening
12 eggs
12 cups flour
4 Tbsps. baking powder
1½ Tbsps. vanilla extract
1 Tbsp. almond extract

CHOCOLATE FILLING
1 cup cocoa
½ cup sugar
¼ cup water

FRUIT FILLING
1 cup candied or dried fruit

NUT FILLING
1 cup coarsely chopped walnuts

GLAZE
1 egg, well beaten
Sugar

USE: 3 baking sheets
YIELDS: 6 loaves

Preheat oven to 375°.

Grease three baking sheets.

In a large mixer bowl, combine almond paste, sugar, salt, margarine, shortening, and eggs. Beat until smooth.

Beat in flour, baking powder, and flavorings. Place dough on a floured surface and knead until a smooth ball is formed. Divide dough into three equal pieces, each to be filled with one of the three fillings.

TO FILL: Roll out each piece of dough into a 24 x 6-inch rectangle. Spoon desired filling in a long ribbon down the center of the dough. Wrap dough around filling and shape into a smooth roll. Cut roll into two 12-inch lengths and place on baking sheet about 4 inches apart.

Repeat process with second and third piece of dough.

GLAZE: Brush all six rolls with beaten egg and sprinkle with sugar.

Bake rolls 45 minutes or until richly browned. Cool loaves on racks, and then slice into ½-inch slices, cutting crosswise.

MANDELBROIT

3 eggs
1 cup sugar
½ cup oil
1 tsp. almond extract
1 tsp. vanilla extract
¼ tsp. cinnamon
2 Tbsps. orange juice
Rind of 1 orange, grated
3 cups flour
3 tsps. baking powder
¼ tsp. salt
1½ cups chopped almonds

OPTIONAL FILLINGS
¾ cup chopped candied cherries, or raisins or chocolate chips

USE: Baking sheet
YIELDS: 3 loaves

Preheat oven to 400°.

Grease baking sheet.

In a large mixer bowl, beat eggs, sugar, and oil. Add the almond extract, vanilla, cinnamon, orange juice, and grated orange rind. Mix well.

Sift flour, baking powder, and salt together and add to bowl. Beat until well blended. Fold in chopped nuts and candied fruits, raisins, or chocolate chips, if desired.

Form into three oblong oval mounds on cookie sheet. Bake at 400° for 25 minutes. Remove from oven and slice into ½-inch slices. To make traditional mandelbroit, return slices to oven and toast at 350° for 10 minutes more until lightly brown.

CRUNCHY PEANUT BARS

1 cup sugar
1 cup margarine, softened
¼ cup molasses or honey
1 egg yolk
1 tsp. vanilla extract
2 cups flour
1 cup semisweet chocolate chips

TOPPING
½ cup semisweet chocolate chips
1 cup raisins
1 cup unsalted peanuts
⅓ cup peanut butter

USE: 9 x 13-inch baking pan
2-quart saucepan
YIELDS: 4½ dozen bars

Preheat oven to 350°.

In a large mixer bowl, mix sugar, margarine, molasses or honey, egg yolk, and vanilla with a spoon. Stir in flour and 1 cup chocolate chips.

Press dough into ungreased 9 x 13-inch pan. Bake until golden brown, 25 to 30 minutes.

TOPPING: Mix chocolate chips, raisins, peanuts, and peanut butter in 2-quart saucepan. Heat over medium-low heat, stirring constantly, until chocolate chips are melted. Spread over baked dough.

Refrigerate at least 2 hours before cutting. Cut into 2 x 1-inch bars.

COCONUT MERINGUE SQUARES

8 eggs, separated
1¼ cups sugar
3 Tbsps. cocoa
1½ cups margarine, softened
1 tsp. baking powder
Pinch salt
1 cup flour
8 ounces apricot jam
1 tsp. vanilla extract
1 cup grated coconut

USE: 9 x 13-inch baking pan
YIELDS: 2 dozen squares

Preheat oven to 350°.

In a large mixer bowl, beat egg yolks, ½ cup sugar, and cocoa. Add margarine, baking powder, salt, and flour. Mix well.

Spread into an ungreased 9 x 13-inch baking pan. Bake for 20 to 25 minutes until dough is slightly set. Remove from oven and cool slightly. Spread top of cake with apricot jam.

In a large mixer bowl, beat egg whites until stiff. Add vanilla, remaining ¾ cup sugar, and coconut. Spread over apricot jam. Bake an additional 20 minutes. Cut into 2-inch squares while still warm and continue to cool in pan.

HERMITS

½ cup oil
1 cup sugar
3 cups flour
1 tsp. cinnamon
½ tsp. nutmeg
½ tsp. salt
1 tsp. baking soda
½ cup apple juice or nondairy creamer
½ cup molasses
¾ cup raisins

USE: 10 x 15-inch jelly-roll pan
YIELDS: 2 dozen squares

Preheat oven to 350°.

Grease 10 x 15-inch jelly-roll pan.

In a large mixer bowl, cream oil and sugar. Add remaining ingredients and mix well.

Spread mixture in jelly-roll pan. Bake for 20 to 25 minutes. Cut into squares while still warm. Then cool in pan.

JAM BARS

¾ cup margarine, softened
¾ cup brown sugar
1½ cups flour
¼ tsp. salt
1 Tbsp. baking powder
1½ cups rolled oats
½ cup chopped almonds (optional)
1½ cups jam or preserves

USE: 9 x 13-inch baking pan
YIELDS: 2 dozen squares

Preheat oven to 350°.

Grease a 9 x 13-inch baking pan.

In a large mixer bowl, cream margarine and sugar. Add remaining ingredients except for jam and mix well. Pat three fourths of dough into bottom of baking pan. Spread jam evenly over top of dough. Crumble remaining dough over jam.

Bake for 30 minutes. Cool in pan, then cut into 2-inch squares.

COCONUT CHEWS

¾ cup solid shortening
¾ cup confectioners' sugar
1½ cups flour
2 eggs
1 cup brown sugar
2 Tbsps. flour
1½ tsps. baking powder
Pinch salt
½ tsp. vanilla extract
½ cup chopped walnuts
½ cup flaked coconut

FROSTING
1½ cups confectioners' sugar
2 Tbsps. margarine
3 Tbsps. orange juice
1 tsp. lemon juice

USE: 9 x 13-inch baking pan
YIELDS: 2 dozen squares

Preheat oven to 350°.

In a large mixer bowl, combine first five ingredients and mix until well blended. Place in ungreased 9 x 13-inch baking pan. Bake for 12 to 15 minutes, until set. Remove from oven.

While baking, combine remaining ingredients in a small bowl. Spread over warm pastry and return to oven an additional 20 minutes.

Cool cake in pan before frosting cake.

FROSTING: Combine all frosting ingredients in mixer and mix well. Spread evenly over cooled cake and cut into 2-inch squares.

OATMEAL BARS

1¼ cups whole-wheat flour
1 cup brown sugar,
firmly packed
½ tsp. baking soda
½ tsp. salt
½ cup margarine or
solid shortening
1 tsp. vanilla extract
1 egg
1 cup rolled oats
½ cup flaked
coconut, optional

TOPPING
½ cup chocolate or
carob chips
¼ cup chopped almonds or
sunflower seeds

USE: 9 x 13-inch baking pan
YIELDS: 2 dozen squares

Preheat oven to 375°.

Grease a 9 x 13-inch baking pan.

In a large mixer bowl, combine first seven ingredients. Beat at medium speed until ingredients are well blended (about 1 to 2 minutes with electric mixer). By hand, stir in oats, and flaked coconut, if desired. Press dough into baking pan. Dough will be very thin.

TOPPING: Sprinkle dough with chocolate chips and nuts. Bake for 15 to 20 minutes or until edges are golden brown (center will be soft).

Cool in pan, then cut into 2-inch squares.

VARIATION
□ When combining the first seven ingredients, add 1½ cup peanut butter and/or ½ cup wheat germ.

MERINGUE-TOPPED JAM SQUARES

½ cup margarine, softened
¼ cup sugar
¼ cup brown sugar
2 egg yolks
1 tsp. vanilla extract
1½ cups sifted flour
Pinch salt
½ tsp. baking soda
½ tsp. baking powder

FILLING
¾ cup raspberry jam
1 tsp. lemon juice
Rind of 1 lemon
1 cup chopped walnuts

MERINGUE
2 egg whites
2 Tbsps. sugar

USE: 9 x 13-inch baking pan
YIELDS: 2 dozen squares

Preheat oven to 350°.

Grease a 9 x 13-inch baking pan.

In a large mixer bowl, cream margarine and sugars. Add egg yolks, vanilla, and sifted dry ingredients and combine until smooth. Pat into baking pan. Bake 12 to 15 minutes until light brown. Cool.

FILLING: Mix filling ingredients in a small bowl. Spread over baked dough.

MERINGUE: In a medium bowl, beat egg whites until frothy; add sugar gradually while beating until whites are stiff. Spread over jam and return to oven for 5 minutes to allow meringue to brown.

Cool in pan, then cut into 2-inch squares.

FUDGY OATMEAL BARS

2 cups brown sugar
1 cup margarine, softened
2 eggs
1 tsp. vanilla extract
2½ cups flour
1 tsp. baking soda
3 cups quick-cooking
or regular rolled oats
12 ounces semisweet
chocolate chips
¾ cup apple or
orange juice
2 Tbsps. margarine
1 cup chopped walnuts
1 tsp. vanilla extract

USE: 10 x 15-inch jelly-roll pan
2-quart saucepan
YIELDS: 4½ to 5 dozen bars

Preheat oven to 350°.

Grease a jelly-roll pan.

Mix brown sugar, margarine, eggs, and vanilla in a large mixer bowl. Stir in flour, baking soda, and oats. Reserve one-third of the oatmeal mixture and press remaining mixture into jelly-roll pan.

Heat chocolate chips, juice, and margarine in a 2-quart saucepan over low heat. Stir in nuts and vanilla.

Spread chocolate mixture over oatmeal dough. With rounded teaspoonfuls, spoon remaining oatmeal dough over chocolate.

Bake until golden, 25 to 30 minutes. While still warm, cut into 1 x 2-inch bars. Cool in pan.

POPPY BARS

A delicious bar for all occasions. A delightful addition to our Purim baking, when poppy seeds, mohn, are traditionally used as hamantash fillings.

FILLING
¾ cup poppy seeds
¼ cup whole blanched almonds
½ cup sugar
⅓ cup nondairy creamer
2 Tbsps. margarine
2 tsps. lemon juice
½ tsp. grated lemon rind
¼ tsp. nutmeg

DOUGH
¼ cup whole blanched almonds
1 cup plus 3 Tbsps. flour
½ cup confectioners' sugar
1 tsp. baking powder
½ cup margarine, chilled
1 egg yolk, chilled
¼ tsp. vanilla extract

USE: 8-inch square baking pan
YIELDS: 16 squares

FILLING: Combine poppy seeds and almonds in a blender. Process until almonds are finely chopped. Place in a small saucepan. Add sugar, nondairy creamer, 2 tablespoons of margarine, lemon juice, lemon rind, and nutmeg to poppy seed mixture. Heat over low flame, stirring until mixture boils. Cook 10 minutes until mixture is very thick. Remove from heat and cool.

Preheat oven to 350°.

DOUGH: In a blender chop ¼ cup of almonds very fine. In a medium mixer bowl, mix flour, confectioners' sugar, and baking powder. Cut in remaining ¼ cup of chilled margarine with two knives or pastry blender until mixture resembles coarse crumbs. Stir in chopped almonds.

Combine egg yolk and vanilla in a small mixer bowl and beat with a fork. Add to crumb mixture and lightly stir with a fork until egg is well distributed but mixture is still crumbly. Divide mixture in half. Press half into a ball and knead a few times on a lightly floured surface. Press into ungreased 8-inch square baking pan and pat in an even layer on bottom of pan.

Spoon cooled poppy seed mixture over layer of cookie mixture. Spread in an even layer. Sprinkle remaining coarse crumb mixture over poppy seed filling.

Bake for 20 to 25 minutes or until topping just begins to turn light brown. Cool in pan, then cut into 2-inch squares.

RASPBERRY SNOW BARS

¾ cup solid shortening
¼ cup sugar
¼ tsp. salt
¼ tsp. almond extract
2 egg yolks
1½ cups sifted flour

TOPPING
1 cup raspberry preserves
2 egg whites
½ cup flaked coconut
½ cup sugar

USE 9 x 13-inch baking pan
YIELDS: 2 dozen bars

Preheat oven to 350°.

Cream shortening, sugar, and salt until fluffy. Blend in almond extract and egg yolks. Mix in flour until mixture is doughy. Pat dough into an ungreased 9 x 13-inch baking pan. Bake for 15 minutes.

TOPPING: Spread preserves over hot baked pastry. In small mixer bowl, beat egg whites until stiff and add coconut and sugar. Spread over preserves.

Bake an additional 25 minutes. Cool in pan, then cut into 2-inch bars.

VIENNESE RASPBERRY-ALMOND BARS

⅓ **cup margarine**
¼ **cup sugar**
1 **egg yolk**
½ **tsp. vanilla extract**
1 **cup flour**
½ **tsp. baking powder**
1 **Tbsp. orange juice**

**RASPBERRY-ALMOND
FILLING**
¼ **cup seedless
raspberry preserves**
¾ **cup ground almonds**
⅔ **cup sugar**
½ **tsp. salt**
1 **egg plus 1 egg white**
½ **tsp. vanilla extract**
¼ **tsp. almond extract**

ICING
1½ **ounces semisweet
baking chocolate**
1 **Tbsp. margarine**
½ **cup confectioners' sugar**
½ **tsp. vanilla extract**
2 **to 3 tsps. hot water**

USE: 8-inch square baking pan
Double boiler
YIELDS: 2 dozen bars

Preheat oven to 375°.

Grease an 8-inch square pan.

In a large mixer bowl, cream margarine and sugar. Add egg yolk and vanilla. Add flour and baking powder and 1 tablespoon orange juice and mix. Pat into baking pan. Bake for 10 minutes.

RASPBERRY-ALMOND FILLING: Spread jam over hot cookie pastry.

In a small mixer bowl, mix the remainder of filling ingredients together. Spread almond filling over jam. Bake another 20 to 25 minutes. Cool and frost.

ICING: Melt chocolate and margarine in the top of a double boiler. Blend in sugar and vanilla and stir in hot water. Spread over filling. Allow to cool 30 minutes before cutting into bars.

NOTE: This recipe can easily be doubled and prepared in a 9 x 13-inch pan. Prepare as above.

YUMMY BARS

¾ **cup solid shortening**
2 **cups minus 2 Tbsps. flour**
⅓ **cup brown sugar**
1 **egg plus 1 egg yolk**

TOPPING
2 **eggs plus 1 egg white**
Pinch salt
2¼ **cups brown sugar**
1½ **cups flaked coconut**
¾ **cup chopped walnuts**
1 **tsp. vanilla extract**

USE: 9 x 13-inch baking pan
YIELDS: 2 dozen squares

Preheat oven to 350°.

Grease a 9 x 13-inch pan.

In a large mixer bowl, cut shortening into flour and mix with brown sugar and egg plus egg yolk, by hand or mixer until crumbly. Pat into 9 x 13-inch baking pan.

TOPPING: In a large mixer bowl, mix 2 eggs plus egg white, salt, brown sugar, coconut, chopped walnuts and vanilla. Spread over dough in pan.

Bake for 45 minutes. Cool in pan, then cut into 2 x 1-inch bars.

Desserts and Confections

Pies
Desserts
Frozen Pareve Specialties
Confections

Dessert is often the course that inspires us to our greatest culinary heights and creativity. Homemade ice cream, fresh fruit sorbet, or light and airy souffles enliven any menu plan. Fruit salad and cobblers are good choices for everyday nutritious desserts, but don't overlook the extravagant and exotic such as our unique recipe for kosher *quindim*, a rich coconut pudding from Brazil.

Fresh fruits in season are always good for a low-calorie sweet. Go for combinations of color as well as taste and texture. Homemade *pareve* ice creams can be made with a variety of delicious ingredients and may be enjoyed after a meat meal. They are easily made in advance. Many ice creams do not need any other equipment than your freezer compartment.

Homemade confections are a special treat. Candy making requires some special equipment as well as practice to develop the touch, but once acquired the results are memorable.

Pies

"As American as Apple Pie" — Perhaps there is nothing so intrinsically American as a pie. European strudels and tortes are elegant desserts. But America has the bounty of its fruit reflected in the variety of its pies. Blueberry, apple, rhubarb, — what would summer and fall be without fruit pies from our local produce?

Make it a deep-dish pie, add a cream base, lattice the top; add a fruit glaze, but a pie is always a pie.

MAKING A PERFECT PIE SHELL/CRUST

- ☐ The basic key to successful pie making is keeping the crust crisp without letting the filling make it soggy.

- ☐ A flaky tender crust is the goal. One must be exact with the ingredients; too much flour toughens the dough; too much liquid makes it soggy, and too much shortening produces a greasy crumbly effect.

- ☐ Mix quickly; overmixing causes crumbling. Chill dough before rolling for easier handling and to prevent shrinkage during baking.

- ☐ The dough should be rolled from the center out. Lift the rolling pin, rather than pushing back and forth. Use a roller stocking to prevent sticking and eliminate the need for extra flour.

- ☐ To bake an unfilled shell: Prick with a fork and weight the bottom of the shell with beans over wax paper to ensure even baking.

- ☐ Try basic pies with a variety of pie crusts — whole-wheat, graham cracker, etc.

PIE CRUSTS

Pie Crusts can be made with a variety of flours and shortenings. There are crumb and sesame seed crusts. Mix and match pie crusts and fillings. Often the pie crust is prebaked to avoid sogginess. To make a deep-dish pie shell, roll out pastry thinner.

PERFECT PIE CRUST

4 cups flour
1 Tbsp. sugar
2 tsps. salt
1¾ cups shortening
½ cup water
1 Tbsp. vinegar
1 large egg

USE: 9-inch pie plate
YIELDS: 4 shells or
2 two-crust pie shells

UNBAKED PIE SHELLS: In a large bowl mix flour with sugar and salt. Cut in shortening with a pastry blender or two knives until crumbly. In a small bowl, beat together the water, vinegar, and egg. Combine both mixtures and stir with fork until moistened. Divide into four portions. Shape each portion into a ball and chill for 30 minutes.

Roll out each on a lightly floured board, place in a 9-inch pie plate and prick dough. Or place two crusts in 9-inch pie plate and use two crusts to cover.

PREBAKED PIE SHELLS: Preheat oven to 450°. Prick shell with a fork and weight the bottom with a sheet of wax paper topped with dried beans. Bake 10 to 15 minutes. Cool.

DECORATIVE PIE CRUST TOPS — ILLUSTRATED

Prepare recipe for a two-crust pie, or a double one-crust recipe. Enhance the presentation of your pie with these simple variations for decorating the top crust.

1 VENTS — for the steam to escape while baking make slashes with a sharp knife.

2 LATTICE — Roll top crust into a 12-inch circle and cut it into strips. Place strips an inch apart across pie; weave in strips at right angle to create a lattice effect.

3 DIAMOND LATTICE — Attach the cross strips on the diagonal to create a diamond effect.

4 TINED EDGING — Press the floured tines of a fork into the pastry at the rim all around the edge.

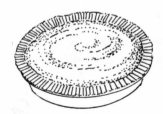

5 FLUTED — Leave a one-inch overhang on top crust. Fold the overhang to make a stand-up edge. Pinch the pastry with the right thumb and index finger. Repeat it every inch. Leave points rounded or pinch again to sharpen.

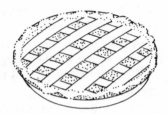

BASIC PIE CRUSTS

9-INCH ONE-CRUST PIE SHELL

1¼ cups sifted flour

½ tsp. salt

6⅓ Tbsps. shortening

3 to 4 Tbsps. ice water

UNBAKED PIE SHELLS: Have all ingredients and utensils cold. Sift the flour and salt into a mixer bowl. Cut in half of the shortening with a pastry blender or two knives until crumbly — shortening should be covered with flour. Cut in the remaining shortening until the size of large peas. Sprinkle 1 tablespoon of water on a small section of the flour mixture. With a fork, lightly mix this portion until it is evenly moistened. Repeat until all flour is moistened. Use as little water as possible. When all water has been added, lightly gather the dough into a ball. Press very gently into a pie plate.

►

8-INCH TWO-CRUST PIE SHELL

2 cups sifted flour
½ tsp. salt
¾ cup shortening
4 to 5 Tbsps. ice water

9-INCH TWO-CRUST PIE SHELL

2½ cups sifted flour
1 tsp. salt
¾ cup shortening
5 to 6 Tbsps. ice water

For two-crust pies, divide ball of dough in half. Roll out first half to form a circle a little larger than pie plate. Roll out second half to place over pie and filling.

PREBAKED PIE SHELLS: Preheat oven to 450°. Prick shell with a fork and weight the bottom with a sheet of wax paper topped with dried beans. Bake 10 to 15 minutes. Cool.

BASIC CRUMB CRUST

This recipe makes a 9-inch pie shell or 8-inch square.

2 cups flour
2 tsps. baking powder
¾ cup sugar
Pinch salt
½ cup margarine, softened
1 egg, beaten
1 tsp. vanilla extract
Confectioners' sugar

USE: 9-inch pie plate or 8-inch square baking pan
YIELDS: 1 pie shell

Preheat oven to 350°.

Grease a 9-inch pie plate or an 8-inch square baking pan.

In a large bowl combine flour, baking powder, sugar, and salt. Cut in margarine. Blend with two forks or a pastry blender with egg and vanilla until crumbly.

Press ⅔ of the dough firmly on bottom of pan. Fill with desired filling. Cover with remaining crumbs of dough sprinkled like a streusel topping. Bake for 45 to 60 minutes. Sprinkle top with confectioners' sugar before serving.

SESAME PIE SHELL

This recipe makes a 9-inch pie shell.

1 cup flour
¼ cup sesame seeds
½ tsp. salt
¼ cup plus 2 tsps. margarine
2 to 3 Tbsps. cold orange juice

USE: 9-inch pie plate
YIELDS: 1 pie shell

UNBAKED PIE SHELL: In a medium mixer bowl, with a fork, mix together flour, sesame seeds, and salt. With pastry blender or two knives, cut margarine into flour until mixture resembles coarse crumbs. Sprinkle orange juice, a tablespoon at a time, over flour mixture, mixing lightly with a fork after each addition until pastry is just moist enough to hold together. Press on bottom and sides of 9-inch pie plate. Pinch to form a high fluted edge and set aside until ready to fill.

PREBAKED PIE SHELL: Preheat oven to 425°. Prick shell with a fork and weight the bottom with a sheet of wax paper topped with dried beans. Bake 10 to 15 minutes. Cool.

WHOLE-WHEAT PIE CRUST

This recipe, made with no sugar and whole-wheat pastry flour, is a tasty, wholesome alternative to the standard pie crust.

**2 cups whole-wheat
pastry flour
Pinch salt
¼ tsp. baking powder
½ cup margarine, softened
3 to 4 Tbsps.
cold orange juice**

USE: 9-inch pie plate
YIELDS: 1 pie shell

UNBAKED PIE SHELL: Combine flour, salt, and baking powder in a mixer bowl. Cut in margarine with a pastry blender or two forks until mixture resembles coarse crumbs. Add the cold juice a tablespoon at a time, mixing with a fork until the pastry is moist enough to hold together.

Divide dough in half. Press dough on bottom and sides of 9-inch pie plate. Roll out second half to place over pie and filling.

PREBAKED PIE SHELL: Preheat oven to 425°. Prick shell with a fork and weight the bottom with a sheet of wax paper topped with dried beans. Bake 10 to 15 minutes. Cool.

PIES

ALL AMERICAN APPLE PIE

**1 unbaked 9-inch
two-crust pie shell
(Pie Crusts, page 445)**

**FILLING
¾ to 1 cup sugar
2 Tbsps. flour
½ tsp. cinnamon
Pinch salt
⅛ tsp. nutmeg (optional)
6 to 7 cups peeled
and sliced apples
2 Tbsps. margarine,
cut in pieces**

USE: 9-inch pie plate
YIELDS: 1 pie

Prepare pie crust of your choice.

Preheat oven to 425°.

In a large bowl combine sugar, flour, cinnamon, salt, and nutmeg. Toss apples with sugar mixture. Spoon apple mixture into pie shell. Dot with bits of margarine.

Place top crust over pie and flute edges of pastry. Cut several vents to let steam escape. Bake for 50 minutes or until crust is browned and apples are tender. Cool.

VARIATIONS
☐ Roll out an extra piece of dough and cut in shape of an apple and a leaf. Attach to pie crust with a little water.

☐ Brush top crust with water and sprinkle with granulated sugar before baking.

APPLE BETTY PIE

**4 cups peeled
and sliced apples
¼ cup orange juice**

Preheat oven to 375°.

Put apples into greased 9-inch pie plate. Sprinkle with orange juice.

▶

CRUMB TOPPING
¼ tsp. salt
1 cup sugar
¾ cup flour
½ tsp. cinnamon
¼ tsp. nutmeg
½ cup margarine, softened

USE: 9-inch pie plate
YIELDS: 1 pie

CRUMB TOPPING: Combine salt, sugar, flour, cinnamon, and nutmeg. Cut in margarine. Mix until mixture is crumbly.

Cover apples with crumb topping. Bake for 45 minutes to 1 hour. Cool.

BLUEBERRY-PEACH PIE

1 unbaked 9-inch
two-crust deep dish
pie shell
(Pie Crusts, page 445)

FILLING
2 cups fresh or
frozen blueberries
4 medium-size ripe peaches,
peeled, pitted and cubed
2 Tbsps. whole-wheat flour
2 Tbsps. brown sugar
Juice of ½ lemon
1 Tbsp. margarine,
cut into pieces

USE: 9-inch deep-dish
pie plate
YIELDS: 1 deep-dish pie

Prepare pie crust of your choice.

Preheat oven to 350°.

FILLING: In a large bowl gently mix blueberries, peaches, flour, sugar, and lemon juice. Pour into pie shell. Dab bits of margarine over the top.

Cover pie with top crust and make slits throughout top; or slice crust into strips and arrange over top of pie in a lattice pattern. Place pie plate on a baking sheet and bake for 45 minutes or until golden brown. The baking sheet will catch any spills. Cool.

VARIATION
☐ Use nectarines, plums, or additional peaches instead of blueberries.

NOTE: If using store-bought shells, they must be marked "deep-dish".

BLUEBERRY PIE

PASTRY SHELL
3½ cups flour
1¼ cups sugar
3 eggs
1 cup margarine, softened
1 Tbsp. baking powder
¼ cup orange juice

FILLING
2 pints fresh blueberries
¼ cup flour
⅓ cup sugar

USE: 9 x 13-inch baking pan
YIELDS: 1 pie

Preheat oven to 375°.

PASTRY SHELL: Combine flour, sugar, eggs, margarine, baking powder, and orange juice in a large mixer bowl, and mix until smooth. With floured hand, pat ⅔ of the dough into the bottom of a 9 x 13-inch baking pan.

FILLING: Gently mix blueberries with flour and sugar in a large bowl. Pour over crust in baking pan.

Roll out remaining dough and cover filling. Bake for 45 minutes or until done. Cool.

CHOCOLATE-ALMOND ANGEL PIE

MERINGUE SHELL
3 egg whites
Pinch of salt
¼ tsp. lemon juice
½ tsp. vanilla extract
¾ cup sugar
¼ cup thinly sliced almonds

FILLING
¾ cup semisweet chocolate chips or one 4-ounce bar of semisweet chocolate, broken up
Pinch of salt
1 tsp. vanilla extract
¼ cup hot water
1 cup nondairy dessert topping

½ cup nondairy dessert topping

USE: 9-inch pie plate
Double boiler
YIELDS: 1 pie

Preheat oven to 250°.

MERINGUE SHELL: In large mixer bowl, combine egg whites, salt, lemon juice, and vanilla. Beat until soft peaks form. Gradually beat in sugar until it is completely dissolved. Spread mixture over bottom and sides of a very well-greased 9-inch pie plate. Build up sides. Sprinkle almonds over bottom of pie shell. Bake for 1 hour. Cool, then refrigerate before serving.

FILLING: Melt chocolate in a double boiler over hot (not boiling) water. Add salt, vanilla, and hot water. Cook, stirring until well blended and smooth. Cool.

Whip 1 cup dessert topping. Fold chocolate mixture into whipped topping. If desired, sweeten with a little confectioners' sugar.

Spoon mixture into shell. Chill for at least 4 hours.

Just before serving, whip ½ cup nondairy dessert topping and use to top pie.

CHOCOLATE CREAM PIE

GRAHAM CRACKER CRUST
9 double graham crackers
⅓ cup margarine, softened
3 Tbsps. sugar

FILLING
3 ounces unsweetened baking chocolate,
½ cup margarine, softened
3 eggs
1½ cups confectioners' sugar
1 cup whipped nondairy dessert topping

USE: 8-inch square baking pan
Double boiler
YIELDS: 1 pie

GRAHAM CRACKER CRUST: Crush graham crackers in blender until finely ground. Place in a large bowl. Add margarine and combine well. Press firmly into pan on sides and bottom.

FILLING: In the top of a double boiler melt chocolate. In a large bowl mix melted chocolate into ½ cup softened margarine, eggs, and sugar. Beat at high speed until smooth. Spoon over crumb crust.

Put the pie in the freezer until the chocolate is slightly hard. Then remove and spread the whipped dessert topping over chocolate.

Keep pie refrigerated.

CHOCOLATE BROWNIE PIE

1 unbaked 9-inch pie shell (Pie Crusts, page 445)

FILLING
2 Tbsps. margarine
2 ounces unsweetened baking chocolate
3 eggs
½ cup sugar
¾ cup light corn syrup
1 tsp. vanilla extract
¾ cup broken pecans

USE: 1-quart saucepan
9-inch pie plate
YIELDS: 1 pie

Prepare pie crust of your choice.

Preheat oven to 375°.

FILLING: In a 1-quart saucepan, melt margarine and chocolate over low heat. Pour into medium-sized bowl of mixer. Cool slightly. Add eggs, sugar, and corn syrup. Beat at medium speed until well blended. Stir in vanilla and pecans, and pour mixture into pie shell. Bake for 35 to 40 minutes. Cool, then refrigerate before serving.

VARIATION
☐ Substitute walnuts or almonds for pecans.

CUSTARD-CREAM PIE

1 baked 8-inch pie shell (Pie Crusts, page 445)

FILLING
½ cup sugar
3 Tbsps. flour
1 Tbsp. cornstarch
Pinch of salt
1½ cups nondairy creamer
3 egg yolks, slightly beaten
1 Tbsp. margarine
1 tsp. vanilla extract

1 container nondairy dessert topping, whipped

USE: 8-inch pie plate
Double boiler
YIELDS: 1 pie

Prepare pie crust of your choice. Bake according to instructions and cool.

Combine sugar, flour, cornstarch, and salt in top of double boiler. Mix well. Gradually stir in nondairy creamer and then egg yolks. Add margarine. Place over boiling water with top pot touching water. Cook, stirring constantly, until smooth and thick, about 7 minutes. Remove from heat and stir in vanilla. Pour into pie shell. Chill. When cool, top with whipped topping.

VARIATIONS
☐ **Banana Cream Pie:** Slice 2 ripe bananas into pie shell before filling with custard.

☐ **Chocolate Frosted Cream Pie:** Mix ½ cup sifted confectioners' sugar with 2 Tbsps. nondairy creamer until smooth. Blend in 1 ounce melted baking chocolate and 2 tablespoons melted margarine. Spread over cooled pie. Garnish with dollops of whipped topping.

☐ **Butterscotch Cream Pie:** Substitute ¾ cup brown sugar for the granulated sugar and add 1 tablespoon margarine.

☐ **Coconut Cream Pie:** Add 1 cup flaked coconut to the filling mixture before pouring into pie shell. Toast some extra coconut and sprinkle it over the whipped topping.

☐ **Maple-Nut Cream Pie:** When pie has cooled, drizzle a little maple-flavored syrup over it. Top with whipped topping and sprinkle with pecans, walnuts, or almonds.

☐ **Chocolate Cream Pie:** When making filling mixture, add 1½ ounces melted baking chocolate. Increase sugar to ¾ cup. Garnish with chocolate curls over whipped topping.

CUSTARD PIE

PASTRY SHELL
1½ cups flour

2 tsps. sugar

Pinch of salt

10 Tbsps. very cold margarine, cut up into small pieces

1 egg yolk

3 Tbsps. ice water

FILLING
½ cup margarine

1 Tbsp. apple-cider vinegar

3 eggs

1½ cups sugar or ¾ cup honey

1 tsp. vanilla extract

1 Tbsp. lemon juice

USE: 9-inch pie plate
1-quart saucepan
YIELDS: 1 pie

PASTRY SHELL: Mix flour, sugar, salt, and margarine in blender. Pour flour mixture into bowl, add egg yolk. Gradually add water — just enough so that the dough comes away from sides of bowl. Shape dough into a ball. Pat into 9-inch pie plate. Put in refrigerator to chill.

Preheat oven to 350°.

FILLING: In a 1-quart saucepan, melt margarine with vinegar. In a medium mixer bowl mix eggs and honey or sugar, beating until mixture is pale. Gradually add margarine mixture, then stir in vanilla.

Pour mixture into chilled pie shell. Bake for 30 to 40 minutes, until knife inserted comes out clean. Cool thoroughly and refrigerate before serving.

LEMON MERINGUE PIE

1 baked 9-inch pie shell, (Pie Crusts, page 445)

FILLING
1½ cups sugar

⅛ tsp. salt

½ cup cornstarch

1 teaspoon grated lemon rind (optional)

2 cups boiling water

3 egg yolks

½ cup lemon juice

2 tsps. margarine

MERINGUE
¼ tsp. salt

3 egg whites

¼ tsp. baking powder (optional)

6 Tbsps. sugar

1 tsp. vanilla extract or lemon juice

USE: 9-inch pie plate
2-quart saucepan
YIELDS: 1 pie

Prepare pie crust of your choice. Bake according to instructions and cool.

FILLING: In a 2-quart saucepan mix sugar, salt, cornstarch, and lemon rind. Add water and stir until well blended. Cook over very low flame for 5 to 7 minutes, stirring constantly and making sure that no lumps form. Beat egg yolks and add 2 tablespoons of sugar mixture to egg yolks. Mix well, then pour eggs into saucepan. Stir in well over low heat. Add lemon juice and margarine and cook until thick. Remove from heat and cool slightly. Pour into pie shell.

MERINGUE: Add salt to egg whites and beat until foamy. Add baking powder and beat until stiff. Gradually add sugar 1 tablespoon at a time. Add vanilla and continue beating until sugar is well blended and mixture can be heaped.

Preheat oven to 325°.

Completely cover pie with meringue, making sure it touches pie crust all around so that meringue will not shrink away. It should have peaks on top.

Bake for 15 minutes or until golden brown. Cool thoroughly and refrigerate before serving.

LEMON-SLICE PIE

**1 unbaked
9- or 10-inch pie shell
(Pie Crusts, page 445)**

**FILLING
1 cup sugar
3 Tbsps. flour
3 eggs
1 cup light corn syrup
¼ cup melted margarine
2 tsps. grated lemon rind
3 Tbsps. lemon juice
1 lemon, peeled
and thinly sliced**

USE: 9- or 10-inch pie plate
YIELDS: 1 pie

Prepare pie crust of your choice.

Preheat oven to 375°.

FILLING: Mix sugar and flour in large bowl of mixer. Add eggs, corn syrup, and margarine. Beat until well blended. Stir in rind and juice. Pour into pie shell. Arrange lemon slices on top in a decorative design.

Bake for 45 minutes or until center is almost set but soft. Cool thoroughly and refrigerate before serving.

PAVLOVA

A favorite Australian dessert.

**MERINGUE
4 egg whites
Good pinch of salt
1½ cups sugar
1 rounded Tbsp. cornstarch
1 tsp. vanilla extract
1 tsp. vinegar**

**FILLING
4 egg yolks
½ cup sugar
2 Tbsps. cornstarch
1 20-ounce can crushed
pineapple, drained**

**1 container nondairy
dessert topping, whipped
1 quart strawberries,
washed, hulled, and dried**

USE: 2-quart saucepan
Pizza tray
YIELDS: 1 pie

Preheat oven to 400°.

MERINGUE: In a large mixer bowl beat egg whites and salt on maximum speed until stiff. Gradually add sugar, about a tablespoon at a time. Quickly add cornstarch, vanilla, and vinegar, and turn beaters off.

On a pizza tray lined with greased foil, make a flat circle with half of the mixture, then heap the other half around the edge to leave a hollow for filling. Place on bottom shelf of oven. Turn down to 200° as soon as Pavlova is in. Bake for 1½ hours. Remove from oven and cool thoroughly.

FILLING: Cook egg yolks, sugar, cornstarch, and crushed pineapple in a 2-quart saucepan over a low flame until thickened. Remove from flame and cool.

Fill cooled Pavlova with pineapple mixture. Top with whipped topping and strawberries. Refrigerate before serving.

CRANBERRY PIE

This easy-to-make pie is a cranberry lover's dream.

1 unbaked 9-inch two-crust deep-dish pie shell (Pie Crusts, page 445)

FILLING
4 cups cranberries
⅔ cup orange juice
1⅓ cups light brown sugar

USE: 3-quart saucepan
9-inch deep dish pie plate
YIELDS: 1 deep-dish pie

Prepare pie crust of your choice.

Preheat oven to 450°.

FILLING: Boil cranberries with orange juice in a 3-quart saucepan 3 to 5 minutes. Stir in brown sugar. Cool slightly and pour into pie shell. Lattice top with extra dough. Chill 30 minutes. Bake at 450° for 25 minutes. Lower heat to 375° and bake 15 minutes more.

NOTE: If using store-bought shells, they must be marked "deep-dish."

SOUTHERN PEANUT BUTTER PIE

1 unbaked 9-inch pie shell (Pie Crusts, page 445)

FILLING
⅔ cup sugar
1 cup dark or light corn syrup
⅓ cup creamy peanut butter
3 eggs
1 cup chopped, salted peanuts

USE: 9-inch pie plate
YIELDS: 1 pie

Prepare pie crust of your choice.

Preheat oven to 375°.

In a large mixer bowl beat sugar, corn syrup, peanut butter, and eggs. Stir in peanuts. Pour into pie shell. Bake for 40 to 50 minutes or until crust is golden brown. Cool thoroughly and refrigerate before serving.

PECAN PIE

This all-American favorite is a treat anytime.

1 unbaked 9-inch pie shell (Pie Crusts, page 445)

FILLING
3 eggs, lightly beaten
1 cup dark corn syrup
½ cup sugar
2 Tbsps. margarine, melted
1 tsp. vanilla extract
1 cup shelled pecans

USE: 9-inch pie plate
YIELDS: 1 pie

Prepare pie crust of your choice.

Preheat oven to 400°.

FILLING: In a large bowl mix by hand eggs, corn syrup, sugar, margarine, vanilla, and pecans. Pour into unbaked pie shell. Bake at 400° for 15 minutes and then at 350° for 35 to 40 minutes. Cool.

STRAWBERRY-RHUBARB PIE

**1 unbaked 8-inch
two-crust pie shell
(Pie Crusts, page 445)**

**FILLING
2 eggs
1 cup sliced strawberries
3 Tbsps. flour
2 tsps. cinnamon
2 cups sliced rhubarb
1 cup sugar
½ tsp. salt**

USE: 8-inch pie plate
YIELDS: 1 pie

Prepare pie crust of your choice.

Preheat oven to 425°.

FILLING: In a large bowl beat eggs with fork and add strawberries, flour, cinnamon, rhubarb, sugar, and salt, and mix well. Pour into pie shell. Top with second crust and flute edges together. Bake for 40 minutes. Cool.

TOFU "CHEESE" PIE

The crust used here is an excellent substitute for Graham Cracker Crust.

**WHOLE-WHEAT CRUST
6 Tbsps. oil
1 cup whole-wheat flour
3 Tbsps. brown sugar
¼ cup shredded cocunut
optional**

**FILLING
1½ pounds soft tofu
½ cup honey
3 Tbsps. lemon juice
¼ cup corn or salad oil
¼ cup water
1 Tbsp. vanilla extract
¼ tsp. salt
½ cup shredded coconut
optional**

USE: 10-inch spring-form pan
YIELDS: 1 pie

Preheat oven to 350°.

WHOLE-WHEAT CRUST: Mix oil, flour, and sugar together in a medium bowl. Add coconut, if desired. Press mixture into bottom of a 10-inch spring-form pan. Bake for 5 to 10 minutes, until lightly browned.

FILLING: Blend tofu, honey, lemon juice, oil, water, vanilla, and salt in food processor until smooth. Pour into pie crust and bake for 40 to 45 minutes until top is golden and pie is firm. Cool.

If desired, add coconut to tofu mixture before baking.

VARIATION
□ Use Graham Cracker Crust (page 469) and press into the bottom of a greased 10-inch spring form pan.

TOFU FRUIT PIE

1 baked 9-inch pie shell
(Pie Crusts, page 445)

FILLING
1½ cups cooked apples,
or fruit compote
or peaches
1 pound soft tofu
2 eggs
1 Tbsp. oil
⅓ cup maple syrup or
honey
2 tsps. vanilla extract

USE: 9-inch pie plate
YIELDS: 1 pie

Prepare pie crust of your choice.

Preheat oven to 325°.

FILLING: Place fruit in bottom of pie shell. Set aside. In a food processor or blender, combine tofu, eggs, oil, syrup, and vanilla. Blend well. Pour over the fruit.

Bake pie for 45 minutes or until set.

VARIATIONS
☐ For crustless pie, grease pie plate well and proceed as above.

☐ Pie can be made without the fruit. Just pour tofu mixture into the crust and bake as above.

☐ Use 1½ cups cooked mashed sweet potato instead of fruit.

DELUXE WALNUT PIE

1 unbaked 9-inch pie shell
(Pie Crusts, page 445)

FILLING
½ cup brown sugar
1 Tbsp. flour
1½ cups light corn syrup
3 Tbsps. margarine
3 eggs
1½ tsps. vanilla extract
1 cup large walnut pieces

USE: 1-quart saucepan
9-inch pie plate
YIELDS: 1 pie

Prepare pie crust of your choice.

Preheat oven to 375°.

FILLING: Mix sugar and flour in 1-quart pan. Add corn syrup and margarine and heat until margarine is just melted. Beat eggs and vanilla in a large bowl. Stir in sugar mixture. Pour into pie shell and sprinkle the walnuts over the top.

Bake for 45 minutes until mixture is set in center. Cool.

Desserts

FRUIT DESSERTS

Fruit desserts are always welcome at the end of a filling meal. They are refreshing and low in calories. Compote, a medley of fruits simmered together, can be made with almost any combination of fruits. Add dried fruit, lemon, lime, or grate a carrot or an apple in for taste. Fresh fruit salad, using fruits as they are available, is both economical and healthful. It has great eye appeal and tremendous variety.

AMBROSIA

3 MacIntosh apples, unpeeled
3 oranges
3 Bartlett pears, unpeeled
2 bananas
½ cup sweet red wine
½ grated coconut

USE: Large bowl
YIELDS: 10 servings

Peel and core apples and cut into thin slices. Peel oranges and pull off outside membrane. Slice crosswise into very thin slices. Peel and core pears and cut into thin slices. Slice bananas.

In a large bowl, layer fruits, ending with oranges. Pour wine over fruit and chill for several hours. When ready to serve top with coconut.

VARIATION
□ In the summer substitute fresh fruit as available, such as peaches, plums, nectarines, or apricots.

APPLE BROWN BETTY

4 cups small (½-inch) fresh white bread cubes
½ cup margarine, melted
½ tsp. cinnamon
¾ cup dark brown sugar, firmly packed
4 cups sliced tart apples

HARD SAUCE
¼ cup margarine
1½ cups confectioners' sugar
1 tsp. vanilla extract
½ tsp. rum, orange or lemon extract
Nutmeg to taste (optional)

USE: 2-quart casserole
YIELDS: 4 to 6 servings

Preheat oven to 375°.

Grease a 2-quart casserole.

In a large bowl combine bread cubes, margarine, cinnamon, and brown sugar. Place one half of bread cubes into casserole, cover with apple slices. Top with remaining bread cubes.

Bake for 50 to 60 minutes or until apples are tender. If crust darkens too quickly, cover loosely with foil. Serve warm, spooned into dessert dishes, topped with Hard Sauce. The sauce will melt on top.

HARD SAUCE: In a small bowl, cream margarine. Gradually add sugar and flavorings.

VARIATION
□ Substitute challah or soft whole-wheat bread for white bread.

OATMEAL APPLE CRISP

1½ pounds Cortland apples
¾ cup flour
¾ cup dark brown sugar
½ tsp. cinnamon
½ tsp. ginger
¾ cup margarine, softened
¾ cup rolled oats
½ cup chopped walnuts

USE: 8 x 8-inch baking pan
YIELDS: 6 to 8 servings

Preheat oven to 350°.

Grease an 8 x 8-inch baking pan.

Peel, core, and slice apples; place in pan. Mix flour, brown sugar, cinnamon, and ginger in a bowl. Mix in margarine until coarse crumbs form. Stir in oats and walnuts. Sprinkle over apples.

Bake for 35 minutes until apples are tender and crumb topping is crisp. Serve warm or cool.

NOTE: Recipe can easily be doubled. Bake in a 9 x 13-inch pan.

PARTY APPLES

Apples coated with ground nuts, baked and topped with a strawberry sauce make an elegant presentation.

10 Cortland apples
2 cups ground almonds
¼ cup sugar
2 egg whites, lightly beaten

STRAWBERRY SAUCE
1 pint strawberries
½ cup confectioners' sugar
2 Tbsps. cherry liqueur

USE: 9 x 13 baking dish
YIELDS: 10 servings

Preheat oven to 350°.

Peel and core apples. In a small bowl mix almonds and sugar. Roll apples in egg white and then in nut mixture until very well coated.

Bake in 9 x 13-inch pan for 30 to 40 minutes, or until apples are soft but not falling apart. Serve apples hot.

STRAWBERRY SAUCE: Rinse and hull strawberries. Place all ingredients in blender and blend for 2 to 3 minutes. Pour over apples and into hollows when ready to serve.

APPLE AND PEAR COMPOTE

10 Cortland apples
6 ripe pears
¼ cup water
1 package unsweetened frozen strawberries
3 Tbsps. sugar to taste, optional
1 package strawberry imitation gel dessert or 1 tsp. lime juice plus ¼ tsp. lime peel

USE: 4-quart saucepan
YIELDS: 10 to 12 servings

Peel and dice apples and pears; combine with water in a 4-quart saucepan. Cook over low flame until mixture is soft, about 35 to 45 minutes. Ten minutes before it is done, add strawberries, sugar if desired, and strawberry gel. If not using gel, add lime juice and peel.

Serve warm or cool.

CRANBERRY-FILLED BAKED APPLES

8 MacIntosh apples

FILLING
1½ cups cranberries, or
1 cup golden raisin, plus
½ cup coarsely chopped
walnuts
¼ cup honey
1 Tbsp. cinnamon

SAUCE
½ cup corn syrup
½ cup orange juice
⅓ cup grape juice

USE: 9 x 13-inch pan
YIELDS: 2-3 cups

Preheat oven to 325°.

Cut out approximately 1-inch deep cavity in top of apple.

FILLING: Combine filling ingredients, using 2 tablespoons per apple. When using raisins, plump first in boiling water to prevent drying out.

SAUCE: Mix together sauce ingredients and coat bottom of pan.

Bake apples in sauce for 30-35 minutes until pulp is soft. Skin should not burst.

Spoon sauce over apples before serving.

CRANBERRY-APPLE SAUCE

1 pound fresh cranberries
2 pounds MacIntosh apples
⅓ cup honey
½ cup water
½ cup orange juice
1 tsp. cinnamon

USE: 4-quart saucepan
YIELDS: 2 cups sauce

Rinse cranberries in a colander. Remove stems and bad berries. Peel and slice apples. In a 4-quart saucepan, combine the fruit with honey, water, orange juice, and cinnamon, and cook on low flame, 30 to 45 minutes. Cool and then strain. Use as relish, dessert, or side dish.

BAKED FRUIT COMPOTE

1 fresh pineapple
4 oranges, sectioned
1 cup pitted prunes
¾ cup dry white wine
¼ cup honey
⅛ tsp. ground cloves
¼ tsp. cinnamon
2 tsps. grated orange rind

USE: 1-quart casserole
YIELDS: 4 servings

Preheat oven to 350°.

Peel, core, quarter, and slice pineapple. Arrange in baking dish with orange sections and prunes. Pour wine over fruit.

In a small saucepan, combine honey, cloves, cinnamon, and orange rind. Heat to boiling. Pour over fruit. Cover and bake until pineapple is tender, about 45 minutes.

Serve warm.

STRAWBERRY PEARS

3 Bartlett or Anjou pears
½ cup sugar
¼ cup lemon juice
3 Tbsps. margarine, melted
1 cup boiling water
2 10-ounce packages
frozen strawberries, thawed
2 Tbsps. sweet red wine

USE: 7 x 11-inch ovenproof
glass baking dish
YIELDS: 6 servings

Preheat oven to 350°.

Peel pears. Cut in half and core. Place in ovenproof glass baking dish, cut side down. Combine sugar, lemon juice, margarine, and boiling water. Pour over pears. Cover and bake 45 minutes until pears are tender. Drain completely.

Puree strawberries in a blender with wine. Pour mixture over pears, turning pears to coat well. Bake at 350° for another 20 minutes. Remove from oven. Serve chilled.

FRUIT CUP

TROPICAL FRUIT CUP
5 Red Delicious apples
5 Golden Delicious apples
5 oranges
3 grapefruits
1 fresh pineapple
1 cup walnut pieces
3 kiwi fruit or 3 limes
1 cup walnut halves

YIELDS: 24 portions

COCONUT FRUIT CUP
8 Red Delicious apples
5 oranges
1 fresh pineapple
1 cup raisins
¼ cup shredded coconut
½ cup lime juice
Light corn syrup or
honey to taste
1 10-ounce container
nondairy dessert topping

YIELDS: 18 portions

TROPICAL FRUIT CUP: Wash and cut apples into chunks. Peel and section oranges and grapefruits. Peel and cut pineapple into chunks. In a large bowl combine fruit and nuts, except for kiwi fruit or lime. Serve in champagne glasses and garnish with slices of kiwi or lime. Sprinkle walnut halves on top.

COCONUT FRUIT CUP: Wash and cut apples. Peel and section oranges. Peel and cut pineapple into chunks. In a large bowl combine fruit with raisins and coconut. Combine lime juice and corn syrup and pour over fruit. Let stand an hour or two.

Whip dessert topping. Spoon fruit salad into small dishes and top with whipped topping just before serving.

FESTIVE CANTALOUPE APPETIZER

CANTALOUPE BASKETS

6 cantaloupes
1 honeydew melon
¼ watermelon
1 pint strawberries

YIELDS: 12 servings

CANTALOUPE QUARTERS

3 cantaloupes
48 watermelon balls
24 honeydew balls
1 pint blueberries

YIELDS: 12 servings

CANTALOUPE RINGS

1 cantaloupe
24 watermelon balls
24 honeydew balls
24 cherries
½ cup blueberries or
½ cup grapes

YIELDS: 6 servings

CANTALOUPE BASKETS: Cut cantaloupes in half and remove seeds. Using a melon ball scoop, scoop out large and small balls of cantaloupe. Even out the insides of the cantaloupe. To decorate cantaloupe, make edges look like crowns by cutting out small V's at ½-inch intervals all around the edges of the cantaloupe halves.

Scoop out balls of honeydew and watermelon. Rinse and hull strawberries and mix with fruit. Fill cantaloupe halves with fruit. Garnish with sprigs of mint and serve chilled.

CANTALOUPE QUARTERS: Cut cantaloupes into quarters and remove seeds.

Scoop out 3 balls from both sides of each quarter — one from each end and one from the middle. Set these balls aside and fill the holes with a watermelon ball at each end and a honeydew ball in the middle. Place blueberries on the top of each serving of melon. Serve chilled.

CANTALOUPE RINGS: Cut top and bottom off cantaloupe; slice cantaloupe into 6 rings. Remove seeds and peel.

Place rings flat on plate. Heap center of each ring with watermelon and honeydew balls, and cherries and blueberries or grapes. Serve chilled.

FRUIT WITH CREAMY PLUM DIP

4 fresh pears
4 oranges
1 grapefruit
1 30-ounce can plums
Grapes, any variety

CREAMY PLUM DIP
1 cup reserved plum liquid
½ cup water
¼ cup sugar
2 Tbsps. cornstarch
¼ tsp. cinnamon
1 Tbsp. lemon juice
5 drops red food coloring
½ cup mayonnaise

USE: 2-quart saucepan
YIELDS: 6 to 10 servings

Cut pears into quarters or eighths. Peel and section the oranges and the grapefruit. Drain plums, and reserve liquid for dip. Arrange fruit on a platter and garnish with grapes.

CREAMY PLUM DIP: Pour plum liquid and water into 2-quart saucepan. In a small bowl, combine the sugar, cornstarch, and cinnamon, and blend into plum syrup and water. Cook over medium heat until mixture boils, lower flame and simmer 1 minute. Remove from heat and stir in lemon juice and food coloring.

Set mixture aside and allow it to cool to room temperature. Blend in the mayonnaise and mix well.

Pour dip into bowl, and place in center of fruit.

ISRAELI FRIED BANANAS

6 firm bananas
⅓ cup margarine
2 Tbsps. sugar
Peel of 1 orange,
finely grated
Peel of 1 lemon,
finely grated
3 Tbsps. rum
2 Tbsps. orange juice
1 Tbsp. lemon juice
½ cup nondairy
dessert topping

USE: 10-inch skillet
YIELDS: 6 servings

Peel bananas and cut lengthwise and then crosswise to quarter them. Melt margarine in hot 10-inch skillet. Add sugar, orange and lemon peels, and stir for several minutes. Fry bananas on both sides.

Add rum to frying pan and bring to a boil. Lower to a simmer. Add orange and lemon juices and simmer several minutes. Whip dessert topping until stiff.

Serve hot with a dollop of whipped topping.

VARIATION
☐ **Dairy:** Serve with a dollop of sour cream, yogurt, or a scoop of vanilla ice cream.

WATERMELON BASKET

When serving a large crowd in summer, treat them to fresh fruit from a watermelon basket. It makes a beautiful centerpiece and is very refreshing to eat.

1 medium to large
watermelon
2 cantaloupes
1 honeydew melon
Grapes, optional
Cherries, optional
Blueberries, optional

USE: Pencil
Sharp knife
Melon scoop
Large bowl

With a pencil, draw a line around the watermelon as shown, with a loop on top for a handle, if desired. Using a sharp knife, pierce outer shell. Carefully cut through the melon and remove top.

Cut out all the watermelon from inside and put on a plate. With a melon scoop, make balls. Remove as many pits as possible and put balls into a large bowl. Then scoop balls out of cantaloupe and honeydew.

To decorate watermelon after the top is cut off, cut ½-inch V's into top of rind, making a crown.

Fill basket with watermelon, cantaloupe, and honeydew balls. Grapes, cherries, and blueberries are optional.

Serve chilled.

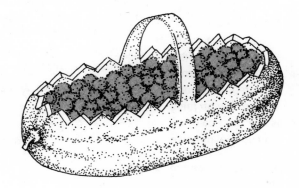

SPECIALTY DESSERTS

Specialty Desserts like Trifle or Quindim require a good deal of work but the result will surpass your expectations.

QUINDIM

A luscious Brazilian coconut custard dessert for the real coconut lover. Well worth your time and effort.

3 cups grated coconut
4 whole eggs plus
5 egg yolks
1 Tbsp. vanilla extract
2 cups sugar
½ cup coconut milk

USE: 1½ quart
ovenproof glass dish
9 x 13-inch pan
YIELDS: 12 servings

Preheat oven to 350°.

Blend all ingredients in a blender for 5 minutes.

Grease ovenproof glass dish. Sprinkle with additional sugar. Pour in batter. Place dish in a 9 x 13-inch pan containing water and put in the oven. Bake about 1 hour until quindim has set and turned a golden color. If water in pan evaporates, add more.

When done, remove from oven and invert onto a cake plate. The bottom, which has become moist from the eggs, will now be on the top and the coconut on the bottom.

Chill and serve cold.

TRIFLE

This lovely dessert should be prepared in a trifle dish or a large glass or crystal bowl to look its best.

½ of a 9 x 13-inch sponge cake
½ cup cherry liqueur
1 package lime imitation gel dessert
1 package lemon pudding
1 package strawberry or cherry imitation gel dessert
1 10-ounce container nondairy dessert topping
1 package chocolate pudding
1 package lemon pudding
1 package frozen raspberries, defrosted
1 10-ounce container nondairy dessert topping
6 walnut halves
Maraschino cherries
1 kiwi fruit, sliced
Chocolate shavings

USE: 1 trifle dish
YIELDS: 20 to 24 servings

Before you begin, all puddings and gels should be prepared separately, and partially set, and the dessert toppings whipped stiff.

Soak the sponge cake in liqueur and place on the bottom of a large clear glass trifle bowl. Begin with lime-flavored gel. Spread over the cake, refrigerate, and let it set further. Follow with the lemon pudding, letting it set a few minutes.

Continue in order, spooning each layer gently over one another until all puddings, gels and topping are used and set.

Decorate top with nuts, cherries, kiwi slices, and chocolate shavings.

BISCUIT TORTONI

½ cup toasted sliced almonds
½ cup crushed
almond macaroons
1 10-ounce container
nondairy dessert topping
¼ cup confectioners' sugar
1 tsp. rum extract or
3 Tbsps. dark rum
4 maraschino cherries

USE: 8 ramekins
YIELDS: 8 servings

Reserve about 1 tablespoon of toasted almonds. Combine remaining almonds and macaroons in small bowl.

In a small bowl, beat dessert topping until thick. Beat sugar and rum into whipped dessert topping. Fold nut and macaroon mixture into whipped mixture. Spoon mixture into ramekins or paper muffin cup liners. Sprinkle tops with remaining almonds. Place ½ cherry in center of each.

Freeze until firm.

CREPES DELUXE

CREPES
6 eggs
1½ cups flour
Pinch salt
1 Tbsp. sugar
2 cups nondairy creamer
Margarine for frying

FILLING
Lemon juice
Confectioners' sugar
Cinnamon

1 cup blueberry, strawberry,
or apricot jam

USE: 10-inch skillet
YIELDS: 10 to 12 pancakes

CREPES: In a large mixer bowl, lightly beat eggs. Beat in flour, salt, and sugar. Blend in nondairy creamer.

Brush skillet with margarine. When hot, pour in ¼ cup of batter — tilt to cover entire pan. When bubbles appear, turn and cook other side for 30 seconds. Remove and set aside. Repeat with remaining batter. See Blintzes Illustrated (page 83).

FILLING: Sqeeze lemon juice over each pancake and sprinkle with confectioners' sugar and cinnamon. Then spread each pancake with jam and roll up like a jelly roll. Sprinkle again with cinnamon and confectioners' sugar.

Serve immediately.

FROZEN PAREVE SPECIALTIES

ICE CREAM *made without dairy ingredients is the classic ending to the elegant dinner or Simchah. Similar to a frozen mousse, your favorite flavor combines well with a crunchy crust or tasty topping.*

SODA FOUNTAIN FAVORITES

These long-time favorites can be made from homemade *pareve* ice cream or commercial dairy or nondairy ice cream. Indulge!

☐ PINEAPPLE COUPE: Place a scoop of vanilla ice cream on a dish. Top with crushed pineapple mixed with brandy and garnish with whipped cream.

☐ COUPE MELBA: Place a scoop of vanilla ice cream into a peach half. Top with pureed raspberries.

☐ PEARS HELENE: For each serving, place a slice of sponge cake on a dessert plate. Top with a scoop of ice cream, then a canned pear half, placed cut side down. Cover with chocolate or hot fudge sauce. Garnish with whipped cream.

☐ BANANA SPLIT: Split a banana in half, lengthwise. Place the halves next to each other flat side down on a dish. Place three different flavored scoops of ice cream on the banana halves. Vanilla is usually in the center with chocolate and strawberry on either side. Cover each scoop with ½-ounce of different topping: hot fudge, pineapple, strawberry, butterscotch, etc. Garnish with whipped cream, chopped nuts, and a maraschino cherry.

☐ HOT FUDGE SUNDAE: Place a scoop of your favorite ice cream in a dish. Top with hot fudge sauce, chopped nuts, whipped cream, and a maraschino cherry.

☐ CHOCOLATE ICE CREAM SODA: Mix 1½ ounces chocolate syrup and 1½ ounces cream or softened ice cream in a 14-ounce glass. Fill three quarters full with club soda. add 2 scoops of chocolate or vanilla ice cream. Mix gently and finish filling with club soda. Top with whipped cream.

☐ MILK SHAKE: In a blender combine 6 ounces milk, 2 scoops of vanilla or chocolate ice cream, and 1½ ounces chocolate syrup. Serve immediately. For extra nutrition, add an egg.

☐ SNOWBALLS: Roll scoops of ice cream in grated coconut. Freeze on baking sheets until ready to serve.

PAREVINE

6 eggs, separated
¾ to 1 cup light corn syrup
2 to 3 Tbsps. confectioners' sugar

FLAVORING
1 Tbsp. vanilla extract or
3 Tbsps. cocoa or
1 Tbsp. instant coffee or
6 to 10 frozen strawberries, defrosted

USE: 1 quart plastic container
YIELDS: 1 quart

In a large mixer bowl, beat egg whites until stiff. Gradually add corn syrup. Still beating, add confectioners' sugar, yolks, and flavoring. Spoon into quart container and freeze until firm.

CHOCOLATE PAREVE ICE CREAM

7 eggs, separated
½ cup honey or
¾ cup sugar
½ cup oil
4 Tbsps. cocoa
Pinch salt
1 tsp. instant coffee
(optional)

USE: 1 quart plastic container
YIELDS: 1 quart

In a large mixer bowl, beat egg whites until stiff. In a separate bowl, combine yolks, honey, oil, cocoa, and coffee if desired. Beat until thick and creamy. Fold whites into yolk mixture until well blended. Spoon into quart container and freeze until firm.

VARIATION
☐ Substitute 1 package frozen strawberries, chopped or blended, for cocoa. Bananas or other fruit may also be substituted.

DELUXE PAREVE ICE CREAM

6 eggs, separated
1 cup confectioners' sugar
2 tsps. vanilla extract
6 Tbsps. light corn syrup
3 Tbsps. cocoa, optional
2 10-ounce containers
nondairy dessert topping

USE: 9 x 13-inch pan
YIELDS: 18 servings

In a large mixer bowl, beat egg whites until stiff, gradually adding confectioners' sugar. Set aside.

In a medium mixer bowl, beat together egg yolks, vanilla, corn syrup, and cocoa if desired. In a separate bowl, beat dessert topping until stiff. Add to yolk mixture. With a spatula, fold in egg whites. Pour into pan, smooth top. Cover with aluminum foil, and freeze completely.

FRENCH VANILLA PAREVE ICE CREAM

This ice cream can be made when you have "nothing" in the house.

2 Tbsps. cornstarch
2 cups water
6 eggs, separated
1¼ cups sugar
2 Tbsps. vanilla extract
2 Tbsps. solid shortening

USE: 1-quart saucepan
9 x 13-inch pan
YIELDS: 10 to 15 servings

In a 1-quart saucepan mix cornstarch into 2 cups of cold water. Cook, stirring, over low heat, until mixture thickens, about 5 minutes. Set aside and let cool.

In a large mixer bowl, beat egg whites until stiff peaks form. Set aside.

In a blender container, combine egg yolks, sugar, vanilla, and shortening and blend for about 10 minutes. Add thickened cornstarch and blend 1 more minute. Pour into a bowl and fold stiff egg whites in by hand. Pour into a 9 x 13-inch pan. Cover with aluminum foil and freeze until firm.

VARIATIONS
☐ **Chocolate Ice Cream:** Add 2 tablespoons cocoa to egg-yolk mixture.

☐ **Coffee Ice Cream:** Add 1 tablespoon instant coffee to egg-yolk mixture.

☐ **Dairy Ice Cream:** Substitute milk for water.

PAREVE NEAPOLITAN ICE CREAM

A beautiful three-layered ice cream, perfect for special occasions!

VANILLA
4 eggs, separated
1 10-ounce container nondairy dessert topping
4 Tbsps. sugar
1 tsp. vanilla extract

CHOCOLATE OR COFFEE
4 eggs, separated
1 10-ounce container nondairy dessert topping
4 Tbsps. sugar
1 tsp. vanilla extract
6 Tbsps. cocoa or
2 Tbsps. coffee

STRAWBERRY
4 eggs, separated
1 10-ounce container nondairy dessert topping
1 package strawberry imitation gel dessert or 16 ounces frozen strawberries and ⅓ cup sugar

USE: 11 x 14-inch pan
YIELDS: 20 servings

VANILLA: In a large mixer bowl, beat the egg whites until stiff. In a separate bowl, beat dessert topping until stiff. In a third bowl, beat egg yolks, sugar and vanilla. Beat egg yolk mixture into dessert topping for 2 minutes. Carefully fold in egg whites. Pour ice cream into an 11 x 14-inch baking pan and freeze about 1 hour.

CHOCOLATE OR COFFEE: In separate bowls, beat egg whites and nondairy topping as above. In another bowl, beat egg yolks with sugar, vanilla, and cocoa or instant coffee. Combine as above. Spread over partially frozen vanilla ice cream and return to freezer for another hour.

STRAWBERRY: Prepare egg whites and dessert topping as above. In another bowl, beat egg yolks with strawberry gel or frozen strawberries mixed with sugar. Combine as above. Spread over partially frozen chocolate ice cream and return to freezer until completely frozen.

VARIATIONS
To make the following recipes prepare each flavor of ice cream using 2 eggs only.

☐ **Ice Cream Cake:** Prepare favorite sponge cake in an 11 x 14-inch baking pan. Carefully cut cake into three layers. To assemble, alternate layers of cake and layers of ice cream to make six layers. Freeze until ice cream is firm. Serve each slice of cake lying down on plate.

☐ **Ice Cream Roll:** Line baking sheet with aluminum foil. Prepare first layer of ice cream and spread it on the foil. Freeze about 1 hour. Prepare second layer and spread it on top of first layer. Return to freezer for another hour. Make third layer, spread on top and freeze.

After the three layers are partially frozen, lift aluminum foil and gently begin rolling like a jelly roll, removing foil from bottom layer as you roll it. Sprinkle roll with ½ cup graham cracker crumbs or chocolate cookie crumbs. Return to freezer.

☐ **Ice Cream Cake Roll:** Prepare Jelly Roll Cake Recipe (page 365). Prepare one flavor of ice cream. Spread on top of cake and slowly roll up. Freeze until ready to serve. Sprinkle with ground walnuts or colored or chocolate sprinkles or powdered sugar.

PRALINE PAREVE ICE CREAM

1 cup sugar
6 tsps. water
1 cup blanched almonds
3 10-ounce containers
nondairy dessert topping
6 eggs

USE: Baking sheet
1-quart saucepan
9 x 13-inch pan
YIELDS: 12 to 15 servings

Lightly oil a baking sheet.

Combine sugar and water in a heavy 1-quart saucepan. Heat over low heat, swirling pan until sugar dissolves. Raise heat and bring syrup to a boil. Brush sides down with damp pastry brush. Cook until mixture is a rich brown, but not too dark. Stir in nuts and continue cooking about 1½ minutes. Immediately pour out onto prepared sheet and cool. Break into 1-inch pieces and grind to a powder in a blender.

In a large mixer bowl, whip dessert topping until thick. Beat in eggs, one at a time; mixture should remain thick. Stir in praline powder.

Spoon into a 9 x 13-inch pan. Cover with aluminum foil and freeze until firm.

VARIATION
☐ This mixture is ideal as filling for ice-cream jelly rolls or cream puffs.

SOY MILK ICE CREAM

1 cup soy milk
¼ cup honey or sugar
2 tsps. vanilla extract
1 egg (optional)
4 tsps. cocoa or
carob powder
1 cup oil

USE: 1 quart plastic container
YIELDS: 1½ pints

Combine all ingredients except oil in a blender container. Begin blending at high speed. Remove glass knob from cover of blender container and slowly dribble oil into soy-milk mixture. Continue adding the oil until mixture thickens and no more oil can be absorbed. Turn blender off.

If a drop of oil remains on top of the mixture, turn blender on and off quickly. Pour mixture into container, cover, and freeze.

VARIATION
☐ **Dairy Ice Cream:** Substitute milk for soy milk.

ICE CREAM NOVELTIES, *fancy and fun, make special desserts.*

PAREVE ICE CREAM SUNDAE PIE

DOUGH
½ cup margarine, softened
2 Tbsps. sugar
1 cup flour

Preheat oven to 350°.

DOUGH: Combine margarine, sugar, and flour. Mix well. Pat into ungreased 9-inch pie plate and bake for 15 minutes. Cool.

ICE CREAM: In a medium mixer bowl, beat dessert topping until stiff. Beat in egg yolks and vanilla.

►

ICE CREAM
**1 10-ounce container
nondairy dessert topping**
3 eggs, separated
2 tsps. vanilla extract
½ cup sugar

SUNDAE FILLING
**3 ounces
semisweet chocolate**
2 Tbsps. light corn syrup
2 Tbsps. water

**Chocolate sprinkles
(optional)**

USE: 9-inch pie plate
Double boiler
YIELDS: 1 ice-cream pie

In a separate bowl, beat egg whites until stiff, gradually adding sugar until stiff peaks form. Gently fold egg whites into egg yolk mixture and combine well.

SUNDAE FILLING: Melt chocolate, corn syrup, and water in top of double boiler over simmering water. Stir frequently. Cool to room temperature.

TO ASSEMBLE: Put half of ice cream in pie shell. Spoon filling over ice cream. Carefully spread remaining ice cream over filling. Decorate edges with sprinkles, if desired. Freeze until ready to serve.

VARIATION
☐ Use your favorite homemade or commercial ice cream, softened slightly for ease of assembly.

DELUXE PAREVE ICE CREAM SANDWICH

27 graham crackers
**6 Tbsps. light red wine or
rum**
3 cups water
2 Tbsps. sugar
**2 packages
chocolate pudding**
9 ounces chocolate chips
**1 10-ounce container
nondairy dessert topping**

GARNISH
**Grated chocolate,
walnuts, or coconut**

USE: 9 x 13-inch pan
YIELDS: 20 servings

Arrange 9 graham crackers in 9 x 13-inch pan. Sprinkle lightly with wine or rum. In a small saucepan, boil water with sugar. Add pudding, then remove from stove. Stir in chocolate chips. Pour ⅔ of mixture over crackers. add another layer of 9 crackers. Sprinkle lightly with wine.

In a separate bowl, whip dessert topping until stiff. Spoon half over graham crackers. Arrange a last layer of 9 crackers on top. Combine remaining topping with remaining pudding mixture. Spread over top layer. Sprinkle with garnish.

Freeze until firm. Cut between crackers to make sandwiches.

SAUCES and CRUSTS *dress up your homemade ice cream. Mix and match above and below.*

GRAHAM CRACKER CRUST

⅔ cup margarine
**3 cups graham
cracker crumbs**

USE: 9 x 13-inch pan
YIELDS: 9 x 13-inch crust

In a small saucepan melt margarine and mix with graham cracker crumbs. Press into the bottom of a 9 x 13-inch pan, reserving 1 cup for topping.

Spread ice cream smoothly on top. Cover and freeze until firm. Cut with sharp knife dipped in cold water.

CRISPY CHOCOLATE CRUST

3 cups crisped rice
½ cup margarine, melted
3 ounces semisweet chocolate, melted

USE: 9 x 13-inch pan
YIELDS: 9 x 13-inch crust

In a medium bowl, combine crisped rice with margarine and chocolate. Press over bottom of 9 x 13-inch pan. Freeze 15 minutes.

Spread ice cream smoothly on top. Cover and freeze until firm. Cut with sharp knife dipped in cold water.

CHOCOLATE CUPS

A special treat when filled with a scoop of ice cream.

1 cup chocolate chips
2 Tbsps. solid shortening

USE: Muffin pan
YIELDS: 12 cups

Melt chocolate and shortening in top of a double boiler. Keep over boiling water. Place cupcake holders in muffin pan. Using a basting brush, brush insides of the cupcake holders with chocolate mixture, making an even thickness all around.

Put entire muffin pan in freezer overnight. To peel off the paper, make a pin prick in the bottom to release the air. Slowly peel the paper from the center to the outside. Replace in freezer until ready to fill.

BUTTERSCOTCH SAUCE

½ cup margarine
½ tsp. white vinegar
1 pound light brown sugar
½ cup nondairy creamer
Pinch salt
1 tsp. vanilla extract

USE: 2-quart saucepan
YIELDS: 2 cups sauce

Combine margarine, vinegar, sugar, nondairy creamer, and salt in 2-quart saucepan. Cook over low heat, stirring occasionally, for ½ hour. Stir in vanilla.

Store in covered jar in the refrigerator.

Serve warm over ice cream.

CHOCOLATE HOT FUDGE SAUCE

2 ounces unsweetened chocolate
¾ cup sugar
⅛ tsp. salt
½ cup light corn syrup
½ cup nondairy creamer
2 Tbsps. margarine
1 Tbsp. vanilla extract

USE: 2-quart saucepan
YIELDS: 2 cups sauce

Combine chocolate, sugar, salt, corn syrup, and nondairy creamer in 2-quart saucepan. Cook over low heat, stirring often, for 20 to 25 minutes or until thickened. Stir in margarine, then vanilla.

Store in covered jar in refrigerator.

Serve warm over ice cream.

STRAWBERRY SAUCE

1 10-ounce package
frozen strawberries
in syrup, thawed
2 Tbsps. sugar
2 Tbsps. lemon juice

USE: 1¼ cups sauce

Combine strawberries, sugar, and lemon juice in blender. Blend until liquified.

SHERBET *and* SORBETS *are frozen desserts appropriate any time of year — for the family or for the fanciest* simchah. *Sherbets are creamier, with more body. Sorbets are lighter in texture, with fewer calories.*

CANTALOUPE SHERBET

2 cantaloupes
¼ cup water
1 package imitation
gel dessert, unflavored
1 cup sugar
1½ tsps. lemon juice

USE: 2-quart freezer container
Ice cream maker
YIELDS: 1½ quarts sherbet

Cut melons in half and remove seeds. Scoop pulp out and puree in blender. You should have 4 cups puree.

In a small saucepan boil water and immediately add the package of gel dessert, mixing well. Add the gel mixture to the cantaloupe puree and blend. Mix in sugar and lemon juice.

Process cantaloupe mixture in ice cream maker according to manufacturer's instructions. Cover and freeze.

Scoop into chilled dessert dishes.

WATERMELON SHERBET

½ small watermelon to make
4 cups watermelon puree
1 10-ounce container
nondairy creamer
1 package imitation
gel dessert, unflavored
1 cup sugar
2 tsps. lemon juice
¼ tsp. nutmeg (optional)

USE: Ice cream maker
YIELDS: ½ gallon sherbet

Scoop out watermelon meat, removing all seeds. Puree in blender or food processor. Keep half of the watermelon puree in the blender container it was pureed in. Pour the other half of puree into ice cream maker. Bring ¼ cup nondairy creamer to a boil and dissolve gel dessert in it. Immediately blend into pureed watermelon in blender. Blend in remaining creamer, sugar, lemon juice, and nutmeg. Pour watermelon mixture into ice cream maker container and combine.

Process watermelon mixture in ice cream maker according to manufacturer's instructions.

Cover and freeze.

VARIATION
❏ This recipe can also be made with honeydew melon.

FOUR-FRUIT FREEZE

⅓ **cup sugar**
1 cup orange juice
**1 8¼-ounce can crushed
pineapple in syrup**
2 Tbsps. lemon juice
1 tsp. vanilla extract
**3 medium-size
ripe bananas, sliced**

USE: 9-inch square pan
YIELDS: 4 to 6 servings

Mix sugar, orange juice, pineapple with syrup, lemon juice, and vanilla in large bowl until sugar dissolves. Puree bananas in blender or food processor until smooth. Add to orange juice mixture and mix well. Turn into 9-inch square pan and freeze until mushy. Remove from freezer and beat until smooth. Return to pan and refreeze.

Remove from freezer about 15 minutes before serving. Scoop into chilled dessert dishes.

ORANGE SHERBET

2 cups sugar
1 cup water
4 cups orange juice
¾ cup lemon juice
1 egg white

USE: 9 x 13-inch pan
YIELDS: 15 servings

Cook sugar and water in small saucepan until syrupy. Pour into bowl and cool. Add orange and lemon juices to syrup. Pour into 9 x 13-inch pan and freeze until mushy.

In a small mixer bowl, beat egg white until stiff. Fold into sherbet and freeze until firm.

Cut into squares to serve.

PINK CLOUD DESSERT

**2 cups fresh strawberries
or raspberries**
¾ cup confectioners' sugar
1 tsp. grated lemon rind
3 egg whites
Pinch salt
Fresh mint or berries

YIELDS: 5 to 6 servings

Hull the strawberries. Wash and drain.

In a large bowl, thoroughly crush berries with potato masher. Combine berries and sugar, lemon rind, egg whites, and salt in large bowl of mixer. Beat at highest speed for about 10 minutes until mixture is thick and fluffy. Pour into sherbet glasses and chill in freezer.

Before serving, top each glass with a sprig of mint or a fresh berry.

STRAWBERRY SORBET

1 cup sugar
2 cups water
2 pints fresh strawberries
8 Tbsps. lemon juice
6 Tbsps. tequila, optional

USE: 2-quart saucepan
Ice cream maker
YIELDS: 1½ quarts

Cook sugar and water in a 2-quart saucepan until sugar is dissolved. Simmer 5 minutes. Cool.

Rinse and hull strawberries. Place in a food processor or blender and puree. Add lemon juice, and tequila if used. Pour into sugar syrup. Cover mixture and chill.

Process strawberry mixture in ice cream maker according to manufacturer's instructions.

Cover and freeze.

MOUSSE is an airy creation of stiffly beaten egg whites combined with egg yolks and flavoring. Like ice cream, there is great variety in flavor.

CHOCOLATE MOUSSE

4 ounces bittersweet chocolate
4 ounces semisweet chocolate
2 Tbsps. margarine
¼ cup rum or orange juice
1 tsp. almond extract
1 Tbsp. instant coffee
5 eggs, separated
½ cup sugar
1 10-ounce container nondairy dessert topping
1 cup chopped almonds

USE: 10-inch spring-form pan
Double boiler
YIELDS: 10 to 12 servings

Melt chocolates, margarine, rum or orange juice, almond extract, and coffee in top of double boiler. In a large mixer bowl beat egg whites until stiff but not dry. Pour into a large bowl and set aside to cool.

In top of double boiler mix egg yolks well with sugar. Cook while beating with whisk over water until thickened and creamy. Add egg-yolk mixture to chocolate mixture.

In a small mixer bowl beat nondairy dessert topping until stiff. Fold egg whites into chocolate-egg yolk mixture. Fold dessert whip into mixture until blended.

Dust greased spring-form pan with almonds. Pour mousse on top of nuts. Refrigerate at least 3 hours until firm to serve. Cut into ¾-inch wedges.

CHOCOLATE MOUSSE CAKE

1 stick margarine
7 eggs, separated
7 ounces chocolate chips
1 cup sugar
1 Tbsp. vanilla extract

1 carton dessert whip
4 Tbsps. confectioners' sugar

USE: Small saucepan
1 tube or spring form pan
YIELDS: 12 servings

Beat egg whites with ¼ cup sugar, set aside.

In small saucepan, melt chocolate chips and margarine. Let cool. Beat·yolks with remaining sugar and vanilla. Add chocolate chip mixture to yolk mixture and mix well. Fold in egg whites. Pour ½ of mixture into greased tube pan or spring form pan. Bake for 30 minutes at 350°. Refrigerate remaining half of mixture. When cake is cooled, pour onto it refrigerated mixture and freeze for a few hours.

Beat dessert whip and sugar. Remove cake from pan and frost sides and top with dessert whip. Sprinkle with chocolate sprinkles and replace in freezer until a few minutes before serving time. Slice and serve.

DIET MOCHA MOUSSE

This dietetic dish will please everyone! It's simple and very chocolaty, and it's hard to belive that it contains only 91 calories per serving. With sugar, just 125! Enjoy!

3 Tbsps. boiling water
2 ounces unsweetened chocolate, cut up
1 Tbsp. liquid noncaloric sweetener or 2 Tbsps. sugar
1 Tbsp. instant coffee
2 eggs, separated

YIELDS: 4 servings

Combine water, chocolate, sweetener, and coffee in blender. Blend on high speed until chocolate is liquid. Add egg yolks. Blend at high speed for 1 more minute. Pour into medium bowl.

In a small mixer bowl beat egg whites until stiff but not dry. Fold into chocolate mixture. Spoon into four small dessert dishes.

Chill and serve.

LEMON GEL MOUSSE

1 package imitation gel dessert, unflavored
2 cups water
4 eggs, separated
⅔ cup sugar
¼ cup lemon juice
1 10-ounce container nondairy dessert topping
½ cup ground walnuts

USE: 2-quart saucepan
YIELDS: 6 servings

In a small bowl, dissolve gel dessert in 2 cups water. In a medium mixer bowl, beat egg whites until stiff. Beat egg yolks together with sugar in a large mixer bowl; stir gel dessert into the yolks. Add lemon juice.

In a small mixer bowl, beat dessert topping until stiff. Fold into egg yolk-gel mixture. Fold egg whites into mixture until just blended. Spoon into six small dessert dishes. Sprinkle tops of each serving with ground walnuts.

Chill and serve.

Confections

Memories of the candied grapefruit peels Grandmother used to make remain with us forever. Real peanut brittle and red candy apples — where are these delectables? If it's been years since you had some real homemade treats, indulge yourself and your family in some candy and confections.

THE ART OF CANDY MAKING

☐ Don't double recipes. Increasing amounts increases cooking time.

☐ Use a wooden spoon for stirring.

☐ Put margarine on the sides of the pot or pan when cooking so that sugar doesn't stick to sides of pan and remain undissolved.

☐ Using a candy thermometer: Make sure bulb is completely covered by boiling mixture but not touching the bottom of the pan. Allow thermometer to cool before washing in dish water.

☐ Cold water test: Have a cup of very cold water ready for testing. Remove the pan of candy mixture from the heat and with a clean spoon, drop about ½ teaspoon of the mixture into the water. The mixture will achieve one of the following stages referred to in candy recipes, to help achieve the perfect texture.

☐ Thread Stage — 230° to 234°F — Syrup spins a 2-inch thread in the air as it falls from spoon.

☐ Soft Ball Stage — 234° to 240°F — Syrup dropped in cold water forms a soft ball that flattens when taken out of water.

☐ Firm Ball Stage — 244° to 248°F — Syrup dropped in cold water forms a firm ball that doesn't flatten when it's taken out of water.

☐ Hard Ball Stage — 250° to 266°F — Syrup dropped in cold water forms a ball which holds its shape, but is pliable when taken out of water.

☐ Soft Crack Stage — 270° to 290°F — Syrup dropped in cold water separates into threads which are hard but not brittle.

☐ Hard Crack Stage — 300° to 310°F — Syrup dropped in cold water separates into threads which are brittle and hard.

CANDY APPLES

12 small Red Delicious apples
12 wooden skewers
2 cups sugar
½ cup light corn syrup
¾ cup water
Several drops
red food coloring

USE: 2-quart saucepan
Baking sheet
YIELDS: 12 apples

Wash and dry apples. Insert wooden skewers into apples.

Combine sugar, corn syrup, and water in a 2-quart saucepan. Heat mixture over medium-low flame until sugar dissolves. When mixture begins to boil, add food coloring until bright red. Boil without stirring for about 20 minutes until reaching Hard Crack Stage, 300°F on a candy thermometer. See The Art of Candy Making. Remove from heat.

Dip apples into syrup one at a time. Turn apples so that syrup covers them immediately. Stand the apples stick side up on an oiled baking sheet and allow to cool completely before eating.

NOTE: Work quickly when coating apples, but if syrup hardens place pan over a very low flame to soften.

CARAMEL APPLES

18 small Red Delicious apples
18 wooden skewers
4 cups sugar
1 cup light corn syrup
2⅔ cups nondairy creamer

USE: 3-quart saucepan
Baking sheet
YIELDS: 18 apples

Wash and dry apples. Insert wooden skewers into apples.

Combine sugar, corn syrup, and ⅔ cup nondairy creamer in a heavy 3-quart saucepan. Mix well. Cook over medium-low heat, stirring until sugar dissolves. Cook to a thick syrup, stirring constantly.

Slowly add remaining 2 cups nondairy creamer. Cook until reaching Firm Ball Stage, 244°F on candy thermometer, stirring constantly. See The Art of Candy Making. Remove from heat. Allow to stand until caramel stops bubbling. Set in a pan of hot water to keep from thickening.

Dip apples, one at a time, into syrup. Remove immediately and twist so caramel covers apples evenly. Stand the apples stick side up on an oiled baking sheet and allow to cool completely before eating.

CREAMY CHOCOLATE FUDGE

2 cups sugar
⅔ cup nondairy creamer
2 Tbsps. corn syrup
3 ounces semisweet baking chocolate
2 Tbsps. margarine
1 tsp. vanilla extract

USE: 3-quart saucepan
8 x 8-inch pan
YIELDS: 16 pieces

Place sugar, nondairy creamer, corn syrup, and chocolate in 3-quart saucepan. Stir over low heat until sugar is dissolved. Cook slowly until reaching Soft Ball Stage, 234°F on candy thermometer. See The Art of Candy Making. Remove from heat and add margarine.

When cooled to lukewarm, add vanilla. Pour into a large mixer bowl; beat with a mixer until thick, 1 to 3 minutes. Pour immediately into greased 8 x 8-inch pan. Chill at least 3 hours and cut into 2-inch squares when firm.

VARIATION
☐ ½ cup nuts, coconut, or chopped cherries can be added with vanilla.

CAROB CONFECTIONS

8 ounces sesame seeds
8 ounces sunflower seeds
12 ounces natural peanut butter, crunchy or creamy
1 cup carob powder
1 cup honey
6 ounces coconut flakes

YIELDS: 40 to 45 pieces

Combine sesame seeds, sunflower seeds, peanut butter, carob powder, and honey in a bowl and mix well. Take a teaspoonful of the mixture and shape into a small ball. Roll in coconut and place in small paper candy holder. Repeat with remaining mixture. Refrigerate or freeze before serving.

NOTE: Be sure utensils are dry.

SUGAR CLOUDS

These candies, also known as Divinity, will not harden if made on a humid or rainy day.

1½ cups light brown sugar, firmly packed
½ cup water
1 tsp. vinegar
1 egg white
Pinch salt
1 tsp. vanilla extract
½ cup chopped pecans

USE: 3-quart saucepan
YIELDS: 1 pound divinity or 40 candies

Combine sugar, water, and vinegar in a 3-quart saucepan, mixing well. Bring to a boil over medium heat, stirring until sugar dissolves. Cover and boil 2 to 3 minutes, then uncover and scrape down sugar mixture from the sides of the pot with a wet pastry brush (or a fork wrapped in a wet paper towel).

Boil without stirring until reaching Firm Ball Stage, 244°F on a candy thermometer. See The Art of Candy Making.

While sugar mixture is cooking, beat egg white in a small mixer bowl with salt until stiff but not dry. Turn on mixer and slowly pour syrup onto the egg white. Beat until creamy. Stir in vanilla and pecans.

Working quickly, drop teaspoonfuls of candy onto a sheet of oiled aluminum foil. When cool, store in an airtight container.

CANDIED FRUIT PEEL

3 oranges or lemons or 1 grapefruit
½ cup light corn syrup
1 cup sugar
1 cup water

GLAZE
½ cup sugar or
3 ounces chocolate, melted
USE: 2-quart saucepan
YIELDS: 36 pieces

Peel oranges or lemons or grapefruits. Remove as much of the white as possible. Cut into ¼-inch strips.

Place peels in a 2-quart saucepan and cover with water. Do not cover pot. Cook for 15 minutes. Drain, add fresh water, and cook for 15 more minutes. Drain, add fresh water, and cook an additional 15 minutes for the third and final time. Drain and set peels aside in a dish.

Boil corn syrup, sugar, and water. When boiling, reduce heat, add peels and simmer for 45 minutes.

GLAZE: Lift peels out of syrup and place on wax paper or aluminum foil and roll in sugar, or dip ends into melted chocolate.

HONEY CEREAL NIBBLES

Delicious low-sodium snack.

6 cups puffed-wheat cereal
2 cups unsalted peanuts
¼ cup toasted sesame seeds
½ cup brown sugar
¼ cup honey
¼ cup unsalted margarine

USE: 9 x 13-inch baking pan
2-quart saucepan
YIELDS: 9 to 10 cups nibbles

In a 9 x 13-inch baking pan, combine cereal, peanuts, and sesame seeds. Set aside.

In 2-quart saucepan, combine brown sugar, honey, and margarine. Stir over low heat until smooth. Pour over cereal mixture, tossing to coat. Bake at 275° for 45 minutes, stirring occasionally.

Allow to cool and store in a covered container.

NOTE: Cereal becomes crisp when cool.

MINT PATTIES

**1 pound
confectioners' sugar
3 Tbsps. margarine,
at room temperature
3 to 5 Tbsps. cold water
13 drops oil of peppermint
Food coloring**

USE: Rubber candy mold
YIELDS: 100 small candies

In a large bowl, mix all ingredients together until dough consistency is reached. Divide into four portions and add a few drops of food coloring to each portion. Knead in color.

Fill rubber candy mold, flatten top and pop out. Allow to dry.

NOTE: Do not substitute peppermint extract for oil of peppermint.

PEANUT BRITTLE

**1 cup sugar
½ cup light corn syrup
¼ cup water
1 cup chopped raw peanuts
1 Tbsp. margarine
½ tsp. baking soda
½ tsp. salt**

USE: 10 x 15-inch cookie sheet
1-quart saucepan
YIELDS: 1 pound

Heat sugar, corn syrup and water in a 1-quart saucepan over low flame until sugar is dissolved. Stir in peanuts. Continue cooking about 20 minutes until reaching Hard Crack Stage, 300°F on candy thermometer. See The Art of Candy Making. Remove from heat and stir in margarine, baking soda and salt, mix well.

Quickly spread out mixture evenly and thinly on a well-greased cookie sheet, using two forks, pulling and lifting into a rectangle the dimensions of the cookie sheet.

Cool and break into pieces.

SESAME-SEED CANDY

These candies will not harden if made on a humid or rainy day.

**1 pound sesame seeds
½ cup flour
¾ cup sugar
1 cup honey
¾ cup water
1 tsp. lemon juice
2 cups sliced
toasted almonds**

USE: 10-inch skillet
2-quart saucepan
Baking sheet
YIELDS: 100 pieces candy

Mix sesame seeds with flour and toast in 10-inch skillet on a small flame until golden brown.

In 2-quart saucepan, bring sugar, honey, water, and lemon juice to a boil. Simmer 20 to 30 minutes until thickened.

Add sesame-seed mixture and almonds to syrup. Simmer 10 minutes more, stirring constantly with a wooden spoon. Allow to cool until mixture can be handled.

Spread mixture on an oiled baking sheet or oiled aluminum foil, patting to about ½-inch thickness. Cool until firm enough to cut. Cut into squares or diamond-shaped pieces.

VARIATION
□ Omit lemon juice. Substitute 1 pound plus 2 cups coarsely chopped walnuts for both sesame seeds and almonds. Add ¼ teaspoon ground ginger to the syrup.

PEANUT BUTTER-CRISPED RICE SQUARES

The perfect birthday party treat. So easy the children can make it themselves.

1 cup dark corn syrup
1 cup peanut butter
1 cup sugar
5 cups crisped rice
4 squares
semisweet chocolate

USE: 3-quart saucepan
9 x 13-inch baking pan
Double boiler
YIELDS: 24 squares

Combine corn syrup, peanut butter, and sugar in 3-quart saucepan and bring to a boil. Remove from flame and add crisped rice. Mix well. Pour into a 9 x 13-inch baking pan. Melt chocolate in a double boiler and spread over the top. Cut into 2-inch squares.

VARIATION
☐ Mix ½ cup cocoa with corn syrup, peanut butter, and sugar.

CHOCOLATY PEANUT BUTTER BALLS

1½ cups
creamy peanut butter
½ cup margarine, softened
1 tsp. vanilla extract
3 cups confectioners' sugar

6 ounces semisweet
chocolate chips
2 Tbsps. solid shortening

USE: Baking sheet
Double boiler
YIELDS: 80 balls

Line a baking sheet with wax paper. In a medium-sized bowl, with your hands, knead peanut butter, margarine, vanilla, and sugar until a smooth dough is formed. Mixture will be very stiff. Shape dough into balls, using 2 teaspoonfuls for each. Place on wax paper and put in refrigerator.

In the top of a double boiler over water which is simmering, not boiling, melt chocolate and shortening together. When smooth, pour into a small bowl or measuring cup. Remove peanut-butter balls from refrigerator. Insert a wooden toothpick into each ball and dip in melted chocolate so that three-quarters of ball is coated. Return to wax paper, chocolate side down, and remove toothpick. Refrigerate on wax paper 30 minute or longer, until chocolate is firm, not sticky.

Store in airtight container with wax paper between layers to separate.

CARAMEL POPCORN

1 Tbsp. margarine
1 cup sugar
1 cup molasses
1 cup popcorn
kernels, popped
(16 cups popped corn)
½ cup shelled peanuts,
salted

USE: 3-quart saucepan
YIELDS: 18 to 20 balls

Combine margarine, sugar, and molasses in 3-quart saucepan. Bring to a boil and remove from heat. Pour over popcorn, add peanuts and mix well. Allow mixture to cool. Wet hands with very cold water and form into 3-inch balls.

SUGARED WALNUTS

1 cup sugar
Pinch salt
¼ cup water
¼ cup honey
½ tsp. vanilla extract
2 cups walnut pieces

USE: 2-quart saucepan
YIELDS: 16 walnut clusters

Combine sugar, salt, water, and honey in a 2-quart saucepan. Bring to a boil and simmer until reaching Soft Ball Stage, 235°F on candy thermometer. See The Art of Candy Making. Remove from heat and add vanilla and walnuts. Stir until thick and creamy. Turn out onto oiled waxed paper and separate into individual nut clusters with two forks. Work quickly.

MAINE SNOWBALLS

½ cup margarine
1 egg, beaten
1 cup chopped dates
1 cup sugar
½ cup chopped raw peanuts
2 cups crisped rice
Pinch salt
1 tsp. vanilla extract

½ cup grated coconut (optional)
½ cup ground peanuts (optional)

USE: 3-quart saucepan
YIELDS: 3 dozen snowballs

Combine margarine, egg, chopped dates, and sugar in 3-quart saucepan. Cook over low heat for 15 minutes, until mixture is smooth. Stir occasionally to prevent scorching. Cool 15 minutes.

Add chopped raw peanuts, crisped rice, salt, and vanilla. Wet hands and shape into 1-inch balls. If desired, roll in coconut or chopped nuts and place in small paper holders. Keep refrigerated.

CHOCOLATE-ALMOND CRUNCH

½ cup margarine
1 cup sugar
Pinch salt
¼ cup water
1½ cups sliced or chopped toasted almonds
2 cups semisweet chocolate chips, melted

USE: 1½-quart saucepan
Baking sheet
YIELDS: 1 pound candy

Combine margarine, sugar, salt, and water in 1½-quart saucepan. Bring to a boil and simmer until reaching Soft Crack Stage, 285°F on candy thermometer. See The Art of Candy Making. Add half of the almonds.

Grease a baking sheet. Line with wax paper. Oil the wax paper. Pour mixture onto wax paper and spread out. Allow to cool.

Cover candy with half the melted chocolate. When candy is firm turn it over and cover the other side with remaining melted chocolate. Spread the rest of the nuts evenly over the chocolate. Chill in refrigerator to harden.

Break into pieces when cold. Store in an airtight container between layers of wax paper.

HALVAH

15-ounce can tahini
Oil drained from tahini,
plus margarine
to make 1½ cups
4 cups flour
1 cup honey
½ cup ground almonds or
sesame seeds
3 ounces melted
chocolate (optional)

USE: 2-quart saucepan
YIELDS: 2½ to 3 pounds

Combine oil and margarine in 2-quart saucepan and heat until margarine melts. Stir in flour and cook over a low flame, stirring often, until light caramel-colored, add tahini and combine.

In a separate pot, heat honey to the Soft Ball Stage, 235°F on a candy thermometer. See The Art of Candy Making. Combine honey with flour mixture and add ground nuts. Mix well.

Pour onto greased flat marble or Formica surface and press into 1-inch-thick rectangle with a wet knife. If desired, cover with a thin layer of melted chocolate. Cut into bars before halvah is completely cool.

EASY MOCK HALVAH

1 cup tahini
2½ to 3 cups
confectioners' sugar

USE: 9 x 9-inch square pan
YIELDS: 20 pieces halvah

Combine tahini and confectioners' sugar in a large bowl. Mixture should be quite thick.

Line a 9 x 9-inch square pan with aluminum foil and spread mixture evenly over it. Refrigerate overnight or 24 hours until firm.

Cut into 20 squares.

A NEW TWIST ON TAYGELACH

These sticky-sweet honey treats are traditionally made for Rosh Hashanah.

3 eggs
2 tsps. sugar
2 Tbsps. oil
½ tsp. baking powder
½ tsp. salt
2 cups flour
¼ tsp. ginger
¼ cup finely chopped
walnuts or almonds
½ cup raisins

SYRUP
1 cup honey
1 cup sugar
1 tsp. ginger
1 Tbsp. ginger (optional)
¼ cup hot water

USE: 4-quart pot
YIELDS: 2 dozen balls

In a mixer bowl combine eggs, sugar, and oil. Stir in baking powder, salt, flour, and ¼ tsp. of ginger to make a soft dough. Knead lightly. Roll dough into a rectangle ¼-inch thick on a lightly floured board. Sprinkle nuts and raisins over dough and gently press in with fingers. Roll from both long edges toward the center and cut down the middle resulting in two long rolls.

Slice each roll into 1-inch pieces and press to seal ends.

SYRUP: In a heavy 4-quart pot combine honey, sugar and 1 tsp. of ginger. Bring to a boil. Once mixture is boiling, lower flame. Drop in taygelach a few at a time until all are added. Cover pot. Simmer ½ hour or until taygelach are golden brown.

Turn them carefully with a wooden spoon. They will sound hollow when done. They will also be dry and crisp inside. If desired add 1 tablespoon of ginger.

Turn off heat and add ¼ cup hot water immediately. Mix well. Cool completely and spoon balls into a storage container, and pour syrup over them.

Shabbat: Light, Blessing and Peace

Celebrating Shabbat
Shabbat and Yom Tov Candles
Observing the Shabbat Laws

Shabbat Shalom . . . *Gut Shabbos* . . . Good Shabbos . . .

Well before sunset on Friday afternoon the approaching mood of Shabbat seems to hover in the air. Stores are closing; steps are hurried. Tantalizing aromas of roast chicken, kugel or tzimmes herald a very special event. The list of Shabbat preparation grows shorter as everything falls into place: last-minute errands run, children dressed in their Shabbat best, cooking finished and the Shabbat stove set up.

Finally the moment of transformation arrives. We light the candles and cover our eyes to say the blessing, often adding a special prayer. It is Shabbat. A spirit of *shalom*, peace and wholeness, now enters the world. All work must be regarded as if complete. There is nothing that has to be done except to enjoy Shabbat, honor it, and "keep it holy."

The best and tastiest of foods and wine, our finest clothing, and a shining house are arrayed as they would be in preparation to receive royalty. And indeed Shabbat is a queen, a royal visitor to our homes each week.

Shabbat has also been called G-d's precious gift to the Jewish people. As one of the Ten Commandments, Shabbat observance is one of the central pillars of the Jewish faith. Observing it is the uniquely Jewish way of acknowledging that G-d created the world in six days and rested on the seventh. In refraining from work on Shabbat, we relinquish our own sense of mastery over the universe and enter a state of peace between man and nature that emulates the actions of G-d on the seventh day of Creation.

Shabbat is the only day given a name in the Torah, for the other days are simply called the first day, the second day, and so on. According to mystical teachings in the *Zohar*, all days of the week are blessed through Shabbat. All the good of the past week is elevated on Shabbat, and Shabbat is the source of all the blessings of the week to come.

Shabbat is a day when we separate ourselves not only from "work" but also from what one Jewish author has called "the busy pleasures of conventional leisure" — from travel, sports, hobbies, television, radio and movies. Imagine a day when the telephone has no hold over us. Business and even talk of business are prohibited. The clamoring world has no power to intrude on our Shabbat peace, and a day of restriction is in actuality a day of freedom.

The Shabbat Perspective

The twenty-five hours beginning at sunset Friday night present an opportunity to savor a way of being that is totally different from our experience the rest of the week. During the six days of the week, when we are involved with one kind of work or another, a weekday mentality reigns. This might be defined as a value system in which we are not only engaged in work, but are also defined by work. Contemporary society categorizes and evaluates people according to their professional and economic status. We, too, judge ourselves by our accomplishments, largely external. On Shabbat, however, all Jews, regardless of profession or social standing, are like royalty. Every man is king and every woman a queen. Shabbat reminds us of a higher reality, and teaches us not to be slaves to the weekday mentality.

Even during the week we can carry with us a bit of the perspective granted by Shabbat. This teaching is found in the verse, "And Moshe gathered all the children of Israel and said to them, "These are the things that G-d has commanded to do: Six days shall your work be done, and the seventh day shall be holy for you." (Exodus 35:1)

The wording in the Torah is always precise. The verse does not say, "six days you shall work," but rather, "six days your work *shall be done*." The passive tense used here indicates that our work should be done with the knowledge that all sustenance and blessings come from G-d, and that in working we are in fact merely creating a vessel to receive G-d's blessings.

As we move from weekday to Shabbat and back again, each influences the other. Our week affects our experience of Shabbat, and our Shabbat affects the coming week. Our weekday thoughts and activities influence Shabbat as our Sages explain, "He who works on *erev* Shabbat will eat on Shabbat." (Talmud Avoda Zorah 3a)

Erev Shabbat, the day before Shabbat, is loosely taken to mean all the days of preparation. "Eating" on Shabbat is the ability to absorb and enjoy the true spiritual nature of the day.

Shabbat has been a source of strength to a people scattered through many cultures across the centuries. In medieval Europe or Arabia, nineteenth-century Russia, or modern-day Israel or America. . . we would have no trouble recognizing Shabbat. The special *mitzvot* of Shabbat make the day a delight and attune us to the spiritual qualities present only on this "day of rest."

Celebrating Shabbat
A Spiritual Oasis

As the week-day consciousness recedes, a new "*Shabbosdik*" state of mind replaces it. Every Jew is granted an "additional soul" on Shabbat, which bestows an extra measure of light, understanding, peace and even appetite to enjoy the delicious Shabbat meals.

Welcoming Shabbat: The Shabbat is welcomed with ceremony and prayer both at home and at synagogue. Before sunset women and girls usher in Shabbat with the lighting of candles (see Shabbat and Yom Tov Candles, page 490). It is a special moment of quiet prayer and meditation. The flickering radiance of the Shabbat candles in their gleaming candelabrum lends brightness and an air of sanctity to the Shabbat table.

The *neshamah yeteirah*, extra Shabbat soul, gives us additional insight and adds depth to our study of Torah. The Torah portion read in *shul* on Shabbat morning often serves as a springboard for further study and lively discussions around the table.

Whether learning, going to *shul*, or sitting down together at the Shabbat table, this is a day when the family is finally united after a busy week. It is like a holiday every seven days, treasured by young and old.

"*Come my Beloved to meet the Bride; let us welcome the Shabbat.*" (Friday evening service.) These words begin L'chah Dodi, a festive song adopted by all Jewish communities to usher in the Shabbat, referred to here as the "bride" of the people of Israel.

THREE SHABBAT MEALS

Enjoyment of delicious food enhances the *mitzvah* of *oneg* Shabbat, Shabbat pleasure. Good food and drink allow the body to participate in what is essentially a spiritual experience. The meal is leisurely and social, a time of being together with family, friends and guests without external distractions. It is a time for stories, for Torah discussion and for encouraging children to share what they have learned about the Torah portion.

Shabbat is a time for the *mitzvah* of *hachnossat orchim*, welcoming guests. Special songs enhance the Shabbat table, some lively and some slow and reflective, some with words and some with melody alone. Most of all, the glow of the candles adds a warmth to the good feeling everyone has at being together in the special atmosphere of *shalom*.

We eat three meals on Shabbat, corresponding to the three times the Torah mentions the word "today" in reference to the miraculous manna that fell from heaven to sustain the Israelites during their wandering in the desert. Each Friday a double portion of manna fell, sufficient for both Friday and Shabbat. The two loaves of challah, *lechem mishnah*, on our Shabbat table are reminiscent of the double portion of manna. They are covered by a cloth above and a board or the tablecloth below, just as the manna was protected and kept fresh by a layer of dew both above and below.

The Friday night meal and the Shabbat afternoon meal begin with the recital of *Kiddush* over a cup of wine. Two traditional songs precede the *Kiddush* on Friday night. The first, *Shalom Aleichem*, is based on a Talmudic passage which describes the two angels who accompany each Jew home from the synagogue on Friday evening.

The second song, *Aishet Chayil*, A Woman of Valor, further describes the feminine aspect of

G-dliness ascribed to Shabbat - as queen, bride, and now the exemplary wife praised by her husband, who exclaims "Many daughters have done well but you surpass them all." *Aishet Chayil* describes the Jewish wife and mother, the foundation and keeper of the home. It also refers to G-d's indwelling presence in the world known as the *shechinah*.

The Kiddush Meal

"The sixth day. And the heavens and the earth and all their hosts were completed. . . And G-d blessed the Seventh Day and made it holy, for on it He rested from all His work..." (Genesis 1:31 -2:1-3)

The melodic words of the Friday night *Kiddush* fill the air as those gathered about the Shabbat table listen attentively and respond "*Amen.*" It is a *mitzvah* to sanctify Shabbat verbally in fulfillment of the Fourth Commandment — to "remember the Sabbath day to keep it holy." (Exodus 20:8)

Kiddush is a prayer of consecration and of distinction between the days of the week and the holy day of Shabbat. It testifies that G-d, the Creator of the world, rested on the seventh day and declared it holy.

Kiddush is recited by the head of the household or any male over thirteen. Those present say "*Amen*" after the blessings of *Kiddush*. When only women are present, one of them may recite *Kiddush* and include other women and children in her *brachah*. It is also customary in many homes for each male over thirteen to make his own *Kiddush* and afterwards to recite the *hamotzi* blessing over two small *challot*.

The *Kiddush* cup, usually made of silver and often beautifully engraved, symbolizes the vessel into which G-d's blessings are poured. The *Kiddush* cup holds four ounces of wine or grape juice. The one who recites the *Kiddush* should drink a little more than half, and distribute the rest among all those who are included in his *Kiddush*.

The Meal: After *Kiddush*, we wash our hands in the customary manner for the *hamotzi* blessing. The head of the household raises the two *challot* and recites the *hamotzi* ("...Who brings forth bread from the earth"), after which we say "*Amen.*" The challah is cut and dipped into salt (three times according to *Chabad* custom). It is eaten right away to avoid interruption between the blessing and eating. The remaining challah is then distributed. According to *Chabad* custom, each person should also recite the *hamotzi* blessing.

The enjoyment of favorite dishes enhances the *mitzvah* of *oneg* Shabbat, Sabbath pleasure. Our finest foods are often saved for Shabbat, including treats for the children and special delicacies. Fish is almost always included as a course in the meal, as are chicken or meat to enhance our enjoyment of Shabbat.

Warm food on Shabbat afternoon is provided by means of the covered stove on which food cooks slowly through the night. We may not light the stove, adjust the flame, or add food to the stove during Shabbat. (See The Shabbat Stove, page 496.) This does not prevent us from enjoying delicious food — but it does free us from the necessity of cooking it on Shabbat.

Cholent is a truly universal Shabbat dish which evolved in many countries to meet the need for a slow-cooking delicacy. Consisting of any combination of ingredients (pages 207-210), it is usually an important feature of the afternoon meal.

Kiddush on Yom Tov: On holidays ushered in by candle-lighting, Yom Tov *Kiddush* is recited followed by a festive meal. For Yom Tov laws applying to food preparation, see page 499.

Shalosh Seudot

The third meal of Shabbat is called *Shalosh Seudot*, or *Seudah Shlishit*. It is eaten in the late afternoon before sunset. The *Talmud* informs us that one who fulfills the obligation of eating three meals on Shabbat will be favorably judged in the world to come.

According to some Rabbinic opinions, *Seudah Shlishit* should be fulfilled with a full meal, beginning with challah or bread. Other authorities allow a lighter repast including foods requiring the blessing of *mezonot*; meat or fish; or at least fruit.

Seudah Shlishit must begin before sunset. If the meal did not begin with challah or bread, it must be finished before sunset.

Each Shabbat meal is imbued with its own particular theme and mood. During the third meal, as Shabbat lingers but a while longer, the feeling is reflective and spiritual. At the table of many Chassidic Rebbes, it was during the third meal that the deepest and most mystical teachings found expression, in both words and song.

On Shabbat we experience a series of levels, the highest of which is reached at the time of *Shalosh Seudot*. The Lubavitcher Rebbe, *shlita*, explains that the three Shabbat meals represent ascending levels of Shabbat rest.

The Friday night meal represents the level of rest that comes directly after work and washes away all traces of fatigue and effort. Concerning this, King Solomon says, "A worker enjoys a sweet sleep." (Ecclesiastes 5:11)

Rest corresponding to the level of the main meal of Shabbat day stems from the knowledge that there is no need to return to work, as the

Midrash says, "Sleep on Shabbat is a pleasure."

Finally there is the level of *Seudah Shlishit*, the highest aspect of Shabbat, "which is all Shabbat and rest." The Kabbalah explains that this third meal reflects the state of the world in Messianic times.

THE CONCLUSION OF SHABBAT

Havdalah

We mark the departure of the Shabbat Queen, as we did her entrance, with wine and blessing. *Havdalah* is a ceremony of separation between "the holy and the profane," between Shabbat and the six days of ordinary activity.

The *Havdalah* prayer includes four blessings. The first, over an overflowing cup of wine, signifies a sign of blessing for the new week.

The second blessing is said upon smelling aromatic spices, such as cloves, which revive the spirit and uplift us now that our extra Shabbat soul has departed.

The third blessing is said upon looking at the flame of a special candle with several intertwined wicks.

The final blessing is the *Havdalah* itself, "...Who makes a distinction between *kodesh*, holy, and *chol*, weekday (secular)."

One should not eat until after *Havdalah*. However, work may be performed after the conclusion of Shabbat and before *Havdalah* if one says the *Ma'ariv* prayer including the additional paragraph for Saturday night, or if one says the shortened phrase, "*Baruch Hamavdil Bein Kodesh L'chol*" - "Blessed is He Who separates between the holy and the secular."

Shavuah Tov... Gut Voch... After *Havdalah* and throughout the evening we wish one another a good week, and the weekly cycle begins anew.

When Yom Tov Occurs On Saturday Night: When the first or second night of Yom Tov is on Saturday night, the holiness of Shabbat is followed not by a weekday but by the holiness of Yom Tov. *Havdalah* for the conclusion of Shabbat is incorporated into the *Kiddush* for Yom Tov, as found in the *siddur*. The blessing for light is said while gazing at the Yom Tov candles, which are lit after dark.

Havdalah After Yom Tov: The conclusion of Yom Tov is also marked by *Havdalah*. However, *Havdalah* after Yom Tov varies from the *Havdalah* following Shabbat in that we do not include the blessings over spices or fire. (However, after Yom Kippur we include the blessing over fire. See page 512.) When Yom Tov ends on Friday night, *Havdalah* is not said until after Shabbat.

Melave Malkah - Escorting The Queen

Shabbat may be over, but the queen's presence lingers while we prolong the atmosphere of Shabbat with a *melave malkah* meal on *motzoai* Shabbat (Saturday night after Shabbat). The *melave malkah*, which means "escorting the queen," may be a feast or simply tea and cake.

Among Chassidim, traditional *melave malkah* foods include herring and whole cooked potatoes in addition to bread or challah — simple fare adorned with stories and good fellowship. People often have a *melave malkah* to celebrate a *simchah* and serve a more elaborate and elegant meal with several courses.

It is said that the Well of Miriam that accompanied the children of Israel in the wilderness flows into some of the world's water supply on *motzoai* Shabbat. We may tap into it by drawing fresh water at this time. It is customary to have a hot drink, such as tea, on *motzoai* Shabbat.

Telling stories about the Baal Shem Tov (the founder of Chassidism) and other *tzaddikim* is a *melave malkah* tradition which is said to bring good fortune. Such stories are a source of faith and spiritual strength that help us to meet many of the challenges we encounter during the week.

The benefit of eating at a *melave malkah* is discussed in the *Talmud*. Food eaten at this meal is the primary source of nourishment for the *luz* bone, a small bone at the top of the spine which never decays and will be the physical basis of resurrection after the coming of *Mashiach*.

Beginning the week with a *melave malkah* allows us to draw the atmosphere and feeling of Shabbat into the days of work, and to approach our week from the spiritual perspective of Shabbat.

Shabbat and Yom Tov Candles
The Blessing of Light

The image of a Jewish woman kindling her Shabbat candles is a timeless symbol of Jewish womanhood. In lighting the candles, she invites peace into the home and infuses the atmosphere with spiritual and physical light. All Jewish women and girls, whether young or old and whether married or unmarried, unite in illuminating the home with *hadlakat hanairot* (lighting the candles). On Yom Tov, too, the candles brighten the atmosphere and grace the table, creating a joyful, festive mood for the meal.

Shabbat candles flickering on a table profoundly affect a family. The candles remind young and old of their Jewish identity, and of the security and sanctity of the Jewish home. The Shabbat candles prevent those who see them from groping and stumbling in the spiritual darkness and confusion in our society. In a world where the distinctions between right and wrong are blurred, the Shabbat candles brightly illuminate the right path.

The *Talmud* explains that candle-lighting enhances *shalom bayit*, family harmony, by providing physical light so that family members don't stumble and fall in the darkness. The candles dispel darkness, creating a more positive environment.

Our Rabbis have compared a *mitzvah* to a candle: "Ki *ner mitzvah v'Torah or*," "A *mitzvah* is a candle and the Torah is light." (Proverbs 4:22) Certainly, a *mitzvah* which produces actual physical light has a particularly powerful spiritual radiance. The flickering flame is like the Jewish soul, ever striving upward to unite with the Creator.

A LIGHT IN EVERY GENERATION

Candle-lighting (*licht bentchen* in Yiddish) has been precious to Jewish women as far back as Biblical times. The candles of our Matriarchs, Sarah, Rivkah, Rachel, and Leah, lit the way for the foundations of the Jewish faith. In their time, idol worship and human sacrifice were a way of life. Their Shabbat lights illuminated a new path, the path of G-dliness, to the heathen world. The Torah relates that Sarah's Shabbat candles miraculously lit up her tent all week, and when she passed away this special light departed. Three years later, this light was rekindled when Rivkah, our second Matriarch, was preparing to marry Yitzchak. Rivkah's Shabbat candles cast the same continuous glow.

Throughout Jewish history, in times of peace or war, prosperity or struggle, Jewish women have held fast to the *mitzvah* of candle-lighting. The candelabra was often a family's most cherished possession, primarily because of the beloved *mitzvah* it represented. During the Spanish Inquisition, women risked their lives in secret observance of candle-lighting. Numerous stories are related of women who escaped with their lives during World War II, leaving behind all possessions except for their cherished candlesticks. Countless others struggled to obtain makeshift supplies in order to keep this precious *mitzvah*.

The Jewish woman is honored with candle-lighting in keeping with her position as *akeret habayit*, the mainstay of the home. She sets the tone and is the primary influence for the entire family. Each Jewish home is a miniature sanctuary, reminiscent of the *Beit Hamikdash* (the Holy Temple).

When the *Beit Hamikdash* was built in Jerusalem, the windows were designed to be narrow on the inside and wide on the outside. This allowed the light from within to spread outward, unlike most windows, whose purpose is to allow light from outside to enter. Similarly, the light of the woman's Shabbat candles spreads a glow of peace upon her household which radiates outward, rather than allowing a multitude of influences to pervade the home. As an *akeret habayit*, her influence begins with those closest to her and eventually extends beyond the home to her community, her people, and her nation. It is this ripple effect to which our Sages referred when they said, "If you will observe the kindling of the Shabbat lights, you will merit to see the light of the redemption of the Jewish people." (Midrash Yalkut Shimoni)

Candle-lighting has always been a special and auspicious moment, one of meditation and quiet prayer. This moment is the culmination of the week's work, the climax of a busy *erev* Shabbat.

The home is neat, the food tastefully prepared, the family dressed in beautiful Shabbat clothes. As a woman stands before the kindled flames, she prays for the well-being of her loved ones, and for the coming of *Mashiach*. The great *Kabbalist* and Torah scholar Rabbi Yitzchak Luria, known as the *Arizal*, writes that a woman's prayer on behalf of her husband and family is especially received by G-d at this moment. Her lights, together with those of her daughters, shine bravely in a world shrouded in darkness and confusion, illuminating the future with hope.

Freedom of religion and our prosperous lifestyle guarantee that in our country a Jewish woman no longer risks her life to light Shabbat candles. Today's Shabbat candles represent a different type of courage — the courage to take a strong stand in favor of Jewish pride and unity, family values, and commitment to Jewish life.

Today, Jewish girls and young women are privileged to participate in their own observance of candle-lighting. Small girls, their teenaged sisters, college students and professional women join homemakers, mothers and grandmothers in a universal observance of candle-lighting.

Young girls are particularly proud to be part of this tradition linking Jewish women throughout the generations. A girl looks forward with pride to the special moment she will share with her mother — a time of peace and of personal connection to G-d. A young girl's face glows with pleasure as she is granted the special opportunity to usher in Shabbat or Yom Tov with her very own candle.

There was a time when the candle-lighting of the mother may have shed sufficient light to preclude the necessity for her daughter to light. Today, an extra measure of light is urgently needed to pierce the dense darkness of a world beset by troubles. It is important, too, for girls in these times to forge their own link in the chain of Jewish womanhood. The sense of participation in *mitzvot* from an early age is an important part of Torah education. When Jewish daughters *bentch licht*, they add happiness to the home and light to the world. Many parents have been so inspired by the enthusiasm with which their young daughter observed candle-lighting that they have strengthened their own observance of Shabbat, *kashrut*, and other *mitzvot*. There can be no greater testimony to the power and importance of a young girl *bentching licht* than this, the return of her entire family to Torah observance.

The Torah's wisdom applies at all times, in every period of history, throughout every land. here are times, however, which demand a ⁺ain emphasis on or fortification of a particular *mitzvah*. For example, prior to the twentieth century, Jewish girls did not receive a formal Torah education. A girl's knowledge of Jewish law and tradition was absorbed at home, as she spent her days with her mother. At the turn of the century, Jewish leaders realized that the "home-style" education for girls had to be supplemented in order to successfully ensure the perpetuation of the strong Jewish home. Jewish leaders of that time established formal institutions of Torah learning for girls, which continue to flourish today.

Similarly, our times demand that every girl now play an active role in Jewish life. Candle-lighting is a most appropriate *mitzvah* for girls to observe. There is certainly nothing new or revolutionary about Jewish girls *bentching licht*; Rivkah, our second Matriarch, was only three years old when her candles cast a week-long radiance upon her tent. It was a common practice in many Rabbinic and Chassidic families for young girls, even as infants, to participate in candle-lighting. When the Jews of the nineteenth century were beset with financial hardships and persecution, it was often extremely difficult for women to produce a few candles, limiting them to the minimum of two candles in honor of Shabbat. Sadly, many women who had the custom of lighting additional candles after the birth of each child relinquished this practice. Reluctantly, unmarried girls were forced to postpone their own candle-lighting.

Today, this precious custom, so central to a Jewish girl's childhood, has been widely revived. Perhaps more than any other *mitzvah*, this practice crosses all lines and diminishes the distinctions between Jewish groups. Candles are lit by girls in homes of every level of observance, in house-

An Added Illumination

holds of numerous Chassidic groups, and in every country and culture where Jewish girls are to be found. This widespread renewal of candle-lighting by girls is the result of a call first made in 1974 (5735) by the Lubavitcher Rebbe, *Shlita*, for participation by all girls and women in the *mitzvah* of candle-lighting.

The candle-lighting campaign recognizes the great power and influence of girls and women. It provides a positive direction for youthful independence, and brings the generations together in Jewish unity. Every Jewish girl has the ability to dispel darkness and sadness and to speed the arrival of the Messianic Age, a time of light and joy.

LIGHTING THE SHABBAT CANDLES: LAWS AND CUSTOMS

Women bring the peace of Shabbat into the home by lighting candles every Friday evening, no later than eighteen minutes before sunset. As sunset varies from one location to the next, candle-lighting time varies from city to city. Jewish calendars provide lists of candle-lighting times for different cities. Sunset times are usually printed in local newspapers. It is strictly forbidden to light the candles after sunset.

As soon as a young girl can understand the significance of Shabbat and say the blessing (approximately three years old), she should kindle her own Shabbat candle. A girl should light before her mother, and is also forbidden to light her candle after the proper time.

Candles are lit on or near the table where the Shabbat dinner will be served, to add to the light and joy of Shabbat.

NOTE: On Shabbat the candles and candlesticks may not be touched or moved until the conclusion of Shabbat.

Procedure and Blessing

When the woman or girl lights candles to usher in Shabbat, she waves her hands toward herself, over the flames, and then covers her eyes with her hands.

She recites the blessing and then uncovers her eyes, gazes at the Shabbat lights and greets her family with "Good Shabbos" or "Shabbat Shalom."

The Blessing For Shabbat

BA-RUCH A-TAH A-DO-NOI ELO-HAI-NU
ME-LECH HA-O-LAM
A-SHER KID-SHA-NU B'MITZ-VO-TAV
V'TZI-VA-NU L'HAD-LIK NER
SHEL SHABBAT KO-DESH.

Blessed are You, L-rd our G-d,
King of the Universe,
Who has sanctified us with His commandments
and commanded us to kindle the light
of the holy Sabbath.

NOTE: When Shabbat and Yom Tov coincide, appropriate words are inserted. See Lighting The Yom Tov Candles, below.

The *mitzvah* of lighting candles for Shabbat and Yom Tov is unique in that the performance of the *mitzvah* precedes the blessing. Ordinarily the recitation of the proper blessing precedes the *mitzvah*. In this case, the *mitzvah* of lighting the candles is performed first, and the blessing is recited afterwards. The reason for this change is that if the blessing were to be recited first, the woman would have at that moment already inaugurated Shabbat. In that case she would not be permitted to light the candles, since kindling lights on Shabbat is forbidden. By gazing at the candles after the blessing is made, the blessing is considered to have preceded the *mitzvah*.

The time of candle-lighting is considered particularly auspicious for private prayer. Women have traditionally prayed, as they stand with eyes closed, for health, happiness, and children who will illuminate the world with Torah. Girls, too, offer their own prayers at this special moment, as they discover the beauty of a practice which will enlighten their entire lives.

Candle-lighting Customs

It is customary to place extra charity into a *tzedakah pushka* (charity box) *before* lighting the candles. This is a very important and beneficial custom, which should not be neglected. It is recommended that during pregnancy, a woman give extra *tzedakah* before candle-lighting. While charity is a daily *mitzvah*, the custom of connecting it to the *mitzvah* of candle-lighting reminds the whole family to consider the needs of others at the advent of Shabbat. Children, too, should be given a few coins of their own to put in the *pushka* before Shabbat. However, the holiness of Shabbat or Yom Tov overrides even this custom; therefore it is never permissible to put coins into a charity box after one has lit candles on Shabbat or Yom Tov.

Although the *mitzvah* of candle-lighting can be fulfilled by lighting only one candle, a married woman lights two candles, corresponding to the two expressions with which the Torah commands us to observe the Shabbat: *Shamor* (guard) and *Zachor* (remember) (Exodus 20:8 and Deuteronomy 5:12). Many women observe the custom of lighting an additional candle with the birth of each child, and continue lighting these additional candles throughout the years. A girl lights only one candle and continues to do so until she is married.

Candle-lighting is obligatory for men and women, although a married man does not light candles, as he is included in his wife's candle-lighting. An unmarried man or boy living with his mother also does not light, as he is included when she lights. A common situation is that of a boy or young man away at school, or a married man travelling away from home. In most cases, if a man lives alone, or if his wife or daughter over Bat Mitzvah (12 years old) is not home, he should light. An Orthodox Rabbi should be consulted for further clarification in each case.

A woman or girl away from home must light candles, either where she is staying or where she is eating. The woman's husband or children at home should also light the candles while she is away. If a woman is in the hospital, she should light candles if she can. If this is not possible, an Orthodox Rabbi should be consulted regarding the use of electric lights for this *mitzvah*.

Special Situations

LIGHTING THE YOM TOV CANDLES: LAWS AND CUSTOMS

It is a *mitzvah* to light candles and recite the appropriate blessing(s) on all Biblical holidays, namely: both nights of Rosh Hashanah, before sunset on Yom Kippur, the first two nights of Sukkot, Shemini Atzeret, Simchat Torah, the first two and last two nights of Pesach, and both nights of Shavuot. In Israel, except for Rosh Hashanah, these holidays are observed for one day.

The candle-lighting procedure for Yom Tov is similar to that for Shabbat. Differences between them concern the time of lighting, method of kindling, and the blessings.

The dates and candle-lighting times of the holidays vary from year to year. Therefore, every Jewish household needs a current Jewish calendar and a schedule of local candle-lighting times. For a fuller understanding of the lunar/solar calendar and of holiday observance, see The Jewish Calendar De-mystified, page 503.

On the first day of Yom Tov, the candles should be lit, as for Shabbat, no later than eighteen minutes before sunset. If they were not lit, one may light the candles after sunset, except on the eve of Yom Kippur or when Yom Tov coincides with Shabbat. When lighting candles past sunset on Yom Tov is permissible, care must be taken not to strike a match but to use a pre-existing flame for lighting (see Method of Kindling, below). However, when the first day of Yom Tov falls on Sunday, necessitating candle-lighting on Saturday night, one must wait until the conclusion of Shabbat before lighting the Yom Tov candles.

When Yom Tov is two days long, candles should be lit after nightfall on the second evening. However, when the second day of Yom Tov coincides with Shabbat, candles must be lit for Shabbat and Yom Tov before sunset on Friday night. (Consult a candle-lighting calendar for correct time.)

Time For Lighting Yom Tov Candles

On Yom Tov, similar to Shabbat, we do not kindle a flame. However, for the needs of Yom Tov we may hold a match or candle to a flame which is already lit — such as a pilot light, 24-hour candle, or a cooking flame which has been left on.

To light the candles once Yom Tov has begun, one must light a candle or match from a pre-existing flame as described above, and use this candle or match to light the Yom Tov candles. On Yom Tov, one may not melt the bottom of the candles before inserting them in the candlesticks. In homes with electric stoves, or where there is no gas pilot light available, it is advisable to light a 24-hour candle in order to have a flame for lighting the Yom Tov candles on the second night. Any flame ignited on Yom Tov may not be directly extinguished, but must be allowed to go out by itself.

Method Of Kindling On Yom Tov

Blessings For Yom Tov Candle-Lighting

The blessing over the Yom Tov candles is the same for Sukkot, Shemini Atzeret, Simchat Torah, Pesach and Shavuot. Only Rosh Hashanah and Yom Kippur differ in the blessings required.

NOTE: When Yom Tov coincides with Shabbat, include the words in brackets in the blessing.

The Yom Tov Blessing

BA-RUCH A-TAH A-DO-NOI ELO-HAI-NU
ME-LECH HA-O-LAM
A-SHER KID-SHA-NU B'MITZ-VO-TAV
V'TZI-VA-NU L'HAD-LIK NER
SHEL [SHABBAT V'SHEL] YOM TOV.

Blessed are You, L-rd our G-d,
King of the Universe,
Who has sanctified us with His commandments
and commanded us to kindle the light
of [the Sabbath and of] the holiday.

Shehechiyanu

A second blessing, *shehechiyanu*, is always said except for the last two nights of Pesach:

BA-RUCH A-TAH A-DO-NOI
ELO-HAI-NU ME-LECH HA-O-LAM
SHE-HECH-I-YA-NU V'KI-MA-NU
V'HI-GI-A-NU LI-Z'MAN HA-ZEH.

Blessed are You, L-rd our G-d,
King of the Universe,
Who has granted us life, sustained us
and enabled us to reach this occasion.

The Rosh Hashanah Blessing

BA-RUCH A-TAH A-DO-NOI
ELO-HAI-NU ME-LECH HA-O-LAM
A-SHER KID-SHA-NU B'MITZ-VO-TAV
V'TZI-VA-NU L'HAD-LIK NER
SHEL [SHABBAT V'SHEL] YOM HA-ZI-KA-RON.

Blessed are You, L-rd our G-d,
King of the Universe,
Who has sanctified us with His commandments
and commanded us to kindle the light
of [the Sabbath and of] the Day of Remembrance.

The *shehechiyanu* blessing is then said.

The Yom Kippur Blessing

BA-RUCH A-TAH A-DO-NOI
ELO-HAI-NU ME-LECH HA-O-LAM
A-SHER KID-SHA-NU B'MITZ-VO-TAV
V'TZI-VA-NU L'HAD-LIK NER SHEL
[SHABBAT V'SHEL] YOM HA-KIP-PU-RIM.

Blessed are You, L-rd our G-d,
King of the Universe,
Who has sanctified us with His commandments
and commanded us to kindle the light
of [the Sabbath and of] Yom Kippur.

The *shehechiyanu* blessing is then said.

Observing the Shabbat Laws

Shabbat is a day of holiness completely elevated above the rest of the week. The special laws pertaining to Shabbat preserve its sanctity and beauty.

The unique quality of Shabbat derives from two types of *mitzvot*: the beautiful *mitzvot* of sanctification such as

candle-lighting and K*iddush*; and the equally important *mitzvot* which require that we refrain from certain activities and work. The prohibitions against "work," far from being negative or burdensome, are an integral part of the experience of Shabbat as a day when body and soul are in true harmony.

These two aspects of Shabbat are reflected in the two expressions found in the two different presentations of the Ten Commandments found in the Torah. "*Remember* the Sabbath to keep it holy..." (Exodus 20:8) and "*Guard* the Sabbath to keep it holy..." (Deuteronomy 5:12) were, according to tradition, heard simultaneously by the Jewish people at Mount Sinai.

Zachor, "remember," refers to the positive commandments of the day — the things we do. "*Shamor*," "guard," refers to the negative commandments — the things we may not do. The latter, including such activities as cooking, writing and turning lights on and off, are described generally by the word *melachah*, a certain type of work.

Melachah: A Unique Definition Of Work

The Hebrew language has two words for "work" - *avodah* and *melachah*. *Avodah* is a general term meaning work, while *melachah* has a very precise *halachic* meaning. On Shabbat, *melachah* is prohibited. Our Sages explain that *melachah* refers to the activities which were necessary for construction of the M*ishkan*, the travelling sanctuary which the Jews took with them throughout their desert wanderings.

The Torah specifically mentions two *melachot*, kindling a fire and carrying. The M*ishnah* further explains that 39 different categories of *melachah* went into building the M*ishkan*. While these categories of labor refer to the construction of the M*ishkan*, they actually encompass all forms of human productivity. These *melachot* are not a haphazard collection of activities, and do not necessarily represent physical exertion. Rather, the principle behind them is that they represent constructive, creative effort, demonstrating man's mastery over nature. Refraining from *melachah* on Shabbat is a strong sign of recognition that, despite our human creative abilities, G-d is the ultimate Creator and Master.

A newcomer to Shabbat observance may be concerned that the numerous laws and their many nuances would present a hindrance to *oneg* Shabbat — enjoying and delighting in Shabbat. However, the unique way in which we pursue ordinary activities on Shabbat actually serves as a constant reminder of the special nature of this day. The changes in the way we cut vegetables, prepare a cup of tea, and engage in other mundane activities all heighten our awareness that Shabbat is totally different from the other days of the week.

Studying The Shabbat Laws

The Shabbat laws are quite complex, requiring careful study and a qualified teacher. Shabbat observers find that there is always more to learn on this subject. Becoming *shomer* Shabbat (Shabbat observant) is often a gradual process rather than an overnight transformation. The best way to become familiar with keeping Shabbat is to spend Shabbat with families who are *shomer* Shabbat and to continue to study the pertinent laws. All specific questions should be asked of an Orthodox Rabbi.

Following is a brief summary of some Shabbat laws, with practical examples of some laws pertaining to food preparation and other basics of Shabbat observance.

Melachah On Yom Tov: Most prohibitions applicable to Shabbat also apply on Yom Tov, except for major differences in the laws of cooking and carrying. The laws of Yom Tov observance pertaining to food preparation and carrying are discussed later.

FOOD PREPARATION ON SHABBAT

Included among the 39 *melachot* are several related to food preparation. In addition to the prohibition against cooking in any form, on Shabbat we are also prohibited from squeezing fruit, selecting, kneading, grinding and mashing. Electrical appliances may not be turned on or off on Shabbat.

Our Shabbat menus reflect our adherence to these various laws. Many traditional Shabbat foods have their origins in the Shabbat laws, including *cholent*, a warm dish which has been cooked prior to Shabbat, and gefilte fish, which has had all bones removed during its preparation.

Our manner of washing dishes, opening food packages, and even using the refrigerator are also different on Shabbat. The observance of Shabbat is greatly enhanced by becoming well-versed in the relevant laws.

Cooking On Shabbat

Cooking is prohibited on Shabbat. This includes boiling, roasting, frying and baking. We may not kindle or extinguish a flame, whether for cooking or any other purpose.

However, there are permissible ways to serve warm food on Shabbat. In fact, it is a *mitzvah* to eat warm food during the Shabbat lunch. This can be accomplished by keeping food hot on a special covering placed over the stove, as explained below. A gas or electric oven regulated by a thermostat should not be used on Shabbat, since opening and closing the oven door may affect the flame or electricity.

The "Shabbat Stove" - Setting Up The Blech

It is permissible to keep food warm on a gas flame or electric burner which has been turned on before Shabbat, as long as the source of heat is covered. This is usually done by covering the stovetop with a thin sheet of aluminum referred to as a *blech* (Yiddish for "tin"). It is preferable for the *blech* also to cover the control knobs for those burners which it covers, to prevent one from adjusting the flame on Shabbat.

A *blech* usually covers two to four burners, of which one or two are left on. If, for example, one wishes to place two pots of food on the *blech*, it is wise to leave only one burner on. The entire *blech* will become hot, but the area directly over the burner will be hottest.

When setting up the *blech*, it is best to use a low flame (or flames) so as not to burn the food. Food can be kept hot effectively even with a low flame.

From a health standpoint, be sure that food kept on the *blech* for more than an hour remains hot, not lukewarm, to prevent spoilage.

Food on the Blech: Food placed on the *blech* for Shabbat must be at least one-third or preferably one-half cooked. All salt, spices and liquid must be added before Shabbat begins.

Keeping Food Warm On The Blech: On Shabbat it is permissible to rearrange only those pots which sit directly on the *blech*, under the following conditions:
- □ the food is completely cooked;
- □ the part of the *blech* on which the pot sits is hot to the touch;
- □ the food has not cooled down to room temperature.

Warming Cold Food: On Shabbat, one may not place cold food, even when fully cooked, into a pot on the *blech*. However, one may place cold food (such as chicken or challah) near the fire but not on the *blech* to take the chill off, as long as it could never become hot (over 113° F) in that spot.

One may not serve food directly from a pot on the *blech*. The pot must first be removed from the *blech*.

Replacing Pots On The Blech: After removing a pot or kettle from the *blech* to serve from it, one may replace it on the *blech* only if all of the following conditions are met:

- When the pot was removed, one intended to put it back;
- The food is fully cooked;
- The food has not completely cooled off and is still slightly warm;
- The food has not been transferred to another pot;
- One holds the pot handle until replacing the pot on the *blech*. It is preferable not to put the pot down. If necessary, the pot may be placed on a table or any dry place except the floor, as long as one continues to hold the pot.

The Use Of A Crockpot: The laws concerning the use of a crockpot resemble those concerning the *blech*. The *cholent* stew, whether it is cooked first in a regular pot and then transferred to a crockpot, or cooked only in the crockpot, should be at least ½ cooked before Shabbat begins, and the temperature knob should be covered with aluminum foil.

The crockpot must have a removable bowl, which should be taken out before serving, just as a pot is removed from the *blech*.

In order to return the bowl to the crockpot on Shabbat, foil or some other material must be placed between the removable serving bowl and the heating element before Shabbat (to serve as a *blech*). See Replacing Pots on the Blech, above, for further guidelines.

When a hot food or liquid is removed from the *blech*, nothing may be added to it in the pot until it is transferred to another cup or bowl. In most cases it must be put into a third vessel, such as when adding salt, tea, croutons, etc. to soup or liquid. In addition, if the food from the *blech* is solid, such as chicken or thick *cholent*, it should also be allowed to cool down before adding anything to it in a third vessel. Further study of these laws is necessary, as the requirements vary according to the types of foods being combined.

Preparing Hot Beverages: If one wishes to prepare tea, coffee, or other hot drinks, one should set up a kettle of boiled water on the *blech* before Shabbat. Regarding the use of an electric urn to produce hot water, consult an Orthodox Rabbi.

One may not pour the hot water from the kettle directly onto an uncooked solid or liquid, since this would be considered cooking. Coffee, tea, and cocoa fall into this category. Therefore, to make tea or coffee on Shabbat, use the following method:

- pour the hot water from the kettle into a clean, dry cup;
- pour the water from this cup into another cup; and
- then add teabag, tea essence, coffee, sugar or milk. If using a teabag, do not squeeze it.

Many authorities recommend that instead of using teabags, a special concentrated "tea essence" be prepared before Shabbat. One cup of tea essence is prepared by allowing six teabags to steep in a cup of boiling water. Use one tablespoon of this concentrate to make a cup of tea.

Adding To Hot Foods and Liquids

On Shabbat we are not permitted to squeeze fruit, select, knead, grind, mash, grate, chop, shred, or cut very finely. There are complex details requiring further study regarding each *melachah*. The following are just a few practical examples:

- Salads must be made immediately before mealtime, and the pieces should not be cut too small.

- When mashing foods such as banana or avocado, one should vary the usual weekday method, and do it right before eating. For example, mash with the handle of a utensil instead of a spoon or fork. Vegetables or fruits that have been cooked can be mashed in the usual way.

- Fruits such as lemons, oranges and grapefruits may not be squeezed for their juice. They may, however, be squeezed directly onto solid foods such as vegetables, salad, or cake, to enhance their flavor.

Borer: On Shabbat it is forbidden to separate or sort out two or more types of items which are mixed together. This *melachah* is called *borer*, which means "selection." Selection may be done under the following conditions:

- Select that which you wish to use from that which you do not wish to use. For example, if a bowl contains both desirable and undesirable fruit, select the desired ones and leave the rest. Do not pick out the pieces of fruit you *don't* want. An easy phrase reminds us of the correct way: choose "good" from "bad," not "bad" from "good."

- The selection should take place only by hand, not by instrument.

- That which is being selected should be for immediate use.

Other Laws Pertaining To Food Preparation

□ When preparing eggs, fruits or vegetables which have inedible shells or peels, these may be removed on Shabbat immediately before the meal, but not with an instrument especially made for that purpose, such as a peeler. A knife, however, may be used. Some authorities permit the use of a peeler only if the peel is edible, as in the case of apples and carrots.

Preparing Food For Children: On Shabbat, there are special ways to prepare formula, warm bottles, mix cereals or mash food for babies or children. Consult one or more of the guides to Shabbat observance available in English or an Orthodox Rabbi.

NOTE: The above *melachot* on food preparation also affect other activities in addition to those directly involving food. Examples are wiping spills with a sponge, playing with modeling clay, mopping, or sorting broken or unwanted articles such as dishes, chairs or clothing.

OTHER IMPORTANT SHABBAT LAWS

Shabbat observance extends to many activities outside the realm of food preparation. Some basic activities from which we refrain on Shabbat are:

□ writing, erasing, and tearing;
□ business transactions;
□ driving or riding in cars or other vehicles;
□ shopping;
□ using the telephone; and
□ turning on or off anything which uses electricity, including lights, radios, television, air-conditioners and alarm clocks.

Lights which will be needed on Shabbat should be turned on before Shabbat. Automatic timers may be used for lights and some appliances as long as they have been set before Shabbat. The refrigerator may be used, but the light should be disconnected before Shabbat by unscrewing the bulb slightly. A freezer whose fan is activated when the door is opened may not be used on Shabbat.

Two other important categories which are not permitted are using or touching items that are considered *muktzeh*, and carrying outdoors. These two laws are explained below.

Muktzeh

On Shabbat, some objects may not be handled in the same way that they are handled during the week. These items are called *muktzeh*. In some cases, *muktzeh* may not be moved or used, even for activities permitted on Shabbat. There are a number of categories of *muktzeh* and many complex laws on this subject. We present only a few practical examples.

Objects which are used for activities forbidden on Shabbat are *muktzeh*. Examples include pens, money, matches and tools. Anything that contains or is a base for *muktzeh*, such as a purse holding money or a schoolbag, may also be *muktzeh*.

A situation that arises each week concerns lighting Shabbat candles on the table. The candlesticks are *muktzeh*, and may not be removed from the table on Shabbat. The table holding the candlesticks may in some cases be considered a base for *muktzeh* — preventing it from being moved if necessary. Therefore it is recommended for *halachic* reasons to place the *challot* or a *siddur* on the table before lighting the candles or before sunset. This makes it permissible to move the table if necessary. However, the candlesticks are still considered *muktzeh*. (After the meal, if the *challot* were eaten, some people set new ones on the table.)

Carrying

On Shabbat one may not carry or transfer objects between a "*reshut ha-yachid*" (private, enclosed domain, such as the house); and a "*reshut ha-rabim*" (public domain, such as the street). Examples of this prohibition include: carrying in one's pocket; carrying anything in the hand; wheeling a baby carriage or shopping cart, going outside with gum or food in the mouth. This prohibition also includes carrying in public hallways or yards of multiple dwellings, unless an *eiruv chatzeirot* is made. An *eiruv chatzeirot* is an arrangement whereby carrying in some of the above situations is permitted. In addition, the area in which one wishes to carry must be enclosed. This enclosure, commonly referred to as an *eiruv*, can occur naturally or be man-made, and must be constructed before Shabbat.

The Jewish community in some cities or neighborhoods constructs an *eiruv* which encloses several blocks. The area within the *eiruv* is considered a private domain where carrying is permitted. If there is an *eiruv*, it is important to know its boundaries so as not to carry beyond them. Some Rabbinic authorities discourage the practice of carrying within an *eiruv* which has been constructed around a neighborhood or city because one may become accustomed to carrying on Shabbat and make an error in a city without an *eiruv*, and for other *halachic* reasons.

For guidance on the laws of the *eiruv* and for other questions regarding an *eiruv*, consult an Orthodox Rabbi.

SOME YOM TOV LAWS

The holiness pervading the atmosphere on Shabbat prevails on Yom Tov as well. The days of Yom Tov are especially festive, and we make special efforts to honor Yom Tov with fine clothes and delicious dishes.

Generally, *melachot* prohibited on Shabbat are also prohibited on Yom Tov, with a few exceptions and alterations.

The Torah tells us regarding the observance of Yom Tov,"...No work may be done on these days, except for that which every person must eat..." (Exodus 12:16). Many of the activities necessary in food preparation are permitted because eating fresh food enhances the joy of the holiday.

___

Cooking On Yom Tov

Food may be prepared on Yom Tov according to the following conditions. (As on Shabbat, electrical appliances such as food processors and toasters may not be used.)

☐ One may cook and bake on Yom Tov as long as some of the food will be eaten on that day.

☐ Many food preparation activities which are prohibited on Shabbat may be done on Yom Tov in the weekday manner, such as kneading, dicing and mashing, and all forms of cooking and baking.

___

The Stove Top on Yom Tov

On Yom Tov, one may not light a new fire. A new flame may be kindled from an existing flame, such as a candle, gas flame, or pilot light. The burners on stoves which use electric starters must be lit without the use of these starters. If it will be necessary to light a new burner on Yom Tov, the stove top should be unplugged before Yom Tov and a small gas flame left on from which new flames may be lit.

A gas flame may be raised on Yom Tov. However, the flame can be lowered but not extinguished, only if another smaller flame is not available or cannot be lit, and the food will burn.

One may not adjust the heat on the burner of an electric stove at all. Whether the heat is raised or lowered, one element is either lit or extinguished, and this is prohibited on Yom Tov.

Since cooking under these conditions is permitted, one need not cover the stove with a *blech*. (However, many find the *blech* useful in keeping food warm on Yom Tov.) It is permissible to use the oven and to turn the heat up.

___

Eiruv Tavshilin

When Yom Tov occurs on Friday, it becomes necessary to prepare during Yom Tov for Shabbat. (Even if all food has been prepared, there are still tasks such as setting up the *blech* and preparing the candles.)

To be permitted to perform these preparations, one must make an *eiruv tavshilin*, (literally, a "mixing of cooking") *before* Yom Tov begins. This is done by taking at least one ounce of cooked food and at least two ounces of baked foods. Foods commonly used for the *eiruv tavshilin* are fish or hard-boiled egg and challah (or matzah on Pesach). A special blessing and paragraph, found in the *siddur*, are said over the two foods, which are put aside to be eaten on Shabbat afternoon.

If one forgot to make an *eiruv tavshilin* before Yom Tov, consult an Orthodox Rabbi.

NOTE: If Shabbat is followed directly by Yom Tov, one may not cook or prepare on Shabbat for Yom Tov. It is necessary to wait until nightfall Saturday night before preparing in any way for Yom Tov.

___

Carrying And Handling Muktzeh

On Yom Tov one may carry items which are needed for the day. Examples are carrying a *siddur* to *shul* (synagogue), carrying keys or personal items, bringing food for Yom Tov to someone's house, or pushing a baby in a stroller.

The laws regarding *muktzeh* on Shabbat also apply on Yom Tov, and in some cases are even stricter on Yom Tov.

Items used for performing an activity forbidden on Shabbat but permitted on Yom Tov, such as candles or candlesticks, are not *muktzeh* on Yom Tov.

___

The Promise of Redemption

Observing the Shabbat and Yom Tov has preserved the unity of the Jewish people throughout the centuries, and is a source of delight and spiritual sustenance each week.

The Talmud tells us "Were Israel to properly observe two Shabbatot, they would immediately be redeemed." (Talmud Shabbat 118b)

We hope this brief guide will serve as an impetus for further study of the Shabbat and Yom Tov laws.

The Jewish Year: The Sanctification of Time

"And you have given us in love Sabbaths for rest, and festivals for rejoicing, holidays and seasons for gladness . . ." (Siddur)

The Jewish holidays we celebrate throughout the year enrich our lives with their spiritual and physical delights. Each holiday brings a theme and a message, as well as a vivid experience which conveys more powerfully than words the beauty of our Jewish heritage. Happy memories of lighting the Chanukah *menorah* or asking the Four Questions at the Seder last a lifetime and form many links in the chain that binds generation to generation.

The Yomim Tovim — Jewish Festivals — emphasize the special historic and continuing bond between G-d and the Jewish people. Pesach (Passover) commemorates our redemption from slavery in Egypt; Shavuot marks our receiving the Torah seven weeks later. Chanukah and Purim celebrate miraculous Jewish victories over seemingly all-powerful enemies.

The Festivals are honored with delicious food and fine clothing, with conversation and song, *mitzvot* and prayer. The family table in the Jewish home complements and completes the synagogue service. The Yomim Tovim specified in the Torah are sanctified with candle-lighting and K*iddush*, as well as festive meals. As on

Shabbat, they are concluded with H*avdalah* (page 489). Chanukah and Purim, established by our Sages for all generations, have their own *mitzvot* and customs.

These holidays are more than a commemoration of long-past events and more than cultural traditions. Each Yom Tov brings a renewal of the Divine forces and influences that were present at the time of the first occurrence of the day. Pesach is thus intrinsically a time of redemption, a time for freeing ourselves from the personal "Egypt" of spiritual boundaries. On Shavuot we each receive the Torah anew and have the opportunity to internalize its message on a deeper level. The spiritual forces available at these times are thus renewed each year, in their season, for all generations.

The Jewish Calendar De-mystified

The dates of the Jewish Festivals are determined by their position in the Hebrew calendar, which is based on the lunar cycle. (The secular calendar is a solar one, based on the position of the earth in relation to the sun.) Each Hebrew month consists of either 29 or 30 days. The year begins with the month of Tishrei in early fall and is numbered according to the number of years from Creation.

Each month begins with Rosh Chodesh, the new moon. In ancient times the beginning of the month was declared by the *Beit Din* (Jewish Court), when two witnesses testified in Jerusalem that the new moon had appeared. The declaration of the new moon determined the dates of the Festivals. The time of Rosh Chodesh and the subsequent dates of the Yomim Tovim were fixed by Hillel Hanassi in the fourth century, based upon calculations handed down in the Oral Torah.

Seven times in every nineteen years, a second month of Adar is added to the calendar before the month of Nissan. This is to compensate for the fact the the lunar year is slightly shorter than the solar year, and to ensure that each Festival falls in its proper month and season designated in the Torah. Without this adjustment, all the months and holidays would move backwards in the year. Eventually Pesach would come in the winter, Rosh Hashanah in the spring, and so forth. The difference between the solar and lunar year also accounts for the fact that the Jewish holidays are sometimes earlier and sometimes later in relation to the secular months.

Although the new year begins with the anniversary of G-d's completion of the world, the month of Nissan is called "the first month" and the months themselves are numbered accordingly. This is because of the importance of the Festival of Pesach, in the month of Nissan, when the Jewish people were redeemed from Egypt.

Many of the Festivals we celebrate for two days are celebrated for only one day in Israel. The practice of observing two days of Yom Tov in the Diaspora originates from the ancient practice of declaring the new moon upon the testimony of witnesses and the subsequent dispatching of messengers to distant locations. Sometimes the messengers were unable to arrive before the Festival itself; therefore it became necessary to celebrate both of the possible days on which the Festival might fall.

A deeper reason for this difference is that in the Holy Land it is possible to absorb and experience the holiness of the Yom Tov in only one day, while in the Diaspora we require more time to accomplish this.

Living in Jewish time means living with an awareness of the weekly and yearly cycle of the special days, anticipating the Festivals, and celebrating them with meals, with wine, with prayer and with song. The year is then more than just a linear span of time; it is an upward spiral that is always meaningful and always a source of connection with the Jewish people and G-d. Actual performance of the *mitzvot* is the key to drawing down the holiness inherent in these days. The following pages provide the background and main observances of each Yom Tov. We hope these chapters will enhance your enjoyment of living Jewishly through the year.

The Jewish Calendar at a Glance

HOLIDAY	DATE	HEBREW MONTH	CORRESPONDING CIVIL MONTHS
Rosh Hashanah	1-2	Tishrei	September-October
Fast of Gedaliah	3		
Yom Kippur	10		
Sukkot (first 2 days)	15-16*		
Chol Hamoed Sukkot	17-21**		
Hoshanah Rabbah	21		
Shemini Atzeret	22		
Simchat Torah	23*		
		Marcheshvan	October-November
Chanukah	25-29(30)	Kislev	November-December
Chanukah (last days)	1-2(3)	Tevet	December-January
10th of Tevet (fast day)	10		
Tu B'Shvat	15	Shvat	January-February
		(Adar Rishon)***	
Fast of Esther	13	Adar	February-March
Purim	14		
Shushan Purim	15		
Fast of the First Born	14	Nissan	March-April
Pesach (first 2 days)	15-16*		
Chol Hamoed	17-20**		
Pesach (last 2 days)	21-22*		
Pesach Sheni	14	Iyar	April-May
Lag B'Omer	18		
Shavuot	6-7*	Sivan	May-June
Shiva Asar B'Tammuz (fast day)	17	Tammuz	June-July
Tisha B'Av (fast day)	9	Av	July-August
Fifteenth of Av	15		
		Elul	August-September

* The second date of these holidays indicate the additional day observed outside of Israel.

** In Israel, Chol HaMoed begins one day earlier.

*** Occurs only in a leap year.

On the Threshold of the New Year

As the summer months draw to a close and the new year approaches, there is a sense of anticipation in the air. Summer relaxation gives way to renewed energy for the coming year, which begins with Rosh Hashanah, the first two days of the Hebrew month of Tishrei.

Tishrei is the month most filled with holidays, special *mitzvot*, festive meals and traditional food customs. It is called a general or all-encompassing month, taking us through a full range of emotional and spiritual experiences, from serious and introspective to joyful and exuberant. From the first solemn blast of the *shofar* on Rosh Hashanah to the final joyful dance around the *bimah* on Simchat Torah, the Festivals of Tishrei give us spiritual strength for the year to come.

Our physical preparations for the new year are extensive; our kitchens are aromatic with delicious *challot* and traditional honey-cakes. By the same token, we must set aside time for spiritual preparation so that when Rosh Hashanah comes, we will feel prepared to proclaim G-d our King and to ask His blessings.

To enable us to enter the new year and its time of judgment in the right frame of mind, we are given the entire month preceding it as a time of preparation. This is the month of Elul.

ELUL

Elul, the month that brings the year to a close, also signifies the beginning of our preparations for the year to come. The sound of the *shofar* each day reminds us that with all the physical preparations we undertake for the approaching holidays, we should also remember that this is a time for spiritual reflection.

The month of Elul, occurring in late August and early September, is a time especially designated for reflection upon the year that is ending, a time for introspection and spiritual stock-taking. A businessman takes account of all his assets and liabilities at the end of his fiscal year; Elul is our month for a *cheshbon hanefesh* (an accounting of the soul).

Through examining our deeds, we can begin to correct what is lacking and effect changes for the better in preparation for Rosh Hashanah, the Day of Judgment.

Elul has been an auspicious time for *teshuvah* since Biblical times. On Rosh Chodesh Elul, Moshe ascended the mountain to spend the next forty days, until Yom Kippur, praying on behalf of the Jewish people.

Although often translated as repentance, *teshuvah* means return — return to the true inner self that is always connected to its source. *Teshuvah* means sincere regret for past misdeeds and the resolve not to repeat the same actions in the future. It also means the desire to come closer to G-d through prayer and the performance of *mitzvot*, particularly the giving of *tzedakah* (charity).

Rabbi Schneur Zalman, founder of the *Chabad* Chassidic movement, used the parable of the "King in the field" to describe the month of Elul: Once a year the king would be out in the fields where all could approach him and he received everyone graciously. G-d — the King of Kings — is also in the field once a year, during Elul. Our prayers and requests are readily received during this time, and the path to G-d is wide open.

This is alluded to by the verse whose initial letters spell out the name Elul, "Ani L'*dodi* V'*dodi* Li" — "I am to my beloved and my beloved is to me" (Song of Songs 6:3) referring to the closeness between G-d and the Jewish people experienced in the month of Elul.

Observances During Elul

Each day during the month, except on Shabbat and the day before Rosh Hashanah, the *shofar* is blown after morning services. We also add Psalm 27, containing allusions to the holidays of Tishrei, to the morning and afternoon prayers. This practice continues until Hoshanah Rabbah. *Chabad* custom is to add to the recital of *Tehillim* (Psalms) from the beginning of Elul through Yom Kippur.

In personal letters and cards one expresses good wishes to friends with the words, "May you be inscribed and sealed for a good year."

In the final days of Elul, in the very early hours of the morning, we highlight our preparation for the new year with *Selichot*, heartfelt prayers for forgiveness. After the *Selichot* prayers, the climax of our preparations for the New Year, we stand ready for the awesome day of Rosh Hashanah.

Rosh Hashanah through Yom Kippur

Days of Awe

The Jewish year begins with the *Yomim Norayim*, Days of Awe. They extend from Rosh Hashanah, the Day of Judgment, until Yom Kippur, the Day of Atonement. These ten days are a time of concentrated spiritual effort, permeated with the knowledge that everything we do

during this time has the power to affect the coming year. The inspiration of these days awakens us to ever new possibilities for conducting our lives on a higher level, and we enter the new year prepared to improve our relationship both with G-d and with our fellow man.

The concept of *teshuvah*, return, that is emphasized during these days is a positive one, permitting us to begin the year with a clean slate and the feeling of new beginnings. Prayer, *tefillah*, is especially important during this time. Our prayers are both individual and communal, underscoring the fact that the fate of each Jew is fundamentally bound up with the fate of all other Jews and that we are all parts of one whole. This concept is also expressed in the giving of extra *tzedakah*, charity, during these days. Thus the

phrase that is a recurrent theme in the holiday prayer book on Rosh Hashanah and Yom Kippur: "*Teshuvah—tefillah — tzedakah* avert the evil decree."

The holiness of the Days of Awe is a prelude to the joy which follows during Sukkot and Simchat Torah, festivals of rejoicing. On Rosh Hashanah, as we affirm G-d's Kingship, we are filled with gladness and confidence that our prayers for a sweet year will be answered. Yom Kippur, the culmination of our days of *teshuvah* and the holiest day of the year, brings the certainty that we have been sealed for a good year.

Honey cake and sweet round challahs, giving charity and going to *shul*, holiday clothing and festive meals — all are part of the special time we call the Jewish New Year and the *Yomim Norayim*. The experience of these days remains with us well into the year, providing inspiration and strength until a new cycle begins once again with another new year, each year bringing a new light and radiance as the cycle continues.

ROSH HASHANAH

"The first day of the seventh month [Tishrei] shall be a sacred holiday to you when you may not do any mundane work. It shall be a day of sounding the (ram's) horn. (Numbers 29:1)

Rosh Hashanah stirs the heart of every Jew. The Jewish New Year is a time of awe and solemnity. On this day we re-establish and intensify our relationship with G-d and are judged, together with all of mankind, as to the events of the coming year.

Throughout Rosh Hashanah, we are attuned to the holiness of the day. All our activities - praying in *shul*, listening to the *shofar*, and partaking of

festive meals are imbued with an awareness of G-d's Kingship.

On Rosh Hashanah we stand before the Almighty, united with Jews everywhere, and pray for a year of health, prosperity and peace. The words we read in the *machzor*, the special holiday prayer book, help us channel our thoughts and prayers upward, shaped by the stirring and incisive words of our great Sages. Our hearts are awakened to the awesome power of the day.

Rosh Hashanah is observed both in Israel and in the Diaspora for two days. Yom Tov candles are lit both nights, with the appropriate blessings, including *shehechiyanu*. A number of special food customs are observed during holiday meals.

Rosh Hashanah means "head of the year." Just as the head contains the brain which controls the entire body, so does Rosh Hashanah contain within it the potential for life, blessing and sustenance for the entire year. Our actions on Rosh Hashanah set the tone for the year to come. For this reason we are careful in all we think, say and do during these two days.

The anniversary of the creation of man is on Rosh Hashanah. The first man, Adam, proclaimed G-d as King over the Universe, calling upon all creatures to worship Him. Each Rosh Hashanah we reaffirm that G-d is our King and renew our commitment to live according to His will. We pray that G-d, in turn, will grant us a good and sweet year. Our wishes for one another are reflected in the words which we say after services on the first night of Rosh Hashanah, L'shanah tovah tikateiv v'teichatem, "May you be written and inscribed for a good year."

The Shofar

"After the blowing of the shofar, a new, more sublime light descends, so sublime a light as has never shone yet since the beginning of the world." (Tanya Iggeret Hakodesh 14)

Hearing the *shofar* blown on Rosh Hashanah is obligatory for men. Women, too, have accepted this *mitzvah*. For the sake of *chinuch* (education), children are also brought to hear the *shofar*.

The *shofar* is blown on both days of Rosh Hashanah, except on Shabbat. One should hear at least the first thirty *shofar* blasts of the hundred which are sounded throughout the Rosh Hashanah services. If one is not able to attend synagogue services, one should make every effort to hear the *shofar* elsewhere, even later in the day. The man who blows the *shofar* must know the *halachot* involved, for there are details which, if incorrect, could invalidate the sounds.

The *shofar* is a ram's horn, the oldest and most primitive of wind instruments. The call of the *shofar* touches the innermost chords of the Jewish soul. Its sound is simple and plaintive — a cry from the heart, like that of a lost child for its parent. The sound of the *shofar* is a call to look into one's soul and improve one's ways, as expressed by the *Rambam*: "Awake you sleepers from your sleep, and you slumberers, arise from your slumber - examine your deeds, return and remember your Creator."

The *shofar* is associated with several other themes. It not only symbolizes the coronation of G-d as King of the Universe but also brings to mind several great events which involved a ram's horn, including the giving of the Torah at Mount Sinai, and the binding of Yitzchak on Mount Moriah. The sound of the *shofar* will also herald the coming of *Mashiach* and the final redemption of the Jewish people.

Tashlich

On the first day of Rosh Hashanah, after the afternoon services, we symbolically cast our transgressions into a body of fresh water containing live fish, in accordance with the words from the *Tashlich* prayer, "And You [G-d] will cast all their sins into the depths of the sea." After reciting this prayer, which is found in the *machzor*, we shake the bottom of our garments. If the first day of Rosh Hashanah is on Shabbat, *Tashlich* is said the second day. If necessary, *Tashlich* may also be said any day until Yom Kippur, except for Shabbat.

Food Customs

Many *mitzvot* and customs of Rosh Hashanah are related to food. The following guide includes most of the traditional dishes. Many groups, especially Sephardic Jews, observe additional customs, including special blessings and foods.

On Rosh Hashanah, we eat round *challot*, which we dip into honey after the *hamotzi* blessing. We also dip an apple into honey. This expresses our wish for a good, sweet year, as does the popular custom of serving sweet dishes such as carrot *tzimmes* and honey cake.

Many food customs on Rosh Hashanah reflect our wishes for the coming year in the form of a culinary pun such as *merren* (Yiddish), which means both "to increase" and "carrots." This is another reason for eating carrot *tzimmes* at the holiday meals.

On the first night of Rosh Hashanah, after we eat the challah dipped in honey, we dip slices of apple in honey. *Chabad* custom is first to say the blessing *ha-aitz* over the fruit and then:

Y'HEE RA-TZON MIL-FA-NE-CHA
SHE-T'CHA-DAISH A-LAI-NU
SHA-NAH TO-VAH U-M'TU-KAH

*May it be Your will to renew for us
a good and sweet year.*

Chabad custom is to serve pomegranates on the first night of Rosh Hashanah, after the apple is dipped in honey. This custom symbolizes the wish that our merits be increased like the seeds of a pomegranate.

The head of a lamb or a fish is often served, signifying our hope to be the "head," outstanding in righteousness and an example for all.

The Blessing Shehechiyanu On The Second Night: The blessing *shehechiyanu*, in which we thank G-d for enabling us to reach a new season, is said on the first and second night of Yom Tov, during candle-lighting or *Kiddush*. On Rosh Hashanah, which is considered "one long day," we need an additional reason to say *shehechiyanu* on the second night. At the time of candle-lighting on the second night, a new fruit which has not yet been eaten that season is placed on the table. When *shehechiyanu* is said during candle-lighting or *Kiddush*, one has in mind that this blessing is also said for the new fruit.

The new fruit is eaten right after *Kiddush*, before *hamotzi* is made on the challah. Popular choices include fresh (not dried) figs, dates, kiwis, mangoes and papayas.

On the second night of Rosh Hashanah it is preferable for the woman to light candles right before eating the meal to diminish the time lapse between her *shehechiyanu* blessing and the time when she will eat the new fruit. Since *shehechiyanu* can also be said over a new garment, she may also have in mind that the blessing is being said over a new garment that she is wearing. (Some authorities recommend the latter practice as preferable.)

Observing Rosh Hashanah

- ☐ Candle-lighting both nights
- ☐ *Kiddush* and festive meals, both nights and both days
- ☐ Hear *shofar* both days, except Shabbat
- ☐ Say *Tashlich* first afternoon, except Shabbat

TRADITIONAL FOODS

- ☐ Round challahs
- ☐ Challah dipped in honey
- ☐ Apple dipped in honey
- ☐ Other sweet foods, such as carrot *tzimmes*
- ☐ The head of a fish or lamb
- ☐ A new seasonal fruit over which *shehechiyanu* is said

THE TEN DAYS OF TESHUVAH

"On Rosh Hashanah they are inscribed and on the fast day of Yom Kippur they are sealed." (Machzor - U'netanah Tokef)

Rosh Hashanah, Yom Kippur, and the days between them are known as the Ten Days of *Teshuvah*. *Teshuvah* means return — a return to good, to *mitzvot*, and to one's true inner self, which is a spark of G-dliness. While Rosh Hashanah is the Day of Judgment, our verdict is not sealed until the final moments of Yom Kippur. Even then, the gates are not fully closed until Hoshanah Rabbah in the following week. Like a fond parent, G-d keeps giving us another chance to do *teshuvah*. Our sincere *teshuvah* is accepted at all times, but these days are particularly opportune for renewing our relationship with G-d.

The seven days between Rosh Hashanah and Yom Kippur represent the first weekly cycle of the new year. This complete week presents a special opportunity to evaluate each day of the week as it was spent in the previous year, and to plan for improvement in the coming year. During this week we increase in Torah study, the giving of *tzedakah*, and observance of *mitzvot*. We may make a special effort to avoid gossip, or observe a stricter level of *kashrut*. For example, those who might eat *pat palter* (see page 26) during the year will avoid doing so during the Ten Days.

During these days it is customary to apologize and seek forgiveness from friends, relatives and anyone whom we may have wronged during the year. This is important because Yom Kippur atones for sins against G-d, but not for those against one's fellow man.

Fast Of Gedaliah: The third of Tishrei, the day following Rosh Hashanah, is a fast day in remembrance of the last Jewish governor of ancient Israel after the destruction of the first *Beit Hamikdash*. His death initiated the decline of Jewish settlement in Israel at that time, and for many years to come.

Shabbat Shuvah: The Shabbat between Rosh Hashanah and Yom Kippur is known as Shabbat Shuvah because of the beginning words of the *Haftorah* which is read this Shabbat: "Return Israel unto G-d." (Hosea 4) Rabbis customarily speak to their congregations on this day about the importance of *teshuvah*. This Shabbat is also referred to as *Shabbat Teshuvah*.

Chabad custom is to light a 24-hour candle prior to lighting the Shabbat candles for Shabbat Shuvah. This candle is referred to as a *teshuvah licht*.

EREV YOM KIPPUR

The day preceding Yom Kippur is an important prelude to Yom Kippur itself. *Erev* Yom Kippur is a busy day filled with customs, traditional foods, and the *mitzvot* that complete our preparation for receiving forgiveness on Yom Kippur.

Kapparot: Before Yom Kippur we observe the custom of *Kapparot* ("atonement"). A man or boy takes a rooster, and a woman or girl a hen. Swinging the fowl over the head, the prayer, "This is my exchange . . .," is recited. The fowl is then given to the *shochet* and the meat, or the value of it, is donated to the poor. The idea of this custom is to evoke sincere repentance by reminding us that we ourselves may deserve a similar fate as the result of our transgressions.

This custom may also be observed by using money instead of a live fowl. While it is preferable to do *Kapporot* on the night or in the early morning before Yom Kippur, it may also be done on any other day between Rosh Hashanah and Yom Kippur, except Shabbat.

Two Festive Meals

It is a *mitzvah* on *erev* Yom Kippur to eat more than usual. Partaking of a festive meal before Yom Kippur demonstrates our faith in G-d's abundant mercy, and our confidence in being forgiven and sealed for a good year. Our Sages say that the merit of one who eats well on *erev* Yom Kippur is as great as one who has fasted for two days. Not only is eating before Yom Kippur a preparation for Yom Kippur, a day of fasting, but it is a *mitzvah* in itself, enabling us to receive forgiveness.

Two meals are served on *erev* Yom Kippur. The first is eaten early in the afternoon, before the afternoon service. The second, final meal before the fast is called the *seudah hamafseket*. This festive meal is eaten after *Minchah*, late in the afternoon.

Both meals begin with challah dipped in honey, but *Kiddush* is not said.

Fish is customarily included in the first meal. Neither fish nor dairy are served at the second meal and meat is not eaten at all on *erev* Yom Kippur. (This includes both red meat and veal, but chicken and other fowl may be served.)

Kreplach are traditionally served on this day. Their closed shape symbolizes the covering of G-d's strictness with loving-kindness.

To ease our fast, we should eat only light, easily digestible foods that are not salty or spicy. Chicken soup and boiled chicken are traditional.

The *seudah hamafseket* must be completed well before sunset.

Other Customs On Erev Yom Kippur

Immersion in a *mikvah* is another preparation for the holiness of Yom Kippur. The *mikvah* is a ritual bath which imparts spiritual purity to those who immerse. Men have the custom to immerse as many as three times on this day. Many women have also adopted the custom of immersing on *erev* Yom Kippur. (This is apart from the *mitzvah* of *mikvah*, one of the three special *mitzvot* that is incumbent upon married women.)

A common custom on *erev* Yom Kippur is to receive a piece of *lekach* (honey cake) from another person, often the *gabbai* or Rabbi of the *shul*. This transaction is a symbolic substitute for any charity a person might be destined to receive in the coming year; it also represents the giver's wish that the recipient have a good year.

After the final meal, parents bless their children, the father putting his hands on the head of each child and reciting a prayer on his or her behalf. The following Biblical words are included: "May G-d make you like Efraim and Menashe" (for a son) or "May G-d make you like Sarah, Rivkah, Rachel and Leah" (for a daughter).

Extra *tzedakah* (charity) is given on this day. Platters representing various charities greet us at the entrance to the *shul* — a timely reminder of the great *mitzvah* of *tzedakah*.

Minchah, the afternoon prayer, is said early, to allow enough time for the second festive meal. The *Viduy*, a confessional prayer said on Yom Kippur, is included.

Extra Candles For Yom Kippur: In honor of this holiday, before we light the Yom Tov candles, every household lights a 24-hour candle called a *lebedik licht* (light for the living). This is lit at home. The flame from this candle is used to light the *Havdalah* candle at the conclusion of Yom Kippur.

Twenty-four hour *yahrtzeit* candles are lit in memory of parents who have passed away. A separate candle is lit for each. According to community customs, these candles may be lit in *shul*.

Observing Erev Yom Kippur

- ☐ Perform *Kapparot*
- ☐ Immerse in *mikvah*
- ☐ Two festive meals (without *Kiddush*)
- ☐ *Lekach*
- ☐ Extra *tzedakah*
- ☐ Parents bless children
- ☐ *Yahrtzeit* candle(s)
- ☐ Candle-lighting before sunset

TRADITIONAL FOODS

- ☐ Challah dipped in honey
- ☐ *Kreplach*
- ☐ No meat
- ☐ Fish at first meal
- ☐ Do not eat spicy or very salty foods, fish or dairy at second meal

YOM KIPPUR

"Each year on the tenth day of the seventh month (Tishrei) you must fast and not do any work... Before G-d you will be cleansed of all your sins. It is a Sabbath of Sabbaths to you, and you must fast. This is a law for all time." (Leviticus 16:29-31)

Yom Kippur, the holiest day of the year, is the culmination of the "Ten Days of Teshuvah." This is the day on which the eternal words, "I have forgiven," were spoken by G-d after Moshe Rabbeinu prayed and fasted for forty days on behalf of the Jewish people after their sin of the Golden Calf. The tenth day of Tishrei is the Day of Atonement for all generations, a day when G-d forgives all our sins. It is a day of fasting and prayer.

Yom Kippur begins before sunset, and is ushered in with candle-lighting and the appropriate blessings, including *shehechiyanu*. On Yom Kippur five activities are prohibited: eating and drinking, anointing with perfumes or lotions, washing (for pleasure), wearing leather shoes, and marital relations.

Fasting on Yom Kippur is such a serious injunction that we fast even if Yom Kippur occurs on Shabbat. (All other fast days are postponed until Sunday in honor of Shabbat.) Yom Kippur is also called Shabbat Shabbaton, the Sabbath of Sabbaths — and activities which are prohibited on Shabbat are also prohibited on Yom Kippur.

Men wear a *kittel*, a special white garment, to *shul*. Women often dress in white to symbolize purity.

On Yom Kippur, free from material concerns, we can devote the day to prayer. The Yom Kippur prayers are found in a special prayer book called a *machzor*, containing some of the most beautiful and moving passages in Jewish liturgy. Many of the prayers are sung to hauntingly beautiful melodies. The prayers direct our thoughts to feelings of *teshuvah*. We pray to receive G-d's greatest gift — His forgiveness — an expression of His eternal, unconditional love. Yom Kippur is the day that most clearly reveals the true essence of the soul of the Jew, which is a spark of G-d and united with Him.

The first prayer of Yom Kippur, as the sun is setting, is *Kol Nidrei*, the annulment of vows. We recite *Kol Nidrei* because the atonement achieved on Yom Kippur does not include the annulment of broken vows. This prayer is especially symbolic

of unity among all Jews.

During each main prayer throughout Yom Kippur, we recite the *Viduy*, confession, tapping our chest near the heart with the right hand and asking G-d for forgiveness as we enumerate the sins we may have committed. The *Viduy* is phrased in the plural ("We have sinned..."), for all Jews are considered as one body, and we are all responsible for one another.

Yizkor, the memorial prayer for the departed, is chanted at the end of the morning service. Only those who have lost a parent remain in the synagogue during this short prayer. (*Yizkor* may be said at home if necessary.) One of the highlights of the Yom Kippur prayers is the recital of the *Avodah*, which recounts the service which took place in the *Beit Hamikdash* on Yom Kippur.

The final prayer of Yom Kippur, as our judgment

Special Prayers

for the coming year is being sealed, is called Ne'ilah, "closing the gate." This is the only service of the year during which the doors of the Aron Kodesh (Holy Ark) remain open from beginning to end, signifying that the gates of prayer are wide open to us at this time. We conclude with Shema Yisrael and other verses said in unison, and the final sounding of the shofar followed by the words, L'SHA-NAH HA-BAH BI-Y'RUSHA-LA-YIM, "Next year in Jerusalem!" Yom Kippur ends on a triumphant note, with greetings of "Good Yom Tov!"

The Conclusion Of Yom Kippur

At the conclusion of Yom Kippur, we recite the Havdalah prayer over a cup of wine. We include the blessing over light because during Yom Kippur, as on Shabbat, we are prohibited from handling fire. The blessing should be said on a flame that was lit before Yom Kippur began, such as a 24-hour candle.

After Havdalah we break the fast with a festive meal. It is customary to begin building the sukkah afterwards, or at least to plan the sukkah. In this way, we go from mitzvah to mitzvah and from "strength to strength."

Observing Yom Kippur

☐ Candle-lighting before sunset
☐ Fast, from before sundown until after nightfall
☐ Observe five prohibitions
☐ Say Yizkor, if applicable
☐ Say Havdalah before breaking fast

Sukkot, Shemini Atzeret and Simchat Torah
Season of our Rejoicing

We end Yom Kippur in an uplifted mood, joyfully anticipating the next Yom Tov. Sukkot is only four days away. Soon after breaking the fast, many people begin to build the *sukkah*, and the sound of hammers is heard well into the night.

In the days following, shopping for a beautiful *etrog* (citron) for the *mitzvah* of the Four Species becomes a primary concern. Jews hurry along the streets carrying the carefully boxed *etrog* and tall slender *lulav* (date palm). The *lulav* is like a scepter; it is symbolic of our faith in having emerged victorious after the days of judgment and atonement, and of our faith in G-d's promise to grant us a good year.

The air is fragrant with the smell of pine needles as we place evergreen branches on the roof of the *sukkah*. Invitations have been issued, guests arrive, ovens are full. Finally, on the fifteenth of Tishrei, the full harvest moon shines down upon the first night of the joyous holiday of Sukkot.

All Yomim Tovim are occasions for rejoicing, but only Sukkot is called *z'man simchateinu*, the Season of Our Rejoicing. The Torah commandment to "rejoice in your festivals" is mentioned more times in connection with this holiday than with any other, and indeed Sukkot abounds with *mitzvot* that enable us to enter the new year with a buoyant spirit and a feeling of unity.

SUKKOT

Sukkot is one of the *Shalosh Regalim*, the three "Pilgrimage Festivals" when all Jews were commanded to travel to Jerusalem at the time when the *Beit Hamikdash* stood. Although this requirement was primarily for men, whole families often dotted the roads in ancient Israel, walking or riding in jubilant anticipation of celebrating the Yom Tov in the proximity of the *Beit Hamikdash*. Sukkot is also known as the Festival of Ingathering, when the produce of the field, orchard and vineyard was harvested. The bounty of the harvest was an additional cause for celebration.

The holiday of Sukkot lasts for seven days. We light Yom Tov candles on the first two nights with the appropriate blessings, including *shehechiyanu*. We recite *Kiddush*, eat festive meals, and observe all holiday laws during these two days. The next five days are known as *Chol Hamoed*, the intermediate days, when some work is permitted. The fifth day of *Chol Hamoed* is called Hoshanah Rabbah, which is a festival in its own right.

During the seven days of Sukkot, we eat meals and spend time in temporary dwellings in fulfillment of the commandment, "In *sukkot* (booths) shall you dwell, seven days." (Leviticus 23:42)

The Sukkah

The *sukkah* is an outdoor structure whose roof consists of vegetation such as evergreen branches, corn husks, or bamboo stalks. This roof, partly open to the sky, is called *s'chach*. Any material may serve as walls. Some people build their *sukkah* out of plywood or other wooden boards; others buy colorful plastic or prefabricated ones. The *sukkah* is often placed on a porch or adjacent to the house, with one wall of the house forming a wall for the *sukkah*. It may be small or large, as long as it meets the requirements of Jewish Law. (Consult an Orthodox Rabbi for details concerning the building of a *sukkah*.) The *sukkah* is completed before Sukkot begins.

The *sukkah* is the only *mitzvah* that actually encompasses us. It symbolizes the "clouds of glory" which surrounded and protected the Jewish people during their forty years in the wilderness after they left Egypt. These clouds of glory, serving as a shade and a shield, were an ever-present reminder of G-d's kindness and love for His children. The fragility of the *sukkah* also reminds us that it is G-d to Whom we must turn for protection, even at the time of the ingathering of the crops, a time of material success and accomplishment, when we might be tempted to think that our well-being is dependent upon our human power and abilities alone.

Although the exodus from Egypt occurred in the spring, we are commanded to celebrate Sukkot in the fall. Dwelling in the *sukkah* is not similar to vacationing in a summer cabin or a bungalow. We enter the *sukkah* for the sake of the *mitzvah*, when the autumn weather is upon us and when strong winds begin to blow and rain to fall.

It is very desirable to have guests in one's *sukkah* for the festive meals, just as we have the *ushpizin* (heavenly guests) who are said to visit every *sukkah*. These heavenly guests are our "Seven Faithful Shepherds" — Avraham, Yitzchak, Yaakov, Moshe, Aharon, Yosef, and David. There is also a Chassidic tradition of *ushpizin* corresponding to the previous generations of Chassidic leaders, beginning with Rabbi Yisrael Baal Shem Tov.

The Four Species

"*On the first day, you must take for yourself a fruit of the citron tree, an unopened palm frond, myrtle branches, and willows that grow near the brook. You shall rejoice before G-d seven days.*" (Leviticus 23:40)

This passage refers to the *mitzvah* of "the taking of the Four Species": the *etrog* (citron, a lemon-like fruit), the *lulav* (palm branch), *hadas* (myrtle) and *aravah* (willow). The *lulav*, *hadas* and *aravah* are joined together prior to Sukkot. This combination of three branches is collectively known as a *lulav*.

Many of the commandments of the Torah, often simple actions performed with physical objects, provide us with philosophical insights which enrich our understanding as we actually perform the *mitzvah*. In this case, four separate species together comprise one *mitzvah*; if one of them is missing then the *mitzvah* is not fulfilled. Our Sages have explained that the holiday of Sukkot, when all of the Jewish people gathered in Jerusalem, expresses the concept of the unity of the Jewish people. This unity is represented by the *mitzvah* of *lulav* and *etrog*.

The *etrog* is a fruit that has both taste and fragrance, and is compared to the person who studies Torah and performs good deeds. The *lulav* (palm) has taste but no fragrance, referring to one who is learned in Torah but lacks good deeds. The *hadas* (myrtle) has fragrance but no taste, like one who practices good deeds but is not learned in Torah. And the *aravah* (willow) has neither fragrance nor taste — a reference to a person who lacks both Torah knowledge and good deeds. The *Midrash* tells us, "G-d says, 'Let them be bound together in one bond, and these will atone for those.' " (Vayikrah Rabbah 30) In other words, when Jews are united, each individual complements and makes up for that which is lacking in his fellow Jew.

The Lubavitcher Rebbe, *Shlita*, explained further that the *mitzvah* of *lulav* and *etrog* teaches us that no one can reach fulfillment unless he joins his fellow man. Even the highest level of perfection, as represented by the *etrog* (which combines both taste and smell), is incomplete. Similarly, no matter how much we develop ourselves as individuals, we cannot reach our true potential without the help of others. Unity among all Jewish people contributes to the growth and progress of every individual.

The Mitzvah of Lulav and Etrog

The enhancement of the *mitzvah* of *lulav* and *etrog* is an essential aspect of its performance. As a result, we go to great lengths to acquire *etrogim* that are considered to be especially *hadar* or beautiful. Many stories are passed down of great sacrifices made by Jews to obtain *etrogim* in times of scarcity or hardship.

The *mitzvah* of *lulav* and *etrog* is performed on all seven days of Sukkot except on Shabbat. It should be done early in the day but is permissible until sunset. While women are not obligated in the *mitzvah*, they have generally accepted the responsibility to perform it throughout Sukkot.

The *lulav* (along with the *hadassim* and *aravot*) is taken in the right hand with the *lulav's* 'spine' facing the person holding it. The following blessing is then said:

BA-RUCH A-TAH A-DO-NOI
ELO-HAI-NU ME-LECH HA-O-LAM
A-SHER KID-SHA-NU B'MITZ-VO-TAV
V'TZI-VA- NU AL N'TILAT LU-LAV.

Blessed are You, L-rd our G-d, King of the Universe,
Who has sanctified us with His commandments
and commanded us concerning the taking of the lulav.

On the first day of Yom Tov, or the first time performing the *mitzvah* of *lulav* for the year, the blessing *shehechiyanu* is also recited.

The *etrog* is taken in the left hand and held to the other three species. All are shaken together. A left-handed person takes the *lulav* and other species in the left hand and the *etrog* in the right hand. When "taking the four kinds," one should have the hands free of gloves, rings, etc. One can fulfill the commandment of the Four Species by simply holding them, but the preferred way to perform the *mitzvah* is to face east and give them a slight shake while extending them in each of the six directions.

We *bentch lulav* (make the blessing on the Four Species) every day of Sukkot until (and including) Hoshanah Rabbah, except on Shabbat.

Eating In The Sukkah

During Sukkot, the *sukkah* becomes like our home. We honor the *sukkah* with sumptuous festive meals, a beautifully set table, and by lighting the Shabbat and Yom Tov candles there. If windy or rainy conditions are likely to extinguish the candles, or if other factors prevent candle-lighting in the *sukkah*, it may be done in the house. The practice of actually sleeping in the *sukkah* has diminished in recent years, especially in cold climates outside of Israel.

Many observe the custom of adorning the *sukkah* with beautiful decorations. *Chabad* custom is not to decorate the *sukkah* because the unadorned walls themselves, as reminders of the clouds of glory, convey the essential character and teachings of the *sukkah*.

All meals and snacks are eaten in the *sukkah* from the first day of Yom Tov through Shemini Atzeret (or Hoshanah Rabbah, depending upon custom), unless it rains. If it rains one should wait for the rain to subside. Men are obligated to eat all meals in the *sukkah*. *Chabad* custom is that men eat and drink everything in the *sukkah*, even water.

Although women are not obligated to eat in the *sukkah*, they often do so. On Yom Tov, even if they cannot eat the entire meal in the *sukkah*, many women hear *Kiddush* and eat at least a *k'zayit* of bread in the *sukkah*. After saying *hamotzi* and before eating the challah, the blessing *laishev basukkah* (see below) should be said. For the sake of *chinuch* (education), children should be trained to eat in the *sukkah*.

The *sukkah* is a place of rejoicing and festivity for the whole family. Several families sometimes share one large *sukkah*, fostering an atmosphere of togetherness and increased *simchah*.

Carrying between the house and the *sukkah* is prohibited on Shabbat during Sukkot unless the *sukkah* adjoins the house or an *eiruv* surrounds the area. An *eiruv* is a special enclosure that permits one to carry on Shabbat. It is advisable to consult an Orthodox Rabbi about whether an *eiruv* is required and how to set it up.

The Blessing Laishev Basukkah: On the first two nights of Sukkot, after saying the *hamotzi* blessing and before eating the challah, we say the following blessing:

BA-RUCH A-TAH A-DO-NOI
ELO-HAI-NU ME-LECH HA-O-LAM
A-SHER KID-SHA-NU B'MITZ-VO-TAV
V'TZI-VA-NU LAI-SHEV BA-SUK-KAH.

Blessed are You, L-rd our G-d, King of the Universe,
Who has sanctified us with His commandments
and commanded us to dwell in the sukkah.

This blessing is said during the entire Festival of Sukkot whenever eating at least 2 ounces of food (two *k'zaytim*) requiring the blessing of *hamotzi* or *mezonot* (bread, rolls, cake, pasta, etc.). On the first night of Sukkot, one can say the blessing *laishev basukkah* even on one *k'zayit*.

Simchat Beit Hashoevah

The Sukkot celebration during the time of the *Beit Hamikdash* was highlighted every evening by the "ceremony of the water-drawing." This ceremony was marked by great public festivity. The *Talmud* says, "Those who have never seen the ceremony of *Simchat Beit Hashoevah* have never truly seen joy." (Sukkah 51b) Huge torches were lit which illuminated the area so brightly that even at night, the *Beit Hamikdash* appeared to be bathed in bright sunlight.

The usual order of worship in the *Beit Hamikdash* involved the pouring of wine on the Altar as a sacrifice to G-d. In addition, on Sukkot, water was drawn in a special ceremony, and poured on the Altar. The pouring of water on the Altar was unique to the holiday of Sukkot. Wine symbolizes wisdom. Clear water, on the other hand, represents a commitment to G-d beyond the limits of our understanding. The joy expressed in this ceremony was the joy of a simple and pure acceptance of G-d's will, as opposed to a service which is based upon and limited to our human comprehension.

Today it is customary in many Jewish communities to "rejoice in the Festival" with celebration and song throughout the week of Sukkot. Joyful singing and dancing often lasts well into the night.

Chol Hamoed

Chol Hamoed means "the weekday of the holiday." It includes the third day of Sukkot through Hoshanah Rabbah, also known as "Intermediate Days." While the sanctity and joy of the Festival prevails, the regular Yom Tov prohibitions do not apply.

We do not recite Kiddush or light Yom Tov candles on these days (except on Shabbat during Chol Hamoed) although additional prayers and Torah readings are said. These days are especially appropriate for family outings.

The Torah has established guidelines for us as to which activities are permitted during Chol Hamoed. Generally, one may go to work if it is necessary to prevent a financial loss. However, certain activities, such as haircuts, sewing, laundry and non-urgent house repairs, are restricted. Consult an Orthodox Rabbi for further guidance.

Hoshanah Rabbah

The seventh day of Sukkot and the final day of Chol Hamoed is called Hoshanah Rabbah. This is the concluding day of the judgment period which began on Rosh Hashanah. It is also the last day we perform the mitzvah of lulav and etrog, and is also the final occasion of the year for reciting the blessing laishev basukkah.

It is customary to stay awake the night of Hoshanah Rabbah, reciting portions of Torah and Tehillim (Psalms).

In the synagogue, during the morning services, special prayers called Hoshanot are said as the worshippers circle the bimah seven times with lulav and etrog in hand. We ask G-d to seal our inscription for a good year, and we beat the aravot (hoshanot) — five willow branches bound together — on the floor five times, symbolically "sweetening" G-d's judgment.

A Holiday Meal: On the afternoon of Hoshanah Rabbah, we eat a festive meal in the sukkah. Kiddush is not recited, but we begin the meal with challah which is dipped into honey. Kreplach are often served, symbolizing the covering of G-d's strictness with loving-kindness.

Celebrating Sukkot

- ☐ Candle-lighting first two nights
- ☐ Kiddush and festive meals first two nights and days
- ☐ Eat all meals in the sukkah, saying blessing laishev basukkah
- ☐ Mitzvah of lulav and etrog
- ☐ On Hoshanah Rabbah: eat festive meal, beat the aravot

SHEMINI ATZERET AND SIMCHAT TORAH

Shemini Atzeret and Simchat Torah are the culmination of the days of rejoicing and of all the Tishrei holidays. The theme of these days is "rejoicing with the Torah."

Shemini Atzeret and Simchat Torah are two distinct holidays in the Diaspora but are celebrated as the same day in Israel. As Yomim Tovim, they are highlighted by candle-lighting, Kiddush, and festive meals. On Shemini Atzeret (the eighth day of Sukkot), the custom of Chabad and others is to eat meals in the sukkah, but without reciting the blessing laishev basukkah. On Simchat Torah, the ninth day of festivities, we resume eating meals indoors.

Shemini Atzeret

In Chassidic congregations it is customary to have hakafot (see below) on the night of Shemini Atzeret, as we do on the night of Simchat Torah. The Musaf service of Shemini Atzeret is marked by the special prayer for geshem (rain). Yizkor, the memorial prayer for departed parents, is recited before Musaf.

Shemini Atzeret means "the eighth day which concludes the Festival." In the time of the Beit Hamikdash, seventy sacrifices were brought to the Beit Hamikdash on behalf of all the nations of the world during the seven days of Sukkot. After these seven days were over, G-d set aside an eighth day of celebration on which only one holiday sacrifice was offered, this one on behalf of the Jewish people.

The distinction between Shemini Atzeret and the rest of Sukkot can be understood by a parable about a king who celebrated for a full week with all his kingdom. After the celebration, he said to his beloved son, "It is difficult for me to part with you. Please stay another day to celebrate." He then held a separate feast in honor of his son.

Similarly, Shemini Atzeret is a day of special celebration between G-d and His people.

On the night of Simchat Torah, the synagogue comes alive in a uniquely joyful way. As we enter the *shul* we are greeted by the lively sounds of singing and clapping.

After the evening service, special verses are recited and then all Torah scrolls are removed from the *Aron Kodesh*. They are carried seven times around the *bimah* (platform) in a lively procession known as *hakafot*. This is a night of special celebration when all Jews, from Torah scholars to those who barely know the alef-bet join to sing and dance joyously with the Torah.

The *hakafot* emphasize that the Torah is the inheritance of all the Jewish people. The Torah scrolls remain inside their embroidered velvet covers during the dancing. This is a time not for study but for pure *simchah*, a celebration of the sublime level of every Jewish soul. Children perched upon their fathers' shoulders wave Simchat Torah flags, joining the celebration. Everyone takes great pleasure in kissing the Torah as it passes.

On the morning of Simchat Torah, the *hakafot* are repeated. Then the final *parsha* (weekly section) of the Torah is read, completing the yearly cycle of reading the entire Torah. Immediately after the final *parsha* is read, we start again with *Bereishit barah*, "In the beginning of G-d's creating..." These are the opening words of the first portion of the Torah. By reading the first *parsha* immediately after we have read the Torah's final words, we demonstrate that one never completes one's learning of Torah and its wisdom.

On Simchat Torah we resume eating meals indoors. Stuffed cabbage, whose rolled shape resembles Torah scrolls, are often served during Simchat Torah.

Celebrating Shemini Atzeret and Simchat Torah

☐ Candle-lighting both nights
☐ *Kiddush* and festive meals both days and both nights
☐ Rejoicing in the *hakafot* celebration in *shul*

Chanukah and Purim
A Time for Miracles

Chanukah and Purim are joyous holidays, instituted by the Sages for all generations to commemorate miraculous events in Jewish history. Both of these Rabbinical holidays reveal the hand of Divine Providence guiding the destiny of the Jewish people. In the stories of both Chanukah and Purim, there was a severe threat to Judaism. In the time of the events leading to Purim, the very lives of the Jews were at stake. In the time before Chanukah, the Jews' spiritual survival was endangered. In both cases, against great odds, the Jewish people victoriously triumphed over their enemies and proudly restored Torah and *mitzvot* to their cherished place in Jewish life.

We celebrate these holidays not merely to remind us of events that occurred long ago, but to relive the events anew. Celebrating Chanukah and Purim, each with their numerous *mitzvot*, customs, and foods, evokes in us a profound joy and deepened faith when we remember the miracles G-d performed for the Jewish people.

We celebrate Chanukah for eight days and Purim for one day. There is no prohibition of *melachah* (work) as on other Festivals and on Shabbat. There is no candle-lighting as on other holidays, except on the Shabbat which is during the week of Chanukah. The menorah is lit each of the eight nights of Chanukah, as detailed below. We do not recite *Kiddush* before eating on Purim or the weekdays of Chanukah. After eating, when we recite *Bircat Hamazon*, we add a special paragraph called *Al Hanissim* which is found in the *siddur*.

CHANUKAH

"We kindle these lights to commemorate the saving acts, miracles and wonders which you have performed for our forefathers, in those days, at this time..." (Siddur)

When the days have grown cold and night descends early, the darkest time of year, the Festival of Chanukah arrives, bringing light and inspiration to Jews everywhere. As we gaze into the brightly flickering lights of the Chanukah menorah, we recall the miracle that took place over 2,000 years ago, when a handful of Jews called the Maccabees were victorious over their enemies, and when a little jar of oil, sufficient to burn for only one day, burned miraculously for eight.

The Menorah

The menorah is probably the best-known Jewish symbol. The menorah we light today is reminiscent of the beautiful, golden seven-branched menorah that was part of the daily service in the *Beit Hamikdash*. The Chanukah menorah has eight branches, plus a ninth place for the *shamash* (servant candle). In Israel, this eight-branched menorah is called a *chanukiah*. The light of the Chanukah menorah, increasing by one flame each day, reminds us not to be satisfied with the previous day's accomplishments; we should always strive to add more goodness and holiness to our lives.

The menorah is a symbol of freedom, not only from a tyrant of long ago, but from a spiritual darkness that is not limited to ancient times. The story of Chanukah is the story of light, and the victory of the light of Torah over its enemies, as we say in the blessing for Chanukah — "in those days at this time."

A Clash of Ideals

The story of Chanukah takes us back to a time during the second *Beit Hamikdash* in the second century B.C.E. Antiochus IV ruled over the Syrian portion of the Greek Empire, which included the Land of Israel. Known to all as an unusually cruel tyrant, Antiochus took steps to bring all nationalities of the area into the fold of Greek civilization. His goal was to bring about their total submission to his rule.

Very little stood in his way, as one by one the nations of the ancient world traded in their gods for the new Greek ones. The sweep of Greek culture, or Hellenism, meant acceptance not only of the pagan gods of the pantheon, but of the Greek philosophy. Belief in the ultimate reliability of human reason and in the ideal of physical beauty for its own sake characterized Greek thought. The human mind with its logic, and the human body with its potential perfection of form, were the epitome of the Hellenic ideal.

In Greek thought the Torah as a work of great wisdom and beauty— as literature, philosophy, history and ethics — was to be admired. But it was not to be considered holy.

Those Jews who were sympathetic to the Hellenist view gained power and prominence as the Greek rulers appointed them to ever more important positions in Jewish government and religious life. The sophisticated and powerful elite consisted of Jews who took Greek names, Greek dress and Greek thought, bowing to the Greek idols that symbolized rejection of their own faith.

Meanwhile, in the hills and villages, the masses of Jews remained loyal to the Torah. Infuriated, Antiochus sent soldiers to wipe out their stubborn "old-fashioned" ways. Ever harsher measures were taken to eliminate the Jewish religion. Many Jewish martyrs, men and women, stood strong to defy the ban on such *mitzvot* as *brit milah* and Shabbat even in the face of torture and death. Heroic deeds include those of Chana and her seven sons, all of whom perished rather than bow down to a Greek idol, and of the aged priest Eliezer who was slain when he refused to eat non-kosher food.

It was then that in the town of Modin that an aged *Kohen* named Matityahu and his five sons rose up and began the rebellion that led to the expulsion of the entire Greek army. They called themselves the Maccabees.

The Search For Pure Oil

Maccabee is a word composed of the initial letters of the four Hebrew words Mi *Komochah* B'*eilim Hashem,* "Who is like unto Thee, Oh G-d." It also means "hammer." The tiny band fought with enormous faith and courage to preserve the Torah. Although they fought against the might of the entire Greek arsenal, the Maccabees ultimately prevailed. They then turned their attention to the center of Jewish life, the Holy Temple in Jerusalem.

When the Maccabees entered the *Beit Hamikdash* to restore what had been pillaged and defiled, they searched for pure oil with which to light the menorah. Careful searching revealed only one small jar of oil that had not been made ritually impure by the Greek soldiers. The oil was sufficient to light the menorah for only one day. Miraculously, the oil burned a full eight days, until newly pressed oil could be obtained. The tiny jar of oil, like the tiny spark of pure *Yiddishkeit* in every Jewish soul, was sufficient to light the way for a complete renewal of Jewish life. The victory of the Maccabees ensured the continued existence of the Jewish people at that time. The forces of assimilation, then as now, could not extinguish the light of Torah.

Lighting The Menorah

A menorah must have eight branches or holders in a straight row and of equal height. There is also a place for the *shamash* (servant candle), which is used to light the other flames and must stand a little higher or lower than the others. It is preferable to use oil in the menorah because of its role in the miracle of Chanukah, but candles may also be used. When using oil, wicks can be purchased ready-made, or made by twisting absorbent cotton. For the *shamash*, a beeswax candle is often used.

An electric menorah may not be used to fulfill one's obligation to light Chanukah lights; however, it may be lit in addition to a candle or oil menorah to publicize the miracle. If no menorah is available, holders such as small metal caps or small cups may be used.

The Chanukah flames are lit by the flame of the *shamash*, rather than directly with a match. On the first night, one lights the flame on the extreme right of the menorah. On each succeeding night, an additional flame is added to the left of the flame(s) lit previously. The new flame is lit first, followed by the one directly to its right, and so on. This pattern is followed nightly until finally, on the eighth night, all eight lights are burning brightly.

There are different customs as to where to place the menorah. *Chabad* and others place the menorah in the doorway, opposite the *mezuzah*, while many people light the menorah in a window facing a public thoroughfare.

The flames are kindled after saying the appropriate blessings at either sunset or nightfall depending on custom. In either case, they must burn for a full half hour after nightfall.

On Friday night, the Chanukah lights must be lit before the Shabbat candles. We are extremely careful about this, since it is forbidden to light any candles once Shabbat has begun. To be sure that the Chanukah lights will continue burning until after dark, fill the cups with much more oil than usual, or use larger candles. On Saturday night the Chanukah lights are lit after *Havdalah*.

The man of the house lights for the household. If he does not light the menorah, the woman lights it. Children are permitted to light their own *menorot*.

Publicizing The Miracle: Our Sages have emphasized the importance of publicizing the Chanukah miracle through lighting the menorah where all can see. Originally this was fulfilled by placing the menorah in the main doorway of the home. Today, *menorot* are often prominently displayed in various public places. Chanukah, whose name is related to the Hebrew word *chinuch*, meaning dedication or education, is a particularly opportune time to spread awareness of our Jewish heritage.

Enjoying The Chanukah Lights: During the time that the Chanukah candles are burning, it is customary to sit near the candles and either study Torah, tell stories of the holiday, or in some other way honor the holiday. This is the opportune time to distribute Chanukah *gelt* to the children. *Dreidel* games, which provide fun for hours, are often begun at this time.

In honor of the lights, work should be avoided in their proximity. Some women have the custom of refraining from household work like sewing, laundry and ironing during the first half-hour that the Chanukah lights are burning in honor of the brave Jewish women who played a role in the miracle of Chanukah.

Chanukah Customs

Chanukah Gelt: Chanukah *gelt* (money) is distributed to the children after lighting the menorah. It was originally given as an incentive for Torah study and observance. Children are also encouraged to give charity with a portion of the *gelt* they receive. It has become common for parents to give the children gifts of books and toys instead of *gelt*; this is acceptable, but the children should be given some *gelt* as well. According to *Chabad* custom, Chanukah *gelt* is given on the fifth night, in addition to *gelt* given on any other night. Chanukah *gelt* is not given on Friday because Shabbat, when money may not be handled, is closely approaching.

The Dreidel: The *dreidel* is a small spinning toy, like a top, with four sides. Each side has one letter: *nun*, *gimmel*, *hai*, or *shin*. These letters stand for the words *Nes Gadol Haya Sham*, "A great miracle happened there." In Israel, the words are, "A great miracle happened here," with a *pay*, for *poh* (here) replacing the *shin* for *sham* (there).

Tradition has it that playing *dreidel* is a reminder of the days when Greek decrees forbade Torah study and children played *dreidel* to disguise their Torah study whenever the Greek soldiers approached.

Traditional Foods: In honor of the miracle which occurred with oil, it is traditional to eat foods fried in oil. Potato *latkes* (pancakes) and *sufganiot* (Israeli-style doughnuts) are the most popular. Dairy dishes such as cheese latkes are also customary.

Cheese latkes on Chanukah recall the deeds of a famous Jewish heroine, Yehudit, in the time of the second *Beit Hamikdash*. Israel was then occupied by the cruel and oppressive Syrian-Greek army. Yehudit helped secure a victory for the Jewish forces by slaying the vicious general of the Greek army, Holofernes. She gave him salty cheese to eat, followed by strong wine to quench his thirst. The wine caused him to fall into a deep slumber. Yehudit then seized his sword and slew him with it. His soldiers fled in fear and confusion. The victory of the Maccabees followed this brave deed.

Celebrating Chanukah

☐ Kindle Chanukah lights all eight nights
☐ Add *Al Hanissim* in *Shemoneh Esrai* and *Bircat Hamazon*
☐ Refrain from certain types of work for the first half-hour that the candles are burning
☐ Distribute Chanukah *gelt* to children

TRADITIONAL FOODS
☐ *Latkes* and *sufganiot*
☐ Dairy foods

PURIM

"...In every province, and in every city, wherever the King's command and his decree reached, the Jews had gladness and joy, a feast and a holiday..." (Megillat Esther 8:17)

When the month of Adar arrives, joy increases. In the days of Mordechai and Esther, the Jewish people experienced total salvation from the decree of annihilation leveled against all of them by the king of Persia. This month was "transformed for them from one of sorrow to gladness and from mourning to festivity." (Megillat Esther 9:22)

To celebrate the miraculous salvation which occurred at that time, our Sages instituted for all generations a holiday of feasting, rejoicing, and sending food portions to one another and giving charitable gifts to the poor. Colorfully costumed children fill the streets on Purim bearing baskets filled with all kinds of treats to deliver to friends, relatives and neighbors.

Rejoicing on Purim is a *mitzvah* that brings us to a very high level. It is even said that Yom Kippur, also called *Yom Hakippurim*, is a day "like Purim" (*ki Purim*). On Purim it is possible to achieve through joy and feasting the lofty spiritual heights accomplished through repentance and fasting on Yom Kippur.

The name Purim means "lots," referring to the lots that the evil prime minister, Haman, drew to determine which day to carry out his plans to annihilate the Jews. His plot backfired, and a bleak situation turned into its opposite, a total victory for the Jewish people. Everything about Purim, in fact, is consistent with sudden reversals, hidden meanings and paradox. This is apparent in the Purim story as it is told in Megillat Esther, the scroll we read on Purim, in the evening and once again in the morning.

Megillat Esther is named for the Jewish woman fated to become queen of the Persian empire so that she might save her people when the need arose. On the surface, the *Megillah* appears to be simply a tale of palace intrigue, ambition, greed, and finally the triumph of innocence over evil. Events unfold naturally without any obvious miracles taking place. The name of G-d is not even mentioned once throughout the entire *Megillah*, the only instance of such an omission in all 24 books of the written Torah!

A closer look at the *Megillah*, however, reveals an unseen hand shaping the story throughout. Seemingly unrelated events ultimately fit together like the pieces of a puzzle. A series of apparent coincidences are really the unfolding of G-d's plan through miracles concealed in the natural order of things, in the workings of Divine Providence. The name Esther (related to *hester*, concealment), alludes to this concealment of miracles within the natural world. The popular custom of wearing masks, disguises and costumes on Purim brings this idea to life.

The Purim Drama

The *Megillah* opens with the words, "And it came to pass in the days of Achashverosh... who reigned from *Hodu* (India) to *Cush* (Ethiopia)..." Achashverosh was the king of Persia, heir to the entire Babylonian empire. He held an extravagant feast in his capital city, Shushan, setting in motion the complicated series of events that would involve the fate of all Jews living in his empire.

The Jews were scattered throughout the Persian kingdom. They had been exiled after the Babylonian armies destroyed the *Beit Hamikdash* and drove them from their land. The Purim story took place during the seventy-year period between the First and Second Temples. King Achashverosh was searching for a new queen. He chose Esther, who did not reveal her Jewish identity.

Haman soon rose to power in the king's court. A hater of Jews, Haman hated one Jew above all: Mordechai, a righteous leader among the Jews in exile and an old adversary of Haman. Mordechai was in fact the uncle and guardian of Queen Esther, and now became an advisor to the king. Mordechai would not bow down to Haman, despite the king's proclamation that everyone must do so.

Haman was filled with rage and sought a way to destroy all the Jews. He approached King Achashverosh with the charge, "There is a certain people scattered abroad and dispersed among the peoples in all the provinces of your realm. Their laws are different from every other people's...it is not befitting the King to tolerate them." (Megillat Esther 3:8) Achashverosh readily agreed to sign a decree of annihilation against all Jews, effective on the 13th of Adar. In saying that the Jews were "scattered abroad," Haman revealed a significant piece of information: The Jews were not unified and were therefore in a weak position, spiritually as well as physically.

How the evil decree was overturned in time and how Haman's plans rebounded against him is the subject of the *Megillah*. Mordechai and Esther were instrumental in awakening G-d's mercies to save the Jewish people. They did not primarily use their political power or influence with the king to try to change the situation but went directly to the Jews themselves.

One of the first things Mordechai did was to call together all the Jewish children and begin learning Torah with them, knowing that in the merit of the children the Jews would be saved. Esther took upon herself a fast of three days and requested that all the Jews do the same. These three days were a time of prayer and repentance, and of uniting the people. The Jews returned

wholeheartedly to Torah and *mitzvot*. No longer a "people scattered," their victory was assured.

And "the Jews had light and gladness, and joy and honor." (Megillat Esther 8:16)

Taanit Esther

The day before Purim, we fast in remembrance of Queen Esther's fast, during which she prayed to G-d to repeal Haman's decree. The fast begins at dawn and we break our fast after the evening *Megillah* reading.

On Taanit Esther, during *Minchah* or before the reading of the *Megillah* in the evening, we give *machtzit hashekel* in *shul*. This is a half-dollar coin which is given to charity in memory of the half-*shekel* given by the Jews in the time of the *Beit Hamikdash* during the month of Adar. The half-dollar coins are made available to exchange in *shul*.

Purim Observances

Hearing The Megillah: On the evening of Purim, and again during Purim day, we gather to listen to the reading of the entire *Megillah*. Men and women over the age of *Bar* and *Bat Mitzvah* are required to hear every word of the reading. Children, too, are encouraged to listen, and to sound *graggers* (noisemakers) when the name of the wicked Haman is mentioned. The *Megillah* reading need not take place in the synagogue. The blessing after the reading is said only with a *minyan*.

Mishloach Manot: Food Gifts. During the day, everyone should send a gift of at least two different ready-to-eat foods (each of which require a different *brachah*), to at least one friend. One may send more foods to as many friends as one wishes.

Women send *mishloach manot* to women and men send to men to fulfill the *mitzvah*. The minimum requirements are a *k'zayit* of food, (approximately 1 ounce), and 4 ounces of liquid. The *mishloach manot* are often generously apportioned and elaborately presented in beautiful baskets. Children, too, should participate in this *mitzvah*, and they are usually thrilled to do so. It is considered preferable to send the *mishloach manot* through a messenger; children often fill this role. Gifts of *mishloach manot* are especially appreciated by Jews who are elderly, housebound, or hospitalized.

Hamantashen are a popular Purim treat. These are three-cornered pastries stuffed with various delicious fillings, such as sweetened poppy seeds or *lekvar*, prune jam. The name *hamantashen* may be read as *mahn* (poppy seeds) *tashen* (pockets). Another version explains that *hamantashen* remind us of Haman's triangular hat. In Israel, these pastries are called *aznei Haman*, "Haman's ears."

Matanot L'evyonim: Gifts (of charity) to the poor. Everyone should give at least a token amount to two poor people. It is praiseworthy to give generously. As we enjoy the holiday of Purim, it is certainly appropriate that we remember the poor and raise their spirits, too. In a place where one cannot find any needy people, one can fulfill the *mitzvah* by giving to charitable institutions or charity boxes designated for organizations that help the needy.

Seudat Purim: We eat a festive meal during the late afternoon of Purim day, often extending into the night. The meal is eaten before noon if Purim is on Friday. The Purim *seudah* is a happy and exuberant feast beginning with the blessing *hamotzi* on challah. Some people shape the challah like a *hamantash*. It is customary to have a lit candle on the table during the meal. The candle is lit without blessings.

Kreplach, chopped meat encased in dough, are served at this meal. Both *hamantashen* and *kreplach*, with their fillings hidden inside, allude to the hidden aspect of the Purim miracle.

Celebrating Purim

☐ Fast on the day before Purim
☐ Hear the *Megillah* at night and during the day
☐ Send food portions to at least one person
☐ Give charity to at least two people
☐ Have a Purim feast in the afternoon

TRADITIONAL FOODS

☐ *Hamantashen* pastry
☐ Serve *kreplach* during the festive meal

Pesach through Shavuot
Birth of the Jewish Nation

The festivals of Pesach and Shavuot celebrate the exodus from Egypt followed by the giving of the Torah on Mount Sinai. With these two events, the Jewish people truly became a nation. We became a people uniquely entrusted with keeping G-d's commandments as "a kingdom of priests and a holy nation."

Pesach is known as *z'man cheiruteinu*, the Season of our Freedom. It commemorates the exodus from Egypt, when G-d fulfilled His promise to the patriarchs Avraham, Yitzchak and Yaakov. G-d had made the promise to Avraham that after 400 years of servitude as "strangers in a strange land," He would redeem them and make of them a great nation. When the time for the redemption arrived, G-d sent Moshe Rabbeinu to lead the Jews to freedom and to challenge the mightiest monarch on earth, Pharaoh of Egypt, with the words: "Let my people go so that they may serve Me [G-d]..." (Exodus 5:1)

On the fifteenth of Nissan the Jews left Egypt amid great miracles and revelations: the ten plagues with which G-d afflicted the Egyptians, the parting of the Sea of Reeds (not the "Red Sea") that allowed them to pass through on dry land, and the closing of the sea over the Egyptian horsemen who pursued them even in their final flight to freedom.

Seven weeks later, they stood before Mount Sinai to receive the Torah. This was the ultimate goal of the exodus from Egypt -"...so that they may serve Me."

At Sinai they camped "as one man with one heart," with a feeling of unity and harmony that brought them together as a nation worthy of receiving the Torah and becoming G-d's people. *Mattan* Torah has been compared by our Sages to a wedding between G-d and the Jewish people. This occurred on the sixth day of Sivan, commemorated by the Festival of Shavuot. Pesach and Shavuot are each one of the *Shalosh Regalim*.

During the seven weeks that elapsed between the exodus from Egypt and *Mattan* Torah, the Jewish people worked to eliminate from themselves the damaging effects of Egyptian bondage and to prepare themselves to become a holy nation ready to stand before G-d. This period of time is known as *Sefirat Ha'Omer*, counting the *Omer*, and is associated with the *Omer* offering that was brought to the *Beit Hamikdash* on the second day of Pesach. (See The Omer.)

PESACH

"In each generation every person is obligated to see himself as if he had personally gone out of Egypt." (Talmud Pesachim 116b)

The Festival of Pesach celebrates the Jewish people's deliverance from bondage in the land of Egypt more than three thousand years ago. The departure from Egypt, recounted in great detail in the second book of the Torah, is the pivotal event in Jewish history. Not only is it the birthday" of the Jewish nation; it also stands as eternal reminder of G-d's special involvement in our fate. The exodus from Egypt is mentioned often in the daily prayers, and the first of the Ten Commandments states: "I am the L-rd your G-d who brought you out of the land of Egypt, out of the house of bondage. You shall have no other gods before Me." (Exodus 20:2-3)

The approach of Pesach on the fifteenth of Nissan brings a sense of renewal as our houses are transformed from top to bottom and declared *Pesachdig*, "kosher for Pesach." This Jewish version of spring cleaning involves more than vacuuming and washing the windows; it is a search and destroy mission directed against *chametz*, leaven, in all its forms, for the Torah commands us, "Eat matzot *for seven days...During these days, no leaven may be found in your homes...you must not eat anything leavened...no leaven may be seen in your possession.*" (Exodus 12:15-20, 13:17)

Weeks of busy, and sometimes frantic, preparation culminate in the event everyone has been looking forward to: the Pesach Seder. Boxes of matzah sit in readiness, the "bread of affliction" that our ancestors ate when they fled Egypt without waiting for their dough to rise. An ample supply of fine, red kosher wine is on hand for the Four Cups we drink at the Seder. The children are busy practicing the Four Questions beginning with "*Mah nishtanah halaylah hazeh--Why is this night different...*" Everything seems to shine with a special *Pesachdig* glow.

The earth almost seems to mirror our mood as its vegetation is liberated from winter dormancy. Nissan is the month of spring, and Pesach the Festival of spring. The time when nature blossoms, however, is the time when a Jew is reminded to look beyond nature to G-d, the source of nature and all blessings, and to give thanks for the miracles He performs for us.

The First of Festivals

The month of Nissan, in which Pesach occurs, is a month associated with redemption. Because of this, the Torah calls it "the first of the months" (Exodus 12:2), even though the new year begins in the month of Tishrei with the anniversary of the creation of the world.

Pesach is the first of the three Pilgrimage Festivals, and the only one for which women as well as men were required to travel to Jerusalem to the Holy Temple. It consists of eight days, seven in Israel. The first two and last two days are Yomim Tovim. We light Yom Tov candles with the appropriate blessings, recite Kiddush, eat festive meals, and observe all holiday laws. The *shehechiyanu* blessing is said only on the first two days. The intermediate days are *Chol Hamoed*.

In the Torah, Pesach is called *Chag Hamatzot* (Festival of *Matzot*). Since *chametz* is prohibited all eight days of Pesach, matzah takes its place at all meals.

A Time of Personal Liberation

Egypt is not only a geographical location but also a state of mind. "Going out of Egypt," in a personal sense, refers to each individual's personal departure from everything that interferes with the full expression of his spiritual potential. The Hebrew word for Egypt, *Mitzrayim*, is related to the word *maitzorim*, boundaries or limitations. Through Torah and *mitzvot*, a Jew can go beyond the limits of his physical existence and become more closely connected to G-d.

Although the inner liberation implicit in the exodus from Egypt is an ongoing spiritual endeavor, it is on Pesach that we receive the strength to carry out this endeavor during the rest of the year. We eat matzah, the "food of faith"-- the only provisions our ancestors took with them in their flight from Egypt, when they faithfully relied upon G-d to provide for their sustenance. The *mitzvot* of the Pesach Seder, including eating matzah and bitter herbs, drinking four cups of wine and telling the story of the exodus from Egypt, enable us to see ourselves as if we had "personally gone out of Egypt."

Laws of Chametz

Chametz refers to all leavened products containing wheat, barley, oats, rye or spelt. During Pesach it is forbidden to eat, own, or derive benefit from *chametz* or any mixture containing *chametz*, even in the smallest amount. The prohibition of eating even a minute quantity of *chametz* on Pesach is of comparable seriousness to that of eating on Yom Kippur. The Torah further prohibits even owning or deriving benefit from *chametz*.

Several weeks before the Festival begins, our activities begin to focus on the all-important task of eliminating all *chametz* from our possession. All locations, including garage, attic, basement, car, and place of business must be free of *chametz*. Most important is the kitchen and any areas of the home where food is eaten or prepared. Dishes and utensils used all year are stored away, with the exception of items that will be *kashered* for Pesach.

The remaining *chametz* is sold, through a legally binding contract, to a non-Jew. An Orthodox Rabbi acts as our agent in effecting this sale and in buying back the *chametz* when the holiday is over. *Mechirat chametz*, selling of *chametz*, is an extremely important aspect of Pesach observance. *Mechirat chametz* contracts can be obtained from an Orthodox Rabbi or by mail. (Allow enough time for the signed contract to reach the Rabbi a few days before Pesach.)

Having completed all cleaning and other preparations by the night before Pesach, there remain three *mitzvot* that involve the elimination of *chametz*. *Bedikat chametz* is the formal search for *chametz* beginning at nightfall on *erev* Pesach. We search for ten designated, wrapped pieces of bread using a lit candle, a feather, a wooden spoon, and a paper bag for collecting any *chametz* found.

Bittul chametz is a verbal statement with which the head of the household disowns any *chametz* inadvertently overlooked. It is found in the *Haggadah* and the *siddur*.

Biur chametz is the burning of *chametz* the following morning. All *chametz* found during the search and any other *chametz* that has not been sold must be burned.

Matzah

Matzah plays an important role in the Seder, and we eat it several times during the evening. At minimum, one must eat at least a *k'zayit* of matzah (approximately 1 ounce) to fulfill the *mitzvah* of eating matzah on the night of Pesach.

Three *matzot* are placed under the Seder plate, one each to represent *Kohen*, *Levi* and *Yisrael* — the totality of all Jews. The middle matzah becomes the *afikoman*, the "dessert" of the Seder meal.

Shmurah matzah is matzah that has been guarded from the time of harvesting to ensure that it has not come in contact with water. Water will cause a leavening action to begin after eighteen minutes. Handmade *shmurah* matzah is round and earthy. *Shmurah* matzah is preferable to other kinds of Passover matzah, especially for the Seder.

We are prohibited from eating matzah on *erev* Pesach so that we may savor the taste of matzah at the Seder. We also refain from eating it before Pesach for a period of time, which varies according to community custom.

The Meaning Of Chametz And Matzah: *Chametz* and matzah are both made of flour and water. The only difference between them is that *chametz* rises, while matzah remains flat. *Chametz* is thus indicative of inflated egotism, arrogance, and self-love. Matzah, which the Torah calls "poor man's bread," (Deuteronomy 16:3) symbolizes the qualities of selflessness and humility.

As we work to remove all traces of *chametz* from our homes, we are aware of the deeper significance of *chametz*, and endeavor to remove the "spiritual *chametz*" from within ourselves. We have an opportunity to go beyond our limitations — to "leave Egypt" — by developing the qualities represented by matzah.

"And You Shall Tell It To Your Children..."

The story of the Jewish people's liberation from Egypt has been handed down from father to child in an unbroken chain ever since the exodus itself. The Torah states that at the Pesach Seder we must relate these events to our children, and that even when there are no children present we must tell the story of *yetziat mitzrayim* to each other — and a person who is alone must tell the story to himself.

When Seder night arrives, the children are especially excited. In many ways, it is their night. According to tradition, we should begin the Seder "right away, as soon as Father comes home from *shul*, so the children will not fall asleep and be unable to recite the *mah nishtanah*..." (Talmud Pesachim 109a)

Many of the unique practices of the Seder table, such as dipping the *karpas* in salt water and the *maror* in *charoset*, are designed to stimulate a child's curiosity so that he will ask why we are doing these things, and, in answering, the father will tell about the exodus from Egypt. The child's queries are expressed formally in the Four Questions.

The *Haggadah* leads us through the stages of the Seder with instructions for the various *mitzvot* and customs, focusing on the Seder plate, which sits atop the three *matzot*. It is either a raised, three-tiered plate or a special cover which encloses the *matzot* and on which the Seder items rest.

Items On The Seder Plate

The special foods we eat on Pesach are also food for thought. Each item on the Seder plate abounds in meaning. These six items, arranged in a special order, require much preparation. It is best to prepare all these items before Yom Tov in order to avoid *halachic* questions.

Zeroah: a roasted chicken neck or shankbone representing the Paschal Lamb eaten on the eve of the exodus from Egypt. It is roasted over an open fire on the stove. As it may not be eaten, most of the meat is removed. The *zeroah* may be re-used on the Seder plate the second night;

Betzah: a hard-boiled egg representing the Holiday Offering in the *Beit Hamikdash*;

Maror: bitter herbs reminding us of the bitterness and slavery of our forefathers in Egypt. Fresh romaine lettuce, endives and horseradish are commonly used. (Romaine leaves must be washed extremely well before Yom Tov begins and care taken to check for insects.) Leaves must be completely dry when used;

Charoset: a mixture of apples, nuts, and wine resembling the mortar and brick made by the Jews when they toiled for Pharaoh;

Karpas: a non-bitter vegetable. The letters of *karpas*, re-arranged, mean back-breaking work. A slice of onion or potato is commonly used;

Chazeret: additional bitter herbs, usually romaine lettuce, used in the *korech* sandwich described in the *Haggadah*.

Minimum quantities of matzah and *maror* must be eaten, as indicated in various Seder guides and handbooks.

NOTE: In order to fully savor the special foods on the Seder plate, we do not eat certain items from *erev* Pesach until the meal of the second Seder, except when using them for their role in the Seder. These items include foods used for *maror* and *charoset*. Roast meat is not served on either Seder night because of its resemblance to the Pesach sacrifice. Consult an Orthodox Rabbi for further guidance.

The Seder

The Seder is a total sensory experience. We not only hear about our bitter years of slavery but taste them in the form of the bitter *maror* that literally brings tears to the eyes. We eat the "bread of affliction" and drink the Four Cups of Redemption. We express our wish to greet Eliyahu Hanavi, (the Prophet Elijah) who heralds the coming of *Mashiach*, by pouring a cup of wine for him and opening the door to the night air and inviting him in. It is said that Eliyahu visits every Seder table on Pesach night.

Although reading the *Haggadah* consists of a formal recitation, he who speaks at great length on Pesach night about the exodus from Egypt is praiseworthy." (Haggadah) A variety of commentaries serve as a springboard for lively discussions at the Seder. On the first night, however, the *afikoman* and all other food should be eaten before *chatzot*, a time corresponding approximately to midnight.

The Seder Meal

After concluding the first part of the *Haggadah*, which relates the story of the exodus from Egypt, we drink the second cup of wine and wash the hands for *hamotzi*. This is followed by the eating of matzah, *maror* and the matzah and *maror* sandwiches, as described in the *Haggadah*.

The long-awaited holiday meal is now served. We begin the meal with a hard-boiled egg dipped in salt water. A festive meal follows, traditionally consisting of fish, chicken soup, and other favorite dishes. We may drink more wine if we wish.

After the meal we eat the *afikoman*, the matzah symbolizing the *Korbon Pesach*. The cup of Eliyahu is now filled and kept full until the end of the Seder. We recite *Bircat Hamazon* and then open the door to greet the Prophet, Eliyahu. The Seder concludes with the words that express our desire for the final redemption and the end of all exile: *L'shanah habah b'Yerushalayim!* "Next year in Jerusalem!"

The Final Days of Pesach

The last two days of Pesach are Festival days marked by candle-lighting (without *shehechiyanu*) and by *Kiddush* meals in which two *matzot* take the place of two loaves of challah. The seventh day celebrates and commemorates the miracle of the splitting of the Sea of Reeds, and marks the total liberation from Egypt. Many people stay awake during this night to learn Torah.

The eighth day of Pesach is called *Acharon Shel Pesach*. This final day of the "season of freedom" celebrates an even higher level of freedom that is more than merely a liberation from servitude. It is devoted to the idea of the future redemption. The *haftorah* of *Acharon Shel Pesach* elaborates on this theme.

In our generation a custom initiated by the Baal Shem Tov has become widely practiced —the custom of eating a meal of matzah immediately before sunset on *Acharon Shel Pesach*. This meal, which also includes four cups of wine, is called "Seudat Mashiach" (the Feast of *Mashiach*). The Baal Shem Tov explained that through participating in this meal we are able to appreciate a glimmer of the Messianic age.

Celebrating Pesach

- ☐ Light Yom Tov candles first, second, seventh and eighth nights
- ☐ *Kiddush* and festive meals on the first two nights and days, and the last two nights and days
- ☐ Seder first two nights according to *Haggadah*
- ☐ Eat matzah first two nights

Observing Pesach

- ☐ Remove all *chametz*
- ☐ Search for *chametz*
- ☐ Sell *chametz*
- ☐ Burn *chametz*

NOTE: Refer to *Body & Soul: A Handbook For Kosher Living* and to *The Spice & Spirit of Kosher-Passover Cooking* for more information on preparing for Pesach.

THE OMER

Connecting Pesach and Shavuot are forty-nine days known as *Sefirat Ha'Omer*, counting the *Omer*. In the time of the *Beit Hamikdash*, the *Omer* was an offering of barley from the first grain of the new crop. It was offered on the second day of Pesach.

The *Omer* period coincides with the time of preparation for receiving the Torah. When the Jewish people went out of Egypt they counted these days in joyful anticipation of the day when they would stand at Mount Sinai as G-d had promised them. During this time they worked to transform themselves from being abject slaves into a people worthy of receiving G-d's great gift, the Torah.

Counting The Omer

We are commanded to count seven weeks from the time of the bringing of the first *Omer* offering until the Festival of Shavuot. (Leviticus 23:15) Each night, we say a blessing and then mention the particular day of the *Omer*. The blessing and the order of the counting are included in the *siddur*.

The *Omer* is counted at night, usually after the evening prayers. If one forgets to count the *Omer* at night, one may do so during the following day but without a blessing, and may resume counting the next day with the blessing. If an entire day has gone by, then one resumes counting the *Omer* without a blessing and continues to do so for the remainder of the *Omer* period.

Seven character traits, or *midot*, are emphasized during these seven weeks. Each week presents an opportunity to perfect another of these qualities within ourselves. The first week, for example, stresses the trait of *chesed*, kindness, and the second week that of *gevurah*, or severity. Each of the *midot* also contain within themselves aspects of the other *midot*. During the week of *chesed*, seven facets of *chesed* are expressed. By the time seven weeks have elapsed, all possible combinations of *midot* have been developed in *Sefirat Ha'Omer*.

A Time of Partial Mourning

Sefirat Ha'Omer became a time of sadness in the days of our great Sage, Rabbi Akiva. Twenty-four thousand of his disciples died during an epidemic that our Sages explain was a result of their not having had sufficient respect for one another. Weddings and haircuts are among the activities restricted during this mourning period. The blessing *shehechiyanu* is customarily not said during this time, although according to *Chabad* custom, it may be said on Shabbat.

Lag B'Omer, the thirty-third day of *Sefirat Ha'Omer*, is a day of celebration arriving like a beacon of light during the solemn days of the *Omer*. The prohibitions that are in effect during *Sefirat Ha'Omer* are lifted. Customs vary concerning the time period of the prohibitions during *sefirah*. One should consult an Orthodox Rabbi for guidance. During the last three days before Shavuot, these prohibitions are lifted in honor of the holiday. *Chabad* custom is to have haircuts only on *erev* Shavuot.

Pesach Sheni

One month after Pesach, on the fourteenth day of Iyar, we celebrate Pesach Sheni, a "second Pesach," by eating some matzah that was put away for this purpose at the end of Pesach. Bread and other *chametz* are not prohibited as on Pesach, and the day is not marked by any of the observances of a Yom Tov.

Our observance of Pesach Sheni has its origins in the days immediately following the exodus from Egypt. Certain men could not bring the Pesach sacrifice at the proper time because they were ritually impure or could not be present. They requested and were given an opportunity to fulfill the *mitzvah* on Pesach Sheni. Pesach Sheni teaches us that there is always another chance when one wishes to serve G-d.

Lag B'Omer

The thirty-third day of counting the *Omer* is treasured by Jewish children as a day for outings and for parades that celebrate Jewish unity and pride. Many of the prohibitions of *sefirah* are lifted. Music is heard once again. In many communities, little boys who have had their third birthday during *sefirah* now receive their first haircut. This ceremony is known as the *upsherin*.

Lag B'Omer commemorates the cessation of the tragic plague in which many thousands of the students of Rabbi Akiva perished. It is also the anniversary of the passing of Rabbi Shimon Bar Yochai, one of Rabbi Akiva's most illustrious disciples. Rabbi Shimon Bar Yochai, known by his initials as the Rashbi, taught and revealed the hidden and inner light of the Torah-mystical teachings which were later written down in the holy Zohar.

He requested that the day of his passing be one of celebration. The end of his life in this world signalled the fact that his work was complete and that the teachings he revealed to his generation would illuminate the path of subsequent generations down through the centuries.

Rabbi Shimon's life was an example of total dedication to Torah and to his fellow Jews. He bravely defied the Roman ban against teaching Torah, as his teacher Rabbi Akiva had done before him. When a sentence of death was decreed against him and his son, Rabbi Elazar, they hid together in a cave for thirteen years. During this time they learned Torah unceasingly. They ate from the fruit of a carob tree which grew miraculously outside the cave. They left the cave only after the decree against them had been lifted after the death of the Roman emperor.

In Israel, many people travel to Meron, the burial place of Rabbi Shimon Bar Yochai on Lag B'Omer. Bonfires are lit and many three-year old boys celebrate their *upsherin* on this site.

When Jewish students leave school on Lag B'Omer to enjoy picnics, parades and fairs, it is for the purpose of bringing a Torah atmosphere to the world at large. The unity and *ahavat Yisrael* displayed at such events remind us that it was at this time that the fault of insufficient mutual respect that was displayed by Rabbi Akiva's students was eradicated from their midst.

SHAVUOT

The month of Sivan signals the approach of warm weather and the summer season. The first ripe fruits have been harvested. The Jews of Israel, in the time of the *Beit Hamikdash*, would now be busy preparing for their grand procession to Jerusalem. Amid great festivity and jubilation, they carried the first fruits of their harvest as offerings to the Holy Temple.

The Festival of Shavuot on the sixth and seventh days of Sivan is both the Festival of the First-Fruits (*Chag Ha-Bikurim*) and the Time of the Giving of the Torah (*Z'man Matan Torateinu*). It is celebrated with candle-lighting with appropriate blessings, including *shehechiyanu*. We recite *Kiddush* both days.

Dairy Foods

We observe the custom of eating dairy foods such as blintzes and cheesecake on the afternoon of the first day. The dairy foods can comprise the main Yom Tov *seudah*, or they may be a light repast followed by a traditional *fleishig* Yom Tov meal after the appropriate waiting time. In some communities, dairy meals are served throughout Shavuot.

One of many explanations for the custom of eating dairy foods is that when the Jews first received the Torah on Shavuot, they were not yet well-versed in the laws of *shechitah*, (kosher slaughtering), so they refrained from meat foods and ate dairy instead.

Many have the custom of decorating the home and synagogue with flowers and greens for Shavuot.

Arriving fifty days after Pesach, Shavuot marks the giving of the Torah by G-d to the entire Jewish people on Mount Sinai. Shavuot means "weeks" and refers to the seven weeks that the Jewish people counted while preparing to receive the Torah. Six hundred thousand men of conscription age, plus their families and others who had joined the Jewish people, totalled several million men, women and children who witnessed the unparalleled revelation of G-dliness. The Midrash teaches that all souls of all generations, past and future, were present at Sinai.

With the words, "Na'aseh v'nishmah — We will do and we will hear," the Jewish people accepted the mission of keeping G-d's commandments, even prior to understanding them. In so doing they established the identity of the Jewish people for all time. The Jews would henceforth be reminders of G-d's presence in the world, carriers of the ideal of ethical conduct and morality based upon G-d's law.

The Torah

The Torah is much more than a book, even a holy book. It contains more than knowledge or wisdom. The word Torah is derived from *horo'ah*, meaning instruction. The difference between instruction and wisdom is that wisdom is abstract knowledge in which conclusions are reached through the processes of human reasoning. They are always subject to revision.

By contrast, the Torah gives us a set of Divine laws and guidelines that are so universal that they have been applied these three millennia by Jews in every country and every culture throughout the world.

The Torah consists of two parts: written and oral. The Oral Torah was given to Moshe along with the written Torah at Mount Sinai. It explains and clarifies the written Torah, which is only superficially comprehensible on its own. The Oral Torah was transmitted from generation to generation until it was finally compiled and written down in what we know as the *Mishnah* and expounded on in the *Gemarah*. The *Mishnah* and *Gemarah* are known as the *Talmud*.

Through the *Talmud*, a continuous chain of tradition connects the scholars of the present day to the revelation at Sinai. It provides us with a framework for daily living based upon the most authoritative moral code in existence. Wherever we may be and whatever the situation, the Torah provides us with a precise and eternally relevant yardstick against which to measure our actions.

The Ten Commandments

Our entire people heard the Ten Commandments proclaimed by G-d at Mount Sinai. The Ten Commandments are known throughout the world as the bedrock of moral existence. They concern both relations between man and G-d and relations between man and man.

The Ten Commandments contain six hundred and thirteen letters which include within them all six hundred and thirteen *mitzvot* of the Torah, plus seven letters in the last two words which allude to the seven Rabbinical *mitzvot*.

Hearing The Ten Commandments On Shavuot: Our Sages have declared that we must always view the Torah as "new, as if we received it today." Each year on Shavuot, in particular, we commit ourselves anew to the observance and study of Torah.

We relive the historic revelation at Mount Sinai by listening as the Ten Commandments are read from the Torah in *shul* on the first day of Shavuot. It is important for all to be present for this reading, including children and infants — whose *neshamot*, souls, will absorb the message even if they cannot as yet understand the words. The importance of children is underscored by the fact that it was the children whom G-d accepted as guarantors of the Torah.

The Children As Guarantors: Our Sages explain that before G-d gave the Torah to the Jewish people He demanded guarantors. The Jews offered many possibilities, from the patriarchs to the prophets and other great men as yet unborn, but G-d was not satisfied until the children were suggested. The Jewish children would be the guarantors and transmitters of Torah; our commitment to their education was and is the best assurance of our continued commitment to Torah and *mitzvot*.

The Women Were Approached First

The Importance Of Jewish Women: At Mount Sinai G-d told Moshe to address himself first to the Jewish women concerning the giving of the Torah: "So shall you say to the House of Yaakov" (referring to the women) was followed by, "Tell to the sons of Yisrael" (Exodus 19:3) (referring to the men). In this way it was assured that the Torah would be readily received and perpetuated for all time.

A woman's influence on her home and surroundings is inestimable. It is she who, primarily instills values in her children, encourages her husband to observe and to study Torah, and often is in a position to affect others through her hospitality, warmth and teaching.

Torah knowledge is obligatory for women as well, in order to fulfill the commandments and live a fully Jewish life. The study of *Chassidut* is an approach to understanding the fundamental *mitzvot* of loving G-d and fearing G-d. To instill this foundation in herself and others, a woman must learn Torah, particularly the inner dimensions of Torah, and the teachings of *Chassidut*.

Megillat Ruth: In many communities Megillat Ruth (the Story of Ruth) is read in *shul* on the second day of Shavuot. Ruth was a modest, righteous woman who converted to Judaism and accepted the Torah. King David was a descendant of Ruth. She merited to become the mother of the kings of Israel because of her love of Torah and *mitzvot* and her lofty conduct.

Shavuot is the anniversary of the passing of King David, who laid the foundation for the first *Beit Hamikdash*, and in whose merit it was built. The line of descent from King David leads ultimately to *Mashiach*, who will redeem us from this final exile and rebuild the *Beit Hamikdash*.

Shavuot is also the *yahrtzeit* of the Baal Shem Tov, founder of the *Chassidic* movement. This is more than coincidential, for through the teachings of the Baal Shem Tov, the world is being drawn closer to achieving the unity between man and G-d that was first initiated with the giving of the Torah at Mount Sinai and which will culminate in the coming of *Mashiach*.

Celebrating Shavuot

☐ Hear the Ten Commandments
☐ Eat dairy foods

Other Significant Days

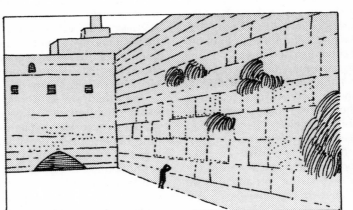

"Everything has its season, and there is a time for everything under the heaven..." (Kohelet 3:14)

A number of significant days in addition to the Yomim Tovim are observed throughout the Jewish year. We have days of remembrance, days of joy, and days of mourning. Some are fast days serving to heighten our awareness of being in a state of exile.

The year has four fast days associated with the destruction of the *Beit Hamikdash* (Holy Temple) in Jerusalem. The 17th of Tammuz and the 9th of Av are the first and last days of a twenty-one day period in the summer known as "The Three Weeks." During this time we not only mourn for the First and Second Temples but also learn about and look forward to the building of the Third, permanent *Beit Hamikdash*.

The weekly occurrence of Shabbat and the monthly occurrence of Rosh Chodesh, the new moon, create a cycle that brings new insights with each year. Each Shabbat has its particular coloration based upon the content of the weekly Torah portion, or *parsha*. Rabbi Schneur Zalman of Liadi, in commenting that "one must live with the times," stressed the importance of reading and studying the weekly *parsha* as it always has relevance to our lives at the particular time when it is read.

Birthdays, too, are important in the Jewish year. The birthday of a great Jewish leader is an occasion for rejoicing. We note the birthday of Moshe Rabbeinu, on the 7th of Adar and of the Baal Shem Tov, on the 18th of Elul and the birthdays of other great *tzaddikim*. Our own Hebrew birth date is also an important day, an occasion for making resolutions for our new year and gathering with friends to celebrate. It is an auspicious time to give extra *tzedakah* (charity) and increase in Torah study.

The anniversary of the passing away (*yahrtzeit*) of a *tzaddik*, a Jewish holy person, is also an occasion for rejoicing since the day of the *yahrtzeit* is a time of new and greater ascent for the soul of that person. (See Lag B'Omer, page 531.)

Many of the calendar's special days are associated with customs, laws and special foods. Certain prayers are added or deleted from the daily service, as indicated in the *siddur*.

SPECIAL DAYS

Rosh Chodesh

Rosh Chodesh is the day of the appearance of the new moon and thus the first day of the Jewish month. In the time of the *Sanhedrin* (Great Court), the new month was proclaimed when two reliable eye witnesses reported that they had seen the new moon, even though this date was also calculated mathematically according to the methods handed down since the giving of the Torah at Mt. Sinai. In this way, the Jewish calendar was made dependent upon the activities of man rather than solely on celestial movements. This is highly significant in that the time for the Festivals was determined in accordance with man's proclamation of the new moon.

Work is permitted on Rosh Chodesh. As a reward for not contributing to or participating in the worship of the golden calf, Rosh Chodesh is a semi-holiday for women. Many women have the custom to refrain from certain work such as sewing on this day. A special Torah portion is read in *shul*, and *Hallel* is included in the morning prayers. "It is customary to feast sumptuously on Rosh Chodesh." (Orach Chaim 419) If Rosh Chodesh occurs on Shabbat, an extra dish should be prepared in its honor.

Lag B'Omer stands out as a festive day occurring in the period between Pesach and Shavuot known as *Sefirat Ha'Omer*, a time of partial mourning. The prohibitions associated with this period are lifted on Lag B'Omer. It is a day of public celebration, especially for children. Jewish schools participate in parades and outings of various kinds. (See The Omer, page 527.)

Special celebrations are held in Meron, Israel, the burial place of Rabbi Shimon Bar Yochai.

The New Year for Trees, on the 15th of Shvat (Tu B'Shvat) marks the beginning of the season in Israel when trees begin to sprout. It is customary to eat fruit, particularly those for which the Land of Israel is praised; olives, dates, grapes, figs, and pomegranates. A new seasonal fruit is customarily eaten for the first time in the year. *Bokser* (carob pods) are a traditional favorite. The blessing *shehechiyanu* is recited and the blessing *ha-aitz* is said over the fruit.

From Tu B'Shvat we learn that just as a healthy tree bears fruit, so must we "bear fruit" by engaging in *mitzvot* and bringing goodness into the world — "For man is a tree of the field." (Deuteronomy 20:19)

IN REMEMBRANCE OF THE BEIT HAMIKDASH

For nearly 2,000 years one theme has been the focus of the aspirations and the prayers of the Jewish people in all parts of the world: our yearning for the ingathering of all Jews and our return to Jerusalem with our righteous *Mashiach*, who will rebuild the *Beit Hamikdash* and end the exile from our land.

In ancient times, while the Jews inhabited the Land of Israel, the *Beit Hamikdash* was the dominant and central feature of Jewish life. It possessed a magnificence we can only begin to imagine when we contemplate the immense stones of the Western Wall, the remnant of the outer wall surrounding the Temple Mount.

In the *Beit Hamikdash* the *Kohanim* (priestly tribe) led the nation in the service of G-d and the songs of the *Levi'im* uplifted the heart. Three times a year Jews traveled from all over to celebrate the Pilgrimage Festivals of Pesach, Shavuot and Sukkot. Nearby the Sages sat and taught from the over-flowing wellsprings of Torah. And once every seven years, in the year of *Hakhel*, the king gathered the people to read to them from the Torah.

The destruction of Jerusalem and the *Beit Hamikdash* was a tragic loss for the Jewish people, initiating the dispersion of Jews throughout the world. The Torah has given us strength and power to survive, long after the great empires that overcame us have crumbled and disappeared. Yet we still mourn our loss. Throughout history, Jews have not forgotten the *Beit Hamikdash* and G-d's promise of a third *Beit Hamikdash*.

Our Sages have taught: "All those who mourn the destruction of Jerusalem will merit to see it rebuilt." (Talmud Taanit 30b) We are confident that with each year and each day we are approaching ever closer to the time of *Mashiach*, when "the earth will be filled with the knowledge of G-d as the water covers the sea." (Isaiah 10:9) With the coming of *Mashiach*, then all days of mourning will be changed to days of rejoicing.

There are four fast days set aside for remembering the destruction of the *Beit Hamikdash*. The object of these fasts is to stir our hearts to repentance, in that by remembering these sad events we will resolve to improve our ways. We are told that the Second *Beit Hamikdash* was destroyed because of the sin of *sinat chinam* - unwarranted hatred. The remedy for this sin is unconditional love. In other words, we must endeavor to excel in the *mitzvah* of *ahavat Yisrael*, loving a fellow Jew, even when we think this love is undeserved.

Fasting is required for all Jews over the age of Bar and Bat Mitzvah. Women who are pregnant or nursing are obligated to fast for the entire fast only on the two major fast days of Yom Kippur and Tishah B'Av. One who is ill or requires medication, or a woman who has just given birth, should consult an Orthodox Rabbi.

On the following fast days, eating and drinking are prohibited from daybreak until nightfall (it is important to check the exact time on a Jewish calendar): the Fast of Gedaliah, the Tenth of Tevet, the Fast of Esther (Taanit Esther), and the 17th of Tammuz. On Yom Kippur and Tishah B'Av the fast begins before sunset and ends the following night. Other restrictions are also in effect on these two days.

The four fast days designated to commemorate the loss of the *Beit Hamikdash* are:

1) The Third Of Tishrei, The Fast Of Gedaliah: This fast is in remembrance of the Jewish governor who attempted to continue the Jewish settlement in Israel after the King of Babylon destroyed the *Beit Hamikdash* and took many of the people into exile. A remnant of Jews in the

Holy Land began to cultivate the land and to prosper somewhat under Gedaliah's wise leadership. After he was treacherously murdered, hope ended for continued Jewish presence in the land.

2) The Tenth Of Tevet: On this day, 850 years after the Jewish people entered Israel, the King of Babylon laid siege to Jerusalem, beginning the chain of calamities that ended in the burning of the Beit Hamikdash. The terrible suffering that the Jews endured during this siege is described in Megillat Eichah (Lamentations).

3) The Seventeenth Of Tammuz And "The Three Weeks": The fast day of the 17th of Tammuz begins the period known as the Three Weeks, or Bein Hametzorim (between the straits) a time that has, throughout history, been a harsh one for the Jews. On this day, Moshe Rabbeinu broke the first set of tablets because of the Jews' worship of the golden calf. On this date, too, the walls of Jerusalem were breached by the enemy before the destruction of the Beit Hamikdash.

Signs of mourning in effect during the Three Weeks include not cutting the hair, not saying the blessing shehechiyanu, not having weddings, and not listening to music. In addition, we are advised to take special care to avoid dangerous situations.

Throughout the Three Weeks it has become customary in many communities to study the laws concerning the building of the Beit Hamikdash. This study reawakens our hope to see the ultimate reconstruction of the Beit Hamikdash. According to our Sages, "G-d has assured us; I will consider their studying this as if they are actually taking part in the reconstruction of My Home." (Medrash Tanchuma Tzav:14)

The Nine Days: During the last days of the Three Weeks, from Rosh Chodesh Av until the Ninth of Av, we observe additional signs of mourning. We do not eat meat or drink wine. Meat and wine are permitted on Shabbat, at the conclusion of a tractate of Talmud, or for a seudat mitzvah such as a brit milah and pidyon haben.

4) The Ninth Of Av, Tishah B'Av: This is the day on which the first Beit Hamikdash was destroyed by Nebuchadnezzar, the king of Babylon in 3338 (420 B.C.E.). It was also the day that the second Beit Hamikdash was destroyed by Titus of Rome in 3828 (70 C.E.). It is a major fast day, lasting from sunset until after dark. On Tishah B'Av there are five prohibitions similar to those of Yom Kippur: eating and drinking, wearing leather shoes, washing for pleasure, using perfumes, and having marital relations.

The Talmud tells of five tragic events that befell the Jewish people on the Ninth of Av. Both Holy Temples were destroyed. The generation that left Egypt was sentenced by G-d to wander and die in the wilderness instead of entering the land of Israel. The city of Betar, a last stronghold against Roman domination, was captured and a terrible massacre was inflicted on its people. And after the destruction of Jerusalem, the site of the Beit Hamikdash was ploughed over and turned into a wasteland.

In addition, many other historic tragedies occured on Tishah B'Av. The decree of expulsion from Spain went into effect on the Ninth of Av, when King Ferdinand and Queen Isabella gave the Jewish community the choice of conversion, death or exile.

Observances of Tishah B'av

On erev Tishah B'Av, the day before Tishah B'Av, it is customary to eat a substantial meal in the afternoon, followed after Minchah (the afternoon service) by a short meal called the seudah hamafseket. This final meal consists primarily of bread and a cold hard-boiled egg. We may not eat more than one type of cooked or pickled food. Fruit and raw vegetables are permitted. We eat this meal while seated on a low stool, a sign of mourning. During the meal we dip a piece of bread in ashes, in memory of the destruction of the Beit Hamikdash. Reciting Bircat Hamazon with a mezuman (the extra blessing said when three men eat a meal together) is forbidden; therefore three men do not eat the seudah hamafseket together.

If erev Tishah B'Av falls on Shabbat, we eat regular Shabbat meals but take care to end them before sunset. If Tishah B'Av falls on Shabbat, the fast is postponed until Sunday.

During the night of Tishah B'Av and in the morning until noon (approximately 1 p.m. during Daylight Savings Time), we sit only on low stools or on the floor. Since Torah study "rejoices the heart," it, too, is prohibited until the afternoon, except for passages describing the destruction of the Beit Hamikdash. At night, after the evening prayer, the book of Eichah (Lamentations) is read in a mournful tune.

Food for the night may be prepared after noon. Some women have a custom to clean the house and sweep the floor after noon in anticipation of the Redemption, for it is a tradition that Mashiach will be born on Tishah B'Av.

Food Before and After A Fast

Eating a good meal before a fast will provide strength for the following day. It is advisable to avoid salty foods and to drink more water than usual to reduce thirst - remember that on Jewish fast days even drinking water is prohibited. Those who drink coffee or other beverages high in caffeine benefit from eliminating them several days before the fast, since caffeine withdrawal increases the discomfort of fasting. Food eaten after the fast should be light and easily digestible.

Seven Weeks Of Consolation

This period of mourning is followed by a time of consolation. On each Shabbat for seven weeks following Tishah B'Av, one of the seven prophetic passages from the prophet Isaiah is read in *shul*.

These passages reflect the theme of rejoicing and hope for the coming of *Mashiach* and the rebuilding of the *Beit Hamikdash*.

Tu B'Av — The Fifteenth of Av

With the fifteenth of Av, Tu B'Av, we have hints of a year ending and a new one soon to begin. It is the last day of planting for the year, with reference to the *shmittah* (Sabbatical) year and the day when the cutting of the wood for the Altar was completed each year. It was the day of forgiveness for the generation of the wilderness; consequently it is a day of purification from sin similar to Yom Kippur. In earlier generations it was marked with festivity and dancing, when Jewish daughters would dance in the vineyards.

The quality of the day itself was a protection against any taint of immodesty. Many engagements came about in this atmosphere of holiness. Our Sages said, "No days were as festive to Israel as Tu B'Av and Yom Kippur."

Tu B'Av is a time to begin to examine one's deeds of the past year, a prelude to the work that will begin in earnest next month during Elul. With the lengthening nights, it is also the time to increase in Torah study at night.

Spices, Spirit and Substitutions

Herbs and Spices
Measurements and Substitutions
Classic Menus for Shabbat and Holiday Meals

Herbs and Spices
The Art of Seasoning

The beauty of herbs and spices lies in the unique taste and aroma they impart to any dish. Spices (usually found in ground form) are derived from the seeds, bark and roots of plants, while herbs are the dried leaves and stems. Herbs should generally be added fairly close to the time of serving, as too much cooking destroys their flavor. Spices, on the other hand, mellow and permeate throughout the food with extended cooking. In light of current concerns about the use of salt, spices are an excellent substitute.

The following list describes some of the most widely used spices and how they are used.

Allspice - *Similar to a blend of cloves, cinnamon and nutmeg.*
Cakes, cookies, fish, fruit, meat, pastry, poultry, soup.

Anise Seed - *Strong licorice flavor and aroma.*
Cookies, fruit.

Basil - *Faintly anise-like flavor and sweet aroma.*
Desserts, fish, soups, vegetables, salads, tomato.

Bay Leaves - *Strong flavor. Ingredient in bouquet garni.*
Fish, meat, poultry, sauces, soup, stuffing.

Caraway Seed -*Warm, sweet, slightly sharp taste.*
Breads, dips, fruit, sauces.

Celery Seed - *Slightly bitter, fresh celery flavor.*
Cheese, dips, eggs, fish, meat, soup, vegetables, salads.

Chervil - *Faintly sweet flavor reminiscent of tarragon.*
Cheese, dips, eggs, fish, meat, sauces, soup, stuffing, vegetables, salads.

Chili Powder - *Dark red powder, mild or hot.*
Cheese, dips, eggs, fish, meat, sauces.

Chives - *Scallion flavor.*
Cheese, dips, eggs, fish, meat, poultry, soup, vegetables, salads.

Cinnamon - *Sweet pungent aroma.*
Beverages, breads, cakes, cookies, desserts, fruit, vegetables, salads.

Cloves - *Pungent, warm, sweet aroma.*
Cookies, desserts, fruit, meat, poultry, sauces, soup, vegetables, salads, cholent.

Coriander Seed - *Slightly lemony.*
Breads, cakes, cookies, fruit, pickles.

Cumin Seed - *Strong, slightly bitter flavor.*
Cheese, cookies, eggs, fish, meat, rice. Used in Meditteranean and other international cuisine.

Curry Powder - *Blend of many spices.*
Cheese, dips, eggs, meat, poultry, sauces, soup, Indian cuisine.

Dill - *Distinctive yet mild caraway-like flavor.*
Cheese, dips, fish, garnishes, meat, sauces, soup, stuffings, pickles, vegetables, salads.

Ginger - *Pungent sweet aroma and hot flavor.*
Cakes, cookies, fruit, meat, pastry, poultry, sauces, soup, vegetables, salads, pies, Asian-style meat and poultry.

Marjoram - *Spicy, slightly bitter flavor.*
Eggs, fish, meat, poultry, stuffing, vegetables, salads, Italian dishes.

Mint - *Strong sweet aroma and cool after-taste.*
Beverages, desserts, fruit, vegetables, salads, jelly.

Mustard Powder - *Pungent taste.*
Cheese, dips, eggs, sauces, vegetables, salads, spreads.

Nutmeg - *Sweet, warm aromatic flavor.*
Beverages, cakes, cookies, desserts, fruit, vegetables, salads.

Oregano - *Similar to marjoram but stronger.*
Cheese, fish, meat, poultry, sauces, soup, vegetables, salads, pizza, Italian, Greek or Mexican dishes.

Paprika - *Sweet aroma and flavor.*
Cheese, dips, meat, poultry, sauces, vegetables, salads, cholent.

Parsley - *Mild flavor.*
Dips, fish, garnishes, meat, poultry, sauces, vegetables, salads.

Pepper, Black - *Sharp, bitter, spicy taste.*
Cheese, dips, eggs, meat, poultry, sauces, soup, vegetables, salads, pickles.

Pepper, Red - *Hot flavor, cayenne is hottest.*
Dips, sauces, soup, vegetables, salads, main dishes, gravies, pickles.

Poppy Seed -*Sweet, mild nutty flavor and aroma.*
Bread, cakes, cookies.

Rosemary - *Pungent tea-like aroma and bittersweet flavor.*
Beverages, eggs, fish, meat, poultry, stuffing.

Saffron - *Deep orange color. Strong aroma. Pleasant taste.*
Bread, fish, poultry, rice.

Sesame Seed - *Slightly nut-like aroma and flavor.*
Bread, cakes, cheese, cookies, vegetables, salads.

Tarragon - *Sweet aromatic flavor and piquant tang.*
Dips, eggs, fish, meat, poultry, sauces, soup, vegetables, salads.

Thyme - *Pungent, aromatic flavor.*
Cheese, poultry, sauces, stuffing, vegetables, salads, dips, eggs, fish, meat.

Turmeric - *Yellow. Pepper-like aroma. Slightly bitter flavor.*
Cheese, dips, eggs, fish, poultry, sauces, relishes.

Substitutions and Measurements

Easy-to-follow kitchen guides

BAKING EQUIVALENTS AND SUBSTITUTIONS

	EQUIVALENTS	SUBSTITUTIONS
Almonds	1 pound unshelled = 1 1/4 cup nut meats	
Apples	1 medium apple, chopped = 1 cup	
Bananas	1 cup = 2 large bananas mashed	
Cocoa		1 cup = 1 cup carob powder
Chocolate	1 ounce = 1 square	3 Tbsps. cocoa + 1 Tbsp. margarine
Cornstarch		1 Tbsp. cornstarch = 2 Tbsps. flour or 2 Tbsps. kuzu (arrowroot)
Eggs	7-8 whites = 1 cup 8-10 yolks = 1 cup	
Flour	1 cup = approximately 5 ounces 3 - 4 cups = 1 pound	1 cup all purpose flour = 7/8 cup whole-wheat flour, or 1 cup whole-wheat pastry flour, or 1 cup plus 2 Tbsps. cake flour
Honey	1 lb. = 1/3 cup	1/2 cup honey = 1 cup sugar
Lemon	1 lemon squeezed = 3 Tbsps. lemon juice 1 grated lemon peel = 1 Tbsp. lemon rind	
Margarine	1 stick = 1/4 lb. = 1/2 cup or 8 Tbsps.	1 stick = 1/2 cup shortening
Milk		1 cup whole milk = 1/2 cup evaporated milk plus 1/2 cup water, or 1/2 cup nondairy creamer plus 1/2 cup water, or 1 cup soy milk
Buttermilk		1 cup buttermilk = 1 cup fresh milk plus 1 Tbsp. lemon juice or vinegar
Nondairy Creamer	1 container = 16 ounces	1 cup = 1 cup soy milk
Nondairy Dessert Topping	1 container = 10 ounces	
Orange	1 orange squeezed = 1/3 cup orange juice 1 grated orange peel = 2 Tbsps. orange rind	
Raisins	1 pound = 3 cups	
Sugar, White	2 1/4 cups = 1 lb.	
Brown	2 1/4 cups packed = 1 lb.	
Confectioner's	3 1/2 cups unsifted = 1 lb.	
Vanilla	1 package = 1/2 oz.	1 package = 2 teaspoons vanilla extract
Shortening	1 cup = 1/2 pound	
Walnuts	1 pound unshelled = 2 cups nut meats	
Yeast		1 cake fresh (2 oz.) = 3 packages dry

STANDARD MEASURES

Liquid or Dry Measurements

3 tsps. = 1 Tbsp.
2 Tbsps. = 1/8 cup
4 Tbsps. = 1/4 cup
5 Tbsps. + 1 tsp. = 1/3 cup
16 Tbsps. = 1 cup

Liquid Measurements

1 oz. = 2 Tbsps.
2 oz. = 1/4 cup
8 oz. = 1 cup
2 cups = 1 pint
2 pints = 1 quart
4 quarts = 1 gallon

METRIC EQUIVALENT MEASURES

Equivalent Liquid Measurements

1/4 tsp. = 1.5 ml
1/2 tsp. = 3 ml
1 tsp. = 5 ml
1 Tbsp. = 15 ml
1/3 cup = 80 ml
1/2 cup = 125 ml
3/4 cup = 200 ml
1 cup = 250 ml
1 quart = 1.25 l
1 gallon = 5.l

CONVERSION FORMULAS

U.S. to Metric

tsps. x 5 = milliliters
oz. x 30 = milliliters
cups x .24 = liters
quarts x .95 = liters
gallons x 3.78 = liters

Metric to U.S.

milliliters x 2 = tsps.
milliliters x .032 = oz.
liters x 4.2 = cups
liters x 1.06 = quarts
liters x .26 = gallons

Equivalent Dry Measurements

1/4 lb. = 125 g
1/2 lb. = 250 g
1 lb. = 500 g
2 lbs. = 1 kg
3 lbs. = 1.5 kg
4 lbs. = 2 kg
5 lbs. = 2.5 kg

CONVERSION FORMULAS

U.S. to Metric

oz. x 28.35 = grams
lbs. x .45 = kilograms

Metric to U.S.

grams x .035 = oz
kilograms x 2.2 = lbs.

Equivalent Length Measurements

Inches	cm	mm
1	2.5	25
2	5	50
3	7.5	75
4	10	100
5	12.5	125
6	15	150
7	17.5	175
8	20	200
9	22.5	225
10	25	250
11	27.5	275
12	30	300
13	32.5	325
14	35	350
15	37.5	375

CONVERSION FORMULAS

U.S. to Metric
inches x 2.54 = centimeters
feet x .304 = meters
yards x .91 = meters

Metric to U.S.
centimeters x .39 = inches
meters x 3.3 = feet
meters x 1.09 = yards

Bakeware Examples
5 x 9-inch loaf pan = 12.5 cm x 22.5 cm
9 x 13-inch baking pan = 22.5 cm x 32.5 cm
11 x 14-inch baking sheet = 27.5 cm x 35 cm

Equivalent Oven Temperatures
(approximate)

200° F = 100° C
250° F = 120° C
275° F = 140° C
300° F = 160° C
325° F = 170° C
350° F = 180° C
375° F = 190° C
400° F = 200° C
425° F = 220° C
450° F = 230° C
475° F = 240° C
500° F = 260° C
525° F = 270° C
550° F = 280° C

CONVERSION FORMULAS

U.S. (Fahrenheit) to Metric (Centigrade)
1. subtract 32,
2. multiply by 5,
3. and divide by 9.

Example: 250° F = ? C
1. 250° F - 32 = 218
2. 218 x 5 = 1090
3. 1090/9 = 121° C

Metric (Centigrade) to U.S. (Fahrenheit)
1. multiply by 9,
2. divide by 5,
3. and add 32.

Example: 200° C = ? F
1. 200° C x 9 = 1800
2. 1800/5 = 360
3. 360 + 32 = 392° F

Classic Menus for Shabbat and Holiday Meals

SHABBAT

The Shabbat and holiday meals provide an arena where creativity blends with tradition. Each festive meal, or *seudah*, begins with *Kiddush*, challah, followed by several courses including fish, soup, meat or poultry, side dishes, and dessert. Within this basic format, each cook's personal style and preferences, as well as the season and number of people to be served, will determine what to serve.

Friday Night

Traditional	Natural	Gourmet
Traditional Challah	Honey and Whole-Wheat Challah	Tasty Challah
Vegetable Eggplant Salad	Tofu-Tahini Dip	Yemenite Zchug
–	–	–
Classic Gefilte Fish	Lemon Fish	Stuffed Whitefish
Leafy Green Salad with French Dressing	Avocado Salad Beet and Wheat Salad	Mimosa Asparagus Vinaigrette
–	–	–
Classic Chicken Soup with Perfect Knaidlach	Vegetarian Lentil Soup	Onion Soup with Croutons
–	–	
Apricot Chicken	Zucchini-Stuffed Chicken	Chicken in Mushroom Sauce
Potato Kugel Spiced String Beans Basic Coleslaw	Deluxe Brown Rice Toasted Almond Butternut Squash Broccoli and Cauliflower Salad	Classic Potato Knish Zucchini-Stuffed Tomatoes Turnip Relish
–	–	–
All American Apple Pie with Perfect Pie Crust	Tofu Fruit Pie	Lemon Meringue Pie

Shabbat Day

Traditional	Natural	Gourmet
Traditional Challah	Honey and Whole-Wheat Challah	Tasty Challah
Turkish Tomato Relish	Guacamole	Tunisian Tomato Paste
–	–	–
Tantalizing Shabbat Fish	"Knoebel" Carp	Caribbean Fish
Waldorf Salad	Garden Chickpea Salad	Sweet-and-Sour Spinach Salad
–	–	–
Hungarian Potato Cholent	Chicken Cholent	Tebeet
–	–	–
Sweet-and-Sour Pot Roast	Meatless Stuffed Cabbage	Sliced Roast in Apricot Mushroom Sauce
Classic Salt and Pepper Lokshen Kugel Cucumber Salad	Pineapple Whole-Wheat Noodle Kugel	Yerushalayim Kugel Zucchini and Carrot Julienne
–	Ratatouille	–
Cocoa Chiffon Cake	–	Strawberry-Rhubarb Pie
	Banana-Peanut Butter Bread	

Seudah Shlishit
(Shalosh Seudot)

(Serving Suggestions)

Challah Rolls

Fish Cocktail Salad - Sardine Salad - Tuna Spread

Cabbage with Spicy Vinaigrette - Classic Potato Salad
Easy Four-Bean Salad - Pasta Salad Vinaigrette

Chocolate-Mint Brownies - Oatmeal Apple Crisp - Napoleons

YOM TOV

Whereas the Yom Tov meals are similar to the Shabbat meals in format, the holiday meals often feature special traditional foods. Other laws and customs pertaining to food are described in the respective sections on each Yom Tov. In addition, the laws regarding food preparation on Shabbat and Yom Tov differ, as detailed in the pertinent sections.

Yom Tov Night

Traditional	Natural	Gourmet
Raisin Challah	Rye-Oatmeal Challah	Half-and-Half Challah
Baba Ganoush	Hoummous	Parsley Dip
-	-	-
Sweet-and Sour Salmon Trout	Steamed Ginger Fish	Pesce Al Cartoccio
Israeli Salad	Winter Garden Salad	Spinach, Egg, and Onion Salad
-	-	-
Chicken Barley Soup	Miso Soup	French Tomato-Onion Soup
-	-	
Honey Breaded Chicken	Basic Baked Chicken with Honey-Soy Sauce	Braised Duck in Orange Sauce
Vegetables for the Discriminating Easy Yom Tov Tzimmes	Tabouli Green Beans and Carrot Salad	Stuffed Zucchini Persian Rice
-	-	-
Classic Chocolate Cake with Chocolate Swirl Frosting Deluxe Pareve Ice Cream	Ambrosia Blueberry-Peach Pie with Whole-Wheat Pie Crust	Berry-Sauced Sponge Cake Dessert Quindim

Yom Tov Day

Traditional	Natural	Gourmet
Raisin Challah Chili-Horseradish Sauce	Rye-Oatmeal Challah Hearty Vegetarian Chopped Liver	Half-and-Half Challah Cranberry Relish
-	-	-
Pickled Carp Waldorf Salad	Ceviche Marinated Mushrooms	Marinated Sweet-and-Sour Fish Stir-Fried Carrots and Celery
-	-	-
Glazed Veal Pot Roast Green Bean Almandine Toasted Barley and Mushrooms	Crown of Lamb Stuffed with Rice and Vegetables Tofu-Vegetable Saute Broccoli and Olive Salad	Pickled Tongue in Apricot Sauce Two-Tone Potato Roll Oriental Mushrooms
-	-	-
Mandelbroit Baked Fruit Compote	Carob-Nut Brownies Soy Milk Ice Cream	Chocolate-Almond Angel Pie Strawberry Sorbet

TRADITIONAL HOLIDAY FOODS

The following list itemizes the particular foods traditionally served on each holiday. They can be included in the above suggested Yom Tov menus.

Rosh Hashanah
Round Challah, Fish Heads, Tzimmes, Honey Cake

Erev Yom Kippur
Kreplach, light foods

Hoshanah Rabbah
Kreplach

Simchat Torah
Stuffed Cabbage

Chanukah
Latkes, Dairy, Doughnuts

Purim
Hamantashen, Kreplach

Shavuot
Blintzes, Cheesecake

Appendix

Glossary
For Further Reading
Credits

Glossary

Ashkenazim - Jews whose culture and origin is that of Eastern Europe and Russia.

Beit Hamikdash - The Holy Temple in ancient Jerusalem. There were two Holy Temples which stood on the same site in different eras. The *Kotel Hama'aravi* (Western Wall) in Jerusalem is a remnant of the wall which surrounded the second *Beit Hamikdash* which was destroyed by Titus of Rome in 70 C.E. In the Messianic Era, the third *Beit Hamikdash* will be rebuilt on the same site.

Bishul Yisrael - Food cooked by a Jew.

Brachah - (Pl. *brachot.*) Blessing. A *brachah* is made before and after eating and drinking. *Brachot* are also said before performing certain *mitzvot*.

Chabad - Acrostic for three Hebrew words: *chochmah* (wisdom), *binah* (understanding), *da'at* (knowledge). Branch of Chassidism based on an intellectual approach to the service of G-d, founded by Rabbi Schneur Zalman of Liadi.

Chalav Yisrael - Milk supervised by a Jew throughout processing, from the beginning of the milking until the end of production. This term also refers to dairy products made from such milk.

Challah - (Pl. *challot.*) 1. Traditional Shabbat and Yom Tov loaves of bread, often braided. 2. Portion of dough donated to the *Kohanim* in times of the *Beit Hamikdash*. Today, *challah* is a small piece of dough which is removed from the entire dough before baking. It is then burned.

Chametz - (lit. "leavening.") All food, drink, and other products made of wheat, barley, rye, oats, or spelt which has come into contact with water, other liquid, or a leavening agent for 18 minutes or longer.

Chol Hamoed - (lit. "weekday of the festival.") "Intermediate Days" of the festivals of Pesach and Sukkot, during which some forms of work forbidden on the Festival itself, may be permitted.

Erev - Day preceding Shabbat or Yom Tov. Thursday night and Friday are *erev* Shabbat.

Fleishig - (Yiddish) Meaty; any food containing meat, fowl, or their derivatives.

Glatt Kosher - 1. Meat which comes from a kosher, properly slaughtered animal, that upon its examination after the slaughtering has been found completely free of any imperfections whatsoever. Simply "kosher" is when some of these imperfections are found, yet declared permissible. 2. The term "glatt kosher" is also commonly used to declare certain foods, restaurants, etc. completely kosher with strict supervision.

Hafrashat Challah - Separating a portion of dough. See Challah.

Haggadah - Traditional book used for the Pesach *Seder*. It includes the order of the *Seder* and various portions from the Torah and the Sages, recounting the story of the Exodus from Egypt.

Halachah - (Pl. *halachot.*) Jewish (Torah) Law.

Hamotzi - (lit. "Who brings forth.") Identifying word in the blessing over bread.

Hashem - (lit. "the name.") G-d.

Hashgachah - Supervision. Usually refers to *kashrut*.

Hechsher - (Pl. *hechsherim.*) Guarantee of *kashrut* given by a supervising authority.

Kashering - Process by which a non-kosher utensil is made kosher.

Kashrut - Torah dietary observances defining which foods are kosher, or permissible for consumption.

Kiddush - (lit. "sanctification.") At the beginning of a Shabbat or Yom Tov meal we proclaim the holiness of the day by saying a special blessing. This is usually done over a cup of wine, or over the two loaves of challah.

Kohen - (Pl. *Kohanim*.) Priest in the *Beit Hamikdash*. Descendant of Aaron, brother of Moses. Many of the laws pertaining to the Kohanim still apply.

Koshering - Process of soaking and salting the meat of a kosher, ritually slaughtered animal.

Levi - (Pl. *Levi'im*.) Descendant of the tribe of Levi who assisted the *Kohanim* in the services and upkeep of the *Beit Hamikdash*.

Ma'aser - Portion to be separated before eating food grown in Israel; in the time of the *Beit Hamikdash* this portion was given to the *Levi'im*.

Machzor - (Pl. *machzorim*.) Prayer book for Rosh Hashanah and Yom Kippur.

Mashgiach - Person in charge of *kashrut* supervision at all levels of production, in a factory, restaurant, caterer, butcher shop, etc. The *mashgiach* should be a G-d-fearing, knowledgeable person.

Mashiach - (lit. "annointed one.") Messiah. The arrival of the Messiah will herald the end of the exile, speedily in our days.

Matzah - (Pl. *matzot*.) Unleavened bread which is eaten on Pesach.

Mikvah - (Pl. *mikvaot*.) Ritualarium. Gathering of natural water in a structure conforming to the laws of ritual immersion, used for spiritual purification.

Milchig - (Yiddish) Dairy. Any food containing milk or milk derivatives.

Midrash - Rabbinical homiletical literature.

Mishnah - The codification of the Oral Law by Rabbi Yehudah Hanassi.

Mitzvah - (Pl. *mitzvot*.) Torah commandment.

Neshamah - Soul.

Nikur - See *Treibering*.

Pareve - Food containing neither meat nor milk derivatives and which may be used at either meat or milk meals, e.g. fish, eggs, juice, fruits and vegetables.

Pesach - Passover holiday. The Festival of *Matzot* observed in the spring. One of the *Shalosh Regalim*.

Rosh Chodesh - (lit. "head of the month.") New moon, beginning of the Hebrew month. Some months have two days of Rosh Chodesh, with the first day occuring on the thirtieth day of the preceding month and the second day occuring on the first day of the new month.

Seder - (lit. "order.") Refers to the ritual gathering and meal which takes place on the first two nights of Pesach.

Sephardim - Jews whose culture and origin is that of countries bordering the Mediterranean Sea, the Middle East, Asia and Africa.

Seudah - Meal, especially a festive or Shabbat meal.

Sha'alah - (Pl. *sha'alot*.) Question in Jewish Law which should be addressed to an Orthodox Rabbi.

Shalosh Regolim - The three pilgrimages when Jews inhabited the Land of Israel, before the current exile. All Jewish males over thirteen were commanded to celebrate the three holidays of Pesach, Shavuot, and Sukkot, first in the place of the M*ishkan* (portable sanctuary) and later in Jerusalem at the Holy Temple.

Shechitah - Torah-prescribed method of slaughtering kosher animals and fowl. The man skillfully trained to perform this is a *shochet*.

Shehechiyanu - Blessing of thanks to G-d for bringing us to a new season, said on holidays, when tasting fruit for the first time in season, and other occasions.

Shemoneh Esrai - (lit. "eighteen.") Name of the silent prayer, originally composed of eighteen blessings, also called the *amidah* (lit. "standing."), which is the main part of the prayer service.

Shmittah - (lit. "unattended.") Torah law requires that every seventh year in Israel there be an agricultural Sabbath, during which there is no harvesting, planting, etc.. One may not eat food grown in Israel during the *shmittah* year.

Shmurah Matzah - (lit. "guarded" matzah.) Matzah which has been made from grain which was guarded from the time of either reaping or grinding so that it never came into contact with water or other liquids.

Shochet - See S*hechitah*.

Shul - (Yiddish) Synagogue.

Siddur - Prayer book.

Simchah - (lit. "joy.") Celebration of a special event, such as a wedding, Bar Mitzvah, etc.

Talmud - Explication of the Oral Law, including M*ishnah* and later teachings, concluded around the sixth century C.E.

Toiveling - The process of immersing food utensils into a *mikvah* before they are used.

Torah - The written and Oral Law. Also used more specifically to refer to the Five Holy Books given by G-d to Moses, which contain in them the happenings of the world from the beginning of Creation until the Jews were about to enter Israel. Every word and even every letter contains many teachings for us as explained by our Rabbis. It also contains the laws by which we live.

Trefah - (lit. "torn.") This refers to 1) an animal which has a torn limb and may not be eaten, and 2) (commonly) non-kosher food or utensils.

Treibering - Yiddish for *nikkur*. Removal of forbidden veins and fats from an animal before *kashering*.

Tzedakah - (lit. "justice, righteousness.") Charity.

Yahrzeit - (Yiddish) (lit. "year time.") Anniversary of a death.

Yizkor - Memorial prayer said on Yom Kippur, Shemini Atzeret, Pesach, and Shavuot, in memory of deceased parent(s).

Yom Tov - A Jewish holiday.

For Further Reading

The hallmark of a Jewish home is a bookcase filled with Jewish books. The increasing availability of excellent books in English enables everyone to begin collecting a Jewish library — for education, pleasure, and inspiration.

Basic Judaism

The following titles are basic texts for every Jewish home.

Chumash - The Five Books of Moses.

Naviim and Ketuvim - Prophets and Writings.

Sefer Hamitzvot - Explanation by Maimonides of the 613 Commandments.

Tanya - Classic text on Chabad Chassidism by Rabbi Schneur Zalman of Liadi.

Code of Jewish Law - Rabbi Solomon Ganzfried. An abbreviated English edition of the *Shulchan Aruch* (authoritative compilation of all laws), provides information about all areas of *halachah*.

Shabbat And Holidays

The Sabbath, Dayan Dr. I. Grunfeld.
    Feldheim Publishers, Jerusalem/N.Y.

Shmirath Shabbath K'Hilchasa, Volumes I, II, Yehoshua Y. Neuwirth.
    Feldheim Publishers, Jerusalem/N.Y.

The Gift, Lubavitch Women's Organization.
    Brooklyn, N.Y.

The Complete Story of Tishrei, Dr. Nissan Mindel.
    Merkos L'Inyonei Chinuch, Brooklyn, NY.

The Complete Festival Series, Dr. Nissan Mindel.
    Merkos L'Inyonei Chinuch, Brooklyn, NY.

The Book Of Our Heritage, Rabbi E. Kitov.
    Feldhiem Publishers, Jerusalem/N.Y.

Kashrut

Body & Soul: A Handbook For Kosher Living,
Lubavitch Women's Cookbook Publications, Brooklyn, N.Y.

Kashrut, Y. Lipshutz.
Mesorah Publications, Brooklyn, N.Y.

The Jewish Dietary Laws, Dayan Dr. I. Grunfeld.
Soncino Press, London.

A Practical Guide To Kashrut, Rabbi S. Wagschal.
Gateshead Foundations For Torah, Gateshead, England.

The Spice & Spirit of Kosher-Passover Cooking,
Lubavitch Women's Cookbook Publications, Brooklyn, N.Y.

Of Interest To Women

Aura, Lubavitch Women's Organization.
Brooklyn, N.Y.

The Modern Jewish Woman, Lubavitch Women's Publications.
Brooklyn, N.Y.

Jewish Women in Jewish Law, Rabbi Moshe Meiselman.
Ktav Publishing House, N.Y.

The Waters Of Eden, Rabbi Aryeh Kaplan.
NCSY, N.Y.

Di Yiddishe Heim, Lubavitch Women's Organization.
Brooklyn, NY.

Psychology

Let Us Make Man, Dr. Abraham Twersky.
Traditional Press, Brooklyn, N.Y.

*E.M.M.E.T.T - A Step-by-Step Guide to Emotional Maturity
Established Through Torah*, Miriam Adahan.
Feldheim Publishers, Jerusalem/NY.

Raising Children To Care, Miriam Adahan.
Feldheim Publishers, Jerusalem/NY.

For a free catalog listing hundreds of additional titles in English for children and adults, write to: Merkos L'Inyonei Chinuch, 770 Eastern Parkway, Brooklyn, NY 11213, (718) 778-0226.

Credits

CONSULTANTS

Production
Yerachmiel Benjaminson
Charles Bloch
Seymour and Harriet Gluckow
Sam Goldman
Ed Goldman
Shlomo Lakein
Yaakov Reich

Marketing
Chaim Clorfene
Barbara Kirschenblatt-Gimblett
Eve Gittelson

General
Rabbi N. Bernstein
Rabbi M. Blau
Rabbi Z. Deitsch
Rabbi S. Duchman
Rabbi S. Light
Rabbi S. Lipsker
Rabbi Y. Pinson

Editorial
Sara Tova Best
Esther Kesselman
Esther Leuchter
Baila Olidort
Chana Sharfstein
Freydie Tiefenbrun
Yerachmiel Tilles

Financial
Esther Tova Dick
Shaina Kahan
Riva Kaplinsky
Henya Laine
Chaya Lang
Zlati Mochkin
Chani Moskowitz
Sara Rosen

Extra Credit
Fruma Weg

RECIPE BOARD

Founding Associates
Fraidie Andrusier
Marilyn Rosenfeld
Frida Schapiro

Advisors
Fayge Sara Friedman
Nechama Hackner
Chaya Freyda Kahan
Leah Lypszyc
Ella Pinson
Ray Schildkraut
Martha Stock
Baila Wilenkin

Stylists
Shayna Ezagui
Chaya Haller
Goldie Litvin
Baila Schwartz
Chana Baila Schwartz
Alessa Wircberg

Typesetting Assistants
Baila Apfel
Baila Gansburg

RECIPE CONTRIBUTORS

Abboudi Family
Rivkah Aisenbach
Esther Alpern
Esther Altman
Sara Andrusier
Reggie Arahanchie
Faige Bassman
Feige Benjaminson
Chana Leah Berger
Brenda Berkowitz
Adela Bernstein
Esther Blau
Shoshana Braun
Fayge Broner
Etta Chaya Brummel
Tzipporah Brusowankin
Mrs. Bukiet
Chana Baila Burston
Rochel Butman
Chani Capland
Ellen Center
Eva Cohen
Chaya Sara Cohen
Bina Cunin
Sara Deitsch
Cyrel Deitsch
Raizy Edelman
Aliza Eisenberg
Arlene Epstein
Fredka Ezagui
Esther Feinstein
Hennie Fialkoff
Yadida Flint
Sara Forer
Tzirel Frankel
Faige Sara Friedman
Simone Gansburg
Barbara Gold
Leah Goldberg
Rochel Goldberg
Fraidel Goldsmid

Seema Goldstein
Lynn Gollurstein
J. Goodman
Miriam Gopin
Miriam Gordon
Josephine Gottleib
Shterna Greisman
Rivkie Grossbaum
Sterna Grunblatt
Baila Guez
Nechama Hackner
Shirley Halon
Sara Hammer
Beila Hayes
Judith Illions
Sara Junik
Chaya Freyde Kahan
Chaya Kaplan
Riva Kaplinsky
Rivkah Katzen
Chaya Klein
Sterka Krinsky
Ruth Krinsky o.b.m
Devorah Kroll
Chava Kuzecki
Henya Laine
Leah Lederman
Nettie Lerner
R. Levi
Shoshana Lifschitz
Cherna Light
Leah Lipszyc
Sterna Maline
Sara Malka
Alice Marks
Vicky Massry
Sue Mischel
Fradel Mishulovin
Zlati Mochkin
Sara Morgenstern
Elisheva Morrison
Chaya Ohana o.b.m

Chanie Piekarski
Chana Devorah Pinson
Elka Popack
Nechama Pruss
Yaffa Rabin
Channie Rapaport
Zeesy Raskin
Chaya Rice
Bluma Rivkin
Rochel Rosenbloom
Rivkah Rothstein
Nina Chaia Sabghir
Rochel Sandman
Racheline Sasson
Naomi Saul
Frida Schapiro
Devorah Scheiner
Doris Schneid
Helen Schneid
Ray Schildkraut
Sara Shollar
Chana Sara Shuchat
Tillie Segelstein
Brenda Sher
Sarah Smith
Randy Soltz
Esther Rochel Spielman
Fruma Yetta Spiller
Gitty Stolik
Esther Tauber
Mashie Taurog
Chaya Teldon
Sterna Tenenbaum
Devorah Tenenbaum
Freydie Tiefenbrun
Miriam Torenheim
Baila Vilenkin
Leah Wagshul
Emma Wang
Alessa Wircberg
Bassie Woonteiler

Index

Subject Index
Recipe Index

Subject Index

Frequently used Hebrew and Yiddish terms are defined in the Glossary (pages 549-551).

Recipe Index

Recipe names followed by (v.) are variations of main recipes.

For further information regarding kashruth,
or if you or anyone you know needs assistance in making a home kosher, contact:

Kashruth Division of Lubavitch Women's Organization
770 Eastern Parkway, Brooklyn, N. Y. 11213
(718) 771-4342 or (718) 493-8581

or contact your local Chabad-Lubavitch Representative

A Letter From The Lubavitcher Rebbe
Rabbi Menachem Mendel Schneerson
The Role of the Jewish Home

...In a Jewish household, the wife and mother, the *akeres habayis*, largely determined the set-up and atmosphere of the entire home.

G-d demands that the Jewish home—every Jewish home—be quite different from a non-Jewish home, not only on *Shabbos* and *Yom Tov*, but also on ordinary weekdays and in "weekday" matters. It must be a *Jewish* home in every respect.

What makes a Jewish household different from a non-Jewish household that it is conducted in all its details according to the directives of the *Torah, Toras Chayim*—meaning that it is the Jew's guide in daily life—given by G-d. Hence the home becomes an abode for G-d's Presence, a home for G-dliness, one of which G-d says: " Make Me a sanctuary, and I shall dwell among them." (Exod. 25:5)

It is a home where G-d's Presence is felt not only on *Shabbos* and *Yom Tov*, but on every day of the week; and not only when *davenning* and learning *Torah*, but also when engaged in very ordinary things, such as eating and drinking, etc., in accordance with the directive, "Know Him in all your ways."

It is home where mealtime is not a time for indulging in ordinary and natural "eating habits" but a hallowed service to G-d, where the table is an "altar" to G-d, sanctified by the washing of the hands before the meal, reciting the blessings over the food, and Grace after the meal, with every item of food and beverage brought into the home being strictly *kosher*.

It is a home where the mutual relationship between husband and wife is sanctified by the meticulous observance of the laws and regulations of *Taharas Hamishpocho*, and permeated with the awareness of the active third "Partner"—G-d—in creating new life, in fulfillment of the Divine commandment: "Be fruitful and multiply." This also insures that Jewish children are born in purity and holiness, with pure hearts and minds that will enable them to resist temptation and avoid the pitfalls of the environment when they grow up. Moreover, the strict observance of *Taharas Hamishpocho* is a basic factor in the preservation of peace and harmony (*Shalom Bayis*) in the home, which is vitally strengthened and fortified thereby—obviously, a basic factor in the preservation of the family as a unit.

It is a home where the parents know that their first obligation is to instill into their offspring from their most tender age on, the love of G-d and also the fear of G-d, permeating them with the joy of performing *mitzvos*. With all their desire to provide their children with all the good things in life, the Jewish parent must know that the greatest, indeed the only real and eternal legacy they can bequeath to their children is to make the *Torah* and *mitzvos* and traditions their life-source and guide in daily life.

In all that has been said above, the Jewish wife and mother the *akeres habayis*—has a primary role second to none.

It is largely—and in many respects exclusively—her great task and privilege to give her home its Jewish atmosphere. She has been entrusted with, and is completely in charge of, the *kashrus* of the foods and beverages that come into her kitchen and on the dining table.

She has been given the privilege of ushering in the holy *Shabbos* by lighting the candles on Friday, in ample time before sunset. Thus, she actually and symbolically brightens-up her home with peace and harmony and with the light of *Torah* and *mitzvos*. It is largely in her merits that G-d bestows the blessing of true happiness on her husband and children and the entire household.

In addition to such *mitzvos* as candle-lighting, challah and others which the *Torah* entrusted primarily to Jewish daughters, there are matters which, in the natural order of things, lie in the woman's domain. The reason for this being so in the natural order is that it stems from the supra-natural order of holiness, which is the source and origin of the good in the physical world. We refer, of course, to the observance of *Taharas Hamishpocho* which, in the nature of it, is in the hands of the Jewish woman. The husband is required to encourage and to facilitate this mutual observance; certainly not hinder it in any way, G-d forbid. But the main responsibility—and privilege—is the wife's.

This is the great task and mission which G-d gave to the Jewish woman—to observe and disseminate the observance of *Taharas Hamishpocho*, and of other vital institutions of Jewish family life. For besides being the fundamental *mitzvos* and the cornerstone of the sanctity of Jewish family life, as well as relating to the well-being of the children in body and soul—these pervade and extend through all Jewish generations to eternity.

Finally, it is to be remembered that the Creator has provided each and every Jewish woman with the capacity to carry them out in daily life in the fullest measure, for otherwise, it would not be logical or fair of G-d to give obligations and duties which are impossible to fulfill.

The points mentioned above—all too briefly in relation to their vital importance for our people Israel, individually and collectively, especially in the present day and age, as discussed at greater length elsewhere—should be the objects of intensive and widespread activity by Jewish women everywhere. There is a crying need to bring them to the attention, and within living experience, of the widest possible Jewish circles. There can be no danger of over-emphasizing these vital aspects of Jewish life, nor of over-publishing on these subjects. Every additional volume is to be heartily welcomed...

DEDICATED TO THE LUBAVITCHER REBBE, MH"M
whose teachings and example are a never-ending source of life for all mankind